For Christopher, David, Joseph, & Ann Elizabeth
Ní grá go dtí muintir
There's no love until there's a family.
(Irish Proverb)

Contents

Preface and Acknowledgments

The idea for this book came to me as I was finishing an earlier work on the Marshall Plan to rebuild Western Europe after the Second World War. In tracking the congressional debates over the Marshall Plan, I was struck by two convictions that ran through the arguments on both sides. The first was the conviction that elements of current policy involved a break with past practice, and not only with the practice of American foreign policy but with related economic and institutional policies as well. The second was the conviction that bad policies could put the United States on the slippery slope to a garrison state dominated by military leaders and devoted to military purposes. Intrigued by these themes, I decided to track them through a variety of related initiatives having to do with military manpower, the modern day defense department, the allocation of resources for defense and international programs, and the mobilization of science and industry behind the national defense.

These and similar initiatives departed from peacetime practice and provoked a good deal of argument among policy makers, politicians, journalists, and ordinary Americans alike. Both sides understood that a peacetime national security state was in the making where none had existed before. Both saw the need to guard against the potentially corrosive effects of this process on the American way of life as they understood it. And both resorted to the metaphor of the garrison state to explain what could happen if American leaders took the country in the wrong direction. The following chapters explore these debates and how they influenced the shape of the national security state that finally emerged.

In organizing these chapters, I found it helpful to cast the debate over national security initiatives as one between two broad groups – those who believed in a new ideology of national security and those who adhered to values rooted in an older political culture. A few words about these two concepts might also help the reader. My concept of ideology owes much to the insights of Clifford Geertz, especially his view of ideologies as formal, coherent systems of belief that usually emerge in periods of crisis, influence the way people make sense of the world, and enable them to act politically. Political culture embraces ideology, as Geertz points out, but can also denote a popular, less coherent set of problem-solving principles, ideas, attitudes, and values that are commonly held but seldom integrated into a formal system of thought. I use the term political culture in this sense, but also to refer to what Raymond Williams called residual culture or what Geertz called "received tradition." I use it, in other words, to refer to the remains of an older way of thinking, to a body of older ideas and traditions that coexists with the new ideology and against which the new ideology must react.

To put these concepts in the context of what follows, the ideology of national security refers to a set of assumptions that emerged from the crises of World War II and the Cold War. This new ideology shaped the way its believers saw the postwar world and America's place within it. It laid the groundwork for a more internationalist foreign policy and for a supportive program of state making, both of which challenged such received traditions as isolationism, antimilitarism, and antistatism. Much that happened in American state making during the first decade of the Cold War can be viewed as a struggle between these new and residual ways of thinking, between the national security ideology and the old political culture, with the outcome in many cases being a program of action that reconciled the differences between them.

I am also grateful to Geertz and others for the notion that ideology and political culture confer on those who share them a common sense of political identity – in this case a sense of what it meant to be an American. Much the same is true of political language, which can be used rhetorically to forge a sense of shared identity, on the one hand, or to define differences, on the other hand. Theorists like Michel Foucault and scholars like David Campbell and Benedict Anderson have noted the constructed nature of national identities – the way, in other words, that language, tradition, and symbols are used to create a sense of collective identity, in part by juxtaposing that identity with its opposite. Because those who subscribed to the new ideology of national security were also byproducts of a residual political culture, it was not unusual for them to use the same political language, including the same symbols and metaphors, as their critics and opponents. But there was a difference, in that each side used these rhetorical tools to mobilize the nation behind a different sense of national purpose, the one toward internationalism, the other toward nationalism, regionalism, or isolationism.

Many of those from whom I have borrowed will wish that I had been more faithful to their theories or had woven their ideas more tightly into the fabric of my narrative. But if I may be forgiven my own interest, it was in other threads of the story, especially in the way American leaders tried to negotiate the process of state making without forsaking their cherished values and convictions. I have been interested in this issue and in the whole process of state making for many years and have benefited greatly from the insights of Ellis W. Hawley, Theda Skocpol, and other scholars who share interests similar to those explored in the following pages. These include to some extent the way political alignments influenced the shape of the state, the way state structures influenced the economy, and the degree to which the state, or at least the military arm of the state, tended toward independent action and autonomy. But above all they include the way state structures are formed. This part of the story emphasizes the role of war and the Cold War as agents of state formation, but also the important part played by ideology, political culture, and party politics, not just as spurs to the process of state making but also as constraints on that process and on the degree of state autonomy that emerged.

In developing the last point, it will become clear to many readers that the national security discourse of the early Cold War continued a debate over the role of the state in American life that dates back to the founding of the Republic. Indeed, one of my great debts is to the many historians who have explored American political thought in the early Republic, especially the concept of republicanism and its long resonance in the history of American politics. The national security discourse is part of that history, even though it is more than just another round in an old debate.

If I am grateful to those scholars and theorists from whom I have learned so much, I am no less grateful to many friends and colleagues who lent very practical help to this enterprise. Like other scholars who have worked on aspects of American history in this period, I am enormously indebted to archivists at the Truman and Eisenhower presidential libraries, the Library of Congress, the National Archives, and other depositories. Their knowledge of the records and patient helpfulness proved invaluable. Although my duties as a journal editor and department chair kept me from taking much leave time, I am indebted to the Ohio State University and especially to the College of Humanities for generous financial assistance in support of my research. I owe a similar debt to colleagues in the History Department, who took the time to talk with me about different aspects of this project, and to the Mershon Center at Ohio State, which kindly funded the help of a research assistant over several quarters.

Several students served in this capacity or otherwise volunteered to help: Glenn Dorn, Darryl Fox, Mary Ann Heiss, Bruce Karhoff, Bruce Khula, Susan Landrum, Amy Staples, Jennifer Small, David Stefacek, Yuji Tosaka, and Paul Wittekind. I also benefited from the help of other students, notably Richard Damms and Paul Pierpaoli, who were kind enough to exchange research notes with me as they did their own dissertations or wrote their own books. Much of the work also benefited from the helpful suggestions of some of the same students, from the copy-editing of Kurt Schultz, from the friendly secretarial assistance of Janice Gulker and Gail Summerhill, from the close reading and critical comments of Ellis Hawley, Gary Gerstle, Carolyn Eisenberg, Burt Kaufman, and Allan Winkler, and from the encouragement of my editor, Frank Smith.

As always, my greatest debt is to my wife, Virginia, for whom each day brings a new appreciation, and to our children, Christopher, David, Joseph, and Ann Elizabeth, to whom this book is dedicated. Now grown and gone away, they continue to give the deepest meaning to my life and to everything I do.

M. J. H.
Columbus, Ohio
October 1997

The National Security Discourse
Ideology, Political Culture, and State Making

"How can we prepare for total war," Hanson Baldwin asked in 1947, "without becoming a 'garrison state' and destroying the very qualities and virtues and principles we originally set out to save?"[1] Baldwin, a military-affairs writer for the *New York Times*, was not the only one asking this question at the start of the Cold War. The same question was on the minds of many Americans as they confronted the prospect of a long and bitter struggle with the Soviet Union. Fighting the Cold War seemed to require peacetime military and diplomatic initiatives that departed from American tradition, and this possibility led some to ask if it was worth the cost, not just in dollars or lives but in the freedoms they held dear. These Americans resisted new initiatives, usually in the name of tradition, while a second group, though hardly indifferent to tradition, tried to reshape the way Americans thought, both about their role in world affairs and about the new initiatives and institutions that national security appeared to demand. The struggle between these two groups, which was fundamentally a struggle to shape the nation's political identity and postwar purpose, forms an important theme in the narrative that follows.

Examining this struggle opens a window on one of the most striking developments in recent American history – the emergence of the national security state in the early years of the Cold War. The process of state making involved long and difficult battles between civilian and military leaders, between different branches of the armed forces, between Congress and the White House, between Democrats and Republicans, and between liberals and conservatives. These battles are delineated in subsequent chapters, but running through all of them was a creative tension between older ways of thinking and a new ideology of national security. This tension pulled the process of state making in different

---

[1] Baldwin quoted in Aaron L. Friedberg, "Why Didn't the United States Become a Garrison State?" *International Security* 16 (Spring 1992): 109–42.

directions. It forced the American people to reconcile old habits with new policies, an older sense of themselves with a new sense of national purpose, and to do so in ways that stopped short of the garrison state. The goal of this brief chapter is to sketch the new world that most Americans perceived, outline the transformations that ensued and the thinking of key groups, and thus set the stage for the chronicle of state making that unfolds in this book.

II

To most Americans, the age of isolationism had gone up in smoke at Pearl Harbor. To be sure, they had earlier grown accustomed to a certain degree of involvement in world affairs. Isolationism had not kept them from opening the door to Asia in the nineteenth century, from the economic internationalism that followed, or from the interventions of 1917 and 1941. Measured by these indicators, the United States had become an active world power long before the Cold War. Still, there was something different after 1945. For most Americans, the peace was more precarious and the United States was more vulnerable than ever before. They could no longer count on friendly powers to carry the burden of battle while they prepared. Nor could they count on the great ocean barriers to ensure their security in an age when long-range bombers, aircraft carriers, and atomic weapons made it possible for potential aggressors to inflict the same devastation on their homeland that two world wars had wrought on much of Europe and Asia.

To most Americans, moreover, the Soviet Union had emerged from the Second World War as just such an aggressor; the United States was the only power able to contain the Soviet threat; and containment required the kind of entangling alliances and permanent defense establishment that earlier generations had abhorred. Guided by these convictions, American policymakers began to discard the last remnants of the country's prewar isolationism. They talked more expansively about the national interest, used the phrase "national security" more frequently than ever before, and engineered a rapid expansion of American power into every nook and cranny of the world.

The initial turning points came on the European front. Beginning in 1947, American leaders worked to shore up the anti-Communist governments in Greece and Turkey and to rebuild Western Europe into an effective counterweight to the Soviet bloc in the East. Similar goals inspired their efforts to reconstruct the western occupation zones in Germany, forge them into a separate West German republic, and defend the new republic against the Soviet blockade of Berlin that began in July 1948. The reconstruction of Western Europe and the formation of the West German republic completed the postwar division of the Continent into rival spheres of influence and set the stage for the North Atlantic Treaty of 1949, an innovative military alliance that committed the United States to the defense of Western Europe for the first time in the country's history.

While Europe was their first priority, American leaders also broke new ground in other parts of the world. They threw their weight against destabilizing influences in the Middle East, solidified American dominance in the Western Hemisphere, brought defeated Japan into the Western orbit, and lent support to the anti-Communist government of South Korea. Indeed, with Western Europe securely divided by 1950, the global reach of American policy turned more decisively toward these other areas of the world, where policy makers were more inclined than ever to see destabilizing developments, such as the war in Korea, as a threat to their interests and to respond accordingly.[2]

At the same time, the national security imperatives that drove Americans from the old isolationism also forced them to build a national security state at home. They unified the armed forces, expanded the defense budget, harnessed science to military purposes, and forged new institutions, many of which, like the National Security Council and the Central Intelligence Agency, are now among the best known and most powerful organs of government.[3] The transformation altered the architectural face of the federal government, as Ernest May pointed out several years ago. The Old Executive Office Building, once large enough to house the Army, Navy, and State departments, now became the new home of the National Security Council. The State Department grew to proportions that required a building of its own, and the armed services took up residence in the newly built Pentagon, a massive five-sided labyrinth with nearly eighteen miles of corridors, more than six million square feet of office space, and as many daily inhabitants as most small towns. The Central Intelligence Agency eventually earned a new building, too, as did the Atomic Energy Commission, while dozens of other defense and

---

[2] For the most detailed survey of the global expansion of American power in the early years of the Cold War see Melvyn P. Leffler, *A Preponderance of Power: National Security, the Truman Administration, and the Cold War* (Stanford, 1992).

[3] These developments are discussed in detail in the text, but for a brief overview see Charles E. Neu, "The Rise of the National Security Bureaucracy," in *The New American State: Bureaucracies and Policies since World War II*, ed. Louis Galambos (Baltimore, 1987), 85–108.

security agencies either sprouted new facilities or squeezed older agencies from the spaces they had occupied for years.[4]

The transformation of the state also gave birth to a new class of national security managers who reproduced themselves as rapidly as American power expanded overseas. These officials, as May has pointed out, were neither elected politicians nor permanent government bureaucrats. To be sure, they included a new breed of professionals in foreign and military affairs, such as George Kennan, Charles Bohlen, and other Soviet specialists in the State Department. But most were "in-and-outers," to use Richard Neustadt's phrase, in effect, a Cold War version of the dollar-a-year men who had left the private sector for government service in the First and Second World Wars. Although some were academic experts recruited from the nation's elite universities, or scientists drawn from corporate and university laboratories, the most prominent figures were lured into government service from corporate board rooms, financial institutions, and Wall Street law firms – men such as W. Averell Harriman, Robert P. Patterson, Robert A. Lovett, John J. McCloy, and James V. Forrestal, to name but a few.[5]

These nonelected experts presided over the largest and fastest growing sector of the federal government. As May has noted, and as the subsequent chapters will elaborate, national security affairs now began to dominate the budget and control the agenda of a government that had given little time or money to such matters only a decade earlier. After shrinking in the first years of the postwar period, defense spending began to grow as a proportion of the budget while nondefense expenditures started to decline. What is more, as the institutions of national security expanded in size and stature, older departments, once the major depositories of federal power and prestige, were quickly eclipsed, as were the political agendas they represented.[6]

Nor was the transformation limited to the executive branch or even to the federal government. Congress reorganized its committee system to

---

4 Ernest R. May, "The U.S. Government, a Legacy of the Cold War," in *The End of the Cold War: Its Meaning and Implications*, ed. Michael J. Hogan (New York, 1992), 217–28; and Jay M. Shafritz, Todd J. A. Shafritz, and David B. Robertson, eds., *Dictionary of Military Science* (New York, 1989), 347–48. See also Alfred Goldberg, *The Pentagon: The First 50 Years* (Washington, 1992).

5 Ernest R. May, "Cold War and Defense," in *The Cold War and Defense*, ed. Keith Neilson and Ronald G. Haycock (New York, 1990), 10. See also the discussion of the national security managers that runs through Richard J. Barnet's *The Roots of War: The Men and Institutions Behind U.S. Foreign Policy* (New York, 1972).

6 May, "Cold War and Defense"; idem, "The American Commitment to Germany, 1949–1955," *Diplomatic History* 13 (Fall 1989): 431–60.

account for the growing demands of national security on its business and on the government's budget. Those in both houses who were associated with the isolationist policies of the prewar period found themselves under attack and often discredited. Congressional careers depended more and more on capturing a share of the defense budget for local contractors and on building a reputation as an ardent defender of the country's military interests internationally. At the same time, local groups began to devote more time and energy to currying favor in the Pentagon, and local economies were increasingly influenced, sometimes in unexpected ways, by the massive infusion of defense dollars. Local newspapers as well as the national press gave more space to international events while journalists who specialized in national security issues, once a backwater for reporters, now began to exercise real influence on both public opinion and policymaking.

III

Although we take most of these transformations for granted, it was not clear at the time that a national security state would actually take shape or how it would function. On the contrary, these issues were hotly contested by competing economic and national security agencies, by civilian officials and military leaders, and by the executive and legislative branches. In addition, state making unfolded in a political context that had ideological, cultural, and party dimensions, with conservatives, especially in the Republican party, often resisting the national security initiatives supported by the Truman administration and its congressional allies, mostly in the Democratic party.

While claiming to speak for the American people as a whole, each of the two parties represented certain interests over others. The Truman administration and its congressional supporters stood atop the New Deal coalition that had formed in the 1930s and that spoke not only for urban populations, ethnic groups, and liberal reformers but also for an alliance of international investment firms, capital-intensive industries, and much of the modern trade union movement. For the most part, these constituencies were committed to a positive role for the state in promoting the general welfare, to economic policies, including low tariffs and multilateral trade, that would open world markets to American business, and to international institutions and alliances that would order the postwar world and guard against destabilizing tendencies.

Republican conservatives, on the other hand, dominated a coalition that also included conservative Democrats, at least on some issues, and a group of older Republican insurgents who were increasingly concerned with the concentration of power and the swollen bureaucracies associated with the modern state. These conservatives were more likely to speak for local interests, including small producers and labor-intensive firms, that found it difficult to shoulder the tax burden required to sustain New Deal social programs, a large military establishment, or expensive foreign aid programs. Nor could they afford the low tariffs and liberal trading policies that would invite more efficient foreign competitors into the American market. On the contrary, if the New Deal coalition had become the agent of internationalism in the 1930s and 1940s, the conservative coalition had remained wedded to an older tradition of American nationalism and isolationism.[7]

The conservative coalition would play an important role in the postwar politics of state making, in part because of the Republican party resurgence in the elections of 1946, in part because of the collapse of left-wing liberalism under the weight of the Cold War, the anti-Communist crusade in the United States, and the government's growing preoccupation with national security rather than social justice. These developments, together with the military burden on the budget, would enable conservatives to curb the growth of social investment and to define the way key issues were approached, including issues having to do with defense spending, the development of airpower, and the purge of alleged Communists or Communist sympathizers from the American government. On all of these issues, moreover, the Republicans could count on some support from the Democratic party, and especially from conservative Democrats who were also concerned about the mounting deficits and the alleged influence of subversive forces on American life.

As this suggests, economic and party groupings would often fray at the edges, in part because each political party contained conservative and moderate factions, and neither could impose a strict party discipline. Liberal Democrats, to give examples taken from the text, would ally with conservative Republicans to defeat a presidential plan for universal military training, just as conservative Democrats would join their

---

7 On the differences between the New Deal and the conservative coalitions on domestic and foreign policies see Thomas Ferguson, "From Normalcy to New Deal: Industrial Structure, Party Competition, and American Public Policy in the Great Depression," *International Organization* 38 (Winter 1984): 41–94; and Michael J. Hogan, *The Marshall Plan: America, Britain, and the Reconstruction of Western Europe, 1947–1952* (New York, 1987), 1–25. For more on the party structure and the role played by an older generation of progressives, particularly in the Republican party, see also David A. Horowitz, *Beyond Left & Right: Insurgency and the Establishment* (Urbana and Chicago, 1997).

Republican counterparts in dealing with the loyalty issue. What is more, individual parties or party factions were sometimes pulled in different directions by competing political values, forcing them to establish priorities and live with the inconsistencies that sometimes resulted. Conservative Republicans, to cite another example, were usually more concerned with Communist subversion than with Soviet aggression, and were therefore less concerned with the political freedoms imperilled by McCarthyism than with the economic freedoms endangered by defense spending. Something similar can be said of their position on the control of atomic energy, in which case they were less inclined to trust liberal planners in the Democratic party than military leaders in the Pentagon, and this despite their fear of militarism and their opposition to big government.

Similar divisions and inconsistencies can also be found in particular individuals, including President Harry S. Truman, who was often pulled in different directions by the growth of the national security state. No one was more responsible for this important development than Truman, and yet no one was more convinced that national security needs, however urgent, could wreck the budget, militarize society, and undermine the welfare state that had grown out of the New Deal. Much the same was true of President Dwight D. Eisenhower, who succeeded Truman in 1953. What is more, both men surrounded themselves with budget balancers who shared their concerns, so that divisions evident in their own thinking, or in the party system generally, were also evident in their administrations, which often looked like a battleground between economizers, on the one hand, and national security managers, on the other.

As the discussion thus far indicates, political divisions of the kind noted above usually involved more than a struggle for power between different individuals, institutions, or political parties. Historians of the national security state must also look for agency in other directions, especially in the interplay of competing ideas and ways of thinking. Indeed, political divisions were usually rooted in a discourse over the nature of the American way, to borrow a phrase from the documents, which was essentially a clash between the new ideology of national security and the values rooted in an older political culture. By summarizing these two ways of thinking we can frame the national security discourse of the early Cold War and establish the ideological and cultural context for the bureaucratic, institutional, and political battles that are addressed in subsequent chapters.

On one side of the national security discourse stood the critics of American policy, mostly conservatives in the Republican party and their allies in the press. Their thinking drew on an American cultural narrative, to

borrow a concept from cultural studies, with a discursive tradition that
stretched from the republican ideology of the Founding Fathers through
the antiwar and antigovernment campaigns of the recent period. The
story of American greatness to which they subscribed was a story of
freedom-loving men and women who had fled the oppression of the Old
World, rebelled against unjust taxes and the abuse of political and military authorities, and founded a new republic with a constitution that
constrained the state, divided authority in a balanced system of representation, and guaranteed civilian over military leadership. These pro-
tections and guarantees had then been combined with a calculated isolationism to produce a nation of virtuous and self-reliant citizens and a
degree of political freedom and economic progress unmatched in human
history.

As conservatives saw it, the welfare state that had emerged with the
New Deal and the warfare state that was taking shape in the postwar
period imperilled the values and traditions that had contributed to this
narrative of national greatness. More likely to be assumed than fully
defined, these values and traditions included a strong antipathy toward
entangling alliances, a large peacetime military establishment, and the
centralization of authority in the national government, especially in its
military arm. These were European rather than American practices, or
so the critics claimed, and they had the potential to waste the nation's resources, create a powerful military caste, and erode the rights of Congress
and the prerogatives of the president. To the critics, in other words, the
rise of the national security state necessarily entailed economic and political adaptations that could undermine the very traditions and institutions
that had made America great. These institutions included the Constitution itself, which seemed to be endangered by the creation of a powerful
military establishment, by the new role that military leaders played in
the civilian side of government, and by the centralization of government
authority at the expense of a balanced system of representation in which
authority was more widely dispersed and decentralized.[8]

Nor were these the only threats to traditional political culture that
conservative critics could discern. In their view, the growth of a powerful

---

[8] The themes outlined in this and the next two paragraphs are developed in the chapters that
follow, but for a good summary of most of them see Senator Robert A. Taft, address to the
Rhode Island Republican Club, 15 January 1948, Robert A. Taft Papers (Library of Congress,
Washington, DC), Legislative File, box 722, folder: National Defense (Speech), 1948; and
Taft, address to the Lincoln Club, Denver, Colorado, 14 February 1948, ibid., box 61b,
folder: Foreign Policy, 1948.

national security state could also weaken other institutions that played a central role as counterweights to federal authority, as engines of economic growth, and as the principle means for educating the nation's youth in the values and habits of democratic politics. Military training and conscription, to give one example, would supposedly undercut the home, the family, and the school, replacing the democratic virtues they taught with a mindless military mentality and a habit of regimentation that were decidedly un-American. These and related concerns had been evident in the antidraft movements that marked earlier periods of American history, and they were evident as well in the debates over military research and development, which dated to the First World War, at least. If carried too far, or so the critics argued, military research would monopolize the scientific manpower on which industry depended. It would corral corporate and university laboratories for military purposes, bring these units into an institutional complex dominated by the Pentagon, and erode their standing as independent sources of authority.

Conservatives made a similar case when it came to defense spending, where they again drew on a discursive tradition that spanned most of American history. By increasing the size of the federal establishment and by concentrating more power in the executive branch, particularly in its military arm, defense spending aroused in conservative critics a traditional distrust of big government, centralized authority, and military rule. It also prompted a vigorous defense of what they viewed as the country's historic commitment to fiscal responsibility and a balanced budget. To the conservative mind, budget deficits would encourage inflation, corrupt the currency, or lead to higher taxes and economic controls that expanded the public sphere at the expense of the private, denied the American people the fruits of their labor, and eroded their capacity for hard work and self-help. In this sense, budget deficits, high taxes, and government controls would not only "militarize our economy," they would also threaten the "survival of our liberties." They would undermine the independence of the virtuous citizen, celebrated in the republican ideology of the Founders, and destroy the habits of perseverance, self-discipline, and initiative on which both economic and political freedom depended.[9]

---

9 In addition to the sources cited in the previous note, and throughout the chapters that follow, see the remarks quoted from congressional leaders in *Congressional Record, 1948*, 94:5399; and in Warner R. Schilling, "The Politics of National Defense: Fiscal 1950," in Schilling, Paul Y. Hammond, and Glenn H. Snyder, *Strategy, Politics, and Defense Budgets* (New York, 1962), 101.

On the other side of the national security discourse stood the administration and its supporters in Congress and in the press. They, too, borrowed from a cultural narrative that celebrated American exceptionalism and American destiny, and from a discursive tradition that dated to the era of manifest destiny in the early years of the nineteenth century. At the same time, however, they were more likely than the conservatives to balance a defense of tradition against appeals to a new ideology of national security that took shape in the period between the start of World War II and the end of the Korean War. This ideology supposedly accommodated the stern realities of international politics and thus made room for the important postwar responsibilities that fell to the United States. Its central components, which can be gleaned from four important documents, will be summarized now to avoid unnecessary repetition later.

The first was the famous long telegram of February 1946, an eight thousand-word missive that George Kennan despatched to the State Department from his post as the American chargé d'affaires in Moscow. The document is treated here together with Kennan's elaboration of its main points in "The Sources of Soviet Conduct," an article he published under the pseudonym "X" in the July 1947 issue of *Foreign Affairs*.[10] Kennan was one of the State Department's most experienced specialists in Soviet history and foreign policy, with roughly two decades in the diplomatic corp to his credit when the long telegram catapulted him to a position of prominence both in the State Department and in the history books. A deeply intellectual man with a scholar's demeanor and a brooding disposition, Kennan viewed the Soviet regime as brutally oppressive at home, ruthlessly aggressive abroad, and a threat that had to be contained. His achievement, however, was not so much in framing the policy of containment as in giving intelligent expression to a policy that was already unfolding. His views, in other words, distilled American thinking in 1946 and 1947, so much so that one of his mentors, Secretary of the Navy James V. Forrestal, reproduced hundreds of copies of the long telegram for distribution throughout the administration and the press.[11]

So far as our story is concerned, Kennan's thinking was less important for what it said about Soviet diplomacy, which other historians have

---

[10] Kennan to the Secretary of State, 22 February 1946, U.S. Department of State, *Foreign Relations of the United States, 1946* (Washington, 1969) 6:696–709 (hereafter *FRUS*); and X [Kennan], "The Sources of Soviet Conduct," *Foreign Affairs* 25 (July 1947): 566–82.

[11] On Forrestal and reaction to the long telegram in Washington see Leffler, *A Preponderance of Power*, 108–9.

elaborated in great detail, than for what it said about American policy and the ideology behind it. Much the same was true of the famous Clifford–Elsey report commissioned by President Truman less than six months after Kennan's long telegram.[12] Dark haired and handsome, a graduate of Princeton and Harvard, George Elsey was a presidential aide and legislative draftsman whose enormous skills as a speechwriter belied his youth and matched in every way the honeyed voice of his principal partner in the famous report of 1946. Captain Clark Clifford was the president's naval aide. A tall and dashing young man, not yet forty years old when he joined the president's staff, Clifford was a lawyer by training and a man of considerable charm, Hollywood good looks, and enough energy, intelligence, and personal finesse to make himself an indispensable member of the White House staff.

In July 1946, President Truman asked Clifford and Elsey to prepare a report on Soviet diplomacy and Soviet-American relations. The resulting document, handed to Truman the following September, ran to more than one hundred thousand words, most of them devoted to a lengthy analysis of the dangers raised by the Soviet Union's military buildup, its alliances with local Communist parties in other countries, and its policy of ruthless aggrandizement in Europe, the eastern Mediterranean, and the Middle East. Although Truman considered the report to be explosive and ordered it locked up, the document did little more than echo what Kennan had said in the long telegram. Indeed, the authors had simply written a report that summarized the thinking of key policymakers, including the thinking of George Kennan, who had reviewed the final draft and pronounced it "excellent."[13]

The third text was President Truman's celebrated speech to Congress in March 1947, announcing what came to be known as the Truman Doctrine. In the background was a Soviet demand for joint control with Turkey of the Black Sea Straits and a British decision to withdraw financial support for the anti-Communist regime in Greece, which was then under pressure from a group of left-wing guerrillas. Communist success in either case would give the Soviets an opening to the eastern

---

[12] The report, "American Relations with the Soviet Union: A Report to the President by the Special Council to the President, September 1946," is printed as Appendix A in Arthur Krock, *Memoirs: Sixty Years on the Firing Line* (New York, 1968), 421–82.

[13] David McCullough, *Truman* (New York, 1992), 543–55. In addition to the source cited in the previous note, see Robert J. Donovan, *Conflict and Crisis: The Presidency of Harry S. Truman, 1945–48* (New York, 1977), 221–22; and Clifford to Truman, September 1946, in Krock, *Memoirs*, 419. For a detailed analysis of the Clifford–Elsey report see Leffler, *Preponderance of Power*, 130–38.

Mediterranean and from there to Western Europe and the Middle East. To contain this danger, Truman asked Congress to fund a massive American program of aid to Greece and Turkey, and in the process outlined some of the major features of the national security ideology delineated below.[14]

The last of the four documents was NSC-68, produced in 1950 by a subcommittee of the National Security Council under the direction of Paul H. Nitze. One of many tough-minded Wall Street investment bankers in the Truman administration, Nitze was then in charge of the State Department's Policy Planning Staff, where he and his colleagues began working on NSC-68 after the Soviets had tested their first atomic device and the Communists had come to power in China. These developments had cast a pall over Washington, not only because they threatened to destabilize the global balance of power but also because they had thrown the United States on the defensive in its struggle with the Soviet Union. Anxious to recapture the initiative and shore up the country's faltering position, Nitze and his collaborators drafted a document that portrayed the Soviet Union in the most aggressive light possible and called, among other things, for a massive American rearmament. Perhaps more than any other document of the period, NSC-68 can claim to be the bible of American national security policy and the fullest statement to that point of the new ideology that guided American leaders.[15]

Unlike the pronouncements of conservative critics, which articulated a cluster of symbols, customs, and assumptions that were widely shared but rarely defined, these four documents and others cited in the text encoded a set of basic convictions in a fashion that was coherent enough to approximate a formal ideology. One of these was the conviction that a new era of total war had dawned on the United States. In total war, the battle was not confined to the front lines but extended to the home front as well, as did the awesome destruction that modern weapons could inflict not only on military combatants but also on industry, urban centers, and civilian populations. Modern war was total war in this sense and in the sense that modern armies depended on the output of citizen soldiers in farms and factories behind the battle line. In total war all of the nation's resources and all of its energy and talent had to be

---

[14] Truman, "Special Message to Congress on Greece and Turkey: The Truman Doctrine," 12 March 1947, _Public Papers of the Presidents of the United States: Harry S. Truman, 1947_ (Washington, 1963), 176–80 (hereafter _Public Papers, Truman_).

[15] For NSC-68 see "United States Objectives and Programs for National Security," 14 April 1950, _FRUS, 1950_ (Washington, 1977), 1:234–92.

mobilized on behalf of the war effort, thereby obliterating the old distinction between civilian and military, between citizen and soldier, between the home front and the front line. When American leaders talked about total war they did so in these terms and also in terms that recognized that modern weapons could bring massive destruction from great distances with barely a moment's notice. In the new age, American leaders would no longer have the time to debate the issue of war or peace or to prepare at a slow pace.[16]

In short, the age of total war seemed to require a degree of military preparedness that was out of step with traditional convictions and old habits, such as the traditional fear of a large standing army that had encouraged rapid demobilization after previous conflicts. The emphasis on military preparedness was another component of the national security ideology, as was the conviction that the United States was now locked in a long-term struggle for survival with the Soviet Union. Not only was it a long-term struggle, which therefore required a permanent program of military preparedness, but also a dangerous struggle against a ruthless enemy whose own level of readiness made American preparedness a matter of urgent concern. According to the Clifford–Elsey report, it was only realistic to "assume that the U.S.S.R. might fight at any time." The United States had to be prepared for this "showdown of force," at least as prepared as the Soviet Union, which was then maintaining its army and air force in a higher degree of readiness and in numbers greater than the American military could muster in places like Germany, Austria, and Korea.[17]

The lack of readiness had serious political and military implications that were clearly articulated in the national security ideology. It would encourage Soviet aggression and undermine the negotiating position of American diplomats, not least because Soviet leaders rarely responded to the give-and-take of conventional diplomacy. According to Kennan, while American policymakers were governed by "Anglo-Saxon traditions of compromise," Soviet leaders were driven by "fanaticism," a "messianic" ideology, and implacable hostility toward the capitalist countries of the world. Their belief in the "innate antagonism" between Russia and the West and their cynicism about the prospects for "happy coexistence" justified "the iron discipline" they imposed on Soviet politics, their "absolute power" and dictatorial policies, and their opposition to serious negotiation with the United States. The Soviets, it was true,

---

[16] Some of the implications of total war are noted in NSC-68 and in the Clifford–Elsey report, while others are spelled out in various documents discussed in subsequent chapters.

[17] Krock, *Memoirs*, 476, 425. See also ibid., 424, 470.

might negotiate agreements whenever they found it expedient to do so, but they were basically "duplicitous" and could not be trusted to honor their commitments. On the contrary, they were fundamentally unresponsive to "normal logic" and incapable of pursuing "a community of aims" with the Western powers.[18]

It followed from this view that negotiations were pointless, if not dangerous, and that only force would produce results in Moscow. Kennan made this point in the X article when he downplayed the prospects for a negotiated settlement and urged instead the "adroit and vigilant application of counter-force at a series of constantly shifting geographical and political points, corresponding to the shifts and manoeuvre of Soviet policy."[19] The Clifford–Elsey report went further. "The language of military power is the only language which [the] disciples of power politics understand," the report said of the Soviets. "The mere fact of preparedness" might be enough to deter Soviet aggression, but if deterrence failed the United States had to be prepared to wage "total" war, including the use of atomic and biological weapons.[20]

In the national security ideology, then, the nature of the Soviet regime put a premium on military preparedness, the immediacy of the Soviet threat made preparedness a matter of urgency, the long-term nature of that threat required a permanent program of preparedness, and the danger of total war dictated a comprehensive program that integrated civilian and military resources and obliterated the line between citizen and soldier, peace and war. Closely linked to these notions was another theme in the new ideology of national security, namely the conviction that peace and freedom were each indivisible. This conviction seemed to leave the American people with little choice but to defend their own security and their own liberty by defending peace and freedom everywhere. Put in reverse, it meant that a threat to peace anywhere in the world also posed a threat to American security, and that a loss of freedom anywhere increased the risk to freedom in the United States. "The United States," according to the Clifford–Elsey report, "should support and assist all democratic countries which are in any way menaced or endangered by the U.S.S.R.," since a failure to do so would only encourage further Soviet aggression and make it more difficult and more expensive to check that aggression later.[21]

[18] Kennan, "Sources of Soviet Conduct," 568, 571–75, 580, 582.
[19] Ibid., 576.
[20] Krock, *Memoirs*, 477–78.
[21] Ibid., 479.

This line of thinking added up to a domino theory of peace and freedom captured best in Truman's appeal for aid to Greece and Turkey. The loss of Greece to "an armed minority," he warned Congress, would be "disastrous" not only for Greece "but for the world." It would have disastrous effects upon Turkey, sow "confusion and disorder" across the "entire Middle East," and discourage the people of Europe who were "struggling against great difficulties to maintain their freedoms and their independence." To avoid such a calamity, the United States had to "take immediate and resolute action" on behalf of "free peoples" everywhere, who "look to us for support in maintaining their freedoms."[22]

Truman's last remark underscored still another theme in the national security ideology, specifically the belief that leadership of the free world was a sacred mission thrust upon the American people by divine Providence and the laws of both history and nature. This theme, which drew on the long history of American expansionism, was evident in Truman's famous speech of 12 March 1947, when he told his audience that "great responsibilities have been placed upon us by the swift movement of events" and emphasized the country's mission as the global defender of democracy.[23] The same theme also appeared in the Clifford–Elsey report, in NSC-68, and in "The Sources of Soviet Conduct." In defense of its recommendations, for example, NSC-68 cited America's historic mission to spread the blessings of liberty on a global scale.[24] And in urging the American people to confront the "implacable challenge" of communism, Kennan told his readers that "Providence" had "made their entire security as a nation dependent on their pulling themselves together and accepting the responsibilities of moral and political leadership that history plainly intended them to bear."[25]

The sense of destiny and mission that suffused these and other documents usually rested on an appeal to authority that was another hallmark of the national security ideology. The authority cited in the Truman Doctrine was the United Nations charter, which the president and others read as a recapitulation of traditional American principles, such as the right of self-determination. Kennan invoked the authority of Providence in the X article, while the authors of NSC-68 wrapped their case in the authority of the Constitution, the Bill of Rights, and the Declaration of Independence. Historical authority not only lent legitimacy to the

---

[22] Truman, "Special Message to Congress," *Public Papers, Truman*, 179, 180.
[23] Ibid., 180.
[24] *FRUS, 1950* 1:238.
[25] Kennan, "Sources of Soviet Conduct," 582.

American mission, it also gave evidence of the calamities that lay ahead if the American people turned their backs on destiny. Not surprisingly, the most common evidence came from the interwar period, when American disarmament and isolationism had supposedly encouraged aggression and set the stage for World War II. The lesson was clear. "If we falter in our leadership," as Truman summed it up in his speech of March 1947, "we may endanger the peace of the world – and we shall surely endanger the welfare of this Nation."[26]

Truman's warning highlighted yet another theme in the national security ideology and in the discursive tradition from which it borrowed – the conviction that the American people had to muster the strength of character, the national will, and the moral fiber, to lead the free world and bear the burdens that leadership entailed. According to Kennan, the Soviet-American struggle was an exercise in moral rejuvenation, an opportunity to recapture the civic virtue and national discipline that had marked earlier periods of American history. It was "a test of national quality," he wrote in the X article, and of "the over-all worth of the United States as a nation among nations." To succeed, the United States only had to "measure up to its own best traditions and prove itself worthy of preservation as a great nation." It had to "create the impression of a country which knows what it wants, which is coping successfully with the problems of its internal life and with the responsibilities of a World Power, and which has a spiritual vitality capable of holding its own among the major ideological currents of the time."[27]

According to the Clifford–Elsey report and the Truman Doctrine, the American people had to be diligent in "helping free and independent nations to maintain their free institutions." They had to take "resolute action" to keep "hope alive," and they had to be "generous."[28] As these documents reveal, and as subsequent chapters will confirm, being generous meant enduring hardships and making sacrifices. The American people might have to transfer a portion of their national wealth to beleaguered governments in Greece, Turkey, or Western Europe. They might have to accept lower living standards than would otherwise be the case, pay higher taxes, live with economic controls, and borrow against the future. As NSC-68 implied, they might even have to compromise some of the blessings of their own liberty, if not liberty itself, in the best interest

---

[26] Truman, "Special Message to Congress," 180. See also ibid., 179; Kennan, "Sources of Soviet Conduct," 582; and *FRUS, 1950* 1:238.

[27] Kennan, "Sources of Soviet Conduct," 581–82.

[28] Truman, "Special Message to Congress," 179–80; and Krock, *Memoirs*, 479.

of peace and freedom worldwide. "There are risks in making ourselves strong," said NSC-68. "A large measure of sacrifice and discipline will be demanded of the American people," who would be "asked to give up some of the benefits which they have come to associate with their freedoms."[29]

As the discussion thus far suggests, the national security ideology framed the Cold War discourse in a system of symbolic representation that defined America's national identity by reference to the un-American "other," usually the Soviet Union, Nazi Germany, or some other totalitarian power. The documents under review typically described the Soviet way explicitly while delineating the American way by implication. The Soviets were hostile and active, usually according to a plan preordained in Communist ideology, while the Americans were friendly, reactive, and usually reluctant. The Soviet Union was animated, much like a "Church," by a "doctrinaire 'rightness'" and "the over brooding presence of 'the word,'" while the United States behaved like a pragmatic nation state. The Soviets rejected "every single ethical value in their methods and tactics," while the Americans negotiated in good faith. The Soviets "recognized no restrictions, either of God or man," while American leaders kept their promises and honored their agreements. The Soviets were equated with aggression and domination, while the Americans were equated with peace and cooperation. The Soviet system was associated with a controlled economy, minority rule, and the oppression of basic liberties, while the American system was associated with free markets, majority rule, and democratic politics. The Soviet way was marked by "forced labor," economic deprivation, and misery, while the American way was characterized by free labor, economic growth, and prosperity. Soviet politics were abnormal, secretive, and driven by the "doctrines and actions of a small ruling clique," while American politics were normal, open, and responsive to the rule of public opinion. The Soviet system was unnatural and ungodly, while the American system dovetailed with natural law and divine Providence.[30]

The logic of this binary system made it difficult for critics to dissent from prevailing policies. On the contrary, as David Campbell has argued, the strategy of otherness drew the boundaries of national identity in a

---

[29] *FRUS, 1950* 1:265.

[30] The quoted phrases are taken largely from Kennan, "Sources of Soviet Conduct," 566–82, but also from Kennan to the Secretary of State, 22 February 1946, *FRUS, 1946* 6:696–709; and Krock, *Memoirs*, 421–82. A similar system of binary representation is also apparent throughout NSC-68.

way that excluded domestic dissent, as well as the Soviet other, and did so by linking the two together.[31] In the Truman Doctrine, for example, the president had declared that people "must choose between alternative ways of life," in effect, the American way and the Soviet way, and this declaration had implied that any criticism of American policy amounted to an act of disloyalty.[32] Not surprisingly, the burden of this implication hung like a millstone around the necks of such left-wing critics as Henry Wallace, who was accused of being soft on communism, and of such conservative critics as Republican Senator Robert A. Taft of Ohio, who was denounced as an irresponsible isolationist. But it did not silence the dissenting voices entirely, particularly the voices of conservative critics who challenged the new direction in American policy and spelled out its most serious implications.

The discourse between the conservative defenders of an older political culture and the national security managers was itself framed in a binary system of symbolic representation. Both sides shared a similar vocabulary and set of symbols, both associated their critics with an un-American other, and both spoke in a language of ideological opposites, such as democracy or totalitarianism, freedom or tyranny, centralization or decentralization, civil or military, free-market capitalism or controlled economy, loyalty or disloyalty, isolationism or internationalism. Both sides understood the need to sacrifice on behalf of the nation's security, but disagreed on how the burden of sacrifice should be distributed. Both summed up the consequences of bad policy in the image of the garrison state, which became the dominant metaphor in the national security discourse. Both used this metaphor to describe a society dominated by military institutions, a military economy, and a military mentality, and both tried to frame a public policy that would protect the American way against the dangers of regimentation.

Captured in the binary oppositions to which both sides resorted was a fundamental contest over the nation's political identity and postwar purpose. For those who defended the old political culture, usually conservatives, the uniqueness of America, its democratic traditions and capitalist economy, derived in part from its historic separateness. If the United States wanted to retain its democratic identity, they said, it could not become enmeshed in foreign intrigue, emulate old world imperialisms and militarisms, or play the game of power politics, all of which would

[31] David Campbell, *Writing Security: United States Foreign Policy and the Politics of Identity* (Minneapolis, 1992), 70–1.
[32] Truman, "Special Message to Congress," 176–80.

corrupt the country's basic institutions and values. Those who spoke for the national security ideology saw things differently. In a world where peace and freedom were indivisible, they said, the United States had no choice but to assume the new role that history had thrust upon it – that of a great military power and defender of democracy globally. Doing so, moreover, would not repudiate the country's destiny but fulfill it, would not corrupt the nation's institutions but defend them, would not compromise liberty but spread its blessings to those threatened by Soviet aggression. While conservative critics invoked the tradition of isolationism and wanted the country to lead by splendid example, national security managers invoked the tradition of manifest destiny and wanted the country to be a missionary of freedom on a global scale.

Yet, despite these differences, as subsequent chapters will show, the line between the administration and its critics was not as hard and fast as might appear to be the case at first glance. More like a bridgeable wall than an unconquerable barrier, it did not prevent the president and many of his advisers from seeking to reconcile their policies with the concerns of their critics. On the contrary, they often spoke in the same political idiom as their opponents, relied on the same historical authorities to legitimize their policies, and inherited the same political traditions, which they valued as well and which led them whenever possible to hammer out the differences that divided the two sides. In this sense, traditional political culture worked like a powerful sluice gate to regulate what American leaders could do, damming the current of public policy in some directions while opening channels that would harmonize the national security state with older ways of thinking.

When it came to military manpower, for example, one of the issues was whether universal military training (UMT) amounted to a dangerous and wrongheaded departure from the nation's traditional antipathy toward a large, standing army, as critics were inclined to argue, or whether it squared with both practical necessity and the tradition of the citizen soldier, as the administration liked to believe. There were similar debates over the degree to which authority should be centralized in the new institutions of national security. Conservatives warned that too much centralization would compromise presidential and congressional prerogatives and pose a threat to the principle of civilian supremacy, while the administration claimed that a certain degree of centralization would guarantee efficiency and guard against the dangers of a military dictatorship. These arguments unfolded in battles over how to unify the armed forces, organize the Department of Defense, control atomic energy, and bring science into a national-security partnership with government, all of which are taken up in the text. In most cases the debate paralleled the struggle over UMT, and in most cases the outcome balanced centralizing and decentralizing tendencies, tradition and necessity, in a way that enhanced the authority of the military but stopped short of the garrison state.

A similar story, as we will see, unfolded in the great budget debates of the early Cold War. In these debates the traditional commitment to a balanced budget collided with the burgeoning price of national security, including expensive foreign assistance programs and the more imposing cost of a large military establishment. The debates indicated how difficult it was to disentangle the defense budget from ongoing arguments over military strategy and unification, from mounting fears of a military dictatorship, and from other fiscal and economic issues, such as the cost of social programs, the fear of inflation, and the desire to reduce wartime taxes. Although both sides were more likely in this area than in others to emphasize the theme of national will and to stress the need for sacrifice, the outcome was usually a politically negotiated compromise similar to those worked out in the debates over military manpower and institution-building. The administration was able to increase the national security budget whenever it seemed essential to do so, the conservatives were able to reduce taxes and curb social spending, but the trade-offs were seldom sufficient to balance the budget or reduce the national debt.

The traditional commitment to a balanced budget and to such older values as antistatism, antimilitarism, and isolationism also had important implications in the realm of grand strategy. They influenced the thinking of conservatives in the Great Debate that began in 1950 and in the Truman–MacArthur controversy of 1951, particularly their support for a hemispheric system of defense that would limit the size and cost of the military establishment. Nor do these two episodes tell the whole story. The same values and traditions also help to explain congressional support for a vigorous expansion of the Air Force at the expense of the Army and the Navy. For Republican conservatives, in particular, such a course, like a hemispheric system of defense, would help to curb defense expenditures, facilitate tax cuts, and limit both the size of the state and the scope of the country's commitments abroad.

Although conservative critics would not prevail in the Great Debate, the traditional values they defended would lead to a system of collective security based on the principle of specialization and on a capital-intensive strategy of deterrence. Under this system, the United States would contribute foreign aid and high-technology weaponry, especially air atomic power, while allied governments would provide much of the military manpower. This strategy would begin to emerge in the early years of the Truman administration, give way temporarily during the Korean War, and then reemerge as the so-called New Look in the 1950s. Indeed, the Eisenhower administration, as the debates over the New Look point out, would wrestle with the same problems of institution-building and budget-making as its predecessor, reach some of the same compromises, and thus consolidate a pattern of state making that had been taking shape since the end of World War II.

IV

At issue in all of these debates was the central question of state making in the first decade of the postwar period: How could the United States wage a long-term battle with the Soviet Union without sacrificing the freedoms it sought to defend? This was the question that Hanson Baldwin asked in 1947, and that is taken up in the following chapters. These chapters focus on civil–military relations and on the political, bureaucratic, and economic battles that influenced the way American state makers managed the defense budget, organized the modern-day military establishment, and tackled the other problems noted above. Always in the background, however, were the cultural and ideological forces sketched in this chapter. These, too, would influence the process of state making and the compromises that often emerged.

All but two of the substantive chapters deal with this process as it unfolded during the Truman administration. They treat Truman as the principle architect of the national security state, and they describe his efforts to strike a workable balance between the old political culture and the new ideology of national security, between the welfare state and the warfare state. Of the two exceptions, one examines the first years of the Eisenhower administration in an effort to show how the new Republican president built on a foundation laid by his predecessor. The other looks beyond the state makers in Washington to the public sphere as a whole, and especially to the way ordinary citizens reacted to the process of state making and to the questions of national identity and postwar purpose that it raised. This chapter supplements the review of media opinion that runs throughout the book, and thus provides a more rounded view of the subject than would be possible through a strictly state-centered analysis.

State making in the early Cold War would never produce an outcome as good as Truman and many liberals had hoped, nor as bad as Taft and most conservatives had feared. Liberals had assumed that national security would add legitimacy to their notions of an activist state and justify a more aggressive role for the government in promoting the general welfare, as well as the common defense. This was not to be the case, however, at least not in the 1950s, when the economic burden of defense put serious limits on the expansion of social-welfare programs and gave conservatives a powerful weapon they could use to halt the forward march of the New Deal. But if the results in this sense would fall short of liberal dreams, neither would they amount to the nightmare that most conservatives had in mind. Although government would grow larger, taxes would go up, and budget deficits would become a matter of routine, none of these and other transformations would add up to the crushing regime symbolized in the metaphor of the garrison state. The outcome instead would be an American national security state that was shaped as much by the country's democratic political culture as it was by the perceived military imperatives of the Cold War. The making of the new state would begin with the National Security Act of 1947, and it is to this part of our story that we now turn.

2

Magna Charta

The National Security Act and the Specter
of the Garrison State

Looking back from a later day it is tempting to conclude that the great American military behemoth lurched without a limp from World War II into the postwar period, though nothing could be further from the truth. Although the Truman administration never retreated to the sleepy peacetime military establishment of the interwar era, it did authorize a substantial demobilization of the armed forces before reassembling them in an organization more appropriate to the long period of armed truce that lay ahead. More time and thought went into this process than is commonly conceded, and the process itself was marked by intense bureaucratic struggles, by competition between the executive and legislative branches, and by different designs for an organizational framework that would meet political as well as military requirements.

In the background, too, was the new ideology of national security that American leaders brought to bear on the task of state making. Usually reduced to the notion of anticommunism or to the doctrine of containment, the new ideology also envisioned a prominent role for the United States in world affairs and included the conviction that national security in an age of total war required some elaboration of the state's authority to organize civilian and military resources behind a permanent program of peacetime military preparedness. As this chapter will show, the national security ideology eventually became the basis for a plan of action in the early postwar period, but not before the Truman administration had also accounted for an older vision of American democracy and an older system of beliefs, such as antistatism and antimilitarism, that had long been rooted in the country's traditional political culture.

In effect, different strategies of state making competed in American thinking and even, at times, in the thinking of individual policy makers. One strategy would concentrate authority in a strong executive or in a series of administrative czars who would manage military affairs on an efficient basis. Those who articulated this strategy drew on a discursive tradition, evident in the recent history of liberal reform, that celebrated the economic efficiencies and political benefits to be gained through centralized direction and expert leadership. The second strategy invoked a different tradition, one that dated from the birth of the nation and one that would preserve the essentials of a liberal-republicanism in which power was divided and controlled through a system of institutional checks and balances. The competition between these two approaches often produced a compromise – essentially a third strategy – that would balance centralizing and decentralizing tendencies in a corporative pattern of decision making. The national security discourse amounted in part to a dialogue between these different visions of the American state. In this sense, it carried forward a debate that had stretched from the founding of the republic through the New Deal of the 1930s, with all sides relying on some of the same rhetorical images, notably the metaphor of the garrison state, to dramatize the danger of untoward transformations and the need to harmonize new developments with old traditions.

As this suggests, those involved in the organizational struggle were concerned about more than the country's chances for success in the battle against communism. At issue were contested questions about America's democratic identity and national purpose, and specifically about its role in world affairs and the deleterious effects that national security policies might have on established institutions, revered traditions, and the American way of life at home. Indeed, the politics of state making were so boisterous precisely because concerns over the fate of the American way were so great. Some wondered if the United States could recast itself as a warrior state without losing its democratic identity, while others believed that a remodeling of sorts was the key to the survival of democracy worldwide. Whatever their differences, the goal on all sides was to deter the Soviets without turning the country into a garrison state, and the search for that goal began with the National Security Act of 1947 – which might be called, with some exaggeration, the Magna Charta of the national security state.

II

The drive for a postwar national security establishment drew its inspiration from several sources. One was the bitter Army–Navy battles over airpower during World War II, which drove home the need for a postwar organization that could discipline and unify the services. Another was Japan's surprise attack on Pearl Harbor, which made it plain to most Americans that disunity and unpreparedness invited aggression and disaster. Still another was the rapid development of strategic airpower, atomic weapons, and modern missiles, all of which accentuated the danger of sudden attack and the need for constant preparedness. Then, too, an emphasis on preparedness seemed especially compelling at a time when the United States could no longer depend on allies to carry the initial burden of a future war. It was the "top dog" now, according to General Carl Spaatz of the Army Air Forces. It was the "No. 1 target" of potential aggressors, and it had to "maintain in constant readiness such military strength" as would deter aggression and command respect for its policies.[1]

These remarks were cast against a background that included the collapse of wartime arrangements for national security planning and decision making. During the war, interdepartmental discussions had been coordinated at the staff level through the State–War–Navy Coordinating Committee and at the policy level through regular meetings of the three secretaries. Agencies like the War Production Board and the Army–Navy Munitions Board worked, often in great friction, to mobilize economic resources for the war effort, while the Joint Chiefs of Staff, organized to expedite Anglo-American war planning, facilitated efforts by the War and Navy departments to collaborate at the strategic level. In addition, Admiral William D. Leahy, the old salt with a pince-nez who presided over the Joint Chiefs, acted as the president's military chief of staff and served in that capacity as a bridge between the armed forces and the White House. Haphazard and jerry-rigged, more informal than institutional, held together by key personalities rather than by law, these wartime arrangements started to break down as soon as the war ended and top policy makers began returning to civilian life.[2]

With nothing to take the place of wartime arrangements, American officials found it increasingly difficult to sort through policy options, harmonize their differences, and plan for the postwar world. The War and Navy departments, to give a good example, found it difficult to meet a presidential request for a comprehensive plan on the overall size and composition of the postwar military establishment, in large part because their planning kept faltering on the overlapping roles and missions of the armed forces in such areas as antisubmarine warfare, over-water

---

[1] U.S. Congress, Senate, *Hearings on S. 84, A Bill to Provide for a Department of Armed Forces, and Hearings on S. 1482, A Bill to Establish a Department of Military Security* (Washington, 1945), 341, 14 (hereafter *Hearings on S. 84 and S. 1482*). See also ibid., 10, 14, 16, 49, 54, 55, 342.

[2] John Morton Blum, *V Was for Victory: Politics and American Culture during World War II* (New York, 1976), 117–46; Townsend Hoopes and Douglas Brinkley, *Driven Patriot: The Life and Times of James Forrestal* (New York, 1992), 320.

reconnaissance, and the protection of shipping. Clearly, the country needed a more effective mechanism for reconciling such disputes, bringing the armed services together in a coherent unit, and responding to the Soviet threat that began to emerge as the wartime alliance gave way to confrontation over the future of Germany and the fate of Eastern Europe.[3] In light of the Soviet challenge, argued Secretary of War Robert P. Patterson, it was no longer possible to base the "nation's security establishment . . . on one organization in peace and another in war."[4]

As Patterson's remark pointed out, national security needs had started to dissolve the usual distinction between war and peace in the minds of American policy makers. Modern war, it was said, had become "total war" and total war necessarily engaged the whole of the nation's resources, civil and military alike, just as modern weapons brought the battle home to citizen soldiers behind the lines.[5] "Wars are no longer fought solely by the armed forces," explained Fleet Admiral Ernest J. King. "Directly or indirectly, the whole citizenry and the entire resources of the nation go to war."[6] This kind of thinking was characteristic of the national security ideology, as was the conviction that total war required a total system of military preparedness, what Secretary of the Navy James V. Forrestal called a "comprehensive and dynamic program" to which all citizens would contribute, whatever the sacrifices involved. Such a program had to involve every agency of government and reach out from the state to the great army of industrial workers and to the nation's farms and factories, its scientific and technological resources, its industrial and university laboratories.[7]

The question was whether the organizational framework appropriate to such a program was also appropriate to the way Americans saw themselves, or whether it would undermine their democratic traditions, subvert their Constitution, and transform their country into a modern-day Sparta. At issue was an old concern over the role of the state in American society. During the New Deal, government leaders had come to accept a positive role for the state, not only in the realm of defense but

---

[3] Laurence J. Legere, *Unification of the Armed Forces* (New York, 1988), 316–22; Walter Millis, ed., *The Forrestal Diaries* (New York, 1951), 116; James F. Schnabel, *The History of the Joint Chiefs of Staff: The Joint Chiefs of Staff and National Policy, 1945–1947* (Wilmington, 1979), 227–47; Leffler, *Preponderance of Power*, 27–30.

[4] *Hearings on S. 84 and S. 1482*, 14.

[5] Ibid., 15. The term "total war" is here cited to Secretary Patterson, but was widely used by other civil and military leaders.

[6] Ibid., 119.

[7] Ibid., 97.

also in regulating the business cycle, expanding foreign trade, promoting full employment, and providing basic social services. The economic theory behind this view derived from the work of John Maynard Keynes and his American disciples, and the political forces that gathered around it included trade unionists, ethnic voters, liberal intellectuals, political reformers, and moderate business leaders, particularly those representing the great, capital-intensive firms that could afford progressive labor policies and still compete in a multilateral system of world trade. Stronger in urban than in rural areas, on the east and west coasts than in the south or midwest, these and allied groups constituted the New Deal coalition that had emerged from the profound political realignment of the 1930s.[8]

Beneath the surface of this consensus, however, lurked considerable doubt about how to harness the state to positive public policies. Most New Dealers favored a system of power-sharing between the different branches of government and between the public sector and private actors. Under this system, government power would expand but would still be constrained by a system of checks and balances and a broad pattern of representation. This line of thought had two branches, one that envisioned an administrative state in which the balance of power tilted decidedly toward the government, especially the executive branch, and one in which power was more widely dispersed and decentralized. By the end of the 1930s, most New Dealers had discarded the strongly statist prescription favored by some liberal reformers and trade unionists. To be sure, this prescription would still find its way into policy debates on different issues, including those dealing with national security, but most had come to favor power-sharing arrangements that left considerable room for local authorities, for policy makers in Congress, and for organized private actors, particularly organized business, labor, and agriculture.

Opposition to these arrangements came primarily from conservative forces, mostly Republicans from the Midwest, the plains states, and the mountain states, together with their allies among old Republican progressives and conservative southern Democrats, all of whom held on like grim death to a national vision at odds with the New Deal. Indeed, their views were grounded not only in a different discursive tradition but also in a competing cultural narrative. The New Deal narrative sketched a picture of modern society capped by huge concentrations of private power

---

[8] Ferguson, "From Normalcy to New Deal," 41–94; Hogan, *Marshall Plan*, 1–25.

that required the oversight of a powerful administrative state, acting on its own authority or in power-sharing arrangements with partners in the private sector. This narrative borrowed from the rhetoric of progressive reform and from the progressive vision of a corporate commonwealth based on economic planning and led by disinterested, professional experts.

The conservative narrative was somewhat different. Adopting the rhetoric of Jeffersonian republicans and late nineteenth-century populists, conservatives shared a political and economic vision in which authority was defused and decision making was scattered among a host of contending forces. In this vision, order was guaranteed by free-market forces and the virtue of independent citizens, who had often been forced to defend their liberties against powerful federal institutions, monster banks, private trusts, and other forms of tyranny. The conservatives, as this suggests, claimed to speak for local governments and regional traditions that were losing out not only to Wall Street but also to Washington, and for small, independent producers who had once been viewed as the bedrock of American democracy. As they saw it, small and medium-size firms were being ground under the heels of powerful labor unions and the modern welfare state, not to mention elite commercial enterprises. They could not afford the higher wages demanded by labor, the higher taxes needed to support liberal social programs, and the lower tariffs required to forge a multilateral system of world trade. In short, conservatives claimed to represent the remnants of a once dominant majority whose opposition to the New Deal was driven in part by traditional American concerns, including the fear of corrupting foreign influences and excessive concentrations of both economic and political power.[9]

These concerns were evident in the work of the Austrian economist Friedrich von Hayek and the Yale political scientist Harold D. Lasswell, both of whom sought to explain how the modern state imperilled the country's democratic habits and institutions. In his classic polemic on the *Road to Serfdom*, published in 1944, Hayek used the concept of totalitarianism to collapse the differences between fascism and communism, arguing that both were aspects of a contemporary collectivism that relied on economic planning and state programs to promote social welfare. It did not matter to Hayek whether the balance of power in the new collectivism tilted more toward the private than the public sector, only that economic planning set in motion a process that would lead, however

[9] In addition to the sources cited in note 8 see Horowitz, *Beyond Left & Right*, 91–161.

unintentionally, to entrenched bureaucracy, heavy-handed regulation, and the loss of political liberties – in short, to totalitarianism.[10]

Hayek's book, which became the bible of conservative commentators and politicians, raised concerns similar to those first expressed by Lasswell. But where Hayek saw totalitarianism arising on the shoulders of the welfare state, Lasswell saw it coming from national security imperatives in an age of total war. In his view, the need to defend the nation through a program of permanent military preparedness would enlarge the size and increase the authority of the state. It would give the state additional authority over manpower, science, industrial production, and the allocation of resources and would throw up a new governing elite, basically a national security elite dominated by military leaders and their allies. "The iron heel of protracted military crisis," Lasswell wrote, would "subdue civilian influences and pass 'all power to the general.'" The outcome over time would be a new brand of totalitarianism, what Lasswell called the "garrison state."[11]

To many observers, Lasswell's concerns had been reinforced by the wartime experience as seen through the eyes of such mobilization chieftains as Donald M. Nelson. In 1946, Nelson published *Arsenal of Democracy*, a controversial account of his work as head of the War Production Board (WPB).[12] The book celebrated the miracle of production that had enabled the United States to overwhelm its enemies without completely sacrificing the civilian economy, but gave little credit for this success to the War Department. On the contrary, Nelson argued aggressively that

[10] Hayek, *The Road to Serfdom* (Chicago, 1944). On the reception of Hayek's book in the United States see George H. Nash, *The Conservative Intellectual Movement in America, Since 1945* (New York, 1976), 4–9.

[11] Harold D. Lasswell, "Sino-Japanese Crisis: The Garrison State versus the Civilian State," *The China Quarterly* 11 (Fall 1937): 643–49. See also idem, "The Garrison State," *American Journal of Sociology* 46 (January 1941): 455–68; and idem, "The Garrison State and Specialists on Violence," in Lasswell, *The Analysis of Political Behaviour: An Empirical Approach* (New York, 1947), 146–57.

[12] Donald M. Nelson, *Arsenal of Democracy: The Story of American War Production* (New York, 1946). For an excellent recent account of Nelson and wartime mobilization see Alan Brinkley, *The End of Reform: New Deal Liberalism in Recession and War* (New York, 1995), 175–200. For the controversy surrounding Nelson's book see Patterson to George W. Healy, Jr., 10 September 1946; Patterson to General Brehon Somervell, 11 September 1946; Julius H. Amberg to Patterson, 16 September 1946; Somervell to Patterson, 16 September 1946; Floyd Odlum to Donald Nelson, 18 and 23 September 1946; and Patterson to Odlum, 26 September 1946, all in Robert P. Patterson Papers (Library of Congress), General Correspondence, box 21, folder: 1945–47, Nelson, Donald; and Ferdinand Eberstadt to Patterson, 12 September 1946, Ferdinand Eberstadt Papers (Seeley G. Mudd Library, Princeton University, Princeton), box 121, folder: 1945–47, Patterson, Robert P.

military planners had tried incessantly to capture the national economy and run it without regard for basic civilian needs. Their efforts had led to a series of pitched battles, basically civil–military contests, and these battles had highlighted in Nelson's mind the importance of civilian control to the survival of democracy.

Such charges lent credence to the fears of those who saw permanent preparedness leading to a garrison state, even though Nelson's basic argument actually pointed in a different direction. Nelson intended his story to celebrate the virtues of a corporative democracy in which the real heroes were not state planners but the workaday leaders in business, labor, and agriculture who had cooperated with each other and with the government to ensure victory in the war against fascism. This was part of Nelson's prescription for success in the postwar period as well, and it drew considerable support from academic specialists who studied civil–military relations and the impact of war on society. Like Nelson, in other words, these specialists envisioned what Harvard scholar E. Pendleton Herring once called "a national symphony" of private groups working together and with the government to manage the nation's economic and defense policies.[13]

Nelson's thinking, when set beside that of Hayek and Lasswell, illuminates the ideological and cultural currents at work in postwar America. Hayek's famous essay expressed a deepening concern in conservative quarters that the tide of New Deal statism was swamping the traditional virtues associated with the individualistic, free-market values of an older day. Lasswell's work added to this concern by raising the prospect of a powerful military state joined to the New Deal, while Nelson's book fused elements of this older way of thinking with new realities. He shared Lasswell's fear of unregulated state power, at least in military hands, but he also saw democratic corporatism as a viable way to contain such power while still achieving the economic planning, managerial efficiencies, and coordinated direction that national security and the modern economy required.

Competing tendencies were thus evident in American thinking. They conjured up different images of how Americans should govern themselves and these images were captured rhetorically in such pairings as statism or power-sharing, federalism or localism, collectivism or individualism, centralization or decentralization, planning or freedom. These

---

[13] My discussion here, including the quote to Herring, is taken from Jeffery M. Dorwart, *Eberstadt and Forrestal: A National Security Partnership, 1909–1949* (College Station, 1991), 96–98.

ideological oppositions and the political visions they evoked would play a major role in postwar planning for national security, particularly in the battle between two broad organizational frameworks, one supported by the Army, the other by the Navy. These two frameworks would illuminate the contested nature of the country's postwar identity, and would work at the same time to both shape and constrain the national security state that finally emerged.

General of the Army George C. Marshall and his colleagues in the War Department wanted to unify the armed forces under a single department of defense. Marshall had suggested a plan drawn along these lines in 1943, as had the Joint Strategic Survey Committee and other agencies working under the Joint Chiefs of Staff. Over the next two years, the War Department had also thrown its weight behind three similar schemes drafted primarily by Lieutenant General Joseph T. McNarney, Admiral James O. Richardson, and General J. Lawton Collins.[14] The three plans differed in detail, but all drew on the Army's organizational tradition, with its emphasis on consolidation and on a straight line of military command emanating from a central authority. They all envisioned a single department of defense headed by a civilian secretary of cabinet rank and composed of army, navy, and air force components, each with its own military chief of staff who would combine with his counterparts to advise the president on military strategy and expenditures. The Richardson report and the Collins plan, which carried the principles of centralization and consolidation the furthest, would put the president's chief of staff at the head of the combined chiefs, provide him with a unified working staff, and give him, rather than the individual chiefs, overall operational control of the armed forces. In addition, the War Department would eliminate the individual service secretaries, or demote them to the rank of undersecretary, and would transfer their responsibilities to the secretary of defense, his various assistants, and the combined chiefs of staff.[15]

If "consolidation" and "centralization" were the Army's watchwords, "coordination" and "cooperation" were the Navy's. Policy makers in

---

[14] Demetrios Caraley, *The Politics of Military Unification: A Study of Conflict and the Policy Process* (New York, 1966), 24–35, 46–49. See also Paul Y. Hammond, *Organizing for Defense: The American Military Establishment in the Twentieth Century* (Princeton, 1961), 186–92, 196–201, 213–14; *Forrestal Diaries*, 60; Legere, *Unification of the Armed Forces*, 235–313; and Secretary of War Henry L. Stimson to Forrestal, 26 May 1945, Eberstadt Papers, box 7, folder: 1945 Armed Services Unification Files: Forrestal, James V.–Files: Correspondence.

[15] Caraley, *Politics of Military Unification*, 24–35, 46–49; Hammond, *Organizing for Defense*, 213–14. The Collins Plan is discussed and debated in *Hearings on S. 84 and S. 1482*.

the Navy Department had dissented from the recommendations of the wartime study groups, arguing instead that decisions regarding the post-war organization of the military establishment should await the end of hostilities. A delay, they said, would avoid the interservice battles that might otherwise ensue and enable military planners to draw more fully on the organizational lessons of the current conflict. Also important was the conviction that unification of the services would come at the Navy's expense in such areas as procurement, and could even mean scrapping the Marine Corps in favor of the Army or curtailing naval aviation in favor of an independent air force.[16]

To avoid these dangers, Secretary of the Navy Forrestal recruited Ferdinand Eberstadt to draft an alternative to the plans coming from the War Department.[17] Eberstadt was a man that Forrestal could trust. The two had been college friends at Princeton and had worked together at Dillon, Read and Company, the legendary Wall Street investment firm that contributed so many national security managers to the Truman administration. Forrestal had become president of the firm before entering government service on the eve of World War II, first as an aide to President Franklin Roosevelt and later as undersecretary and secretary of the navy. Eberstadt had left Dillon, Read a multimillionaire, launched his own investment and consulting firm, and then served during the war as chairman of the Army-Navy Munitions Board and vice chairman of the War Production Board. Needless to say, he brought his experiences in government and in the field of corporate reorganization to bear on his assignment for the Navy, not to mention his longtime friendship with Forrestal.

Eberstadt's first order of business was to assemble a group of experts to help prepare his report to the secretary. As Jeffery Dorwart has pointed out, the group consisted largely of naval reserve officers who had graduated from Ivy League universities, were on the faculty of these universities, or were connected with the leading Wall Street investment firms and law offices. These experts in turn leaned for information and advice on leading scientists, journalists, and trade unionists, and especially on such prominent figures in business and banking as Bernard M. Baruch, Owen D. Young, Paul G. Hoffman, Nelson Rockefeller, John Foster Dulles, John Hancock, and Eric Johnston. Many of these business and banking leaders had served in various war mobilization agencies, and most were

---

[16] Caraley, *Politics of Military Unification*, 28, 30, 33–34, 36–39; *Forrestal Diaries*, 60, 64; Forrestal to Eberstadt, 6 October 1945, Eberstadt Papers, box 7, folder: 1945 Armed Services Unification Files: Forrestal, James V.–Files: Correspondence.

[17] *Forrestal Diaries*, 63.

committed to corporative schemes of decision making in which responsibility was shared among government agencies and between public and private leaders. All urged a permanent program of postwar preparedness, and all wanted that program to be implemented through a set of national security institutions run by skilled experts and linked to the private sector through a system of advisory committees. These institutions would mobilize the nation's resources for defense, coordinate military and civilian requirements, and harmonize national security policies across the government.[18]

These ideas shaped the report that Eberstadt presented to Forrestal in September 1945. The report called for increasing the number of national security agencies and "institutionalizing desirable lines of coordination" between them. In addition to the War and Navy departments and continuation of the Joint Chiefs, Eberstadt envisioned an independent air force; a national security resources board to manage industrial mobilization; an updated version of the wartime Munitions Board to standardize military contracting and production; a central intelligence agency to oversee government operations in the field of intelligence; and a research and development board to coordinate military research in government, industry, and the university. Envisioned as well was a national security council to coordinate the work of these other bodies, formulate military and foreign policies, and advise on the defense budget.[19]

Eberstadt's plan for a postwar national security state differed in two important ways from the proposals current in the War Department. Although Marshall, Forrestal, and others had talked since 1943 about a mechanism, similar to the British War Cabinet, that could oversee national security policies, the War Department's proposals focused largely on unifying the armed forces and reorganizing the military establishment.[20] Eberstadt and Forrestal, on the other hand, were among the first to see the need for an organizational framework equal to the postwar responsibilities of the United States in an era of total war. They wanted to mobilize all of the nation's resources behind this task, including every branch of government, civil and military alike. Already

---

[18] Dorwart, *Eberstadt and Forrestal*, 90–107.

[19] U.S. Congress, Senate, *Report to Honorable James Forrestal, Secretary of the Navy, on Unification of the War and Navy Departments and Postwar Organization for National Security, October 22, 1945* (Washington, 1945).

[20] Alfred D. Sander, "Truman and the National Security Council: 1945–1947," *Journal of American History* 59 (September 1972): 369. The Richardson Committee had suggested a national defense council. See Hammond, *Organizing for Defense*, 200.

in 1944, Forrestal had warned that something like the Joint Chiefs of Staff would be needed to mobilize the civilian side of government for national security purposes.[21] A year later, Eberstadt was calling for "a complete realinement [sic] of our governmental organizations to serve our national security in the light of our new world power and position, our new international commitments and risks."[22] In the Eberstadt report, this realignment would be achieved primarily through the national security council and the national security resources board.

If the emphasis on total organization for total war separated the Navy Department's thinking from that of the War Department, so did the emphasis on coordination rather than consolidation. In this case, moreover, both sides of the unification debate summoned arguments that ran deep in American political thought and culture. Drawing on the ideology of efficiency that had long been central to liberal visions of an administrative state, Marshall and his colleagues stressed the importance of economy, centralized direction, and strong leadership by professional managers. To their way of thinking, the current system of coordination by committee, which the Navy wanted to expand, fostered destructive competition between the services. It discouraged rational planning, delayed decision making, and led inevitably to an unnecessary duplication of functions. Marshall and Patterson were convinced that wasteful duplications had contributed to the Army's financial "starvation" in the interwar period, and had cost the country "billions" of dollars during World War II. Unification, they argued, would be a "businesslike" way to "bring economy" to the field of national security and the only "financially practicable" way to shoulder the burden of a permanent peacetime military establishment. General Dwight D. Eisenhower concurred. Unification would "promote efficiency," he wrote the War Department, and "avoid unconscionable duplications" at a time when "economy" must be the "watchword" of national defense.[23]

Like Marshall and his colleagues, Eberstadt and Forrestal were self-conscious state makers whose thinking drew on well-established traditions in American political culture. This was particularly apparent when the War Department implied that unification would ensure civilian

[21] *Forrestal Diaries*, 19. See also Sander, "Truman and the National Security Council," 369–70.

[22] Eberstadt quoted in Hammond, *Organizing for Defense*, 205.

[23] *Forrestal Diaries*, 60; *Hearings on S. 84 and S. 1482*, 14, 55; Eisenhower to War Department, 25 July 1945, Records of the U.S. President's Advisory Committee on Government Organization (Dwight D. Eisenhower Presidential Library, Abilene, KS), box 18, folder: No. 136, Defense – Reorganization 45.

control of the armed forces, an idea that quickly became a major source of contention between consolidators in the Army and the advocates of cooperation in the Navy.[24] According to Forrestal and others, Eberstadt's plan, with its emphasis on coordination between separate services, was similar to arrangements that had worked well during the war and had maintained civilian supremacy. They saw no reason to tamper with success, especially when Eberstadt's scheme embraced such key principles of democratic government as the supremacy of civilian leadership, decentralized decision making, and a voice for all relevant parties in a balanced system of representation.

This was a line of argument to which the War Department was vulnerable. Most of its plans would centralize decision making in a "super secretary" of defense and a "supreme commander" of all military forces, thereby creating what the Navy saw as something akin to the German General Staff of World War II. They would provide the "supreme commander" with a "superior general staff," make him the coequal of the civilian secretary, and give him and the service chiefs direct access to the president and a controlling influence over the defense budget. Nor were these the only problems apparent to the Navy. By eliminating or demoting the individual service secretaries, the Collins plan and the other War Department proposals would also permit the service chiefs rather than civilian officials to administer the armed forces. Such arrangements would undermine the normal checks and balances that inhered in a system where power was more dispersed and decision making was more widely shared. They would put too much authority in the hands of a single individual or group, Forrestal and his assistants told Congress. At best, they amounted to a "weakening of civilian control"; at worst, they ran the risk of creating a "man on horseback." Either way, said Admiral Ernest King, they were "incompatible with our concept of democracy."[25]

Assistant Secretary of the Navy H. Struve Hensel also attacked the Collins plan on this basis in testimony before the Senate Military Affairs Committee in late 1945. The plan's "main effect," Hensel argued, "seems to be the reduction of civilian control over the armed services."

---

[24] Hammond, *Organizing for Defense*, 216–17; *Hearings on S. 84 and S. 1482*, 172–73; Maxwell Rabb to Eberstadt, 30 October 1945, Eberstadt Papers, box 8, folder: 1945–46, Armed Services Unification Files: Rabb, Maxwell M.

[25] *Hearings on S. 84 and S. 1482*, 120, 145, 121, 122. See also ibid., 100–101, 150; James V. Forrestal Diary, 10 May 1945, James V. Forrestal Papers (Mudd Library), vol. 2, box 1; Rabb to Eberstadt, 23 October 1945, Eberstadt Papers, box 87, folder: 1945–46, Armed Services Unification Files: Rabb, Maxwell M.; Hammond, *Organizing for Defense*, 195; and Caraley, *Politics of Military Unification*, 30.

It removed power from the civilian secretaries, concentrated administrative control in the hands of military men, and made the chief of staff the "dominant power" in everything from military strategy to the defense budget. All of this was "directly contrary to the philosophy of our form of government" and a "source of real danger" to the country.[26] Eberstadt made the same points in denouncing the "dangerous experiments" cooked up in the War Department.[27] "We believe," said the Eberstadt report, "that any organizational set-up which tends to dilute or obstruct the free flow of civilian authority is foreign to our system of government." The postwar national security state must not "obstruct the authority of Congress" or create "a military personage or hierarchy whose control over the armed forces could dominate the civilian Secretaries."[28]

The Navy's critique suggested how the search for security could raise basic questions about the nature of the American state. At issue was the connection between new institutions and old traditions, between the process of state making and the preservation of basic values, between the nation's security and its democratic identity. The danger the Navy foresaw was in a national security organization that subverted some of the fundamental principles by which Americans governed themselves – an organization, in effect, that was more appropriate to German totalitarianism than to American democracy. Indeed, by raising the specter of the German General Staff, the Navy was relying on a strategy of otherness to advance its case and discredit its rivals. It was inscribing the country's political identity in a way that embraced its own thinking, excluded the Army's alternative, and equated its critics with the un-American other.

Yet in different ways Eberstadt's report would take the country as far in the wrong direction as any plan hatched in the War Department. The report would safeguard the Navy against the dangers of centralization by ruling out a single department of defense with a single civilian secretary and military chief of staff. It looked instead to a national security system cast in a corporatist mold. This system would include a variety of coordinating boards and advisory committees that were supposed to harmonize civil–military relations and interservice disputes but would, in reality, give

---

[26] *Hearings on S. 84 and S. 1482*, 244–45. See also ibid., 246–50; Rabb to Eberstadt, 7 November 1945, Eberstadt Papers, box 8, folder: 1945–46, Armed Services Unification Files: Rabb, Maxwell M.; and Caraley, *Politics of Military Unification*, 50–54.

[27] Eberstadt quoted in Caraley, *Politics of Military Unification*, 41. For Forrestal's thinking see *Hearings on S. 84 and S. 1482*, 603.

[28] Quoted from Hammond, *Organizing for Defense*, 207.

enormous power to the military departments, if not to military officers. For example, both the munitions board and the resources board would be dominated numerically by the military departments, putting those departments in a position to control industrial mobilization, research and development, strategic stockpiling, and other functions critical to the civilian economy. Much the same could be said of the national security council. In theory, the council would be advisory to the president, who would chair its meetings; but in practice, as Paul Hammond pointed out years ago, the president's participation would make it difficult for him to ignore the advice of the council, half of whose members were to come from the military departments. Even though the Navy denied it, the president would be in a position where collective deliberation led inevitably to shared responsibility and decision making, which could pose a serious threat to the principle of civilian leadership and to the constitutional authority of the chief executive.[29]

This possibility was very much on the mind of President Truman, whose ideas on how to deal with the military establishment fed directly into the Army–Navy debate. A veteran of the First World War and a charter member of the Tirey J. Ford Post of the American Legion, Truman had a lifelong fascination with military history and with pietistic biographies of great military figures. Hero-worship came close to describing his admiration for men like General Omar Bradley and General George C. Marshall, whom Truman once called the greatest American of his day. Yet, at the same time, Truman had a long-standing fear of "political cliques" in the military and a visceral dislike of swashbuckling commanders, from General George Armstrong Custer to "Mr. Prima Donna, Brass Hat, Five Star [General Douglas] MacArthur."[30] Two strands of thought thus competed in the president's mind, and they were similar in some respects to the two that characterized the Army and Navy positions on unification and that ran like rich veins through the country's political culture.

Truman's challenge was to eliminate wasteful duplication in defense spending while safeguarding the country's democratic institutions and the authority of his own office against would-be dictators in a military uniform. Initially, at least, his wartime experience on a Senate committee that investigated waste in defense procurement had tilted him toward the Army's plan for a full-scale consolidation of the armed forces, a position

29 Ibid., 210–13.
30 Truman quoted in *Forrestal Diaries*, 88; and Donovan, *Conflict and Crisis*, 141–42.

he announced in a much-cited article published in 1944.[31] Once in the White House, moreover, Truman was soon telling his budget director how important it was to hold the armed forces to a strict accounting, lest they "spend every nickel they could get their hands on."[32] Determined to accomplish this goal without diminishing the powers of his office, he urged Congress in December 1945 to unify the armed services in a single military establishment.

Truman's speech drew a tight connection between national purpose and organizational imperatives. The war, he told Congress, had demonstrated the need for a national security organization that could use scarce resources efficiently, reconcile competing claims in an integrated budget, and coordinate military and foreign policies. All these goals were essential if the United States was going to deter aggressors and shoulder its postwar responsibilities at a reasonable cost. And all were attainable through a single department of defense with a cabinet-level secretary, an undersecretary, several assistant secretaries, and a military chief of staff. The new department would be comprised of three "coordinate branches," including an independent air force, each with a civilian assistant secretary and a military commander who would join the chief of staff to advise the president on military strategy and defense spending.

Truman took pains to stress how such a scheme would ensure security without undercutting one of the key attributes of American democracy – the principle of civilian control over the military. The service secretaries, he said, had been captives of competing military branches, but under his proposal the armed forces would be accountable to a single secretary and military chief of staff, whose powers would derive from the president. There was no need to worry that a concentration of military power would lead to militarism, or so Truman concluded, at least not so long as the chief of staff was responsible to the president as well as to Congress.[33]

Truman's initial proposal did not include a central intelligence agency or an organization to foster military research and development. The administration was then laying separate plans for a governmentwide

---

[31] Truman, "Our Armed Forces Must be Unified," *Collier's* (26 August 1944): 63–64.

[32] Harold D. Smith, "Conference with the President," 19 September 1945, Harry S. Truman Papers (Harry S. Truman Presidential Library, Independence, MO), President's Secretary's File, Subject File, box 150, folder: Excerpts of the Diary of Harold D. Smith (hereafter, Truman Papers, PSF-Subject File).

[33] Truman, "Special Message to the Congress Recommending the Establishment of a Department of National Defense," 19 December 1945, *Public Papers, Truman, 1945* (Washington, 1961), 546–60.

intelligence group and for a science foundation that had as one of its responsibilities the promotion and coordination of defense research. Nor did Truman call for a national security council as favored in Eberstadt's report. His proposal dovetailed instead with the War Department's strategy, which meant centralizing authority for the sake of greater efficiency and greater presidential control than would be possible under the Navy's concept of shared responsibility.

With this proposal, Truman would give a certain cast to the architecture of the national security state that he and others were designing. But it is unclear whether the president fully understood how national security needs were prompting a choice between unattractive alternatives – one that concentrated power at the top of the defense establishment and one that decentralized decision making at the expense of presidential prerogatives. If not, there were others in the White House who appreciated the president's dilemma, and among them were Clark Clifford and George Elsey.

By the end of 1945, this dapper duo had begun to play an important role in national security affairs. Clifford was starting at the bottom of a ladder that he would climb over the next two decades, eventually becoming head of the Defense Department he helped to establish. His claim to fame was that of a deal maker in the bureaucratic politics of the executive branch, not to mention the perennial negotiations between Congress and the White House. Elsey was his ally in this enterprise. Both subscribed to the new ideology of national security and would demonstrate as much in the famous Clifford–Elsey report of 1946. Both favored a strong peacetime military establishment to countervail Soviet power. Both had a certain sympathy with the Navy's point of view, as might be expected of naval aides to the president. But both also saw the need to harmonize the Navy's position with the president's prerogatives, the national security ideology with the country's traditional political culture.

Yet this kind of compromise was not easily arranged, as the two first discovered when working on the unification proposal that Truman submitted to Congress in December. In shaping that proposal, Clifford and Elsey had started with a draft prepared in the War Department and supported to some extent by Director of the Budget Harold D. Smith. As one of its principal responsibilities, the Budget Bureau was to oversee the organization of the executive branch, with a view to protecting the rights and obligations of the president. Smith took this responsibility very seriously and denounced Eberstadt's plan for dispersing presidential powers among a wide array of coordinating committees dominated by the armed forces. He urged Truman to centralize authority in a single chief of staff directly responsible to the president. This was the route to efficiency, he said, and the best way to safeguard the president's prerogatives and civilian control of the military. It was also the way that prevailed, at least temporarily.[34]

Clifford's position had been somewhat different. Although he, too, wanted a clear line of authority proceeding from the president and "overall civilian responsibility for the armed forces," these goals, he argued, could easily be undone by concentrating too much power in a military strongman who might then be free to ignore the individual services or to "override" civilian authority. To preclude such "dangerous" developments, Clifford envisioned a national security system that combined elements of the Navy and War department plans. While agreeing to a military chief of staff, he wanted to define the chief's responsibilities and delineate more clearly his relationship to the president and secretary of defense. In addition, Clifford would establish a system of checks over this office by creating an independent military adviser to the president, retaining the Joint Chiefs, and establishing something like Forrestal's security council to coordinate foreign and military policies.[35]

Most of Clifford's ideas failed to find their way into the plan that Truman sent to Congress in late December, but his thinking underscored again the dawning realization that national security needs could alter fundamentally the country's basic institutions, and not necessarily in a fashion compatible with its commitment to democratic principles and civilian rule. Nor was this an idle concern, as became apparent in the Navy's aggressive challenge to presidential leadership in the unification controversy. Although this challenge raised the specter of a garrison state dominated by the military, or at least by the civilian heads of the military departments, basic values embedded in the country's political culture also made it difficult for the president to respond effectively. Americans remained committed to freedom of speech, a system of checks and balances, a degree of decentralization, and, ironically, a degree of antimilitarism, all of which worked to contain what the president could do and to force a settlement that gave the military more authority and autonomy than many thought desirable.

---

34 Smith "Report on a Conference with the President," 13 December 1945, Truman Papers, PSF-Subject File, box 150, folder: Excerpts from the Diary of Harold D. Smith; Dorwart, *Eberstadt and Forrestal*, 122–23.

35 Clifford memorandums for Judge Samuel I. Rosenman (special counsel to the president), 13 and 18 December 1945, George M. Elsey Papers (Truman Library), box 93, folder: Postwar Military Organization – Memoranda, Primary Source Material.

III

After Truman submitted his proposal to Congress, officials in the Navy Department reopened negotiations on the unification issue with their army counterparts and leaders on Capitol Hill. The goal was a compromise that would preclude a public confrontation when congressional hearings got under way in April. By late March, all sides had agreed that new agencies, including a national security council, were needed to harmonize foreign and military policies, supervise intelligence, oversee industrial mobilization, and bring scientific research into the defense effort.[36] Truman agreed to write these additions into a revised version of his original proposal, but at that point the negotiations broke down.

The Navy still wanted the armed forces to retain their administrative autonomy; the Army still sought to merge them. The Navy envisioned a weak secretary of defense with coordinating rather than administrative responsibilities; the Army favored a supersecretary. The Navy wanted the individual service chiefs to retain their current powers and work collaboratively in the Joint Chiefs of Staff; the Army envisioned a single chief of staff with his own general staff and substantial authority.[37] Running through all of these differences was the issue of centralization, to which Forrestal and the admirals had been opposed from the start. Nor would they relent when Truman decided to stand by the revised version of his proposal. Forrestal told the president at a meeting on 18 March that the proposal was "completely unworkable." It could not get through Congress without the Navy's backing, the secretary said, and he more or less implied that such backing would not be forthcoming.[38]

In effect, Forrestal had decided to defy the president's policy on unification, even though he and the admirals had professed their loyalty and had pledged not to criticize Truman in public. The catch was their simultaneous claim that naval leaders were bound to express their reservations

---

[36] Hammond, *Organizing for Defense*, 375; Caraley, *Politics of Military Unification*, 128–29; Sander, "Truman and the National Security Council," 375.

[37] Eberstadt to Forrestal, 5, 11, and 13 March 1946, Eberstadt Papers, box 61, folder: Forrestal, James V.–Files: 1946-; Forrestal to Truman, 12 March 1946, Truman Papers, PSF-Subject File, box 158, folder: Navy, Secy of; General Lauris Norstad memorandum for the record, 14 March 1946, Lauris Norstad Papers (Eisenhower Library), Pentagon Series, box 31, folder: Memos for the Record; Eberstadt memorandums, 14, 18, 19, 20, and 21 March 1946, Eberstadt Papers, box, 4, folder: 1946 Armed Forces Unification Research Compromise and Discussion; minutes of War Council meeting, 10 April 1946, Patterson Papers, General Correspondence, box 23, folder: 1945–47, War Council Meeting; *Forrestal Diaries*, 147–48.

[38] *Forrestal Diaries*, 148–49.

if asked to do so by Congress. That qualification rendered any promise of loyalty more or less worthless and enabled Forrestal and the admirals to hide their defiance behind congressional coattails.[39] Reluctant to instruct military leaders to withhold information from the legislative branch, the president found himself maneuvered into a position where he had to tolerate something close to a naval mutiny against his authority as commander-in-chief – the first of many challenges that eventually established for the military a new degree of independence from presidential control.[40]

Already in November, Forrestal had organized a group of naval officers to wage an intense public relations campaign on behalf of the Navy's case. To head the group he chose Rear Admiral Arthur Radford, a naval aviator who had commanded carrier forces in the Pacific. Radford recruited Rear Admiral Forrest P. Sherman and other hard-boiled naval partisans, who then worked with Eberstadt to sink the president's plan. Eberstadt regretted that unification had become a "fight," but nevertheless threw himself into the battle with a relish befitting his conviction that Truman's plan spelled "national disaster." Together with the admirals, he and Hensel sought to boost the Navy's position among powerful friends, whose support qualified them in Eberstadt's book for the lofty title of "statesmen." These included John L. Lewis, George Meany, and other trade union leaders who represented workers in the country's navy yards. They also included friends in the investment banking community and the Navy Industrial Association, as well as Congressman Carl Vinson of Georgia, who chaired the House Committee on Naval Affairs. Vinson's longtime support of the Navy had earned him the accolade of "Admiral" and the somewhat self-inflated reputation as father of the modern American fleet. It was in his committee that Navy leaders would wage their last battle if Truman's plan could not be stopped in the Senate.[41]

So far as the Senate was concerned, Forrestal, Hensel, and Eberstadt made every effort to orchestrate the right mix of witnesses before the

39 Ibid., 118–19; Caraley, *Politics of Military Unification*, 129; Robert H. Ferrell, ed., *Truman in the White House: The Diary of Eben A. Ayers* (Columbia, MO, 1991), 106; Hoopes and Brinkley, *Driven Patriot*, 329; Robert Greenhalgh Albion and Robert Howe Connery, *Forrestal and the Navy* (New York, 1962), 268–69.

40 *Forrestal Diaries*, 118–19; Caraley, *Politics of Military Unification*, 129; Clark M. Clifford, *Counsel to the President: A Memoir* (New York, 1991), 149.

41 Eberstadt to Forrestal, 20 December 1945, Eberstadt Papers, box 7, folder: 1945 Armed Services Unification Files, Forrestal, James V.–Files: Correspondence; Clifford, *Counsel to the President*, 147–48. See also Hensel to Eberstadt, 5 December 1945, Eberstadt Papers, box 7, folder: 1945–46, Armed Services Unification Files: Hensel, H. Struve; Albion and Connery, *Forrestal and the Navy*, 266; and Hoopes and Brinkley, *Driven Patriot*, 325.

Military Affairs Committee. This was a task in which the Navy had gained substantial experience during earlier hearings on the Collins plan, when both the Army and the Navy had maneuvered like chess champions to counter each other's initiatives.[42] Leaving nothing to chance, Forrestal and Eberstadt also worked relentlessly to have Truman's plan considered by the Naval Affairs Committee of the Senate and to secure seats on the committee for reliable friends and allies. That committee, like its counterpart in the House, could be counted on to support the Navy's point of view, as could senators with an interest in the well-being of naval yards in their states.[43]

The Senate hearings opened in April and dragged on into July. A long line of generals and admirals paraded up Capitol Hill to testify, most of them celebrated veterans of the recent war: Marshall and Eisenhower for the Army, Spaatz for the Army Air Forces, King and Admiral Chester W. Nimitz for the Navy, General Alexander A. Vandegrift for the Marine Corps. Their tunics weighted down with battle ribbons, their views infused with service pride and parochialism, the leaders of each branch adhered resolutely to positions hammered out over many years of interservice warfare. Each side resembled "a punch-drunk 'has-been,'" as an Army memorandum described the scene, "shadow-boxing before a group of admiring relatives in the presence of the Local Press."[44] Under these circumstances, there was little reason to believe that old differences would finally be composed, not even to alleviate the fear of militarism that hung over the hearings, like a dark cloud over the horizon.

The Senate hearings again brought to light one of the major themes in the national security discourse of the early Cold War – the contested nature of state formation and state identity, and specifically the conflict between values rooted in an older political culture and the new ideology of national security, between the country's democratic traditions and its international obligations. All of those involved seemed to assume that America's postwar security, not to mention its global responsibilities, demanded a substantial mobilization of its civilian and military resources. For the first time in history, the United States had to maintain a large peacetime national security establishment, perhaps on a permanent

[42] For this maneuvering see the series of memorandums on the hearings from Maxwell Rabb to Eberstadt of October and November 1945, Eberstadt Papers, box 8, folder: 1945–46, Armed Services Unification Files: Rabb, Maxwell M.

[43] Eberstadt to Forrestal, 20 December 1945, Eberstadt Papers, box 7, folder: 1945, Armed Services Unification Files, Forrestal, James V.–Files: Correspondence; *Forrestal Diaries*, 121.

[44] Unsigned memorandum on S. 2044 [probably Norstad], 4 May 1946, Norstad Papers, Pentagon Series, box 31, folder: Memos for the Record.

basis. The question was whether the country could be prepared militarily without being militarized, and on this score several committee members expressed great alarm. They were especially worried about concentrating too much power in the hands of a single individual, particularly a military leader, thereby subverting the principle of civilian rule and setting the stage for what Senator Warren R. Austin of Vermont called "a military dictatorship."[45]

The fear of authoritarianism and militarism ran through all of the congressional deliberations, as it had the earlier debates in the Truman administration. Key witnesses captured their fear in the usual metaphor of the garrison state, compared American democracy to the authoritarian other, usually Germany, and expressed their misgivings through a rhetorical strategy that relied on such familiar dichotomies as civilian/military, unification/collaboration, consolidation/coordination, centralization/decentralization. Charles E. Wilson, president of the General Electric Company (GE) and former vice chairman of the War Production Board, was on hand to share his experience as a manager of large-scale organizations. Wilson agreed with other witnesses that national security in an age of total war required a comprehensive program of permanent preparedness, including something like a peacetime WPB to mobilize the country's industrial, scientific, technological, and manpower resources. Together with Eberstadt and Forrestal, however, he disputed the War Department's tendency to equate centralization with efficiency and economy. He claimed instead that giant corporations like GE had succeeded by decentralizing decision making in divisions that were coordinated, not controlled, by the "top man." Excessive centralization led to rigidities and waste, according to Wilson. This was one reason to avoid the "big superman" concept favored by the War Department, another being that such an approach invited "authoritarianism" as well as inefficiency.[46]

Playing on this concern, Admiral King also reminded the committee of what had happened in other countries where control of the armed forces meant control of the government. It was not enough to say that "'it can't happen here,'" King argued. Congress had to make sure that neither civilian nor military leaders were in a position to seize control

45 U.S. Congress, Senate, *Hearings on S. 2044, A Bill to Promote the Common Defense by Unifying the Departments and Agencies of the Government Relating to the Common Defense* (Washington, 1946), 60 (hereafter *Hearings on S. 2044*). See also ibid., 61, 69, 70–71.

46 For Wilson's testimony see ibid., 146–63. The quotes are from 149 and 152. See also Hoopes and Brinkley, *Driven Patriot*, 320–21.

of the armed forces. In particular, it had to prevent an "all-powerful" chief of staff from molding "military and possibly national policy to suit his ends," which was exactly the danger that King saw in any plan that eliminated or reduced the War and Navy departments, denied cabinet status to their secretaries, put administrative control in the hands of a single civilian secretary, or permitted a "supreme" military chief of staff to fix strategy and frame the budget. Nor was one-man military rule the only danger. By elevating one service over the others, such a plan would also preclude a proper balance between the armed forces and create what Eberstadt termed a "Maginot Line psychology."[47]

As the congressional deliberations wore on, Truman found it increasingly difficult to tolerate the Navy's challenge to his leadership. He had stood up to Stalin at the Potsdam conference in 1945 and had lectured the Soviets on their postwar responsibilities, so it was not surprising that his anger mounted in proportion to the Navy's insubordination and his own inability to do much about it. At a news conference in April, Truman delivered a bitter tirade against the Navy's die-hard opposition to his position, and on a subsequent occasion he became positively apoplectic when told that naval leaders were not confining their dissent to the congressional hearings, as Forrestal had promised, but were using newspapers, magazines, and other forums as well.[48]

In truth, both the Navy and the War departments had launched substantial public relations campaigns on behalf of their positions, which Truman's thundering did little to curb. Each department was conducting what Forrestal called a "lawsuit" against the other, and each stuck with positions that left little room for compromise.[49] Patterson still wanted to unify the armed forces in a single department under a supreme military commander and civilian secretary with direct administrative control of the military services. The Army believed in "local autonomy," he said, but only to a degree consistent with "efficient and economic operation," which was the "*sine qua non*" of any plan and the essence of unification. Forrestal, on the other hand, still saw the rhetoric of efficiency as a ruse to destroy the Navy's air arm and Marine Corps. Meeting with the president in mid-April, he celebrated the principle of home rule and would go no further than a civilian secretary who would coordinate rather than

---

47 *Hearings on S. 2044*, 128, 109, 44, 32, 37–38, 172.

48 The president's news conference of 11 April 1946, *Public Papers, Truman, 1946* (Washington, 1962), 191–95; Caraley, *Politics of Military Unification*, 129–30.

49 Forrestal to Patterson, 12 December 1945, Eberstadt Papers, box 121, folder: 1945–47, Patterson, Robert P.

control the military departments, referee their disputes, and formulate a coherent defense budget.[50]

If this kind of interservice bickering raised doubts about the dominance of civil over military authority, these doubts seemed to be confirmed in May and June, when the services were unable to reach an agreement man dated by the president. The idea behind such a mandate came from Clark Clifford, who had continued to negotiate with the War and Navy departments after the Forrestal–Patterson talks broke down. In the background, too, was the nagging failure of the Joint Chiefs to agree on the postwar size and composition of the armed forces, without which they also found it difficult to hammer out a joint strategic concept and war plan.[51] These failures had led Clifford to open talks with Major General Lauris Norstad, Rear Admiral Forrest Sherman, and other military officials, out of which came a compromise that would continue the Joint Chiefs and establish a single department of defense, but would rule out a supreme military commander and allow each of the services to retain its own civilian secretary. This was a compromise between centralization and decentralization that Clifford thought he could sell to "the Boss," as he called the president, who would then dictate similar terms to Forrestal, Patterson, and other top policy makers in the War and Navy departments.[52]

Following this script, Truman summoned his service secretaries and military advisers to a meeting at the White House on 13 May. Forrestal arrived with his admirals in tow, Patterson with his generals, and both sides had supporters on the president's staff. The Army had Major General Harry H. Vaughan, the president's old chum and military aide whose matchless ineptitude and crude ethics would eventually embarrass the White House. The Navy could count on Captain Clark Clifford and

---

[50] For Patterson's thinking see his exchange of letters with Bush dated 23, 26, 27, and 30 April and 1 May 1946, Patterson Papers, General Correspondence, box 18, folder: 1945–47, Bush, Vannevar. The quotes are from Patterson to Bush of 30 April 1946. On Forrestal see *Forrestal Diaries*, 151–53; and Forrestal's notes to be discussed at a conference with the president, 17 April 1946, Forrestal Diary, Forrestal Papers, vol. 4, box 2.

[51] See JCS series 1478/8-18 for an exchange of service memorandums between March and May 1946 on the issue of roles and missions, Records of the Joint Chiefs of Staff, Record Group 218 (National Archives, Washington) (hereafter RG 218). See also Legere, *Unification of the Armed Forces*, 316–22.

[52] Norstad record of meeting with Symington and Clifford, 8 May 1946, Norstad Papers, Pentagon Series, box 31, folder: Memos for the Record; Clifford memorandum for the president, 13 May 1946, Elsey Papers, box 93, folder: Postwar Military Organization – Magazine Articles and Clippings.

Admiral Leahy, who still served as the president's chief of staff. Clearly, the Navy had the advantage.

Truman began the meeting with blunt words and an ultimatum. He said that interservice squabbling prevented an integrated budget for the armed forces and a balanced system of national defense, both of which weakened the country's security. He then gave Forrestal and Patterson two weeks to hammer out a compromise on unification or present a list of their agreements and disagreements to the White House, where the president would resolve all issues.[53] George Elsey, who had worked with Clifford on the White House meeting, apparently considered the "pow-wow" a good indication that Truman was going to bull the Navy into line with his thinking. The president, Elsey scribbled in a memorandum, had "had it out" with the services, especially the Navy, which thought "it had licked the Boss" on the unification issue.[54]

In truth, though, Truman had been reduced to a supplicant, pleading with the Army and the Navy for support he should have received much earlier. Nor was that the whole story, for the president's tough talk also concealed a retreat from his original support for a supreme military commander. In his negotiations with Norstad, Clifford had agreed that a commander with such authority might threaten civilian leadership. Leahy had also declared against the Army's proposal for a "'great military commander'" and the two had apparently persuaded the president to abandon that part of his proposal. At the White House meeting of 13 May, Truman announced that he, too, had developed "misgivings" about "vesting so much authority on such a high level to a military man." He had come to the conclusion that such an idea was "too much along the lines of the 'man on horseback' philosophy," and was therefore "dangerous." Patterson responded that he would not be "unyielding" on this point and would "give if necessary."[55] No doubt he had been cued by Norstad that opposition was futile, and perhaps he expected that Forrestal would reciprocate by finally consenting to a single department with a strong civilian secretary.

Truman and Clifford probably saw their concession as consistent with larger policy objectives, not as a reversal of the president's position.

---

53 Norstad record of a meeting with the president, 13 May 1946, Norstad Papers, Pentagon Series, box 31, folder: Memos for the Record; *Forrestal Diaries*, 160–62.

54 Unsigned [Elsey] memorandum, 13 May 1946, Elsey Papers, box 93, folder: Postwar Military Organization – Magazine Articles and Clippings.

55 Norstad record of a meeting with the president, 13 May 1946, Norstad Papers, Pentagon Series, box 31, folder: Memos for the Record; *Forrestal Diaries*, 160–62.

Clifford was aware of concerns on Capitol Hill regarding a single military chief of staff and was convinced that Truman's proposal had little chance of passing with this provision included.[56] At the same time, Truman's suspicion of "prima donna" generals probably made him more amenable to a modification that would safeguard civilian authority against the menace of a military dictator. After all, protecting the president's prerogatives had been one of his goals all along, and discarding the idea of a supreme military commander might help to achieve that goal. Then, too, it was still possible to unify the services under a strong civilian secretary rather than a supreme military commander, and thus to achieve a higher degree of centralized control as well as greater economy and efficiency.

As it happened, however, a compromise along these lines was more remote than either Truman or Clifford appreciated, in part because centralization itself, whether in civilian or military hands, was the real issue for Forrestal. Indeed, discussions following the White House meeting actually saw a hardening of the Army–Navy divisions, rather than a reaffirmation of the agreement that Clifford, Norstad, and others had worked out earlier. Although Patterson would forgo the idea of a single military chief of staff, he still wanted a single department of defense with three subsidiary departments, each with its own civilian secretary and military commander, but with only as much administrative autonomy as was consistent with efficiency, economy, and their subordinate status. In effect, service secretaries would operate as agents of the secretary of defense, who alone would have cabinet rank.

To Forrestal and the admirals, Patterson's plan, even without a single chief of staff, still raised the ugly prospect of concentrating too much authority in the hands of a powerful civilian secretary who might achieve efficiencies at the Navy's expense. They demanded guarantees on the issue of roles and missions, cabinet status for the service secretaries, administrative autonomy for the departments, and strict limits on the authority of the secretary of defense. Although these demands were at odds with what Truman had in mind, the Navy still hoped to prevail, in part by refusing to support an independent air force on any other terms, rejecting the idea of a single department with its own civilian secretary, and calling instead for interdepartment coordination through a presidential deputy who would head the national security council. Two weeks of talks had come to this and no more, with the differences now so great and the acrimony so bitter that Patterson and Forrestal even found it difficult to agree on the language of a letter outlining their disagreements to the president.[57]

Truman had failed to assert his authority over the armed forces. Despite a presidential mandate, the letter that Forrestal and Patterson sent to the White House on 31 May embraced only the principles and organizational components on which the two men had earlier agreed, including the need for a security council and resources board. The failure to resolve other issues raised serious concerns about civil–military relations in the Truman administration, and especially about the president's ability to defend the principle of civilian supremacy that was central to the country's democratic politics and constitution. What is more, there were similar concerns about the proposed security council and resources board, both of which Forrestal wanted to establish immediately. The Budget Bureau and the Treasury Department sounded the alarm on these two issues, and their warnings again highlighted the contested nature of state making and state identity in the early Cold War, and specifically the palpable tension between civilian authorities and military officials, between democratic visions and the nightmare of the garrison state.

Budget Director Smith thought it essential to overcome the "disunifying effect of having three powerfully-organized, autonomy-minded, and mutually jealous organizations," but saw nothing but trouble in plans for a security council and resources board.[58] These "highly dangerous" plans would divest the president "of authority and responsibility which he cannot lose and still be President," and would lodge them instead with the service secretaries and chiefs of staff. In effect, the president's subordinates would enjoy what amounted to "a veto power over foreign policy" and the ability to dictate national decisions "under the guise of a civilian committee structure." Smith warned the president that something like this was already happening in "national planning

---

[57] *Forrestal Diaries*, 163–65; Norstad record of a conversation with Patterson, 14 May 1946, Norstad Papers, Pentagon Series, box 31, folder: Memos for the Record; Eberstadt memorandum of a meeting with Patterson, Forrestal, and Nimitz, 14 May 1946, Eberstadt to Captain Frank Nash, 23 May 1946, with enclosed memorandum of conversation of 21 May 1946, and Eberstadt memorandum re Patterson–Forrestal negotiations, 29 May 1946, all in Eberstadt Papers, box 61, folder: Forrestal, James V.–Files, 1946-; Patterson and Forrestal to Truman, 31 May 1946, Eberstadt Papers, box 11, folder: May-June 1946, Armed Services Unification Files, Truman, Harry S.–Files. See also Hoopes and Brinkley, *Driven Patriot*, 333.

[58] Smith to Truman, 22 May 1946, Truman Papers, PSF-Subject File, box 145, folder: Military: Army-Navy Unification.

for industrial preparedness and mobilization." In this case, he said, the Army–Navy Munitions Board was slowly taking over a job that concerned "the entire civilian side of the Government."[59]

Smith did not want the administration to build a national security state that would protect the American people at the expense of their democratic traditions. To his way of thinking, the search for security must not subvert the Constitution, militarize the economy, or permit the War and Navy departments to dominate the government. Similar advice came from James R. Newman, Richard Bissell, and other officials in the Treasury Department. In a long memorandum to Treasury Secretary John Snyder, they drew the same conclusions about national security in an age of total war that others had reached earlier, but went on to recommendations that echoed more traditional American thought.

"The problem of defense is no longer a military problem," Newman and the others agreed, because "modern warfare" affected "the entire organism of the state" and every aspect of the nation's "economic, social and political life." In this sense, "planning and mobilizing for the common defense are inseparable ... from planning and mobilizing for the general welfare of the nation."[60] Such statements encapsulated major themes in the ideology of national security, namely the notion that modern war was total war and that total war engaged all facets of national life. Yet also apparent in the document was a kind of thinking that was hostile to militarism and excessive concentrations of power. This line of thinking aimed to keep military power within proper bounds through a system of checks and balances in a more comprehensive scheme of representation, and was generally at odds with proposals being discussed by the Army and Navy. Newman and his colleagues were dead set against a resources board that usurped functions properly performed by other government agencies and that bent these functions to the single goal of national security. They felt the same way about presidential prerogatives in an era of total war, when the government's responsibilities, as they told Snyder, were "so basic and so far-reaching" that only the president should exercise them. They must not be parceled out to various agencies, and especially not to a security council that would be dominated by the State, War, and Navy departments. If there was to be such a council,

---

59 Ibid. See also Dorwart, *Eberstadt and Forrestal*, 143.

60 Richard Bissell, Thomas I. Emerson, James E. Newman, and Harold Stein to Snyder, 24 May 1946, with attached memorandum of the same date, John W. Snyder Papers (Truman Library), box 9, folder: Congress – Unification Bill, 1946.

it must represent the full "range of governmental functions," because only such an agency could consider fairly the nonmilitary aspects of national security or balance civilian and military needs in a "comprehensive defense program."[61]

Despite the severity of their concerns, Smith, Newman, and other critics were not at the White House on 4 June when Truman opened another meeting with Forrestal, Patterson, and their military advisers. Both sides went over the same ground covered in their letter of 31 May and then left the president to decide unresolved issues, which he tried to do in a subsequent letter that more or less straddled the differences between the two departments. Truman agreed to safeguard the Marine Corps and concede each of the services its own civilian secretary. But he also called again for a single department of defense under a cabinet-level secretary with general authority over the subordinate services. The services would retain their "autonomy," Truman said, subject "to the authority and overall control" of the secretary of defense.

Smith may have been happy with that declaration, but neither he, nor Newman, nor other civilian critics could have been pleased with Truman's renewed support for a resources board and security council. To be sure, the security council would consist of civilian rather than military officials, notably the head of the resources board, the secretary of state, the new secretary of defense, and the three service secretaries. But this membership hardly represented the full range of government departments involved in national security. On the contrary, despite all of the talk of balancing civilian and military needs, Truman envisioned a security council composed almost entirely of policy makers from various national security agencies and dominated by officials from the military establishment.[62]

Patterson was quick to endorse the new compromise and pledge his support on Capitol Hill; Forrestal was less forthcoming.[63] Besides eliminating the chief of staff, Truman had agreed to safeguard the Marine Corps and establish much of the national security system that Forrestal

---

[61] Ibid.

[62] Truman to Congressman Andrew J. May (chairman, House Military Affairs Committee), 15 June 1946, Clark Clifford Papers (Truman Library), box 16, folder: Unification – Correspondence, General. See also Forrestal to the president, 4 June 1946, Eberstadt Papers, box 158, folder: Harry S. Truman; Norstad notes on a conference at the White House, 4 June 1946, Norstad Papers, Pentagon Series, box 31, folder: Memos for the Record; and *Forrestal Diaries*, 165–68.

[63] For Patterson's reaction see Patterson to Truman, 17 June 1946, Truman Papers, PSF-Subject File, box 157, folder: War, Secy of.

had envisioned. At the same time, however, he had settled one dispute over roles and missions by allotting to the proposed air force land-based operations involving antisubmarine warfare, over-water reconnaissance, and the protection of shipping. These were missions that Forrestal and the admirals had claimed for themselves and about which they were "fanatic," as Forrestal told the president at a subsequent meeting. There must be a parallel role for naval aviation, he said, and guarantees that he could "run his own Department without kibitzing from above." The last demand seemed to indicate that Forrestal was still reluctant to support a single department under a strong secretary. What is more, he continued to assume that he and his aides were free to criticize "particular parts" of the president's program in Congress, and he suggested for the first time that ongoing disagreements might prompt his resignation.[64]

Forrestal's continuing opposition posed a serious obstacle to the success of the president's program. The secretary and his allies had already stalled action on that program past the date needed to get approval in the current session of Congress, and they were determined to draft new legislation to fit the Navy's needs.[65] After the White House meeting in June, they pressed without reserve for an office of national defense, rather than a department, to be headed by a presidential deputy, rather than a cabinet secretary, with limited powers to coordinate the armed forces, rather than overall authority to administer their affairs. They again urged Truman to issue an executive order establishing such an organization, along with the other agencies to which the War and Navy departments had agreed.[66] Nor would they relent when Truman warned, at another meeting in September, that executive action on a "piecemeal" approach might preclude congressional support for a comprehensive plan. The president still wanted his own unification bill to be "the doctrine of the administration," but Forrestal would agree to no other doctrine than his own."[67]

By now a prisoner of the hard-nosed admirals around him, especially Radford, Forrestal marshalled his waning energy for another struggle

[64] *Forrestal Diaries*, 168–70. See also Hoopes and Brinkley, *Driven Patriot*, 334–35.

[65] Patterson to Senator Robert A. Taft, 18 November 1946, Taft Papers, Legislative File, box 842, folder: Unification of the Armed Forces, 1946–47.

[66] *Forrestal Diaries*, 200–202; Budget Director James E. Webb notes on a conference with the president, 5 September 1946, James E. Webb Papers (Truman Library), box 3, folder: Bureau of the Budget, Conference Notes; Forrestal to Clifford, 7 September 1946, Clifford Papers, box 16, folder: Unification – Correspondence, General; Eberstadt memorandum, 13 September 1946, Eberstadt Papers, box 61, folder: Forrestal, James V.–Files, 1946-.

[67] Webb notes on a conference with the president, 5 September 1946, Webb Papers, box 3, folder: Bureau of the Budget, Conference Notes; and *Forrestal Diaries*, 203–4.

against his opponents. He threw the Navy's public relations operation into high gear against any undesirable legislation, and again threatened to resign if such legislation became law. He also tried to outflank the president by working through Wall Street friends with close ties to the War Department and by drafting his own bill for a coordinating rather than an administrative authority.[68] Once more he tangled with the War Department over the Navy's role in land-based aviation for reconnaissance, submarine patrols, and the protection of shipping. And once more he circled his wagons on Capitol Hill and in the press. Forrestal had worked hard to cultivate reliable allies in both quarters to whom he could turn for support, as he did in late December, after three additional months of negotiations had only contributed to what he and Patterson saw as a deepening "mood of bitterness and hatred" between the services.[69]

Perhaps it was their concern with this swelling bitterness, or with the "serious damage" it was doing to the national defense, that finally drove Patterson and Forrestal toward an accommodation.[70] Perhaps it was yet another plea for sweet reasonableness from the president, who urged both secretaries in the first days of the new year to rise above the perspective of their admirals and generals and to see the "whole picture."[71]

[68] *Forrestal Diaries*, 203–4; Albion and Connery, *Forrestal and the Navy*, 274–75; and Eberstadt memorandum of a meeting with John J. McCloy and Robert A. Lovett, 26 September 1946, and Eberstadt to Assistant Secretary of the Navy W. John Kenney, 30 September 1946, Eberstadt Papers, box 3, folder: Armed Services Unification Files Re Agreement between Army and Navy, September 1946. See also Kenney to Eberstadt, 27 September 1946, Eberstadt Papers, box 3, folder: Armed Services Unification Files Re Agreement between Army and Navy, September 1946; Dorwart, *Eberstadt and Forrestal*, 140–41; and Hoopes and Brinkley, *Driven Patriot*, 338–40.

[69] *Forrestal Diaries*, 228–29. See also Norstad memorandum for the record [November 1946], Norstad Papers, Pentagon Series, box 31, folder: Memos for the Record; Admiral Forrest Sherman (deputy chief of naval operations) memorandum for the secretary of the navy, 12 November 1946, Forrestal Diary, Forrestal Papers, vol. 6, box 3; Patterson to Taft, 18 November 1946, Taft Papers, Legislative File, box 842, folder: Unification of the Armed Forces, 1946–47; War Council meeting, 21 November 1946, Patterson Papers, General Correspondence, box 23, folder: 1945–47, War Council Meeting; Norstad memorandum for the record, 21 November 1946, with attached paper on unification of the services, 20 November 1946, Norstad Papers, Pentagon Series, box 31, folder: Memos for the Record; R. J. W. to Norstad, 4 December 1946, with attached undated paper by Norstad, ibid., box 33, folder: Unification Correspondence, Memos for the Record, Misc.; and *Forrestal Diaries*, 223–28.

[70] *Forrestal Diaries*, 228–29.

[71] Truman to Forrestal, 8 January 1947, Truman Papers, PSF-Subject File, box 156, folder: Defense, Secy of – National Defense.

Or perhaps it was Truman's renewed willingness to make concessions to the Navy's point of view. For whatever reason, a new set of agreements finally emerged in mid-January.

One agreement settled the issue of roles and missions in a way that safeguarded the Marine Corps, especially its role in amphibious assaults, and kept intact the land-based operations of naval aviation. Another concerned the organizational structure of the national security state, which, as now envisioned, would include the security council, resources board, intelligence agency, and Joint Chiefs of Staff, on all of which the Army and Navy had already agreed. Envisioned as well was a joint staff of approximately one hundred officers to implement decisions by the Joint Chiefs, and three military departments, including a department of the air force, to be administered as individual units under the "over-all direction" of a secretary of defense. In addition, the agreement contemplated an office of the secretary of defense, not a department of defense, with functions that were to be coordinating, not administrative, as were those of a proposed war council consisting of the secretary of defense, the service secretaries, and the military chiefs.[72]

As Eberstadt wrote a friend, the agreement favored the Navy's position more than the Army's.[73] Truman had been pulled in different directions, not only by perceived national security needs or the bureaucratic battles between the Army and the Navy but also by contending traditions in American politics and culture. The pull from one direction was toward a centralization of authority in order to promote efficiency, guarantee economy, discipline the services, and protect the prerogatives of the president. The pull from the other was toward a more decentralized and corporative scheme of decision making that would guard against militarization, undue concentrations of power, and policies that might put the country on a slippery slope to the garrison state. By early 1947, the pull of these two positions had produced a compromise that contained some of the worst features of both alternatives: a relatively decentralized system of decision making that might be dominated by the military departments.

---

[72] Forrestal and Patterson to Truman, 16 January 1947, Norstad Papers, Pentagon Series, box 25, folder: Roles and Missions. For an earlier draft of this letter, dated 15 January 1947 and including a draft executive order on the roles and missions of the armed forces, see the Eberstadt Papers, box 121, folder: 1945–47, Patterson, Robert P. See also *Forrestal Diaries*, 229–31.

[73] Eberstadt to Julius Adler, 18 January 1947, Eberstadt Papers, box 3, folder: Armed Forces Unification Files: Includes Executive Order of January 16, 1947.

IV

Truman announced the Army-Navy agreement at a press conference in mid-January, shortly after the two sides had come to terms. The reaction was mixed, though generally sympathetic, especially among elite journalists whose views could shape public policy as well as report it. The American press in the early Cold War had a fair share of such opinion makers and they had followed the unification debates very closely. In the process, moreover, they played an important part in disseminating the national security ideology to a wider audience and in calling attention to the potential conflict between that ideology and older values. Hanson W. Baldwin, the influential military-affairs commentator for the *New York Times*, and columnists such as Joseph and Stewart Alsop, Ernest R. Lindley, Walter Lippmann, and Arthur Krock, all agreed that the country could not return to its prewar military system or level of preparedness. The Soviet menace and the nation's new responsibilities required a permanent national security establishment, including a central intelligence agency, an independent air force, and new mechanisms to coordinate military and foreign policies and to harness the country's economic resources to the cause of national security.

They also supported unification of the armed forces, although the Alsops were critical of the Navy's position, Krock was more sympathetic, and none of the commentators thought that Truman's latest proposal amounted to anything like a real merger of the services. It was a "happy compromise," to use Baldwin's phrase. It would give the president additional authority to control the military and to integrate military and civilian resources, but without increasing the power of the armed forces to the point where the American people would sacrifice their freedom to a garrison state. Judged by this standard, most of the commentators seemed to agree that Truman's latest proposal was a step in the right direction, though there was some concern that he might have gone too far in diluting civilian authority, especially the authority of his own office.[74]

---

74 Baldwin, "New Defense Set-Up Faces Obstacles," *New York Times*, 24 July 1947. See also the Alsops, "Ground-Air Forces Feud is Seen Hindering Truman Merger Plan," 6 January 1946; "U.S. Still Lacks a Defense Plan, 6 Months After Atom Bomb Fell," 30 January 1946; and "Navy–Air Forces Rivalry is Seen Jeopardizing Atomic Bomb Test," 11 February 1946, all in *New York Herald Tribune*; Baldwin, "Defense Improvements," 6 February 1946; "Service Merger Battle," 14 April 1946; "Many 'Ifs' are Left in 'Unification' Blueprint," 19 January 1947; and "Forrestal Faces Trials," 21 September 1947, all in *New York Times*; Krock, "Defense Plan Revives Old Cabinet Questions," ibid., 9 January 1947; Lippmann, "For Better Commanders-in-Chief," *Washington Post*, 27 May 1947; and Lindley, "What's at Stake in Unification," *Newsweek* 29 (2 June 1947): 30.

In truth, the agreement was a major victory for the military, or at least for the Navy, over the president's civilian advisers. Besides Clifford, Elsey, and other members of the White House staff, few policy makers outside of the military departments had been involved in the negotiations to this point. Officials in the Treasury Department and the Budget Bureau had expressed their views, to be sure, but only occasionally, and only as outsiders to the negotiations. Nor had the negotiations involved top officials in the State Department, a surprising oversight given the important role that agencies like the proposed security council were to play in the formulation and coordination of foreign and military policies.

The documents are silent on the reasons for this oversight, though it may have had something to do with the sour relationship between the White House and the State Department. Truman had not cultivated close relations with Secretary of State Edward Stettinius and his colleagues at Foggy Bottom. Nor had relations improved under Stettinius's successor, James F. Byrnes, who spent much of his time out of the country and had lost the president's confidence by early 1946. Truman's low esteem for the nation's diplomats stood in sharp contrast to the high regard he had for key officials in the War Department, from Marshall and Eisenhower to Secretary of War Henry Stimson and his successor, Robert Patterson. Perhaps it was inevitable under the circumstances that Stettinius and Byrnes had next to nothing to do with the unification negotiations in 1945 and 1946. In any event, the outcome in mid-January 1947 was an Army–Navy agreement that would revolutionize the American state, and would do so by challenging the tradition of civilian leadership and especially the constitutional rights and responsibilities of the president and the secretary of state.

This became clear after Clifford, Elsey, and their counterparts in the War and Navy departments had worked through several drafts of a bill based on the agreement, at which point they began circulating copies to officials in other areas of government, including George Marshall, who had replaced Byrnes as secretary of state. Marshall responded with a withering critique. The proposed bill, he warned Truman in February, assigned a new intelligence agency powers that were "almost unlimited" and duties that overlapped with the State Department's National Intelligence Agency. There were similar problems with the resources board and especially with the proposed security council, which would set policy on matters of common interest to the military establishment and the State Department and coordinate action among the agencies involved. Such an arrangement, Marshall warned, would "dissipate the constitutional responsibility of the President," who would become an "automaton" of the council in the conduct of foreign affairs. Something similar would happen to the secretary of state. Though a member of the council, the secretary would be "numerically subordinated to the heads of the military establishments," who would thus enjoy "predominance in the field of foreign relations," just as their voice on the resources board would give them considerable influence over the nation's nonmilitary assets.[75]

All of this was more than law or custom allowed, and much more than Marshall could tolerate. The control of the president and the secretary of state over foreign affairs, he wrote to Truman, was "deeply rooted" in the Constitution and in the "sentiments of the people," as was the conviction that both foreign and domestic policy "should be dominated by the non-military branches of the Government." To safeguard these rights and traditions, he urged Truman to confine the legislation to unification of the armed forces and to scrap for now all plans for a national security council, a central intelligence agency, and a resources board.[76]

Marshall's critique echoed earlier warnings from the Budget Bureau, which the bureau repeated when the generals and admirals asked for "technical" advice on the draft legislation. Bureau officials were "shocked" and "dismayed" by the proposed bill, especially Donald C. Stone, the bureau's majordomo in matters regarding the organization of the executive branch. It "destroys what is left of unification," Stone complained. It also "undermines the constitutional position of the President" and "substantially decreases civilian control over the Army, Navy, and Air Forces," indeed "over large non-military areas of the Government, all in the name of national security." Stone and his colleagues knew that Truman had made a "steady series of concessions" to Forrestal and that more concessions had been embodied in the agreement of mid-January. As they saw it, however, "even this watered-down solution" had been further "perverted" in the draft legislation. In effect, the War and Navy departments were "writing a bill" that would establish "a form of military veto over foreign policy" and determine the "structure" by which "the President may control them." No one had stood up for the president, Stone lamented, even though "his very position is being cut out from under him."[77]

75 Marshall memorandum for the president, 7 February 1947, Elsey Papers, box 82, folder: National Defense – Armed Forces Unification.

76 Ibid.

77 Stone memorandum to the director, 30 January 1947, Records of the Bureau of the Budget, Record Group 51 (National Archives), Series 39.32, box 72, folder: Development and History of the National Security Act of 1947 (hereafter RG 51).

From the bureau's point of view, the basic problem lay in the Navy's rejection of a single executive department in favor of an "office" of the secretary of defense with limited staff and virtually no power to administer the affairs of the armed services. An executive department, as the bureau pointed out, carried with it "150 years of law, custom, and tradition," all of which gave its head a "definite position" in the cabinet, a place in the line of succession, and esteem in the eyes of the public. No comparable body of law applied to an "office" that coordinated the work of several executive departments. Its secretary would have no recognized place in the administrative and political structure of government. His standing would derive solely from the authorizing legislation and his authority would be constantly contested by the service secretaries as they asserted their normal prerogatives. "To move toward the objectives of unification," the bureau concluded, the secretary of defense had to be "the head of an Executive department" with enough authority, however limited and decentralized, to do his job. The task was to ask the service secretaries to delineate the specific powers they wished to retain, rule out those that might impede the job of unification, and include the remainder in the bill.[78]

This was easier said than done, since Forrestal really wanted the service secretaries to have all powers of any consequence. At one point in the negotiations, he even objected to provisions that would give the secretary of defense real authority to integrate the budgets of the armed forces into a common budget that he would control. "Money is power in this town," Admiral Sherman explained on Forrestal's behalf; if the service secretaries could not control the budgets of their departments, they could not control their departments. More was at stake "than just [the] Budget," in other words, as Forrestal also revealed when he objected to the proposed post of undersecretary of defense and to paying even assistant secretaries of defense salaries comparable to their counterparts in the service departments. In this case, he might have said, power was money.[79]

---

[78] Webb memorandum for Clifford, 17 February 1947, RG 51, Series 39.32, box 72, folder: Development and History of the National Security Act of 1947. See also Arnold Miles (Budget Bureau) memorandum to Stone, 17 February 1947, ibid.

[79] Memorandum of a telephone conversation between Admiral Sherman and Colonel Steele, 19 February 1947, Norstad Papers, Pentagon Series, box 31, folder: Memos for the Record. See also Stone memorandum to the director, 21 February 1947, RG 51, Bureau of the Budget (BOB) Records, Series 39.32, box 72, folder: Development and History of the National Security Act of 1947.

By the end of February the Army and Navy negotiators, with help from Clifford and Elsey, had finally settled on the terms of a bill that Truman submitted to Congress. In essence, the Navy was successful in defeating last-minute efforts to establish the department of defense as an executive department. Instead, the final bill established the office of the secretary of defense, who would preside over a national military establishment that included the air force as an independent department on a par with the Army and Navy. It also provided for a national security council, a national security resources board, a central intelligence agency, a war council, a joint chiefs of staff, and a joint staff with its own director. Included as well were provisions for a munitions board and a research and development board to coordinate procurement, research, and development policies for military purposes. Both boards were to be headed by civilians but would include representatives from each branch of the armed forces.

The bill contained some meager concessions to critics of the earlier drafts. One provision included vague language giving the secretary of defense general "authority, direction, and control" over the service departments and other agencies in the defense establishment. Another would empower the secretary to "supervise and coordinate" the budget estimates of the service departments and to present the results to the Budget Bureau. The bill did not scrap the proposed security council and resources board, as Marshall had wanted, or alter the military's numerical advantage on the former agency, but it did seek to safeguard the president's constitutional prerogatives by making these advisory rather than policy setting bodies.[80]

The debate on Capitol Hill lasted from March to July 1947, filling page upon page of the *Congressional Record*, not to mention testimony running to hundreds of pages in the House and Senate hearings. Because the War and Navy departments had reached an accord, their initial strategy was to present a united front behind the bill and its benefits. One of these was supposed to be greater economy in defense spending. Patterson and Forrestal seemed reluctant to make lavish promises on this score, realizing perhaps that an independent air force meant triplification, not unification, and hence additional expenditures.[81] Such caution did not

---

[80] Caraley, *Politics of Military Unification*, 155–56.
[81] War Council meeting, 6 March 1947, Patterson Papers, General Correspondence, box 23, folder: 1945–47, War Council Meeting; U.S. Congress, Senate, *Hearings on S. 758, A Bill to Promote the National Security by Providing for a National Defense Establishment*

extend to the bill's congressional supporters, however, most of whom sold the measure as a way to save "billions" at a time when Congress was trying hard to balance the budget, cut taxes, and reduce the national debt. "Huge money savings" were possible, they said, by eliminating redundancies, curtailing competition between the services, and making the defense organization more efficient.[82]

While arguments about economy were clearly appealing, the administration and its allies tried even harder to sell the bill as essential to national defense in an age of "total war." Their arguments in this regard encapsulated the national security ideology that was quickly becoming the common currency of American politics in the early Cold War. "Remember Pearl Harbor!" was a favorite refrain, because that disaster had underscored the need for better intelligence, for teamwork between the services, and for permanent preparedness.[83] "One must be ready when the whistle blows," as one senator explained, particularly in the "atomic age," a phrase that was now synonymous with "total war," and being prepared meant mobilizing the resources of the nation and of every government agency.[84] As usual, Forrestal captured this theme best when he told the Senate Armed Services Committee that "military strength today is not merely military power." It "is economic and industrial strength" and "fiscal strength" and "technological resourcefulness," which meant that "every department of Government" was involved in "modern total war" or in war preparation and that "some form of civilian–military coordination" was "essential."[85] Through coordinating agencies like the security council and the resources board, as Senator Gurney noted, the proposed bill would lay the "foundation" for "total national effort in the event of total war."[86]

As in the past, debate centered on whether the demands of national security, especially the centralization of authority, could be reconciled with the country's democratic traditions and commitments. A determined

---

(Washington, 1947), 47–48 (hereafter *Hearings on S. 758*); U.S. Congress, House, *Hearings on H.R. 2319, A Bill to Promote the National Security by Providing for a National Defense Establishment* (Washington, 1947), 572 (hereafter *Hearings on H.R. 2319*).

[82] *Congressional Record, 1947* 93:2057, 8295. See also ibid., 2067, 2068, 8296, 8298, 8306, 8503, 9398–99, 9401, 9403.

[83] Ibid., 8299, 9409, 9416.

[84] Ibid., 8304, 9409. See also ibid., 8302, 8502, 9429.

[85] *Hearings on S. 758*, 24–25.

[86] *Congressional Record, 1947*, 93:8299. See also ibid., 9410, 9415; and *Hearings on S. 758*, 558.

band of congressional leaders, mostly conservatives and former isolationists, worried that national security imperatives were leading the nation down the primrose path to a military dictatorship. The outcome they foresaw was more un-American than American, a contrast they captured in a variety of German images and in the usual metaphor of the garrison state. Though most conceded that military preparedness in an age of "total war" had to involve every agency of government and every aspect of American life, this very reality, they insisted, made it all the more imperative that power be dispersed and that key agencies be dominated by civilian rather than military leaders. They referred to the Founding Fathers, citing their fear of concentrated power, their faith in a system of checks and balances, and their belief in the supremacy of civilian authority. And relying on a strategy of otherness to carry their case, they contrasted the system envisioned by the Founders to the one under Hitler, going from there to explain how the national security arrangements spelled out in the bill pointed more toward the German than the American ideal.

To Republican Senator Edward V. Robertson of Wyoming, these arrangements would tip the balance of power into the hands of military leaders or departments. The joint staff, said he and other critics, amounted to an "embryonic" general staff similar to the one that dominated civil and military affairs in Nazi Germany. The bill also established what they saw as an "all-powerful super Secretary for National Defense" and gave the military departments and other national security agencies a disproportionate influence in the security council. Even worse, it did not preclude the new intelligence agency from becoming an "American gestapo" and allowed the armed forces to influence a substantial segment of American industry, in part through the munitions board, which they alone would control, and in part through the influence they could bring to bear on the resources board.[87]

So far as the intelligence agency was concerned, all sides agreed that such a body was essential, particularly in light of the fiasco at Pearl Harbor, which was widely attributed to a failure by the Army and Navy to share intelligence about Japanese plans and operations. This consensus had led Truman in January 1946 to establish the Central Intelligence Group, an interdepartmental organization designed to coordinate

---

[87] *Congressional Record,* 1947, 93:5246, 5247, 8320. See also the sources cited in the next two notes.

intelligence operations across the government. Under General Hoyt
S. Vandenberg, its second director, the group had absorbed operations
formerly under the control of other agencies, added substantially to its
budget, collated information from across the government, and started to
collect intelligence on its own – a task not officially within its purview.
By 1947, Vandenberg was working with Clifford and Elsey to draw up
the provisions for an independent intelligence agency that were included
in the legislation considered by Congress in 1947.[88]

The proposed agency attracted surprisingly little attention on Capitol
Hill, perhaps because the tragedy at Pearl Harbor made it seem so essential, but one question that did come up had to do with whether it
could meet an essential need without undermining basic civil liberties.
To provide assurances on this score, the bill's drafters had denied the
agency any policy making, subpoena, or law enforcement powers and
had confined its operations to the collection and evaluation of foreign,
as opposed to domestic, intelligence. Nevertheless, critics still considered
the bill flawed in at least two respects. They thought it a mistake to have
the same agency collect and evaluate intelligence, when these functions
should be separated, and they objected to a provision that permitted a
military officer to serve as the director of central intelligence. It was the
last provision that raised concerns about a "military Gestapo" and that
made it possible for critics to see the proposed agency as part of a pattern of creeping militarism that would also reach through the munitions
board to the American economy as a whole.[89]

In truth, the relationship between the munitions board and the resources board left much to be desired. In theory, at least, the munitions
board would report to the secretary of defense and deal only with military programs. The resources board, on the other hand, would report
to the president and would integrate civilian and military requirements
by drawing up a balance sheet of natural and human resources, drafting
blueprints for industrial mobilization, and arranging for the stockpiling
of strategic materials. As an operating agency, however, the munitions

---

[88] Clifford to Vandenberg, 12 July 1946, and Elsey memorandum for the file, 17 July 1946,
Elsey Papers, box 56, folder: Central Intelligence; Phillip S. Meilinger, *Hoyt S. Vandenberg:
The Life of a General* (Bloomington, 1989), 66–77; and Christopher Andrew, *For the
President's Eyes Only: Secret Intelligence and the American Presidency from Washington
to Bush* (New York, 1995), 149–69. For a documentary history of the origins of peacetime
foreign intelligence operations see U.S. Department of State, *FRUS, 1945–1950: Emergence
of the Intelligence Establishment* (Washington, 1996).

[89] *Congressional Record, 1947*, 93:9421. For the debate over the intelligence provisions of
the bill see also ibid., 9404, 9410, 9412, 9430, 9444–52.

board would do most of the work of the resources board and would be largely responsible for establishing the military determinants of industrial mobilization. In almost every way, judging from the testimony of the administration, the resources board would amount to little more than a figurehead in an arrangement that entrusted real authority to the munitions board, which the military departments would control. Slight wonder that critics in Congress saw the munitions board as a military wedge into the civilian economy and economic policy. Nor were supporters of the bill reassuring when they admitted that under the proposed organizational scheme "all phases of American life are integrated into our military planning."[90]

Taken together, according to the critics, the bill's provisions could only lead to "the eventual domination by a group of professional militarists" of all civilian agencies of government, of foreign policy, of industry, and of natural and human resources.[91] "We must not let our fear of Communism blind us to the danger of military domination," warned Robertson, the most vocal of those who saw a "Frankenstein monster" in the making. He and others embellished their case with an American cultural narrative that celebrated two centuries of democratic struggle against military domination and big government. Robertson cited Donald Nelson's discussion of how close the country had come to military domination during World War II, while Republican Congressman Clare Hoffman of Michigan connected that part of the story backwards to the founding of the Republic. The United States, Hoffman said, had not become the richest, most democratic country in the world by forfeiting congressional governance to the military or to nonelected bureaucrats at the top of some "superorganization" in the executive branch. On the contrary, one generation of Americans after another had trod the same path to greatness blazed by the Founders, who came to the New World to escape repression, resisted unfair taxation, and safeguarded their liberties through a constitution that constrained the state and guaranteed civil over military authority. Let military "bureaucrats" set national security policies, he concluded, and they would squander the country's resources, regiment every area of American life, and take the United States down the road to ruin already traveled by Germany, Japan, and the Soviet Union.[92]

---

[90] *Hearings on S. 758*, 295. See also ibid., 201–2, 215–16, 290–91, 295, 313–15; and *Congressional Record, 1947*, 93:8391.

[91] *Congressional Record, 1947*, 93:5247.

[92] Ibid., 8310, 8318, 9435, 9433. See also ibid., 5246–47, 8308–10, 8316, 8319–95, 9432, 9436–38.

Supporters of the bill tried to be reassuring, in part by drawing on the same rhetorical symbols and citing the same traditions and values to make their case. They explained how the superstructure of the national security state would rest on a solid democratic foundation. According to Forrestal, the bill squared with "our democratic" or "representative-republican form of government," which had no place for "dictators – military or civilian." It stopped short of a single department, rejected the idea of a military chief of staff, and severely limited the powers of the civilian secretary of defense. What is more, all other powers had been reserved to the service secretaries, who were denied cabinet status, to be sure, but who retained the right of direct appeal to the president and Congress. When critics complained of military domination, supporters pointed out that all seats on the security council were to be occupied by civilians and that civilians would also head the service departments, the new office of the secretary of defense, and the resources board. In addition, when critics warned of a supersecretary who might encroach on the responsibilities of the president and Congress, supporters said that his authority would derive from that of the president and that Congress would retain the ultimate power of the purse. They did not worry about re-creating in the United States anything like the "Junker system" in Germany, not with a bill that carefully delineated the duties of the secretary of defense and divided power among a variety of agencies headed by civilian leaders. On the contrary, some wondered whether the bill went too far in the right direction by leaving the secretary of defense with too little power to eliminate waste, forge an integrated budget, and coordinate civil and military policies.[93]

The debate over the powers of the secretary of defense fed directly into the issue of roles and missions. Forrestal and Patterson had not addressed this issue in the bill, settling instead for a side agreement that Truman would approve by executive order. But this agreement began to break down when General Eisenhower told the Senate Armed Services Committee that he hoped someday to see the appointment of a single military chief of staff, and when Undersecretary of the Army Kenneth C. Royall took the position that the secretary of defense had enough authority under the bill to harmonize the operations of the individual services, including their roles and missions. These statements piqued the special concern of Senators Harry F. Byrd and Robertson of Virginia.

---

[93] *Hearings on H.R. 2319*, 96; *Congressional Record, 1947* 93:9401. See also *Hearings on S. 758*, 543; *Hearings on H.R. 2319*, 100–101, 134–35; and *Congressional Record, 1947* 93:8297–98, 8306, 8309, 8311, 8496–99, 8519, 8594, 9428, 9430.

Both were avid defenders of the Navy and of naval yards in their state, and both began to question the Army's commitment to the agreement hammered out by Forrestal and Patterson.

Royall's testimony also led to complaints from Forrestal and to renewed demands from General Vandegrift, the Marine Corps commandant, that Congress include provisions in the final bill specifically protecting the traditional functions of the Marine Corps and naval aviation. Forrestal thought such provisions unnecessary in light of the executive order to which the services had agreed. He also worried that reopening the issue in Congress would scuttle the chances for favorable action on the proposed bill. By the time the hearings were over, however, the secretary had lost control of the admirals who advised him. They had joined Vandegrift and their friends in Congress to demand protection for both the Marine Corps and naval aviation – and they got it by writing into the bill the statement on roles and missions that Truman had promised to issue by executive decree.[94]

The National Security Act of 1947, as the final measure was called, established the modern mechanisms of the national security state. These included the Office of the Secretary of Defense, the Joint Chiefs of Staff, the National Security Council (NSC), and the Central Intelligence Agency (CIA). Established as well were the National Security Resources Board (NSRB), the Munitions Board, the War Council, and the Research and Development Board, and spelled out in some detail was a system of checks and balances that would supposedly reconcile the new agencies with established traditions and the country's liberal-democratic heritage. The act, for example, provided for three independent services, but with protection for traditional naval missions. It gave the CIA access to intelligence information generated by other agencies, including the Federal Bureau of Investigation (FBI), but only upon written request and only to the extent recommended by the NSC. It allowed a military officer to serve as CIA director, a provision that critics deplored, but provided that any officer in that post would not be accountable to his military superiors. In other provisions, the act also made it clear that both the NSC and the NSRB were advisory rather than policy making bodies, that the secretary of defense enjoyed no more than "general" authority over the three

94 Norstad to W. Barton Leach (professor of law, Harvard University), 7 April 1947, Norstad Papers, Pentagon Series, box 33, folder: Unification Correspondence, Memos for the Record, Misc.; *Forrestal Diaries*, 269–72, 274. See also *Hearings on S. 758*, 349–53, 412–13; *Hearings on H.R. 2319*, 101–2, 596; Caraley, *Politics of Military Unification*, 175–77; and Legere, *Unification of the Armed Forces*, 343–47.

services, and that individual service secretaries would retain administrative control over their departments.

These and other provisions grew in part from concern over the dangers a national security system might pose to the country's democratic institutions and traditions. Yet those who warned of such dangers had also been defeated on a number of issues. The CIA was not denied access to the records of the FBI and the Atomic Energy Commission, as some had hoped, and its director did not have to come from civilian life. In addition, critics were unable to alter the relationship between the Munitions Board and the NSRB. Nor could they guarantee that civil and military requirements would be balanced by winning a place for the Agriculture, Commerce, Interior, and Labor departments on the NSC and the NSRB.[95]

V

The National Security Act ended the first round of state making in the early days of the Cold War. It laid the institutional foundations of the national security state, although the final results were not exactly what policy makers had envisioned at the start. Everyone was ready to accept a permanent blurring of the usual distinctions between war and peace, citizen and soldier, civil and military. They seemed to agree that American security in an age of total war demanded a program of constant preparedness, that civilian and military resources had to be integrated into this program, and that new government agencies were needed to meet these requirements. These agreements, however, did not lead to consensus on the institutional innovations and adaptations that were needed. On the contrary, the process of state making was pushed in different directions, in part by the bureaucratic struggles between the Army and the Navy, in part by the need to reconcile the security state with traditional values, in part by contending traditions in the country's political culture.

The Army's plan, initially favored by the president and other key officials, looked to the centralization of authority in a straight line of command proceeding from the president to the secretary of defense, the supreme military commander, the subordinate service chiefs, and the civilian secretaries. This chain of command squared with Army thinking

---

[95] The legislative history of the bill, including the amendments accepted and rejected, is summarized in *Congressional Quarterly, 1947* 3:457–63. See also Caraley, *Politics of Military Unification*, 178–82; and Legere, *Unification of the Armed Forces*, 349–61.

and practice, but also drew support from civilian officials who considered it essential to real unification of the services. Equally important was their conviction that consolidation and centralization were the best ways to achieve efficiency and economy, discipline the armed forces, and preserve the constitutional rights and responsibilities of the president as commander in chief. In this sense, the Army's plan actually appeared as a guarantee against militarism. It would help to safeguard civilian leadership, according to its champions, and thereby reconcile perceived national security needs with traditional democratic principles.

The Navy and its supporters saw things differently. They equated consolidation with inefficiency and rigidity, centralization with militarism and the garrison state. Both sides claimed to champion the principle of civilian leadership, but where the Army evoked the constitutional responsibilities of the president and the ideology of efficiency, the Navy celebrated the benefits of shared decision making and a system based on checks and balances. In Eberstadt's plan and its many variations, the Navy and its supporters envisioned a corporative system of specialized institutions, each performing a task essential to the nation's security. They argued that such a system would encourage innovation and provide a comprehensive mechanism for assessing foreign threats, coordinating foreign policy with military capability, and integrating civilian and military resources. In this system national security institutions would be linked to each other through agencies like the NSC and would be led by national security elites drawn from civilian rather than military life. Besides reconciling the search for security with the principle of civilian supremacy, this arrangement had the advantage of fostering cooperation while preventing an excessive concentration of power in a single individual, group, or agency.

The fear of a garrison state, of centralized authority that could threaten traditional service functions, civilian leadership, or democratic principles, had shaped the debate over the national security state from the beginning. It had led Truman to abandon his original plan for a military chief of staff and had reinforced the Navy's opposition to a consolidation of the armed forces into a single department of defense. The same fear had also led Congress to add further amendments to the watered-down bill that Truman had submitted. In reality, the president's bill did not create a supersecretary, as the critics had feared. Nor did it provide for anything like the German General Staff, establish the CIA as an American Gestapo, or turn policy making over to the military. But the fears reflected in such images were still important in shaping policy, and not always in a way that led to good results.

On the contrary, the fear of centralization so deeply rooted in American political culture operated as a barrier to real unification of the armed forces, to a civilian secretary with enough authority to control the services, and thus to the efficiencies and economies that all sides thought desirable. It also led, ironically, to an institutional arrangement dominated by national security agencies. Even though policy makers conceded the need to balance economic and military requirements and to integrate civilian and military resources, they had refused to create a security council that broadly represented all areas of government. In the end, as some critics had feared, the military departments, particularly the Navy, played a major role in creating the national security system through which the president and other civilian leaders would control them.

The result was a system that gave the armed forces considerable autonomy and that institutionalized the National Military Establishment as a major rival to the State Department in the field of foreign policy. Similar challenges to civilian authority would follow, especially when it came to the defense budget. Indeed, the budget battles of the early Cold War constituted another important episode in the politics of state making, not only pitting civilian leaders against military officials but also traditional values against the new ideology, older democratic visions against the nation's new role as the champion of democracy worldwide. The outcome of these battles would determine the financial foundation of the national security state, with results that we will now begin to investigate.

3

The High Price of Peace
Guns-and-Butter Politics in the Early Cold War

Few principles of traditional public policy were so sacrosanct as that of a balanced budget, and few were so compromised by the national security state that emerged in the early years of the Cold War. Although the principle had been challenged during the Second World War, with the forced expenditures on national defense, and during the Great Depression, when declining revenues and New Deal social programs led to persistent deficits, neither of these experiences had driven the American people from their strong attachment to a balanced budget. This was a value buried deep in the country's political culture, with roots reaching back to the republican ideology that early American leaders had borrowed from English country thought, and from there to the tradition of classical republicanism and civic humanism.

The depth and persistence of this attachment owed as much to moral and political as to fiscal considerations. In the cultural narrative to which most Americans subscribed, individual initiative, fiscal prudence, and a common concern for the public good had combined to make the United States a unique success – a rich and powerful nation in which the virtue of individual citizens and a high standard of living had worked to curb social conflict and sustain democracy. In this narrative, budget deficits corrupted public policy and private lives alike. They contributed to the growth of state power, with its potential for abuse, and they unleashed inflation and debased the currency, which discouraged private savings, robbed citizens of the incentive to produce, and undermined the public welfare. Seen in this light, deficit spending was symptomatic of profound moral and political decay, while a balanced budget affirmed America's historic identity as a nation of righteous citizens and self-reliant producers.

Much of this narrative and the values it embodied survived the New Deal into the postwar period. Most conservatives continued to celebrate the balanced budget as a bulwark against waste and corruption, as a barrier against the growth of big government, and as a symbol of the public virtue deemed essential to the success and survival of democratic institutions. The great problem for them was in harmonizing an older definition of America as a model of republican rectitude with the new ideology of national security, which defined the country as a great power with an expensive military machine and global responsibilities. A similar problem confronted many liberals, including President Truman. They, too, had to reconcile the country's global mission with their sense of civic duty at home, notably their commitment to the New Deal, and they had to do so without busting the budget, corrupting the currency, and running up the national debt.

This chapter deals with the first budget battles of the early Cold War and with the problem of national identity to which they were linked, but also treats related questions of state making, especially the question of whether defense and international programs would alter the American state and how undesirable changes might be avoided. As with the National Security Act, this question provoked a powerful debate in which all sides drew on some of the same symbols and rhetorical devices. Senator Robert A. Taft and other conservative Republicans entered the postwar period determined to dismantle the New Deal, only to discover the foreboding specter of a garrison state thrown up by the Cold War. To these conservatives, the garrison state was a political metaphor for what the country would become if defense and international programs drained a disproportionate share of its resources, and if too much power shifted from the private to the public sector or from civilian to military authorities. Concerns of this sort help to explain why some Republicans wanted to limit the country's commitments overseas, and why others wanted to rely on airpower rather than manpower to guarantee its security.

The conservative position stood in contrast to alternative strategies supported by competing elements inside the Truman administration. Whereas conservative leaders envisioned a small state wedded to traditional values and only marginally involved in global affairs, Secretary Forrestal and his colleagues in the military establishment spoke in the ideological language of the national security state, with its image of America as a defender of democracy in a troubled world. Stressing the importance of total preparedness in an age of total war, they resisted the pace of postwar demobilization, warned of a growing gap between the country's overseas commitments and its military capabilities, and urged Americans to make the sacrifices that world leadership required, even if these entailed higher taxes, cuts in domestic programs, or an unbalanced budget.

Economizers in the Budget Bureau and the Treasury Department staked out another position. Together with the president, they tried to strike a sustainable balance between the warfare and the welfare states, between guns and butter, between the nation's goals internationally and its responsibilities at home. Like Forrestal and his allies, they often drew on the ideology of national security to justify an expansion of state power, specifically in the area of deficit financing. But they tried at the same time to reconcile the new ideology with older values and to forge a system of checks and balances that would preclude abuses and preserve both public virtue and individual liberties. In theory, government would be constrained by limiting the growth of national security programs, and deficits would be curbed by expanding the economy and accepting a permanently higher level of taxation.

In short, the budget battles of the early Cold War fueled a series of conflicts over the size of the state, the purposes to which it would be put, and the resources to support it. In these battles, congressional conservatives defended the balanced budget and all that it symbolized, Pentagon policy makers sought to maximize the resources at their disposal, and officials in other parts of the administration struggled against rising odds to reconcile domestic and international requirements. Interservice rivalries made these conflicts more acute, as did a string of international crises, but out of them eventually emerged a set of politically negotiated compromises that embodied elements of all positions – and that moved the country toward what would later become a familiar pattern of public policy and state making.

II

When it came to the budget, Harry S. Truman seemed to prove the ancient adage that "you can't teach an old dog new tricks." The Keynesian revolution did not disturb so much as a hair on his neatly combed head, at least until 1950, when he would turn to the new economics more out of expediency than conviction. Truman believed deeply in a balanced budget and in all the old values it represented. His memoirs, which elaborated the same cultural narrative that other Americans found convincing, made the familiar connection between a prudent fiscal policy and individual responsibility, at one point comparing the federal budget to a household budget that "sets the normal limit of expenses against the expected income." Overseeing the federal budget, Truman recalled, had been a "thoroughly fascinating" responsibility and one of his "more serious hobbies." He noted the "intense personal interest" he had taken in every detail of the budget and bragged about the three budgets he had balanced, about his efforts to reduce the national debt, and about his careful management of discount rates, bond issues, and similar matters that seldom made the headlines. On these successes, he sermonized, depended "the financial soundness of the government and the prosperity of countless individuals."[1]

Truman's belief in a balanced budget stemmed from his vision of the postwar state as well as his commitment to values embedded in American political culture. In truth, the two were tightly linked in the president's mind. Although he subscribed to the national security ideology, he did not want to remake the country into a warfare state, with military preparedness near wartime levels, military needs dominating the economy, and military leaders challenging civilian authority. Instead, he sought to return political authority to civilian agencies, reallocate resources to peaceful pursuits, and balance these pursuits against the demands of national security. Elements of change and continuity thus competed in his thinking and shaped his definition of both the American state and its mission in the postwar period.

Fear of a garrison state that would subvert the budget, not to mention civilian authority, influenced Truman's decision to demobilize the armed forces far more rapidly than most of his national security managers thought desirable. Secretary of the Navy Forrestal complained repeatedly that demobilization was proceeding too quickly, as did Secretary of War Patterson and Secretary of State Byrnes. According to Patterson, the current rate of demobilization would leave the Army with only four hundred thousand troops in Europe by the spring of 1946 – enough, he thought, to constitute a "police force" adequate to the Army's occupation duties, but hardly enough to exert "effective influence" over European affairs. The story was the same in Japan and no better in China. At the present rate, Forrestal argued, demobilization would denude the armed forces of the trained men they needed to operate efficiently in most parts of the world. He was sure that the Soviets were not demobilizing as quickly and were doing more to retain their commissioned officers. National security required no less of the United States, he insisted, and with this requirement in mind he urged the president to speak publicly of the Soviet threat and do what he could to reverse the pace of demobilization.[2]

[1] Harry S. Truman, *Memoirs*, vol. 2, *Years of Trial and Hope, 1946–52*, paperback ed. (New York, 1956), 47, 53, 62.

[2] *Forrestal Diaries*, 110. See also ibid., 101–2, 106–7, 128–29.

Forrestal's advice, which embraced the new ideology of national security, went more or less unheeded in the White House. To be sure, Truman understood the need for military force levels that exceeded prewar standards. If demobilization went too far, he said on several occasions, it could undermine his diplomacy and the country's strategic position. He made this point in September 1945, after the London Foreign Ministers' Conference had failed to resolve Soviet-American differences over a host of outstanding issues, and he came back to the same point at a cabinet meeting in late October, when he complained about "people in the world who do not seem to understand anything except the number of divisions you have." But despite this bit of brass-knuckle strategizing, Truman had no intention of supporting the force structure that Forrestal had in mind. He announced in mid-September that two million troops would be home for Christmas and that twenty-five thousand would be discharged daily by the first of the year. At that rate, the Army alone would be reduced to fewer than two million soldiers by the spring of 1946.[3]

Truman was determined to get the military establishment and the budget on a peacetime basis as quickly as possible, and that meant sustaining the pace of demobilization and driving down military expenditures. This became clear in meetings with Budget Director Smith in September and October 1945, primarily on the Navy's current expenditures. Given the obligations outstanding at the end of the war, Smith told the president, the best they could do in the present budget was to trim the Navy's expenditures by a few billion dollars. Truman "expressed great concern as he looked over the figures, frequently shaking his head and knitting his brow." He had told the Joint Chiefs only weeks earlier that defense spending should constitute no more than 20–25 percent of the peacetime budget, which he and Smith hoped to reduce to approximately $25 billion.[4] To achieve those targets required cooperation from the armed forces, especially from the Navy, which the two men accused of dragging its feet on demobilization. It was time to "crowd the Navy budgetwise," Truman said, so as to speed its "lagging" demobilization.[5]

Aggravating the debate over demobilization were differences over the size and cost of the postwar military establishment, differences that barely concealed a still more fundamental clash between the welfare state, the

---

3 Record of a conference with the president, 5 October 1945, Truman Papers, PSF-Subject File, box 150, folder: Excerpts from the Diary of Harold D. Smith. See also *Public Papers, Truman, 1945*, 327–28; and Donovan, *Conflict and Crisis*, 127–28.
4 Records of conferences with the president, 13 September 1945 and 18 February 1946, Truman Papers, PSF-Subject File, box 150, folder: Excerpts from the Diary of Harold D. Smith.
5 Record of a conference with the president, 5 October 1945, ibid.

warfare state, and the values that each embodied. When it came to
the postwar military, the president viewed the matter primarily from
the perspective of fiscal responsibility, whereas Forrestal and his allies
applied the same national security yardstick they were using to assess the
pace of demobilization. Forrestal envisioned a postwar Navy of approximately five hundred thousand sailors, fifty-eight thousand officers, and
more than one hundred thousand marines. So did Congressman Carl
Vinson, chairman of the House Naval Affairs Committee, who introduced a concurrent resolution for a postwar fleet that would include
thirty-seven aircraft carriers, seventy-nine escort carriers, eighteen battleships, eighty-two cruisers, two hundred submarines, and nearly seven
hundred destroyers. This fleet, according to Forrestal, was the minimum
size compatible with the Navy's mission, which he defined as defending
the United States and its overseas possessions, protecting the Western
Hemisphere, and honoring the country's larger if less precise obligation
to "preserve the peace of the world." The Navy asked the Budget Bureau
to approve a $6.3 billion appropriation bill for this purpose, and Vinson
made arrangements, no doubt with Forrestal's support, to introduce such
a bill in Congress.[6]

The Navy had not evaluated its proposal from the "fiscal side" but
in terms of the new ideology of national security, not from an economic point of view but from "the standpoint of the new role of the
United States in world affairs." The country had entered a new era
of semiwar, Forrestal said, borrowing language from the new ideology.
It was engaged in a permanent struggle for peace and freedom on a
world scale and it had to be prepared to meet its obligations. These
facts had to be acknowledged in the budget, and the American people, Forrestal concluded, had to make the sacrifices their global mission
required.[7]

Truman, however, approached the subject from a perspective that
left room for the country's domestic goals as well as its international

[6] Forrestal, undated "Agenda for Discussion between the President, the Secretary of the Navy,
Senator Walsh and Congressman Vinson," attached to record of a White House conference
on the postwar navy, 14 September 1945, ibid. See also JCS memorandum, "Basis for the
Formulation of a Military Policy," enclosed in Leahy memorandum for the secretary of war
and the secretary of the navy, 19 September 1945, Forrestal Diary, Forrestal Papers, vol. 3,
box 2; unsigned memorandum, 14 March 1946; and Smith "Highlights of Estimates of Naval
Appropriations, Fiscal Year 1947," in Smith memorandum for the president, 20 March 1946,
Truman Papers, PSF-Subject File, box 158, folder: Navy, Secy of – Postwar Navy.

[7] Record of a White House conference on the postwar navy, 14 September 1945, Harold D.
Smith Papers (Truman Library), box 1, folder: Daily Record, September 1945.

obligations. In going over the proposed budget for fiscal year 1947, both he and Smith were struck with how domestic expenditures had shrunk since fiscal year 1940, while those for defense and other war-related programs had grown severalfold. Both men wanted to reduce such expenditures in fiscal year 1947, which the armed forces estimated at nearly $22 billion, and combine the savings with the Treasury's current cash balance to cover a projected deficit without adding to the national debt – a piece of good news "that'll get 'em" in Congress, as Truman told Smith. With a little more effort, the two men even thought it possible to eventually drive defense spending down to $5 billion for the War and Navy departments, plus an additional $8 billion for occupation costs and other war-related expenses – for a total of approximately $13 billion.[8]

Viewed against these estimates, it was evident that Forrestal's postwar plans were too ambitious, as Truman and Smith explained in a meeting with the secretary, Congressman Vinson, and other officials in mid-September. It was his job, they told Forrestal, to balance military against civilian requirements in a way that bore "some reasonable relationship to our national income" and to the peacetime budget target of $25 billion. For this reason, they would not consider any proposal without a price tag and without some indication of its place in an integrated budget for the armed forces as a whole. Already in August, Truman had asked the Joint Chiefs to consider the postwar size of the Navy in relation to the overall size of the military establishment and to present a comprehensive plan for his approval. Without such a plan, he now insisted, the administration would neither commit itself to Forrestal's vision of the postwar fleet nor throw its weight behind the resolution that Vinson was pushing through the House of Representatives. On the contrary, the president urged the Senate to stall that measure until the Joint Chiefs had outlined a "coordinated" and "complete Military, Air and Naval program."[9]

Truman summarized his thinking again in a combined budget and state of the union message of late January 1946. He still envisioned what

---

[8] Record of a conference with the president, 4 January 1946, Truman Papers, PSF-Subject File, box 150, folder: Excerpts from the Diary of Harold D. Smith. See also the record of a conference with the president, 19 December 1945, Smith Papers, box 1, folder: Daily Record, September 1945.

[9] Record of a White House conference on the postwar navy, 14 September 1945, Smith Papers, box 1, folder: Daily Record, September 1945; Truman to Senator Alben W. Barkley, 30 October 1945, Truman Papers, PSF-Subject File, box 158, folder: Navy, Secy of – Postwar Navy. See also memorandum from the acting director of the Budget Bureau to the president, 25 October 1945, Smith Papers, box 1, folder: Daily Record, September 1945; and Truman memorandum to Leahy, 21 August 1945 attached to unsigned memorandum, 14 March 1946, Truman Papers, PSF-Subject File, box 158, folder: Navy, Secy of – Postwar Navy.

amounted to a war budget for fiscal year 1947, with approximately 42 percent of estimated expenditures devoted to defense, demobilization, and occupation and with another 30 percent for veterans' benefits, payments on the national debt, and additional costs inherited from the war. In all, expenditures for national defense, war liquidation, and occupation totaled $15 billion, which was ten times what the government had spent on national defense prior to the war but still substantially less than wartime highs or the $22 billion originally requested by the armed forces. What was still a war budget, moreover, did reflect the beginnings of a shift from wartime to peacetime priorities. The president pointed with pride to the progress he had made in demobilizing the armed forces and to a total budget that had declined from $67 billion for fiscal year 1946 to $38.5 billion for fiscal year 1947, and that actually included small increases for social security, education, farm subsidies, and other programs unrelated to war and defense.[10]

However modest, these were the first real increases since Pearl Harbor, and they underscored the president's conviction that domestic obligations need not be abandoned to military necessity, the welfare state to the warfare state. To be sure, Truman understood that national security demanded substantial sacrifices of the American people, notably in the large proportion of the budget that was still being siphoned from social and economic investment into military purposes. The need for such sacrifices was emerging as a major theme in the new ideology of national security and in the president's pronouncements as well. Nevertheless, Truman was determined to weigh the hardships that national security required against other claims on the budget and the values they embodied. His goal was a peacetime balance of economic and security concerns, and to achieve this goal he clearly considered it necessary to shift some resources from military programs to social investment and to use more of these resources to eliminate the deficit and reduce the national debt.

Almost immediately, however, the president's effort to balance different priorities ran into difficulties. The Joint Chiefs expressed new alarm about demobilization, claiming that current force levels were barely enough to manage a "minor localized" crisis in Europe and arguing for defense appropriations much larger than the president had in mind. Their recommendation did not amount to the comprehensive plan that Truman had requested in August. Such a plan was impossible to develop

---

[10] Truman, "Message to Congress on the State of the Union and on the Budget for 1947," 21 January 1946, *Public Papers, Truman, 1946*, 378–87.

without first delineating service roles and missions, which in turn awaited agreements on the future status of the air force and unification under a single department of defense. Instead of a comprehensive plan the Joint Chiefs presented an interim proposal that merely combined the separate requests of the armed services, including the Navy's demand for 500,000 sailors by the end of June 1947, as well as 58,000 officers and a Marine Corps of 109,000 troops. These manpower levels, when translated into carriers, battleships, and other naval vessels, amounted to a fleet twice as large as the British navy and "five times larger than the combined navies of all the other powers."[11]

Meanwhile, Congressman Vinson had pushed his resolution, which called for a Navy of this size, through the House of Representatives. The resolution appropriated no funds but its passage did create a prejudice in favor of appropriations that Forrestal put at approximately $5.1 billion in fiscal year 1947, more than $800 million above the sum allotted to the Navy in Truman's proposed budget. Making matters worse, ongoing expenditures on the Navy and on the federal housing program were outpacing what the Budget Bureau had expected, which meant that additional budget cuts would be needed if the administration was going to stay within the deficit that Truman had projected for the fiscal year. Harold Smith and Paul Appleby, assistant director of the Budget Bureau, gave Truman the bad news at a meeting on 18 February and were encouraged when the president barely flinched. "Hold the budget line," was his command, even if it meant larger military cuts than the bureau had anticipated.[12]

The Budget Bureau acted on this order immediately, as did Truman himself. Appleby sent Admiral Leahy, the president's chief of staff, a "rough budget forecast for a true post-war year," his intention being to remind Leahy and the Navy Department of the model budget to which Truman was committed. The forecast predicted a total federal budget

[11] Unsigned memorandum, 14 March 1946, Truman Papers, PSF-Subject File, box 158, folder: Navy, Secy of – Postwar Navy. See also Truman to Smith, 27 November 1945, enclosing Leahy's undated memorandum to the president with attached memorandum by the Joint Chiefs to the president of 23 November 1945, and Leahy memorandum to Truman, 12 March 1946, ibid., box 145, folder: Military: Army–Navy Unification; and record of a conference with the president, 28 November 1945, ibid., box 150, folder: Excerpts from the Diary of Harold D. Smith.

[12] Record of a conference with the president, 18 February 1946, Truman Papers, PSF-Subject File, box 150, folder: Excerpts from the Diary of Harold D. Smith. See also David I. Walsh (chairman, Senate Committee on Naval Affairs) to Truman, 16, February 1946, unsigned memorandum, 14 March 1946, and the enclosures in Smith memorandum for the president, 20 March 1946, ibid., box 158, folder: Navy, Secy of – Postwar Navy.

of $25–27 billion, which included expenditures for the Army and Navy of $5–7 billion plus $8.7 billion for veterans' benefits, interest on the national debt, and other war-related costs. The total for national defense exceeded earlier projections, but Appleby predicted that Congress would put the "squeeze" on these expenditures. Seven billion dollars for the Army and Navy, he concluded, constituted the most "ambitious" figure and the "top possibility" that could be considered. Truman made a similar point when he told the chairman of the Senate Naval Affairs Committee that Vinson's plan would drive the Army–Navy budget to the unacceptable figure of $8.548 billion. He did not want Congress to authorize more than $6 billion, the president said, or to fix the size of the Navy until the armed services had agreed on a comprehensive force structure and the distribution of peacetime duties.[13]

Nor would Truman and Smith give much ground in subsequent talks with Forrestal, who continued to measure the president's budget by a national security yardstick. Forrestal told Smith that Truman's estimates were inadequate "in the face of the Russian situation," the powerful geopolitical argument that drove his demands for more money, and he threatened to say as much in congressional hearings. The threat enraged Smith, who clearly saw it as a Navy challenge to the president's leadership and domestic agenda. He believed that Forrestal was bound to support Truman and that any other course would lead to the "rapid erosion of governmental discipline," particularly to the erosion of civilian control over the armed forces. Truman agreed. When Forrestal protested to him as well as to Smith, he found the president still miffed that the Pentagon had yet to get him a unified defense plan. Without such a plan he was reluctant to bust the budget by approving a peacetime Navy of much more than four hundred thousand sailors.[14]

The deadlock finally produced a compromise that gave Forrestal only some of what he wanted. The two sides agreed to raise the Navy's budget estimate by $200 million, which would allow it to have an average strength of 500,000 sailors over the new fiscal year, but not more than 437,000 at the year's end. Smith and Appleby viewed the compromise as politically necessary, since the Navy had been "negotiating

[13] Appleby to Leahy, 19 February 1946, and unsigned draft letter from Truman to Senator Walsh, 21 February 1946, Truman Papers, PSF-Subject File, box 158, folder: Navy, Secy of – Postwar Navy.

[14] Record of a conference with the president, 28 February, 1946, Truman Papers, PSF-Subject File, box 150, folder: Excerpts from the Diary of Harold D. Smith. See also records of conferences with the president, 4 and 7 March 1946, ibid.

a lot of policy on the Hill," but complained bitterly that it was costing the administration $200 million to buy "something we really shouldn't have to buy – top Navy agreement to support the budget." Still worse, the Budget Bureau was not sure that Forrestal would honor the compromise, especially after he proposed a separate discretionary appropriation of $500–750 million to help the Navy meet its global responsibilities.[15]

With the unification battle building at the same time, the secretary's insubordination was bound to incite fears of a garrison state dominated by military leaders and monopolizing economic resources. Such a development would not only wreck the budget and subvert the government's responsibilities at home, it would also constitute a fundamental redefinition of the state itself. Slight wonder that Truman was beside himself with frustration, which only mounted as Forrestal, Admiral Chester W. Nimitz, and other Navy officials spoke publicly and in congressional hearings about their need for more money than the president's budget allowed. Truman began to see himself as besieged by disloyal insubordinates and a rebellious Congress, much like other presidents before him. Smith and Appleby discovered as much when they visited the White House near the end of March, only to find a dejected president poring over an article, "Truman's Unhappy Year," in a recent issue of *Collier's* magazine.

With this title as a starting point, Truman told his visitors that he had recently finished Marquis James's biography of Andrew Jackson and Bennett Champ Clark's book on John Quincy Adams. There then ensued a discussion that led from Adams and Jackson to the impeachment proceedings against President Andrew Johnson to Truman's recent blow-up with Interior Secretary Harold Ickes, who had impugned the president's integrity in recent congressional testimony. The episode, which resulted in Ickes's dismissal, had embarrassed Truman, who now compared it with the insubordination of the Navy. He "was seriously offended" by the Navy's behavior, he told Smith. He thought that "discipline had been badly upset," "talked about 'firing' Nimitz," and threatened to

---

[15] Record of a conference with the president, 7 March 1946, Truman Papers, PSF-Subject File, box 150, folder: Excerpt from the Diary of Harold D. Smith. See also Forrestal memorandum for the president, 8 March 1946; and Smith memorandum for the president, 20 March 1946, with enclosed draft, "New Expenditures in Relation to President's Budget for Fiscal Year 1947," 20 March 1946, ibid., box 158, folder: Navy, Secy of; and Forrestal memorandum for the president, 12 March 1946, Eberstadt Papers, box 4, folder: 1946 Armed Forces Unification Re Compromise and Discussion.

veto any appropriation that squared with the Navy's demands rather than his own.[16] The Navy's position, he told a press conference shortly thereafter, was "not in line with the facts," by which he meant his own support for a modest increase in domestic spending and some progress toward a balanced budget and reduction of the national debt.[17]

Truman became even more adamant when he learned in April that expenditures for fiscal year 1946 were less than had been expected while revenues were higher. This development promised a budget deficit much smaller than projected just three months earlier, so long as Truman could resist the Navy's incessant demands. His resolve to do so stiffened as the possibility of a balanced budget loomed, and when it also became clear that the War Department was being far more reasonable than the Navy in tailoring its needs to the president's budget. To Truman's way of thinking, the ease with which the Budget Bureau and the War Department had reached agreement was proof of the Navy's intransigence. "I have spent more time on" the Navy's budget, he lamented, than on the budgets of all other agencies "put together."[18]

By the end of May, Truman had won the first postwar battle of the budget. Despite Vinson's support for Forrestal's position, the bill coming from the House of Representatives added barely $100 million to the Navy's budget for fiscal year 1947. Nor was the president yielding elsewhere. In mid-May he again told the armed forces that peacetime defense spending must eventually be capped at no more than one-third of the federal budget, not including payments on the national debt. And in August, he drove his priorities home by fixing defense expenditures for fiscal year 1947 at a sum lower than the amount budgeted by Congress.[19]

---

[16] Record of a conference with the president, 20 March 1946, Truman Papers, PSF-Subject File, box 150, folder: BOB, Smith Diary.

[17] The president's news conference of 21 March 1946 *Public Papers, Truman, 1946*, 164.

[18] Records of conferences with the president, 2 and 29 April 1946, Truman Papers, PSF-Subject File, box 150, folder: BOB, Smith Diary. See also the president's news conference of 11 April 1946 and the statement by the president announcing the revised budget estimates, 11 April 1946, *Public Papers, Truman, 1946*, 191–96.

[19] Record of a conference with the president, 22 May 1946, Truman Papers, PSF-Subject File, box 150, folder: BOB, Smith Diary; press releases of 1 and 2 August 1946 of Truman's letter to the heads of various executive departments and agencies, including the secretaries of war and the navy, ibid., folder: Bureau of Budget, Budget – Misc. 1944–53; Patterson to Truman, 6 August 1946, ibid., box 157, folder: War, Secy of; Forrestal to Truman, 21 August 1946, and James E. Webb (director, Budget Bureau) undated memorandum for the president, ibid., box 158, folder: War, Secy of; and *Forrestal Diaries*, 160, 162–63.

Truman's decision was part of an effort to arrest inflationary pressures at a time when congressional conservatives had weakened the Office of Price Administration and the system of wartime price controls.[20] But however sensible as an antiinflation measure, the decision triggered another clash between traditional values and the national security ideology, another challenge to the principle of civilian rule, another round in the struggle to define the country's political identity and postwar purpose. Forrestal again led the charge. Viewing the nation as a great power with a global mission to contain communism and defend democracy, he told anyone who would listen that American leaders could not succeed with a Navy that had been "stripped down" to a "dangerously low point of efficiency." He was especially concerned about reductions in defense spending so shortly after the allied foreign ministers, meeting in Paris, had failed to reach agreement on the terms of a postwar peace treaty. "The state of the world and the happenings in Paris," he wrote a friend, "do not make me feel like putting the pistols away just yet."[21] On the contrary, he persuaded British and American leaders to open informal talks on how to meet any "emergency in Europe," and then sought with some success to win support for his position in the War Department.[22]

The War Department complained bitterly when Truman decided to limit defense expenditures to a sum lower than Congress had approved for fiscal year 1947. General Eisenhower warned that Truman's decision would make it "practically impossible for the Army to operate," while Secretary Patterson told the president that he needed more money, not less, if the Army was going to meet its occupation responsibilities in Japan, Germany, Italy, and Austria, let alone assume new responsibilities with respect to displaced persons or the defense of South Korea.[23] The Army now saw the budget problem as its "no. 1 priority," and both the Army and the Navy resorted to high-pressure tactics to reverse what Forrestal saw as "a gathering drive to cut down our Armed Forces" and

---

[20] Donovan, *Conflict and Crisis*, 235; James T. Patterson, *Mr. Republican: A Biography of Robert A. Taft* (Boston, 1972), 307–10.

[21] *Forrestal Diaries*, 196–97. See also Forrestal to Truman, 21 August 1946, Truman Papers, PSF-Subject File, box 158, folder: Navy, Secy of.

[22] *Forrestal Diaries*, 196. See also ibid., 198; and Forrestal Diary, 5 September 1946, Forrestal Papers, vol. 5, box 3.

[23] *Forrestal Diaries*, 199. See also Patterson to Truman, 20 September 1946, Truman Papers, PSF-Subject File, box 158, folder: Navy, Secy of.

"haul out of Europe and out of China as well." The Army threatened to terminate its services in the occupied areas, dumping them on the State Department, while the Navy, which had been trying to build public support by taking community leaders for joy rides on naval vessels, raised the prospect of recalling its fleet from the Mediterranean.[24]

None of these threats fazed Truman, who now had the staunch backing of James E. Webb, the new director of the Bureau of the Budget. Webb was a North Carolina lawyer and successful businessman who had made millions in the oil and aviation industries. A tough-minded and pragmatic professional manager, he understood, as Harold Smith had before him, that the bureau's principal responsibility was to protect the president's budget policies and institutional prerogatives. This both men did with unrelenting energy, not to mention a commitment to peacetime priorities and to a balanced budget that was not always compatible with perceived national security needs.

With the Treasury now showing a deficit for the year of just $2 billion, both Truman and Webb were convinced that "further pressure" might "close that gap." Guided by this goal, they refused to consider the Pentagon's requests for additional funding, regardless of the consequences threatened by the Army and the Navy. "They do not have to bring back the Mediterranean fleet to make the necessary savings," Truman said of the Navy. "All they have to do is close down a few Navy Yards." In a letter to Omar B. Ketchum of the American Legion, the president said that he would "make the income meet the outgo" by forcing the Pentagon to "take a substantial cut." And in line with that threat, he even required Forrestal to report the Navy's expenditures each month to the Budget Bureau, much like an ex-convict reporting to a parole officer.[25] In the end, moreover, Truman's resolve paid off. The limits he imposed on spending combined with higher-than-expected tax revenues to produce a balanced budget in fiscal year 1947, and even a small surplus.

[24] Record of a War Council meeting, 17 October 1946, Patterson Papers, General Correspondence, box 23, folder: 1945–47, War Council Meeting; *Forrestal Diaries*, 215. See also Webb notes on a conference with Truman, 11 October 1946, Webb Papers, box 3, folder: Bureau of the Budget, Conference Notes.

[25] Webb notes on a conference with Truman, 11 October 1946, Webb Papers, box 3, folder: Bureau of the Budget, Conference Notes; Truman to Ketchum, 12 November 1946, Truman Papers, PSF-General File, box 112, folder: Appropriations. See also Truman to Forrestal, 9 October 1946, Truman Papers, PSF-Subject File, box 158, folder: Navy, Secy of.

III

Truman's victory in the 1946 budget battle set a pattern that lasted through the next year. Still concerned about inflation and still determined to get government spending on a peacetime basis, the president wanted another surplus in fiscal year 1948, which he could use to reduce the national debt and achieve a better balance between the government's international obligations and its domestic responsibilities. With these goals in mind, he decided to drive defense spending lower, and to do so over the resolute opposition of officials in the national security establishment. More concerned with military than with civilian needs, these officials were still determined to impose their priorities on the budget, even if it meant raising another challenge to civilian authority, and even if it meant substituting the warfare state for the welfare state.[26]

The War and Navy departments initially submitted budgets totaling more than $22 billion for fiscal year 1948, a sum that Webb considered "so fantastic and unrealistic" that he questioned the integrity of the budgeting process in the Pentagon.[27] Disgusted with what he saw, Webb promptly ordered the military departments to regear their estimates to the president's priorities, which were also his own. Like Truman, in other words, he seemed to assume that national security was taking a greater share of the budget than necessary and that more resources should be allocated to other needs. As it was, defense spending amounted to almost 35 percent of the estimated total expenditures for the new fiscal year, with other war-related and international programs bringing the total to nearly 80 percent. "In such a budget," Webb and his colleagues lamented, "very little room is left for such purposes as education and general research, public health, housing, and development of industry, agriculture, transportation, and our national resources." These would continue to receive "only trivial amounts," with results over the long term that would do great harm to "national objectives, including military strength."[28]

---

[26] Press release of a statement by the president at the budget seminar, 8 January 1947, Truman Papers, PSF-Subject File, Bureau of the Budget, box 150, folder: Budget – Misc., 1945–53.

[27] Agenda for a conference by the director with the secretaries of war and navy, the chief of staff of the army, and the chief of naval operations, 9 October 1946, Webb Papers, box 15, folder: Federal Budget – 1948. See also the notes of a conference with the secretary of war and chief of staff, secretary of the navy, and chief of naval operations, and Leahy, 9 October 1946, ibid.

[28] Unsigned comments on the size of the military defense budget, 8 October 1946, ibid.

Webb was raising again the question of priorities in peacetime budget making, which was essentially a question about the nation's political identity and postwar purpose. He was asking if the country was going to define itself as a welfare state or as a warfare state, if education, housing, health, and other programs were going to be sacrificed to military requirements. While the Pentagon wanted defense spending large enough to meet almost every military contingency, Webb sought to reconcile the claims of defense with the president's domestic agenda, including a balanced budget and all of the values it represented. With this goal in mind, he and his colleagues convinced the armed forces to reduce their demands to slightly less than $16 billion, and then complained that even this figure was too high. They still wondered how long the American people could stand an annual defense budget that matched the amount they spent on clothing, doubled their spending on housing, and was five times what they spent on medical care. Convinced that taxpayers would revolt against such skewed priorities "in the third year after the end of active combat," Webb trimmed the defense budget still further before Truman submitted it to Congress in January 1947.[29]

Truman's proposed budget estimated defense expenditures at slightly more than $11 billion in fiscal year 1948, an amount that required $9.6 billion in new obligatory authority. Estimated expenditures in the major budget categories, including defense, international affairs, interest on the national debt, and veterans' benefits, still stood at more than $29 billion, or four-fifths of the total budget, while expenditures for social welfare, health, and education amounted to only $1.7 billion; housing to slightly more than $500 million; natural resources, communications, and transportation to $2.6 billion; and agriculture to $1.4 billion. National spending still favored defense and international programs, as Truman admitted. But the budget was balanced and there was a real prospect of liquidating a small portion of the public debt, so long as Congress continued wartime taxes for another year or two.

In addition, Truman noted that defense spending had dropped to one-eighth of its wartime high and that spending on domestic programs continued to show modest gains, including much needed investment in conservation, agriculture, education, and social programs. He hoped eventually to see national health insurance, a higher minimum wage, expanded Social Security benefits, and passage of the Taft–Ellender–Wagner housing bill. He made it clear that further reductions in the defense

[29] Ibid.

budget would enable the government to reallocate a larger share of its resources to these and similar programs, and he promised additional reductions and reallocations in the years to come. In short, the president envisioned a postwar reconstruction of the welfare state within the framework of a balanced budget, a goal he considered both a practical necessity and a moral good, and one he would achieve through a further downsizing of the military establishment.[30]

Truman's decision to reduce the defense budget was a clear disappointment to senior officials in the Pentagon, who were determined to avoid even deeper cuts in Congress. With this in mind, both the War and Navy departments launched a "strong campaign" on Capitol Hill and in the press. Forrestal lobbied Congress on behalf of the Navy's budget and sought support at the same time from Secretary of State Marshall, a former military man with enormous prestige in Washington. As in the past, Forrestal drew on the ideology of national security to make his case, stressing in particular the country's commitment to the defense of freedom around the world and the widening gap between this commitment and its military capabilities. He was all for economies, the secretary said, but "not at the expense of our ability to move, and move fast," in the event of an emergency. "When the stakes are as high as they are," he concluded, it would be a "grave decision" to deny national security managers "the cards to play."[31]

Forrestal's appeals did not sound as convincing as they would only a short time later, in large part because the United States had clear air and naval superiority over the Soviet Union, intelligence estimates gave no indication of Soviet military aggression, and the Joint Chiefs had yet to produce a war plan to justify their force requirements. They had been trying to draft such a plan since the end of the war, but their efforts had faltered on the same interservice squabbles that had also stalled a comprehensive agreement on postwar force levels. Indeed, the Joint Chiefs could not even agree on relative American and Soviet military capabilities, on service roles and missions, or on the utility of atomic weapons. The best they could do was to outline an emergency war plan,

---

30 Truman, "Annual Message to Congress on the State of the Union," 6 January 1947, "Special Message to Congress: The President's First Economic Report," 8 January 1947, and "Annual Budget Message to the Congress." 10 January 1947, *Public Papers, Truman, 1947*, 1–12, 13–39, 55–97; Susan M. Hartmann, *Truman and the 80th Congress* (Columbia, MO, 1971), 22–25.

31 War Council meeting, 15 January 1947, Patterson Papers, General Correspondence, box 23, folder: 1945–47, War Council Meeting; *Forrestal Diaries*, 237–40. See also Patterson, *Mr. Republican*, 372–73.

which the armed forces would use for planning purposes only, and even this much progress was still a year away.[32]

Nor did it help Forrestal's case that Congress as well as the White House was racing to reestablish peacetime priorities. The Republicans, who captured control of Congress in the elections of 1946, had hardly mentioned foreign policy and national security during the course of the campaign. They ran against big government, which they promised to cut down to size by curbing public expenditures, eliminating the vestiges of wartime economic controls, and reducing taxes – all while balancing the budget and paying off the national debt.

Determined to redeem these pledges, the Republicans envisioned a further reduction in defense spending as part of a larger plan to trim $6 billion from the $37.5 billion budget that Truman had projected for fiscal year 1948. To achieve this target, they allowed the wartime Selective Service Act to expire without regard for the level of military manpower and cut Truman's defense budget from $9.6 billion to $8.7 billion in new appropriations. These and other reductions, together with those already effected by the administration, laid the groundwork for an anticipated budget surplus of nearly $5 billion in fiscal year 1948. The surplus was larger than Truman had expected, thanks to the congressional reductions, and both he and the Republicans wanted others to follow. Indeed, when the president announced the expected surplus in August, he also announced his intention to shrink the budget still further, chip away at the national debt, and allocate more resources to domestic programs that had been starved during the war.[33]

At the time of Truman's announcement, however, the government's fixed charges were making it virtually impossible to cut the budget much more. Webb told the president that his model peacetime budget of $25 billion was out of the question and that the best he could expect was a budget of $30–35 billion.[34] Then, too, the closer Truman came to a budget surplus the more the Republicans pushed for a tax cut. Denouncing the president as "high-spending-high-taxing Harry," they argued that any peace dividend should go to individual consumers, not to nondefense

[32] Kenneth W. Condit, *The History of the Joint Chiefs of Staff*, vol. 2, *The Joint Chiefs of Staff and National Policy, 1947–1949* (Wilmington, 1979), 22, 283–92.

[33] Ibid., 20, 191; Truman press release, 19 August 1947, Truman Papers, PSF-Subject File, box 150, folder: Bureau of the Budget, Budget – Misc., 1945–53.

[34] Webb notes on a conference with the president, 28 October 1946, Webb Papers, box 3, folder: Bureau of the Budget, Conference Notes.

programs.[35] Finally, events abroad were also conspiring to forestall additional cuts, at least in defense spending. On the contrary, if developments in Greece and Turkey were any indication, the international situation appeared to portend an expansion of national security expenditures, not a reduction.

In February 1947 the financially strapped government in London had decided to withdraw support from the repressive, corrupt, but decidedly pro-British government of Greece, which was then locked in a life-and-death struggle with a coalition of left-wing guerrilla fighters and their Communist supporters in neighboring countries. A rebel victory, the administration believed, would open the door to an expansion of Soviet influence through Greece to the Mediterranean. The same would be true if the government in Turkey gave in to Soviet pressure for joint control of the Black Sea Straits, yet another gateway to the Mediterranean. On 12 March, Truman addressed the international situation in a speech to Congress, arguing that both Greece and Turkey were imperiled and pledging, in what came to be known as the Truman Doctrine, American aid to contain communism worldwide, beginning with $400 million in economic aid to the two beleaguered countries.[36]

The Greco-Turkish aid program, which Congress approved while debating the budget for fiscal year 1948, clearly underscored the growing demands on the budget and the competition for resources. By requiring new sacrifices in the name of national security, it challenged the president's ability to reconcile the needs of the warfare state with those of the welfare state, the government's global mission with its domestic obligations, including a balanced budget. Forrestal stressed this point when he told the House Appropriations Committee that Congress faced a "lot of colliding objectives," including "the five-day week, six-hour day, high wages, low prices for manufactured goods, reduced taxes, a balanced budget, debt reduction, a large and strong Army and Navy, [and] a firm foreign policy." If government tried to tackle all of these objectives, he said, it would wreck the economy and "stumble into state socialism just as successfully as if we had marked our course for that harbor."

---

35 Press release of a joint statement by Senator Harry Bridges and Representative John Taber, 21 August 1947, Truman Papers, PSF-Subject File, box 150, folder: Bureau of the Budget, Budget – Misc., 1944–53.

36 For differing accounts of the Truman Doctrine and aid to Greece and Turkey see Bruce R. Kuniholm, *The Origins of the Cold War in the Near East: Great Power Conflict and Diplomacy in Iran, Turkey, and Greece* (Princeton, 1980); and Lawrence S. Wittner, *American Intervention in Greece, 1943–1949* (New York, 1982).

Additional sacrifices had to be made, and it seemed clear that Forrestal wanted his fellow citizens to defer domestic gains in favor of "a firm foreign policy."[37]

Although others had a different set of priorities, it was soon evident that global developments were tilting the debate in Forrestal's favor. The best indication of this came not in the Greco-Turkish aid bill but in subsequent efforts to reconcile the administration's plan for the reconstruction of Western Europe with a Republican plan to cut taxes by nearly $4 billion. When Congress first took up the tax bill its implications for national security were not initially apparent and did not figure prominently in the debate. Instead, most Democrats complained that the Republican proposal would spur inflation and benefit the wealthy few rather than the average income earner. Besides, they said, the administration had cut expenditures as much as possible, a balanced budget was in the offing, and any surplus should go to reduce the national debt, not individual income taxes.[38]

The Republicans, on the other hand, along with their allies among conservative Democrats, complained about a federal budget that had not been balanced in sixteen years. Government, they said, was spending four times more than it had in the prewar period, and more every three or four years than it had in the first 140 years of the Republic. It had become a "Frankenstein" monster, as one of them put it, with so much power, a debt so large, and spending so vast that democracy and national solvency were in danger of giving way to socialism and bankruptcy. These trends had to be reversed, the Republicans argued. Truman's budget had to be trimmed and the savings passed on to the American people in the form of a tax cut.[39]

As this summary of the debate suggests, neither side at this point had much to say about national defense and international programs. Although some Republicans thought it possible to shrink these programs to cover the cost of a tax cut, most of the debate revolved around other issues and continued to do so as the bill passed by substantial margins. Thereafter, everything changed. New developments abroad again raised questions about the sacrifices that national security required and about how these sacrifices would be distributed across the economy.

[37] *Forrestal Diaries*, 249–50.
[38] *Congressional Record, 1947* 93:2062. For the arguments over the tax debate in Congress see also ibid., 809–15, 894–95, 2627–84, 2738–75, 5588–96, 5605–8, 5635–45, 5781–5803, 5943–49, 6196–6205, 6240–44.
[39] Ibid., 2603. In addition to the sources cited in the following note see also Patterson, *Mr. Republican*, 373–74.

In early June, only a week after the Senate had passed the Republican tax bill, Secretary Marshall announced what would become the European Recovery Program, or Marshall Plan. By that time a combination of exchange problems, a severe winter in 1946–47, and Soviet-American quarrels over Germany were threatening to reverse the progress that European governments had made in rebuilding their war-torn economies. Convinced that Communist parties stood to benefit from worsening economic conditions on the continent, Marshall proposed a massive foreign aid program to rebuild Europe and harness Germany to the cause of containment.[40]

Marshall's proposal clearly influenced the legislative priorities in Congress and in the White House. Determined to protect their plans for a tax cut and a balanced budget, the Republicans in Congress used the proposal as a strong argument for curbing public investment in the domestic programs that Truman had recommended. Indeed, by the time the first session of the Eightieth Congress had adjourned in July, the Republicans had succeeded in tabling or rejecting the president's proposals for social legislation as well as his plans for additional economic controls and new investments in land reclamation and power projects.[41]

In the White House, on the other hand, Marshall's proposal influenced Truman's decision to veto the Republican tax bill. Arguments by the administration repeated those raised earlier by the bill's critics in Congress. A tax cut would short-circuit plans for a more fundamental reform of the tax system, the administration insisted, and would also eliminate any chance of reducing the government's debt, encourage inflation at a time when the Republicans were hell-bent on decontrolling the economy, and leave the Treasury with no surplus to cover unexpected expenses relating to the country's international obligations. The bill, as Truman said in his veto message, was "the wrong kind of tax reduction, at the wrong time," since it would wipe out a budget surplus that he intended as a "bulwark" against inflation at home and as a "reserve against emergencies" abroad.[42]

[40] Hogan, *Marshall Plan*, 26–53.
[41] Hartmann, *Truman and the 80th Congress*, 38.
[42] Press release of Truman's message to the House of Representatives, 16 June 1947, Truman Papers, Clark M. Clifford Files, box 2, folder: Bills of the 80th Congress, HR 3950. See also the message by the Council of Economic Advisers to the president, 5 June 1947; Marriner S. Eccles (chairman, Federal Reserve Board) to Truman (with enclosure), 6 June 1947; Marshall to Truman, 10 June 1947; Patterson to Truman, 11 June 1947; Secretary of the Treasury John W. Snyder to Webb, 15 July 1947; and undated memorandum, "Some Suggested Themes for Veto Message on Tax Bill," all in ibid.

As the Republicans saw it, Truman had decided to relieve the war-torn countries of Europe rather than the hard-pressed taxpayers of the United States. As a result, the debate about overriding the veto, unlike the original debate on the tax bill itself, focused almost entirely on this decision. It raised important questions about the kind of postwar state the Americans would build, and marked another round in the guns-and-butter politics that would characterize so much of the Cold War. Democrats defended the veto by arguing, in effect, that Europe was essential to the country's military security and economic well being, that it must therefore have the first claim on any budget surplus, and that such a priority was one of the sacrifices that national security had forced on the American people. The Republicans, on the other hand, denounced the Democrats and the "internationally minded me-too Republicans" for putting Europe ahead of the United States. "America first" was their motto, as opposed to Truman's program of "tax-and-borrow-and-spend-in-other-countries," which was leading the American people down the road to "national bankruptcy."

Led by Congressman Harold Knutson of Minnesota, who had sponsored the tax bill in the House, the Republicans also expressed utter contempt for "the one-worlders, the do-gooders, and the internationalists" who ignored George Washington's admonition against entangling alliances. Clearly, these "give-away-boys" did not understand that international welfare programs like the Marshall Plan were stripping the country of the economic muscle it needed to safeguard freedom in a totalitarian world. Nor did they see that Truman's high-handed veto robbed Congress of its control over the country's purse strings and put the United States itself on the slippery slope to totalitarianism.[43] With arguments like these, the Republicans overrode the president's veto in the House of Representatives but fell short of the two-thirds required in the Senate. A slightly revised version of the same bill met a similar fate one month later.[44]

In the course of the debate, both sides had come to the conclusion that the country could not afford to contain communism while at the same time expanding the New Deal, reducing taxes, and balancing the budget – at least not without redefining itself as a garrison state, which both sides wanted to avoid. In what was becoming one of the keynotes in the national security discourse, everyone agreed that sacrifices had to

---

[43] *Congressional Record, 1947* 93:7146. For the debate over Truman's veto see ibid., 7143–48, 8436–60, 9260–82.
[44] *Congressional Quarterly, 1947,* 340, 507–9.

be made. But the sacrifice that Truman envisioned, namely higher taxes, was the very one that conservative Republicans refused to accept. While Truman saw higher taxes as a way to reconcile the government's international obligations with its responsibilities at home, the Republicans, who put a premium on the traditional values associated with low taxes and a balanced budget, had come to the conclusion that domestic expenditures needed to be curtailed. The final result was a combination of these two sets of priorities. The president held the line on tax cuts and the Republicans on social expenditures, while developments in Europe, as Forrestal confided to his diary, forced Congress to think more seriously about the country's "position as the great stabilizer in international affairs."[45]

It remained to be seen if this more serious thinking would translate into Republican support for the Marshall Plan. In the months following Marshall's proposal, a succession of foreign crises would lend more credibility to the new ideology of national security, captured in Truman's assertion that peace and freedom were threatened everywhere and were everywhere indivisible. But at the same time, the cost of containment and the growing influence of the military services, coupled with their tendency toward self-aggrandizement and their bold defiance of civilian authority, would raise again the specter of a "Frankenstein" government that could wreck the economy and subvert democracy. For conservatives, in particular, this possibility reinforced the need to cut taxes and trim the New Deal. It also made them reluctant to support programs like the Marshall Plan, and it sparked their enthusiasm for a capital-intensive defense that emphasized airpower over a more costly expansion of the Navy and the Army.

IV

In the first half of 1948, Congress debated another major tax bill and appropriations for defense, as well as expenditures for the Marshall Plan. Policy makers in both political parties and in the White House knew that difficult choices had to be made, but could not agree on what those choices should be. Truman announced his priorities at the start of the year, when he presented budget estimates for fiscal year 1949 totaling $39.7 billion. He earmarked 79 percent of that amount for national security and other war-related purposes and also called for additional

---

45 *Forrestal Diaries*, 250.

spending on education, housing, health insurance, the conservation of natural resources, and farm supports. The president would pay for these domestic gains as well as the Marshall Plan by capping the defense budget and reducing expenditures on a variety of international programs. Through such devices, he would hold the total budget increase to only $2 billion over the previous year and try to produce a surplus of nearly $5 billion, which he would use to reduce the national debt.[46]

Once again taxes loomed as a major issue between the two political parties, although the tax debate, like the debate over the Marshall Plan, would be the occasion for a more important struggle over how the American people would define themselves and their postwar purpose. In his annual message on the state of the union, Truman warned against reducing tax revenues at a time when the government was trying to liquidate its debt, expand essential services, and aid in Europe's recovery. He was in favor of a cost-of-living tax credit, but the credit would be modest and the lost revenue would be made up by raising corporate income taxes.[47] The Republicans, however, quickly replaced Truman's proposal with a bill that would cut income taxes by nearly $4 billion a year. Invoking traditional Republican ideology, they argued that such cuts were the best way to contain the state and eliminate a host of New Deal programs that were politically corrupt and morally repugnant.

In debating the bill, both parties repeated arguments rehearsed the previous year. Democrats claimed again that Republican tax policy favored the wealthy over the average taxpayer and would preclude a much-needed reform of the tax code. Even more important was the risk that a tax cut posed to price stability and a balanced budget, and especially to the nation's new role as the champion of democracy worldwide. After all, the president had earmarked three-quarters of his budget for defense and international programs, and the cost of these programs, according to the Democrats, could not be reduced without lowering barriers to the spread of communism. The Republicans, on the other hand, argued that current tax rates were so excessive as to stifle investment and discourage production. They thought it was possible to reduce taxes while balancing the budget and paying off the public debt, so long as

---

[46] Truman, "Annual Message to the Congress on the State of the Union," 7 January 1948, and "Annual Budget Message to the Congress, Fiscal Year 1949," 12 January 1948, *Public Papers, Truman, 1948* (Washington, 1964), 1–10, 19–59. See also McCullough, *Truman*, 586.

[47] Truman, "Annual Message to the Congress on the State of the Union," 7 January 1948, *Public Papers, Truman, 1948*, 1–9.

they shaved down the president's estimates, not only for domestic programs but for the Marshall Plan as well. Informed by these convictions as to the choices before them and the sacrifices that had to be made, the Republicans rammed their tax bill through Congress and succeeded this time in overriding a presidential veto.[48]

The debate on tax policy overlapped congressional consideration of the Marshall Plan, and the two were quickly linked in the minds of Republicans, especially those from western and midwestern states that had long been bastions of fiscal conservatism, economic nationalism, and isolationism. Led by Senator Taft, these Republicans and their allies among conservative Democrats were convinced that democracy had to be saved at home before it was saved abroad. With this priority in mind, they launched a concerted attempt to facilitate tax cuts by limiting the amount appropriated for the European Recovery Program. Supporters had envisioned approximately $5.3 billion for the first twelve months of the program. But conservatives argued that aid on such a scale would exhaust the Treasury, generate shortages, and trigger inflation, all problems that would surely grow worse if the administration tried to deal with them by raising taxes or imposing coercive economic controls.

As these arguments suggest, conservatives like Taft worried that a European aid program would vitiate their success in decontrolling the economy, reducing taxes, and curbing government power. In operation, they argued, it might actually foster the very totalitarianism it was intended to prevent. This was the danger of a garrison state, the rhetorical symbol that conservatives invoked repeatedly, and it was evident not only in the United States but also in Europe, where American aid would supposedly nurture socialist regimes, waste resources on debilitating welfare programs, and discourage private initiative. From Taft's point of view, in other words, the Marshall Plan was the wrong kind of state making both at home and in Europe, and it would be best, under the circumstances, if Congress slashed the amount proposed by more than $1 billion.[49]

The administration and its allies in Congress reversed the arguments mounted by their opponents, claiming, in effect, that Marshall aid would

---

[48] The tax battle in 1948 can be followed in the *Congressional Record, 1948* 94:789–822, 688–711, 888–926, 3037–42, 3177–3222, 3229–33, 4051–53, 3399–3401, 4020–26. See also *Congressional Quarterly Almanac, 1948* 4:344–50; and Leon H. Keyserling (vice chairman, Council of Economic Advisers) to Truman, 31 March 1948, and Truman's veto message to Congress, 2 April 1948, Elsey Papers, Subject File, box 79, folder: Legislation – 80th Congress, 2d Session, Tax Legislation.

[49] Hogan, *Marshall Plan*, 89–101. See also Taft's address to the Economic Club of Detroit, 23 February 1948, Taft Papers, Legislative File, box 616, folder: Foreign Policy, 1948.

prevent the country's democratic identity from giving way to the garrison state. Drawing on a number of impressive studies, they maintained that American resources were equal to the Marshall Plan and that inflationary pressures could be minimized through voluntary measures of conservation and by proper fiscal management, by allocating items in short supply, and by licensing exports. This was particularly true if existing taxes were maintained, although Truman and his supporters continued to argue, even after the tax cut had passed, that economic growth would make it possible to underwrite the Marshall Plan without deficit spending and its attendant consequences, such as rising prices or economic controls.[50]

Indeed, to hear them tell it, the Marshall Plan was the most cost-effective way to safeguard democracy and avoid regimentation in both Europe and the United States. Marshall aid would help to restart the wheels of industry in Europe, cut the ground from under Communist parties there, and end the pressure for dangerous experiments with socialist enterprise and government controls. It would bring similar benefits in the United States, in large part by preventing the economic dislocations and "government control of business" that might result from the loss of European markets or from the country's economic isolation in a Communist world. In such a world, government monopolies and state trading would become common practice, compelling a similar organization of the American economy and forcing the United States into a military buildup so large as to create a permanent war economy, including a measure of government regulation that was incompatible with private enterprise and democratic politics. In summary, both sides used the same rhetorical device to encapsulate their arguments and defend their recommendations. But while conservatives saw the garrison state emerging from the Marshall Plan, supporters saw the plan as the only way to safeguard democracy at home and in Europe.[51]

In early 1948, it seemed that Taft and his associates stood a good chance of greatly reducing the amount of aid involved. They had organized a Senate group known as the Revisionists and had enough strength among Republicans and conservative Democrats to pose a serious threat to the administration's national security agenda. But the threat evaporated in February and March 1948, when the Communists seized the

---

[50] Hogan, *Marshall Plan*, 89–101.

[51] Ibid.; *Congressional Quarterly Almanac, 1948* 4:106–10, 172–92. The quotation is from 176. See also Truman's annual budget message to Congress, 12 January 1948, *Public Papers, Truman, 1948*, 21.

government of Czechoslovakia – the last outpost of democracy in Eastern Europe. The Czech crisis sent a war scare through the Western world and especially through Washington, where it was widely regarded as prelude to coups d'etat in Italy and other countries with powerful Communist parties. Addressing Congress on 17 March, Truman cast the recent developments in Prague as a threat to "our national security" and demanded quick action on the Marshall Plan as a weapon in the war against communism. His speech immediately threw the Republican revisionists on the defensive. Half of them broke ranks and the Marshall Plan sailed through Congress with overwhelming support.[52]

Together with the tax cut, the European Recovery Program made a balanced budget less likely than Truman had been willing to admit. The administration had achieved one of its priorities, but the Republicans had achieved one of theirs as well, and the possibility of reconciling the two within the framework of a balanced budget began to diminish. This was particularly true because the Czech crisis also prompted an increase in defense spending in fiscal year 1949. The budget debates that followed raised serious concerns about military strategy, and about the success of military unification, the principle of civilian rule, and the tendency toward economic and political regimentation. As with earlier debates, moreover, they also involved difficult decisions about the sacrifices that national security required and revealed different strategies for protecting American democracy against the dangers of a garrison state.

In planning for the new fiscal year, Truman had been as determined as ever to force defense spending into line with his budget priorities. In July 1947, he had authorized the Budget Bureau to establish a "dollar ceiling" under which the Army and Navy were to calculate their estimates for fiscal year 1949, whereupon the bureau mandated a ceiling that did not exceed the level of the previous year.[53] The ceiling led policymakers in the Pentagon to raise the usual hue and cry about the gap between the country's overseas commitments and its military capabilities. The Joint Chiefs warned that a partial mobilization might be necessary to enforce a

---

[52] Hogan, *Marshall Plan*, 89–101; *Congressional Quarterly Almanac, 1948* 4:177; Truman, "Special Message to Congress on the Threat to the Freedom of Europe," 17 March 1948, *Public Papers, Truman, 1948*, 182–86.

[53] Forrestal to Secretary of the Army Kenneth C. Royall, 14 August 1947, Records of the Office of the Secretary of the Army, Record Group 335 (Washington National Records Center, Suitland, MD), General Correspondence, file: 111 (hereafter RG 335). See also the undated letter from Eisenhower to Truman, probably August 1947, Hoyt S. Vandenberg Papers (Library of Congress), box 43, folder: Chief of Staff.

presidential policy statement declaring the security of the Middle East and the eastern Mediterranean vital to American interests. They expressed similar concerns about using additional American forces to strengthen the anti-Communist government in Italy, as suggested by the NSC in October 1947, and about the manpower shortage that emerged when Congress ended selective service.[54] As of January 1948, the Army pointed out, its strength had dwindled to 552,000 troops, well below its authorized strength of 667,000.[55]

Secretary of the Army Kenneth C. Royall and Army Chief of Staff General Dwight D. Eisenhower wanted a combined Army–Air Force budget of nearly $8.5 billion in fiscal year 1949, an amount roughly $2.5 billion above the ceiling fixed by the Budget Bureau. Merely meeting their basic responsibilities would require at least $7.3 billion, they argued, and even more would be needed to avoid "calculated" risks to the national security. Stuart Symington, the hot-headed Missouri businessman and newly nominated secretary of the Air Force, was even more adamant. He would rather fight the Budget Bureau tooth and nail than "take the rap" for a budget he considered grossly inadequate, especially when the Navy's air wing was sucking up funds that he thought belonged to the Air Force. Nor was Symington the kind of man who allowed inexperience to check his opinion. In a phone conversation with General Hoyt S. Vandenberg, for example, it quickly became clear that Symington knew next to nothing about such procurement items as the R5F, the C-119, the PBM-5, and other planes. Nevertheless, he was prepared to defend requests for them anyway, because, as he explained, "the more we fight for the more we're going to end up getting."[56]

The complaints coming from the Pentagon, as Symington's remark about the Navy suggests, had as much to do with interservice disputes as with the perceived gap between the country's commitments and capabilities. As noted in the last chapter, Congress had written a statement on

54 Condit, *Joint Chiefs of Staff*, 2:25–28, 66–67.

55 Steven L. Rearden, *History of the Office of the Secretary of Defense: The Formative Years, 1947–1950* (Washington, 1984), 316–17.

56 Royall to Webb, 16 December 1947, RG 51, Series 47.3, box 22, folder: G1-81; records of telephone conversations between Vandenberg and Symington, 26 and 27 September 1947, Vandenberg Papers, box 1, folder: Daily Diary Kept of Office of Deputy Commander. See also undated Eisenhower letter to Truman, Vandenberg Papers, box 43, folder: Chief of Staff; and Eugene M. Zuckert (special assistant to the assistant secretary of war for air) memorandum for Symington, 5 September 1947, Stuart Symington Papers (Truman Library), box 8, folder: Correspondence File, 1946–50: Memoranda – General. The R5F was a helicopter, the C-119 was a troop carrier, and the PBM-5 was an amphibious patrol bomber used for air–sea rescue.

service roles and missions into the National Security Act of 1947, and the White House had issued an executive order on the same subject. But the resulting documents defined service functions too broadly to be of much help when an ad hoc committee representing each branch of the armed forces tried but failed to reconcile the differences between them. Nor were these differences harmonized when the committee referred the whole matter to the Joint Chiefs, who found it impossible to assign "roles and missions" without a joint strategic concept, on which the services had yet to agree.[57]

The problem stemmed from the reluctance of the services to accept any limits on their operations, a phenomenon especially apparent in the Navy's claim to a major role in the field of strategic warfare. The Air Force was determined to dominate that field with a new fleet of B-36 bombers, while the Navy sought support for a big flush-deck carrier, the so-called supercarrier, from which heavy bombers could launch air–atomic attacks against the Soviet Union. The two sides squabbled like children over the relative merits of their cases, and then over who started the squabble in the first place. And with each new round of the conflict, an agreed statement on roles and missions became less probable, as did an agreed budget and strategic concept.[58]

Forrestal finally sequestered the feuding chiefs on a naval base at Key West, Florida, where he won support for an agreement that permitted the Navy to push ahead with a flush-deck carrier while giving the Air Force primary responsibility in the area of strategic bombing.

---

[57] Forrestal memorandum for the secretaries of the army, navy, and air force, 3 February 1948, Records of the Office of the Secretary of Defense, Record Group 330 (National Archives), CD 12-1-26 (hereafter RG 330). See also John H. Ohly (Forrestal aide) memorandum for Forrestal, 15 October 1948, RG 330, CD 12-1-8; JCS 1478/20, 22 January 1948, enclosing Forrestal memorandum to the Joint Chiefs and secretaries of the army, navy, and air force, 20 January 1948, JCS 1478/21, Report by the Ad Hoc Committee to the Joint Chiefs, 28 January 1948, with enclosures, chief of naval operations memorandum to the Joint Chiefs, 30 January 1948, RG 218, CCS 370 (8-19-45), Sec. 6; and General Wedemeyer memorandum for the army chief of staff, 10 February 1948, ibid., Sec. 1. See also Condit, *Joint Chiefs of Staff*, 2:165–75.

[58] Norstad memorandum for the record, 18 February 1948, Norstad Papers, Pentagon Series, box 21, folder: Memorandums for the Record; Royall memorandum for Forrestal, 28 February 1948, ibid., box 25, folder: Roles and Missions. Also Lt. Gen. LeR. Lutes memorandum for Forrestal, 9 March 1948; Royall memorandum to Forrestal, 12 March 1948; Symington memorandum for Forrestal, 12 March 1948; Symington memorandum for Forrestal, 15 March 1948, with enclosed Symington memorandum for Secretary of the Navy John Sullivan, 15 March 1948; and Symington memorandum for Forrestal, 22 March 1948, with enclosed Symington memorandum to Sullivan of 22 March 1948, RG 330, CD 12-1-26. See also Condit, *Joint Chiefs of Staff*, 2:175–81.

Carrier-based aircraft might play a role in that area, too, but only as determined by the Joint Chiefs acting on recommendations from the Air Force. The Joint Chiefs wrote these agreements into a "functions" paper that Forrestal sent to the White House, at which point the president accepted the paper as a substitute for the mission statement he had ordered earlier.[59]

Supposedly, the Key West agreements would make it easier for the armed forces to reconcile their differences and live with the president's budget priorities. As submitted to Congress in January 1948, Truman's defense budget for fiscal year 1949 totaled only $11 billion, including $9.8 billion in new obligatory authority. This figure meant that Truman was holding the line to virtually the same amount and the same 28 percent of the total budget as in the previous fiscal year. Given the rate of inflation, moreover, the figure would limit the Air Force to only fifty-five regular groups and require a reduction in military personnel. Over the long term, Truman hoped to offset that reduction through a program of universal military training (UMT) for able-bodied young men, which he saw as less expensive than a regular military establishment and therefore more in line with his efforts to balance the budget and allocate additional funds to health, education, and the Marshall Plan. "All these programs," Truman told Congress, "directly support the twofold objective of building economic and individual strength and health in this Nation, and of better preparing this Nation to discharge its increased responsibilities in the family of nations."[60]

But while Truman was still trying to balance the government's domestic responsibilities against its global obligations, the Pentagon was arguing that equilibrium was all but impossible. When the NSC considered using force to safeguard American interests in Greece and Italy, the Joint Chiefs

---

[59] Diary entry, "Meeting with the President-Key West Conference Report," 15 March 1948, Forrestal Diaries, Forrestal Papers, vols. 9–10, box 4. Also, Minutes of a meeting between Forrestal and the Joint Chiefs of Staff, 20 March 1948, with attached Forrestal "Notes for Friday-Opening of Meeting," 11 March 1948; Gruenther memorandum for Leahy and the Joint Chiefs, 26 March 1948, with attached Gruenther memorandum for the record of the same date; Forrestal press release, "Results of Key West Conference," 28 March 1948, RG 218, CCS 370 (8-19-45), Sec. 7. And Forrestal to Truman, 27 March 1948; and Clifford memorandum for the president, 13 April 1948, with attached draft letter (approved by the president) from Clifford to Forrestal of the same date, Elsey Papers, box 83, folder: National Defense-Armed Forces Unification. Also Norstad memorandum for the record, 6 April 1948, Norstad Papers, Pentagon Series, box 21, folder: Memorandums for the Record. See also Condit, *Joint Chiefs of Staff*, 2:181–89.

[60] Truman, "Annual Budget Message to the Congress, Fiscal Year 1949," 12 January 1948, *Public Papers, Truman, 1948*, 21.

reiterated their warning that a substantial deployment would require a partial mobilization in the United States.[61] The Army also spoke up, insisting in February that it was operating at subsistence levels and was now more than one hundred thousand soldiers short of what it needed to fulfill its basic responsibilities.[62] UMT might help in the long term, but in the meantime the Army wanted additional resources or help from the other services. Otherwise, it would have to reduce the number of troops in areas essential to American interests, thereby eroding the country's international position both militarily and politically.[63]

Considering all the services together, Forrestal said in words that echoed the Joint Chiefs, there were barely enough troops in the emergency reserve to meet a sudden crisis abroad without partial mobilization at home. The same point came up at a cabinet meeting on 12 February and at a White House briefing for the president six days later. It was the opinion of the Joint Chiefs, discussed on both occasions, that personnel shortages had forced the Navy to lay up more than one hundred ships and had left the Army more than ten thousand troops short in Korea and more than one hundred thousand overall. The Joint Chiefs argued again that partial mobilization would be required if the administration was going to dispatch more than a division anywhere in the world.[64]

These warnings notwithstanding, Truman continued to resist the Pentagon's pressure for a larger defense budget and won support for his position from Senator Taft and other fiscal conservatives in the Republican party. Although Taft and Truman parted company on the Marshall Plan and the tax issue, they had a common interest in capping the defense budget. Taft saw such a cap as one way to offset the Republican tax cut; Truman saw it as a way to cover the cost of the Marshall Plan; and for both it was a way to get what they wanted without driving the budget into deficit. In addition, Taft shared the president's conviction that absolute security was a pipe dream and could be achieved, if at all, only by transforming the country into a garrison state. The United States, he

---

[61] Condit, *Joint Chiefs of Staff*, 2:43–44, 69–70.

[62] See the memorandum to Forrestal's special assistant Wilfred J. McNeil from his aide John W. Martin, 2 February 1948, RG 335, file: 111.

[63] JCS 1829, 20 January 1948, chief of naval operations to the Joint Chiefs, 28 January 1948, and JCS 1829/1, 4 February 1948, RG 218, CCS 370 (8-19-45), Sec. 6. See also *Forrestal Diaries*, 369–70.

[64] Forrestal draft letter to General Douglas MacArthur, 13 February 1948, RG 330, CD 100-1-13; *Forrestal Diaries*, 371–74.

argued, could not be armed for every contingency without maintaining a permanent war economy, including economic controls and defense budgets equal to those of the Second World War, which would lead inevitably to national bankruptcy, the loss of political and economic freedoms, and the destruction of the very "America we are trying to preserve." For Taft and his allies, the challenge was to spend less money without losing any military capability, a challenge they wanted to meet by eliminating waste of all kinds and picking the right military strategy.[65]

In their determination to reduce costs, Taft and his colleagues were critical of the Pentagon for its failure to achieve the economies promised by unification and to agree on a joint strategic plan that could guide the defense budget. They also tended to favor a military strategy that would emphasize air–atomic power, which led them to endorse the findings of the Air Policy Commission that Truman had established in the summer of 1947.[66] Headed by Thomas K. Finletter, the commission had held a series of well-publicized hearings that quickly degenerated into an acrimonious debate over the relative merits of the Navy's plan for a flush-deck carrier and the Air Force's plan for a new fleet of B-36 bombers. The response of the Joint Chiefs had been to embrace both sides by endorsing a seventy-group air force and a comparable expansion of the other services. In its report to the president in January 1948, the Finletter Commission also came down in favor of seventy regular air groups, as did a subsequent report by the Joint Congressional Aviation Policy Board.[67]

To Taft, a military strategy keyed to the Air Force had several things to recommend it. Because the United States could not match the Red Army man for man, he thought it was better to counter Soviet strength on the ground with American strength in the air, particularly in air–atomic power. Such asymmetry had financial as well as military advantages. Although a seventy-group Air Force might add to the budget, the extra cost could be offset by eliminating the Navy's supercarrier and ending forever its wasteful attempt to duplicate the strategic mission of the Air Force. Further cost reductions could be achieved by reducing the regular Army and canceling Truman's proposal for universal military training. Over

---

[65] Taft address to the Rhode Island Republican Club, 15 January 1948, Taft Papers, Legislative File, box 722, folder: National Defense (Speech), 1948; Taft address to the Lincoln Club, Denver, 14 February 1948, ibid., box 61b, folder: Foreign Policy, 1948.

[66] In addition to the sources cited in the previous note see Bonner Fellers to Taft, 19 January 1948, ibid., box 722, folder: National Defense (Speech), 1948. Fellers was a long-time adviser on airpower, intelligence, and similar subjects to Taft, General MacArthur, and other conservative Republicans.

[67] Rearden, *Formative Years*, 313–16.

time, this kind of military posture could actually save money, as expensive ground and sea forces gave way to cost-effective airpower, and the money saved could be used to support tax cuts and balance the budget.

For Taft, however, the air–atomic strategy that he had in mind possessed advantages that went well beyond the budget, and well beyond Truman's position, which also relied heavily on atomic bombs as a cost-effective deterrent. There was an isolationist subtext in his song of support for the Air Force, and it drew heavily on a familiar cultural narrative about the sources of American greatness. In other words, Taft's enthusiasm for airpower was linked to his sense of America as a nation apart with a democratic identity that would only be lost if it violated the ancient taboos against a large standing army, entangling alliances, and the stationing of American troops abroad. Americans must not emulate European ways and practices, he explained. They must not become "imperialists," anxious to take a "provocative stand on every controversial issue" and ready to attack "every" other people "in the world." Limited resources mandated limited commitments, and in Taft's mind "national defense" must be the country's "primary purpose."[68]

Although Taft and Truman would distribute defense spending differently, they were both determined to limit that spending to achieve other priorities and close the door to the garrison state. Truman wanted a balanced budget, a European aid program, and additional expenditures on domestic programs. Taft wanted a balanced budget and a tax cut. What is more, each looked for ways to respond to the Czech crisis of February and March 1948 without giving up his priorities. Besides higher taxes, Truman urged Congress to enact a program of universal military training, arguing that UMT would create a pool of trained citizens on which the armed forces could draw in major emergencies. For Taft, however, the seventy-group Air Force became what UMT was for Truman – the key to a credible military deterrent without the enormous expense associated with a large army and navy. Each now had, in effect, another priority, with Truman thinking of UMT as a substitute for a seventy-group Air Force and Taft viewing such a force as rendering UMT superfluous. Nor was this an idle difference. It reflected larger philosophical disagreements, not just those over war-fighting strategy, the use of American

---

[68] See the sources cited in the previous two notes. The quotations are from Taft's address to the Lincoln Club of Denver, 14 February 1948, Taft Papers, Legislative File, box 61b, folder: Foreign Policy, 1948. See also Fellers to Taft, 26 February 1948, ibid., box 721, folder: 1948, National Defense.

troops abroad, and the best way to manage the defense budget. Involved as well were basic differences over the country's postwar purpose, and thus over the shape of the national security state that was emerging in the early Cold War.[69]

As the battle over the budget continued, Truman was also being plagued by the growing gap between his limited national security program and the hyperventilating rhetoric that he used to sell it. In addition to UMT and selective service, his program in the wake of the Czech crisis called only for the defense budget he had requested in January plus a supplemental appropriation of $1.5 billion. The latter sum was barely enough to cover the cost of operating selective service and building the armed forces to their previously authorized manpower levels. Yet in his speech to Congress of 17 March, Truman had cited the "tragic death" of the Czech republic as the latest example of a "ruthless" Soviet policy that would destroy "the independence and democratic character of a whole series of nations in Eastern and Central Europe." Forrestal and others struck a similar theme in congressional hearings on the president's program, pointing to the dangerous expansion of Soviet power across Europe and comparing it to German expansion on the eve of both world wars. Unless stopped, they warned, the Soviets would soon control the economic and strategic assets of Europe and leave the United States "isolated in a Communist world."[70]

The minor revisions in the defense program that Truman sought did not seem to justify such breathless rhetoric. On the contrary, the revised program indicated that Truman and other key officials did not view the Czech crisis as prelude to a Soviet attack or to any substantial alteration in the global balance of power. They wanted essentially to signal American resolve in an unstable world and reassure nervous allies in Europe. These were modest goals and required only modest revisions in the president's budget. But as we will see, the gap between these revisions and the administration's public pronouncements played into the hands of Pentagon policymakers who wanted much, much more.[71]

---

[69] See the following chapter for the story of UMT.

[70] Truman, "Special Message to Congress," 17 March 1948, *Public Papers, Truman, 1948,* 182–86; U.S. Congress, Senate, *Hearings on Universal Military Training* (Washington, 1948) 4, 328 (hereafter Senate, *Hearings on UMT*). See also Senate, *Hearings on UMT,* 6, 326–27, 330, 340.

[71] Leffler, *Preponderance of Power,* 205, 209, 223. See also Hoopes and Brinkley, *Driven Patriot,* 374.

V

The Czech crisis gave policy makers in the Pentagon an opportunity to break the restraints on their budgets and move the country closer to a warfare state at the expense of the priorities that Truman had established earlier in the year. Webb later remembered how the armed forces launched "an all-out drive for appropriations" following the president's fiery speech of 17 March. Edwin G. Nourse, chairman of the Council of Economic Advisers, had a similar recollection. The military and civilian heads of the services, he recalled, were determined "to make the most of" the "war scare" that swept through Washington after Truman spoke to Congress. They sought "the utmost expansion" of their budgets rather than the modest increases envisioned by the president.[72] They were also prepared to defy civilian authority to get what they wanted, and their willingness to do so raised new concerns about a garrison state that could undermine American democracy.

Each of the three services immediately presented a laundry list of essential needs. The Army said again that it needed additional manpower to meet its responsibilities in the occupied areas. Secretary Royall wanted to increase the Army's authorized strength from 669,000 to 822,000 troops. The Navy had a sob story and a wish list of its own, as did the Air Force, which continued to demand seventy air groups. Symington talked in bleak terms about the emerging superiority of Soviet airpower, especially in the field of jet aircraft, and said that funding for the Air Force must have the first claim on supplemental appropriations. Unable to agree on priorities, the three services followed the usual procedure. They submitted the combined total of their individual requirements, only then to discover that it was larger than Truman and his economic advisers would allow.[73]

The new requirements envisioned in the Pentagon would add $8.8 billion to the defense budget that Truman had submitted in January, including $5.8 billion in new obligatory authority, mainly for tanks and aircraft, and $3 billion in direct appropriations. The amount stunned Truman and his budget director, James Webb, who advised Forrestal that anything more than $1.5 billion would be inflationary and would

[72] David E. Lilienthal, *The Journals of David E. Lilienthal*, vol. 2, *The Atomic Energy Years, 1945–1950* (New York, 1964), 350; Nourse memorandum for the record, 10 May 1947, Edwin G. Nourse Papers (Truman Library), box 5, folder: Daily Diary.

[73] Minutes of the 8th meeting of the National Security Council, 23 March 1948, Truman Papers, PSF-National Security Council Meetings, box 203, folder: NSC Meeting #8, 3-23-48.

not take account of the nation's limited resources or the cost of the European Recovery Program, which had first claim on the national security budget.[74] Lengthy negotiations over the size of the supplemental appropriation followed, with Webb's advice playing like a broken record in the Budget Bureau, the Council of Economic Advisers, and the Treasury Department. Officials in these agencies warned repeatedly that supplemental funding for defense, together with appropriations for the first year of the Marshall Plan, would add substantially to the budget, aggravate existing shortages, and raise prices. There was a strong possibility that additional costs would wipe out the budget surplus, particularly when combined with the Republican tax cut, and that a deficit would feed inflationary pressures and require new controls over wages, prices, and credit.[75]

A different kind of criticism came from Secretary of State Marshall, easily the most respected member of the Truman administration. Marshall was a military statesman, maybe the last of his breed in Washington. A man of great probity and personal selflessness, not to mention sound judgement and a distinguished record of service, he had made a habit of putting the needs of the armed forces, even those of his beloved Army, into a larger context. Even while Army chief of staff, he had consistently urged his colleagues in the Pentagon to be practical in their budget demands and to consider the impact of these demands on the economy as a whole. This view explains his support for UMT, which he thought would indicate American resolve to the world at a price the country could afford. It also explains his consistent opposition to Forrestal's efforts to inflate the defense budget, the latest expression of which came at an NSC meeting near the end of March.[76]

Marshall, who presided over the meeting, echoed Taft's conviction that the United States could not be prepared for all contingencies at all times. He wanted the supplemental defense program to stop short of

---

74 In addition to the source cited in the previous note see the record of the luncheon meeting called by the Secretary of Defense, 20 March 1948, RG 218, CCS 370 (8-19-45), Sec. 7; and Rearden, *Formative Years*, 319.

75 Council of Economic Advisers to Truman, 24 March 1948, Nourse Papers, box 4, folder: Daily Diary; J. Weldon Jones (Budget Bureau) to Budget Director Webb, 24 March and 2 and 5 April 1948, and W. F. Schaub and Arthur Smithies (Budget Bureau) to Webb, 25 March 1948, Webb Papers, box 18, folder: Bureau of the Budget: Mobilization; Keyserling to Truman, 31 March 1948, Elsey Papers, box 79, folder: Legislation – 80th Cong., 2d sess. – Tax Veto.

76 James Schnabel, *History of the Joint Chiefs of Staff: The Joint Chiefs of Staff and National Policy* (Wilmington, 1979), 1:229. See also Chapter 4 for Marshall's views on universal military training.

anything like an all-out effort to rearm, which was unnecessary and did not have the support of the president. Marshall's more limited goal was to rearm only to the extent necessary to make American containment credible. Going beyond that limited goal would in all probability lead to congressional opposition and could provoke the kind of Soviet aggression that the administration wanted to discourage. According to the minutes of the meeting, Marshall "cautioned against trying to get such a load of powder that the gun itself would blow up."[77]

Guided by these financial and strategic considerations, Forrestal began to think in terms of a $3 billion defense supplemental, a sum smaller than the services had in mind, especially if the objective was a seventy-group Air Force. In truth, Forrestal had come to the conclusion that the Army had the greatest need, particularly if the United States was called upon to send even a limited force to Greece, Palestine, or other hot spots around the world. Of the $3 billion that he was ready to propose, only $775 million would be used to purchase new aircraft, with the Air Force getting only enough to fill out the fifty-five air groups that Truman had authorized earlier. The decision infuriated Symington and Air Force Chief of Staff General Carl Spaatz, both of whom broke ranks with Forrestal when Congress opened hearings on the supplemental appropriation in late March.

Symington and Spaatz not only challenged the authority of the secretary of defense and the president on the size of the Air Force, they also argued with Forrestal over the cost of a seventy-group program and the need for a balanced military force structure. Symington said that jumping from fifty-five to seventy groups would add no more than $800 million to the budget. Forrestal disagreed. National defense, he said, required a balanced force structure, so that any addition to the Air Force would necessarily entail a comparable expansion of the other services. He put the total cost in the peak year of expansion at $18 billion, a figure he apparently pulled from his hat, but one he later asked the Joint Chiefs to confirm.[78]

77 Minutes of the 8th meeting of the National Security Council, 23 March 1948, Truman Papers, PSF-National Security Council Meetings, box 203, folder: NSC Meeting #8, 3-23-48.

78 *Forrestal Diaries*, 400–2; press release, Office of the Secretary of Defense, 25 March 1948, and Forrestal to Senator Chan Gurney, 2 April 1948, RG 218, JCS Records, CCS 452 U.S. (8-1-47), Sec. 4; Forrestal to the Joint Chiefs of Staff, 27 March 1948, and Forrestal to Gurney, 31 March 1948, RG 335, file: 111. See also Symington to Senator Harry F. Byrd, 11, 12, and 13 March 1948, Symington Papers, box 2, folder: Correspondence File, 1946–50, Budget Memos.

Forrestal also asked the chiefs to determine whether the administration should advocate a balanced military establishment commensurate with a seventy-group Air Force. In doing so, he apparently wanted them to wrestle with the economic as well as the military aspects of national defense, much as Taft, Truman, and the Budget Bureau had been urging all along. No doubt he hoped thereby to isolate the Air Force and win support for the smaller supplemental he had suggested to Congress. But if this was his strategy, it backfired when the Joint Chiefs began considering his request while also responding to inquiries from the State Department and the NSC for opinions on the emergency deployment of American troops to a number of trouble spots around the world. The chiefs took advantage of each inquiry to explain how the "world situation has deteriorated to such a degree" as to require greater appropriations for the armed forces and legislative authorization for industrial mobilization. Until the armed forces were beefed up, they warned, the administration had no choice but to avoid any commitments that were likely to result in military involvements. Having issued this warning, the chiefs then answered Forrestal's request by demanding a mammoth expansion of the armed forces at the expense of the budget. This was the essence of the report they submitted in mid-April.[79]

As usual, the Joint Chiefs had found it easy to justify their budget demands by drawing on the national security ideology and enumerating the global responsibilities that it assigned to the United States. But they could not agree on how large the different branches of the armed services should be, so that each service estimated its own size in a balanced force built around a seventy-group Air Force. The Army asked for 837,000 troops by the end of fiscal year 1950, the Air Force for 502,000, and the Navy for 560,000, plus another 108,000 Marines. The chiefs fixed the cost of such a program at $19.3 billion in new obligatory authority for fiscal year 1949. This sum would add roughly $9 billion to Truman's original estimate of January, and the addition itself was three times greater than Forrestal's proposed supplemental. Grounding their recommendation on military considerations alone, the chiefs had completely ignored the economic issues that Forrestal wanted them to confront, but which they said were beyond their competence and responsibility.[80]

More than two weeks before the Joint Chiefs issued their report, Truman had approved Forrestal's initial estimate of $3 billion for the

79 Condit, *Joint Chiefs of Staff*, 2:48–49, 71–72, 94–96; *Forrestal Diaries*, 410–11.

80 JCS 1796/14, "The Cost of a Balanced Armed Forces Program," 11 April 1948, RG 218, CCS 452 U.S. (8-1-47), Sec. 5. See also Condit, *Joint Chiefs of Staff*, 2:204–6.

defense supplemental, with $775 million of this amount earmarked for the procurement of aircraft.[81] The report thus appeared as a challenge to both the president and the secretary and promptly took its place as the latest in a series of such challenges in matters pertaining to the size and distribution of the defense budget. Symington and Spaatz had earlier thrown their weight against UMT and other initiatives that might siphon defense funds from the Air Force, and they were also collaborating with friends on Capitol Hill to win additional support for their seventy-group program. These friends now included Taft and other Republican conservatives who saw the Air Force as a substitute for a more expensive standing army, as well as influential Democrats such as Congressman Carl Vinson, who had become an Air Force partisan after losing his chairmanship of the Naval Affairs Committee.

The efforts of this group began to pay off in April, when Truman's supplemental defense appropriation bill reached the floor of both houses of Congress. Over opposition from the White House, airpower enthusiasts introduced an amendment to increase the Air Force's procurement budget by $822 million above the $775 million recommended by the administration. The additional funds would cover the first year of a five-year program to build a seventy-group Air Force and would come in part, as everyone understood, by shifting appropriations away from the president's plan for UMT. What is more, with the Air Force lobbying hard for the additional funding, it was not long before the other services adopted similar tactics. At that point, all semblance of order began to break down, as each of the armed forces started to pitch its own proposals in Congress without reference to a comprehensive strategic plan and without regard to the total costs involved.[82]

It took Forrestal several weeks to convince the Joint Chiefs to pare their supplemental requests to a combined figure of nearly $3.5 billion, which was sufficient to give the Navy and Marines together 552,000 men, the Army 790,000, and the Air Force 453,000, enough to maintain sixty-six air groups.[83] Truman thought that Congress should consider the combined figure, but he could not have been pleased with a recommendation that was half a billion dollars more than he had approved

[81] Truman to Forrestal, 26 March 1948, RG 335, file: 111.

[82] *Forrestal Diaries*, 412–17; Symington to Gurney, 13 April 1948, RG 335, file: 111; and diary entries for 13 and 14 April 1948, Forrestal Diary, Forrestal Papers, vols. 9–10, box 4. See also *Forrestal Diaries*, 388–89, 425–29.

[83] JCS 1796/12, "The Cost of a Balanced Armed Forces Program," 20 April 1948, RG 218, CCS 452 U.S. (8-1-47), Sec. 6; *Forrestal Diaries*, 418–21.

in late March. Even Forrestal was expressing some concern about the overall costs of the country's national security program, which now included additional defense expenditures, selective service, UMT, atomic energy, the Marshall Plan, and a contemplated $3 billion a year in military assistance to Europe. Another "blow" might "bust the bungs," Forrestal feared, by which he meant that national security expenditures would do little good if they left the country "economically and socially impotent."[84]

Nor was Truman pleased with his subordinates in the Pentagon. He had earlier criticized Symington's opposition to UMT, and he must have been very disappointed when each of the services lobbied Congress for advantages the administration had not approved. After all, the president had made a decision, only to find the Joint Chiefs asking for more and Forrestal unable to control them. He was "damn sore," Truman told a White House aide. He and his staff thought Symington and Forrestal were behaving like "small boys." Truman called the service secretaries "muttonheads." He was tired of their constant bickering and of Forrestal's pusillanimous behavior, not to mention his independent dealings with members of Congress. He was thinking of getting a new secretary of defense, but in the meantime he would rely on allies in other government agencies to countervail pressure from the Pentagon.[85]

While Congress was looking over the defense supplemental, Truman asked the Budget Bureau for its assessment as well. The bureau reduced the amount from $3.5 to $3.1 billion almost immediately and then recommended a target of $2.5 billion to be achieved by going back to the president's original plan for fifty-five air groups and by curbing new expenditures for naval air, antisubmarine warfare, and army reequipment. The goal, according to Webb, was to cap defense spending at approximately $15 billion in fiscal year 1950. To keep below this ceiling it was necessary to limit supplemental expenditures in the current fiscal year, especially on programs that might grow automatically in the months ahead. Officials in the Budget Bureau warned again of untoward economic consequences, especially shortages and inflationary pressures, if Congress and the Pentagon ignored their advice. They were more convinced than ever that economic controls would be needed, and their view received strong support from the National Security Resources Board, which was urging a comprehensive system of wartime controls, and from Bernard

---

[84] *Forrestal Diaries*, 429, 425.
[85] *Diary of Eben A. Ayers*, 253–54. See also Truman to Symington, 25 March 1948, Truman Papers, PSF-Subject File, box 157, folder: Air Force, Dept of – General.

Baruch, the Wall Street tycoon turned wartime administrator thirty years earlier.[86]

Drawing on the new ideology of national security, Baruch told Congress that the age of total war required a program of total security, including a substantial mobilization of the economy. Needed in particular was a system of priorities and allocations; stand-by controls on wages, prices, and rents; taxes sufficient to cover the cost of defense; a vigorous effort to stockpile strategic materials; an intensive program of research and development in military science; expanded intelligence and information services; industrial decentralization to reduce the country's vulnerability to air attack; and a national security czar to superintend this pyramid of total preparedness and to balance "our growing commitments against our resources." Even without war, Baruch argued, "there is no peace." Demands on the economy were growing, what with the Marshall Plan, aid to Greece and Turkey, new spending for defense, and plans to withdraw thousands of additional workers from the labor force into the military services. The country was entering a period of mobilization that might be permanent, Baruch concluded, and would require a system of planning and controls in order to avoid "wrecking" the economy.[87]

Once again, though, these kinds of recommendations called forth the dark specter of the garrison state, of a nation that would surrender freedoms at home in order to fight communism around the world. This was a prospect that both Taft and Truman wanted to avoid, Taft by boosting the Air Force, Truman by holding the line on tax cuts, capping defense expenditures, and instituting UMT. "We must be very careful that the military does not overstep the bounds from an economic standpoint domestically," Truman wrote Edwin Nourse. "Most of them would like to go back to a war footing," and "that is not what we want."[88]

Truman was preaching to the converted. Nourse was a professional economist with a quiet manner, a studious appearance, and little stomach for politics. He, too, was committed to the cultural narrative that

---

[86] *Forrestal Diaries*, 429–31; Jones to Webb, 19 April 1948, Webb Papers, box 18, folder: Mobilization; "Outline of Action Taken on Questions Raised by Director Webb," [6 May 1948], Forrestal Diary, vols. 11–12, box 5, Forrestal Papers; Nourse memorandum for the record, 10 May 1948, Nourse Papers, box 5, folder: Daily Diary. See also Jordan A. Schwarz, *The Speculator: Bernard M. Baruch in Washington, 1917–1965* (Chapel Hill, 1981), 508–21.

[87] Senate, *Hearings on Universal Military Training*, 405–7.

[88] Truman to Nourse, 25 March 1948, Truman Papers, PSF-Subject File, box 143, folder: Council of Economic Advisers.

Truman would later recount in his memoirs – one that located the country's success in the economic and political values celebrated by the Founders, including the personal rectitude, fiscal prudence, and concern for the public welfare that were hallmarks of good government and good citizenship. What is more, Nourse had the courage of his convictions, at least to the point where he would overcome his distaste for politics and join other presidential allies in the struggle to build a security state that balanced the government's global obligations against its domestic responsibilities.

Like Webb, Nourse consistently urged Truman to keep a lid on defense spending, lest the pursuit of open-ended ambitions discourage growth and undermine the traditional values associated with a balanced budget, including the individual initiative and hard work that would contribute to private gain and the public good alike. Defense expenditures could be a short-term prop to a sagging economy, he admitted, but in the long run they entailed sacrifices in the levels of production and consumption the country might otherwise enjoy. "We can't eat our cake and have it too," was his summary of the situation. The Pentagon could not withdraw $15 billion in goods and services from the economy annually "and still leave the real income of consumers as high as it would otherwise be."[89]

In addressing the question of what sacrifices national security demanded, Nourse was repeating arguments made earlier in the Council of Economic Advisers' first quarterly report to the president. And like the council, he was particularly critical of those who thought it possible to expand defense spending while cutting taxes, a combination that he saw as a sure-fire prescription for economic disaster. Nor did Nourse think it possible to pay for defense by shrinking other parts of the budget, such as public works, a favorite target of conservatives. After all, the budget for fiscal year 1949 allotted only $2.6 billion for public works, a paltry amount that was considerably less than the combined cost of the administration's defense supplemental and the Republican party's tax cut. What is more, public works had already been cut to the bone and further cuts would be counterproductive. How, asked Nourse, are we "to keep up the quality of our working force and keep up our traditional standards of education if we do not soon make up the under-maintenance of our public school plant and expand it in step with population growth?"

[89] Nourse address to the alumni meeting of the Illinois Institute of Technology, 19 May 1948, Nourse Papers, box 5, folder: Daily Diary.

For Nourse, then, the needs of the public sector and the dream of higher living standards were reasons enough to support the president's modest defense program instead of "the war machine proposed in some quarters." But equally important was the grim possibility of a garrison state that would become a reality if a reckless rearmament program led, as it surely would, to spiraling rates of inflation, ever-higher taxes, and rigorous government controls, with all their negative influence on traditional economic freedoms and on such traditional values as individual incentive and hard work.[90]

In addition to his economic advisers, Truman also turned again to Secretary Marshall for support against the Pentagon, and was not disappointed. At a meeting in early May, Marshall repeated much of what he had said two months earlier. He told Forrestal that war was neither inevitable nor even probable at the moment. Hence, the defense supplemental need not become a war preparedness program, especially when such a program might actually provoke what the administration wanted to prevent. Forrestal was not persuaded by these arguments, nor by those mounted by the Budget Bureau. Although he was showing some concern about the weight of defense expenditures on an overburdened economy, he was still more convinced than Marshall that Soviet-American relations were entering a particularly dangerous phase and that anything less than $3.2 billion in supplemental defense spending was irresponsible. Nor would Forrestal budge when Webb reminded him of the many other national security burdens on the budget, such as the Marshall Plan, atomic energy, and the merchant marine.[91] In the end, nothing less than Truman's personal intervention would bring the secretary into line.

The president's intervention came in mid-May at a White House meeting with Forrestal and his top aides, followed by a series of blunt directives to key officials in the Pentagon. At the meeting, Truman pulled together the lines of policy emanating from the State Department and the Budget Bureau. Echoing Marshall, he declared that it was not his intention to put the country on a war footing. The goal instead was to signal American resolve to the world, especially to the Soviet Union, and this could best be done through gradual rearmament and limited appropriations. He had initially hoped for a supplemental of

---

90 Ibid. See also in the same folder, Nourse's memorandum for the files of 10 May 1948 and his address to the third annual conference of the Association of State Planning and Development Agencies, 20 May 1948.

91 *Forrestal Diaries*, 430–33.

$1.5 billion, had then accepted $3 billion, and would now agree to slightly more than $3.1 billion in new obligatory authority – but only if the services promised to commit the additional funds in ways that did not drive the defense budget above $15 billion in the next fiscal year. "We all recognize that military strength is dependent on a strong economic system," Truman said, and anything beyond what he was recommending would mean deficit financing and increased taxation. The administration had to present a "solid front," he concluded, and this meant subordinating "personal and service preferences to the broader interests of the national program" that he was supporting.[92]

By this time, however, it was already too late for a solid front to do much good. Each of the services had spent weeks lobbying Congress for more than the administration was recommending, and the resulting damage could not be undone at the last moment. The Air Force was particularly successful, although its gains came largely at the expense of UMT, which Congress refused to approve. The big decision came when Congress adopted the amendment favored by Vinson, Taft, and others, adding $822 million for additional aircraft procurement in hopes of building to a seventy-group Air Force.

The amendment passed with bipartisan support. To be sure, some legislators expressed concern that additional defense spending, on top of the Marshall Plan, ran the risk of overtaxing the country's resources. Their fear was of a garrison state in which large defense budgets would "militarize our economy," creating shortages, inflation, and government controls over wages, prices, and scarce commodities.[93] But most came to the conclusion that the Czech crisis and tensions building over Berlin required additional spending on defense, especially on the Air Force. In addition, conservatives in both parties were convinced that government expenditures, if they became too great, could then be reduced by further

[92] Truman to Forrestal, 13 May 1948, Vandenberg Papers, box 49, folder: Hoyt S. Vandenberg – Budget, 1947–48; Truman to Symington, 13 May 1948, with attached statement by the president of 13 May 1948, Truman Papers, PSF-Subject File, box 157, folder: Air Force, Dept of – Secy of War for Air – W. Stuart Symington; Truman to chief of staff of the air force, 13 May 1948, Vandenberg Papers, box 60, folder: Secretary of the Air Force; Truman to the secretary of the army, 15 May 1948, RG 51, Series 47.3, box 22, folder: G1-79. See also *Forrestal Diaries*, 435. Truman later placed limits on the expenditure of defense funds in certain categories during the first quarter of fiscal year 1949. He did so to make sure that rearmament proceeded at a gradual rate and did not entail heavy forward commitments that might drive the budget for the next fiscal year above the $15 billion ceiling he had established. See Truman to Symington, 3 June 1948, Symington Papers, box 4, folder: Correspondence File, 1946–50, Declassified Documents.

[93] *Congressional Record, 1948* 94:5399. See also the sources cited in the following note.

shrinking the domestic budget and scrapping the Marshall Plan, which they still viewed as little more than a public works project promoted by New Deal bureaucrats. "Let us have more planes and fewer bureaucrats," was their theme. More typical was the conviction that investment in the Air Force would be cost-effective over the long term. It would enable the United States to spend less on the other services, especially on the Army, by moving to a strategy where American airpower would work in combination with allied ground forces to contain the Soviet Union.[94]

These arguments drew enough support to pass a defense budget that was even larger than the one sought by the Joint Chiefs prior to the White House meeting of mid-May. Truman had proposed $12.964 billion in new obligatory authority, a sum that included the regular defense budget of $9.8 billion, which he had requested in January, plus the supplemental budget of $3.159 billion. Congress, in the measure finally passed, authorized approximately $13.942 billion, which was slightly more than $4.1 billion above the president's January proposal and about $1 billion above the new amount he requested in the wake of the Czech crisis. In the process, moreover, Congress had voted down UMT and had allocated $822 million more for the procurement of airplanes than the administration had recommended – prompting an angry president to impound the money over the noisy complaints of airpower enthusiasts in Congress and the Pentagon.[95]

VI

James Webb finished the latest round of budget negotiations feeling very discouraged. To be sure, Forrestal had said again that a "busted benefactor" was of no use to the world. Somehow the United States had to finance its national security and aid Europe while still remaining "socially sound and financially solvent."[96] Symington had also conceded as much, though in the final analysis he was like other Pentagon officials in picturing his department's requirements as reasonable while lamenting

---

94 Ibid., 4254. For the floor debates over the defense budget, including the supplemental and the amendment on behalf of a seventy-group air force, see ibid. 3004–5, 3423–25, 4254, 4442–58, 4530–48, 4564–65, 4796–4800, 5395–5408, 5586, 5598.
95 Condit, *Joint Chiefs of Staff*, 2:210–11. As Condit points out, of the $13.942 billion provided by Congress, nearly $3.1 billion was made available for fiscal year 1948, the balance for fiscal year 1949. See the following chapter for details on the debate over UMT.
96 *Forrestal Diaries*, 444.

waste, duplication, and fraud everywhere else.[97] The truth of the matter was that each of the services tried to maximize its share of the defense budget, each identified its mission with the nation's security, and each wanted economies to come at the others' expense. They could be told to evaluate the defense budget in economic as well as military terms, but their thinking continued to be driven by bureaucratic imperatives, by unbridled military scenarios, and by the national security ideology that was emerging in the early days of the Cold War.

Marshall and Truman wanted a military establishment large enough to signal America's resolve and make the policy of containment credible. Although the country could build on such a force in the event of an emergency, it would not otherwise require a large-scale rearmament that might overburden the budget, interfere with the pursuit of peacetime priorities, or change the country from a welfare to a warfare state. Military planners, on the other hand, counted up the country's commitments abroad, noted the gap between these commitments and their military capabilities, and demanded a military establishment large enough to meet all contingencies. This was the case even though unresolved differences over their respective roles and missions and over Soviet capabilities, the strategic war plan, and the use of atomic weapons robbed their position of considerable credibility, except in the eyes of their partisans on Capitol Hill.

This was the pattern of behavior that Webb found so discouraging, as he did the Pentagon's tendency to "scare the country" into supporting a vast rearmament and the readiness of officials there to question the resolve, if not the patriotism, of their critics. Just as bad, he thought, was the willingness of the Joint Chiefs to challenge the authority of civilian leaders, notably the president but also the secretary of defense, and to appeal over their heads to Congress. Forrestal had "lost control completely," Webb concluded. He was "so bulldozed" by the Joint Chiefs that he had even refused to distribute presidential directives. "With this kind of situation," Webb told his friend David Lilienthal, chairman of the Atomic Energy Commission, "the idea of turning over custody of atomic bombs to these competing, jealous, insubordinate services, fighting for position with each other, is a terrible prospect."[98]

---

97 Symington, of course, never tired of pointing out how the Navy's air arm was a wasteful duplication of the Air Force. See Symington to Truman, 24 May 1948, with attached memorandum of 21 May 1948, Symington Papers, box 13, folder: Correspondence File, 1946–50: Truman, Harry S.; and Symington to William Allen (president of Boeing Airplane Company), 7 June 1948, Symington Papers, box 1, folder: Correspondence File – 1946–50.
98 Lilienthal, *Atomic Energy Years*, 350–51.

Webb's lament raised the prospect of power shifting from civilian to military hands, which was one way to the garrison state, another being the transfer of resources from civilian to military consumption. Here, too, Truman, Webb, and others had cause for concern. In 1946 and 1947, Truman had struggled with considerable success to bring defense spending into line with his postwar priorities, especially his determination to balance the budget, reduce the national debt, and revitalize domestic programs that had languished during the war. After the Czech crisis, however, the tide had begun to turn against the president. The pressure of that event drove defense spending beyond the limit he had set, and the new figure had then combined with the Republican tax cut to puncture the president's hopes for a balanced budget and his plans to reallocate resources from military to civilian purposes. Contrary to his wishes, Congress had decided to pay for the defense supplemental by torpedoing the most important items on his domestic agenda, including federal housing, national health insurance, broader Social Security coverage, an increase in the minimum wage, and additional aid to education. In effect, Congress had exchanged these and similar gains for a stronger military policy, as Forrestal had urged, and for a reduction in individual income taxes, as the Republicans had proposed.

Did Taft have more reason to celebrate than Truman? Not really. No one worried more than Taft about the dangers of a garrison state, which he saw as a large, national security bureaucracy grafted on to the New Deal state and consuming resources that properly belonged in the private sector. Because Taft thought that good government was small government, he must have been pleased with the Republican tax cut and with most of the cuts in Truman's domestic agenda. Both were blows to the New Deal. In addition, Congress had gone along with his support for a larger Air Force and his opposition to UMT, two decisions that squared with his isolationist instincts and his desire to contain the budget. At the same time, however, Congress had appropriated more for the Marshall Plan than Taft thought desirable, and the total cost of national security, together with the tax cut, would finally result in a budget deficit that he as well as Truman had hoped to avoid.

Truman and Taft had been unable to reconcile their priorities within the framework of a balanced budget, and the significance of this failure was not lost on some of the country's most important journalists and commentators, most of whom subscribed to key tenets of the national security ideology. Virtually every leading commentator assumed that the United States could not disarm after World War II as it had after World War I. Although most were sympathetic to the president's efforts to put the defense budget on a more reasonable foundation, they also assumed that the old distinction between war and peace had disappeared, that Soviet imperialism stood in the way of "real peace," and that the country had no choice but to maintain what Walter Lippmann called an "impressive level of preparedness." No matter how expensive, all agreed, preparedness was cheaper than another world war.[99]

This agreement notwithstanding, liberal commentators at first seemed reluctant to admit what their conservative colleagues argued from the start – that a period of prolonged preparedness might entail difficult choices between different national identities and in the allocation of national resources. Conservative publications such as *U.S. News* and conservative commentators such as Henry Hazlitt invariably sided with Taft and the Republicans. Hazlitt saw the Marshall Plan as an international welfare program, complained about extravagance in the Pentagon, and wanted to reduce taxes, balance the budget, and cover the cost of national security by eviscerating the social welfare programs coming out of the New Deal. Arthur Krock of the *New York Times* expressed a milder version of the same thinking, whereas liberal publications like *The Nation* and liberal commentators like Marquis Childs and Ernest K. Lindley generally supported Truman's efforts to balance the needs of the warfare state against those of the welfare state.[100]

That changed in 1948, however, when the cost of the Marshall Plan and the defense supplemental added substantially to the budget. To be sure, some commentators, such as Lippmann and Krock, were disturbed

---

99 Arthur Krock, "Two Pillars of Our Foreign Policy," *New York Times*, 14 March 1946, and Walter Lippmann, "Postscript," *Washington Post*, 23 March 1946. See also Lippmann, "Stalin Speaking," and "Military Discussions with Russia," *New York Herald Tribune*, 12 and 19 February 1946; idem, "An Educational Cruise," *Washington Post*, 21 February 1946; and Hanson W. Baldwin, "Military Funds Studied," and "New Military Budget," *New York Times*, 4 September 1946 and 27 January 1947.

100 Hazlitt, "Inflation and the Forthcoming Budget," *New York Times*, 7 January 1946; Arthur Krock, "Some Old Friends of a Balanced Budget," "The Spending Account of the Government," and "Many Issues Involved in Marshall's Warning," *New York Times*, 5 and 8 March 1946 and 16 February 1947; Marquis Childs, "Admiral's Line," "Taxes and the Debt," and "Scalpel Vs. Ax," *Washington Post*, 27 March 1946, 10 January, and 18 February 1947; David Lawrence, "The Spending Goes On," *U.S. News* 22 (17 January 1947): 24–25; "G.O.P. Budget Problem," *The Nation* 164 (18 January 1947): 60–61; Ernest K. Lindley, "Long Haul to Peace," *Newsweek* 29 (10 February 1947): 30; and Hanson W. Baldwin, "A Warning on Budget Cut," and "Military Budget Caution," *New York Times*, 20 February and 9 March 1947.

by the open-ended anticommunism spelled out in the Truman Doctrine. They wanted to know where the country's commitments would end and how much they would cost. But they were even more disturbed by the reluctance of both political parties to face up to the critical choices and the substantial sacrifices that an expansive foreign policy entailed. They were dismayed by the president's efforts to expand the New Deal in 1948 while reversing the downward trend in defense expenditures. They did not believe that the country could have its cake and eat it too, at least not without going to something like a wartime mobilization, complete with economic controls and much higher taxes. On the other hand, they also rejected the ostrich-like posture of Taft and other isolationists, and refused to believe that taxes could be reduced and the budget balanced without cutting defense and international programs more than was desirable.[101]

Clearly the Cold War was forcing choices in the allocation of resources and in the shape of the state that neither Taft nor Truman really wanted. As was the case with the National Security Act, the process of state making was being pushed in different directions by those who articulated the new ideology of national security, by those who defended the values of an older political culture, and by those who sought to balance traditional values against new imperatives, domestic priorities against national security needs. In the background, too, was the widespread fear that meeting these needs would subvert the country's democratic identity and give rise to a garrison state that was more German than American.

This fear, together with the weight of traditional culture, put some limits on how far Forrestal and other national security managers could go,

---

[101] Arthur Krock, "Some Questions Arising over the Truman Doctrine," "A Slight Undercurrent of Party Politics," "Some Specifications that are Overdue," "Everything, Including the Kitchen Stove," "Truman Shy of Target," and "The Two Impulses for Tax Reduction Now," *New York Times*, 20 and 25 March and 20 June 1947, 8 and 14 January, and 19 March 1948; Marquis Childs, "Politics and World Responsibility," "Core of Isolation," and "Push-Button Fantasy," *Washington Post*, 9 and 17 June 1947, and 6 March 1948; Walter Lippmann, "Generalities Won't Help," "Measures for the Crisis," and "A Few Brass Tacks," *Washington Post*, 12 June 1947, and 22 March, and 26 October 1948; Ernest K. Lindley, "Progress of the 80th Congress," *Newsweek* 30 (4 August 1947): 31; Lindley, "Republican Travail," and Henry Hazlitt, "Back to Police-State Controls," *Newsweek* 30 (1 December 1947): 27, 72; Hazlitt, "Blueprint for Disruption," *Newsweek* 31 (19 January 1948): 76; Lindley, "The Meaning of Our Military Plans," *Newsweek* 31 (5 April 1948): 25; and Hanson W. Baldwin, "Defense Analysis Urged," "Daft Action Advances Vast Security Scheme," "Thrift Urged on Services," and "Nation's Armed forces Facing Wide Expansion," *New York Times*, 2 May, and 13, 20 and 27 June 1948.

although the mix of competing priorities that emerged from the budget battles, as from the battle over the National Security Act, came closer to their vision of the postwar state than it did to the more traditional thinking of Taft, or even to the kind of equilibrium that Truman wanted to strike. It had become more difficult to move toward the small state and the budget surplus that Taft had in mind, or to achieve the balance between warfare and welfare that Truman envisioned. Indeed, there was a widespread view that something of a turning point had been reached with the Czech crisis. Many began to wonder if it was still possible to address the nation's security within the framework of a fiscal policy that provided for a balanced budget, substantial social welfare expenditures, and lower taxes. National security now seemed to require greater sacrifices, including the loss of social services and of the balanced budget that Truman, Taft, and other Americans held dear.

4

The Time Tax
American Political Culture and the UMT Debate

Between 1945 and 1948, as we have seen, Truman had tried to strike a balance between the warfare state and the welfare state. He wanted to equip the country for its new role as the global defender of democracy, but on terms that squared with American tradition and with his own domestic agenda, including a balanced budget and a modest expansion of the social programs that had grown out of the New Deal. With these goals in mind, he had begun to redirect resources from wartime to peacetime purposes and had made some progress in unifying the armed forces and creating a national security organization that dovetailed with the principle of civilian leadership. But progress had been slow, some ground had been lost after the Czech crisis, and the same issues would have to be refought in the years ahead. Nor were they the only issues. The Truman administration also had to mobilize the military manpower and the economic and scientific resources needed to sustain a credible deterrent. The story of American state making included major battles in these areas, too, and of these battles none was more hard fought than the one over universal military training (UMT).

Truman waged this battle, the subject of little scholarship thus far, even as he was struggling to reduce the defense budget and bring the armed forces under better control, and the battle itself revealed themes that were also evident in these concurrent struggles.[1] In part, the debate

---

[1] Most of the literature on military manpower policy deals primarily with the draft, although there are similarities between the arguments on both sides of the UMT debate after 1945 and those on both sides of the debates over selective service. The best works dealing with the draft and the issue of military manpower include James M. Gerhardt, *The Draft and Public Policy: Issues in Military Manpower Procurement, 1945–1970* (Columbus, OH, 1971); J. Garry Clifford, *The Citizen Soldiers: The Plattsburg Training Camp Movement, 1913–1920* (Lexington, KY, 1972); J. Garry Clifford and Samuel R. Spencer, Jr., *The First Peacetime Draft* (Lawrence, KS, 1986); John Whiteclay Chambers II, *To Raise an Army: The Draft Comes to Modern America* (New York, 1987); and George Q. Flynn, *The Draft, 1940–1973* (Lawrence, KS, 1993). The published literature on the UMT movement after 1945 is very limited, but for a good overview see Robert D. Ward, "The Movement for

revolved around how best to meet America's new responsibilities as the defender of democracy worldwide. On one side stood Truman and other policy makers for whom UMT was the right way to close the gap between the country's overseas commitments and its military capabilities. On the other stood a group of dissenters who saw UMT as an obsolete, labor-intensive instrument of containment in a new era of high-technology warfare. As noted in the previous chapter, these critics wanted to scuttle UMT and divert resources to the Air Force.

In the case of UMT, however, as in other cases, the national security discourse focused as much on political values as on military strategy and weaponry. Truman and his allies articulated the new ideology of national security, with its conviction that total war compelled the integration of civilian and military resources into a program of constant preparedness. UMT was part of that program and also functioned in the same ideological context as a powerful symbol of the nation's resolve to accept the destiny that history had thrust upon it, as a test of whether the American people could muster the strength of character to lead the free world, and as a way to reconcile the needs of national security with an older set of values.

Truman, in particular, sought to defend UMT by calling on an American cultural narrative that stretched back to the republican ideology of the revolutionary period and from there to the political thinking of the British Whigs. At the center of this narrative was a set of interconnected ideals, including the ideal of the citizen-soldier as a font of public virtue, of the citizen's militia as a guardian of liberty, and of military service as a duty owed the nation in periods of crisis. In line with these ideals, Truman and others would cast UMT as both a "time tax" that young men exchanged for the blessings of freedom and as a program of moral renovation that would democratize American life, equip young workers with useful skills, and improve their general health, their moral vitality, and their commitment to civic duty.[2]

The critics of UMT, including liberal Democrats and conservative Republicans, followed the same narrative to a different conclusion. This

---

Universal Military Training in the United States, 1942–1952" (Ph.D. diss., University of North Carolina, 1957). See also the relevant sections in the books by Gerhardt and Flynn cited above.

[2] The quote is from U.S. Congress, Senate, *Hearings on S.1, A Bill to Provide for the Common Defense and Security of the United States and to Permit the More Effective Utilization of Manpower Resources of the United States by Authorizing Universal Military Service and Training, and for other Purposes* (Washington, 1951), 470.

rare combination shared a common commitment to a set of political values that could also be traced to the Founding Fathers and to the oppositional ideology of the British Whigs, who saw a threat to liberty in the expanding powers of the state, especially in its power to assemble an army and wage war. From their perspective, UMT would arrogate to the state responsibilities that properly belonged to other institutions, make individual citizens more dependent on the government, and threaten the ideal of a balanced system of representation based on the tradition of civilian leadership. For these critics, UMT was not American but un-American, not a builder of democracy but of totalitarianism, and not a wellspring of republican virtue but a danger to democracy. As in other debates, this danger was conveyed in the rhetorical symbol of the garrison state, by which the critics meant a society dominated not only by military institutions but also by military values that were fundamentally incompatible with the practice of democratic politics.

In addition, there had always been an economic dimension to the fear of a garrison state, and this dimension, too, found expression on both sides of the UMT debate, as it had in the debates over defense spending and the National Security Act. Truman and his collaborators supported UMT in part because it coincided with their legislative priorities. They saw it as a substitute for a more expensive professional army and therefore as a way to buttress American security without abandoning their plans to balance the budget, reduce the national debt, and reinvest in domestic programs. Viewed this way, UMT was part of a larger effort to avoid the deficits, the inflationary pressures, and the economic controls that were often regarded as hallmarks of the garrison state.

A similar economic dimension was apparent in the thinking of those who opposed UMT. Those on the right, like Senator Taft, viewed UMT as an impractical alternative to a less expensive air force, and thus as a barrier to lower taxes and a balanced budget. Those on the left calculated its cost in what it could buy in housing, education, and other social programs that had gone wanting since the war. But linking both sides together was the common conviction that military preparedness could pose a real danger to the economy, not to mention established institutions and traditional values.

As the above suggests, the UMT debate opens another window on the guns-and-butter politics of the early Cold War and on the struggle to define the country's postwar purpose and national identity. Those on both sides of the debate captured the stakes involved in the usual rhetorical pairings, such as American or un-American, democracy or

totalitarianism, freedom or oppression, civil or military, public or private, isolationism or internationalism. Critics worried that UMT would
waste precious resources and take the country down the same path trod
by totalitarian states; supporters said that it would save money and
reconcile the nation's commitment to democracy at home with its new
role as the champion of freedom around the world. Seen in this light,
the struggle over UMT was another important chapter in the story of
American state making, another attempt to forge the instruments of national security without creating a garrison state on the ruins of American
democracy.

II

As the Second World War came to an end, key military and civilian leaders had looked to universal military training as a way to connect ends
and means in the country's postwar foreign policy. President Franklin D.
Roosevelt, speaking in January 1945, urged congressional action on a
program of universal training. A special congressional committee opened
hearings on the subject several months later, and shortly thereafter President Truman began circulating a plan of his own among members of
the cabinet. Truman's goal was to supplement a small but well-equipped
force of professional soldiers with a large pool of trained manpower on
which the nation could draw in the event of a crisis. To achieve this
goal, he proposed that all able-bodied young men undergo a brief period of military training in the months after their eighteenth birthday
or high school graduation, followed by a more extended period of part-
time service in the organized reserves or National Guard. Some officials
wanted the training program in place before the war ended, and almost all
hoped to achieve their goal before demobilization had proceeded too far,
wartime patriotism had declined, and opposing forces had crystallized.
Whatever their differences, they wanted to avoid the folly of American
policy after the First World War, when rapid demobilization and continued disarmament had made it difficult to deter German and Japanese
aggression.[3]

---

3 *Forrestal Diaries,* 9; Truman, "A Plan for Universal Military Training Under Postwar Conditions," 23 June 1945, Truman Papers, PSF-Subject File, box 146, folder: Military Training;
Matthew J. Connelly minutes of cabinet meeting, 31 August 1945, Matthew J. Connelly
Papers, (Truman Library), box 2, folder: Notes on Cabinet Meetings – White House File,
1945, August 17 & 31; Connelly minutes of cabinet meeting, 7 September 1945, ibid.,
folder: Notes on Cabinet Meetings – White House File, 1945, September 7, 21, 28; Eliot A.
Cohen, *Citizens and Soldiers: The Dilemma of Military Service* (Ithaca, 1985), 156.

In cabinet discussions on the subject, President Truman, Secretary of War Stimson, Secretary of the Navy Forrestal, and other top policy makers drew on the ideology of national security to emphasize UMT's role in making American power more credible. In an age of total war, they said, it was essential to maintain the armed forces in a state of constant readiness. UMT would provide that readiness, thereby enabling the country to meet its global commitments, discourage aggression, and defeat aggressors if deterrence failed. We need "stones in our pockets," Secretary of the Treasury Fred M. Vinson explained in words similar to those that Truman used in an exchange with Leo Crowley of the Foreign Economic Administration. Must the United States "police the world?" Crowley asked. The "courts must have Marshalls [*sic*]," Truman answered.[4]

No one felt more keenly on the subject than Secretary Stimson, a long-time champion of military training who had been involved in the Plattsburg Training Camp Movement before World War I. The arguments that he advanced were long rehearsed, as were those of such colleagues as William J. Donovan, John J. McCloy, Lewis Douglas, and Robert Patterson, all of whom were former Plattsburgers or members of the interwar Military Training Camps Association. Patterson, who would succeed Stimson as secretary of war, always carried the belt of a German soldier he had killed in the First World War, using it to symbolize the tough bravado affected by current leaders of the movement and by many of their illustrious forerunners, including General Leonard Wood, former President Theodore Roosevelt, and other members of a cosmopolitan group of internationalists and interventionists who had championed the cause of military preparedness between 1914 and 1917.[5]

In a speech to the cabinet in 1945, Stimson himself sounded very much like Theodore Roosevelt when he stressed the themes of individual sacrifice and national resolve that were central to the national security ideology. People all over the world, he said, had the mistaken impression of the United States as a "frivolous, selfish, pleasure loving country which did not take the stern business of living in a rough international world

4 Connelly minutes of cabinet meeting, 7 September 1945, ibid., folder: Notes on Cabinet Meetings – White House File, 1945, September 7, 21, 28. See also Connelly minutes of cabinet meeting, 31 August 1945, Connelly Papers, box 2, folder: Notes on Cabinet Meetings – White House File, 1945, August 17 & 31; Stimson statement at cabinet meeting, 7 September 1945, Truman Papers, PSF-Subject File, box 146, folder: Military Training; and *Forrestal Diaries*, 83.
5 Clifford and Spencer, *First Peacetime Draft*, 15–29; and Chambers, *To Raise an Army*, 73–101.

seriously." UMT would dispel that "dangerous misconception," he said, which had twice in his lifetime led other countries to underestimate "our patriotism and our ability to fight." It would let all countries know that the American people took the "duties of citizenship in the family of nations seriously enough to stand a year of training."[6]

Adding urgency to the administration's thinking was the conviction that UMT was the right kind of state making in a democratic society and the only alternative to a large professional force that might well become an economic burden and a political danger. UMT, as Truman and others saw it, would provide a cheap supply of trained manpower without overburdening the budget or creating a large gap in the pool of tax-paying workers. It was also a way to reconcile the need for military strength with public pressure for rapid postwar demobilization and with traditional opposition to a large standing army based on peacetime conscription. According to the president's advisers, Congress was not likely to make the draft a permanent feature of American life. Nor was it likely to strengthen the position of an officer elite that might challenge civilian authority. But with UMT, they said, it was possible to be prepared militarily while avoiding both of these dangers and creating at the same time a better, more democratic republic.[7]

Truman was especially enamored with the citizen-soldier as a symbol of public virtue and as an instrument of democratic reform and social betterment, ideals that were reinforced by his own experiences in World War I and his well-known antipathy toward "brass hats" and braided admirals. Drawing on these ideals, the president saw universal training as the key to a "citizens' army" that would be supervised by a small corps of officers recruited from "regular" schools and commissioned after serving at least one year in the ranks. By these means, he hoped to break up the "political cliques that run the Army and Navy" and forge a "democratic" fighting force trained in "republican" principles and invulnerable to the "personal aggrandizement of some dictator." In addition, Truman and his colleagues thought of UMT as an appropriate mechanism for educating young men in the duties of citizenship, improving

---

[6] Stimson statement at cabinet meeting, 7 September 1945, Truman Papers, PSF-Subject File, box 146, folder: Military Training. See also Connelly minutes of cabinet meeting, 7 September 1945, Connelly Papers, box 2, folder: Notes on Cabinet Meetings – White House File, 1945, September 7, 21, 28; and *Forrestal Diaries*, 93.

[7] In addition to the sources cited in the last three notes see General Dwight D. Eisenhower telegram to the War Department, 25 July 1945, Records of the U.S. President's Advisory Committee on Government Organization (Dwight D. Eisenhower Library, Abilene, KS) box 18, folder 136: Defense – Reorganization Proposals and DOD Reorganization Act of 1958; and *Forrestal Diaries*, 89–90.

their physical fitness, equipping them with useful skills, and disciplining their character, all of which would make for a better workforce, a more productive economy, and a healthy democracy. In short, UMT was to be a democratic crucible from which young men would emerge, bodies hardened, skills honed, minds steeped in republican virtue, and values attuned to the defense of democracy in a dangerous, Darwinian world.[8]

Such arguments became the order of the day in June 1945, when the House Select Committee on Postwar Military Policy met to consider a program of universal military training. Secretaries Stimson and Forrestal joined military leaders from the Army, Navy, and Marine Corps to make the case for UMT. The United States, they warned, must not enter another war with an empty reserve of trained manpower, if only because it could not count on future allies to engage aggressors while it rearmed, as was the case between 1939 and 1941. Nor should it be forced into a defensive strategy, as it had been in the months after Pearl Harbor, but should build instead the military strength needed to guarantee its safety and meet its responsibilities as a world power. Because voluntary enlistments would not produce a force of sufficient size, and because a permanent system of compulsory military service neither squared with American tradition nor had the support of the American people, the only alternative left was some system of universal military training.

Those making the case for UMT also emphasized its capacity to meet national security needs in a way that would protect the country from the dangers posed by a large standing army, a swollen military budget, and undemocratic militarization. In short, UMT would help to safeguard democracy at home as well as abroad, or so its proponents argued, and to clinch their case they emphasized again its important value as a symbol of American resolve and of the willingness of the American people to make the sacrifices that world leadership required. UMT, they said, would lend credibility to the country's commitments around the world and to the negotiating position of American diplomats.[9]

---

[8] *Forrestal Diaries*, 88–89; Truman, "Plan for Universal Military Training," 23 June 1945. See also Connelly minutes of cabinet meeting, 31 August 1945, Connelly Papers, box 2, folder: Notes on Cabinet Meetings – White House File, 1945, August 17 & 31; Secretary of Commerce Henry A. Wallace to Trumen, 5 September 1945, Truman Papers, PSF-Subject File, box 146, folder: Military Training; Connelly minutes of cabinet meeting, 7 September 1945, Connelly Papers, box 2, folder: Notes on Cabinet Meetings – White House File, 1945, September 7, 21, 28; and Stimson statement at cabinet meeting, 7 September 1945, Truman Papers, PSF-Subject File, box 146, folder: Military Training.

[9] U.S. Congress, House, *Universal Military Training, Hearings and Statements Pursuant to H. Res. 465, A Resolution to Establish a Select Committee on Postwar Military Policy* (Washington, 1945), 1–5, 479–83, 491–92, 498–505, 525–27, 531–33, 546–51, 556–79 (hereafter House, *Universal Military Training*).

These arguments won support from a variety of private officials, particularly those representing the American Legion, the Veterans of Foreign Wars, the National Guard Association, and the Reserve Officers
Association.[10] Support also came from the U.S. Chamber of Commerce,
from distinguished private citizens like President Karl T. Compton of the
Massachusetts Institute of Technology, and from the Citizens' Committee
for Military Training, a private group that claimed chapters in forty-two
states.[11] Like Forrestal, Stimson, and the military leadership, these witnesses stressed the diplomatic and national security advantages of UMT,
including its utility as a deterrent to aggression. As one witness put it,
"Few people rush up to Joe Louis or Jack Dempsey and slap them in the
face."[12]

If anything, however, witnesses drawn from the private sector were
even more inclined than their government counterparts to emphasize the
political and social benefits of universal training. They said that UMT
would help to eliminate illiteracy, improve the health and physical fitness
of the nation's youth, and provide them with vocational training. They
were even more convinced that UMT would give the next generation
"a new baptism in the principles of democracy," to borrow the words
of one witness.[13] It would improve understanding between boys from
different backgrounds and thereby overcome prejudices of all sorts, ef-
face class distinctions, and encourage teamwork and a greater sense of
community purpose. It would also instruct young men in their responsibilities to the nation, give them a new respect for authority, and create a
generation infused with traditional republican values and better prepared
in the duties of citizenship.[14]

These sentiments, however, were not shared by most of those who
testified. Opposition to UMT grew naturally out of the long history of
popular resistance to any form of military conscription, a resistance that
had been evident most recently in the bitter fights against the draft on
the eve of both world wars. What is more, if support for UMT came
from some of the same corporate, government, and military leaders that
had earlier backed the draft, then a similar continuity was evident in
the opposition as well, which included the same combination of conservative Republicans, midwestern insurgents, trade unionists, pacifists,

[10] Ibid., 35–48, 51–52, 57, 62–63.
[11] Ibid., 6–10, 191–95, 462–66.
[12] Ibid., 6.
[13] Ibid., 49.
[14] Ibid., 10, 43, 47, 50, 462–64. For similar thinking by military leaders and other government
   witnesses see ibid., 556–79.

radicals, religious groups, and women's organizations that had earlier rallied against conscription.[15]

The oppositional alliance included bastions of cultural conservatism, like the Young Men's Christian Association, as well as radical, liberal, and civil libertarian groups, like the Socialist Labor Party of America, the Liberal Party of New York, the National Association for the Advancement of Colored People (NAACP), and the American Civil Liberties Union (ACLU). Business support for UMT was offset by strong opposition from labor and farm groups, most notably the American Federation of Labor, the Congress of Industrial Organizations, the National Grange, and the National Farmers Union. Church groups were another part of the oppositional alliance, represented particularly by witnesses speaking for the United Lutheran Church of America, the Disciples of Christ, the Federal Council of Churches of Christ in America, the National Catholic Welfare Conference, the Evangelical and Reformed Church, the Presbyterian Church of the United States, the Rabbinical Assembly of America, and the American Friends Service Committee. And next to church groups the alliance's strongest representation came from a variety of prominent educational associations. The National Education Association spoke against UMT, as did the American Association of University Professors, the American Council on Education, the National Commission of Christian Higher Education, the Association of American Colleges, the American Association of Teachers' Colleges, and the National Congress of Parents and Teachers.

To some degree, each of these organizations had its own agenda. Educators feared the removal of students from the schools, although they usually denied it, while labor leaders worried that business and the military would use UMT to inculcate antilabor values in a national reserve of union busters. The ACLU argued that UMT would violate personal liberties, something that was acceptable only in a national emergency, and the NAACP complained that it would do nothing to overthrow the pattern of racial segregation in the armed forces.[16] Whatever their special concerns, however, groups comprising the anti-UMT alliance shared a set of assumptions that guided their attack on the proposal and led to more general arguments.[17]

[15] Chambers, *To Raise an Army*, 103–24; and Horowitz, *Beyond Left & Right*, 25, 170–71.
[16] Ibid., 111, 113–17, 209.
[17] For a summary of the arguments leveled against UMT in 1945 see Elsey memorandum for Commodore Jake Vardaman (White House, naval aide), 18 August 1945, Elsey Papers, box 90, folder: National Defense – Universal Military Training.

On one level, their assault struck directly at the national security arguments raised on behalf of UMT. Given the imminent end of the war, they said, it was best to meet short-term military manpower requirements through a temporary extension of selective service. Postwar requirements would depend on international commitments that had yet to be determined and could be satisfied, in any event, by tapping the enormous pool of returning veterans. In addition, critics denied that UMT would help to prevent aggression and maintain peace in the postwar period, any more than it had helped the Belgians, the French, and the Soviets to deter German aggression in the 1930s. Its more likely result, they said, would be to encourage a reckless foreign policy that aroused suspicion among friends and foes alike, diminished the possibility of international cooperation, and provoked another in a long line of military competitions that had always been a source of war. Nor did critics believe that UMT would enhance the credibility of the country's commitment to the United Nations, as some of its proponents claimed. On the contrary, as one witness testified, it would be "declaring in advance that we have no faith in collective security" and that "World War III is inevitable."[18]

On another level, critics challenged the view of UMT as an agency of social betterment and democratic training, seeing it instead as a source of social destruction and the demise of democracy. They agreed that young men should be schooled in citizenship, that their health and moral character had to be nurtured, and that vocational training and education required constant attention. But to their way of thinking these goals could be achieved more easily and at less expense through the traditional community institutions of family, church, and school. They worried that UMT would allow the military to weaken or replace these institutions and to delay, or even distort, the moral instruction and practical education of American youth. To buttress their point, critics cited the moral hazards of a regimented, segregated camp life, including the higher rates of suicide and the greater risk of venereal disease and alcoholism in such an environment.[19] UMT did not build character, they insisted, and especially those attributes of character associated with a democratic political system. On the contrary, it was bound to re-create the military pattern of regimentation, rigid hierarchy, and unthinking obedience to authority that had characterized a similar system in prewar Germany, and had led

---

[18] House, *Universal Military Training*, 107. See also ibid., 92, 110, 112–13, 118, 119, 130, 139, 144–56, 165–68, 227–32, 339–44, 362, 391–95.
[19] Ibid., 110, 119, 131, 163–64, 158–59.

the young men of that country to perpetrate the most horrible crimes against humanity.[20]

As this suggests, arguments on both sides focused to a large extent on whether UMT was compatible with the country's democratic identity and postwar purpose. Supporters saw UMT as a source of democratic renewal at home and as essential to success in the struggle against communism around the world. Dissenters saw it as a threat to the American way. Each side resorted to an emotionally charged language that conveyed its claim to be the one true defender of democracy. Supporters talked of civic duty, of the citizen soldier, and of a democratic fighting force. Critics defined the American way by reference to the totalitarian "other" and captured the distinction in such binary oppositions as freedom/regimentation, voluntary/compulsory, civil/military, us/them, American/German. UMT, they argued, was a European institution particularly associated with fascist states. It was "not American," declared Dr. Gould Wickey, representing the Association of American Colleges, because the "American way is one of freedom and not of compulsion."[21] Dr. William J. Miller, a Catholic priest and president of the University of Detroit, made a similar point on behalf of the Michigan Council to Oppose Peacetime Military Conscription, as did Norman Thomas on behalf of the Postwar World Council. Nothing was "more dangerous to democracy," said Miller, "than the conditioning, regimentation, and uncritical obedience to arbitrary authority that most compulsory military training induces."[22] Routine obedience to authority, Thomas agreed, was the essence of militarism and UMT was a step in that direction.[23]

Hubert Klemme of the Evangelical and Reformed Church also worried that UMT would lead to the "militarization of our democracy," as did Eric Hass of the Socialist Labor Party, who saw UMT as an effort by the War Department to "Prussianize America."[24] The military, he and others claimed, wanted to indoctrinate the nation's youth, "control [its] civilian life," and transform it into a "warlike country" that would be dominated, like the "tragic examples" of Germany and Japan, by "military cliques, military dictatorships, and the military mind."[25] To "adopt the essence

---

[20] Ibid., 165–68.
[21] Ibid., 119. See also ibid., 165–68, 410–13.
[22] Ibid., 108.
[23] Ibid., 227–32.
[24] Ibid., 158–59, 349.
[25] Ibid., 120, 110. See also ibid., 158–59.

of the system we are fighting to destroy," one witness declared, was "to be victimized by victory."[26]

Critics also focused on the cost of UMT compared with other, more effective programs. According to union leaders, in particular, a strong and stable economy was a better defense against aggression than a large standing army. After all, they said, unemployment and other social and economic problems had fueled class hatred, suspicion, and violence and had thereby paved the way to power for Hitler and Mussolini. And because these problems were the primary breeders of war and aggression, they wanted Congress to direct its efforts toward measures that promoted employment and greater growth, such as multilateral trade, free collective bargaining, and passage of a full employment bill. It must not support initiatives that actually pointed in the opposite direction and had the potential to "disorganize our peacetime economy, gear us to an armament economy, reduce our productivity and reduce our national income." Indeed, if the resources required for homes, food, and other basic necessities were to go instead for tanks and guns, taxes would increase, living standards would decline, and social tensions would escalate.[27]

These arguments notwithstanding, the House Select Committee on Postwar Military Policy recommended a program of universal military training, at which point the president drafted a plan for training young men between eighteen and twenty years of age. Under Truman's plan, submitted to Congress in October 1945, these young men would constitute a general reserve of military manpower to supplement the National Guard, the organized reserves, and a small professional Army, Navy, and Marine Corps. The plan had been heavily influenced by General of the Army Marshall, Acting Secretary of War Patterson, and other officials in the Navy and War departments. It was at their urging that Truman recommended a year of continuous military training, rather than a few months, and gave first billing to the program's national security advantages. The United States needed military strength, the president declared, if it was going to lead the world into a new era of peace and justice. To those who said that UMT would move the country closer to militarism, he replied that a citizens reserve was the best alternative to a large, standing army. To those who would draw on the pool of trained veterans to meet a national emergency, he cited the inequity of asking these men and women to serve again. And to those who hoped to delay action until

[26] Ibid., 107. See also ibid., 92, 165–68, 361, 410–13.
[27] Ibid., 412. See also ibid., 363, 410–13, 419–23.

more was known about the country's international obligations, including its UN commitments, he said that it was better to prepare now and retrench later.[28]

At congressional hearings on a variant of Truman's proposal held in November and December 1945 and again in February 1946, testimony focused on the major issues that had arisen earlier, including the cost of UMT, the sacrifices that such expenditures entailed, and whether these funds could bring a greater degree of security if invested in other areas.[29] Supporters of the measure still assumed that military force would be needed to guarantee the country's postwar security and that UMT was much preferable to a large standing army, which they considered too expensive. According to Patterson, speaking for the War Department, the administration had a plan to reduce the regular army and to rely on UMT to train seven hundred thousand men a year, at an annual cost of $2.4 billion for the regular army and $1.8 billion for UMT. Without UMT, Patterson warned, a much larger standing army would be required at an annual cost of $8.4 billion. This figure stunned some members of the committee and added emphasis to the administration's claim that UMT offered the best defense at the lowest price.[30]

Nevertheless, the claim failed to convince the administration's critics, who included representatives of the same groups that had earlier testified before the House Committee on Postwar Military Policy. They still insisted that UMT was unnecessary, impractical, and misguided, and they added new arguments to support their case. The country's industrial power and monopoly of atomic weapons made it virtually immune to attack, or so the critics now argued, and any war that did break out would be fought with atomic bombs, missiles, rockets, and robots, for which no defense was possible. Under these circumstances, the critics worried that UMT would give the country a false sense of security, much as the Maginot Line had deluded the French, while actually

---

[28] Acting Secretary of War Patterson memorandum for Truman, 21 September 1945, Truman Papers, PSF-Subject File, box 146, folder: Military Training; Harry S. Truman *Memoirs*, vol. 1, *Year of Decisions*, paperback ed. (New York, 1965), 562; Truman address before a Joint Session of the Congress on Universal Military Training, 23 October 1945, *Public Papers, Truman, 1945*, 404–13; Donovan, *Conflict and Crisis*, 136–37; Cohen, *Citizens and Soldiers*, 156–58.

[29] U.S. Congress, House, *Hearings on H. Res. 515, An Act to Provide Military or Naval Training for All Male Citizens Who Attain the Age of 18 Years, and for Other Purposes* (Washington, 1945). H.R. 515 has been introduced by Representative Andrew J. May of Kentucky, a Democrat and chairman of the House Military Affairs Committee.

[30] Ibid., 3–8.

provoking another arms race leading to another world war. If an army was necessary, they contended, it would be better to recruit a small, volunteer force and better still if the country used its defense dollars to raise a professional army of scientists, rather than conscripts, and to fund a comprehensive program of research and development in the technology of modern war.[31]

To most critics, however, the real choice was not between UMT and an army of volunteers but between military and nonmilitary expenditures. At issue was the purpose to which the nation's wealth would be put and whether these expenditures would define the country as a warrior state or as a welfare state. The Chamber of Commerce, complained Nathan Cowen of the CIO, would spend billions on the military but was the first to say that government could not afford an additional $400 million per year in aid to education, that spending for school lunches had to be reduced, and that an adequate program of child care was financially impossible. But it was just such expenditures, he and others argued, that would advance democracy and eradicate the social and economic problems that had set the stage for fascism in the 1930s and world war in the 1940s.[32]

Donald DuShane of the National Education Association illustrated the relative cost of UMT in a dramatic presentation to the committee. By his calculations, the annual bill for UMT would cover the college expenses of nine hundred thousand undergraduates or ten thousand graduate students. It would provide a free education for three million children or $750,000 for a trade and technical school in every congressional district in the United States. And for every county in every state of the union, he concluded, it would buy ten modern school buses each year, provide ten full-time recreation and juvenile guidance workers, meet the payroll of one junior college with ten instructors, or construct a ten-room school building, a small hospital, a library, or a psychiatric clinic.[33]

As this suggests, the cost of UMT relative to other government programs involved a larger debate over state making and state identity, and specifically over the degree to which UMT might alter the nation's traditional institutions, customs, and priorities. Supporters still insisted that

---

31 Ibid., 4–5, 8, 89–117, 312, 378–79, 381, 417–60, 469–72, 474, 572, 593, 604.
32 The U.S. Chamber of Commerce was a strong supporter of H.R. 515, as it had been of other UMT proposals, and consistently emphasized the social as well as national security benefits of such training, including its utility in providing a better, more reliable, more disciplined workforce. See the testimony of Dunlop C. Clark of the Chamber of Commerce in ibid., 327–35. For the arguments of the bill's opponents see the sources cited in the following note.
33 Ibid., 311–14, 472, 582, 594–95, 598, 605–6.

UMT would affirm a tradition of national service, instill in young men the habits that made for good citizenship, and promote both democracy and a military system that was less militaristic. It would do all this, they said, while enabling the American people to fulfill their new duty to defend democracy abroad.[34] Critics, on the other hand, still insisted that UMT would remake America in a totalitarian mold. In their view, the armed forces would use it to indoctrinate young men in military values, drive out the spirit of fair play, tolerance, and equality associated with democracy, and instill a mean-spirited regimentation and a blind obedience to authority. In addition, UMT would enable the military to manipulate the labor market and forge an alliance of industrial and military interests with a vested stake in defense expenditures, the arms race, and war. Nor were its other effects likely to be beneficial, since it would also produce a political bloc composed of trainees and professional soldiers to which Congress would feel obliged to cater, just as it did to existing veterans' groups. It was this corruption of politics by the military and allied private interests that critics saw as a danger to democracy – not to mention UMT's equally corrosive effects on the economy and on such traditional bulwarks of democracy as the home, the school, and the church.[35]

Although public opinion polls consistently registered support for UMT, the intense opposition on Capitol Hill finally led the House Military Affairs Committee to suspend its hearings in favor of a resolution, introduced by Republican Minority Leader Joseph W. Martin, Jr., of Massachusetts, that called for an international agreement prohibiting any form of compulsory military service in peacetime. During hearings on the resolution in February 1946 the committee heard the same divided testimony from many of the same groups that had earlier testified on the administration's proposal. These divisions kept the committee from reporting the measure and apparently had a similar effect on Truman, who decided to suspend his efforts on behalf of UMT until after the fall elections.[36]

At the same time, however, the rapid pace of postwar demobilization had persuaded the administration that UMT was more essential than ever. The Pentagon was planning to demobilize over five million soldiers by July 1946, and was convinced that new volunteers and reenlistments

---

[34] In addition to the sources cited in notes 12 and 13 above see ibid., 7–9, 332.

[35] Ibid., 311–13, 417–60, 469–74, 580–81, 596, 603–7.

[36] *Congressional Quarterly, 1946* (Washington, 1946), 718–20. For a convenient summary of the public opinion polls see Appendix 8 of the Report of the President's Advisory Commission on Universal Training. *A Program for National Security* (Washington, 1947), 225–42.

would not permit the armed forces to meet their global responsibilities. Demobilization would hit the War Department especially hard, and Secretary Patterson counted on UMT to close the gap between the Army's capabilities and the country's commitments, particularly in Japan and Germany, where he anticipated difficulties in providing replacements for the occupation troops.[37]

But if UMT remained the goal, the deadlock in Congress at least prompted changes in strategy. The Army set up an experimental UMT program at Fort Knox, Kentucky, and spent substantial sums to advertise the program's cultural, education, and recreational benefits, as well as its military value.[38] In addition, people on both sides of the issue had been urging the appointment of a citizens' committee to study the matter and make recommendations. Opponents were convinced that such a study would demonstrate how new developments, especially the atomic bomb, had rendered UMT unnecessary, while supporters saw the same study as a way to dramatize the importance of an integrated program of national security in which UMT would be a major component.[39] Truman now turned to this idea as well, deciding near the end of 1946 to establish the President's Advisory Commission on Universal Training composed of nine distinguished citizens led by President Compton of MIT.

Meeting with the new commissioners in late December, the president made an appeal based squarely on the ideology of national security, with its emphasis on "total war," its blurring of the line between war and peace, and its clarion call for a disciplined and virtuous citizenry. He reminded the commissioners that America now lived in an age of constant danger in which all citizens had to contribute to the national security, if not as part of the regular forces then as members of the industrial army or of the general reserve of trained manpower created by UMT. He also stressed again his belief that UMT would educate young men to their civic duty and improve their mental health and physical conditioning. Of those drafted during the war, the president claimed, nearly 30 percent

---

37 *Forrestal Diaries*, 106–7; Connelly minutes of cabinet meeting, 31 August 1945, Connelly Papers, box 2, folder: Notes on Cabinet Meetings – White House File, 1945, August 17 & 31; minutes of War Council meeting, 7 November 1945, Robert P. Patterson Papers (Library of Congress, Washington, DC), General Correspondence, box 23, folder: 1945–47, War Council Meeting.

38 The Army's expensive publicity campaign, including the cost of the Fort Knox experiment, provoked outrage among the anti-UMT forces around the country and led to a critical congressional investigation. See Gerhardt, *The Draft and Public Policy*, 60.

39 See, in addition to the sources cited in note 36, Wallace to Truman, 5 September 1945, Truman Papers, PSF-Subject File, box 146, folder: Military Training.

were unfit for military service, a record that he found alarming, particularly since he assumed that great republics always crumbled when "their peoples became prosperous and fat and lazy." The United States must not go the way of Greece and Rome, Truman concluded, both of which had collapsed because their citizens were unwilling or unable to sacrifice for the national good.[40]

Truman was again lecturing to the converted. The commissioners might not have shared his theory of history, but they did subscribe to the national security ideology and were sure to use it to defend a program of universal training that came close to what the president and the military establishment wanted.[41] The problem was that the commissioners could not finish their work in time to influence legislation in the current session of Congress, which discouraged the administration from submitting a bill of its own. The only bill considered was a measure drafted by the American Legion and supported by other veterans' groups. The Legion worked through its local posts and more than five million members to deluge Congress and the press with petitions, letters, and editorials on behalf of UMT. The campaign seemed to pay off in that public opinion polls showed that 65 percent of the American people favored UMT, while only 31 percent were opposed. Still, the measure encountered enough opposition from labor, religious, and education groups that Congress again decided to postpone action.[42] Nor were these groups swayed by the Compton Commission's final report, which reached the president in May 1947.

As expected, the report used the ideology of national security to defend a "balanced security system," in effect, a program of state making that included the stockpiling of critical materials, a plan to mobilize industry and science, a coordinated intelligence service, a powerful air force, and a system of universal military training. The report lamented the rapid demobilization and continued deterioration of the country's military forces at a time when war could strike without warning and

[40] Truman informal remarks to the Advisory Commission on Universal Training, 20 December 1946, Records of the President's Advisory Commission on Universal Training (Truman Library), box 3, folder: Commission Kit. – 2d meeting, 12-28-46.

[41] The Joint Chiefs conveyed their views to the commission through the president. See Truman to Compton, 17 January 1947, RG 218, Records of the U.S. Joint Chiefs of Staff, Records of the Chairman, Admiral Leahy, 1942–48, box 20, folder: Correspondence Signed by the President.

[42] *Forrestal Diaries*, 244; minutes of War Council meeting, 6 March 1947, Patterson Papers, General Correspondence, box 23, folder: 1945–47, War Council Meeting; *Congressional Quarterly, 1947* (Washington, 1947), 58, 310–11, 468.

when the American government had committed itself to a position of leadership around the world. The United States had only 2.3 combat divisions available for duty, according to the commissioners, while its air and naval strength had shrunk so rapidly as to imperil a viable defense, encourage new aggressors, and cause friendly governments to lose faith in America's ability to defend democracy against competing ideologies. Needed, said the commissioners, were measures such as UMT that would "lend authority to our voice in international affairs," reassure allies, and discourage aggression.[43]

In arguing for UMT, the commission embraced many of the usual arguments. It disputed the notion that atomic bombs and other instruments of mass destruction had eliminated the need for a large supply of military manpower in wartime, arguing instead that trained troops would still be needed for home defense, for counterattack, and for ultimate victory, and that UMT was the only way to provide this training short of "overburdening the country's economy" with a permanent military of substantial size. In addition, UMT would enable the War and Navy departments to mobilize quickly in the event of war, provide the basis for a wartime system of selective service, and feed manpower to the National Guard and the organized reserves. It would also function as a giant sifting and sorting machine, enabling the defense establishment to inventory the country's skills and aptitudes and to channel qualified young men into programs of scientific and vocational training in fields essential to national security. Nor were its benefits limited to national security. The commission still insisted, though in muted tones, that UMT would improve the health and education of the nation's young men, give them a shared experience in good citizenship, and contribute to national unity.[44]

With these goals in mind, the commission recommended that every young man undergo a period of military training upon reaching the age of eighteen or upon completing or leaving high school. The program would begin with six months of basic training, to be followed by a longer period of part-time service in the National Guard, the organized reserves, or in some other capacity. To reassure those who worried that UMT would increase the power of the military establishment, the commission urged that it be operated under a presidential commission consisting of one military and two civilian representatives and that further safeguards

---

[43] *Program for National Security*, 90, 5. See also ibid., 3, 90–91.
[44] Ibid., 93. See also ibid., 89–92.

be provided by an advisory board of private citizens and by civilian inspection of training camps on a regular basis.[45]

In June and July the House Armed Services Committee held hearings to consider the commission's recommendations, the proposals coming from the American Legion and other sources, and the views of the War Department, which now had UMT on its list of "must" legislation. As in the past, the hearings also became a forum for those who considered UMT unnecessary and un-American, with both sides repeating their previous arguments.[46] One side insisted that atomic bombs made UMT unnecessary; the other that only a "disciplined citizenship" could survive a modern war. One side predicted that UMT would trigger an arms race and lead to another world war; the other claimed that military strength was the key to deterrence and peace. One side charged that UMT threatened the prospects for collective security; the other retorted that military power would enable the United States to honor its UN commitments. One side believed that UMT had contributed to the rise of German militarism and aggression; the other blamed German aggression on the lack of military preparedness in the West. One side pointed to the high incidence of alcoholism, prostitution, and venereal disease on wartime military bases; the other argued that UMT would improve the spiritual and physical health of the nation's youth. One side complained that UMT contradicted the country's historic opposition to a large standing army; the other thought it squared with the individual's traditional duty to defend the nation.[47]

As in past debates, the core of the discussion revolved around the cost of UMT, the purposes to which American resources should be put, and the effects of military training on the country's political identity and institutions. The administration and its supporters estimated the cost at no more than $1.75 billion per year, which they said was less than the alternative of a large standing army and much less than the cost of a third world war that might otherwise result. Critics put the budget at $3 to $5 billion per year and argued again that money set aside for UMT would do more to promote peace if used to stimulate economic growth at home and abroad. In the previous fiscal year, by their calculations,

---

45 Ibid., 93–94.
46 *Congressional Quarterly, 1947*, 467–68.
47 U.S. Congress, House, *Full Committee Hearings on Universal Military Training* (Washington, 1947), 4230. See also ibid., 4176–77, 4198–4200, 4222, 4236–39, 4242, 4341–42, 4337, 4344–46, 4366–67.

the United States had spent only 1.5 percent of its budget for education while spending 34 percent for military purposes, including more than a billion dollars for the pay of officers alone. This disparity had to be corrected, they said, and again they calculated what the money for UMT would buy in housing, education, and health care and how expenditures in these areas would eradicate the economic and social problems that fed aggression and war.[48]

As in earlier stages of the debate, disagreements over the cost of UMT brought to the fore more fundamental differences over threatened changes in American political life and culture. Once more, critics summoned the image of the garrison state and used it to attack the national security initiatives recommended by the Compton Commission, including UMT, industrial mobilization, and the stockpiling of critical raw materials, all of which they saw as part of a trend toward the militarization of American society. With the adoption of these initiatives, they argued, the "power of the military" would extend to "every facet of our national life." Colleges would be forced to adopt ROTC programs, "industry would be tightly geared to the military machine," and "huge vested interests in military production" would form. Military men would play an increasingly important role in shaping the nation's foreign policy and the armed forces would enjoy a substantial voice in almost every university and industrial laboratory in the country. The result over time would be a "permanent war economy," the critics said, and this economy would drain resources from civilian investment, drive up taxes, and lower living standards.[49]

The proponents of UMT accused their critics of exaggerating the degree of military influence in American life, but they also drew on the ideology of national security to argue that America's democratic political identity and traditional values had to be adapted to its new responsibilities in an age of total war. Some changes were essential, they said, and not just more spending on defense and new programs like UMT. Recent developments in "international relations" brought about "by total war" and the Communist challenge also required changes in "societal forms" and in the country's political culture. The obligations of defense now reached "deeper and deeper into the community," and the duties of citizenship had to be enlarged accordingly. These were the views of

[48] Ibid., 4176, 4337, 4340, 4342–43, 4367–69.
[49] Ibid., 4338, 4336.

the Compton Commission and particularly of commissioner Edmund A. Walsh, a Catholic priest and vice president of Georgetown University. "In modern conditions," Walsh proclaimed, "we can no longer speak of the battle front or of a theater of operation. That is over. Every city and every town of the United States is now involved in any global war," and this development necessitated a "corresponding expansion" of the "moral obligation" of citizenship. Citizenship must go beyond the conventional duty "to defend one's country" in time of danger to embrace the "obligation of preparedness," including universal military training.[50]

Talk of a new citizenship was frequently linked to talk of a new America, which had finally become a Great Power seasoned by two world wars and now obliged to assume its duties as guardian at the gate of civilization. To those who spoke for UMT, the new America was America the strong, America the world leader, America the defender of freedom that could not escape the part that history had written for it. Americans had no choice but to face up to realities, rather than repeat the mistakes of the past, and to make the sacrifices that world leadership required. It would be good to have full employment and lower taxes, explained Daniel A. Poling, editor of the *Christian Herald* and another member of the Compton Commission. But the country also had to invest in "war risk insurance," by which he meant UMT and other measures to secure the world community against aggression. Surely this investment was worth some adaptations and some modest sacrifice of basic comforts. UMT would only cost "one-tenth of what the country each year spends on liquor, tobacco, chewing gum, and cosmetics," or so Compton told the Armed Services Committee, and every "patriotic citizen" should be willing to give up these little "luxuries" for the "security of our country."[51]

By the time the hearings ended, the debate had spread from Congress through the national press. Liberal journals like the *New Republic* opposed UMT, as did some conservative commentators, but most of the country's leading newspapers supported it, even while disagreeing on the details of a workable plan. Much the same was true of the most prominent syndicated columnists and editorial writers, whose opinions we have tracked in the arguments over military budgets and the National Security Act. Their thinking echoed the views of those who testified for UMT in

---

[50] Ibid., 4195–96.
[51] Ibid., 4222, 4176.

the congressional hearings and was more likely to reach a much wider audience, which may account for the gap between the vigorous opposition to the measure on Capitol Hill and the strong support it garnered in the public opinion polls.[52]

The most important exception to the rule was Hanson Baldwin, the influential military-affairs editor of the *New York Times*, who testified against UMT in Congress and devoted considerable space to the subject in his columns. To him the whole issue turned on the measure's "military utility," and in this regard he considered it a "backward step." He was convinced that large standing armies would become a thing of the past over the next ten years. During that period the armed forces would have a pool of trained veterans on which to draw in the event of an emergency, and thereafter the nation's security would rest primarily on its airpower, its missiles, and its stockpile of atomic weapons, all of which would "starve" for investment if funds were diverted to the kind of "Maginot line" defense envisioned in UMT.[53]

In the end, however, the Armed Services Committee sided with Compton rather than Baldwin, reporting a bill that required all able-bodied young men between eighteen and twenty years of age to undergo six months of basic training in a National Security Training Corps, followed by another six months in the corps, enlistment in the regular forces, or service through the National Guard, the organized reserves, the military academies, or the Reserve Officers Training Corps. Although every member of the committee supported the bill, it came too late for congressional action in 1947, so both sides in the debate began gearing up for a major battle in the new year. By that time, moreover, new international crises and worsening conditions in Europe would make the administration more determined than ever to enact UMT. It only remained to be seen if these world-shaking events would also shake the administration's critics from their relentless opposition to a program they viewed as militarily useless, economically counterproductive, and a threat to basic American values.[54]

[52] For press reaction on UMT see the survey of editorial opinion in *U.S. News* 22 (10 January 1947): 30; and the more comprehensive survey in *Program for National Security*, 240–42. For the liberal view see the editorial, "Universal Military Training," in *The New Republic* 117 (23 June 1947): 11. For typical arguments in support of UMT see Marquis Childs, "Universal Military Training," *Washington Post*, 26 February 1947; and Ernest K. Lindley, "The UMT Report," *Newsweek* 29 (9 June 1947): 32.

[53] Baldwin, "UMT's Value Weighed," *New York Times*, 4 May 1947; and idem, "Why I Oppose Peacetime Conscription," *Reader's Digest* 51 (July 1947): 103–7.

[54] *Congressional Quarterly*, 1947, 468, 658–59.

III

By the time Congress reconvened in 1948, the liberal opponents of UMT had gained a powerful ally in Senator Robert Taft, the conservative Ohio Republican who had opposed selective service in 1940 and 1941.[55] Taft tied his assault on UMT to a general attack on the cost of defense and the administration's defense strategy. He believed that UMT could serve no function whatsoever, except perhaps as a spur to similar initiatives in other countries and thus as an "obstacle to peace." If established, it would train about a million men per year, according to his estimate, but their training would be superficial and actually out-of-date by the time they were called to active duty in a national emergency.[56]

Taft also found it difficult to grasp why the country needed such a reserve, which would be too large for defensive purposes and too small to counter the Soviet Union's massive conventional forces in Europe. The United States, in his opinion, would be better advised to maintain a small force of volunteers trained in the newest technology and backed by the greatest air force in the world. As noted in the previous chapter, the President's Air Power Commission had reached a similar conclusion in a report, issued in January 1948, that called for a seventy-group air force. Such a force would add approximately $2 billion to the annual budget for airpower, according to Taft, but that much and more could easily be recovered by scaling back the Army and the Navy and by canceling Truman's plan for universal military training – the cost of which he estimated at substantially more than the $2 billion per year projected by the administration. "I believe the increase in the Air Corps is less expensive" than the increase for UMT, he said, "and ten times as important."[57]

In Taft's view, moreover, good military strategy must always dovetail with the country's free economy and democratic political system, which he identified with the values of an older political culture, not the new

55 Taft would support selective service bills in 1948, 1950, and 1951, but never a bill for UMT. See Patterson, *Mr. Republican*, 240–41, 392–93.

56 Taft remarks on Universal Compulsory Military Training, 1 October 1947, Taft Papers, Legislative File, box 722, folder: National Defense (Speech), 1948. See also the sources cited in the following note.

57 Taft address to the Rhode Island Republican Club, 15 January 1948, Taft Papers, Legislative File, box 722, folder: National Defense (Speech), 1948; Taft address to the Lincoln Club of Denver, Colorado, 14 February 1948, and summary of remarks by Senator Taft to a Republican party meeting in Springfield, Ohio, 20 March 1948, ibid., box 616, folder: Foreign Policy, 1948. Taft was coached in his thinking on these matters by Bonner Fellers. See Fellers to Taft, 27 January 1948, ibid., box 722, folder: National Defense (Speech), 1948; and Fellers to Taft, 26 February and 4 April 1948, ibid., box 721, folder: 1948, National Defense.

ideology of national security. It was important to guard against foreign enemies, he said, but it was also important to build a national security state that did not destroy "the America we are trying to preserve." Pursuing the pipe dream of total defense would require long-term expenditures on a level comparable to wartime, and such a course would bankrupt the Treasury, make a reasonable standard of living impossible, and snuff out the economic and political liberties on which future growth and security depended. Taft reminded anyone who would listen that America's success in the last war had rested largely on its great "productive power, developed primarily to improve the conditions of the civilian population." And conserving that power required defense policies that would not waste resources on UMT and other ineffective measures.

Waste was not the most serious problem, of course, at least not to Taft, who was convinced that UMT flew in the face of time-tested traditions that distinguished the United States from other powers and accounted for its democratic character. The American people had never been "imperialists," he insisted, in language that defined the United States by comparison with the un-American other. Nor were they prepared at this point to support a "provocative" foreign policy with a reserve of ten million soldiers ready "at the drop of the hat to march around the world." In Taft's book, moreover, wresting a boy from his home, education, or occupation and forcing him "to serve for a year under the direction of the Federal Government" amounted to the "greatest limitation on individual freedom yet proposed." It was "the weapon of a totalitarian state," very much in line with the New Deal idea of government coercion but completely at odds with the traditional "concept of American liberty."[58]

Taft's reference to the New Deal highlights the strange coalition that took shape against UMT. At one end were Taft and other conservatives who saw UMT extending the New Deal's emphasis on coercive state power to the field of national security, and who were also concerned that military spending, when added to the cost of social welfare, ran the risk of debasing the currency, increasing the debt, and threatening the very foundations of American democracy and capitalism. At the other end

---

[58] Taft address to the Rhode Island Republican Club, 15 January 1948, ibid., box 722, folder: National Defense (Speech), 1948; Taft address to the Lincoln Club of Denver, Colorado, 14 February 1948, Taft Papers, Legislative File, box 616, folder: Foreign Policy, 1948. See also Taft address to the Economic Club of Detroit, 23 February 1948, ibid., folder Foreign Policy, 1948.

were Henry Wallace, Norman Thomas, and a variety of left-wing critics who thought that World War II had choked off a promising program of political reform and who now recoiled at the prospect of a permanent battle forever blasting their dream of a better world at home and abroad. In their constant refrain, military initiatives such as UMT subtracted from the resources otherwise available to enlarge the social welfare programs of the New Deal and to foster economic recovery and growth on a global scale.

Despite their differences, however, the two ends of the spectrum continued to be linked by a shared belief that UMT was impractical and provocative and by the conviction that it was the wrong kind of state making in a democratic country. It would centralize too much power in the military arm of the state and thus challenge the tradition of civilian supremacy embedded in the Constitution. This was what the critics were getting at when they spoke of UMT in binary oppositions as a foreign, not an American, institution, as the instrument of totalitarianism, not of democracy – a rhetorical strategy that had the advantage of inscribing the country's political identity in a way that excluded not only UMT but also its supporters, who were equated instead with the un-American other. As in totalitarian systems, the critics argued, peacetime military training diminished the individual by compelling a service best secured by voluntary means, and by crushing initiative, prohibiting free thought, and reducing the conscript to a cog in a regimented system. Nor was that the worst of it. By entrusting the military with functions normally and properly performed by the family, the church, and the school, UMT would enhance the powers of the state while diminishing the authority of these traditional institutions, not to mention the individual's capacity for self-help and independent thinking, all of which were essential to good citizenship.

But if the stakes were high for Taft and other critics on the left and the right, they were no less so for officials in the Truman administration, whose thinking was influenced not only by the national security ideology but also by the need to reconcile the requirements of defense with other priorities and older values. These officials expected Soviet-American tensions to run through "the next decade" at least, and they were convinced that neither Congress nor the American people would stay on a "draft basis" for that long or accept the financial burden of maintaining a large standing army. Truman told a meeting of his staff that government lacked the capacity over the long term to support a military establishment worth $11 billion annually, the figure that he was projecting for fiscal year 1949. But with UMT, he and others believed, it might be possible to reduce that expense to a reasonable level while at the same time getting the administration "off the hook of the Selective Service."[59]

The United States could not have an "adequate defense without" universal training, concurred Secretary Marshall, a long-time champion of UMT who seized every opportunity to speak with "great vigor" on the subject. Marshall was convinced that UMT meant savings to the country in the long run and was a better investment than the National Guard, which absorbed a "great amount" of money and "produces nothing" in return.[60] From his point of view, however, UMT had been "damned by too much arithmetic" of this kind, not to mention educational, health, and other "collateral considerations," all of which obscured the program's real necessity in light of "conditions in the world today." If the United States was going to reestablish a global balance of power, the secretary explained in words that echoed Stimson's thinking of two years earlier, it was essential to convince the world that "we did not propose to abdicate our responsibilities in Europe or anywhere else in combating the rising and spreading tide of Communism."[61]

What bothered Marshall, in other words, was his conviction that the country's current military strength could not support its global responsibilities. "We are playing with fire," he told the NSC on 12 February, and "have nothing with which to put it out." Marshall's remark came in a discussion of whether the Pentagon should reinforce the Greek government with American troops, an action, however desirable, that present force levels would not permit without a "partial mobilization." That was Marshall's opinion, and it was shared by the Joint Chiefs and Secretary of Defense Forrestal.[62] Nor was Greece their only problem. Speaking for the Joint Staff, Major General Alfred M. Gruenther also identified Italy, Palestine, and Korea as "explosive points" where the United States had interests it could not easily protect and commitments it could not easily honor. Indeed, manpower shortages were so acute, according to

59 *Forrestal Diaries*, 400. See also Eben A. Ayers Diary, 26 December 1947, Eben A. Ayers Papers (Truman Library), Diaries, box 16, folder: Diary, 1947.

60 Connelly minutes of cabinet meeting, Connelly Papers, box 2, folder: Notes on Cabinet Meetings – White House File, 1948 January 9–December 31. See also *Forrestal Diaries*, 368–69.

61 In addition to the sources cited in the previous footnote see diary entry for 4 March 1948, Forrestal Diary, Forrestal Papers, vols. 9–10, box 4.

62 *Forrestal Diaries*, 371–78.

the Pentagon, that neither the Army nor the Navy could implement the emergency war plan, let alone deploy a substantial force to any of the trouble spots that Gruenther listed.[63]

If Taft's thinking was pulled in one direction by the weight of traditional political culture, Marshall's thinking was pushed in a different direction by assumptions rooted in the new ideology of national security. In line with these assumptions, he and others worked assiduously to educate Congress on the need for additional military manpower, repeating the usual arguments that UMT would create a citizens' reserve for national emergencies while encouraging voluntary enlistments in the regular forces, the National Guard, and the organized reserves. Before mid-March, however, UMT's prospects on Capitol Hill seemed no better than in previous years. Ordinary citizens, Forrestal lamented, were complacent about the Soviet menace and not anxious to support new measures of defense, UMT included. In addition, conservatives in both parties were giving first priority to reducing taxes and balancing the budget, and were therefore inclined to question new expenditures on UMT, which Taft and Senator Harry F. Byrd, a conservative Democrat from Virginia, estimated at nearly $4 billion per year. When that sum was added to the billions of dollars that Truman requested for the regular defense establishment, the combined figure, by Byrd's calculations, would drive the government's budget for fiscal year 1949 to $50 billion, a sum so large that it would "wreck the country" for sure.[64] Under the circumstances, Byrd agreed with Taft and with officials in the Air Force that it was much wiser to rely on airpower rather than manpower to defend the country.[65]

As it turned out, it took action by the Soviet Union to brighten the prospects for UMT. What appeared to be a turning point came in March 1948, when a Communist coup in Czechoslovakia led the Senate to open hearings on a UMT bill that it had been reluctant to consider earlier. "Events are making progress for us," said Forrestal, who had been talking for some time about a concerted campaign to marshal popular and congressional opinion behind UMT and related initiatives. The Czech coup lent credibility to the case that he and others wanted to make, and they were quick to seize the opportunity to push for UMT as part of a necessary response to dangerous developments abroad. The time

---

[63] Ibid., 374–77.
[64] Ibid., 388. See also 384–86.
[65] Ibid., 373–77, 384–85, 388–89.

was ripe, Forrestal believed, and so did Truman, who prepared a mighty speech on which his program could sail through Congress.[66]

In his famous speech to Congress of 17 March, as in other elaborations of the national security ideology, Truman again drew on a system of symbolic representation to define America's national identity by comparison with the Soviet other. This and concurrent documents demonized the Soviet Union. They compared Stalin to Hitler, said the "tragic death" of the Czech republic was only the latest example of worldwide Communist aggression, called upon the American people to accept their mission as defenders of democracy everywhere, and urged them to make the sacrifices that such a mission required, including the sacrifice of time and money for a larger military establishment. Specifically, Truman demanded immediate passage of the Marshall Plan, a temporary reenactment of the draft, and a program of universal military training, not to mention a supplemental defense appropriation to cover the cost of increasing military force levels.[67] Truman wanted Congress to increase the Army's authorized strength to 782,000 troops, a level that could be reached partly through a temporary reenactment of selective service and partly through UMT's effect on enlistments.[68]

As in the past, the administration's position drew strong support from a parade of individuals and organized private groups. Representatives of the American Legion, the Veterans of Foreign Wars, the National Guard, and the Reserve Officers Association all urged the Senate Armed Services Committee to adapt the country's defenses to the danger it confronted in Europe, its democratic traditions to its global responsibilities. Drawing on the national security ideology, they argued that weakness compelled appeasement and encouraged aggression, and that only military strength would reassure allies and enable the United States to negotiate from strength. All favored a comprehensive national security program beginning with selective service and UMT. All saw selective service as the only way to quickly overcome the shortfall of military manpower and meet the current crisis. And all thought of UMT as the best long-term solution to the manpower problem. Similar thinking also came from Clem D. Johnston of the Chamber of Commerce and Charles E. Wilson

---

[66] Ibid., 389. See also ibid., 392–94; and diary entry for 11 March 1948, Forrestal Diary, Forrestal Papers, vols. 9–10, box 4.

[67] *Public Papers, Truman, 1948*, 182–86. See also Truman, *Years of Trial and Hope*, 278–79; *Forrestal Diaries*, 397–98, 400–401; Donovan, *Conflict and Crisis*, 357–58; and McCullough, *Truman*, 603.

[68] Senate, *Hearings on Universal Military Training*, 8, 33–34, 343–44.

of the General Electric Company, as well as from university presidents Isaiah Bowman and Arthur Compton, whose brother had chaired the President's Advisory Commission on Universal Military Training.[69]

What was most surprising, however, especially in light of the war scare whipped up by the administration, was the widespread opposition that greeted the president's program on Capitol Hill, particularly his proposal for UMT. If anything, the debate over national security issues since 1945 had enabled the opposition to grow and to become better organized and more entrenched. This was not borne out by opinion polls, to be sure, which continued to show strong support for some form of UMT, but it was plainly evident in the long list of individuals and organizations that testified against the measure in Congress.

Nor were the critics cowed by the hysteria that rushed through Washington in the wake of the Czech crisis. On the contrary, many of the witnesses accused the administration of manufacturing the crisis in order to mobilize support for an unpopular and unnecessary program. The administration, they said, wanted the American people to believe that free elections in Italy represented a threat to American democracy or that Soviet armies, still weak and exhausted from the war, were poised to overrun Central and Western Europe. If a threat existed, the critics found it in Europe's failure to recover economically from the ravages of war and from various social and economic problems that strengthened indigenous Communist parties and were best resolved through programs like the Marshall Plan. In their view, military initiatives would only diminish the resources available for these civilian needs while at the same time wrecking the chances for collective security through the United Nations, provoking an arms race the country could not afford, and increasing the risk of another world war.[70]

For the critics, moreover, any preparedness measures that might be needed bore no relationship to UMT. They continued to view the next war as a technological battle fought with airpower, rockets, and atomic bombs, not one involving millions of young soldiers trained "to shoot rifles, dig trenches, and scramble across fields under fire." If manpower shortages actually existed, they were due, the critics argued, to antiquated practices that discouraged enlistments and could be overcome through such practical reforms as higher pay and a greater promise of advancement. Some critics were even willing to reinstitute selective service as a

[69] Ibid., 161–62, 268–72, 284, 443–44, 787, 789, 815, 869.
[70] Ibid., 117, 122–23, 212–24, 233, 267, 244, 418, 421, 425, 500, 511–15, 525, 542–44.

temporary expedient, but under no circumstances would they support UMT. They could not see the sense in competing in an area of Soviet strength when doing so subtracted resources from the development of military science and technology, where the United States enjoyed a natural advantage. Any additional defense spending, they said, should go not for UMT but to enlarge the Air Force, expand the arsenal of atomic weapons, and promote a vigorous program of research and development in rockets, missiles, and other weapons of the future.[71]

As in the past, much of the debate came down to the most efficient use of American resources, with all sides passing themselves off as economizers. The supporters of UMT continued to claim as their goal a security system that was "bearable financially," would "not bankrupt the country," and could be "continued at a minimum of cost" over a number of years.[72] These goals, they held, could be realized by opting for UMT rather than a seventy-group Air Force that would destroy an effective balance between land, sea, and airpower, require a substantial expansion of both the Army and the Navy, and thus produce a much larger military establishment than the country needed or could afford.[73]

Forrestal resorted to such arguments repeatedly, although his testimony often raised some of the very concerns it sought to dampen. While claiming success at keeping defense costs at a bearable level, he was also prone to wax on about the need for national discipline and for the willingness to make tough choices – both central themes in the national security ideology. The American people, he conceded, would have to accept substantial hardships if they wanted to increase defense expenditures without wrecking the economy. When Senator Leverett Saltonstall noted that military spending accounted for 34 percent of the proposed budget, Forrestal admitted that it was possible to "inflate ourselves into defeat as well as through loss of war." The government was doing a lot, he said, what with defense expenditures and the Marshall Plan, while at the same time the American people wanted "lower taxes, big incomes, high dividends and high wages, the 4-day week and week ends at Palm Beach." There would have to be "a resolution of those [conflicting] desires," he confessed. The American people would have to sacrifice something if they hoped to maintain a free and "sound economy" without a system of "absolute control."[74]

71 Ibid., 145. See also ibid., 146, 153–54, 212–24, 230–33, 285–91, 453, 500–501, 552, 687, 842–43, 848, 856–57, 890–94, 1015, 1034.
72 Ibid., 5.
73 Ibid., 395–97, 1111–15; *Forrestal Diaries*, 402–3.
74 Senate, *Hearings on Universal Military Training*, 336. See also ibid., 7–9, 332, 337, 446.

Forrestal argued that Truman's proposal managed to balance these desires without risk to the economy; but others were not so sure. Senator Wayne Morse of Oregon and Charles Wilson of GE agreed that estimated defense expenditures, including those for UMT, fell within the country's capacity to pay, but both viewed the total as borderline and both assumed that military expenditures much beyond that amount would require sacrifices elsewhere, including some controls over wages, prices, and profits.[75] As noted previously, Bernard Baruch took this assumption even further, arguing that preparation for total war required a substantial mobilization of the nation's resources, including a mobilization czar, higher taxes, and government controls over the economy.[76]

As Baruch's remark pointed out, debates about funding and about the best use of American resources continued to feed concerns over the fate of democratic politics and traditional institutions. Baruch, to be sure, did not see his proposals leading to a "police state," but it was just this prospect that many critics feared the most. Relying again on a rhetorical strategy of otherness, they warned of the "perils of Prussianism," in Pearl Buck's felicitous phrase, and doubted that much good could come from the kind of state making that Baruch had in mind. Mrs. Alexander Stewart of the Woman's Committee to Oppose Conscription was convinced that "such strict government planning and control" would mean "giving up most of those values which we have considered worth defending." Democracy, she said, "would be lost in the preparation for a war of retaliation."[77] Similarly, Don Willner of the Students for Democratic Action warned that Baruch's approach would increase the dangerous degree of control that military leaders already exerted over the American economy, American universities, and American science. Russell Smith of the National Farmers' Union compared this control to the great military bureaucracies that had throttled free enterprise and individual initiative in many European countries. Not only would more military spending "Prussianize" the economy, he and others argued, it would also add to the national debt, increase the cost of living, and curtail the resources available for constructive investment in the civilian economy or in a wide range of social programs.[78]

Repeatedly stressed as well was what William Green of the American Federation of Labor called "the sacrifice of a considerable share of production for civilian use." Walter P. Reuther of the United Auto

[75] Ibid., 446–51.
[76] Ibid., 405–7.
[77] Ibid., 416, 452, 425.
[78] Ibid., 148–49, 231–32.

Workers figured that UMT would divert about two billion man hours per year from civilian production to military purposes. Seymour Linfield of the Wallace-for-President Committee estimated the cost in terms of lost goods and services to be about $2 billion annually. And both drove their point home by tabulating what the country could buy each year in homes, schools, and medical services with the $5 or $6 billion needed to cover the direct and indirect costs of UMT. Linfield even underscored his argument by maintaining that resources ought to be reallocated in the other direction. By his calculation, the government already spent more on the Army's office equipment than on national health care and more on military transportation than on education. Military expenditures already consumed 30 percent of the projected budget for fiscal year 1949, while social programs, including education and housing, consumed less than 5 percent, or $25 million less than the cost of UMT alone.[79] Such a balance sheet had an inescapable logic that Henry Wallace tried to capture rhetorically: "Butter and guns," he said, "are followed by guns and butter and finally by guns and dry bread."[80]

Government controls and the loss of goods and services to military purposes were only two aspects of the garrison state that critics saw emerging from Baruch's national security agenda and even from Truman's more modest plan to reinstitute the draft and launch UMT. They also worried that such initiatives would militarize the American mind, as well as the American economy. Repeating a major point made by earlier critics, they argued that military institutions would be strengthened to the same degree that UMT weakened the home, family, and school – all counterweights to the growing power of the federal government and the very institutions that traditionally socialized young people in the habits and values of democracy. As a result, young men would be educated in martial values, individual initiative and independent thinking would be discouraged, equal opportunity would give way to a "caste system," diversity would yield to regimentation, and civil rights would be replaced by arbitrary rule. The American people wanted the "nation to keep its primary emphasis on the home, the school, the church, and the community," argued Mrs. Stanley Cook on behalf of

---

79 Ibid., 845. See also ibid., 252–53, 1035–36. Other witnesses made similar points. See the testimony of Frederick J. Libby of the National Council for the Prevention of War, former vice president Henry Wallace, Paul Elicker of the National Association of Secondary School Principals, Bishop Hugh L. Lamb of Philadelphia, and Leon Henderson of Americans for Democratic Action, ibid., 192–202, 549, 887, 1015, 1033.
80 Ibid., 545.

the National Congress of Parents and Teachers. They did not want to let a period of "enforced" military service undermine the religious and educational training of America's young men, undercut the family's influence on their character, and encourage them to drink, smoke, and consort with lewd women. Such a program would pose a real "danger to our Republic."[81]

Nor were these the only dangers to civic virtue and republican institutions. Although the administration and its supporters claimed that UMT would "breed a truer democracy" by bringing young men from different regions and social classes together, critics like Walter Reuther argued that Truman's proposal was actually biased against boys from working-class backgrounds who could not afford a college education.[82] These boys would get the full UMT treatment of one year in the training camps, followed by additional service as enlisted men, while college-bound trainees could substitute ROTC for several months of UMT training and then emerge from college as members of the officer corps. No matter how you looked at it, Reuther said, a "class stratification" based on income would separate officers from regular soldiers and would be extended by UMT throughout the adult life of the male population.[83]

Other critics, pointing to the long history of racial segregation in the military services, argued that UMT would indoctrinate a generation of young men in the practice of Jim Crow. Democratic Senator Richard B. Russell of Georgia added weight to this charge by suggesting that every draftee be permitted to serve in a unit of his own race. The Armed Services Committee rejected Russell's proposal, but not before it had reinforced what the critics had suspected all along. Henry Wallace and his supporters attacked UMT as racially biased. So did J. T. Sanders of the National Grange and other witnesses, but none more so than Jesse Dedmon of the NAACP and A. Philip Randolph of the Brotherhood of Sleeping Car Porters. Randolph, in particular, warned congressional leaders that blacks were in no mood to shoulder a gun for democracy abroad when they were denied its rights at home. They would resist, he said, as Ghandi was resisting British imperialism in India.[84]

---

[81] Ibid., 1037, 891, 122–23. See also ibid., 148, 231–32, 421–22, 440, 452, 842, 845–47, 856.

[82] The quote is from Karl Compton in ibid., 282. See also Baruch's remarks in ibid., 408. For Reuther's views, see ibid., 1036.

[83] Ibid., 1036.

[84] Ibid., 232, 246, 662–87; *Congressional Quarterly Almanac, 1948*, 236; *Forrestal Diaries*, 439.

Those who feared that UMT was one step toward the militarization of American life were hardly reassured by some of its defenders, who did speak in the language of social control and who saw UMT as a way to deal with existing institutional failures. One such defender was Mrs. Leslie Boudinot Wright, representing the General Federation of Women's Clubs. She pointed to the lack of home training in spiritual values as one of the major problems confronting American youth and then went on to argue that a boy whose family had failed him in this regard deserved a second chance with military tutors. Baruch made the same connection between the plight of handicapped young men who had been rejected by local draft boards during the war, only to be turned back to a community that had usually ignored them. Now these youths would have another chance to be rehabilitated as part of their service in UMT. Clem Johnston of the Chamber of Commerce made still another such connection between UMT and the public schools. He accused the modern high school of concentrating on the curriculum needs of college-bound students and argued that UMT would correct this distortion by offering vocational training for young men who were not going past the twelfth grade. At the same time, it would provide them with health instruction not provided in the public schools and make up for similar deficiencies in moral, religious, and civic education and in the teaching of what Arthur Compton called "national aims." In Compton's view, the public schools offered little instruction in "the responsibilities of citizenship and the needs of defense necessary to maintain our democratic freedom" – all failures that UMT would remedy.[85]

Also linked to this idea of better education for citizenship was the notion that universal training would make young people less vulnerable to Communist propaganda. Those who thought this way were also resorting to a strategy of otherness that portrayed their critics as un-American agents of the Communist party, which also opposed UMT. James O'Neil of the American Legion, for example, accused Henry Wallace of adopting the Soviet line in opposing UMT, while Senator Chan Gurney, who chaired the Armed Services Committee, grilled Seymour Linfield regarding reports of his earlier membership in the Young Communist League.[86]

Charges like this infuriated Walter Reuther, who implored the committee to distinguish between Communist opposition to UMT and the opposition of loyal citizens, like himself, who feared the "militarization"

---

[85] Senate, *Hearings on Universal Military Training*, 282–84. See also ibid., 167, 407, 459.
[86] Ibid., 239–67, 784.

of America." Any Communist propaganda, he said, was dwarfed by that coming from military leaders in the Pentagon, whose campaign to promote UMT and whose tendency to impeach the loyalty of opposing forces were good indications of how an excessive concern with "national security" threatened American democracy. UMT would amount to another step down this dangerous path, he said, until "in the end, we would have not only a garrison state but a military state in which our lives would be ordered by the military, not the civilian, mind."[87]

The strength and depth of the opposition had its effects. As the hearings drew to a close, UMT's prospects were not good in the Senate, and were even less favorable in the House. Worse, from the administration's point of view, the public hysteria associated with the Czech crisis was slowly fading. A "growing apathy" was spreading across the country, Forrestal complained, fed by conciliatory gestures from the Soviet Union and by the speeches of Henry Wallace and others who blamed American rather than Soviet foreign policy for the war scare of March. A new mood had taken shape, and coming with it was a reawakening of earlier concerns about the cost of defense and earlier hopes for disarmament.

Under these circumstances, Forrestal began to wonder if selective service, let alone UMT, could make it through Congress. Others in the administration agreed with his assessment, Truman included, and the eventual result was a decision to leave UMT out of a new legislative program negotiated within the administration and between the administration and congressional leaders. That program called instead for reestablishing selective service, raising the authorized strength of the military forces by approximately 25 percent, compensating somewhat for the loss of UMT by increasing the pool of trained manpower in the National Guard and the organized reserves, and covering the cost of these initiatives through a supplemental defense budget of approximately $3 billion.[88]

With UMT sidetracked, selective service became the issue revealing the nation's anxieties about the fate of democracy and the danger of a garrison state, and those on each side were soon repeating arguments

---

[87] Ibid., 1037–40.

[88] Forrestal memorandum of conversation with Senator Taft, 31 May 1948, Truman Papers, PSF-Subject File, box 157, folder: Defense, Secy of – James Forrestal – Special Letters. See also *Forrestal Diaries*, 445–47; and Gerhardt, *Draft and Public Policy*, 94–106. The specifics of Truman's legislative program remained in doubt for some time. This was especially the case with the amount of the supplemental defense appropriation and thus with the number of additional troops that this appropriation would support, both of which were subjects of considerable controversy within the administration. For a handy summary of this controversy and how it was resolved see *Forrestal Diaries*, 435–39.

already rehearsed in earlier debates.[89] Supporters of the new legislative agenda argued again that only the United States could defend democracy and contain the Soviet Union, and then only if it possessed a military strength equal to its commitments abroad. This meant adding to the defense budget and reestablishing the draft, they insisted, but both of these measures were clearly affordable and certainly less expensive than another world war. Indeed, the proposed legislation seemed so sensible to its supporters that they found it difficult to take their critics seriously and were more inclined than ever to dismiss them as "Wallacites," as Soviet lackeys, or as pacifists and isolationists whose naïveté had earlier left the nation unprepared for war. "Isolation, isolation, oh what crimes have been committed in thy name?'" crowed Representative Harold D. Cooley, a Democrat from North Carolina, who went on to deride the normal distinction between wartime conscription, which the critics considered acceptable, and peacetime conscription, which they saw as a dangerous departure from tradition. "We are not living in normal times," he said, in a reference to how the Cold War had obliterated the usual distinction between war and peace.[90] In the new age, agreed Democratic Congressman John D. Dingell of Michigan, it was necessary "to stack our buckshot and be ready."[91]

On the other side, opponents of the revised legislative agenda still drew the boundaries of the country's political identity in a way that branded both the draft and its supporters as un-American. They accused the administration of exaggerating the Soviet threat and were inclined to find the real enemy in the Pentagon, where military leaders had an insatiable appetite for more money, more men, and more power, whatever the cost to democracy. With the force levels being proposed, said Republican Senator William Langer of North Dakota, there would be more soldiers on the federal payroll than civilians in the postal and civil services combined.[92] He and others also argued that large standing armies and military conscription added up to a "Maginot line" that would be as useless in the next war as it had been in the last. To their way of thinking, which continued to build on a strategy of otherness, defense dollars were

---

[89] The debate in both houses of Congress can be followed in the *Congressional Record, 1948* 94:1643–45, 6997–7008, 7139–54, 7257–61, 7528–53, 7578–95, 7659–81, 8341–47, 8502–23, 8652–8713, 8778–8817, 8828–29, 8969–99, 9268–77. The discussion in the text draws largely on these sources. Additional references are provided only when necessary to identify other sources, quoted material, or the remarks of particular individuals.

[90] Cooley cited in Gerhardt, *Draft and Public Policy*, 108.

[91] *Congressional Record, 1948* 94:8675.

[92] Ibid., 7139.

better spent on airpower and atomic weapons than on an un-American institution like peacetime military conscription, which they saw as "aping the military clique of Hitler" and leading to a "complete militarization of the country." Peacetime conscription, they said again, would create "a permanent military caste," "exalt the military over the civil branches of the Government," and undermine the home, family, and school.[93]

The critics also repeated the usual complaint that defense spending gobbled up a substantial portion of the budget and deflected public attention, as well as public funds, from serious domestic problems. Conservatives like Taft worried that new defense spending, when added to the cost of the Marshall Plan, would feed inflation, increase the national debt, and keep taxes high. Liberals complained that defense expenditures benefited military contractors while diverting tax dollars from such pressing needs as public housing and broader social security coverage. In their view, moreover, Congress should take steps to prohibit any form of discrimination, particularly racial discrimination, in the armed forces, a position that also won support from Republican conservatives like Langer.[94]

The debate raged over several days, including a last-minute filibuster in the Senate, before the final votes in both houses produced a solid victory for the champions of selective service. The principal features of the act required all young men between eighteen and twenty-six years of age to register for the draft; allowed eighteen-year-olds to volunteer for one year of duty, to be followed by six years in the reserves; and made all those between nineteen and twenty-five years of age liable for twenty-one months of service in the regular forces. The act came very close to what the Truman administration had proposed, the only substantial difference being a decision by Congress to limit the period of induction to twenty-one months, instead of the twenty-four months that Truman had suggested.[95]

The administration's most serious setback did not involve selective service but UMT, which was the centerpiece of the legislative program that Truman had presented to Congress in his speech of 17 March. Truman had urged Congress to reinstate the draft as a short-term solution to the

---

93 The quotations are from ibid., 8509, 8520, 8505, 8508.

94 Ibid., 7139–51, 7260. See also Gerhardt, *Draft and Public Policy*, 117–18; and *Congressional Quarterly Almanac, 1948*, 236.

95 *Congressional Quarterly Almanac, 1948*, 235; Marx Leva (special assistant to the secretary of defense) to Elmer Staats (assistant director, Legislative Reference Branch, Bureau of the Budget), 21 June 1948, Truman Papers, White House Central File, General File, box 136, folder: Selective Service System.

immediate danger raised by the Communist coup in Czechoslovakia, and had offered UMT as the long-term answer to the military's manpower requirements. But only the first part of this formulation won sufficient congressional support, primarily, it seems, because some of those opposed to UMT saw the draft as a needed emergency measure that would be administered on a selective basis by civilian authorities on a local level. In these ways, the advocates of selective service were able to make a case that it squared with the American principle of civilian supremacy and with such other American ideals as individualism and localism.[96] When it came to UMT, however, the president's opponents were united in their conviction that a permanent system of compulsory training was a threat to American democracy, and it was their united front that handed the administration another defeat on the issue.

IV

The discourse on UMT revolved around familiar rhetorical formulations and brought to the surface many of the major themes that have informed our story thus far. The garrison state was the central metaphor to which both sides resorted, as they did to a rhetorical strategy that captured the issues in a binary system of symbolic representation. In this system, the choices were between the American way or the foreign way, a free economy or a command economy, civilian rule or military domination, democracy or totalitarianism, virtue or corruption, sacrifice or self-indulgence, internationalism or isolationism, will power or weakness, greatness or decline.

These choices emerged as the two sides debated UMT's military, economic, and political utility, including its influence on traditional values and whether it would redefine the country as a garrison state. Supporters were convinced that UMT would lend credibility to the policy of containment without the need for a large standing army, which many viewed as a danger to democracy and a threat to the budget. They called upon the American people to sacrifice on behalf of national greatness, but they were also reluctant to demand sacrifices in higher taxes, economic controls, or reduced social expenditures that might bring on the garrison state, or to ask for more than most Americans were willing or able to give. UMT offered an escape from these dilemmas: It would allow the United States to assume its new identity as the global defender

---

[96] Chambers, *To Raise an Army*, 253–54.

of democracy, but at a cost it could afford, and was politically less dangerous and more acceptable than a large professional army.

Critics had little time for these arguments. On the contrary, they denounced UMT as militarily outdated, as a waste of money that was better used to develop the weapons of the future, and as diverting resources from the kind of economic and social investment that would remedy the underlying causes of conflict. In addition, the critics held that UMT would undermine the prospects for collective security and disarmament, would lead to another arms race and another world war, and would militarize the American economy, regiment American youth, and undercut traditional institutions. The church, the home, and the school, according to the critics, were healthy counterweights to the growing power of the federal government and the very institutions that had historically tutored American youth in the moral values and republican principles that sustained democratic government. The supporters of UMT might celebrate the need to sacrifice in the name of freedom and destiny, but what this meant, so far as the critics were concerned, was the subversion of traditional liberties that had made America great.

As in the budget debates and the debates over the National Security Act, the discourse on UMT drove both sides toward a middle ground. Even the supporters of UMT were forced to cite tradition itself in order to defend departures from the past. This was the case when Truman invoked the image of the citizens' militia in defense of UMT and the first truly peacetime draft in the country's history. And it was also the case when he and others said that UMT would not only improve the health and moral vitality of American youth, and equip them with useful skills, but would also dampen their tendency toward self-indulgence and instill in them the classic republican virtues and the spirit of good citizenship on which democracy depended.

Those on the other side of the debate made similar concessions. Critics would not bend on the issue of UMT, which they successfully defeated, but they were willing to accept a peacetime draft. They did so because the draft would be a temporary expedient, or so it seemed, would be less universal than UMT, and would be administered at the local level, where private citizens rather than military officials could account for community needs. Like Truman, moreover, they equated the draft with the republican tradition of citizen service in periods of national emergency, and they saw the Czech crisis as just such an emergency.

In short, the battle over UMT not only brought into the open the guns-and-butter politics that we see in other parts of our story. It also revealed how the national security ideology accommodated an older political culture, and how this accommodation influenced the process of state making. The opposition to higher taxes, the concern with social investment, and the fear of deficit spending, inflation, and coercive government controls all influenced the administration's decision to back UMT, rather than a large standing army, just as similar influences accounted for much of the opposition on both the left and the right. What is more, while older American values and traditions did not halt the drive for a military manpower policy that took account of the country's global commitments, they did influence the shape of the national security state that was emerging, in this case by ruling out UMT in favor of a system of selective service that seemed more in line with traditional notions of the citizen-soldier. As we will see, moreover, this bargain would remain intact even after the outbreak of the Korean War, and similar bargains would be struck in other areas of national policy, including those having to do with the budget, with new efforts to reorganize the defense establishment, and with the mobilization of economic and scientific resources – all aspects of our story to which we now turn.

5

"Chaos and Conflict and Carnage Confounded"

Budget Battles and Defense Reorganization

By the time James V. Forrestal became the country's first secretary of defense, he was showing the strains of nearly eight years of government service. As his biographers point out, Forrestal had become something of an automaton, a workaholic who could neither relax on the job nor retreat to the haven of a happy family. He and his wife led essentially separate lives. She was a schizophrenic whose bizarre behavior, including vulgar language, chronic breakdowns, and alcoholism, grew worse with each year of their marriage. He was a promiscuous Lothario whose private affairs revealed a cynical and secretive personality that became increasingly unstable in the Machiavellian world of the National Military Establishment.[1]

As secretary of defense, Forrestal worked with a small staff to administer the affairs of military departments that behaved more like hostile sovereigns than a unified force. The National Security Act, which he had shaped, made it difficult for him to succeed in his new assignment, and the struggle to succeed exhausted him both physically and mentally and left him increasingly nervous and irresolute. Only days after taking office he was complaining about the difficult tasks before him and telling a friend that he would soon need "the combined attention" of the "entire psychiatric profession." He was right.[2]

From the start, Forrestal had trouble making up his mind. Or perhaps he was of several minds, one that sought greater control over a burgeoning military establishment and one that saw centralized authority as a threat to democracy; one that cherished traditional rights and freedoms and one that saw them as roadblocks to security; one that would pay any price to contain the Red menace and one that worried about the damage a large defense budget could do to the American economy. On one occasion, shortly after the arrest of Communist party leaders in the

---

[1] Hoopes and Brinkley, *Driven Patriot*, 47, 131–35.
[2] *Forrestal Diaries*, 300.

United States, Forrestal explained to the National Security Council how important it was for the government to coordinate its domestic and foreign policies with a view to their influence on Soviet diplomacy. But in America, he admitted, almost as a lament, the separation of powers made it difficult to achieve that kind of coordination, and the government itself had little control over the free play of ideas.[3] There were "no easy black and white solutions for the problems which face this country," he confided to a friend on another occasion, no easy formula for building a "military organization sufficiently formidable to give any other country reason to stop, look and listen, without at the same time its eating our national heads off."[4]

This dilemma, which had troubled Forrestal since the end of the war, came up again and again as he and others wrestled with the defense budget for another fiscal year and pondered the problem of reorganizing the military establishment. These were important topics in the national security discourse of 1949, which was concerned, as it had been in the years since 1945, with the central challenge of state making in the early Cold War. That challenge was to advance the nation's security and its new role as the defender of democracy everywhere without at the same time subverting democracy at home and transforming the republic into a garrison state.

In addressing this challenge, public officials continued to speak in two languages. One was the language of the national security ideology, a language sometimes superheated by international crises, such as the Soviet blockade of Berlin, or by changes in the balance of power, such as the Soviet explosion of an atomic bomb in late 1949 and the virtually simultaneous seizure of power by Communist forces in China. In this language, the emphasis was on America's new identity as a global leader in a world where peace and freedom were indivisible, on the threat of communism and the danger of total war, on squaring the country's military capabilities with its commitments around the world, on mobilizing civilian and military resources behind a program of permanent preparedness, on making the sacrifices that such a program entailed.

The other language stressed the country's traditional democratic identity and its endangerment, not only by the Communist threat but also by efforts to contain it. Once again, those who spoke in this language

---

3 NSC-23, "A Report to the National Security Council by the Secretary of Defense on Domestic Activities and Foreign Relations," 27 July 1948, Truman Papers, PSF-National Security Council Meetings, box 204, folder: NSC Meeting #17, 8/5/48.
4 *Forrestal Diaries*, 512.

invoked a cultural narrative that began with the Founders, including the ancient conviction that concentrations of power invariably posed a threat to political and economic freedoms, especially when power was concentrated in military departments that commanded a disproportionate share of the nation's resources. Such developments raised concerns about the corruption of politics on a grand scale, as would be apparent in the B-36 controversy, and about a military threat to civilian rule, as would be apparent in the budget battles and in the famous "Revolt of the Admirals." Both were cases that fostered new efforts to reform the military establishment only a year after the National Security Act became law.

If the national security state threatened important attributes of the country's democratic character, including the tradition of civilian rule, not to mention a free economy, then democracy itself also offered a solution. The rhetoric of reform celebrated the old democratic values, including the old wisdom that good government was one in which power was limited or at least divided between different branches and departments. The goal of reformers was to devise a national security framework that would confirm civilian supremacy over the military and ensure that authority was dispersed and balanced between different groups and agencies. The problem came in striking a proper balance between domestic and national security requirements, between civilian and military authority, between centralized and decentralized decision making. Public discussion centered on these issues, and those involved, like James Forrestal, were often pulled in different directions.

II

As the Truman administration set its sights on the defense budget for fiscal year 1950, economizers in the White House, the Treasury Department, and the Budget Bureau still held the upper hand, as might be expected when they counted the president as one of their number. Since the Cold War amounted to a crisis of indefinite duration, they envisioned a program of military preparedness that balanced the needs of the warfare state against those of the welfare state, and specifically one that could be sustained without stifling investment, neglecting social programs, and wrecking the economy. Truman had been working toward this goal since the end of the war, and his efforts had succeeded in reducing the debt and balancing the budgets for fiscal years 1947 and 1948.

To be sure, the Republican tax cut threatened a new deficit in fiscal year 1949, but this threat only stiffened the president's resolve to hold the line on government spending, especially defense spending, in fiscal year 1950. So did the possibility of inflation, which economizers saw as a continuing danger, and the reluctance of almost everyone to deal with this danger through higher taxes or economic controls.[5] With such considerations in mind, Truman and his economic advisers had decided by the end of May 1948 to cap defense spending at $15 billion in the budget for fiscal year 1950. That ceiling would deny Forrestal and his lieutenants an opportunity to draft a budget that squared with their national security assessments rather than the president's economic concerns. In theory, at least, they were to distribute no more than $15 billion within an integrated, single budget for the National Military Establishment, instead of separate, overlapping budgets for each of the military services.

Forrestal, however, could not "take hold" of a process that made fiscal constraints rather than national security considerations the major budget determinants. He thought that defense planners should begin by assessing the threats to American security, identify the military assets required to contain those threats, and conclude by drafting a budget large enough to embrace those assets. With this goal in mind, he asked the NSC to render expert advice on how best to match the country's military capabilities to its security requirements and commitments around the world. The NSC was the logical vehicle for such an investigation, having produced a similar report in the past, and Forrestal clearly hoped that its advice would give him the leverage he needed to reverse the president's position on the budget.[6]

Truman had his own experts, of course, as well as his own opinions on the budget, and he was not shy about invoking them. When he authorized the NSC study that Forrestal had suggested, he also told the secretary that defense planning for fiscal 1950 could not await the results of that endeavor. It had to proceed, he insisted, on the basis of the budget ceiling established earlier with due regard to national security.[7] Truman then turned for support to Edwin Nourse, chairman of the Council of

---

[5] Ibid., 430, and Edwin Nourse, "What Effect Will Armament Spending Have on the Business Outlook?" *U.S. News & World Report*, 10 December 1948, copy in Nourse Papers, box 10, folder: National Military Establishment.

[6] Lilienthal, *The Atomic Energy Years*, 386. See also Forrestal to Truman, 10 July 1948, with enclosed Forrestal memorandum to the NSC, 10 July 1948, Truman Papers, PSF-Subject File, box 156, folder: Cabinet: Defense, Secy of, Misc.; Forrestal to Truman, 10 July 1948, ibid., box 150, folder: Bureau of the Budget, Budget – Military, 1945–53; and Condit, *Joint Chiefs of Staff* 2:215–16.

[7] Truman to Forrestal, 15 July 1948, RG 330, CD 5-1-20.

Economic Advisers, and James Webb, director of the Budget Bureau, both of whom were consistent allies in struggles of this kind. Nourse defended Truman's budget proposals in a speech at the Pentagon. Webb did the same in correspondence with Forrestal, and from other officials in the Budget Bureau came the argument that Truman's ceiling was based not only on all available intelligence regarding the international situation but also on the availability of resources and the impact of military spending on civilian requirements. Such ceilings, their argument ran, gave Pentagon planners a fair "indication" of presidential "priorities" and had proven their "usefulness" in balancing the "security program" against the other "major functions included in the Budget."[8]

Achieving that balance would do more than forestall inflation and other economic problems; it would also shield the country's economic and political liberties against the dangers of a different course. As in earlier debates over the budget, these dangers were captured in the familiar symbol of the garrison state and similar rhetorical devices. Webb and his counterparts in other economic agencies warned repeatedly that additional defense spending could feed inflation and that government action to contain inflation, such as higher taxes and economic controls, could transform the country's tradition of economic freedom into a new pattern of economic regimentation.[9] Others, such as David Lilienthal, who shared similar fears for somewhat different reasons, summed up those fears in other metaphors of militarism. Lilienthal saw military spending as the most important issue of the day, in part because it influenced prices, taxes, and the state of the economy as a whole, but also because it strengthened a "conservative" military bureaucracy and fostered a dangerous coalition between that group and the private arms producers who lived off the defense budget.[10] Similar expressions came from Truman himself, who thought that ordinary voters worried about a "military clique in Washington," and from Walter Lippmann and other

---

[8] J. Weldon Jones (Budget Bureau) memorandum to Leo C. Martin (Budget Bureau), 5 October 1948, RG 51, Series 47.8a, box 47, folder: A-2 1950 Budget – Basic Documents. See also Webb memorandum to Forrestal, 16 July 1948, ibid., box 46, folder: FY 1950 – Correspondence; Nourse, "What Effect Will Armament Spending Have on the Business Outlook?"

[9] In addition to the last source cited in the previous note see Council of Economic Advisers memorandum for the president, "The Government's Anti-Inflation Program," 19 July 1948, and Nourse's statement before the Cabinet Committee on Anti-Inflation, 16 December 1948, Nourse Papers, box 5, folder: Daily Diary.

[10] Lilienthal, *Atomic Energy Years*, 430.

journalists, for whom fears of the garrison state had become a "continual theme song."[11]

As in the past, Truman could also count on strong support from Secretary Marshall. At meetings with Marshall in July and October, Forrestal and the Joint Chiefs warned again that America's military assets were inadequate to deal with unfavorable developments in different parts of the world, including Europe, where only one division would be ready in the event of a major war. From Marshall's viewpoint, however, the United States was immeasurably better prepared than it had been in 1940. In addition, the secretary knew full well that neither the CIA nor the State Department had evidence of a rapid Soviet military buildup or of Soviet plans for aggression, not even in Europe, where the Berlin blockade had created an air of tension and confrontation. Still later, when Forrestal asked if the international situation warranted a defense budget that exceeded Truman's ceiling, Marshall responded coyly that it was "neither better nor worse insofar as it affects the ceiling of our military establishment."[12]

These exchanges were symptomatic of a profound gap between Marshall's thinking and the views of his former colleagues in the Pentagon. To defend their budget claims, the Joint Chiefs repeatedly invoked the new ideology of national security, with its emphasis on total war and total preparedness in an age when peace was indivisible. They made a habit of pointing to hot spots around the world, stressing military rather than economic or political threats, and planning for worst-case scenarios. Regardless of the cost, they wanted to be prepared for all contingencies, to have on the shelf, as it were, all the military hardware required at the outset of another world war. Marshall, on the other hand, was more alert to economic constraints and more inclined to think of peacetime military power in political and psychological terms. What mattered to him was whether the United States had a force large enough to discourage aggression and lend credibility to its foreign policies.

Nor did Marshall expect the United States to shoulder the burden of containment alone. Whereas Pentagon planners were reluctant to count on allies when forging their military strategy, or their defense budgets, Marshall was equally reluctant "to build up US ground forces for the express purpose of employing them in Western Europe." He envisioned a common defense based on the principles of specialization and division of

---

[11] *Forrestal Diaries*, 502.
[12] Marshall to Forrestal, 8 November 1948, RG 330, CD 5-1-25. See also *Forrestal Diaries*, 459–60, 502, 508–11; and Leffler, *Preponderance of Power*, 262–63.

labor, specifically a European army operating under the North Atlantic Treaty and supported by American air and naval power, an American arsenal of atomic weapons, and an American program of military assistance. Such a strategy, which anticipated the New Look of the 1950s, was more economical than what the Joint Chiefs had in mind and more in line with the president's budget ceiling.[13]

Not surprisingly, then, NSC planners who took their cue from Truman were quick to make the State Department primarily responsible for the study that Forrestal had requested. Under Marshall's guidance, the department was to estimate future threats to American security and outline policies to counter those threats. Nor is it surprising that both the State Department and the NSC took their time in completing these tasks, or that the final results squared more with Marshall's thinking than with Forrestal's.[14]

The NSC report, adopted by the council in November, elaborated views coming from the State Department's Policy Planning Staff, led by George Kennan, whose "Long Telegram" of 1946 had defined an American way of life by reference to the Soviet other. Much the same was true of NSC-20/4, as the council tagged its new report, which spoke of a Soviet threat that was primarily ideological, economic, and political, not military; it was the threat of subversion, the report said, not the threat of aggression. To be sure, the Soviets had the military capability to overrun Western Europe and much of the Middle East, but NSC-20/4 saw no danger of an imminent attack or another world war, and hence no need for a policy much different from the one that Marshall had urged on Forrestal. This policy would combine economic and military assistance to Europe with a level of American military preparedness calculated to deter Soviet aggression without "impairing our economy and the fundamental values and institutions inherent in our way of life."[15]

The phrase "our way of life" was yet another of the rhetorical devices that recurred in the budget debates of the early Cold War. It encapsulated an older sense of American identity, one often inscribed in the documents by comparison with Nazi Germany, Communist Russia, or some other

---

[13] See the sources cited in the previous note. The quote is from Marshall to Forrestal, 8 November 1948, RG 330, CD 5-1-25.

[14] Minutes of the 17th Meeting of the NSC, 5 August 1948, Truman Papers, PSF-National Security Council Meetings, box 204, folder: NSC Meeting #17; *Forrestal Diaries*, 492–93.

[15] NSC-20/4, "Report by the National Security Council on U.S. Objectives with Respect to the USSR to Counter Soviet Threats to U.S. Security," 23 November 1948, U.S. Department of State, *FRUS, 1948* (Washington, 1976), 2:662–69; and Condit, *Joint Chiefs of Staff* 2:219–26.

totalitarian power, and one associated with a set of traditional values that appeared to be endangered, not only by Communist subversion or Soviet aggression but also by the country's global mission and the national security ideology that guided so much thinking in the State Department and the Pentagon. This was the danger of constantly accumulating deficits that would drive up the national debt, spur inflation, and debase the currency, and through such afflictions would impoverish the population and rob citizens of their incentive to work hard and be productive. Nor could the threat be overcome by using economic controls to manage inflation and higher taxes to cover the cost of defense. As we have seen, Webb and other economizers worried that such measures would only fatten the state while emasculating the private sector and robbing producers of the incentive to produce. From such thinking could be inferred a "way of life" that put the private sector over the public, valued the individual over the state, and celebrated private initiative and industry as two of the keys to democratic politics and free-market capitalism.

Needless to say, such thinking made it difficult for Forrestal and others to create a new identity for the nation as a great military power and defender of democracy everywhere, at least so long as key officials in the White House, the State Department, and the NSC saw no immediate threat to world peace and American security. It enabled these officials to side with Truman's economic planners in the Treasury Department, the Budget Bureau, and on the Council of Economic Advisers against his military planners in the Pentagon, whose more expansive ambitions were driven by the ideology of national security and especially by the need to match the country's military capabilities to its growing commitments around the world. "We are being more and more restricted by budgetary and manpower ceilings," explained Air Force Chief of Staff Hoyt S. Vandenberg in words that bespoke the Pentagon's point of view, "yet at the same time we are faced with ever-increasing commitments on an international scale."[16]

Bereft of support outside the Pentagon, Forrestal had in the meantime asked the Joint Chiefs to draft their own program of military preparedness for fiscal year 1950, including recommendations as to the size of the military establishment and how resources should be allocated among the services. These tasks were sure to be divisive, as they had been in the past, especially if Forrestal enforced the president's budget ceiling,

---

[16] Vandenberg to General George C. Kenney, 13 December 1948, Vandenberg Papers, box 32, folder: Vandenberg Files, 1948.

which he ultimately refused to do. Perhaps he was unwilling to drive the chiefs into line with a ceiling he could not support himself, or perhaps he counted on their views to leverage Truman into a larger defense budget. Whatever his motives, Forrestal instructed the chiefs in July 1948 to base their recommendations on military considerations rather than budgetary constraints.[17] The outcome was predictable. Responding to Forrestal in late July, the chiefs painted a bleak picture of imposing Soviet military strength and a steady military buildup that added weight to the Kremlin's foreign policy. Although Soviet aggression was still unlikely, according to the chiefs, these dangers had to be countered with a further expansion of American forces. As in the past, the chiefs were not prepared to gear that expansion to an agreed strategic concept, a joint war plan, or to the needs of the civilian economy. Nor had Forrestal's instructions obliged them to do so. Instead, they had simply allowed the services to draw up their individual requirements and then combine these requirements into a budget of $30 billion, twice what the president's ceiling permitted. What is more, even though the chiefs had sought to justify their demands with the kind of strategic assessment that Forrestal expected from the NSC, their budget included a substantial duplication of resources and functions, which plainly belied the notion that military considerations alone had guided their thinking.[18]

If the Joint Chiefs were going to frame a budget under Truman's ceiling, they clearly required more explicit instructions than Forrestal had provided. Marx Leva, one of Forrestal's principal assistants, had made this point in commenting on a draft of the secretary's instructions, which indicated, he said, that Forrestal did "not intend to exercise any personal judgement over the 1950 budget." It was "all right for the Joint Chiefs of Staff to consider exclusively military factors," Leva told Forrestal bluntly, but "not all right for you to fail to consider economic factors in making your recommendations to the President." Even the Joint Chiefs, Leva concluded, should "face the reality that there is no point in building a military establishment of such a size that the national economy will be wrecked thereby." Air Force General Joseph T. McNarney, who headed the secretary's budget advisory committee, or McNarney board, filed a

[17] Forrestal memorandum for the secretaries of the army, air force, and navy, 17 July 1948, RG 218, CCS 370 (8-19-45), Sec. 9; Forrestal memorandum for the Joint Chiefs, 19 July 1948, RG 51, Series 47.8a, box 47, folder: A-2, 1950, Budget – Basic Documents.
[18] JCS 1800/9, Formulation of the Fiscal Year 1950 Budget for National Defense, 22 July 1948, RG 218, CCS 370 (8-19-45), Sec. 9; *Forrestal Diaries*, 492–93; and Condit, *Joint Chiefs of Staff* 2:229–32.

similar critique several weeks later. It was the secretary's job, he pointed out, to establish priorities, identify military functions that had a first claim on resources, and target those to be eliminated or reduced.[19]

This was good advice that Forrestal, unfortunately, found difficult to follow. To be sure, the secretary finally instructed the chiefs to recommend an allocation of funds under the president's ceiling of $15 billion, minus $600 million for stockpiling strategic materials. But he did not rule out a budget that exceeded the ceiling or provide the chiefs with the guidance that McNarney thought necessary. The outcome was just as predictable as it had been in the first round of the budget exercise. Working with the McNarney board in August and September, the chiefs were able to reduce their request by only $6.4 billion, from $30 billion to $23.6 billion. Their proposed budget was still swollen by overlapping functions and still more than $8 billion above the president's ceiling.[20]

Much of the problem stemmed from the fact that old disputes over service roles and missions had not abated with passage of the National Security Act and subsequent negotiation of the Key West agreement. No sooner had that agreement been concluded than the Joint Chiefs began to argue over what it meant. Would the Air Force or the Navy control the Armed Forces Special Weapons Project, an interservice agency that explored the military uses of atomic energy? Would the Navy's air arm have priority in funding over the Air Force? And which of the two services would act as agent for the Joint Chiefs in matters involving atomic warfare? Forrestal took these questions up with the Joint Chiefs during a meeting at the Naval War College in Newport, Rhode Island. The conferees resolved some of the issues, at least temporarily, but the agreement quickly began to break down under the weight of the budget restrictions imposed by the White House.[21]

One clash concerned the best strategy for countering Soviet aggression in Europe. The Air Force would rely on atomic reprisals from air bases in England and would forgo any attempt to secure the Mediterranean line of communications to the Middle East, which, it said, would cost more than the president's ceiling permitted. The Navy, on the other hand, objected to a strategic concept that succeeded financially at the expense

[19] Leva memorandum for Forrestal, 22 June 1948, RG 330, CD 9-2-41. See also McNarney memorandum to Forrestal, 1 October 1948, Symington Papers, box 8, folder: Correspondence File, 1946–50, Memoranda, General.

[20] *Forrestal Diaries*, 499; Condit, *Joint Chiefs of Staff* 2:232–33.

[21] *Forrestal Diaries*, 476–77; Office of the Secretary of Defense memorandum for the record, 23 August 1948, RG 330, CD 9-2-50.

of its carrier forces in the eastern Mediterranean. Operating from these carriers, according to the chief of naval operations, naval air forces could stop invading Soviet armies, launch strategic attacks against the Soviet Union, and prepare the ground for a counteroffensive. Nor would the Navy relent on its position, not even when manpower reductions by the Air Force and the Army ruled out a balanced force structure in the Mediterranean.

The result was a split recommendation that reached Forrestal in the first days of October. The chiefs agreed that $15 billion was not enough to implement the administration's national security policy, but while the Army and the Air Force recommended a budget of $15.8 billion, the Navy's plan added up to $16.5 billion. The difference amounted to several carriers that would allow the Navy to assume important assignments in the Mediterranean, especially in strategic air operations, that were claimed by the other services. The budget numbers changed somewhat as discussions continued, but the basis of the conflict always remained the same. Each of the services sought to adapt Truman's ceiling to a strategic concept from which it would benefit the most. The Navy wanted carriers that could hold the eastern Mediterranean; the Air Force stressed air–atomic attacks from Great Britain; the Army generally supported the Air Force. If the budget did not permit a balanced force in the Mediterranean, the Army and the Air Force seemed to say, then the only alternative was no force at all.[22]

McNarney and the other members of the budget advisory committee tried to put a good face on these differences. They noted that a truly "scientific" budget depended on an approved statement of national goals in relation to military strength, an agreed strategic concept, a joint mobilization plan, and other requirements that had never been established. The Joint Chiefs, they argued, had done the best they could given these shortcomings, although Forrestal's judgment came closer to the mark.[23] He concluded that budgetary restraints, notably the president's budget ceiling, had aggravated interservice differences and produced discussions that had quickly "degenerated into a competition for dollars."[24]

---

[22] Leahy memorandum to Forrestal, 6 October 1948, RG 330, CD 5-1-25; Bradley memorandum to Forrestal, 7 October 1948, Vandenberg Papers, box 40, folder: Budget 1948 (50 Group Program); Vandenberg memorandum to Forrestal, 7 October 1948, ibid., folder: Budget 1948; Forrestal memorandum to the Secretary of the Army, 14 October 1948, RG 51, Series 47.8a, box 46, folder: FY 1950 – Correspondence; Condit, *Joint Chiefs of Staff* 2:233–43.

[23] McNarney et al., memorandum to Forrestal, 14 October 1948, RG 330, CD 5-1-25.

[24] See the source cited in the following note.

Nonetheless, Forrestal sought to make good use of the interservice conflicts in meetings with the president. As the secretary knew full well, the Army and Navy were generally opposed to a strategic plan that put all of their "eggs in one basket," and for this reason had never regarded an air–atomic offensive as the most "acceptable concept." To Forrestal, however, the concept's utility lay in its very "absurdity." It allowed him to denounce the president's ceiling as impractical and to argue for a larger budget based on a more conventional military strategy. He must have been surprised when such arguments failed to sway the president, who promised to revisit the issue only if the international situation deteriorated to a point where supplemental defense appropriations were required. Until that point, Truman concluded, the administration would stand by the ceiling of $15 billion.[25]

Under the circumstances, Forrestal again asked the Joint Chiefs to consider the force levels that could be supported "in the general area of 14.4 billion." Only then could they recommend levels appropriate to a budget somewhere between the president's ceiling and the top figure favored by the chiefs – an intermediate amount that Forrestal put at approximately $17.5 billion.[26] But if the chiefs were going to squeeze their expectations under Truman's ceiling without relying wholly on air–atomic warfare, they would have to whittle away at individual service requirements until they reached something like a balanced force. With this strategy in mind, General Omar Bradley, the army chief of staff, urged his colleagues to take another stab at reducing their expectations. He was ready to cut the Army's budget by delaying the development of a new rifle or by settling for fewer than seven pairs of pants per soldier. The Army could get along without a "better gun," Bradley said, if the Navy could "get along without a better destroyer."[27]

For the Navy, of course, aircraft carriers rather than destroyers were the real issue, which meant its role in air–atomic warfare. The Navy was determined to expand that role. The Air Force and the Army were just as determined to curtail it and increasingly convinced that Forrestal, a long-time champion of the Navy, had rigged the budget process to their disadvantage.[28] What is more, so long as the Joint Chiefs disagreed over

[25] *Forrestal Diaries* 498–99, 502–5.
[26] Forrestal memorandum to the Joint Chiefs, undated, RG 51, Series 47.8a, box 47, folder: A-Z 1950 Budget – Basic Documents. See also Forrestal memorandum to the Joint Chiefs, 29 October 1948, RG 330, CD 5-1-25.
[27] *Forrestal Diaries*, 502–5.
[28] Symington memorandum to Forrestal, 22 October 1948, Vandenberg Papers, box 40, folder: Budget 1948; Royall memorandum to Forrestal, 25 October 1948, RG 330, CD 5-1-25.

the role of naval aviation it was impossible for them to agree on force requirements, or for that matter on a strategic concept, even after they had hammered out their differences over the size of the defense budget and how to allocate it. At that point, in other words, the Navy still wanted to use part of its allocation to maintain a carrier force in the Mediterranean, the Army and the Air Force still refused to approve this course without a comparable expansion of their own forces in the area, and such an expansion would cost far more than the president's budget ceiling of $15 billion.

These differences disappeared under a budget of $23 billion, the amount the chiefs equated with an adequate program of national security. They even disappeared under the intermediate budget that Forrestal had requested and the chiefs eventually put at $16.9 billion. In each case, the higher figure permitted the services to balance their forces at a level acceptable to the Navy, which explains why Forrestal kept urging the intermediate figure on the president. He did so at a White House meeting on 9 December, when he joined the Joint Chiefs to justify the intermediate figure by pointing to the continuing crisis in Berlin and the emerging crisis in China. Still later, he even suggested that defense expenditures might be increased by approximately $700 million through a variety of simple bookkeeping strategies, such as returning to the defense budget all $200 million in taxes paid by American military personnel.[29]

Despite these entreaties, the president stuck to his budget ceiling. By early December, Truman was fresh from his dramatic triumph at the polls, following a campaign that had featured strong attacks on a "do-nothing" Republican Congress for bestowing tax breaks and other benefits on the "gluttons of privilege," and an equally strong defense of his own efforts to balance the budget and redirect government expenditures from the "interests" to the people, from wartime to peacetime purposes. This was a record that Truman had promised to expand if reelected and that he therefore defended in meetings with Forrestal and the Joint Chiefs of Staff.[30]

Truman told his military advisers that his priorities, not theirs, would determine the size and shape of the defense budget. Global conditions

[29] Admiral Louis Denfeld memorandum to Forrestal, with enclosures, 8 November 1948, Vandenberg Papers, box 40, folder: Budget 1948; Forrestal memorandum to the Joint Chiefs, 9 November 1948, RG 330, CD 5-1-25; Joint Chiefs memorandum to Forrestal, 15 November 1948, RG 218, CCS 370 (8-19-45), Sec. 11; Forrestal memorandum to the Joint Chiefs, 17 November 1948, RG 330, CD 5-1-25; Forrestal to Truman, 1 December 1948, Truman Papers, PSF-Subject File, box 150, folder: Bureau of the Budget, Budget – Misc., 1944–53; *Forrestal Diaries*, 535–37; Condit, *Joint Chiefs of Staff* 2:245–52.
[30] McCullough, *Truman*, 642, 653–719; Donovan, *Conflict and Crisis*, 417–31.

were not worsening, he insisted, but had stabilized and might even be improving, which meant that $15 billion was an adequate defense budget and more than he hoped to spend in the future. Over the long run, he said in what was becoming a familiar refrain, the country could not afford to spend such large amounts on defense – not if it wanted to balance the budget, manage inflation without government controls, and shift more resources to civilian needs and purposes. The president, Forrestal reported, was "determined not to spend more than we take in in taxes." He was "a hard-money man if ever I saw one" and was not about to "wreck our economy in the process of trying to fight the 'cold war.'" Nor would Truman buckle under pressure from the Joint Chiefs. In Forrestal's eyes, he was "the most rocklike example of civilian control that the world has ever witnessed."[31]

Truman's budget for fiscal year 1950, which he submitted to Congress in January 1949, estimated total government expenditures at $41.9 billion, only $1.7 billion above the budget for fiscal year 1949. Of this total, the president earmarked $21 billion for international and national security programs, and another $11 billion for veterans' benefits, atomic energy, and other defense or war-related programs. Only $10 billion, or 24 percent of the budget, would be left for all other expenditures.

The National Military Establishment accounted for the largest single category of expenditures. It claimed roughly $15.3 billion, of which amount Truman slotted $13.7 billion for the armed forces, including $4.6 billion for the Air Force, $4.5 billion for the Army, and $4.6 billion for the Navy. The balance would support the Office of the Secretary of Defense and cover such items as military pay and housing, strategic stockpiling, and universal military training. In addition, Truman announced that he would later seek funding for a program of military aid to the countries that were then negotiating the North Atlantic Treaty.[32]

The projected expenditures for the National Military Establishment would support an Air Force of 412,000 officers and airmen organized in 48 groups; an Army of 677,000 soldiers organized in 10 divisions and 59 battalions; and a Navy and Marine Corps of 527,000 men, 7,540 aircraft, and 731 ships, including 288 combat ships. Although the combined forces would reach 1,616,000 officers and troops, the total fell short of the targets established in the supplemental defense appropriation of the previous spring. The current goal, as Truman explained it, was "relative

---

[31] Schilling, "Politics of National Defense," 199; *Forrestal Diaries*, 536–37.

[32] Truman, "Annual Budget Message to the Congress: Fiscal Year 1950," 10 January 1949, *Public Papers, Truman, 1949* (Washington, 1964), 44–97.

military readiness," meaning a level of "military strength which can be sustained for a period of years without excessive strain on our productive resources, and which will permit rapid expansion should the need arise." That goal was consistent with the country's "traditional concept of military strength for purposes of defense" and with the "proper relationship between our security requirements and our economic and financial resources."

As his last remark suggested, Truman was still trying to reconcile the needs of the warfare state with those of the welfare state. He was trying to do so within the framework of a balanced budget and was hoping to achieve these goals by restraining defense expenditures and raising taxes. The budget he submitted to Congress envisioned a deficit of $873 million, which Truman blamed on the Republican tax cut of the previous year and which he planned to wipe out by increasing taxes on some of the special interests that had earlier benefited from the Republican-controlled 80th Congress. With the additional revenue, estimated at $4 billion per year, the president could not only balance the budget but also reduce the national debt and cover the increased costs of both national security and domestic programs.[33]

To Truman's way of thinking, national welfare and national security, domestic and international programs, were inextricably linked. It was not merely that America's economic power contributed to its military power, its position in the global marketplace, and its ability to assist allies through programs like the Marshall Plan – all that was taken for granted. It was also that America's success abroad required improvements in education, housing, and health care at home, if necessary through expanded federal programs. "Our domestic programs are the foundation of our foreign policy," he explained. "The world today looks to us for leadership because we have so largely realized, within our borders, those benefits of democratic government for which most of the peoples of the world are yearning."[34]

For Truman, in other words, the country's political identity and postwar purpose were the same at home as they were abroad and were mutually reinforcing. It could not advance the cause of freedom on a global scale without advancing those aspects of its own national life that marked the United States as a truly democratic country. Truman's thinking on

---

33 Ibid., esp. 55–56 and 47 for quoted material. See also "Special Message to the Congress: The President's Economic Report," 7 January 1949, ibid., 13–26.

34 Truman, "Annual Message to the Congress on the State of the Union," 5 January 1949, ibid., 6.

this score was consistent with his ongoing efforts to shift more of the nation's resources into domestic programs, and with what he had promised in his reelection campaign. Anxious to redeem his pledges with additional initiatives, however constrained by the goal of a balanced budget, the president's budget for fiscal year 1950 envisioned more support for a wide range of social programs, including an enlarged system of social security, a new program of national health insurance, and increased aid for education, housing, and slum clearance.[35]

Edwin Nourse articulated perhaps better than anyone else the economic and political philosophy behind the president's budget, its connection to a set of traditional values that both held dear, and the danger that defense spending could pose to those values. As chairman of the Council of Economic Advisers, Nourse had wrestled with the problem of defense spending for three years. He was not a White House insider, but his well-developed views clearly captured the president's thinking and the main current inside the administration, at least prior to the Korean War. Nor was Nourse shy about presenting his views, even walking into the lion's den to lecture military and civilian leaders at the regular orientation seminars that Forrestal convened in the Pentagon.

There his message invariably addressed some of the major issues in the national security discourse of the early Cold War – the connection between state making and state identity, between the country's global mission and its commitment to democracy at home, between the sacrifices that national security required and the danger to democracy if these sacrifices went too far. Permanent preparedness in an age of "total war," Nourse noted repeatedly, entailed substantial sacrifices, including fundamental changes in the "structure of economic society." All elements of society, "workers and farmers, citizens as a whole," had to be "convinced" that their sacrifices were worthwhile, that "theirs was a political, social, and economic system that is worth defending." Mobilizing this popular support required effective responses to what Nourse called the "ideological" challenge of preparedness, and among these responses was a preparedness program that balanced the claims of national security against those of the civilian economy. Maintaining that balance would prevent a serious decline in civilian consumption and preclude government controls, excessive taxes, and mounting deficits – developments, according to Nourse, that could undermine democracy, transform the

---

35 See the sources cited in note 33.

country into something resembling a garrison state, and rob the American people of the will to sacrifice on behalf of national security.[36]

Nourse lamented that defense spending and the Republican tax cut were making it difficult to achieve such a balance. He pointed repeatedly to areas that had been starved for investment, especially to the "accumulation of deferred maintenance in our total school system," in streets and highways, in housing, and in other "public facilities." Even four years after the war, the president's proposed budget for fiscal year 1951 envisioned expenditures of $300 million per week for defense, as compared with $300 million per year for education, about the same for rural electrification, a little less for public health programs, and barely three-quarters of that amount for housing and slum clearance. Nourse assumed that national well-being, including the future of democracy, required greater expenditures in these areas, less in the area of defense. "The country that advances the welfare of the nation," he also intoned, "lays a foundation of preparedness that the garrison state never can."[37]

At the same time, however, Nourse wanted to increase public investment without resorting to budget deficits or government controls over wages, prices, or other areas of economic life. His thinking in this regard reflected his own commitment to the older values associated with a balanced budget and his determination to defend them, as well as the budget, against the demands of national security. It was not simply that deficits encouraged inflation and diminished the value of investment. Like government controls, they were also "habit-forming" and fundamentally corrosive of the public virtues that Nourse considered essential to the success of democratic capitalism. They either extended the authority of the state "over larger and larger areas of life," thereby weakening "the reliance of the people on free bargaining," or they encouraged citizens to defy duly "constituted authority." Under the circumstances, Nourse was willing to support proposals for a new program of military assistance to Europe, but only if the administration covered the cost of that program out of funds already earmarked for the Pentagon. He also encouraged legislators to adhere to the president's budget in other respects, increase

[36] Nourse speech before the American Ordinance Association, "The Impact of Military Preparedness on the Civilian Economy," 16 February 1949, Nourse Papers, box 10, folder: American Ordinance Association. In addition to the sources cited in note 40 see also Nourse, "What Effect Will Armament Spending Have on the Business Outlook?"

[37] Nourse speech before the American Ordinance Association, 16 February 1949, Nourse Papers, box 10, folder: American Ordinance Association.

taxes if they wanted to spend more, force the Pentagon to eliminate waste, and redirect the savings into social programs.[38]

III

Following his budget presentation, Truman kept pressure on the military to support his recommendations on Capitol Hill.[39] But the armed forces were more concerned with their own priorities and could count on powerful allies in the press and in Congress to put their interests ahead of the president's recommendations. As noted in an earlier chapter, virtually every leading journalist and commentator covered the annual budget debates from their inception inside the Truman administration through final action in Congress. Almost all of them accepted the need for a substantial military establishment and for costly economic and military aid programs. To be sure, conservatives like Henry Hazlitt, who wrote for *Newsweek* magazine, constantly lamented wasteful expenditures in the Pentagon and give away programs like the Marshall Plan. Interested in low taxes, a balanced budget, and small government, they urged Congress to achieve these goals by reducing expenditures in every category, including defense. In this camp as well, though more moderate in their views, were columnists like Raymond Moley and Arthur Krock, who blasted Truman's spending on social welfare programs and his support for higher taxes, but were more supportive of the administration's national security initiatives.[40]

Others were more hopeful that economic and security considerations could be balanced, though, as usual, they could not agree on how balance should be achieved. Ernest Lindley, a liberal commentator who

---

[38] Ibid. See also Nourse's speech to the Pentagon's Second Joint Orientation Conference, "The Impact of Military Preparedness on the Civilian Economy," 5 April 1949, Charles S. Murphy Papers (Truman Library), box 21, folder: Council of Economic Advisers; and Nourse's speech to the Third Joint Orientation Conference, "Economic Implications of Military Preparedness," 13 June 1949, Nourse Papers, box 10, folder: National Military Establishment.

[39] Unsigned memorandum, "Points for Discussion Between the President and Civilian Heads of the Military Establishment," 4 March 1949, Truman Papers, PSF-Subject File, box 145, folder: Military – President's Program – Army, Navy, Air Appropriations.

[40] Moley, "Can We Afford to be Free?" *Newsweek* 33 (10 January 1949): 80; Hazlitt, "Paradise on a Platter," ibid. (17 January 1949): 64; Hazlitt, "Balance Whose Budget?" ibid. (24 January 1949): 62; Krock, "Pressures on Budget Stir Capital Debate," "A Strange Way to Promote Economy," "Or, Putting the Message Another Way," and "Truman Economic Plan Has Wide Implications," *New York Times*, 24 April, 13 May, 12 July, and 17 July 1949; Hazlitt, "Arms and the Money," and Moley, "Grim Alternatives" *Newsweek* 33 (30 May 1949): 68, 88; and Hazlitt, "The Economics of Arms Aid," ibid. 34 (8 August 1949): 58.

generally supported the Truman administration, sympathized with Nourse's call for additional public investment, but was reluctant to see it come at the expense of defense and international programs that he considered essential for national security. In the end, Lindley, like other liberals, tried to reconcile his guns and butter priorities by endorsing a Keynesian approach to the budget, which meant that he would tolerate budget deficits, especially after a midyear recession reduced government revenues and ruled out a tax hike. Stewart Alsop also thought that most Americans were willing to tolerate persistent budget deficits and make the government increasingly responsible for the public welfare. These had become permanent features of American politics, he argued, and were even supported to some extent by conservatives such as Taft.

Of all the major columnists, Joseph Alsop was the only one to become something of a shill for the Pentagon, especially for the Air Force. While Walter Lippmann and others urged Congress to take more responsibility for curbing excesses and eliminating waste in the defense budget, Alsop was inclined to view economizers as little more than isolationists. He said that Truman was not spending enough on defense, criticized most efforts at economy in the Pentagon, and rejected the idea that military assistance should be covered out of the defense budget. In the middle of this fray was Hanson Baldwin, who thought that some savings were possible in every aspect of the budget, including military spending, and who warned against a search for "absolute security" that had transformed other countries into "garrison states or bankrupt states."[41]

On Capitol Hill, Alsop found an ally in Democratic Congressman Carl Vinson, who was an avid champion of the seventy-group Air Force. Vinson and his allies had won support for their position in the budget battle of the previous year and were still smarting under Truman's

---

[41] Baldwin, "Budget Arms Set-Up Hit," *New York Times*, 16 January 1949. See also Stewart Alsop, "The Social Welfare State," *Washington Post*, 8 January 1949; Joseph Alsop, "The Missing Keystone," ibid., 12 January 1949; Stewart Alsop, "Tying Our Haymaker in a Sling," ibid., 16 January 1949; Lippmann, "The Dream of Troubled Spirits," Stewart Alsop, "The CIO and the White House," and Childs, "A People's President," ibid., 20 January 1949; Childs, "Democratic Outpouring," ibid., 21 January 1949; Joseph and Stewart Alsop, "Congress and the Pact," ibid., 23 March 1949; Joseph Alsop, "The New Isolationism," ibid., 11 April 1949; Joseph Alsop, "George Likes Pact, Not Tax Hike," ibid., 17 April 1949; Lindley, "What Dr. Nourse Really Meant," *Newsweek* 33 (18 April 1949): 30; Lippmann, "Budget of the Cold War," *Washington Post*, 18 April 1949; Baldwin, "Military Economy," *New York Times*, 7 May 1949; Lindley, "Fair-Weather Test of Congress," *Newsweek* 33 (9 May 1949): 24; Baldwin, "The Atlantic Pact," *New York Times*, 5 June 1949; Lindley, "Which Way will Truman Turn?" *Newsweek* 34 (11 July 1949): 24; and Lindley, "The President's New Stance," ibid. (18 July 1949): 20.

decision to impound the extra $822 million they had appropriated for aircraft procurement. In hearings before the Appropriations Committee and on the floor of Congress, they mounted a new effort to amend the president's budget and were successful in attaching another $800 million for additional aircraft in the new fiscal year. Of that amount roughly $600 million would come from an overall increase in the president's budget, and the balance from cuts in other programs. The additional funds would enable the Air Force to expand from forty-eight groups, the number called for in Truman's budget, to fifty-eight groups, which Vinson and Alsop saw as the first step toward a seventy-group Air Force.

Vinson made a similar though less successful effort to increase spending for the Navy, most notably for the so-called supercarrier, the floating behemoth that was the Navy's entry into the field of strategic warfare. Together with Republican Congressman Gerald R. Ford of Michigan, he argued that a balanced force structure required additional funding for carrier-based aircraft, which, to hear them tell it, could provide a superior strategic alternative to the Air Force's growing fleet of land-based B-36 bombers. Such arguments brought inevitable rebuttals from Air Force partisans and touched off a debate in Congress similar to the one among the Joint Chiefs of Staff. According to Republican Congressman Francis Case of South Dakota, the country could not afford two air forces. According to Congressman Lloyd Bentsen of Texas, a Democrat who flew B-24s in World War II, the new fleet of B-36 bombers provided the only strategic airpower the country needed. And according to other partisans, the proposed carrier forces would be too limited in range and too vulnerable to attack to be of much use in a war against the Soviet Union.[42]

The debate over airpower, like other chapters in the national security discourse, focused as much on questions of state making and national identity as on military strategy. The issue was how to reconcile the national security ideology with the values rooted in an older political culture. How could the American people assume their new role as the defenders of freedom worldwide without at the same time destroying the economic and political principles that sustained democracy at home? Airpower enthusiasts were at one end of this discourse. They tried to legitimize their demand for additional funds by linking it to the evolving ideology of national security, with its notion that peace was indivisible and its stress on the burdens of leadership, the danger of total war, and

---

[42] *Congressional Record, 1949* 95:4428, 4430–33, 4440, 4498–4500, 4501–2, 4521–25.

the need for constant preparedness. They pointed to the continuing crisis in Berlin, the new commitments to be assumed under the North Atlantic Treaty, and the worsening conditions in the Far East, where, according to Charles A. Plumley, a Republican congressman from Vermont, the United States had to "take on the white man's burden." The country was neither at peace nor at war, they said, but in a dangerous in-between state that required constant vigilance and the will to sacrifice on behalf of the nation's security – especially in a world where the United States could neither bank its security on the United Nations nor count on strong and stable allies.[43]

At the other end of this discourse were those members of Congress whose ideas ran parallel to Edwin Nourse's. They sought to discredit the demands for more military spending by invoking the antistatist and antimilitarist values associated with an older political culture, and by re-sorting to a discursive strategy that identified these values with American democracy and their opponents with the totalitarian other. In this camp, some supported the president's recommendations, while others did not, but all were concerned that cherished traditions might be imperilled by what they repeatedly called the largest peacetime budget in American history. Among these critics, all could be counted on to complain about the inefficiencies and duplications built into the defense budget, to blame these shortcomings on interservice rivalries, and to call for cuts to elim-inate waste and for reforms to regulate the Pentagon. But some had concerns that ran much deeper. Behind the interservice disputes, they worried, lurked the danger of a military challenge to civilian authority. To Congressman Robert L. Coffey, a Pennsylvania Democrat, it was time to stand up to the "brass," to tell the Navy that it was no longer the first line of American defense, and to insist that all of the services stop padding their operations and start looking for ways to economize. These reforms required organizational adjustments that went beyond the National Se-curity Act of 1947, the shortcomings of which were plainly evident in the interservice bickering over the budget. For Coffey and other reformers, they required nothing short of greater authority in the hands of leaders who would reassert the principle of civilian control.[44]

Fear of militarism went hand-in-hand with concern about the delete-rious effects of a large defense budget on the character of the American people and their economy. In giving weight to this concern, Coffey and other critics were again repeating arguments made earlier by Nourse and

[43] Ibid., 4432–33.
[44] Ibid., 4524, 4509–10.

other economizers in the Truman administration. They were amazed that military appropriations still absorbed more than a third of the budget some three years after the war. Republican Congressman James L. Dolliver of Iowa wondered if the United States was marching down the same path to perdition taken by other countries whose governments had constructed a vast war machine. He worried that national security managers, especially military leaders, would be seduced by the resources at their disposal and would multiply the country's commitments around the world, ignore peaceful strategies, and rely too heavily on military might. In addition, he and others were appalled by the prospect of investing vast sums in military hardware over an indefinite period of time. Such investment, they said, was economically unreproductive and would require a rate of taxation that was bound to discourage individual incentive and other habits essential to a productive, free-market economy.[45]

Coffey, Dolliver, and like-minded critics found it difficult to believe that defense expenditures alone were nearly double what it had cost to run the whole government a decade earlier. The comparison was even more startling if one added to these expenditures the other national security allocations in the budget, including $5 billion for the European Recovery Program and large sums for veterans' benefits and interest on the national debt. Taken together, these national security expenditures amounted to a stupendous burden on the American economy, which Congressman Frederick Coudert, a New York Republican, tried to reduce through a motion that would restore the president's estimates for the Air Force. Coudert rallied nearly two dozen supporters behind his initiative, in part by arguing that the "economic life of the United States is at stake." And though his motion ultimately failed, even supporters of the final budget conceded that Congress could not afford to spend such "astronomical sums" for very long – not without staggering deficits, higher taxes, and economic controls, and not without eroding the country's diplomatic and military position around the world.[46] Nothing would make the Soviet Union happier, explained Congressman George H. Mahon, a Texas Democrat, "than to have us bankrupt our country and destroy our economy by maintaining over a period of years complete readiness for armed conflict."[47]

The Senate debate saw similar arguments expressed with even greater vigor and to better results. As in the past, Harry F. Byrd of Virginia,

[45] Ibid., 4441–42.
[46] Ibid., 4427–28, 4525; Schilling, "Politics of National Defense," 101.
[47] Mahon quoted in Schilling, "Politics of National Defense," 105.

Robert A. Taft of Ohio, and other conservatives took the lead, although much of what they had to say received a sympathetic hearing across the political spectrum. The warfare state, they argued, involved the same dangers as the welfare state. Both led to a powerful, oppressive government that overhung the private sector; both corrupted the political process; both threatened the economy; and both were driven to expand by organized interest groups, ranging from the military services to the advocates of national health insurance. These groups were determined to turn the government into "a gigantic money mill" and were already responsible for the fact that Congress had "caught the habit of spending so badly" that current revenues were never enough. Fiscal year 1949 would end with a budget deficit of $1.7 billion; Truman's January estimates anticipated another deficit of $873 million; and given a deteriorating economy even this estimate was likely to be too low. Estimates on Capitol Hill ran to $3 billion and Senator Byrd, a perennial pessimist, set the figure at between $5 and $8 billion.[48] He and others were sure that such large deficits would lead to what one congressman called "national insecurity." They would constitute, in the words of another, "a much greater threat from within to both the security and survival of our liberties than does the military threat of communism from without."[49]

Few wanted to curb the deficit by raising taxes, as recommended by Truman. Opposition to higher taxes increased substantially after the economy began to slip into a recession, but was always strong among conservatives like Taft, who had fought hard for the Republican tax cut just a year earlier. Taxes, they believed, supported a corpulent government bureaucracy that endangered free-market capitalism. And since federal, state, and local taxes already took $61 billion of the national income, any more would make private enterprise unprofitable and open the door to government ownership, as had happened in England.[50] There was "a point at which free enterprise must go on a downward path," Taft lectured his colleagues, a point where the country would "turn to a socialist form of government."[51]

Given these sentiments, and the mounting recession, it was not surprising that Truman's proposed tax bill never got off the ground on Capitol Hill. And with higher taxes ruled out, the alternative seemed to be a harsh program of spending cuts to which Republicans like Taft and their

---

[48] *Congressional Record, 1949* 95:12418, 12389–93.
[49] Both conservatives are quoted in Schilling, "Politics of National Defense," 100, 101.
[50] *Congressional Record, 1949* 95:12410.
[51] Taft quoted in Schilling, "Politics of National Defense," 102.

allies among conservative Democrats quickly turned. They backed the so-called McClellan amendment, which would direct the president to cut between 5 and 10 percent of estimated expenditures from the final budget for fiscal 1950. The reduction would be at the president's discretion, to be sure, but it was evident where the deepest cuts would come. As noted by Senator Hubert H. Humphrey, a liberal Democrat from Minnesota, roughly 60 percent of the budget consisted of fixed costs and only 40 percent of costs that could be controlled, which meant that an overall reduction of 5 to 10 percent would translate into a cut of 10 to 20 percent in controllable expenditures. A cut of this magnitude would eviscerate agencies like the Post Office and the Federal Works Administration, as well as the agricultural conservation program and farm price supports.[52] It would also mean crippling reductions in social security, school aid, and other social programs, not to mention substantial cutbacks in the national security portion of the budget, including foreign aid and national defense. Indeed, Senator Byrd, who spelled out the reductions in some detail, envisioned savings of $2.5 billion in defense and proportionate cuts in foreign aid and other areas.[53]

The prospect of such cuts made the amendment attractive to legislative leaders like Taft, Byrd, and McClellan. They were convinced that social welfare programs had contributed to a dangerous growth of state power, and they had similar misgivings about the national security programs that were now being grafted onto the New Deal state. They also added to the power of the state, overburdened the budget, and undermined the dollar. Then, too, conservatives were convinced that national security initiatives like the Marshall Plan propped up socialist enterprises abroad and promoted welfare policies on a global scale. Together with collective security arrangements like the North Atlantic Treaty, they overextended American power, made the country more vulnerable, and fostered wasteful bureaucracies and a powerful military elite. To the conservative way of thinking, the McClellan amendment would strike a blow against all these dangerous tendencies by forcing the administration to curb both domestic and international programs.

Although it failed on procedural grounds, the McClellan amendment drew support from a large number of senators – more than half of those voting. Clearly, the concerns expressed by conservatives like Taft were widely shared, which helps to explain why the Senate initially rejected

---

52 *Congressional Record*, 1949 95:12589–92, 12403–5. See also the remarks by Democratic Senator Scott Lucas of Illinois in ibid., 12416–17.
53 Ibid., 12392–95, 12416.

the House's proposal for a fifty-eight-group Air Force at a cost of roughly $800 million more than the forty-eight groups that Truman had requested. The debate over this issue filled nearly fourteen pages of the *Congressional Record*, focusing not only on the relative merits of a balanced or unbalanced force structure but also on whether economy or security should have the top priority. The House had been willing to invest more in the Air Force at the expense of the Army and the Navy, while the Senate seemed to favor a balanced force structure at a lower cost to the taxpayer.[54]

Although the Senate eventually reversed course and threw its weight behind a fifty-eight-group Air Force, the change of direction was not easily achieved and did not necessarily signal the triumph of security over economic considerations. To be sure, the Senate's action was prompted in part by news that the Soviet Union had successfully tested an atomic device, a development that appeared to portend a dangerous deterioration of the strategic balance.[55] At the same time, however, Truman had signaled his decision to impound extra funding for the Air Force rather than drive the budget further into deficit, and both houses of Congress had taken steps to reduce national security expenditures in other areas.[56] What is more, Taft and other conservatives still believed that a more expensive Air Force would save money in the long run, and would do so by making it possible to reduce the size of the standing army and scrap Truman's proposal for universal military training.

The final budget came close to what Truman had recommended, in large part because Taft's concerns were widely shared in both houses of Congress. Truman had recommended a budget of $13.7 billion for the armed forces, plus additional funds for such items as military pay and strategic stockpiling, for a total of roughly $15.3 billion. Congress appropriated slightly less than $15.6 billion. The buildup to a fifty-eight-group Air Force accounted for the extra funding, which Truman vowed not to spend in any event.[57] Seen in this light, Truman's budget strategy in the area of defense turned out to be largely successful. The failure came in the reluctance of Congress to increase taxes by $4 billion to balance the budget while allowing new expenditures on health care, education, housing, and other domestic programs. As in the past, conservatives in

---

[54] Ibid., 12301–15.

[55] Ibid., 14144.

[56] The Senate concession came in conference negotiations between the two houses. For the debate over the conference report see ibid., 14136–59, 14352–55, 14854–59, 14920–23.

[57] *Congressional Quarterly Almanac, 1949* 5:220–25.

Congress led a movement to balance the budget by curbing expenditures in these areas, and by mid-October 1949, when work on the budget came to an end, appropriations for fiscal year 1950 totaled approximately $37.8 billion, about $4 billion below the president's estimate of the previous January.[58]

IV

The danger of persistent deficits was not the only specter haunting the country in 1949. The interservice squabbles that threatened the budget also culminated in an astonishing challenge to civilian control of the armed forces. The revolt of the admirals, as it became known, raised anew the prospect of American democracy giving way to a garrison state dominated by military leaders, or at least by military departments. In this case, moreover, the fear of militarism went hand-in-hand with a conviction in some quarters that military leaders were at the center of a circle of corruption that could destroy the moral fabric of American politics. This circle was characterized not only by what some saw as a pattern of bribery and patronage but also by a conspiracy of privilege that embraced party leaders and private elites. Again, such concerns built on a cultural narrative that had a long history in American politics, from Jackson's war on the "monster" bank, to Roosevelt's attack on the "trusts," to Truman's assault on the "gluttons of privilege." These concerns typically sprang from the conviction that concentrations of power led inevitably to a loss of public virtue, and they often ended, as in the revolt of the admirals, with new efforts to limit or delineate that power.

The revolt of the admirals has been described many times, but a brief summary is required here to indicate how far the services would go to advance their interests, the resources they could bring to bear, and their willingness to challenge civilian authority.[59] The brouhaha began with another round in the old debate over the relative merits of the B-36, the Air Force's long-range bomber, and the Navy's so-called supercarrier. Each side had mounted a campaign for additional funds to cover its program. Each was touting its own advantages and belittling the claims of the other, and each was working with private-sector allies. The Navy was helping the Navy League, a private organization, run a half-million dollar publicity blitz on behalf of naval aviation. The Air Force, according

---

[58] Ibid., 183.
[59] For the best recent study see Jeffrey G. Barlow, *Revolt of the Admirals: The Fight for Naval Aviation, 1945–1950* (Washington, 1994).

to rumors circulating in Washington, was "working with big aviation companies and others to lobby for a large Air Force regardless of the position of the Administration."[60] Symington denied these rumors, but not reports that his office operated its own publicity campaign, racing to set new distance records for the B-36 and bragging about new in-flight refueling techniques. Both sides had lobbyists combing Capitol Hill and feeding information to friends in the press. The situation was "chaos and conflict and carnage confounded," wrote David Lilienthal.[61]

By the end of April the Air Force had gained the upper hand in this struggle. It was slated to get additional funding from Congress, and Secretary of Defense Forrestal, who supported the Navy's supercarrier, had been forced to retire. The job had finally overcome him, what with the Joint Chiefs constantly "at each other's throat" so that no decisions could be made. Even General Eisenhower, in his capacity as informal chairman of the Joint Chiefs, became ill under the stress and was "ordered South for a rest," while Forrestal's condition grew much, much worse.[62] Ground down by the bickering and backstabbing in the Pentagon and under constant attack from the admirals and generals he supposedly commanded, Forrestal had also come under severe criticism in the press, especially from radio and newspaper commentators. Walter Winchell and Drew Pearson, in particular, led a campaign of vilification against the secretary, calling him a liar and a coward, accusing him of mismanaging the Pentagon, and attacking his alleged anti-Semitism and his supposedly pro-Nazi bias during the war. Under the circumstances, Forrestal had become increasingly nervous and paranoid. He began to scratch the top of his head raw and to see plots everywhere, usually Communist and Zionist conspiracies.[63] He also found it more difficult to make decisions on his own, which is one of the reasons that Truman finally dismissed him.

After leaving office, Forrestal suffered a complete breakdown. He spent several weeks under psychiatric care at Bethesda Naval Hospital, where his paranoid delusions grew worse. He kept his blinds closed to guard against spies and had Sidney Souers, the executive secretary of the NSC, search his room for listening devices. In the early morning of 22 May

[60] Symington to Webb, 13 December 1948, Webb Papers, box 8, folder: President.
[61] Lilienthal, *Atomic Energy Years*, 493. See also Condit, *Joint Chiefs of Staff* 2:311–24; Rearden, *Formative Years*, 411; Paul Y. Hammond, "Super Carriers and B-36 Bombers: Appropriations, Strategy and Politics," in *American Civil–Military Decisions: A Book of Case Studies*, ed. Harold Stein (Birmingham, 1963), 491, 505.
[62] Lilienthal. *Atomic Energy Years*, 493. See also *Forrestal Diaries*, 547–49.
[63] *Forrestal Diaries*, 547; and McCullough, *Truman*, 737.

1949, Forrestal, despondent and sleepless, read Sophocles's classic poem "The Chorus from Ajax," in which the hero contemplates suicide. He copied several lines of the poem onto a notepad and then walked quietly from his room to a small pantry across the hall. There he tied one end of his bathrobe sash to a radiator, the other around his neck, and slipped silently out the pantry window. He apparently hung helplessly for a few terrifying seconds, scratching desperately at the brick wall of the building until the sash gave way and he plunged thirteen stories to his death. Forrestal had once described himself as a "victim of the Washington scene." After his death, others were more specific, counting the secretary as a casualty of the Cold War and the national security state he had helped to build.[64]

Forrestal's replacement, Louis Johnson, came to office determined to do what his predecessor could not: save money and whip the services into shape. A millionaire lawyer from West Virginia, past commander of the American Legion and one-time assistant secretary of war, Johnson was a tall, bulky, tough-talking goliath with a great dome head and square jaw. He weighed 250 pounds, and liked to throw every ounce of it around. His first major step was to halt construction of the Navy's supercarrier, a decision he made under pressure from economizers in the White House and Congress and after learning that the Army and Air Force favored the decision, as did General Eisenhower. Still, Johnson had acted without giving the Navy a full hearing, and there was some reason to believe that he was less concerned with the strategic implications of his decision than with boosting his reputation as an economizer and his prospects for a presidential nomination in 1952.

Johnson's decision brought a chorus of complaints from the Navy, especially from Secretary of the Navy John Sullivan, who resigned in a huff, and from a host of top-ranking admirals who refused to take "no" for an answer. The admirals set out to reverse Johnson's decision. They launched a full-scale publicity campaign that aimed in part to educate Congress and the public about the merits of the supercarrier, in part to denigrate the value of the B-36, which the Navy considered its rival for funding in the field of strategic warfare. The Navy's friends on Capitol Hill also played a part, especially Representative James Van Zandt, a Republican from Pennsylvania and a captain in the Naval Reserve.

Van Zandt aired rumors that Johnson's decision had stemmed from a cozy financial relationship between the Democratic party, the Air Force,

---

[64] Ibid., 544. See also Hoopes and Brinkley, *Driven Patriot*, 460–66.

and Consolidated Vultee Aircraft Corporation, which manufactured the B-36 bomber. According to these rumors, Floyd Odlum, who headed Consolidated, had contributed large sums to the president's reelection campaign in 1948, when Truman's major fund raiser had been none other than Louis Johnson, also a Consolidated shareholder, a member of its board of directors, and head of its principal law firm. Johnson's partner in this enterprise was rumored to be Air Force Secretary Symington, who supposedly rewarded Odlum's generosity with a promise of greater government support for the B-36. Then, once the election was over, or so the reports had it, Symington delivered on his promise by canceling contracts with Boeing, Northrop, and other aircraft companies in order to shift more resources into the B-36 program. There were even rumors that he was going to resign as air force secretary to feather his nest as the head of a huge aircraft conglomerate that he and Odlum planned to establish.[65]

Although the Air Force may have accelerated B-36 production to increase its stake in strategic warfare and preempt any role for the Navy, it had not, according to a subsequent investigation, played politics or showed favoritism when awarding contracts. On the contrary, the charges against Symington, Johnson, and others had been trumped up in a propaganda office operated by an assistant to Undersecretary of the Navy Dan Kimball and encouraged by one of Consolidated's disgruntled competitors. This revelation embarrassed the Navy, but did not deter the admirals from their unrelenting assault on the B-36. Contrary to explicit orders from the civilian leadership, especially from the new secretary of the navy, Francis P. Matthews, the Navy brass opened another front in a congressional committee investigating service roles and missions.

On this front, Vice-Admiral Arthur W. Radford led a phalanx of sailors who attacked the B-36 as "a billion-dollar blunder," arguing again that even an upgraded version of the bomber was too slow and too vulnerable to be of much use in a war with the Soviets. At best it would be useful only if the strategy was one of saturation bombing with atomic weapons, and this, in their view, was both morally bankrupt and an ineffective deterrent to Soviet aggression. The need instead was for a strategy in which naval

[65] Ayers Diary, 75–76, Ayers Papers, Diaries, box 17, folder: Diary, 1949; Vandenberg memorandum to Johnson, 26 April 1949, Vandenberg Papers, box 52, folder: Navy vs. Air Force; undated "Dirt Sheet," Symington Papers, box 6, folder: Correspondence File, 1946–50: Investigation; Norstad memorandum on the B-36, 19 July 1949, and Norstad memorandum to Dr. Leach, 11 August 1949, Norstad Papers, Pentagon Series, box 22, folder: Official File, 1949–50 (2); *Congressional Quarterly Almanac, 1949* 5:499–500; Rearden, *Formative Years,* 412–13; Hammond, "Super Carriers and B-36 Bombers," 493–97.

air would play a prominent role, namely one that relied more heavily on tactical air strikes to prevent Soviet forces from overrunning Western Europe and other areas in the early stages of a conflict.[66]

According to the admirals, moreover, the willingness of the Air Force and the Army to support an "obsolete" airplane had wrecked the chances for cooperation among the services as envisioned in the National Security Act of 1947. Instead, it had illustrated how genuine cooperation required greater representation for the Navy, which was outnumbered by the Air Force and the Army, and additional limits on the authority of the Joint Chiefs to dictate roles and missions and to determine how the defense budget would be expended. The Navy must have the right to choose the weapons and forces appropriate to its mission, including the supercarrier, which the admirals asked Congress to support.

Spokesmen for the Army and the Air Force responded by defending the deterrent power and performance capabilities of the B-36, questioning the value of naval aviation, denouncing the supercarrier, and raising doubts about the integrity and loyalty of the admirals. Symington came close to accusing the admirals of treason by revealing too much about American military strategy and thereby giving the Soviets an "advantage in developing their [own] strategic plan." Army General Omar Bradley agreed. He said the Navy had done "infinite harm" to the nation's security and compared the admirals to "fancy Dans" who refused to play ball unless they could "call the signals."[67]

As Bradley's remark suggests, personal animosity ran like a muddy river through the debates over military strategy and service functions. Symington was critical of Admiral Radford and others in the Navy for organizing a campaign of vilification against the Air Force and its secretary, accusing him of financial misconduct in the case of the B-36 and of ripping off government contracts during the war. Symington was convinced that Radford and his group were working through the Navy's biggest contractors to influence editorial opinion across the country, a tactic he considered "un-American." On the other hand, Symington was not above threatening Navy Assistant Secretary Kimball, who had come to

---

[66] *Congressional Quarterly Almanac, 1949* 5:500–502; Condit, *Joint Chiefs of Staff* 2:332–34; Hammond, "Super Carriers and B-36 Bombers," 499–500; Rearden, *Formative Years*, 413–15. For the congressional investigation see also U.S. Congress, House, *Hearings on H. Res. 234, Investigation of the B-36 Bomber Program* (Washington, 1949).

[67] *Congressional Quarterly Almanac, 1949* 5:500–2. See also Condit, *Joint Chiefs of Staff* 2:334–51; Hammond, "Super Carriers and B-36 Bombers," 507–48; and Rearden, *Formative Years*, 415–19.

Washington from firms that did a substantial business with the Air Force and the Army. At a cocktail party in Washington, Symington warned Kimball that his firms ran the risk of losing half of their business if he continued to criticize the Air Force. In addition, there is reason to believe that the Air Force hired private investigators to follow high-ranking Navy officials during the controversy.[68]

All in all, the revolt of the admirals amounted to a remarkable display of military insubordination that culminated in the dismissal of Admiral Louis Denfeld, the chief of naval operations, who had not done enough to keep his subordinates in line. Involved as well were numerous charges of personal malfeasance and political corruption, which were allegedly the result of a conspiracy of profit linking the armed forces, arms makers, and political elites in actions that wasted public resources. Congress discredited the worst of these reports, but there was no denying the Navy's "open rebellion against civilian control," as General Bradley called it. Taken together with the interminable battling in the Pentagon and the reluctance of the services to live with presidential policies, the Navy's rebellion brought to a boil long-simmering concerns that the Cold War was subverting the nation's traditional democratic politics and laying the groundwork for a garrison state.[69]

These concerns were widely shared by popular commentators who followed the admirals' revolt with increasing alarm and a mounting resolve to extract some meaningful lessons for the future. Hanson Baldwin was appalled by the Navy's "persecution complex" and its "open defiance" of civilian control. The Alsops also denounced the "insubordination" of the admirals and demanded immediate reforms, as did Marquis Childs and other commentators. As they saw it, the revolt was only the latest indication that the National Security Act had not gone far enough to control an increasingly powerful military establishment. Without further reforms, they agreed, it would be impossible to achieve real economies in the defense budget, to guarantee the principle of civilian rule, or to

---

[68] Symington to Forrestal, 22 November 1948, Vandenberg Papers, box 52, folder: Navy vs. Air Force. See also Kimball memorandum of conversation with W. Stuart Symington, 20 May 1949, Dan A. Kimball Papers (Truman Library), box 2, folder: Kimball, Dan A. (Diary Notes), Symington to Congressman Vinson, 2 June 1949, and undated "Dirt Sheet," Symington Papers, box 6 folder: Correspondence File, 1946–50: Investigation; Hammond, "Super Carriers and B-36 Bombers," 504.

[69] Bradley quoted in Rearden, *Formative Years*, 419. On the dismissal of Admiral Denfeld see Secretary of the Navy Francis P. Matthews to Truman, 14 October 1949, Truman Papers, PSF-Subject File, box 158, folder: Navy, Secy of – Misc.; and Matthews to Truman, 27 October 1949, Clifford Papers, box 11, folder: National Military Establishment – Navy.

solve the interservice disputes that kept "arising, like Banquo's ghost, to plague" the secretary of defense. It was time, as Baldwin, the Alsops, and others pointed out, to defend the constitutional basis of American democracy, dismiss some of the current participants in the revolt, and further reorganize the National Military Establishment.[70]

V

Indeed, as the admirals' revolt ran its course, serious consideration was being given to just such a reorganization, one that would help the United States fulfill its new world mission while also producing rational budgets, ensuring presidential prerogatives, and protecting the other values associated with good government and the country's democratic tradition. The issue again was one of state making, of civilian versus military rule, of democracy versus the garrison state, and the question was whether traditional values and institutions could be adapted to national security needs or whether these needs required basic changes in the American pattern of government.

As in the past debates over the National Security Act, those involved resorted to an emotionally charged rhetorical style, including the usual binary oppositions and metaphors of militarism, that captured their concerns and aspirations. As in the past, they relied on a strategy of otherness to delineate the country's political identity in a way that dismissed opposing points of view as more un-American than American, more authoritarian than democratic, more in keeping with the German way or the Soviet way than with the American way. And as in the past, the new debates set the stage for a pattern of state making that balanced centralizing against decentralizing tendencies, the need for greater authority against the fear of statism, militarism, and totalitarianism.

One center of the new movement for organizational reform was the Office of the Secretary of Defense, which Forrestal had once called a "cemetery for dead cats."[71] In the debates over the National Security Act,

[70] Baldwin, "Navy is Freudian Study" and "Navy Wars With Itself," *New York Times*, 16 October and 8 October 1949; Joseph and Stewart Alsop, "The Angry Admirals," *Washington Post*, 7 October 1949; Baldwin, "Unification Full Circle," *New York Times*, 7 October 1949. See also Childs, "Bickering as Usual," *Washington Post*, 28 September 1949; Alsops "The Grain Among Chaff," and "Facts For Admirals," *Washington Post*, 10 and 14 October 1949; and Baldwin, "The War of Unification," "Bradley Bombs Navy," and "Bradley's Charges Upset Washington," *New York Times*, 13, 20, 21 October 1949.
[71] *Forrestal Diaries*, 299.

Forrestal had worked for an organizational structure that decentralized authority and preserved the identity of the separate services, his goal at that point being coordination rather than control. But Forrestal was nothing if not proof of the old adage, once popular among students of bureaucratic politics, that where you sit determines how you stand. After he had moved from the Office of the Secretary of the Navy to the Office of the Secretary of Defense, he and his aides began to see the need for more authority and assistance than they had anticipated, and especially for impartial advice they could not get from the armed services.[72]

Forrestal got a chance to make improvements when the Commission on Organization of the Executive Branch of the Government, established in 1947 under the leadership of former president Herbert Hoover, decided a year later to form a special task force to evaluate the country's national security establishment. Hoover's choice to head the task force was Ferdinand Eberstadt, who had been Forrestal's agent in the negotiations leading up to the National Security Act. As a result of this connection, Eberstadt was regarded by the Air Force and the Army as being strongly committed to an independent Navy and hence likely to recommend greater coordination rather than real unification of the armed forces. Both Royall and Symington complained about Eberstadt's appointment, both eventually swallowed their objections, and both lived to regret it.[73]

Forrestal quickly communicated his views to Eberstadt's task force. He needed more authority than his office could exercise under the National Security Act, but his thinking still balanced precariously between the Navy's position and the one staked out by the Army and the Air Force – between fears of concentrated power and visions of greater authority.

---

[72] For a critique of the National Security Act from the point of view of the Office of the Secretary of Defense see the working paper "Revisions of the National Security Act Essential to More Rapid Progress Toward Presidential Objectives," enclosed in the memorandum from Forrestal's aide Marx Leva to the director of the Bureau of the Budget, 3 December 1948, RG 51, Series 39.32, box 74, folder: National Security Act Amendments of 1949 – To Establish a Department of Defense, Legislation and Staff Memos, January 1948–January 1949.

[73] Hoover to Eberstadt, 24 April 1948, Eberstadt memorandum, 10 May 1948, and Secretary of the Army Kenneth Royall to Hoover, 25 May 1948, Eberstadt Papers, box 72, folder: Hoover Commission Files: Correspondence and Related Materials, 1948–49: Hoover, Herbert; Eberstadt Diary, 20 and 22 May 1948, Eberstadt Papers, box 146, folder: Royall, Kenneth C., 1946, 1948–49; and Eberstadt to Hoover, 21 May 1948, with enclosed memorandums from Symington and Royall to Forrestal of 21 May 1948, Symington Papers, box 4, folder: Correspondence File, 1946–50, Declassified Documents. Eberstadt accepted his appointment only after telling Hoover that he would not commit himself to a single military department. See Eberstadt's memorandum of 10 May 1948 cited above.

To help carry the burdens of his office, Forrestal now thought that he needed a military adviser, an undersecretary, and three or four assistant secretaries who might also double as heads of the Munitions Board and the National Security Resources Board. In addition, Forrestal wanted the Joint Staff to be enlarged, the Joint Chiefs to be chaired by one of its members, and the secretary's authority over the military departments to be more specific. To achieve the last goal he would remove the word "general" from section 202 of the National Security Act, because that section limited the secretary of defense to "general direction and control" of the armed forces.

Yet even as he sought more resources and greater authority, Forrestal still thought that each of the services should retain its "autonomy." He did not want a strong man as military chief of staff or the overconcentration of power that he associated with authoritarian governments or with a garrison state. Nor did he want the service secretaries to be demoted or the chairman of the Joint Chiefs to dominate that agency. To hear him tell it, the innovations he was proposing aimed at nothing more than a greater degree of coordination among the service departments and other elements of the National Military Establishment.[74]

Officials in the Army and the Air Force did not share the ambivalence that marked Forrestal's thinking. They paraded their views aggressively before Eberstadt's task force, attacking the Navy's position and launching a concerted campaign for the same reforms they had pushed during debates over the National Security Act. With typical hyperbole, Symington promised "fantastic savings" from real unification rather than "triplification" of the armed forces, while Air Force Chief of Staff Hoyt Vandenberg said that economies adding up to 30 percent of the defense budget could be achieved without any loss of military effectiveness.[75] For the most part, of course, these economies would come by consolidating airpower in the hands of the Air Force. Both Symington and Royall

---

74 *Forrestal Diaries*, 465. See also ibid., 300–1, 497; excerpts from a telephone conversation between Forrestal and Marx Leva, 16 September 1948, RG 330, CD 12-1-1; Forrestal memorandum to the Eberstadt Committee, 30 September 1948, Eberstadt Papers, box 121, folder: 1948–51, Patterson, Robert P.; and Symington memorandum to Forrestal, 7 October 1948, Symington Papers, box 5, folder: Correspondence File, 1946–50, Forrestal, James V.

75 Symington to Eberstadt with attached record of his testimony before the Eberstadt Committee, 30 June 1948, Patterson Papers, General Correspondence, box 30, folder: 1947–1952, Commission on the Organization of the Executive Branch, June-September 1948; Eberstadt Committee, Minutes of Meeting, 29 June 1948, Vandenberg Papers, box 49, folder: Eberstadt (Navy vs. Air Force). See also, for the point of view of Symington and the Air Force, Symington to Forrestal, 14 September 1948, RG 330, CD 12-1-1.

made this point, as did former Air Force Chief of Staff Carl Spaatz and other partisans, including retired General Jimmy Doolittle, the hero of the daring bomber raid on Tokyo in 1942. According to Doolittle, military leaders were almost wholly indifferent to issues of economy. Those in the Navy spent money like drunken sailors, especially in their effort to build a second air force the country could not afford without destroying "our economy and eventually our form of government." His solution: abolish the Navy's air arm.[76]

Symington had refrained from denigrating the value of aircraft carriers in his first meeting with Eberstadt's task force; Navy officials were not so polite. They came to the task force armed with the conviction that the best defense was a good offense. Once again, they attacked the B-36 bomber as a suicide plane that could not evade Soviet fighters or cover the distance to the Soviet Union and return safely. On the other hand, they said, carrier bombers could take the war to the enemy. Launched from the Mediterranean, they could make the round-trip flight to targets in the Soviet Union and would have the advantage of a fighter escort. In the Navy's hyperbolic rhetoric, which was deep enough to float a battleship, its fast carrier task forces amounted to mobile air bases and were virtually invulnerable, even to atomic attack.[77]

News of the Navy's testimony sent Symington into a rage. He accused Eberstadt of turning his committee into a forum for Navy propaganda. The Navy's attack on the B-36 violated instructions from the secretary of defense, he said, and flew in the face of the Newport agreements, which supposedly gave the Air Force priority in the field of strategic bombing. Nor was Symington long in mounting a rebuttal. Not one to hold the high ground, he was ready for a "public brawl," said a colleague, even if it undermined the military establishment and compromised the "security of the country."[78] Within weeks he had reconvened Eberstadt's group to hear additional testimony from himself and other officials about the

---

[76] Doolittle to Eberstadt, 20 September 1948, Symington Papers, box 4, folder: Correspondence File, 1946–50, D – General. See also Doolittle to E.P. Curtis of Eastman Kodak Company, 27 August 1948, ibid.; Royall to Forrestal, 7 September 1948, and Leva to Forrestal, 10 September 1948, RG 330, CD 12-1-26.

[77] Unsigned (J.B.M.) memorandum to Symington, 19 October 1948, Symington Papers, box 4, folder: Correspondence File, 1946–50, Declassified Documents. See also Norstad to Admiral Forrest Sherman, Norstad Papers, Pentagon Series, box 22, folder: Official – Classified – 1948.

[78] Norstad to Sherman, 2 November 1948, Norstad Papers, Pentagon Series, box 22, folder: Official – Classified – 1948, and Symington to Eberstadt, 25 October 1948, Patterson Papers, General Correspondence, box 30, folder: 1947–1952, Commission on the Organization of the Executive Branch, Oct. 1948–June 1950.

Newport agreements, the role of the Air Force in strategic bombing, and the ineffectiveness of carrier-based aircraft.[79]

The exchange of tantrums between the Air Force and the Navy, not to mention the revolt of the admirals, underscored the complete failure of the National Security Act. The military establishment had not been able to dampen interservice disputes or work out a reasonable assignment of roles and missions. Its failure to do so made Pentagon policy makers look foolish and raised doubts about the nation's security and the ability of civilian authorities to control the military. It also called into question the efficacy of the Joint Chiefs of Staff and fed the demand for organizational reform, even while it created a situation that made reform very difficult. After all, the shape of such a reform depended on the goals pursued, and the services could not agree on what these goals should be.

The Navy had nothing to gain from organizational reforms that might restrict its role in strategic warfare or its ability to develop the aircraft and the carriers it considered essential to that mission.[80] The Air Force and the Army, on the other hand, wanted to capitalize on their majority in the Joint Chiefs of Staff. Symington considered the National Security Act a "phoney" piece of legislation because the need for unanimity by the Joint Chiefs gave the Navy a veto over military policy. He wanted to strengthen the Office of the Secretary of Defense by removing the service secretaries from the NSC, appointing an undersecretary of defense, and designating one of the Joint Chiefs to chair that agency. These views had strong support from the Army leadership and from Air Force Chief of Staff Vandenberg and Major General Lauris Norstad, who handled reorganization matters for the Air Force.[81] Norstad acknowledged the opposition in a democratic country to investing military leaders with

---

[79] William H. Strong, Minutes of Committee on National Security Organization Meeting, 5 November 1948, Patterson Papers, General Correspondence, box 30, folder: 1947–52, Commission on the Organization of the Executive Branch, Oct. 1948–June 1950.

[80] Leva to Forrestal, 4 September 1948, RG 330, CD 12-1-1; unsigned (J.B.M.) memorandum to Symington, Symington Papers, box 4, folder: Correspondence File, 1946–50, Declassified Documents.

[81] Minutes of Meeting of the Eberstadt Committee, 18 October 1948, Vandenberg Papers, box 49, folder: Eberstadt (Navy vs. Air Force). See also Minutes of Meeting of the Eberstadt Committee, 29 June 1948, ibid.; Symington to Eberstadt, 30 June 1948, with attached record of Symington's testimony before the Eberstadt Committee, Patterson Papers, General Correspondence, box 30, folder: 1947–52, Commission on the Organization of the Executive Branch, June-Sept. 1948; and Norstad memorandum for the record, 2 November 1948, Norstad Papers, Pentagon Series, box 21, folder: Memorandums for the Record.

substantial authority. But there was "a big job to be done," he argued, and it required "central control and authority if the services are to be used effectively and economically."[82]

In the end, however, these arguments were not particularly persuasive to most members of the Eberstadt task force and the Hoover Commission, both of which issued documents that sounded some of the central themes in the new ideology of national security. Peace, they argued, was no longer the normal condition of national life, interrupted only occasionally by wars of short duration; nor was the government's responsibility for the common defense an intermittent obligation. The United States had entered a new era of "relentless struggle" in which national security was a continuous and "in many ways controlling" responsibility of the federal government. What was more, the new age of total war required a total system of security in which "all of our national resources" had to be integrated into a "comprehensive" peacetime security organization, the likes of which had never existed before.[83]

The Hoover Commission admitted that such a system was bound to raise concerns among a people who had always been "fearful of military cliques" and whose constitution included provisions to safeguard democratic government against the threat of military rule. But it also insisted that a "proper relationship" between the elements of national policy and between military and civilian authority would enable the country to guarantee its security without damaging its democratic traditions or free economy. It was particularly important in this connection that "the military arm of the Government, in its new strength, will not grow up a thing apart" but remain "unequivocally under the direction of the executive branch and fully accountable to the President, the Congress, and the people."[84]

That a proper relationship had yet to be achieved was evident in the waste that typified military budgets and expenditures, in arrangements that permitted the Joint Chiefs to act as "virtually a law unto themselves," and in military departments where "centralized civilian control scarcely

[82] Minutes of Meeting of the Eberstadt Committee, 29 June 1948, Vandenberg Papers, box 49, folder: Eberstadt (Navy vs. Air Force).

[83] Committee on the National Security Organization, *Task Force Report on National Security Organization* (Washington, 1949), 28, 29–30 (hereafter the Eberstadt report). See also the source cited in the next note.

[84] *The National Security Organization: A Report to the Congress by the Commission on Organization of the Executive Branch of the Government, February 1949* (Washington, 1949), 1–2 (hereafter the Hoover report).

exists."[85] The country was paying more for defense than it was getting in security, according to the Eberstadt and Hoover reports. The armed forces were "prodigal" with government funds and did not understand that "every waste of resources is an impairment of our national strength." Reforms were necessary to guarantee more economy and better management, and the reforms they recommended would give the secretary more authority over the military budget and allow him to select one member of the Joint Chiefs to chair that agency. In addition, both reports would remove the word "general" from section 202 of the National Security Act and revoke the right of service secretaries to appeal decisions directly to the president, sit on the NSC, or retain all powers and responsibilities not specifically assigned to the secretary of defense. To help the secretary shoulder his responsibilities, the Hoover report also called for an undersecretary of defense, and both reports recommended three assistant secretaries and a military assistant junior in rank to the Joint Chiefs.[86]

These reforms, however extensive, stopped short of the general staff system favored by the Army and the Air Force, chiefly because Eberstadt and others were loath to foster anything like "a military 'party line'" or "one-man military control of the armed forces." Relying on a rhetorical strategy of otherness, they associated such a system with the "Third Reich" and said it would put too much power in military rather than civilian hands and thus pose a "danger to our democratic institutions," as it had to democracy in Germany. For similar reasons, Eberstadt would not allow the chairman of the Joint Chiefs to be superior in rank to his colleagues or to make military decisions on his own, exercise command, or establish a military staff.[87]

From Eberstadt's point of view, it was better to live with some organizational confusion, even some conflict, than to have issues resolved "by dictate." After all, these issues usually involved difficult questions of military theory, technology, and national policy. They were issues that should not be resolved by the "arbitrary decisions of a 'strong man' at the top," if only because there were "dumb strong men as well as wise ones" and they were "as likely to reach the wrong settlement as the right one." Should the administration allow controversial issues to be decided

---

[85] Ibid., 2–17. The quotes are from 11, 8.
[86] Eberstadt report, 5, 18. See also ibid., 3, 4, 11–13, and Hoover report, 1–2.
[87] Eberstadt report, 53–60. See also ibid., 13, 55.

by fiat, Eberstadt wrote to Walter Lippmann, it would be "one of the most dangerous things that could happen to the country."[88]

The Eberstadt and Hoover reports became central documents in a continuing controversy that ran through both committees and through the administration as well. They forced Forrestal to make up his mind about the reforms he favored, which in the end came closer to the "Navy pattern" than to the "Army pattern," closer to his original vision of the National Security Act than to the tortured lessons he had learned as secretary of defense. The secretary's authority would be enhanced only slightly under Forrestal's scheme, mainly by scratching the word "general" from section 202 of the National Security Act, providing for an undersecretary, detaching the Joint Chiefs from the individual services, appointing one of the chiefs to chair that agency, and increasing the size of the joint staff. In what could be seen as mere "tinkering," Forrestal rejected the idea of a powerful chief of staff to act as agent for the president and the secretary of defense. Nor would he merge the armed forces into a single department. The service departments would remain intact and the service secretaries would retain their rank as cabinet officers, if not their representation on the NSC, and their right to appeal any decision to the president.[89]

Not surprisingly, officials in the Army and the Air Force greeted these reports and recommendations with dismay and disappointment. According to Eisenhower and Vandenberg, the military establishment was at "low ebb" and something "drastic had to be done to rehabilitate" the Joint Chiefs and overcome "inherent service desires for self-sufficiency." By ruling out a military chief of staff, however, the recommendations left intact a system whereby each of the Joint Chiefs could exercise what amounted to a veto over military strategy and policy, and thus guaranteed that current disputes would continue, that strategic planning would

---

[88] Eberstadt to Lippmann, 7 March 1949, Eberstadt Papers, box 103, folder: Lippmann, Walter, 1945–47, 1951, 1958–59.

[89] C.B. Stauffacher (Budget Bureau) memorandum to the director, 6 January 1949, Frederick J. Lawton Papers (Truman Library), box 7, Correspondence – Director – Staff Memoranda; Budget Bureau staff memorandum on the proposals by the secretary of defense, 30 November 1948, RG 51, Series 39.32, box 74, folder: National Security Act Amendments of 1949 – To Establish a Department of Defense, Legislation and Staff Memos, January 1948–January 1949. See also W.F. Schaub (Budget Bureau) memorandum to the director, 29 November 1948, RG 51, Series 39.32, box 74, folder: National Security Act Amendments of 1949 – To Establish a Department of Defense, Legislation and Staff Memos, January 1948–January 1949; and *Forrestal Diaries*, 539–40.

entail substantial waste, and that defense budgets would be much larger than needed. Vandenberg was disgusted. At the very least, he thought, the Joint Chiefs should act by majority vote and should have a chairman, perhaps a fourth member who did not represent a particular service. Eisenhower agreed. He "sounded off in very strong language about the Eberstadt report and about Eberstadt's wisdom and personal judgment in presenting such a report."[90]

Similar complaints came from dissenting members of both the Eberstadt task force and the Hoover Commission. These included Dean Acheson, who served as vice chairman of the Hoover Commission, and former Secretary of the Army Robert Patterson and former Assistant Secretary of the Army John J. McCloy, both of whom served on the Eberstadt task force. Neither Patterson nor McCloy thought that Eberstadt's reforms went far enough to stop the interservice feuds, the empire-building, and the self-aggrandizement that was so detrimental to efficiency and security. Patterson still envisioned a single department with a military chief of staff and a civilian secretary whose authority was comprehensive. McCloy recommended a chief of staff who would preside over the Joint Chiefs, supervise his own general staff, serve as principal military adviser to the secretary of defense, and sit on the NSC, where he would learn more about the role that economic considerations must play in the formulation of defense policy. Neither man worried about concentrating too much power in the hands of a military chief of staff. McCloy thought that fears of a "man on horseback" amounted to a "complex," and both he and Patterson were more concerned about the current system, under which a pattern of divided authority precluded economies and left the United States vulnerable to disasters like the one at Pearl Harbor.[91] Acheson reached similar conclusions, arguing that a single chief of staff would bring economies and actually result in a clear line of authority

---

[90] Vandenberg memorandum for the record, 5 January 1949, and Vandenberg memorandum to Symington, 17 January 1949, Vandenberg Papers, box 43, folder: Chief of Staff; Stauffacher memorandum for the director, 6 January 1949, Lawton Papers, box 7, folder: Correspondence – Director – Staff Memoranda. See also Vandenberg to Symington, 12 January 1949, Clifford Papers, box 11, folder: National Military Establishment – Hoover Commission Recommendations on National Security Organization; and Vandenberg memorandum to Symington, 21 March 1949, Vandenberg Papers, box 32, folder: Vandenberg Files, 1949.

[91] McCloy to Eberstadt, 1 November 1948, and Patterson to Eberstadt, 9 November 1948, Patterson Papers, General Correspondence, box 30, folder: 1947–1952, Commission on the Organization of the Executive Branch, Oct. 1948–June 1950. See also McCloy to Eberstadt, 18 November 1948, Eberstadt Papers, box 72, folder: Hoover Commission Files; Correspondence and Related Materials, 1948–49: McCloy, John J.

for carrying out presidential decisions. "We believe," read the dissent that embraced his views, "that a single chief of staff will strengthen, not weaken the tradition of civilian control of the military, a tradition which is held most closely by our people and one which we think needs reaffirmation by action."[92]

Thinking in the White House and the Budget Bureau coincided to some extent with these dissenting views. The president was so unhappy with Forrestal's recommendations that he warned the secretary against publishing them in his annual report.[93] He also thought that Eberstadt's report did not go far enough, and he ordered his colleagues in the White House and the Budget Bureau to formulate a response. As they did so, they found nothing to change their earlier view that the National Security Act of 1947 had not done enough to equip civilian leaders with the authority they needed to produce a coherent defense program within the framework of the president's budget priorities. On the contrary, it had dispersed authority through the military establishment, so that the president depended on several service secretaries and the Joint Chiefs for guidance. What is more, by establishing such arrangements and by giving each of the services a seat on the NSC, it had created the appearance if not the substance of military predominance.[94]

George Elsey, Clark Clifford, and their allies in the White House and the Budget Bureau wanted to correct these problems by shifting more resources and more authority to the secretary of defense, even if the service departments and the Joint Chiefs remained intact. Like Eberstadt and Forrestal, they would remove the service secretaries from the NSC, eliminate the word "general" from section 202 of the original act, and appoint an undersecretary of defense. But they would also add at least three assistant secretaries and appoint a military chief of staff at the head of an integrated general staff, a position that was particularly important to them, as it was to the dissenters on the Eberstadt committee and the Hoover Commission. To "dodge" that appointment was "to toy with

[92] Hoover report, 25–30. The quotes are from 25, 28.

[93] Truman memorandum to Forrestal, 3 December 1948, RG 51, Series 39.32, box 74, folder: National Security Act Amendments for 1949 – To Establish a Department of Defense, Legislation and Staff Memos, January 1948–January 1949.

[94] Elsey memorandum to Clifford, 17 November 1948, Elsey Papers, box 83, folder: National Defense – Armed Forces Unification. For a critique of the National Security Act coming from the Budget Bureau see the statement by Frank Pace, Jr., before the Hoover Commission, 6 October 1948, RG 51, Series 39.32, box 70, folder: Recommendations of the Hoover Commission re Organization for National Security, 1948–49. See also the sources cited in the following note.

the national security" and to stop short of real unification and effective civilian control of the military. There was irony, these officials would concede, in the idea of vesting civilian control in a military chief of staff. But to their way of thinking, only such an official could bring order to the Joint Chiefs and reassert the president's authority. To do all of this would take a "military agent through whom civilian control of the military will be maintained."[95]

VI

By the end of January 1949, Eberstadt and Hoover, Forrestal and the military services, the White House and the Budget Bureau had all staked out positions on how to revise the National Security Act. The time for a resolution had come, and Clifford took the lead by opening negotiations with Forrestal, the service secretaries, and Frank Pace, Jr., who had replaced Webb as director of the Budget Bureau. By mid-February the negotiators had hammered out an accord on some but not all of the key points. They agreed to convert the National Military Establishment into a single executive department, called the Department of Defense, with the Army, Navy, and Air Force becoming military rather than executive departments within the new agency. They also agreed to enhance the secretary's authority by removing the word "general" from section 202 of the National Security Act, as well as language reserving to the military departments all powers and responsibilities not vested in the secretary. In addition, the accord would provide for an undersecretary and three

---

95 Budget Bureau staff memorandum on the proposals by the secretary of defense for amendment of the National Security Act, 30 November 1948, and BOB staff working paper on unification of the armed forces, 22 November 1948, RG 51, Series 39.32, folder: National Security Act Amendments of 1949 – To Establish a Department of Defense, Legislation and Staff Memos, January 1948–January 1949. For thinking in the Budget Bureau and the White House on reorganization of the military establishment and the proposals coming from Forrestal, the Eberstadt Committee, and the Hoover Commission see also Budget Bureau working paper, 18 November 1948, unsigned draft memorandum on changes in the National Security Act suggested by the secretary of defense, 29 November 1948, unsigned memorandum, "Legislative Changes Needed to Improve the Administration of the National Military Establishment," 8 December 1948, and unsigned discussion memorandums on national security, 8 and 9 December 1948, RG 51, Series 39.32, box 74, folder: National Security Act Amendments of 1949 – To Establish a Department of Defense, Legislation and Staff Memos, January 1948–January 1949; unsigned memorandum, "Proposals by the Secretary of Defense for Amendment of the National Security Act," Elsey Papers, box 88, folder: National Defense – Armed Forces Unification; and undated, unsigned memorandum "Recommendations of the Hoover Commission in its Report on National Security Organization," RG 51, Series 39.32, box 70, folder: Recommendations of the Hoover Commission re Organization for National Security, 1948–49.

assistant secretaries, remove the service secretaries from the NSC, eliminate their right of appeal directly to the president, and do away with any limitations on the size of the joint staff. The president would have the right to appoint a chairman of the Joint Chiefs, who would take precedence over all other officers in the armed forces, head the joint staff, and function as principal military adviser to the president and secretary of defense.[96]

The agreement did not measure up to what reformers like Acheson, McCloy, and Patterson had envisioned or to what the Army and Air Force had expected. It did not merge the armed forces into a single department, reduce the service secretaries to undersecretaries, provide a military staff to the secretary of defense, or establish a powerful chief of staff. Clifford was doubtful that a general staff system could win support in Congress or would actually strengthen civilian control of the military, and Forrestal was still leery of the "Army pattern," by which he meant one department and a military chain of command that proceeded from a single, powerful chief of staff. In a speech to the National Press Club, delivered just as he was negotiating terms with Clifford and Pace, Forrestal said again that what the secretary of defense required was a single military leader who would do little more than advise him on military policies and decide split decisions in the Joint Chiefs of Staff. In no way did he envision a powerful military official who might, in his view, undermine civilian control of the military, which both tradition and the Constitution had reserved to the president.[97]

The president felt the same way. Truman had gone on record over the years as supporting a greater degree of military unification within the framework of a single executive department. He had even endorsed the idea of a single chief of staff during the early debates over what became the National Security Act. But as we have seen, a deep streak of antimilitarism also ran through his thinking and had contributed to his decision in 1947 to abandon the idea of a military chief of staff. Much the same thing happened when Truman wrestled with the agreement

---

[96] Forrestal, Pace, and Clifford, memorandum to Truman, 10 February 1949, Truman Papers, PSF-Subject File, box 194, folder: NSC – Miscellaneous Data.

[97] For a record of the Navy's dissent see the marginal comments on two drafts of the Forrestal, Pace, and Clifford memorandum to Truman, 4 and 8 February 1949, Elsey Papers, box 83, folder: National Defense – Armed Forces Unification. On Forrestal's speech see the Budget Bureau memorandum (M.W.A.) for the files on the views of the secretary of defense to the National Press Club, 4 February 1949, RG 51, Series 39.32, box 74, folder: National Security Act Amendments 1949 – To Establish a Department of Defense, Legislation and Staff Memos, February–March 1949.

negotiated by Forrestal, Clifford, and Pace. Meeting in the White House with these and other officials, he again decided against a single chief of staff, despite strong support for the idea from the Budget Bureau. He opted instead for a chairman of the Joint Chiefs on the assumption that such an official would actually facilitate civilian control while a military chief of staff might weaken it.

At the same meeting, on 16 February, the president also assured the services that neither the secretary of defense nor the chairman of the Joint Chiefs would have the authority to transfer administrative or military functions arbitrarily from one service to another or from the services to the office of the secretary. Marx Leva, one of Forrestal's aides, thought that Truman had gone a long way toward addressing concerns in the Navy Department, where the admirals still wanted an arrangement that reserved for the services a certain degree of autonomy. Leva was right, of course, although Truman's decisions were driven less by a concern for the Navy than by a deep-seated suspicion of brass hats, to use his term, and by a strong desire to frame a proposal that squared with the tradition of civilian control and the constitutional prerogatives of the president.[98]

On 5 March, three weeks after the White House meeting, Truman asked Congress to amend the National Security Act in order to keep our "security organization abreast of our security requirements," which he said was a lesson of the last war. He stressed the need to reconcile the organizational imperatives of national security with the tradition of civilian control, and recommended the reforms hammered out at the White House meeting of 16 February. These reforms, Truman said, would further progress toward unification of the armed forces, make for greater efficiency and economy in the defense budget, and strengthen "civilian authority and control over the military forces." He cited Eberstadt's report on the last point and then urged Congress to rectify the problem by putting more authority in the hands of top Pentagon officials, including the proposed chairman of the Joint Chiefs of Staff.[99]

Although Truman's proposal stopped short of satisfying reformers like Royall, it went too far for those like Eberstadt, who wanted to improve but not discard the existing system of decentralized and coordinated

---

[98] For a summary of Truman's position see Forrestal, Pace, and Clifford memorandum to Truman, 4 February 1949, Elsey Papers, box 83, folder: National Defense – Armed Forces Unification. For the White House meeting see Leva memorandum to Forrestal, 17 February 1949, RG 330, CD 12-1-1.

[99] Truman, "Special Message to the Congress on Reorganization of the National Military Establishment," 5 March 1949, *Public Papers, Truman, 1949*, 163–66.

decision making. Still worse, while Royall was prepared to swallow his reservations, Eberstadt was not. He did not think that centralizing authority was compatible with good government. Nor could he understand how such authority in the hands of military officials would safeguard civilian rule. For these reasons, he rejected Truman's proposal for three assistant secretaries of defense. He also doubted the wisdom of granting precedence to the chairman of the Joint Chiefs and of making him rather than the chiefs as a group the principal military adviser to the president and the secretary. These changes, together with an unspecified expansion of the Joint Staff, amounted in Eberstadt's mind to the creation of a dangerous general staff system.[100]

The Joint Chiefs took the same position, but for reasons that had less to do with the principle of civilian rule than with protecting their own powers and prerogatives. They did not want the proposed chairman to exercise command over other members of the Joint Chiefs, to function as an independent military adviser to the president and the secretary of defense, or to have the joint staff under his control. In these respects, the chiefs sought to retain their own authority rather than enhance that of others. Forrestal, moreover, agreed with most of their argument, although he did balk at proposals that were intended to maximize their influence over other agencies while minimizing their accountability to civilian authorities.[101]

These differences came to light when the Senate opened hearings on a bill that embodied the president's recommendations. In the resulting testimony, all sides were anxious to reorganize the military establishment and give the secretary of defense more authority and assistance. But Hoover and Eberstadt again warned that concentrating too much authority in a single man or office was "an extremely dangerous thing to do." For this reason, they remained sharply critical of proposals to appoint assistant secretaries, demote the service secretaries, or make the proposed chairman, rather than the Joint Chiefs as a group, the principal military adviser to the president and secretary of defense. On the other side, predictably, were Secretary of the Army Royall, Secretary of the Air Force Symington, and former Secretary of War Patterson, all of whom wanted everything that Hoover and Eberstadt opposed, namely,

---

[100] Acting Secretary of the Army William H. Draper to Clifford, 13 February 1949, RG 330, CD 12-1-1; and Eberstadt to Hoover, 30 March 1949, Eberstadt Papers, box 72, folder: Hoover Commission Files; Correspondence and Related Materials, 1948–49.

[101] Denfeld to Forrestal, 25 March 1949, and Forrestal memorandum to the Joint Chiefs, 26 March 1949, RG 218, CCS 040 (11-2-43), Sec. 6.

a secretary of defense and a chairman of the Joint Chiefs who had clear authority over the armed forces.

The differences were sharply contested and personal. Eberstadt constantly traded insults with Royall, Symington, and other Pentagon policy makers. He thought the armed forces were led by narrow-minded men who fought the same battles over and over again. He said that Symington was rude, contentious, and insubordinate, and was especially hard on the Air Force for permitting its plan for seventy air groups to dictate national policy. Royall, for his part, never overcame his conviction that Eberstadt had been a Navy partisan from the start and was utterly incapable of rendering objective advice. Symington, who liked to brag about his success as an industrialist, dismissed Eberstadt as a "private citizen" who "had little operating experience" and was consistently hostile to the military.[102]

After several weeks of hearings, the Senate committee finally reported a bill that struck something of a compromise between the two factions. The bill would transform the National Military Establishment into an executive department – the Department of Defense – and the service departments into military departments. It would give the secretary rights and responsibilities similar to those of other cabinet officers, in part by eliminating the word "general" from section 202 of the National Security Act. Under this arrangement, the military departments would still be administered by their own secretaries but under the unqualified direction and control of the secretary of defense, who would now be assisted by an undersecretary or a deputy secretary, by special assistants, and by a chairman of the Joint Chiefs who was superior in rank to his colleagues. In addition, the service secretaries would be deprived of their seats on the NSC and their right to appeal decisions directly to the president.

The compromise went some distance toward enhancing the authority of the secretary of defense while scaling back the independence and stature of the individual services. But by no stretch of the imagination did it merge the services into a single department with an all-powerful secretary and a military chief of staff. As finally reported, it retained the individual service secretaries, capped the size of the joint staff at

---

[102] Symington to Senator Millard Tydings, Eberstadt Papers, box 102, folder: Leva, Marx, 1947–50. See also Royal to Hoover, 27 April 1949, Eberstadt Papers, box 146, folder: Royall, Kenneth C., 1946, 1948–49; Eberstadt to Secretary Johnson, 20 May 1949, Eberstadt Papers, box 102, folder: Leva, Marx, 1947–50; Eberstadt to Senator Byrd, 20 May 1949, Eberstadt Papers, box 71, folder: Hoover Commission Files, Correspondence and Related Materials, 1949: Byrd, Harry F.; and *Congressional Quarterly Almanac, 1949* 5:477. See also the sources cited in the following note.

210 officers, and restricted the powers of the proposed chairman of the Joint Chiefs by making him a nonvoting member of that body, limiting his term in office, and denying him military command of the armed forces.[103]

On the Senate floor, the committee's compromise ran into strong objections from Republican Wayne Morse of Oregon, who offered a series of amendments that again aimed at greater centralization of decision making. Those who supported the amendments spoke once more of the need for strong leadership if economic liberties and democratic traditions were going to be protected. Under the compromise bill, according to Morse, the proposed chairman would be a mere "figurehead." Neither he nor the secretary would have enough authority to really "knock heads together," which to Morse was the best way to ensure civilian over military rule and avoid bankrupting "our free economy." Those on the other side of the debate again resorted to a strategy of otherness to discredit their opponents, in effect, turning Morse's arguments upside down and warning against a German general staff that gave too much power to too few people. In the end the opponents prevailed, and the measure passed the Senate without the amendments.[104]

The Senate bill might have sailed through the House had it not been for the B-36 controversy, which reached its furious peak just as the Senate was acting. The controversy led the House to set the Senate bill aside pending congressional investigations into the controversy and the subsequent revolt of the admirals. These investigations could have worked to the advantage of those who wanted to subject defiant generals and revolting admirals to greater presidential control through a stronger secretary of defense and a new military chief of staff. But just the opposite seems to have happened. While the Navy's revolt strengthened the case for reform, it also drove home the danger of concentrating substantial power in any government official or agency, especially in the government's military arm. The constant interservice feuding reinforced the conviction of those who believed with Eberstadt that admirals and generals were all muscle and no gray matter, "weight-lifters," as Eberstadt called them, who could not be trusted with too much power. Reacting in this manner,

---

[103] For the hearings see U.S. Congress, Senate, *Hearings on S. 1269 and S. 1843, A Bill to Convert the National Military Establishment into an Executive Department of the Government* (Washington, 1949). The Committee's report, *National Security Act Amendments of 1949*, Report No. 366, 81st Cong., 1st sess., is printed in ibid.

[104] *Congressional Quarterly Almanac, 1949* 5:478–79. See also *Congressional Record, 1949* 95:6094–97, 6621–35, 6703–18, 6725–26, 6781–88, 6871–79.

for example, Lewis Strauss, who had served on Eberstadt's committee, began to wonder whether the committee's conservative recommendations had gone too far toward centralizing authority in the Pentagon – whether in military or civilian hands. Even liberal critics and well-known centralizers like David Lilienthal began to develop misgivings. After watching the blust and blunder that typified Johnson's management style, especially his high-handed cancellation of the supercarrier, Lilienthal came to the conclusion that vesting a "terrific" amount of power in the wrong individual would be "a strain for democracy."[105]

In the end, the balance tipped in favor of those who were convinced that concentrating substantial new authority in the national security establishment was the kind of state making that would imperil democracy. To be sure, they wanted to discipline the armed forces and promote economy, but not at the expense of decentralized decision making, which they associated with good government and democracy. They would not give the secretary of defense unrestricted authority over the military departments and other agencies of the national security establishment. Nor would they support a military chief of staff in the name of civilian rule. This kind of thinking had guided the proposal that Truman and his aides presented in March, and much the same was true of the bill passed by the Senate, of a second reorganization plan that Truman outlined in the summer of 1949, and of the reorganization bill that finally passed the House. The House's version added a series of provisions to improve budgeting and accounting procedures in the Pentagon, but otherwise failed to alter the Senate's bill in ways favored by reformers in the Army, Air Force, and Budget Bureau. A House–Senate conference committee then endorsed the amalgam and both houses approved the final bill shortly thereafter.[106]

VII

Under the National Security Act, the military establishment had not been able to harmonize interservice differences, produce a coherent strategic plan, eliminate waste, or save money. It had failed to meet expectations, and one result was to call into question the competence of the armed

---

[105] Eberstadt to Lippmann, 7 March 1949, Eberstadt Papers, box 103, folder: Lippmann, Walter, 1945–47, 1949, 1951, 1958–59; Lilienthal, *Atomic Energy Years*, 508–9.

[106] *Congressional Quarterly Almanac, 1949* 5:479–81; Walter Millis, with Harvey C. Mansfield and Harold Stein, *Arms and the State: Civil–Military Elements in National Policy* (New York, 1958), 233–34.

forces and the supremacy of civilian authority. Another was to trigger demands for organizational reform, which raised again the central issue of state making in the early Cold War. The country's security as well as its solvency seemed to require a system of centralized decision making that did not at the same time compromise the principle of civilian rule, including presidential and congressional prerogatives. In particular, it seemed essential to endow the secretary of defense and his aides with more authority than most had thought desirable in 1947. But just how this could be done without compromising constitutional principles remained at the center of a continuing debate.

One group of policy makers, including those in the Army and the Air Force, as well as reformers such as Acheson and McCloy, saw no problem with concentrating considerable power in the hands of a military leader, so long as he operated as an agent of civilian authority. On the contrary, they were convinced that such an arrangement was the only way to eliminate waste, regulate interservice rivalries, prevent the abuses associated with the admirals' revolt, and bring effective civilian control. But a second group saw things differently. To this group, which included Eberstadt, the arrangements proposed by Acheson, McCloy, and others actually ran the risk of tilting the balance too far in the direction of centralized decision making and military rather than civilian rule. It was this group that led the way to a compromise that involved a greater degree of centralized decision making but without draining all authority from the military departments or the Joint Chiefs into the hands of the secretary of defense and his agents.

Familiar dichotomies characterized this debate over defense reorganization, including centralization versus decentralization, civilian versus military, democracy versus the garrison state, and the same rhetorical tensions were evident in the battle over the budget for fiscal year 1950. In the case of the budget, policy makers in the Pentagon, especially those in the armed forces, relied on the new ideology of national security to justify ever-expanding budgets, just as that ideology had undergirded some of the demands for more centralized decision making in the National Military Establishment. They stressed the dangers inherent in the new age of semiwar, when the traditional distinction between wartime and peacetime had disappeared. They pointed to the Soviet menace and the need to contain it, the gap between the country's global commitments and its military capabilities, the danger of total war and the need for perpetual preparedness and for a comprehensive security system that embraced all aspects of American life.

Drawing on an older political culture, however, critics of the national security state, especially economizers in Congress and in various government agencies, emphasized the danger that perceived national security imperatives posed to the "fundamental values and institutions inherent in our way of life." The resulting discourse revolved around such familiar dichotomies as relative security versus total security, the individual versus the state, private versus public, balanced budgets versus budget deficits, economic liberties versus regimentation, the "claims of national security against those of civilian economy."

Seen in this light, traditional values and older ways of thinking operated as a check on the development of the national security state. They drove policy makers at both ends of the national security discourse toward a set of compromises that would supposedly balance the needs of security against those of economy and democracy. Truman had gone a long way toward establishing this balance in his budget policies, and the same kind of compromise had shaped the defense reorganization that Congress approved in 1949. It only remained to be seen if the desired balance could be sustained as the Cold War heated up.

6

Preparing for Permanent War
Economy, Science, and Secrecy in the National Security State

In the ideology of national security, the distinction between war and peace had disappeared in a new era of permanent preparedness that embraced every segment of the nation's society and economy. Needed were plans to harness essential assets to the nation's security and government agencies with enough authority to implement these plans, including plans for the mobilization of science and scientific manpower. Not only that; government had to safeguard economic and scientific secrets by regulating the exchange of information, ensuring the loyalty of federal employees, and guarding against the dangers of internal subversion. In all these areas the national security discourse was essentially a discourse in state making, and the challenge, as in building a new military establishment, was to remake existing institutions or create new ones without wrecking the democratic foundations on which they were erected.

This was a difficult task, in part because national security planners had to take account of established interests, older values, and cherished traditions. Indeed, their quest for authority often challenged the prerogatives of more traditional agencies and groups, not to mention free-market principles and normal government procedures, with results that led to bitter quarrels over how power should be divided, distributed, and held accountable. Economic mobilizers envisioned an operating as well as a planning agency with enough power to override the rights and interests of established authorities. Leading scientists sought a partnership with government on terms that shielded their work from congressional oversight and presidential control. The armed forces demanded similar terms when it came to mobilizing the nation's resources, including those essential to the development of atomic energy. At the very least they wanted a high degree of autonomy from civilian authority; at most they wanted independent control of the resources required for military preparedness and modern warfare.

What security planners, scientists, and military leaders had in mind raised basic questions about the nature of the national security state, particularly about the connection between traditional values and new institutions, and the debate that ensued highlighted again the contested nature of state making and national identity in the early Cold War. President Truman hoped to reconcile the search for security with democratic principles and constitutional guarantees, but his efforts in this direction brought him into conflict with those who sought a high degree of independence from government control or favored security measures that would sacrifice civil liberties in the name of national defense. This was the case with plans to mobilize science and the economy behind the defense program, bring atomic energy under civilian control, and guarantee the loyalty of federal employees. In all these areas, public policy raised the dark specter of the garrison state, which remained the dominant rhetorical symbol in the national security discourse. In all these areas, the president found himself in a bitter battle with congressional conservatives, especially in the Republican Party. And in all these areas, that battle led eventually to a set of negotiated compromises similar to those that had emerged in the debates over budget policy, military training, and organization of the defense establishment.

II

When it came to peacetime mobilization planning, the problem was how to prepare the country for total war without surrendering to military domination or undermining the economic liberties associated with a free-market system. In wartime, the government had necessarily exercised extensive control over the national economy, the result during World War II being a centralized system of economic coordination administered through the War Production Board and the Office of War Mobilization. But what kind of organization was appropriate for peacetime mobilization planning in a country with constitutional principles and democratic traditions? This was the question, and the way in which it was answered would indicate the degree to which the new ideology of national security had displaced an older way of thinking.

When Congress passed the National Security Act of 1947 it established the National Security Resources Board (NSRB) to advise the president on mobilization policies "in the event of war." Like other agencies created by the act, the NSRB was the brainchild of James Forrestal and Ferdinand Eberstadt, both of whom were convinced that the United States had entered an era of permanent struggle, for which it had to be prepared on a permanent basis. The NSRB was to be one of the mechanisms for achieving preparedness. It was to provide, "for the first time in the country's history," a peacetime agency to coordinate mobilization plans across the government, assess military readiness and the availability of essential commodities, and advise the president on strategic resources and the proper balance between civilian and military requirements. Forrestal envisioned an agency with considerable prestige and operating authority, much like the War Production Board or the Office of War Mobilization. Sounding a major theme in the ideology of national security, he told a congressional committee that modern war was total war, and that total war involved every segment of society. Needed, he said, was a permanent agency with a skilled professional staff and enough authority to mobilize all of the country's resources and every branch of government behind the nation's security.[1]

As legislated into existence, however, the NSRB was less powerful than Forrestal and Eberstadt had recommended, in part because Truman was determined to preserve his prerogatives as commander in chief and the constitutional system of checks and balances. As others have shown, the same determination had led the president to establish the National Security Council as a relatively weak organization, one that would meet irregularly, use a staff borrowed from other agencies, and coordinate the concerns of these agencies, not displace them. To be sure, different circumstances could produce different results, as when Truman sought to unify the armed forces under an organizational scheme that concentrated considerable authority in the hands of a strong secretary of defense. But in each instance, the president's goal was an organizational arrangement that could reconcile the nation's security needs with its political values and established institutions.[2]

In the NSRB case, the Budget Bureau recommended an organizational set-up similar to that of the NSC. It urged the NSRB to organize a joint staff, rather than one of its own, and to otherwise rely on the resources

[1] Unsigned Budget Bureau memorandum, "Organization of the National Security Resources Board," 10 October 1947, Webb Papers, box 18, folder: Bureau of the Budget: Mobilization. See also Webb memorandum for the president, 8 August 1947, Truman Papers, PSF-Subject File, box 156, folder: Defense, Secy of National Defense; undated Bureau of the Budget memorandum, "The National Military Establishment Explanatory Statement," RG 51, Series 47.8a, box 45, folder: 1949 Budget – General; Ralph J. Watkins, "Economic Mobilization," *American Political Science Review* 43 (June 1949): 555–63; Rearden, *Formative Years*, 129; and Forrestal testimony in U.S. Congress, Senate, *Hearings Pursuant to S. Res. 46, A Resolution Authorizing and Directing an Investigation of the National Defense Program* (Washington, 1948), 25581–613.

[2] Unsigned Budget Bureau memorandum, "Organization of the National Security Resources Board"; Sander, "Truman and the National Security Council," 347–88; Anna K. Nelson, "President Truman and the Evolution of the National Security Council," *Journal of American History*, 72 (September 1985): 360–78.

available in other government departments. It was to be headed by its own civilian chairman but was to include representatives of the various departments with a role in wartime mobilization. It was to work so far as possible through these departments, coordinating rather than controlling their efforts, and was to connect itself to the private sector through a variety of advisory committees, including those organized by the participating departments. In theory, at least, this was to be a corporative system of administration over which the president would preside. It was to balance centralizing and decentralizing tendencies, and it had the advantage of involving all interested parties without entrusting too much authority to any one of them.[3]

This system of administration came under attack almost immediately. Though similar in many respects to the organizational set-up that Forrestal and Eberstadt had proposed for the defense establishment, it had little support from the new secretary of defense, who apparently believed that it went too far in the direction of decentralized administration and would therefore blunt civilian leadership over the military in the important field of economic mobilization. Arthur M. Hill, whom Forrestal selected as the NSRB's first chairman, had similar reservations. President of the Greyhound Corporation and a personal friend of the secretary, Hill was a stubborn man with a prickly personality and a low tolerance for teamwork. He agreed with Forrestal that mobilization planning could work only if the NSRB had more authority, and he set out to acquire that authority without regard for the interests of other agencies.

Hill's first encounter in his effort to strengthen the NSRB was with a rival mobilization agency, the Munitions Board, which had also been established by the National Security Act of 1947. Formerly the Army–Navy Munitions Board, this agency was supposed to advise the secretary of defense on the human and material resources required by the armed forces in war and peace. Its first chairman was Thomas J. Hargrave, the president of Eastman Kodak Company and another of Forrestal's friends, and its responsibilities overlapped to some extent with those of the NSRB.[4] The NSRB was responsible for a coordinated industrial, military, and civilian mobilization scheme, while the Munitions Board

---

3 Unsigned Budget Bureau memorandum, "Organization of the National Security Resources Board"; Rearden, *Formative Years*, 129–30; Harry B. Yoshpe, *The National Security Resources Board, 1947–1953: A Case Study in Peacetime Mobilization Planning* (Washington, 1953), 11.

4 Unsigned Budget Bureau memorandum, "Organization of the National Security Resources Board"; Yoshpe, *National Security Resources Board*, 11; and Rearden, *Formative Years*, 90–91.

planned the military aspects of mobilization and was more or less an advocate of the armed forces. There were other redundancies as well. As the newest incarnation of an older agency, the Munitions Board had a substantial staff, considerable experience, and well-established relationships with other government agencies, not to mention an extensive network of private advisory groups to help it translate military requirements into plans for the utilization of manpower and the production of essential supplies.[5]

This is not to say that the Munitions Board had already developed a capacity to perform its assigned tasks well. Despite the National Security Act, it still had to deal with a fractious military establishment in which the armed forces resisted every effort to unify their functions. Under these circumstances, the board found it difficult to speak for the armed services as a whole or to develop joint policies. On the contrary, as an agent of the secretary of defense rather than the individual services, the board tended to arouse more suspicion than enthusiasm from the Joint Chiefs and other military leaders, who did their best to hamstring its operations or bend them to their purposes.

The armed forces, for example, successfully opposed Forrestal's plan to strengthen the board's authority by transforming Hargrave's chairmanship from a part-time to a full-time position. Their success left the board's day-to-day operations largely under the control of an executive committee of military officers who saw themselves as representing their respective services rather than the Office of the Secretary of Defense. They wanted the board to function as a planning rather than as an operating agency, and the planning they envisioned would consist primarily of coordinating the mobilization schemes dreamed up by the individual services. With this idea in mind, they also resisted efforts to strengthen the board by appointing a full-time deputy chairman. Forrestal eventually prevailed on this question and also managed, in June 1948, to issue a directive giving the Munitions Board a more unified staff under the leadership of a permanent director. But the services were able to keep the new staff under their control, and they succeeded at the same time in preventing the board from playing much more than a coordinating role when it came to planning for wartime mobilization.[6]

The armed services were even more reluctant to see their autonomy trimmed in favor of a strictly civilian agency like the NSRB. Indeed,

---

[5] Unsigned Budget Bureau memorandum, "Organization of the National Security Resources Board."
[6] Rearden, *Formative Years*, 91–93.

they used the Munitions Board as a shield against what they saw as an intrusion of civilian authority into the realm of military affairs. The most desirable relationship, they said, was to confine the NSRB "to planning rather than to operations" and to have all "contacts with industry occur through ... the Munitions Board." Clearly their goal was to preserve the autonomy and freedom of the armed forces, and to achieve this goal they wanted to assign as many responsibilities as possible to the Munitions Board, instead of the NSRB, and to bring the board under their control.

The struggle between the Munitions Board and the NSRB took place on two fronts. On one front, the battle concerned the definition of civilian and military requirements, with the NSRB arguing for a mobilization plan that balanced the two requirements and the Munitions Board calling for one that specified minimum civilian needs while leaving all other resources to military purposes. The struggle on the second front developed when the Pentagon pushed for a mobilization scheme that gave the military establishment, through the Munitions Board, the job of economic planning. Under this proposal, the NSRB would be reduced to reviewing the board's work, which meant that civilian officials would do little more than advise their military counterparts on the economic aspects of mobilization.[7]

Clearly the NSRB needed considerable power if it was going to prevail in these battles, or so Forrestal believed, but his efforts to enhance the board's power kept running up against the bureaucratic interests and corporatist strategies supported in other government agencies, not just the Pentagon. In late 1947, Forrestal and Hill asked the White House to approve a presidential directive ordering all government departments to provide the NSRB with whatever information it required. In the background was the work of a Senate committee headed by Republican Owen Brewster of Maine. Set up to investigate the wartime defense program, the committee also heard testimony on postwar policies and issued a report calling for a "super-czar" with a presidential mandate to oversee the development and implementation of a comprehensive mobilization plan.[8] As Forrestal saw it, Congress had commissioned the NSRB to

---

7 *Forrestal Diaries*, 329–30. See also Vandenberg, "Meeting of the Three Secretaries with Secretary Forrestal," 13 October 1947, Vandenberg Papers, box 52, folder: National Security Resources Board; Yoshpe, *National Security Resources Board*, 49–55; and Rearden, *Formative Years*, 130–31.

8 Arnold Miles (Budget Bureau) to Webb, 30 April 1948, Elsey Papers, box 83, folder: National Defense – Armed Forces Unification. See also *Hearings Pursuant to S. Res. 46*, 25581–634, 25634–57, 25735–83, 25787–89; [Brewster Committee], *Report on Industrial Mobilization for War* (Washington, 1948); and *Forrestal Diaries*, 332.

perform these functions, which made Hill the logical choice for the job of super-czar. This proposal, however, drew fire from key members of the cabinet, who correctly perceived it as a threat to their own authority as department heads. They said that Hill could do no more than "request" the information he desired and argued that whatever authority he possessed derived indirectly from the president through the NSRB, which is to say through themselves as board members. Truman apparently agreed, and no presidential directive was forthcoming.[9]

Hill and Forrestal were still reeling from this setback when Truman dealt them another blow. This came in the aftermath of the communist coup in Czechoslovakia, when Hill asked the White House to include a provision in the proposed selective service bill giving him the authority to set manpower policies. As he saw it, the old distinction between war and peace was little more than a "technicality" in an age when the United States had to be prepared for war on a permanent basis, which could only be done if the NSRB had complete authority to bring selective service into line with policies pertaining to the mobilization of manpower. This argument appealed to Forrestal, but got nowhere with the Budget Bureau, where officials still saw a difference between war and peace. Budget Director James Webb absolutely refused to surrender to the NSRB policy prerogatives that properly belonged to the president, laying out a case that Truman then recapitulated in a blunt letter to Hill. The NSRB, Truman said, must not assume "executive functions." The president's "authority and necessary freedom to direct the Executive Branch would be attenuated by statutory provisions requiring any agency to adhere to policy determinations of the Board."[10]

Similar issues arose as the war scare continued to deepen in the spring and summer of 1948. The Munitions Board, which was still dominated by the armed forces, began talking about an overall control agency that would direct the mobilization activities of the government as a whole. The board conveyed these ideas to the NSRB, where they found their way into a report to the president and then into a study commissioned by Hill and drafted by Ferdinand Eberstadt. Both documents again contemplated an addition to the board's authority. They noted the burden that preparedness placed on the civilian economy, called for a

9 *Forrestal Diaries*, 332. See also Miles to Webb, 30 April 1948, Elsey Papers, box 83, folder: National Defense – Armed Forces Unification.
10 Hill to Truman, 24 March 1948, and Truman to Hill, 1 April 1948, Webb Papers, box 18, folder: Bureau of the Budget: Mobilization. See also undated Webb letter to Hill, ibid., folder: Bureau of the Budget; and Yoshpe, *National Security Resources Board*, 22–23.

governmentwide program of production and allocation priorities, and urged the creation of a "final authority" to oversee such a program. The NSRB was the "final authority" that Eberstadt had in mind, as did Hill, who would also eliminate other restrictions on the NSRB's ability to operate as a full-scale mobilization agency with the power to direct all government departments.[11]

According to Edwin Nourse, Hill and Eberstadt had erred by starting "from the premise that we now enter a stage of preliminary mobilization or a war economy rather than a peace economy." Along with Webb, Nourse assumed that a line could still be drawn between war and peace, which meant that the NSRB should confine itself to advising the president on mobilization policies.[12] In addition, Webb and his colleagues in the Budget Bureau were as jealous as ever of the president's prerogatives and just as determined to maintain a decentralized and representative pattern of administration. They saw no reason to believe that a concentration of authority had done much good in World War II, and they were convinced that Hill had fallen under the "bad influence" of Eberstadt and his friends in the "military departments," who were milking the war scare for everything they could get. Instead of grasping for power, they said, Hill should be attending to the administrative tasks necessary to make the NSRB an effective source of expert advice to the president.[13]

The possibility that Pentagon planners were behind Hill's proposal raised the prospect of military domination that Donald Nelson had complained about in World War II. This was a real prospect to Webb, and it strengthened his resolve to forge a method of mobilization management that safeguarded presidential prerogatives and included other

[11] Draft NSRB document #28, "Recommendations to the President from the National Security Resources Board Relating to the Steps and Measures Essential to the Fulfillment of the National Security Program," 23 April 1948, Elsey Papers, box 82, folder: National Defense – Armed Forces Unification; and *Forrestal Diaries,* 428–29. See also NSRB R-7, "A Recommendation to the President by the National Security Resources Board," 30 April 1947, Truman Papers, PSF-Subject File, box 146, folder: Agencies – National Security Resources Board; Eberstadt report to Hill, 4 June 1948, ibid., folder: National Security Resources Board – Miscellaneous; Yoshpe, *National Security Resources Board,* 23–26; Nourse memorandum, 31 May 1948, Nourse Papers, box 5, folder: Daily Diary; Dorwart, *Eberstadt and Forrestal,* 160–62; and Robert Cuff, "Ferdinand Eberstadt, the National Security Resources Board, and the Search for Integrated Mobilization Planning, 1947–1948," *Public Historian* 7 (Fall 1985): 37–52.

[12] Nourse to Hill, 29 April 1948, Webb Papers, box 18, folder: Bureau of the Budget: Mobilization.

[13] Nourse memorandum, 10 May 1948, Nourse Papers, box 5, folder: Daily Diary.

government departments. Truman shared these views as well. Despite the hysteria in Washington, which he had helped to inspire, the president was determined to keep the country on a peace footing and the NSRB in line with his policies. Given these goals, he organized an ad hoc group to determine whether the current military effort required the allocation and price controls that Hill demanded. This action took some of the steam out of Hill's demand, as did the group's conclusion that more strenuous efforts to expand the stockpile of strategic materials, along with voluntary measures of conservation, would be sufficient to meet anticipated requirements without debilitating inflation or unpopular controls. In addition, Webb accelerated efforts to move the NSRB from the Pentagon to the Executive Office Building, where it would work directly under presidential oversight, and also laid plans to replace Hill with a chairman who was more likely to take his lead from the White House than from the Pentagon.[14]

In his direct reply to Hill's proposal, moreover, Truman amplified the position he had taken previously. Current government policy, he told Hill, was not "one of mobilization for war" but of "preparedness on which a more rapid mobilization could be based." Accordingly, the president did not want to vest the NSRB with "directive authority over any department or agency" or with "a final power of decision." Instead, the board "must consider itself as a Presidential advisory agency," perform this role with the smallest possible staff, and rely so far as possible on other government agencies.[15] Leaving nothing to chance, Truman then followed through by relieving Hill of his position and appointing John R. Steelman, a presidential assistant, as acting chairman of the NSRB. Steelman was a true-blue Truman loyalist who took on the NSRB chairmanship while maintaining his office in the White House and his position as the president's special assistant. There was little danger that he would behave like Hill, who had acted "as though he were the head of an

[14] R. W. Zehring (Budget Bureau) memorandum for the director, 14 May 1948, Webb Papers, box 18, folder: Bureau of the Budget: Mobilization. See also Steelman to Hill, 3 June 1948, ibid.; and Nourse memorandums, 10 and 31 May 1948, Nourse Papers, box 5, folder: Daily Diary.

[15] Truman to Hill, 24 May 1948, Webb Papers, box 18, folder: Bureau of the Budget: Mobilization. Truman's letter to Hill was drafted in the Budget Bureau and closely followed Webb's advice. See Webb memorandum for the president, 24 May 1948, Webb Papers, box 18, folder: Bureau of the Budget: Mobilization. See also Yoshpe, *National Security Resources Board*, 27–28; and Cuff, "Eberstadt, the National Security Resources Board, and the Search for Integrated Mobilization Planning," 50.

independent agency, with only the slightest sense of responsibility to the president."[16] Nor was there any danger that he would take a back seat to the Pentagon or accede to any demands for military domination in the field of economic mobilization.

On the contrary, the new chairman quickly asserted presidential prerogatives in a quarrel with Forrestal. In early 1949, Steelman received a document in which the Munitions Board laid out its role in economic mobilization and its relationship to both the NSRB and the Joint Chiefs of Staff. The document argued specifically that the Joint Chiefs should be solely responsible for strategic planning, the Munitions Board should determine whether strategic plans were economically feasible, and the NSRB should advise the board of available resources and minimum civilian requirements. The arrangement seemed to assume that all elements of the nation's war effort were subsidiary to strategic planning, and that all agencies were subordinate to the "command" responsibilities of the Joint Chiefs of Staff.[17]

The board's proposal set the stage for a new round of attacks against Truman's position on economic mobilization. Leading the way were Ferdinand Eberstadt and Bernard Baruch, two longtime friends and allies of both Forrestal and Hill. Eberstadt had earlier taken advantage of his leadership of the Hoover Commission's task force on national security to criticize the administration for not making better use of the NSRB and to endorse the mobilization scheme that Hill had proposed several months earlier. Only such a scheme, his task force had asserted, could actually ensure civilian control of mobilization, which would otherwise fall by default to the Munitions Board and its military bosses in the Pentagon. Baruch elaborated on similar ideas in a speech to the Industrial College of the Armed Forces. Once again, he played on his reputation as the great sage of economic mobilization, and once again he criticized the administration for not doing more to forge a comprehensive mobilization scheme directed by the kind of civilian czar that he had been in World War I. Like Eberstadt, Baruch saw Truman's decision to reject the NSRB plan of 1948 as a missed opportunity. It conceded far too much authority to the armed forces, especially to the Munitions Board, and left the United

---

[16] Elsey to Clifford, 17 November 1948, Elsey Papers, box 83, folder: National Defense – Armed Forces Unification. Truman had originally nominated an old friend, Mon C. Wallgren, to replace Hill, but the Senate had refused to confirm the nomination on the ground that Wallgren was wholly unqualified for the job.

[17] Undated Steelman memorandum for the president, Truman Papers, PSF-Subject File, box 156, folder: Defense, Secy of National Defense.

States vulnerable in the event of another war. Baruch's criticism led to a nasty public exchange between the old mobilizer and the president, and to a good deal of press commentary, especially by Hanson Baldwin, the military-affairs commentator for the *New York Times*, who had a close relationship with Baruch and was generally sympathetic to his position.[18]

This sympathy was not shared by John Steelman. Steelman resisted efforts by the Munitions Board to put economic mobilization under military control. Nor would he counter these efforts by turning the NSRB into a super agency with enough power to dominate other government departments and undermine the president's command authority. The Munitions Board, he told Forrestal, had absolutely no business deciding whether strategic plans were economically feasible, as it would then be setting "the direction and the limits of the entire economy." Authority of this sort belonged to a civilian agency like the NSRB, which was to represent other government departments, not replace them, act as the president's agent, not as an independent authority, and advice him on how to coordinate basic policies across the government.[19]

Building on proposals circulated earlier, Steelman then proceeded with plans for a fundamental reorganization of the NSRB. Finally implemented in mid-1950, these plans concentrated the NSRB's responsibilities in its chairman. The board as a whole became advisory to the chair while the chair became an adviser to the president. Through these and other changes, the NSRB finally emerged as the presidential staff agency that Truman had wanted all along. In addition, it made a start toward collecting relevant technical information, assembling a permanent staff, establishing contacts with academic experts, and appointing advisory committees of officials from private industry. The Truman administration had thus made some progress on mobilization planning, had wrested the planning process from the military, and had beaten back efforts to transform the NSRB into an independent operating agency.[20]

---

[18] On Eberstadt, Baruch, and press commentary see: Baldwin, "New Plans Now Unite Strategy and Industry," *New York Times,* 26 September 1948; Marquis Childs, "Resources Board," *Washington Post,* 22 February 1949; Arthur Krock, "The Dispute Over the Mobilization Plan," *New York Times,* 1 July 1949; and Baldwin, "Status of Security," "Plan for War Action," and "Mobilization Plans Wait," ibid., 2 and 4 July and 22 September 1949.

[19] Undated Steelman memorandum for the president, and Steelman to Forrestal, 4 March 1949, Truman Papers, PSF-Subject File, box 156, folder: Defense, Secy of National Defense.

[20] Cuff, "Eberstadt, the National Security Resources Board, and the Search for Integrated Mobilization Planning," 50–51; Rearden, *Formative Years,* 131. See also Elsey to Clifford, 17 November 1948, Elsey Papers, box 83, folder: National Defense – Armed Forces Unification; and Yoshpe, *National Security Resources Board,* 31.

Although the NSRB would be replaced by another agency after the outbreak of fighting in Korea, its history to this point is a good illustration of American state making in the early Cold War. Borrowing from the new ideology of national security, most American officials could agree that national security in an age of permanent struggle required a permanent government agency to mobilize the economy in the event of war. But if such an agency was to be created without destroying the economic and political foundations of American democracy, it had to take account of traditional institutions and values that were firmly rooted in the country's political culture. This explains why Truman and his advisors were reluctant to centralize power and responsibility in an organization that was largely independent of the White House, especially one that might be under military control. Instead, they envisioned an executive agency under the president's control and a system of decision making in which power was dispersed and a range of government agencies were represented. Such a system would safeguard presidential prerogatives, recognize the rights of established departments, and guarantee civilian control. It was this kind of system that Truman had started to build before the Korean War overtook his efforts, and it was also the kind of system that he envisioned when it came to mobilizing science and technology behind the cause of national security.

III

American leaders emerged from the Second World War absolutely convinced that science had saved the day by achieving dramatic breakthroughs in military technology. With government support, scientists had developed new or improved systems of navigation, bomb targeting, and submarine detection, not to mention the atomic bomb, which became the preeminent symbol of the successful wartime partnership between science and the state. No group was more impressed with science as an instrument of national power than were military leaders, and none was more determined to harness that power to its own purposes in the postwar period.

Military leaders did not step into a vacuum, however. On the contrary, their hopes for a considerable degree of autonomy in military research and development did not always square with presidential prerogatives, the tradition of civilian control, and the prewar relationship between science and the state. In addition, civilian leaders had their own ideas about how a partnership with science should be structured and to what purpose it should be directed. And beyond the issue of civilian versus military leadership were important questions about the role that civilian scientists should play in military research and the extent to which science, like the military, should be held accountable to public authority. The answers to these and similar questions would have a lot to say about how Americans governed themselves, and specifically about the nature of the national security state they were building.

Collaboration between science and the state had a history that stretched back beyond the Second World War. Congress had established the National Academy of Sciences in 1863, in part to provide scientific advice to the government. Certain government departments, the Department of Agriculture being the best example, had a long tradition of supporting research and making the results available to private groups and interests. In the First World War, the Navy and War departments had enlisted scientists and engineers in military research, with one result being the Navy Consulting Board established under Thomas Edison to solicit research proposals from civilian scientists. At the same time, President Woodrow Wilson had urged the National Academy to form what came to be known as the National Research Council, which sought to develop a national research agenda and mobilize civilian science, first behind the country's preparedness campaign and then behind its war effort. At the end of the war, President Wilson turned the Research Council into a permanent agency under the aegis of the National Academy, and a decade later President Franklin Roosevelt created a Science Advisory Board to bring American science and technology to bear on the economic problems of the Great Depression.[21]

In the 1920s the collaboration between science and the state had been strongly influenced by the associational philosophy of Secretary of Commerce Herbert Hoover, in effect the kind of corporatism that would later influence the postwar debates over defense reorganization, economic mobilization, and the mobilization of science. In the 1920s, in other words,

---

[21] For the standard survey of the relationship between science and the government before World War II see A. Hunter Dupree, *Science in the Federal Government: A History of Policies and Activities to 1940* (Cambridge, MA, 1957). See also Lewis E. Auerbach, "Scientists in the New Deal: A Pre-War Episode in the Relations between Science and Government in the United States," *Minerva* 3 (Summer 1965): 457–82; Carroll W. Pursell, Jr., "The Anatomy of a Failure: The Science Advisory Board, 1933–1935," *Proceedings of the American Philosophical Society* 109 (December 1965): 342–51; Daniel S. Greenberg, *The Politics of Pure Science* (New York, 1967), 63–65; Daniel J. Kevles, *The Physicists: The History of a Scientific Community in Modern America*, paperback ed. (New York, 1979), 111–38, 252–58; and Bruce L. R. Smith, *American Science Policy since World War II* (Washington, 1990), 22, 29–32.

leaders from government, industry, and science envisioned a decentralized system of science administration, one in which power was divided and dispersed in a public–private partnership that relied on individual initiative and voluntary action to harmonize the different interests involved. But a division of labor concentrated most applied research in government and industry, leaving basic research to universities that were hard-pressed for financial resources. The National Research Council tried to rectify the situation by raising funds for a National Research Endowment to underwrite basic research in university laboratories. But that effort collapsed in the Great Depression, when corporate leaders became more reluctant than ever to subsidize research that might benefit competitors or never produce a practical payoff.

University scientists and administrators also had reasons for limiting the terms of their partnership with industry and the state. Prizing their institutional and scientific independence, they worried that too much government support would restrict academic freedom and hamper their efforts to raise endowments from private donors. Nor was government always sensitive to these concerns. In World War I, for example, the National Research Council had been unable to play a central role in mobilizing science behind the war effort, in part because the Army and Navy had established their own sphere of military research. By commissioning scientists directly into the military services, they had circumvented the council, negotiated terms for a partnership with science that assured their control, and set an important precedent for the future.[22]

The 1930s brought a new generation of leadership to the scientific community, and new enthusiasm for a partnership with industry and the state. Unlike their predecessors, the members of this generation accepted a larger role for government and saw science as having important responsibilities in the fields of social policy, economic planning, and national defense. Isaiah Bowman and Karl Compton symbolized the new leadership and embodied in their own careers, as Robert Kargon and Elizabeth Hodes have shown, the partnership envisioned by their generation. Bowman, a distinguished geographer, had advised President Wilson at the Paris Peace Conference of 1919, had later helped to found the Council on Foreign Relations, and had directed the American Geographical Society, chaired the National Research Council, and was instrumental

[22] Dupree, *Science in the Federal Government*, 340–43; Greenberg, *Politics of Pure Science*, 63; Lance E. Davis and Daniel J. Kevles, "The National Research Fund: A Case Study of Industrial Support of Academic Science," *Minerva* 12 (April 1947): 207–20; Kevles, *The Physicists*, 186–89; Smith, *American Science Policy since World War II*, 30–31.

in persuading President Roosevelt to appoint a Science Advisory Board. Compton, a physicist who became the board's first chairman, had similar credentials. After wartime service in the Science and Research Division of the Army Signal Corp, he had built a successful career as an industrial consultant and academic scientist before assuming the presidency of MIT, one of the premier components of the scientific triad that he and Bowman had in mind. At the helm of MIT, Compton had forged even closer ties between the university and the leading, science-based industries. He had also played a prominent part in the National Research Council, and had cultivated a following among younger scientists who shared his conviction that science must play a prominent part in a new era of economic growth and stability.[23]

These scientists had a rough row to hoe in the 1930s. They wanted a partnership with government that would provide federal support but without the kind of government control or accountability that could politicize science and hamper progress. As they saw it, government support should be administered through programs with independent budget lines that scientists themselves would control with only a minimum of legislative or executive oversight. For some of the older, more conservative scientists, even this arrangement ran the risk of compromising their intellectual freedom. They were unwilling to support the sort of partnership their colleagues had in mind, just as key officials in the Roosevelt administration were reluctant to surrender public responsibilities to private experts. Concerns on both sides undercut some of the initiatives that Bowman and Compton tried to promote, notably the Science Advisory Board, which was so ineffective that Roosevelt allowed it to lapse at middecade. Nor was Compton successful in his subsequent attempt to replace the board with a National Research Administration that would channel government funds into private research and development projects.[24]

By the end of the decade, however, the outbreak of war in Europe had given new life to those who would harness science to the service of public policy, particularly defense policy. Compton was joined by James

---

[23] Robert Kargon and Elizabeth Hodes, "Karl Compton, Isaiah Bowman, and the Politics of Science in the Great Depression," *Isis* 76 (September 1985): 301–18. See also Richard V. Damms, "Scientists and Statesmen: President Eisenhower's Science Advisers and National Security Policy, 1953–1961" (Ph.D. diss., The Ohio State University, 1993), 26–27.

[24] Auerbach, "Scientists in the New Deal," 457–82; Pursell, "Anatomy of a Failure," 342–51; Greenberg, *Politics of Pure Science*, 64–65; Kevles, *The Physicists*, 252–58; Kargon and Hodes, "Politics of Science in the Great Depression," 301–18; and Smith, *American Science Policy since World War II*, 30–32.

B. Conant, a chemist and the president of Harvard University, and by Vannevar Bush, an electrical engineer who had risen through the ranks at MIT before becoming president of the Carnegie Institute in Washington. The group, eventually led by Bush, transformed Compton's proposal for a national research administration into one for a National Defense Research Committee. Established by President Roosevelt in 1940, the committee was to coordinate research in the Army and Navy and allocate military research contracts to university and industrial laboratories. In 1941, the committee gave way to the Office of Scientific Research and Development (OSRD), which Bush directed and which came close to the kind of organization that Compton and Bowman had always envisioned.

An independent federal agency, the OSRD was led by civilian scientists, had its own budget line from Congress, and operated by awarding research contracts to industrial and university laboratories. It cooperated closely with the armed forces, geared its work to military needs, yet remained essentially free of military control. Its apparent success, together with the conviction that science was essential to security in an age of total war, convinced many scientists and military leaders that something like it had to continue into the postwar period. For military leaders, such an arrangement would keep the armed forces on the cutting edge of new military technologies. For scientists, it would allow them to play a useful role in the nation's defense while providing government support for science education and basic research.[25]

Such were the conclusions emerging from a government study commissioned by the OSRD and the armed forces in the last year of the war. The study recommended a postwar Research Board for National Security to replace the OSRD and help the government recruit civilian scientists for military research. For a time, however, two competing schemes vied for support. In one scheme, the board would operate under the auspices of the National Academy of Sciences, rather than government auspices, and would apply for research and development funds from the armed forces.

---

[25] For a general history of the OSRD see Irvin Stewart, *Organizing Scientific Research for War: The Administrative History of the Office of Scientific Research and Development* (Boston, 1948). See also Greenberg, *Politics of Pure Science*, 79–96; Daniel J. Kevles, "Scientists, the Military, and the Control of Postwar Defense Research: The Case of the Research Board for National Security, 1944–46," *Technology and Culture* 16 (January 1975): 20–47; Carroll W. Pursell, Jr., "Science Agencies in World War II: The OSRD and Its Challengers," in *The Sciences in the American Context: New Perspectives*, ed. Nathan Reingold (Washington, 1979), 359–78; Daniel J. Kevles, "Cold War and Hot Physics: Science, Security and the American State, 1945–1956," *Historical Studies in the Physical and Biological Sciences* 20 (1990): 239–42; and Damms, "Scientists and Statesmen," 41–49, 116–17.

This scheme drew support from conservatives who thought it would isolate science from political controls, but was strongly criticized by those who feared military domination. In the version supported by the critics, the board would be an independent federal agency, much like the OSRD, with civilian leaders and its own budget line.

The outcome of this dispute was a short-lived compromise: The board was to operate initially under the auspices of the National Academy of Sciences but evolve eventually into an independent agency with its own research agenda and the authority to coordinate research programs across the government. The problem was that the compromise satisfied no one. The Army opposed the idea of civilian control over its research programs while the Budget Bureau objected to an arrangement that put the board under the aegis of the National Academy, rather than a public authority responsible to the president. Given the bureau's objections, the White House refused to fund the board, and those involved began to look to a more ambitious plan for a national science foundation that would include a division of national defense.[26]

The new plan owed much to Vannevar Bush, whose ideas were grounded on assumptions he had long shared with Bowman, Compton, Conant, and other wartime leaders of American science. Bush had outlined his thinking in *Science – The Endless Frontier*, a report to the president completed just as the Second World War was coming to a close. In the report, he had touted the blessings that modern science could bring to medicine and to the country's economic well-being and military security. He had warned that gains in all these areas were threatened by a shortage of scientific manpower and funds for basic research, and had argued for a national research foundation to foster scientific education, promote basic research, and harness civilian scientists to the cause of national defense. Although government would charter the foundation, Bush saw it as essentially an independent agency linked in a corporative partnership with the state but basically free of political control. It would be run by a director, various division heads, and a part-time board of civilian scientists; and while the president would appoint board members, the board itself would select the director and the division heads in consultation with the National Academy of Sciences. Envisioned as well was a science advisory board that would link the foundation to scientists in the private sector and advise the government on science policy and budget priorities. Taken together, Bush argued, the advisory board and the

---

[26] Kevles, "Scientists, the Military, and the Control of Postwar Defense Research," 20–47.

foundation would give scientists a substantial role in government policy, including military research and development, which would come under the direction of the foundation's division of national defense.[27]

By the end of 1945, Bush's thinking had been incorporated into a bill introduced by Democratic Senator Warren Magnuson of Washington, while a different philosophy had found its way into a rival bill drafted by Senator Harley Kilgore, a New Deal Democrat from West Virginia. Kilgore's bill also called for a national science foundation to support basic and applied research, promote scientific training and education, and coordinate the government's research and development activities. In addition, it would, like Bush's proposal, create a corporative pattern of public–private collaboration structured through a national science board of representatives from industry, labor, education, and government. But unlike Bush's board, Kilgore's would be appointed by the president, as would the foundation's director, and this arrangement would mean greater presidential control, less autonomy for the board, and less influence for the scientists.

There were other differences as well. Kilgore wanted the government to control patents growing out of federally funded research, whereas Bush saw private control as the price that government had to pay for a partnership with corporate laboratories. In addition, Kilgore's scheme would give science a social purpose and prevent a handful of universities and corporations from establishing a monopoly in this important area. With these goals in mind, his measure would provide federal support for the social sciences as well and would do more to distribute federal research contracts beyond the so-called elite institutions.[28]

The two bills drew support from different parts of the executive branch. The Army and Navy endorsed Magnuson's bill, in part because of their happy wartime relationship with Bush and the OSRD, in part because they saw the bill's lenient patent policy as an incentive for industry's continued collaboration in military research. In the Budget Bureau, on the other hand, Director Harold Smith asserted the same position he had taken in connection with the Research Board for National Defense. If the

---

[27] Bush, *Science – The Endless Frontier: A Report to the President on a Program for Postwar Scientific Research* (Washington, 1945). See also James L. Penick, Jr., et al., eds., *The Politics of American Science: 1939 to the Present* (Chicago, 1965), 58–64; and Kevles, *The Physicists*, 347.

[28] Penick et al., *Politics of American Science*, 54–58; Kevles, *The Physicists*, 344–47; Bush to Harold D. Smith, 13 August 1945, Records of the President's Scientific Research Board (Truman Library), box 2, folder: Office of Scientific Research and Development.

foundation was going to coordinate government programs and distribute government funds, Smith insisted, it must not be exempt from "the regular controls and procedure of the Federal government." Although its directors might cooperate with industrial, labor, and educational institutions, they must be agents of the president and directly accountable to the chief executive, not to private scientists and industrial groups. Truman felt the same way and was also sympathetic with Kilgore's desire to support the social sciences and have public control over the patents derived from federally funded research.[29]

Congress was unable to reconcile the two approaches in 1945, and Truman vetoed a revised version of Magnuson's bill a year later. Negotiations stalled over the next two years, so that it was not until 1950 that Congress passed a bill establishing the National Science Foundation. The bill, which Truman signed in May, contained compromises on patent policy and the distribution of research contracts that were more favorable to Bush's position than to Kilgore's. But Kilgore and Truman did prevail on the issue of presidential control; the director of the Science Foundation would be appointed by the president, with Senate confirmation, and would be responsible to public officials rather than private groups.

As for military research, however, the two-year delay had rendered the victory for presidential control less than meaningful. Under the final bill, the National Science Foundation was limited to science education and basic research with little or no military applications. It would not include a division of defense research, function as an instrument of civilian control over military research, or play an important part in coordinating the research agendas of the armed forces. On the contrary, the armed forces had taken advantage of the delay in congressional action to develop their own programs of military research, and the White House had responded by looking elsewhere for new instruments of civilian control.[30]

Near the end of the war the Navy had considered a plan for a new office that would supervise its independent research, contract for research projects proposed by civilian scientists, and be advised by a committee

[29] Smith to Bush, 1 October 1945, Records of the President's Scientific Research Board, box 2, folder: War Department. See also Smith diary, 27 August 1945, Smith Papers, box 1, folder: Daily Record, August 1945; Penick et al., *Politics of American Science*, 72–79; and Kevles, *The Physicists*, 344–48.

[30] For histories of the origins of the National Science Foundation see J. Merton England, *A Patron for Pure Science: The National Science Foundation's Formative Years, 1945–57* (Washington, 1982), 3–110; and Carl Milton Rowan, "Politics and Pure Research: The Origins of the National Science Foundation, 1942–1954" (Ph.D. diss., Miami University, 1985).

representing the interests of the country's scientific community. Nothing came of the proposal so long as Congress seemed likely to establish a national science foundation with a division of defense research. But when the foundation bill foundered in 1946, the Navy went to Congress and won support for a new Office of Naval Research and a Naval Research Advisory Committee. Besides coordinating military research in the Navy's own facilities, the new office was to negotiate contracts with a variety of corporations and universities to train scientific manpower, conduct basic research, and develop new weapons technologies. By the end of 1949, the Office of Naval Research had already established a very close connection to "the university life of this country," and had done so by negotiating $20 million worth of contracts with more than two hundred institutions.[31]

In the meantime, the Army, too, had begun to organize for scientific research and development. Army Chief of Staff Eisenhower had been convinced during the war that "long range military planning can be done only in the light of predicted developments in science and technology." The same man who would later warn against the dangers of a military–industrial–scientific complex began urging the Army to utilize the country's "industrial and technological resources as organic parts of our military structure." The "close integration of military and civilian resources," he said, including educational institutions and industrial corporations, would engender better understanding, benefit the Army, and enhance the nation's security. Guided by these goals, the Army proceeded to establish its own Research and Development Division, which, like its Navy counterpart, was to coordinate the Army's research programs, seek the counsel of scientists in the private sector, and advise the chief of staff and the secretary of war on matters relating to science and technology. At the same time, the Army also began contracting for research with university and industrial laboratories, especially research on guided missiles and airpower, which the Air Force would later continue and expand.[32]

---

[31] Acting Secretary of the Navy John Nicholas Brown to Steelman, 19 August 1947, Records of the President's Scientific Research Board, box 2, folder: Navy Department. See also The Bird Dogs, "The Evolution of the Office of Naval Research," *Physics Today* 14 (August 1961): 30–35; Kevles, *The Physicists*, 353–55; and Harvey M. Sapolsky, "Academic Science and the Military: The Years since the Second World War," in *Sciences in the American Context,* 379–99.

[32] Eisenhower to directors and chiefs of the War Department general and special staff divisions and bureaus and the commanding generals of the major commands, 4 April 1946, attached to Symington to E. L. Vowles, 23 August 1946, Symington Papers, box 11, folder: Correspondence File, 1946–50, Research and Development. See also Eisenhower to Harold

Bush's dream of an independent and authoritative role for civilian scientists was slipping away. As in World War I, the Army and Navy had decided to establish a separate sphere of military research and to negotiate their own terms for a partnership with civilian scientists. These developments made it difficult for civilian scientists to forge the kind of comprehensive research program that Bush thought would eliminate waste and serve the national interests. On the contrary, as the separate sphere grew, the result was increased military control over science, which Bush had wanted to avoid, plus a serious threat to presidential prerogatives and the principle of civilian leadership. Although Truman would eventually establish his authority in the battle over the National Science Foundation, he and his successors would be far less successful when it came to asserting civilian control over the research agendas of the armed forces.

IV

The Army and Navy took the first step toward a unified research and development program in 1946, when, at Bush's suggestion, they replaced the wartime OSRD with the Joint Research and Development Board. The new board, which Bush agreed to chair, arose from his concern that each of the services was moving in its own direction, without coordinating their activities or eliminating costly duplications. The Navy was doing a great deal to support basic research while the Army concentrated on developmental work. Their research agendas overlapped in certain fields, such as guided missile development, and they were both acting in ways that drained the pool of scientific manpower without concern for the civilian economy. Under the new arrangement, each service would still manage its own research programs, but there would now be an agency to coordinate areas of "joint interest" and to promote a reasonable balance between military and civilian requirements.[33]

Smith, 16 April 1946, and Eisenhower to Patterson, 27 April 1946, in *The Papers of Dwight David Eisenhower*, vol. 7, *The Chief of Staff*, ed. Louis Galambos (Baltimore, 1978), 1004–7, 1045–46; Patterson to Senator Chan Gurney, 12 May 1947, Records of the President's Scientific Research Board, box 7, folder: War Department, General; and Damms, "Scientists and Statesmen," 122–23.

33 Unsigned memorandum for the president, "Coordination of Scientific Research in the Federal Government," no date, Records of the President's Scientific Research Board, box 2, folder: President's Scientific Research Board; Charter, Joint Research and Development Committee, 6 June 1946, ibid., folder: National Research Council; General H. I. Hobbs (assistant deputy chief of staff), War Department General Staff Circular No. 5–6,

The National Security Act of 1947 took this corporative arrangement another step forward. It replaced the Joint Board with a new Research and Development Board, consisting of Bush as chair and two representatives from each of the military services. Like its predecessor, the Research and Development Board was to coordinate the research activities of the armed forces, eliminate wasteful duplication, and build links between military research and the civilian scientific community. More specifically, the new board was to design a master plan for military research and development and then implement the plan by assigning responsibility for projects of common interest, facilitating the exchange of information between the services, coordinating their research and development budgets, and evaluating the connection between strategic plans and new weapons technology. There was, however, an important difference between the new board and its predecessor. Whereas the old board had been responsible to the armed forces, which had created it, the Research and Development Board would report to the secretary of defense. In theory, at least, it would be the agent of civilian leadership and the symbol, ultimately, of the president's authority as commander in chief. The reality, as it turned out, would be somewhat different.[34]

Within a year, the Research and Development Board had elaborated a corporative scheme of organization, establishing a host of committees and panels, composed of military and civilian experts, that were to take up research and development issues in areas ranging from aeronautics to electronics. It employed a full-time secretariat, a staff of more than two hundred employees, and roughly fifteen hundred university and industrial consultants who linked military research to private groups and institutions throughout the country. In practice, however, such a fragmented structure hampered efforts to rationalize the board's work, while the inability of the Joint Chiefs to agree on force levels or on a joint strategic plan made it difficult for the board to correlate weapons technology with grand strategy in a master research and development scheme. Nor were these the only disappointments. Bush had counted on objective, civilian scientists to overcome the parochialism of the armed forces and guide military research into efficient, useful paths. But as it turned out, military officers dominated the board as well as its various panels and committees, partly because civilian scientists served under contract to the

"Organization: Research and Development Division, War Department General Staff," 11 June 1946, Symington Papers, box 11, folder: Correspondence File, 1946–50, Research and Development.
34 Kevles, "Cold War and Hot Physics," 246–47; Rearden, *Formative Years*, 97–99.

military, usually on a part-time basis, while their military counterparts were engaged full-time and were more likely to represent the needs of their services than the interests of science. The outcome tended to be military rather than civilian control over the research projects that fell within the board's jurisdiction.[35]

What is more, the board's jurisdiction was limited at best. It did not have administrative control over the research and development work of the armed services and could do little to implement its decisions concerning joint enterprises. The secretary of defense and the board chairman could make recommendations, but compliance by the services was more or less voluntary. As a result, the board's efforts to coordinate military research across the armed forces, or to deal effectively with areas of joint interest, were plagued by the same interservice struggles that also made it difficult to produce an integrated defense budget or an agreed strategic concept. Each branch promoted research that justified or enlarged its own role in American defense strategy, and the overall results added up to waste and duplication of staggering proportions.

Secretary Forrestal tried to deal with the problem of duplication at the Key West and Newport conferences of 1947 and 1948, but to no avail. At Bush's suggestion, the secretary then established the Weapons Systems Evaluation Group, composed of leading civilian as well as military scientists, to advise the Joint Chiefs on new technologies and on the best way to integrate research programs and eliminate waste. As in the past, however, efforts at integration kept foundering on familiar disputes over service roles and missions. The group had virtually no success in consolidating the guided missile projects launched by each of the services, of which there were nearly forty by the end of 1948. Nor was it taken seriously when it questioned the effectiveness of the B-36 bomber or the potential success of an air–atomic assault on the Soviet Union. In these and other cases, its views were ignored whenever they challenged the interests and priorities of particular services.[36]

Much the same was true of budget advice emanating from the Research and Development Board. Bush had wanted the board to evaluate the research and development budgets of the armed forces and advise on funding priorities, thus helping to eliminate waste and unnecessary

---

35 Don K. Price, *Government and Science: Their Dynamic Relation in American Democracy* (New York, 1954), 146–58; Rearden, *Formative Years,* 99–102; Damms, "Scientists and Statesmen," 124–25.

36 Rearden, *Formative Years,* 99, 401–5, 409–10; Damms, "Scientists and Statesmen," 126–28.

duplications. But while he expected the board to work as a "coequal" partner with the Joint Chiefs in this sphere, he quickly discovered that his partners viewed the relationship in a very different light. To his dismay, the Joint Chiefs went about developing the research budget for fiscal year 1950 by asking their military deputies to survey current research, develop new programs, and advise them accordingly. They denied the Research and Development Board any part in the process, which amounted, in Bush's opinion, to a "clear invasion by the Joint Chiefs of Staff into the affairs of the Board." He wanted redress, but what he got was an argument from the Joint Chiefs, who told Forrestal that it was within their charge to evaluate current military research and development programs.[37]

Another mandate which the board could not fulfill was its obligation to provide the president with scientific advice independent of recommendations coming from the Pentagon. This had been an issue of interest to the White House since late 1946, when Truman appointed the President's Scientific Research Board under Steelman's direction and asked it to address his concerns about the proportion of the budget invested in military research, the duplication of research in the armed services, and the relationship between civilian and military requirements for scientific resources.[38] Through much of 1947 the board had held hearings, soliciting the views of prominent scientists and collecting information from the military establishment and from various business groups.[39] Then, in a special report to the president, it had urged the Budget Bureau to create a new division to advise the chief executive on matters regarding the organization and budgeting of government research programs. In addition, it had endorsed the president's proposal for a National Science Foundation as another source of advice on which the president could draw in shaping science policy. Some members of the board and the experts they consulted even recommended a separate, presidentially appointed commission of scientists, or at least a single distinguished

37 Bush to Forrestal, 8 September 1948, and unsigned memorandum for the Secretary of Defense, 28 October 1948, RG 218, CCS 334, Research and Development Board (2-28-46), Sec. 3.
38 Minutes of the first meeting of the President's Scientific Research Board, 2 January 1947, Records of the President's Scientific Research Board, box 3, folder: Minutes of 1st Mtg; record of a National Research Council conference, 4 March 1947, ibid., box 2, folder: National Research Council.
39 Steelman to Bush, 12 March 1947, Records of the President's Scientific Research Board, box 2, folder: Joint Research and Development Board; Lyman Chalkey, Scientific Research Board, to Walter Chamberlin, National Association of Manufacturers, 21 March 1947, ibid., box 1, folder: General Correspondence; Charles V. Kidd, Scientific Research Board, to Steelman, 18 June 1947, ibid., box 8, folder: unknown.

scientist, to advise the president and serve as his link to scientists outside of government.[40]

Nothing would come of the board's most important recommendations; nor would the Research and Development Board emerge as a source of scientific advice to the president. To be sure, the Budget Bureau would become more involved in federal research policy and Congress, as noted earlier, would finally establish the National Science Foundation. But the foundation did not include a division of national defense, had no authority to balance civilian research needs against those of the military, and was hampered by a budget that paled by comparison with the much larger sums invested in military research and development. What is more, the idea of a presidential science commission or White House science officer did not bear fruit until the Eisenhower administration, which meant that Truman never enjoyed a source of advice on military science and technology independent of the Pentagon, where research and development policy had been captured by the individual services.

By the time of the Korean War, each branch of the armed forces had organized its own research and development division and had successfully resisted all efforts to coordinate its work with that of the other services. Neither the Research and Development Board nor its predecessor had the authority to impose its recommendations on the military. On the contrary, the services had taken control of both boards, the National Science Foundation had little to say in matters of military research, and the president had yet to appoint a White House science adviser, as some had urged.

When it came to military research and development, then, national security and the ideology behind it had begun to displace other needs and older ways of thinking. The armed forces had established a great deal of autonomy for themselves in this area and had done so at the expense of other values, including the prerogatives of the president and the principle of civilian rule. On the contrary, they were in a position to dominate the nation's research and development program without effective control by civilian scientists or political leaders, and without regard for the influence of their policies on the larger economy. Already

[40] Warren Weaver (chairman, Naval Research Advisory Committee) to Forrestal, 7 March 1947, Records of the President's Scientific Research Board, box 1, folder: unknown; unsigned conference notes, 22 April 1947, ibid., box 9, folder: Notes of Meetings – Chalkey; Chalkey to J. Donald Kingsley, Scientific Research Board, 2 May 1947, ibid., box 2, folder: Kingsley, Donald; Kidd to Steelman, 18 June 1947, ibid., folder: John Steelman; and Chalkey to J. Robert Oppenheimer, 19 June 1947, ibid., box 1, folder: General Correspondence.

by 1948, the Pentagon accounted for 62 percent of all research and development expenditures, including 60 percent of all federal grants to universities for nonagricultural research.[41]

V

The other major source of federal support for research and development was the Atomic Energy Commission, where the drama of state making was also unfolding, and where we again discover themes similar to those appearing in other theaters of the civil–military conflict. In this case, too, we see a strong emphasis on military research and development, specifically on the development of atomic energy for military rather than civilian purposes. We see the armed forces seeking a substantial degree of control over the commission's work, if not a high degree of autonomy in the field of atomic energy. We see scientists struggling to maintain their independence of military control and political influence. We see Truman and his allies trying to protect traditional presidential prerogatives and uphold the principle of civilian control. In short, we see again the central challenge of state making in the early Cold War, which was to prepare for permanent struggle without surrendering constitutional principles and democratic traditions to the garrison state.

Planning for the control of atomic energy began in July 1944, when the Office of Scientific Research and Development, under Vannevar Bush, called for a postwar atomic energy commission of two army officers, two naval officers, and eight private citizens, five of whom would be distinguished scientists nominated by the National Academy of Sciences. The commissioners would be appointed by the president, but the commission itself would be largely independent of presidential or congressional control and would have substantial authority over the country's atomic energy program, including research, development, and production. At the heart of the OSRD scheme were ideas also evident in Bush's thinking about a national research foundation, including an emphasis on corporative collaboration between scientists in government and the private sector, a faith in private experts rather than political authorities, and a conviction that scientific research had to be insulated from political influences.

Within a year of the OSRD proposal, the War Department had countered with a plan of its own, calling for a commission of nine members

---

[41] Kevles, "Scientists, the Military, and the Control of Postwar Defense Research," 20.

serving on a part-time basis, including four civilian experts and four military officers. Although appointed by the president, the commissioners would exercise enormous authority largely independent of presidential or legislative oversight. They would appoint a full-time administrator and deputy administrator, who would select and supervise the commission's permanent staff, and would control all nuclear facilities, all atomic weapons, all production of fissionable materials, and all atomic research, except for military research by the armed forces. The proposal was similar to the OSRD scheme, in that it emphasized control by so-called experts and sought to balance centralizing and decentralizing impulses in a system of administration where power was dispersed, divided, and shared. As might be expected, however, it gave the armed forces greater proportional representation on the commission and thus more power to regulate private research.[42]

Subsequently, the War Department made some modest revisions intended to satisfy Bush and the State Department, whereupon it persuaded Representative Andrew Jackson May, a Democrat from Kentucky, and Senator Edwin C. Johnson, a Democrat from Colorado, to introduce the proposal in Congress. The May–Johnson bill immediately generated a heated reaction outside the War Department. Although Bush, Conant, Compton, and other members of the wartime scientific elite promptly endorsed the bill, many rank-and-file scientists were beginning to wonder if their eminent colleagues had fallen under the spell of the War Department. From their point of view, the bill overemphasized the military uses of atomic energy, to the detriment of its industrial or medical uses, left too much control of this awesome resource in military hands, and included such strenuous security controls that civilian scientists would be reluctant to participate.

Similar objections came from Don K. Price in the Bureau of the Budget and James R. Newman in the Office of War Mobilization and Reconversion. Price was an expert in public administration and Newman was a liberal lawyer who had developed an expert's grasp of the principles and practice of modern science. Both thought the May–Johnson bill put too much emphasis on the military applications of atomic energy, too little

---

[42] Richard G. Hewlett and Oscar E. Anderson, Jr., *A History of the United States Atomic Energy Commission*, vol. 1, *The New World Order, 1939–1946* (University Park, PA, 1962), 408–9 (hereafter cited as *New World*); Donovan, *Conflict and Crisis*, 133; Kevles, *The Physicists*, 349; Gregg Herken, *The Winning Weapon: The Atomic Bomb in the Cold War, 1945–1950*, paperback ed. (New York, 1982), 117; Peter Douglas Feaver, *Guarding the Guardians: Civilian Control of Nuclear Weapons in the United States* (Ithaca, 1992), 90–91.

on industrial and medical uses; and though both wanted to grant the commission a virtual monopoly over atomic energy, they also wanted a greater degree of legislative oversight and presidential control, fewer restrictions on research, and fewer military representatives on the proposed commission.[43]

Among their allies, moreover, Newman and Price could count the president himself, who again threw his weight behind the principles of civilian leadership and presidential control. They could also count on Senator Brien McMahon, a young Democrat from Connecticut who had recently taken charge of a special Senate committee on atomic energy, and on Budget Director Harold Smith, Interior Secretary Harold Ickes, Commerce Secretary Henry Wallace, and Director of War Mobilization and Reconversion John Snyder. All these civilian officials wanted a bill that gave more attention to the nonmilitary applications of atomic energy, included fewer security restrictions, and held the proposed commissioners accountable to the president. They made these points at a White House meeting near the end of 1945, only to learn that their counterparts in the Pentagon were still clinging to the idea of a nearly autonomous commission led by the military. That idea struck Newman and others as little more than a cover for military domination, and their suspicions were enhanced when the War Department defied a congressional request for classified nuclear information and openly challenged Truman's support for a commission composed entirely of civilians.[44]

Working with Price and with Senator McMahon, Newman and his aides drafted a bill that would bring the military to heel by adhering strongly to the principle of civilian control. The bill would create an atomic energy commission of five full-time civilian members and would authorize the president to appoint these officials as well as the commission's general manager and division heads. Besides exercising a government monopoly over fissionable material and patents relating to the production of that material, the commission, rather than the armed forces, would have custody of the nation's stockpile of atomic weapons, control all research and development in the field of atomic weapons, and supervise the production of all such weapons. Finally, the bill would put fewer restrictions on the exchange of scientific information than was the case with the May–Johnson bill, and would also include a much greater

43 Hewlett and Anderson, *New World*, 413–14, 431–33, 437–43, 445–48; Kevles, *The Physicists*, 349–51; Herken, *Winning Weapon*, 118–22; Feaver, *Guarding the Guardians*, 93–94.
44 Hewlett and Anderson, *New World*, 443–45, 449–53; Truman, *Years of Trial and Hope*, 15; Donovan, *Conflict and Crisis*, 133–34; Herken, *Winning Weapon*, 122–23.

emphasis on basic scientific research to be conducted by the commission or by private laboratories under contract to the commission.

Such provisions were not to the liking of the military, but they did appeal to rank-and-file scientists who were increasingly well organized and lobbying their case vigorously on Capitol Hill. They also appealed to the president and his civilian allies in the administration. Secretary Wallace endorsed McMahon's bill, stressing how important it was to adhere "to the traditional principle of civilian control" and to "avoid any possibility of military domination or dictatorship." Truman also endorsed McMahon's bill, first in a letter to the senator that emphasized "civilian administration, not military administration," and then in a memorandum to the service secretaries. The atomic energy commission, he told the secretaries, "should be exclusively composed of civilians," as this principle accorded "with established American tradition" and had "found its way into statutory provisions which expressly prohibit members of the Armed Forces on active status from serving in other Governmental posts."[45]

In the debates over McMahon's bill, the clash between civilian and military authority appeared as the central theme in a larger debate over the influence of atomic energy on American values and institutions. McMahon and his colleagues in both houses of Congress wrestled at length with the idea of a government monopoly in the field of atomic energy, including government control of fissionable materials, patents, and production. Leading newspaper commentators hit the same theme, with Joseph and Stewart Alsop telling their readers that McMahon's bill contemplated a "revolution in our society and political structure," in that "government control of fissionable material from mine to use will include government control of a huge segment of the national economy."[46]

Conservatives were particularly disturbed by this assault on the principle of private enterprise, which they defined, usually by comparison to the un-American other, as at the heart of the way Americans defined themselves. Republican Congressman Charles Elston of Ohio, who

45 Wallace quoted in Hewlett and Anderson, *New World*, 490, Smith, record of a conference with the president, 21 January 1946, Truman Papers, PSF-Subject File, Smith Diary, box 150, folder: Excerpts from the Diary of Harold D. Smith; Truman memorandum for the secretaries of war and navy, 23 January 1946, Truman Papers, PSF-Subject File, box 199, folder: NSC – Atomic, Atomic Bomb – Cabinet. See also Hewlett and Anderson, *New World*, 482–89, 491; Truman, *Years of Trial and Hope*, 15–18; and Donovan, *Conflict and Crisis*, 134, 170–71.

46 Alsops, "Atom Issue's Urgency Seen in Death of Young Scientist," *New York Herald Tribune*, 3 February 1946. See also the sources cited in the following note.

considered the bill "one of the most dangerous" ever submitted, argued that it would "deprive the American people of their liberties." According to another conservative, the bill's patent provisions would give the commission "absolute authority over American industry," thereby destroying "one of the fundamentals of a free enterprise system under a free government." They amounted, added Republican Congresswoman Claire Boothe Luce of Connecticut, to a "radical new departure" that might have been charted by "the most ardent Soviet Commissar."[47]

Despite their concern for economic liberties, however, and their fears of militarism and big government, conservatives were more willing in this area than in others to give the military arm of the government substantial authority and to tighten the bill's security provisions. They would rather trust atomic energy to military officials than to New Deal bureaucrats, and they viewed the security provisions as too lenient in light of recent disclosures that a Canadian spy ring had revealed atomic secrets to the Soviet Union – not to mention the persistent rumors that a similar ring had penetrated the Manhattan Engineering Project. Besides military control of atomic energy, they favored the severe security restrictions in the original May–Johnson bill and sought strict limits on the dissemination of scientific information. Although scientists saw these limitations as an infringement on their traditional freedoms and waged a vigorous counter offensive on Capitol Hill, the Senate created a large category of "restricted data," permitted the commission to define that data, and specified penalties for violating the commission's decisions. The House went even further, writing into the final bill provisions that seriously limited the international exchange of scientific information, gave the FBI more authority to investigate commission employees, and applied strict penalties to those who violated the commission's restrictions and decisions.

Still another battle developed over military membership on the proposed commission. Although Truman had ruled this out, Secretary Forrestal called openly for military representation, as did Secretary Patterson, whose office prepared a twenty-two-page critique of McMahon's

---

47 The quotations are from Hewlett and Anderson, *New World*, 522–23, 519. The following discussion of the McMahon bill is based largely on the excellent account in ibid., 493–530. See also *Congressional Quarterly* 2 (1946): 339–40, 504–14; Arnold A. Rogow, *James Forrestal: A Study of Personality, Politics, and Policy* (New York, 1963), 169; Alice Kimball Smith, *A Peril and a Hope: The Scientists' Movement in America, 1945–47* (Chicago, 1965), 128–275, 342–436; Kevles, *The Physicists*, 350–52; Herken, *Winning Weapon*, 124–36, 147–48, 242, 243, 262–63; and Feaver, *Guarding the Guardians*, 96–104.

bill even after the president had endorsed it. The War Department urged amendments that would permit a military officer to direct the commission's division of military application and allow the armed forces to conduct their own research on atomic weapons. It also favored amendments that would give the Joint Chiefs a veto over the commission's work and establish a military-dominated advisory board through which the commission would consult with the armed forces on atomic energy matters. Fearful that he would appear to be muzzling his advisers, Truman allowed Patterson to present the War Department's case to Congress and then permitted a similar presentation by General Leslie Groves, whose aggressive support of military research and obsessive concern with security had come to symbolize for scientists the dangers of military influence and control.

The resulting melee got nasty, to say the least. Republican Senator Burke Hickenlooper, a conservative from Iowa, questioned the loyalty of American scientists, while Henry Wallace warned of "military fascism" and Senator McMahon accused the Pentagon of trying to undermine "the Bill of Rights." Rank-and-file scientists also stepped up their campaign for a civilian commission, and Donald Nelson joined with other liberals to organize the Committee for Civilian Control of Atomic Energy, which was committed to blocking a "determined drive underway to vest permanent control of atomic energy in military hands, contrary to [the] historic constitutional principle of civilian control over all phases of American national policy." Both Nelson and the scientists were convinced that military domination would stifle creative research in nonmilitary fields, raise doubts about the American commitment to international control of atomic energy, and thus lead to a global arms race. These were ideas that military leaders and the service secretaries denounced as "absurd," to use Patterson's word, although Admiral Leahy lent credibility to Nelson's critique when he told Truman how ridiculous it was to "turn over the making of one of the most effective weapons of war to a civil commission which would dole out its product, if it decided to make any, as it saw fit."[48]

The issue of military versus civilian control also provoked considerable commentary in the nation's press. Marquis Childs may have gone too far in dismissing the May–Johnson bill as "fascist," but leading

---

[48] McMahon and Wallace quoted in Hewlett and Anderson, *New World,* 504, 506; Nelson to Stimson, 27 March 1946, enclosed in Stimson to Patterson, 28 March 1946, and Patterson to Stimson, 29 March 1946, Patterson Papers, General Correspondence, box 22, folder: 1945–1947, Stimson, Henry L.; and *Forrestal Diaries,* 133.

commentators seemed to agree that strictly military control of atomic energy would be "contrary to American tradition." "This is peace not war," Childs argued, "and in peace we must devise controls to take over from the military if we are to have a strong democracy." The May–Johnson bill went in the other direction. It represented the "military mind" of the War Department and the security obsessions of General Groves and would, in operation, alienate the very scientists whose support was essential to a successful atomic energy program. But if the May–Johnson bill represented the views of "extremists" in the War Department, as Arthur Krock said, then McMahon's bill went to the opposite extreme by denying the military any voice whatsoever in the atomic energy program. Common sense seemed to dictate a middle course, according to Krock, Childs, Baldwin, and other commentators, who eventually threw their weight behind the so-called Vandenberg amendment as a workable and judicious compromise.[49]

That amendment, sponsored by Republican Senator Arthur Vandenberg of Michigan, would establish a military liaison committee to be appointed by the service secretaries and to consult with the commission on matters relating to the military applications of atomic energy. If the committee disagreed with the commission on such matters, it might appeal to the service secretaries, who might then appeal to the president. This was enough to satisfy the Senate. But in the House the bill's critics were also successful in adding provisions that would allow military officers to serve on the commission's staff, though not on the commission itself, and to head its division of military applications.

The final bill, which Truman signed into law on 1 August 1946, called for five civilian commissioners appointed by the president with the consent of the Senate. On this point, Truman and his allies had prevailed. But in doing so they had been forced to yield considerable ground in other areas. The act put more emphasis on military research and less on the peaceful uses of atomic energy than they had wanted. It also included strict security provisions and restrictions on the international exchange of atomic information that many scientists viewed as threats to individual

---

49 Childs, "Atomic Material," "Gen. Groves' Power," and "Groves' Pattern," *Washington Post,* 4, 8 January and 2 March 1946; Arthur Krock, "Broken Alignments on the Atomic Issue," *New York Times,* 15 March 1946. See also Childs, "Atomic Secrecy," "Atoms During Peace," "Progress on Atomic Energy Control," "Scientists vs. Army," and "Vandenberg Move," *Washington Post,* 5, 9, 28 January and 8, 15 March 1946; Hanson Baldwin, "Feud on Atom Control Centers on Authority," *New York Times,* 17 March 1946; and Arthur Krock, "A Meeting of Minds on the Bomb," "Wrangling Over Atom is Eased in the Capital," and "Moves Toward a Sound Atomic Policy," ibid., 19, 31 March and 4 April 1946.

liberty, intellectual freedom, and scientific progress. In addition, Truman and his allies had to accept the Military Liaison Committee and agree that active duty officers could serve on the commission's staff and direct its division of military applications. The armed forces did not come out of the battle with the degree of autonomy they had wanted. But they would have more influence than Truman and the scientists thought desirable, and they would use that influence in a continuing effort to assert their dominance in the field of atomic energy.

"The Army will never give up without a fight," Truman told David Lilienthal, the liberal Democrat and head of the Tennessee Valley Authority (TVA) who had helped to prepare the so-called Acheson–Lilienthal report recommending international control of atomic energy. That report had been set aside in favor of a more stringent recommendation prepared by Bernard Baruch and eventually rejected by the Soviets. But in Truman's mind, Lilienthal's background made him the logical man "to get the whole atomic energy business in civilian hands completely," and thus help "people in this country and all over the world" to get over their "great fear about it." He asked the former TVA head to chair the new Atomic Energy Commission (AEC), but warned him at the same time of the War Department's determined opposition to the exercise of AEC powers. The Army "will fight you on this from here on out," he said, and "in all sorts of places."[50]

An early skirmish came when General Groves and others began raising objections to the smooth transfer of the Manhattan District's properties from the Army to the new Atomic Energy Commission. Groves hoped to exempt raw-materials procurement from the transfer, as well as the Army's established intelligence operation on atomic energy. In addition, and perhaps most importantly, he wanted to exempt all atomic weapons, weapons parts, storage facilities, and fissionable materials ready for assembly. Such exemptions did not square with the Atomic Energy Act, as Lilienthal and the other commissioners interpreted it, and their view seemed to prevail when Truman signed the official order of transfer on the last day of 1946.[51]

Although Truman's order was an important victory for the principle of civilian control, the battle on this front had just begun. At the same time, the Senate hearings on Lilienthal's appointment to the AEC turned

[50] Lilienthal, *Atomic Energy Years*, 118–19.
[51] In addition to the source cited in the previous note see Lilienthal to Patterson, 27 December 1946, Clifford Papers, box 1, folder: Atomic Energy – Atomic Energy Act; Hewlett and Anderson, *New World*, 651–55; and Feaver, *Guarding the Guardians*, 110–11.

into a three-ring circus in which conservatives openly wondered whether the country's atomic secrets could be entrusted to a liberal New Dealer, a champion of public power, and a Jew whose parents had been born in Eastern Europe. Hickenlooper expressed such doubts to a sympathetic Forrestal, who confided to his diary that Hickenlooper and his "Senate associates are very much concerned about a pacifistic and unrealistic trend in the Atomic Energy Commission." As the hearings proceeded, Democratic Senator Kenneth D. McKellar, an aging southern conservative from Tennessee, joined a phalanx of Republican conservatives led by Senators Taft and John W. Bricker of Ohio, Styles Bridges of New Hampshire, Kenneth S. Wherry of Nebraska, and Homer Ferguson of Michigan to call into question Lilienthal's personal integrity and loyalty. They dug up old and discredited charges that he had Communist connections or had accepted payoffs years earlier as a member of the Public Utilities Commission of Wisconsin; they attacked his TVA chairmanship, saying that he represented an elitist, pro-statist philosophy; and they raised questions about the Acheson–Lilienthal plan for international control of atomic energy, saying that it was too quick to surrender the country's atomic secrets to the Soviets.[52] It was "politics in its most primitive form," Cabell Phillips wrote for the *New York Times*. He and Marquis Childs denounced the Senate conservatives, especially McKeller, for "taking out [their] personal spleen on a loyal public servant." So did other commentators, including Arthur Krock, who had no love for liberals like Lilienthal but still found it hard to deny that McKeller and his allies were going too far.[53]

The charge that Lilienthal was soft on communism was at the heart of the attack and explains why conservatives turned out to be reliable allies in the Army's effort to leverage as much room for the Military Liaison Committee (MLC) as possible. Hickenlooper, Taft, and others, including Baruch, condemned complete civilian control, praised Groves, and demanded that the MLC sit with the commission during its meetings. Once it became clear that it had this kind of support, the military

---

[52] *Forrestal Diaries*, 240–41. See also Lilienthal, *Atomic Energy Years*, 139–51; Richard G. Hewlett and Francis Duncan, *A History of the United States Atomic Energy Commission*, vol. 2, *Atomic Shield, 1947–1952* (University Park, PA, 1969), 1–14, 48–53; Donovan, *Conflict and Crisis*, 273–74; Patterson, *Mr. Republican*, 344–45; and McCullough, *Truman*, 536–39.

[53] Phillips, "Lilienthal Case," *New York Times*, 16 February 1947; Childs, "Lilienthal and Brandeis," *Washington Post*, 19 February 1947. See also, Krock, "Senate Imputes its own Sin to Lilienthal," *New York Times*, 18 February 1947; and Childs, "Atomic Security and Democracy," *Washington Post*, 16 July 1947.

began staking out a larger role for itself than Lilienthal thought desirable. Lieutenant General Lewis H. Brereton, the MLC's first chairman, told Lilienthal that his committee would be serving "with" and "as part of the Commission." And Rear Admiral Thorwald A. Solberg, another member of the MLC, insisted imperiously that "no plan, policy or decision which may affect the national security *or the interests of the Armed Forces* could be actually put into effect *or even initiated* by the Commission prior to the Committee being informed in time for it to give the matter reasonable consideration."[54]

Military highhandedness of this sort became commonplace in the early days of the commission. Brereton, for example, drew up plans for producing and storing nuclear weapons and for weapons research and development, as if these were his responsibilities rather than the commission's. He also appeared to assume that the MLC was less a liaison to the commission than an operating agency in its own right, which was the same assumption that informed the Army's view of the AEC's Division of Military Applications. According to the Atomic Energy Act, this division was to be headed by an active-duty military officer selected by the commission from nominations submitted by the War Department. But in an effort to preempt the commission's choice, the department submitted only one nominee, Colonel Kenneth D. Nichols, who was one of Groves's closest associates and had sided with him in urging military custody of atomic weapons. In Nichols's view, the Division of Military Applications should work as an operating agency, more or less independent of the commission's authority, even though such an arrangement would have the effect of putting weapons research and development under military rather than civilian control. It was a view that made Nichols persona non grata to the commission.[55]

Perhaps the best example of the War Department's contempt for the commission, and for the whole idea of civilian control, was Patterson's decision to appoint General Groves to the MLC. Patterson made the decision without fully consulting Lilienthal, who claimed to be "flabbergasted" when he heard the news. Since Congress had decided on a civilian Atomic Energy Commission, and since Truman had selected

---

54 Lilienthal, *Atomic Energy Years*, 110; Solberg to Lilienthal, 15 April 1947, RG 330, CD 3-1-3 (emphasis added). See also Lilienthal, *Atomic Energy Years*, 133, 139–51. Lilienthal turned the tables in his reply to Solberg, saying that the AEC would go as far toward collaboration as would the armed forces, and implying that they had been less than helpful in this regard. See Lilienthal to Solberg, 17 April 1947, RG 330, CD 3-1-3.
55 Hewlett and Anderson, *New World*, 649–52.

civilian commissioners, Lilienthal naturally assumed that the Pentagon would select MLC representatives who were comfortable with the principle of civilian control, not someone like Groves who had fought the AEC legislation tooth and nail and considered it his sworn duty to reverse the results.

The problem was bigger than Groves, of course, in the sense that the AEC was viewed with suspicion in every corner of the Pentagon. Brereton, Solberg, and Nichols had already shown their colors; Patterson had never reconciled himself to the principle of civilian control; and Forrestal, who was "positively dangerous" on the subject of atomic energy, had "cussed" out Lilienthal for thinking that the AEC should do anything but manufacture bombs. Nevertheless, Groves's appointment took on a special, symbolic significance, given his association with the Manhattan Project. It struck Lilienthal as "a vote of no confidence by the Joint Chiefs in the Atomic Energy Commission." Nor was Lilienthal wrong, as Secretary of the Army Kenneth Royall admitted in defending the appointment. Royall had earlier drafted the May–Johnson bill. He and Groves had supported that bill in Congress, Royall told Lilienthal, and both men still believed that McMahon's alternative "had been a mistake."[56]

The constant tension between the commission and the MLC, together with Lilienthal's constant complaints, finally led to Groves's resignation. It also helped that Lilienthal had threatened to refer the issue to the president, who promised his support, and that Conant, J. Robert Oppenheimer, and other scientists had told Royall that Groves must go, no doubt to clear the way for better relations between military and civilian scientists. Groves resigned in late February, but not before he had unburdened himself of a scathing attack on the AEC. The "atomic bomb," he wrote the Joint Chiefs, "will never be a truly military weapon until it is turned over to the military for custody and stockpiling." The Joint Chiefs should drive this point home until it was settled satisfactorily, and should also support legislation giving the military establishment representation on the commission and wider participation in the atomic energy program as a whole. For Groves, it was "axiomatic that the Armed Forces must have control over the weapons upon which our National Security so largely rests." Denying this control posed a "serious hazard to the preparedness of the Nation" and could only "lead to

---

[56] Lilienthal, *Atomic Energy Years*, 136, 261–63, 249–52. See also ibid., 203, 247–48.

confusion and delay at a time when prompt retaliatory action will be vital to our country."[57]

Groves had taken his leave, but not without raising an issue that would plague the AEC in the months ahead. Just months before his departure, the MLC had gone on record in favor of military custody of atomic weapons, the position that Groves had held from the start. The service secretaries followed suit, claiming that military custody was essential to national security, and Admiral Leahy had weighed in as well. Echoing arguments now heard up and down the military chain of command, he told Forrestal that it would be impossible to ensure the prompt and effective employment of atomic weapons unless they were in the custody of the armed forces.[58] The AEC's earlier decision meant nothing to these officials; nor did the president's executive order transferring all Manhattan District properties to the new commission. The Pentagon would not take "no" for an answer on an issue that was presented as a matter of custody but actually involved the president's responsibilities as commander in chief and the question of civilian versus military control.[59]

No doubt sure of Truman's backing, Lilienthal wanted the whole matter referred to the White House, whereupon Forrestal, fearing the outcome, decided to delay presidential action pending completion of a special study by Donald Carpenter, who had succeeded Brereton as head of the MLC. A civilian, Carpenter wanted to establish a cooperative relationship with the AEC. He investigated the custody issue, met with the commissioners, and came to the conclusion that a workable compromise was possible, particularly if the military began training qualified technicians and if the AEC would be willing to transfer atomic weapons to their care in the event of an emergency. Such an arrangement would make actual military custody less important and allow the issue to be postponed until military technicians were better prepared. The Armed Forces Special Weapons Project, created to train troops in the handling

57 Groves to General Spaatz, 28 February 1948, Symington Papers, box 4, folder: Correspondence File, 1946–50, Declassified Documents. Groves sent similar letters to Admiral Denfeld and General Bradley, both of 28 February 1948. See JCS 1859, 31 March 1948, RG 218, CCS 471.6 (8-15-45), Sec. 9. See also Lilienthal, *Atomic Energy Years*, 249–52, 287–88; and Herken, *Winning Weapon*, 242–43.

58 Secretaries of the Army, Navy, and Air Force to Forrestal, 13 March 1948, Truman Papers, PSF-Subject File, box 202, folder: NSC Atomic – Atomic Weapons – Stockpile; Rearden, *Formative Years*, 427.

59 Lilienthal, *Atomic Energy Years*, 306–7; and Rearden, *Formative Years*, 428.

of atomic weapons, seemed to agree with this thinking. It concluded that nothing in the current international scene warranted the immediate transfer of atomic weapons to the military establishment. The issue thus appeared to be on its way to a successful solution, so much so that Carpenter could tell the Hoover Commission that his committee and the AEC were beginning to develop a harmonious working relationship.[60]

Carpenter, though, was unduly optimistic, since his position did not have the support of the armed forces and their allies on Capitol Hill. Forrestal told Truman shortly after Carpenter's appointment in April 1948 that the Joint Chiefs still wanted military representation on the AEC, a larger role in the design and testing of atomic weapons, control over intelligence relating to atomic energy, and military custody of stockpiled atomic bombs. If anything, the Czech crisis, the Soviet blockade of Berlin, and the war scare that accompanied these events had made the Pentagon and others even more determined to wrest custody of the atomic stockpile from the AEC. Putting the stockpile in military hands, Hickenlooper told Carpenter, was an "item of extreme importance to existing conditions." Senator Wherry agreed. Seizing on the emergency, he introduced a motion to return the atomic energy program to the military. At the same time both the Armed Forces Special Weapons Project and Donald Carpenter reversed their earlier positions.[61]

Carpenter and others on the MLC still hoped to send the president a joint AEC–MLC recommendation on military custody. But Lilienthal dashed this hope in a long and tense meeting with the MLC on 18 June. He would not agree to a joint recommendation to the president, as it would deny Truman his right to consider all sides of the issue. Nor would he surrender the stockpile of atomic weapons to the military, in part because the armed forces still lacked the technical staff to manage the stockpile and continue with important development work. In addition, Lilienthal implied that the issue of custody involved larger questions, such

[60] Carpenter memorandum of conversation with Senator Hickenlooper, 16 April 1948, and Carpenter memorandum for the secretary of defense, the service secretaries, and the Joint Chiefs of Staff, 21 April 1948, RG 330, CD 12-1-30; unsigned memorandum of a meeting of the Hoover Commission Subcommittee Investigating the National Military Establishment, 9 June 1948, RG 330, CD 3-1-47; JCS 1848/3, 14 July 1948, RG 218, CCS 471.6 (8-15-45), Sec. 11.

[61] Carpenter memorandum of conversation with Senator Hickenlooper, 16 April 1948, RG 330, CD 12-1-30. See also Forrestal to Truman, 6 April 1948, RG 218, Records of the Chairman, Admiral Leahy, 1942–48, box 20, folder: Correspondence Signed by the President; Lilienthal, *Atomic Energy Years*, 311–12, 362; minutes of the 29th meeting of the Military Liaison Committee and the Atomic Energy Commission of 18 June 1948, 25 June 1948, and JCS 1848/3, 14 July 1948, RG 218, CCS 471.6 (8-15-45), Sec. 11.

as the president's prerogatives as commander in chief and the principle of civilian control, that could not be decided without public discussion and full deliberation by the president.[62]

Lilienthal covered the same ground twelve days later in a meeting with Forrestal and others at the Pentagon. Both sides arrived with such an army of aides that it was difficult to squeeze them all into Forrestal's office. Forrestal had Carpenter, Nichols, Royall, Eisenhower, and Vannevar Bush by his side, while Lilienthal appeared with all the other commissioners. The conferees quickly recapitulated the arguments they had made earlier, but this time the "shadows of the current troubles with the Russians in Berlin" hung like a shroud over the group, especially over Secretary Royall, who "came and left the meeting to get the latest word." Royall seized on the Berlin crisis to emphasize how important it was to resolve such basic questions as whether atomic weapons would be used in an international emergency, when they should be used, and on what targets. Lilienthal had the impression that Royall was asking essentially rhetorical questions to which the armed forces already had the answers, as they did on the custody question. But pushing these presumptions aside, he insisted that all such questions, including the question of custody, involved basic issues of policy that required decision by the president.[63]

Once again Lilienthal was calling the Pentagon's bluff. He was gambling that Truman would support the AEC, and he had good reason to be confident. Indeed, after the meeting in Forrestal's office, he had reported the results to Clark Clifford, who had conveyed them to Truman, who had then responded that so long as "I am in the White House I will be opposed to taking atomic weapons away from the hands they are now in." A few days later Lilienthal got more good news. He saw Budget Director James Webb at a cocktail party and the two fell into a discussion of the custody issue and the views of Secretary of State Marshall, who was reluctant to see the atomic stockpile transferred to the armed forces. Marshall did not want his military friends to know it, Webb reported, but he considered it bad policy to transfer custody in the middle of a major international crisis. Webb also considered the transfer a bad idea, if only because the armed forces were "so hopelessly 'out of control' under

---

[62] Lilienthal journal entry, 18 June 1948, Lilienthal, *Atomic Energy Years*, 362; and minutes of the 29th meeting of the Military Liaison Committee and the Atomic Energy Commission, 18 June 1948, 25 June 1948, RG 218, CCS 471.6 (8-15-45), Sec. 11.

[63] Lilienthal, *Atomic Energy Years*, 373–77. See also Hewlett and Duncan, *Atomic Shield*, 167–69.

Forrestal and engaged in such fights among themselves that to add this 'at this time' would be wrong."[64]

Armed with this support, Lilienthal probably assumed that Forrestal would back down on his threat to take the issue to the White House, as he had backed down before. But he was wrong. Under pressure from the Joint Chiefs, the secretary told Truman in mid-July 1948 that he intended to raise the issue of custody at a meeting with the president the following week. There was "a very serious question," he explained, as to whether the AEC could "assure the integrity and usability" of atomic weapons when it would not be the "user" of such weapons.[65] The "showdown" came at a White House meeting on 21 July with another big crowd on hand.[66] On one side sat Forrestal, Carpenter, Royall, Symington, and William Webster, who was about to replace Carpenter as MLC chairman. On the other side sat Lilienthal, the other AEC commissioners, and their advisers. The president was in the middle, looking grim and irritated at being asked to decide again an issue he had decided twice already.

The showdown began with a small procedural "skirmish" over which side would present its case last, which Lilienthal won in an omen of what was to follow. The full-scale engagement then commenced with Carpenter's long-winded presentation of the Pentagon's case. Reading from a document that Truman had before him, Carpenter explained that the armed forces had to learn how to store and design atomic weapons and how to operate and maintain them if they were going to meet a surprise attack without confusion and delay. The document added nothing to the Pentagon's case, and Carpenter's decision to read it annoyed Truman no end. "I can read," he told Carpenter, in another omen of what was to come.[67] Lilienthal followed with brief, informal remarks that defended the AEC's management of the atomic stockpile and called into question the technical competence of the armed forces. Mostly, though, he explained how the atomic bomb was not just another weapon of war, no matter what some military officials were saying. It was an instrument of mass destruction having broad diplomatic as well as military implications, and decisions concerning such a weapon therefore involved the constitutional responsibilities of the president and the principle of civilian control, both of which could be compromised if the armed forces prevailed on the custody issue. Lilienthal then reminded the president that

[64] Lilienthal, *Atomic Energy Years*, 373–77, 385. See also, ibid., 384.
[65] *Forrestal Diaries*, 458.
[66] Lilienthal, *The Atomic Energy Years*, 387–88.
[67] Ibid., 388–91.

he had fought for these principles in the past, at which point Truman responded that he was "'still having to fight to save those principles.'"[68]

The president's remark was yet another omen of the way things were going, and Lilienthal could "feel the temperatures among the defense establishment gents around me go down considerable." Nor did they warm up when Symington and Royall tried to save the day. With all the bluster he could muster, which was considerable, Symington talked about how "our fellas" thought "they ought to have the bomb. They feel they might get them when they need them and they might not work." When Truman asked if they had failed to work so far, Symington had to say no, whereupon Royall made things worse by talking about the money that had been invested in atomic weapons. "Now if we aren't going to use them," he announced, that investment "doesn't make any sense." Lilienthal could hardly believe his ears. "If what worried the President," he recorded in his journal, "was whether he could trust these terrible forces in the hands of the military establishment, the performance these men gave certainly could not have been reassuring." Truman must have had a similar reaction. He had already told the meeting that the atomic bomb was not really "a military weapon," that it was used to destroy women and children and not strictly for military purposes. And after Royall's reckless declarations, he referred to the international crisis growing out of the Berlin blockade and concluded that it was "no time to be juggling an atom bomb around."[69]

The day after the White House meeting, Webb weighed in with his own recommendation. In a detailed memorandum for the president, he carefully summarized the arguments on the custody issue and then sided with the AEC. He was convinced, first of all, that the AEC had done an excellent job and that the armed forces were not likely to do better. On the contrary, they could hardly expect to take custody of the atomic stockpile when they had yet to devise an agreed strategic plan and were constantly squabbling over their respective roles and missions, including which of them had primary responsibility for an atomic attack. In addition, Webb noted "the provocative utterances of certain highly-placed officers" and concluded that such indiscretions were hardly calculated to inspire public

---

[68] Ibid.

[69] Ibid. See also *Forrestal Diaries*, 460–61; Forrestal to Truman, 21 July 1948 and Lilienthal to Truman, 21 July 1948, Truman Papers, PSF-Subject File, box 202, folder: NSC Atomic – Atomic Weapons – Stockpile; and Forrestal diary entry, 22 July 1948, Forrestal Diary, Forrestal Papers, vols. 11–12, box 5; Hewlett and Duncan, *Atomic Shield*, 169–70; and Feaver, *Guarding the Guardians*, 121–22.

confidence in military custody. On the contrary, granting such custody might be interpreted abroad as the start of "secret preparations for war" and could therefore make a "delicate international situation" even worse. Finally, Webb was absolutely convinced that the AEC had laid adequate plans for a quick and smooth transfer of the atomic arsenal to the armed forces on the command of the president, who had ultimate authority in such a matter. The custody issue was therefore more "symbolic" than substantive, and the AEC's jurisdiction should be retained as a symbol of the president's prerogatives and the principle of civilian control.[70]

When Truman decided in favor of the AEC, he did so in terms that stressed his responsibilities as commander in chief and the principle of civilian control. Because "a free society places the civil authority above the military power," he announced on 24 July, "the control of atomic energy properly belongs in civilian hands." He admitted that civil–military cooperation was essential in the field of atomic energy, but added that Congress had recognized the president's special responsibilities in this area and that, as president, he regarded "continued control" of atomic energy to be the "proper function" of civil authorities.[71]

Forrestal took the news badly. He thought that Truman's public announcement had humiliated him. Nor did military leaders respond any better. In the weeks that followed Truman's announcement, some of them, according to Webb, began "spreading stories all over the place deprecating the commission" and trying to build a new case for military custody.[72] Some also appealed to friends on Capitol Hill and tried to build a case indirectly by getting Congress to raise the custody issue once again. One such friend was Senator Millard E. Tydings of Maryland, a conservative Democrat and member of the Joint Congressional Committee on Atomic Energy, who wrote Truman in March 1949 that current custody arrangements could only impede the military's ability to respond effectively in the event of a sudden emergency. Responsibility for the atomic arsenal was divided, he said, and such a division could lead to another Pearl Harbor. Tydings also believed that atomic bombs were just like any other weapons and therefore belonged in the hands of potential users, particularly because the AEC knew

[70] Webb to Truman, 22 July 1948, Truman Papers, PSF-Subject File, box 200, folder: NSC–Atomic, Atomic Energy – Budget.

[71] Truman statement reviewing two years of experience with the Atomic Energy Act, 24 July 1948, *Public Papers, Truman, 1948*, 414–16.

[72] Lilienthal, *Atomic Energy Years*, 406. See also ibid., 392; editor's note, *Forrestal Diaries*, 461; JCS 1848/4, 30 July 1948, RG 218, CCS 471.6 (8-15-45), Sec. 11; and Forrestal to Carpenter, 28 July 1948, and Truman to Forrestal, 6 August 1948, RG 330, CD 12-1-30.

absolutely nothing about the "higher strategy and detailed tactics of waging war."[73]

In responding to Tydings, Truman's advisers rejected the Pearl Harbor analogy and argued instead that tested arrangements for the wartime transfer of atomic weapons to the military and the opportunities given the armed forces to become familiar with the atomic stockpile were all assurances that national security was being effectively maintained. Having mobilized these arguments, Truman's advisers then went on to a vigorous defense of the president's prerogatives as commander in chief, which in their minds were linked to the principle of civilian control. The AEC, they said, was the instrument through which the president exercised his responsibilities under the Atomic Energy Act, and its use for this purpose was in line not only with the country's security needs but also with American political tradition.[74]

Truman must have been annoyed at how difficult it was to make his decisions stick with the Pentagon. Talking with his AEC advisers about Tydings's letter, he said that he had decided the question of custody more than once, that it would stay decided "as long as he had anything to do with it," and that "he believed firmly in the civilian control of atomic energy." He made the same points in a subsequent meeting with Lilienthal, who was upset by the continued "aggressiveness" of Nichols and other military leaders on the production and custody of atomic weapons. "I want to be frank," Lilienthal told the president, "there are elements in the military establishment – not the whole of it at all, but strong elements – that don't agree with you" on the custody issue, "are pretty outspoken about it, and are causing some difficulties." In response, Truman stiffened up, "practically sticking his chin into my face," and said: "Well, I'm the Commander in Chief." Lilienthal then expressed regret that military officials kept forcing the issue on the president, like children running to "Papa" with troubles they should be able to settle themselves, to which Truman replied, a grin on his face spreading into a "full-scale laugh": "Well, Papa won't hesitate to use the strap if that's what it takes."[75]

Truman's resolve at last forced the Pentagon into something of a retreat. In the summer of 1949, the secretary of defense and the Joint Chiefs

---

[73] Tydings to Truman, 2 March 1949, Truman Papers, PSF-Subject File, box 202, folder: NSC Atomic – Atomic Weapons – Stockpile. See also Russell Andrews to Steelman, 14 March 1949, Truman Papers, White House Central File, Confidential File, box 4, folder: Atomic Bomb and Energy, 1948–49.

[74] Unsigned memorandum of 14 March 1949, Truman Papers, PSF-Subject File, box 202, folder: NSC Atomic – Atomic Weapons – Stockpile.

[75] Lilienthal, *Atomic Energy Years*, 501–2, 527–28.

finally stipulated that only a civilian, rather than a military officer, could head the MLC. They also seemed satisfied with arrangements that recognized the principle of civilian control while allowing the military to work more closely with the AEC in maintaining the atomic stockpile; that envisioned military custody of nonnuclear components; and that channeled military recommendations regarding the production of atomic weapons through the NSC before presentation to the president. The last arrangement was particularly important to Lilienthal, since it would open the Pentagon's recommendations to analysis by the civilian agencies represented on the NSC as well as by the AEC. The president would no longer be forced to accept or reject "a kind of ultimatum" from the military, but could make decisions "on the basis of a rounded staff picture and with real freedom of discretion."[76]

VI

As of 1949, Lilienthal and Truman had prevailed in their battles with the military for control of the atomic energy program. The armed forces had been less successful in this field than in the field of military research and development, at least when it came to establishing a high degree of autonomy for themselves at the expense of presidential prerogatives and such traditional democratic values as the principle of civilian control. But in other areas it was Truman and Lilienthal who were less successful, and not only in the field of military research and development but also when it came to beating back the onerous security restrictions that threatened to impinge on scientific freedoms and individual liberties.

In this area, Truman was again challenged by congressional conservatives whose commitment to individual liberties and the principle of civilian control became attenuated when the civilians were New Deal liberals or other government bureaucrats. Once again, conservatives such as Hickenlooper and Taft joined with Groves, Patterson, Royall, Forrestal, and others in the Pentagon, this time to demand tough restrictions on the exchange of scientific information and strict security requirements for AEC personnel. And once again, Lilienthal was portrayed as the enemy and as a potential subverter of both the nation's security and its basic values. His New Deal liberalism, his support for international control of

---

[76] Ibid., 552–53. See also JCS 1871/2, 21 July 1949, and JCS 1871/3, 26 July 1949, RG 218, CCS 471.6 (8-15-45), Sec. 16; and JCS 1840/8, 29 November 1949, RG 218, CCS 471.6 (8-15-45), Sec. 18.

atomic energy, and even his ancestry were invoked as evidence that he was soft on communism, could not be trusted, and was therefore unfit to serve.

In this case, moreover, the conservative assault on Lilienthal coincided with an increasingly hysterical fear of communism that dated back to the Red Scare of 1919 but had been given new life by the Cold War. International crises, the policy of containment, and revelations of Soviet espionage all worked together to create a national security mentality that fostered demands for loyalty oaths, security investigations, and other measures to rid the government of suspicious elements, including liberal Democrats whose social and political agenda had supposedly set the stage for Communist subversion of traditional values. Conservatives had made Communist subversion and the loyalty question major issues in the 1946 campaign and had emerged from the election in control of both houses of Congress, at which point the door was thrown open to a reckless drive against allegedly disloyal elements in American politics, the American government, and other institutions. Conservative Republicans demanded a new commission to investigate the loyalty of federal employees, and congressional committees promptly opened hearings on a variety of bills to outlaw the Communist party.[77]

Truman, too, saw a way of life at stake in the struggle against communism and was much concerned about internal security. But in his discourse on loyalty, as in his discourse on other aspects national security, he tried to reconcile the need for security with democratic liberties and constitutional guarantees that conservatives often saw as safeguards for sabotage. Whereas conservatives worried most about an alliance between Communists and the government to destroy a way of life they held dear, Truman also saw danger in an unregulated anticommunism that could wreck the very foundations of American democracy. He tried to strike a "balance between internal security and individual rights," and his efforts resulted in a number of familiar measures that need only a brief summary here.[78]

Shortly after the election of 1946, apparently in the hope of heading off congressional initiatives that went further than he thought desirable,

---

[77] For a recent, balanced overview of the McCarthy era in American politics see Richard M. Fried, *Nightmare in Red: The McCarthy Era in Perspective* (New York, 1990).

[78] Charles Murphy (special counsel to the president) and Stephen Spingarn (presidential aide) to Truman, 16 May 1950, in Athan G. Theoharis, ed., *The Truman Presidency: The Origins of the Imperial Presidency and the National Security State* (Stanfordville, NY, 1979), 331–32.

Truman appointed a special commission on employee loyalty that for him would have unintended consequences. To begin with, the appointment lent credibility to conservative charges that the government was riddled with subversives and thus fueled the anti-Communist hysteria that Truman had hoped to contain. Then, too, the commission's investigations and reports added to the effects of the superheated rhetoric that the president used to sell the Greco-Turkish aid program and other measures of containment. Much the same was true when Truman decided on 21 March 1948 to establish a federal employee loyalty program – a decision that many conservatives viewed as further proof of a Communist conspiracy against the American system at home and American interests abroad.[79]

As established, Truman's loyalty program was intended to rationalize the wartime measures he had inherited from the Roosevelt administration, in part by creating uniform procedures for screening prospective employees and for dealing with employees whose loyalty had been questioned. Under its rules, individuals could be denied employment or dismissed from federal service if there was "reasonable" doubt of their loyalty to the government, a term that embraced not only evidence of sabotage, espionage, or treason but also evidence that a federal employee advocated the violent overthrow of the American government or performed his or her duties in a way that served the interests of another state. To implement the program, individual agencies were to appoint their own loyalty panels operating in accordance with the prescribed procedures. At the top would be a Loyalty Review Board to coordinate and supervise the agency panels and guarantee accused employees the benefit of counsel, the right to a hearing, and the right to present evidence on their own behalf. In addition, employees had the right to appeal unfavorable decisions, first to the agency head, and then to the Loyalty Review Board.[80]

The evidence indicates that Truman was interested both in greater security and in precluding more aggressive action by congressional conservatives whose constitutional scruples were less evident than his own. He confided to several colleagues that he was concerned about civil liberties and wrote to a prominent labor leader that the loyalty program

---

[79] Truman's Executive Order 9835 establishing the federal employee loyalty program, 21 March 1948, is reprinted in Theoharis, *Truman Presidency*, 257–61. See also Richard M. Freeland, *The Truman Doctrine and the Origins of McCarthyism: Foreign Policy, Domestic Politics, and Internal Security, 1946–1948* (New York, 1972), 123–150; Fried, *Nightmare in Red*, 67–68; Donovan, *Conflict and Crisis*, 292–94; and McCullough, *Truman*, 550–53.

[80] See the sources cited in the previous note.

had been drafted so "that the Civil Rights of no one would be infringed upon." He also instructed the Loyalty Review Board to avoid a witch hunt and sought to limit the role of the Federal Bureau of Investigation, whose director, J. Edgar Hoover, was more concerned with the Communist threat than with constitutional guarantees. The president was "very strongly anti-FBI," in the words of Clark Clifford. He was "afraid of a 'Gestapo'" and wanted to "hold [the] FBI down." "It's dangerous," is how Truman described the bureau.[81]

Still, the loyalty program was deeply flawed and quickly careened out of control. It was not limited to those areas of federal service involving the national security; was prone to rely on unverified information; did not allow those accused to confront their accusers; and accepted as grounds for dismissal any past association with any organization that the attorney general listed as Communist, fascist, or subversive. In addition, some of the president's colleagues in the executive branch did not share his concern for civil liberties. J. Edgar Hoover and others in the FBI leaked confidential information to congressional conservatives, while Attorney General Tom C. Clark wanted to prosecute the leaders of the Communist party, establish a more vigorous loyalty program, and secure passage of the "toughest anti-spy laws in American history," including laws to legalize wiretaps. Before long, the FBI and the Justice Department were playing a role similar to that of the armed services in the field of national defense: They were resisting presidential policies and trying instead to create a high degree of autonomy for themselves. The FBI literally duped the president into authorizing illegal wiretaps, and the Justice Department began pursuing its own legislative agenda, which showed little concern for civil rights and was developed, without reference to the White House, by officials who were "inclined to resolve all doubts in favor of security."[82]

---

[81] Truman and Clifford quoted in Donovan, *Conflict and Crisis*, 296–97. See also Francis H. Thompson, *The Frustration of Politics: Truman, Congress, and the Loyalty Issue, 1945–1953* (Rutherford, NJ, 1979), 34–39; Lilienthal journal entry, 15 November 1947, Lilienthal, *Atomic Energy Years*, 255. The FBI's role in loyalty investigations was a subject of some debate in the Truman administration. In addition to Thompson's book noted above see the documents in Theoharis, *Truman Presidency*, 262–64.

[82] Clark is quoted in Thompson, *Frustration of Politics*, 106, and the second quote is from Spingarn to Murphy, 1 February 1950, in Theoharis, *Truman Presidency*, 329–30. See also Fried, *Nightmare in Red*, 70–73; Thompson, *Frustration of Politics*, 46–61; Freeland, *Truman Doctrine*, 205–18; Athan G. Theoharis, *Seeds of Repression: Harry S. Truman and the Origins of McCarthyism* (Chicago, 1971), 123–40; and Theoharis, *Truman Presidency*, 325–31.

The Republican-controlled Congress posed an even greater problem. Congressional conservatives were determined not to follow Truman's leadership on the loyalty issue. They provided only limited funding for his program, gave the FBI more responsibility for the investigative process than the president wanted, and pushed constantly to extend the hunt for subversives into every nook and cranny of American life. The House Committee on Un-American Activities, for example, led by the notorious J. Parnell Thomas of New Jersey, opened hearings on Communist penetration of the film industry, demanded the personnel and loyalty files of federal employees, and urged the FBI to investigate the character and the associations, as well as the loyalty, of presidential appointees. In addition, congressional conservatives pressed relentlessly to outlaw the Communist party, deport party members, and deprive Communists born in the United States of their American citizenship. With each succeeding international crisis, moreover, and with each new revelation of Communist subversion, the agitation for these and other measures grew.[83]

Confronted with such pressures, Truman showed a strong reluctance to give way. He refused to release confidential loyalty files to congressional committees, despite the substantial political cost involved; he opposed legislation to ban the Communist party in the United States as being "entirely contrary to our principles"; he was against measures to summarily deport and detain aliens; and he did not want the FBI to investigate the character and associations of his appointees to the AEC. In addition, Truman tried to get renegades in the Justice Department under control, asking them to clear their legislative initiatives with the White House and warning them that "excessive security" was "as dangerous as inadequate security." It "brings normal administrative operations to a stand-still," he said, "prevents the interchange of ideas necessary to scientific progress, and – most important of all – encroaches on the individual rights and freedoms which distinguish a democracy from a totalitarian country." The president's words were less measured in addressing other aspects of the anti-Communist hysteria and the people who promoted it. He proclaimed the House Un-American Activities Committee to be "more un-American than the activities it is investigating," repudiated wiretapping in similar terms, and denounced what Clifford called "the hysteria-mongering branch of the Republican party" – to which he nonetheless lost ground, as the AEC experience indicated.[84]

---

[83] Fried, *Nightmare in Red*, 73–92; Thompson, *Frustration of Politics*, 70–116.
[84] Truman quoted in his news conference of 13 May 1948, *Public Papers, Truman, 1948*,

The conservative attack on Lilienthal's appointment to the AEC, on his personal integrity and loyalty, was the beginning of an unrelenting pattern of harassment. Both military leaders and conservatives on Capitol Hill used the security issue in an effort to discredit the commission and reestablish the principle of military control. They attacked the investigative procedures that Lilienthal and the other commissioners had established, especially the AEC's power to evaluate the results of FBI investigations of commission personnel and make the final decisions on clearance. For this purpose the commission had set up its own system of decentralized review panels, although the commissioners themselves took personal responsibility for difficult cases.[85]

From the beginning, Lilienthal had found the task distasteful, in part because FBI files were full of unsubstantiated information, in part because a wrong step by the commission could easily ruin an individual's career or impair the commission's ability to recruit top-flight scientists. Too often, Lilienthal confided to his journal, the commission was called upon "to play God and decide on ex parte evidence of FBI detectives whether Mr. A.'s or Mrs. B.'s loyalty, character, or associations are such as to justify permitting them access to commission work and facilities." If a scientist was denied clearance it was like having "a police record," except that it was grounded on "hearsay, most of it opinions" collected by young FBI agents. If "ten years ago a scientist contributed to the defense of the Scottsboro boys," or if he "believes in collective bargaining or the international control of atomic energy," such "solemnly reported" bits of information could be "regarded as 'derogatory' " and "lead to a star-chamber summary determination" that might end his "career and make his whole life unhappy." The entire process made Lilienthal "sick at the stomach."[86]

Judicious restraint seemed to be in order, which is why Lilienthal persuaded his fellow commissioners to establish a special five-man security board led by Owen J. Roberts, former associate justice of the Supreme Court. The Roberts Board was to devise investigative procedures with an eye to harmonizing concerns about security with "our traditions

255; in Truman to Attorney General Howard McGrath, 19 May 1950, Theoharis, *Truman Presidency*, 332; and in Thompson, *Frustration of Politics*, 91, 106. See also Truman's directive on the need for maintaining the confidential status of employee loyalty records, 15 March 1948, and his veto of a bill requiring character investigations of Atomic Energy Commission nominees, 15 May 1948, *Public Papers, Truman, 1948*, 181–82, 262–63; and Thompson, *Frustration of Politics*, 74–90.

[85] Hewlett and Duncan, *Atomic Shield*, 88.

[86] Lilienthal, *Atomic Energy Years*, 189–92. See also ibid., 180–81, 223, 412–14.

of civil liberties and the need for the sustained confidence and active cooperation of the scientists." Unfortunately, there was not as much support for such a course among congressional conservatives.[87]

Not long after the commission had gone into business, congressional conservatives, together with their supporters in the Army, the FBI, and the conservative press, had begun to circulate reports of lax security and disloyal employees at the AEC's facilities in Oak Ridge, Tennessee, and Los Alamos, New Mexico. The most serious charge, reported without explanation by the FBI, held that two army sergeants had stolen classified documents from Los Alamos. Subsequent investigation revealed that the sergeants had taken the documents as souvenirs at a time when the atomic energy program was under the control of the Army, whose wartime security system, as it turned out, had left much to be desired. Still, the Los Alamos story and other charges of lax security gained wide coverage in the conservative press, where the tendency was to treat them as proof that only the Army could run a competent security system. Lilienthal and his colleagues suspected, probably correctly, that General Groves, Congressman Thomas, and other opponents of the AEC were behind the leaks and were hyping the incidents to build a case for returning the atomic energy program to military control. Indeed, Thomas admitted as much in public statements, while Groves wasted no time in demanding explanations at an emergency meeting of the AEC and the Military Liaison Committee. The whole "disgraceful performance" made Lilienthal "a bit vomity." Nevertheless, he took advantage of the emergency meeting to deny that any documents of significance had been taken from the AEC, which, he also pointed out, had inherited flawed security procedures from the Army and was doing all that it could to improve them.[88]

Lilienthal's explanation defused the crisis temporarily, but not before the commission's credibility had suffered unnecessarily. What is more, Lilienthal was clearly on notice that conservative critics had little faith in civilian control of the atomic energy program, at least as long as he was in charge, and that security questions would be the weapon of choice in their efforts to return the program to the military. Thomas drove these

---

[87] Ibid., 176. See also ibid., 267–68; and Walter Gellhorn, *Security, Loyalty, and Science* (Ithaca, 1950), 84–85.

[88] Lilienthal, *Atomic Energy Years*, 189–92. See also Lilienthal to Joint Committee on Atomic Energy, 21 July 1948, Clifford Papers, box 1, folder: Atomic Energy – Joint Committee on Atomic Energy; and Hewlett and Duncan, *Atomic Shield*, 88–95.

points home in the Condon affair that surfaced during the war scare of 1948 and continued through the crisis produced by the Soviet blockade of Berlin. Involved were charges by the House Committee on Un-American Activities that Edward U. Condon, a physicist who had worked at Los Alamos and subsequently directed the National Bureau of Standards, had social and professional associations with Communist officials and thus posed a security risk to the United States.

The AEC had supposedly granted Condon a security clearance despite an FBI report that stressed his unreliability and his previous association with Henry Wallace, Truman's former secretary of commerce who had been fired in 1946 for criticizing the administration's foreign policy. Lilienthal viewed the charges as a "new idea of justice," but was convinced that congressional conservatives would use them to discredit the AEC and prevent the commissioners from extending their appointments. He thus sought to disarm the critics by agreeing to share the results of AEC security investigations, including FBI reports, with the Joint Committee on Atomic Energy. The agreement, which Truman approved, helped to defuse the crisis, as Lilienthal had hoped, but it also amounted to a retreat from the president's decision, announced in the executive order of 13 March 1948, to protect personnel records from congressional scrutiny.[89]

Another retreat would come in 1949, following a debate over the AEC's fellowship program and specifically over its decision in mid-1948 that fellowship applicants would not be denied on the basis of party affiliation, including membership in the Communist party, so long as their research did not involve restricted data. The decision squared with sentiment in much of the scientific community. The AEC's General Advisory Committee and the Federation of American Scientists had both warned that unreasonable security procedures could wreck the working relationship between science and the state, while the National Research Council had held that security clearances for graduate study would violate the tradition of academic freedom. The principles also had the support of President Truman, who joined Lilienthal in defending the idea of unfettered scientific inquiry in speeches to the American Association for the Advancement of Science. But others, including AEC commissioner

---

[89] Lilienthal, *Atomic Energy Years*, 180–81. See also AEC Commissioner Sumner T. Pike of March 1948, Clifford Papers, box 1, folder: Atomic Energy – Joint Committee on Atomic Energy; Hewlett and Duncan, *Atomic Shield*, 325–32; Fried, *Nightmare in Red*, 80–81; Theoharis, *Seeds of Repression*, 131; and Thompson, *Frustration of Politics*, 72–74.

Lewis Strauss, thought it was silly, given the shortage of scientists for work on national security projects, to invest government funds in graduate students who would never be eligible for such employment. Senator Hickenlooper went even further, expressing his steadfast opposition to using any government money to educate a Communist.[90]

Despite such objections, the AEC's decision stood until mid-1949, when two developments set the stage for a renewed assault by congressional conservatives and their allies in the Pentagon and the press. One was the commission's decision to publish what critics viewed as important military information. Lilienthal had decided to include the information in the commission's semiannual report because much of it had been published earlier, none of it was classified, and making it available would accord with democratic principles. None of this made sense to conservative critics, however, including some military leaders, who were convinced that such principles as open inquiry and the free exchange of information had to be abandoned if there was any chance that they might work to the advantage of the Soviet military.[91]

The other development was the disclosure that 289 grams of uranium were missing from a storage vault at the AEC's Argonne Laboratory near Chicago. The incident was soon blown out of proportion, since all but four grams were quickly recovered. But along with the brouhaha over the AEC's semiannual report, it helped conservatives in Congress and their allies in the media to discredit the AEC and its efforts to reconcile security considerations with such traditional principles as academic freedom.[92]

Lilienthal tried to take the high ground in congressional hearings that he described as "mean, ugly," and "nasty." He told the Joint Committee on Atomic Energy that security investigations and loyalty tests for graduate fellowships doing unclassified research amounted to an unwarranted government intrusion into the educational process. Similar arguments came from other members of the commission and from most of the scientific community. But despite this testimony, Congress added a rider to the commission's annual appropriation requiring that

[90] Lilienthal, *Atomic Energy Years,* 528–29; Federation of American Scientists, "Implications of the Atomic Energy Commission Fellowship Program," 10 June 1949, and AEC General Advisory Committee Statement Regarding the Fellowship Program, 13 June 1949, Clifford Papers, box 1, folder: Atomic Energy – Appropriations for AEC; Hewlett and Duncan, *Atomic Shield,* 340–42, 352.

[91] Lilienthal, *Atomic Energy Years,* 452–53, 461–62, 464–65, 484–87, 488–91; Hewlett and Duncan, *Atomic Shield,* 352–53, 355.

[92] See the sources cited in the following note.

all fellows be subjected to such investigations and tests. In effect, the rider meant that political conviction and party affiliation were now to be criteria for deciding whether graduate students would receive AEC fellowships.[93]

In the weeks that followed, Lilienthal survived still another assault, this one in the form of charges by Hickenlooper of gross mismanagement of everything from cost containment to weapons production to security procedures. The Joint Committee looked into the charges and issued a majority report that fully vindicated the commission. Nevertheless, Hickenlooper kept repeating his accusations and demanding Lilienthal's resignation, thus continuing a pattern of harassment by congressional conservatives that kept the AEC on the defensive.[94] Lilienthal's journal recorded the constant conservative bombardment, not only from Hickenlooper but also from "Hollering Homer Ferguson" of Michigan and "Wherry the Embalmer" of Nebraska. Even Senator Vandenberg, who was usually more supportive, thought Lilienthal was not tough enough on security issues and would no longer defend him against the conservative onslaught. Disillusioned and exhausted, Lilienthal began to think about a retreat to private life.[95]

Lilienthal also got mixed, though generally sympathetic, reviews in the national press. The mainstream conservative press, such as *Reader's Digest* and *Nation's Business*, which was published by the U.S. Chamber of Commerce, became outlets for critics in the Pentagon and in Congress who routinely leaked information that would embarrass Lilienthal and discredit the commission. Other publications, such as the *New York Times*, the *Washington Post*, and *Newsweek*, along with most of the country's leading columnists, expressed a more balanced point of view.

Few went as far as the conservative commentator Arthur Krock, who accused Lilienthal of using a veil of secrecy to hide lax security procedures. Most seemed to believe that he was guilty of no more than a few

93 Lilienthal, *Atomic Energy Years*, 531–32. See also ibid., 360–61, 528–29, 530, 532–34, 538–40, 558; James B. Conant to Senator McMahon, 18 May 1949, Lilienthal to McMahon, 13 June 1949, Federation of American Scientists, "The O'Mahoney Rider," 14 July 1949, Spingarn to Clifford, 27 July 1949, and unsigned, undated memorandum, "Comments on Proposed Amendments to Atomic Energy Commission Appropriation Act," all in Clifford Papers, box 1, folder: Atomic Energy – Atomic Energy Act; and Gellhorn, *Security, Loyalty, and Science*, 189–202.

94 Lilienthal to McMahon, 25 May 1949, Truman Papers, PSF-Subject File, box 182, folder: Lilienthal, David E.; Lilienthal, *Atomic Energy Years*, 535–36; Hewlett and Duncan, *Atomic Shield*, 358–60.

95 Lilienthal, *Atomic Energy Years*, 538–40. See also ibid., 532–34.

"borderline judgments," as Joseph Alsop put it. In their opinion, the charges of lax security were grossly overblown while the accusations of gross mismanagement flew in the face of an AEC record of great effi- ciency and achievement. To Alsop, Hanson Baldwin, Marquis Childs, Harold Hinton, Ernest Lindley, Walter Lippmann, and Cabell Phillips, among others, Hickenlooper and his conservative allies were cultivat- ing an "unwholesome air of partisanship" and were using it to vent their loathing of New Deal liberals and their resolve to recapture the atomic energy program for the armed forces. According to Baldwin, moreover, the vilification of Lilienthal was the latest example of how the "bloodhounds" in politics and in the conservative press sought to "hound men to the death," as they had "hounded" James Forrestal. He viewed this phenomenon as a sad indication of the profound anxiety that had overtaken the country in the early Cold War and of the false belief that only the atomic arsenal could safeguard the nation's secu- rity. Alsop and Lippmann made a similar point. Alsop saw the attack on Lilienthal as evidence of an "ostrich-minded national security obsession" that was gripping American politics, and both he and Lippmann worried that such vicious assaults would do great harm by driving the best sci- entists and business leaders from the scientific work on which national security actually depended.[96]

VII

The conservatives had scored a victory on the issue of AEC fellowships and had forced Truman and Lilienthal to compromise their plans to pro- tect personnel files. Their attacks, moreover, had clearly made the AEC itself more security-conscious. In dealing with trade unions, for example,

---

[96] Alsop, "The Secrecy Nonsense," *Washington Post,* 13 June 1949; Ernest K. Lindley, "McMahon vs. Hickenlooper," *Newsweek* 33 (20 June 1949): 24; and Baldwin, "Congress and the Bomb," *New York Times,* 26 May 1949. See also Krock, "A State of Mind in the Atomic Commission," and "One Instance where the Law is Plain," *New York Times,* 20 May 1949 and 5 August 1949; Alsop, "AEC's Been Wanting a Forum," "The Irrespon- sibles," and "The Atomic Madness," *Washington Post,* 29 May 1949, 3 June 1949, and 22 July 1949; Harold B. Hinton, "Fight Over Atom Control Renews Old Controversies," *New York Times,* 29 May 1949; Lindley, "The Communists and Atomic Energy," *Newsweek* 33 (30 May 1949): 23, and "The Atomic Enterprise," ibid. (6 June 1949): 22; Marquis Childs, "Politics and the Atom," "Atomic Fishing Expedition," "Atomic Cooperation," and "Atomic Relations," *Washington Post,* 2 and 8 June and 12, 20 July 1949; Cabell Phillips, "Deep Issues Underlie the Lilienthal Inquiry," *New York Times,* 5 June 1949; Baldwin, "Two Great Delusions About the A-Bomb," ibid., 10 July 1949; and Lippmann, "Senators, Scientists and Secrecy," *Washington Post,* 23 August 1949.

the commission had adopted policies at its own facilities that compromised the traditional rights of labor, including the right to strike, in order to eliminate alleged Communist influences and guarantee production. Nor was the commission always sympathetic with scientists who complained that strict security procedures would encourage ignorance and hamper progress. Despite appeals from the scientific community, to give another example, the commissioners decided on security grounds to limit the international exchange of radioactive isotopes, in part because congressional critics were convinced that any such exchange could compromise the nation's security.

Just as the AEC retreated, so did Truman err in handling certain aspects of the loyalty issue. His loyalty program did not sufficiently protect the rights of federal employees; his aggressive foreign policy pronouncements contributed to the anti-Communist hysteria; and his tendency to dismiss his liberal critics as Communists justified similar tactics by congressional conservatives. Even more important, Truman was reluctant to campaign aggressively against anti-Communists zealots in Congress and unable to control the FBI and the Justice Department, both of which had struck an alliance with congressional conservatives harmful to the president's policies.[97]

There had been setbacks in other areas as well. Although Truman had established his authority over the National Security Resources Board and the National Science Foundation, he was only partially successful in countering efforts by the armed forces to gain control of atomic energy, make their own plans for economic mobilization, subordinate civilian requirements to strategic planning, and perpetuate the waste involved in program duplication. When it came to military research and development, moreover, the services had taken advantage of the long congressional deadlock over the National Science Foundation to stake out an independent sphere of military research and development, thereby turning Bush's dream of science controlling the military into military control of science. In effect, the armed forces had negotiated their own terms for a partnership with civilian scientists, brought most federal support for scientific research under their control, and left the president without a source of scientific advice outside the Pentagon.

---

97 Lilienthal, *Atomic Energy Years*, 189–92, 259–60, 540–42; Oppenheimer to Truman, 31 December 1947, Truman Papers, PSF-Subject File, box 200, folder: NSC – Atomic – Atomic Energy – Budget; Hewlett and Duncan, *Atomic Shield*, 80–81, 97–98, 109–110, 342–48; Theoharis, *Truman Presidency*, 324. For standard critiques of Truman's policy on the loyalty/security issue see Theoharis, *Seeds of Repression*; and Freeland, *Truman Doctrine*.

By 1950, the process of state making had begun to chip away at the country's democratic identity and institutions. The nation had established a permanent peacetime military establishment for the first time in its history and the armed forces enjoyed an unparalleled degree of autonomy. Presidential prerogatives and the principle of civilian control had also lost ground to the military, particularly in such areas as military research and development. In addition, the search for security had compromised traditional civil liberties and had led the nation to devote a major share of its budget to military purposes, even before the Korean War, which, as we will see, would add immeasurably to the resources under military control.

7

Turning Point
NSC-68, the Korean War, and the National Security Response

Every story has a beginning, a middle, and an end. This chapter tells the middle part of our story – the turning point at which Truman's long struggle to contain postwar spending finally buckled and broke under the weight of a major military buildup. As we have seen, the war scare and the Republican tax cut of 1948 had stymied the president's initial efforts to downsize the military and redirect resources to peaceful purposes, the result being a budget deficit in fiscal year 1949. As the war scare dissipated, however, Truman tried again to rein in the defense budget by putting more emphasis on air–atomic power as a deterrent to Soviet expansion, by stressing mobilization potential rather than forces in being, and by using economic and military aid to help allies shoulder more of the burden of their own defense. In major respects, the administration's strategy foreshadowed the "New Look" of the Eisenhower era, which also envisioned a collective security system that the country could sustain over the long haul.

Truman's strategy had strong support from economizers who wanted to safeguard an "American way of life" they associated with a balanced budget. They still worried that national security needs would alter the American state, in effect redefining the country's postwar purpose to include defense and international obligations that were not easily reconciled with its free market values and democratic traditions. The armed forces, on the other hand, wanted a comprehensive system of deterrence that would resolve their differences at the budget's expense. Driven by the new ideology of national security, the Joint Chiefs and their allies in the State Department saw the Cold War as a permanent struggle of global proportions in which peaceful pursuits had to take a back seat to military rearmament. Instead of a mobilization base on which the country could build in case of an emergency, they wanted to prepare for all contingencies, or at least for several contingencies at once, and were sorely disappointed when the president rejected their advice in preparing the budget for fiscal year 1951. Indeed, Truman and the economizers seemed on the way to victory when hostilities erupted in Korea and quickly created a situation in which concerns about the budget finally succumbed to a major military buildup.

As this suggests, the budget story stands as subtext to a larger narrative of transformation in which national security leaders constructed a new identity for the American state – a process that unfolded over the determined opposition of economizers, and then only with the aid of a major military crisis. In this transformation, the New Deal state gave ground to the national security state, the older ideology of antistatism, antimilitarism, and isolationism gave ground to the new ideology of national security. It was a story of winners and losers, to be sure, but to a remarkable extent the two sides shared a similar language and common set of symbols, of which none was more prominent than the metaphor of the garrison state. Some saw the garrison state as an inevitable outgrowth of the New Deal and the country's ambitious overseas commitments, while others saw it as the logical consequence of isolationism and its emphasis on fortress concepts and internal security. Despite these differences, however, both sides invoked images of a government behemoth that would erode the nation's economic strength by running up deficits, debase public virtue by debasing the currency, and rob ordinary citizens of their capacity for independence by saddling them with government controls and high taxes.

The central question was how the country could safeguard its security without losing its soul. For President Truman and his allies, the answer was to be found in a mix of deterrents, including atomic weapons and foreign aid, that could be sustained without undue economic or social costs. But for Senator Taft and other conservatives, the cost of these deterrents, when added to the cost of continuing the New Deal, would be more than the country could bear. They wanted greater savings, to be achieved by building a less expensive security system around air–atomic power and by holding the defense budget hostage to cuts in social spending. Between these two camps eventually emerged a third alternative, one that blended old ways of thinking with the new ideology of national security, and one that used established values and traditions to set the nation on a new course. By the end of 1950, this alternative had begun to dominate the national security discourse and to shape rationales that would allow a nation undertaking new Cold War obligations to claim that it could still save its soul.

II

In January 1949, when President Truman submitted his budget for fiscal year 1950, he told Congress that it established a ceiling on defense spending for "the foreseeable future." The ceiling was approximately $14.5 billion in new obligatory authority, excluding the cost of stockpiling critical raw materials. This was the figure that military planners, who were then drafting the defense budget for fiscal year 1951, had to work with if substantial deficits were to be avoided and money was to be found for domestic programs and for such fixed charges as veterans' benefits and interest on the national debt. Although peacetime military preparedness was something Truman took for granted, he remained convinced that national security requirements had to be balanced "against the economic and fiscal burdens of large military expenditures." The goal was a "military defense structure which will maintain national security and which, at the same time, can be supported by the country on a continuing basis."[1]

In the debate that followed, Truman would not concede that the Cold War amounted to a real war or that the distinction between war and peace should be abandoned entirely. He argued that international tensions had abated since Congress added $3 billion to the defense budget for fiscal year 1949, and that it was therefore possible to scale back current expenditures, live safely within the ceiling he had established for fiscal year 1950, and use the same ceiling as the basis for planning the new budget for fiscal year 1951. That ceiling, to be sure, would require some reduction in the number of active duty military personnel and would slow the pace of modernization, particularly for the Air Force. But the country had to take "calculated risks," according to Truman, because it could not afford "absolute security" within the framework of a "peacetime budget."[2]

Similar arguments came from officials in the Budget Bureau. They, too, expected fiscal constraints to limit the scope of military programs in

---

[1] Truman, Annual Budget Message to the Congress: Fiscal Year 1950, 10 January 1949, *Public Papers, Truman, 1949*, 56; "Statement of the President before the National Security Council, the Joint Chiefs of Staff, Chairman of the Council of Economic Advisers, the Economic Cooperation Administrator, and Director of the Bureau of the Budget," no date, RG 51, Series 47.8a, box 51, folder: 1951 Budget – Basic Documents. See also Condit, *Joint Chiefs of Staff* 2:56.

[2] "Statement of the President before the National Security Council, the Joint Chiefs of Staff, Chairman of the Council of Economic Advisers, the Economic Cooperation Administrator, and Director of the Bureau of the Budget."

the new fiscal year, and they, too, envisioned a system of deterrence that could be sustained financially over the long haul. With these goals in mind, they urged Pentagon planners to evaluate military requirements in relation to the Marshall Plan and the military assistance program. Both of these initiatives were calculated to meet a Communist threat that was primarily political rather than military, to help allies to help themselves, and thus to reduce their dependence on American resources and military forces. Bureau officials doubted if the United States could afford to invest heavily in supercarriers and other expensive military hardware whose costs would increase dramatically in the years ahead. They even suggested that some overseas military bases might have to be deactivated. Given a "restrictive" budget, they asked, can "we continue to hold and maintain our present far flung and extensive network of facilities?"[3]

In the Pentagon, meanwhile, each service continued to jockey for special advantages in planning the budget for fiscal year 1951, with the Air Force getting the best of this maneuvering, at least initially.[4] To begin with, interservice bickering kept the Joint Chiefs from preparing a new war plan in time to influence the budget. They decided instead to work off an older, emergency plan, and this plan gave strategic air power a major role in the defense of the Western Hemisphere, the United Kingdom, and the Cairo-Suez area.[5] In addition, General Eisenhower, who was still presiding over the Joint Chiefs, rejected an effort by the Navy to protect its share of the budget by making current force levels the basis for future decision. Eisenhower agreed with the Air Force that fiscal constraints, not existing force levels, should shape the new budget, told the services to plan accordingly, and warned them to expect no more than 80 percent of what they wanted.[6]

In the planning that followed, each of the services estimated its own force level, so that the individual totals could not be integrated into a single, coherent budget and the combined figure exceeded the financial

---

[3] Budget Bureau, "Military Planning under a Restrictive Budget," 16 March 1949, RG 51, Series 47.8a, box 50, folder: FY '51 General (I).

[4] The maneuvering involved efforts by each service to win support for a war plan that would work to the advantage of its budget. See Army Chief of Staff General Omar Bradley to the Joint Chiefs, 7 January 1949, and Chief of Naval Operations Admiral Louis Denfeld to the Joint Chiefs, with attachment, 8 February 1949, RG 218, CCS 330 (8-19-45), Sec. 13; and Air Force Chief of Staff Hoyt Vandenberg to the Joint Chiefs, with attachment, 11 February 1949, ibid., Sec. 14.

[5] This plan was known at different times as Halfmoon, Fleetwood, and Trojan. See Condit, *Joint Chiefs of Staff* 2:288–94.

[6] Secretary to the Joint Chiefs to Major General Alfred M. Gruenther, 2 March 1949, RG 218, CCS 300 (8-19-45), Sec. 14.

constraints established by the president. Eisenhower worked himself into exhaustion trying to devise a system that kept spending below the president's ceiling, but his efforts failed, in large part because the Air Force and the Navy kept attacking each other's proposals. As in past debates, Admiral Louis Denfeld, the chief of naval operations, was the odd man out, since the Army and the Air Force both agreed on the importance of strategic air power. General Omar Bradley, the Army chief of staff, envisioned an Air Force of sixty-seven groups, only three less than what General Hoyt Vandenberg, the Air Force chief of staff, had in mind, but substantially more than the forty-eight groups that both the Navy and the White House favored. In addition, whereas Denfeld wanted a Navy of ten large carriers, Vandenberg and Bradley would eliminate these carriers altogether, or at least reduce their number, and would also do away with marine aviation, trim the number of naval cruisers, and cut the Marine Corps by half. Denfeld and his colleagues were infuriated by these recommendations, which they said would render the Navy unable to meet its responsibilities under the National Security Act. They considered the whole process of Pentagon decision making unfair, and they kept trying to get the budget grounded on a strategy that would limit the Air Force to forty-eight groups while protecting the Navy's fleet of large carriers.[7]

These interservice tensions only grew worse as military planning continued into June. Denfeld still wanted each service to calculate the forces it needed and to allow these forces to determine the budget, whereas Eisenhower kept urging the services to accept the president's budget ceiling and fix their force levels accordingly.[8] Adding to these old problems was the dawning realization that Truman's budget ceiling was more restrictive than had been expected in January. Rising costs, particularly for aircraft, and the introduction of expensive new technologies, such as the jet engine, required additional expenditures or substantial cuts in aircraft procurement, ship construction, research and development, industrial mobilization, and public works. According to the secretary of defense, simply maintaining American forces at current levels would

---

7 Condit, *Joint Chiefs of Staff* 2:260–64. See also Vandenberg to the Joint Chiefs, 21 March 1949, and unsigned memorandum for the Joint Chiefs, 4 May 1949, RG 218, CCS 370 (8-19-45), Sec. 15; Vandenberg to Eisenhower, 23 May 1949, and Bradley to the Joint Chiefs, with enclosure, 25 May 1949, Vandenberg Papers, box 41, folder: Budget, 1949–50; and unsigned [Norstad] memorandum for the record, 31 May 1949, and undated, unsigned [Norstad] memorandum on the 1951 budget discussions, Norstad Papers, Pentagon Series, box 20, folder: Budget FY 1951.

8 Condit, *Joint Chiefs of Staff* 2:264–71.

require increases from $14.5 billion in fiscal year 1950 to $16.5 billion in fiscal year 1951 and to $17 billion in fiscal year 1952, not to mention another $1 billion annually if the administration went along with congressional pressure for a seventy-group Air Force.[9]

As usual, these facts elicited very different responses from military planners in the Pentagon and economizers in the Budget Bureau. Despite an "apparent easing" of international tensions, the Soviet Union, according to the Joint Chiefs, had not altered its "basic objectives and military capabilities." Under these circumstances, any decrease in U.S. force levels would imperil national security and adversely affect the international situation.[10] In the Budget Bureau, on the other hand, policy makers were less concerned about the international situation. Outside of Southeast Asia, they argued, the security outlook had improved, due largely to the success of the Marshall Plan and the growing strength of America's allies in Europe. It thus seemed possible to reduce military expenditures "without improperly reducing the Nation's relative readiness," especially if the administration continued to build the national guard and other civilian components into a ready reserve on which the country could draw in an emergency.[11]

Officials in the Budget Bureau worried more about the economic situation than the international situation, and by the end of June 1949 their economic forecasts had grown gloomy. The economy was sliding into a recession and tax revenues were falling off, just as federal expenditures under current programs were expected to increase. They anticipated a budget deficit of $3–5 billion in fiscal year 1950, rising to $6–8 billion in fiscal year 1951. New taxes were unlikely politically and would be counterproductive economically. Nor was it possible to reduce expenditures by an amount equal to the projected deficit, or to find a place where even modest savings might be accomplished. Although spending for domestic programs had been increasing, the gains were marginal, the programs operated at minimum levels, and some of the expenditures, such as those to maintain public buildings, had been deferred so long that further

---

[9] Unsigned memorandum, "Assumptions Underlying Projections of the Obligational Authority for Fiscal Year 1951 and 1952," 10 May 1949, and Wilfred J. McNeil (special assistant to the secretary of defense) to Louis Johnson, with enclosure, 11 May 1949, RG 330, CD 5-1-46; Johnson to Pace, 10 May 1949, RG 330, CD 5-1-43; unsigned memorandum to the director of National Security Branch, Budget Bureau, 11 May 1949, and director, National Security Branch, to Pace, 24 May 1949, RG 51, Series 47.8a, box 50, folder: 1951 Budget Review – Projections.

[10] Johnson to Pace, 10 May 1949, RG 330, CD 5-1-43. See also Denfeld to Johnson, 18 May 1949, RG 330, CD 5-1-43.

[11] Pace to Truman, 30 June 1949, RG 51, Series 47.8a, box 51, folder: 1951 Budget – Basic Documents. See also Pace to Truman, 22 June 1949, ibid.

delays would entail substantial losses to the government. The Marshall Plan and other international programs could not be trimmed by very much, either, as these programs involved American commitments that had to be honored. The same was true of veterans' benefits, interest on the national debt, and other fixed charges on the government, which left military spending as "the only major area where significant reductions can be made."[12] According to Frank Pace, Jr., the new director of the budget, national defense accounted for one-third of all government expenditures and thus stood out as "the major problem in the budget outlook" for fiscal year 1951.[13]

Given the improved international situation and the impending deficits, Pace and his colleagues in the Budget Bureau wanted to cap defense spending at $13 billion in fiscal year 1951, a figure that was $1.5 billion below the budget expected for fiscal year 1950 and $2.5 billion below the amount required to maintain the force levels and procurement plans outlined in that budget. A budget cut of this magnitude would entail substantial adjustments in current military programs. It would mean slowing the rate at which air power was modernized; trimming active military strength by approximately two hundred thousand soldiers and sailors; and reducing the funds available for shipbuilding, industrial mobilization, military public works, and military research and development.[14] Anticipating this trend, the bureau also wanted to hold military spending in fiscal year 1950 below the amount requested by the president or appropriated by Congress, especially in those areas where rising costs threatened to drive future budgets through the roof. As a consolation, it again urged Pentagon planners to put defense spending in the context of other "quasi-military" programs, such as the Marshall Plan, the stockpiling of strategic materials, and the Atomic Energy Commission. Together with the country's air power and atomic weapons, these programs, according to the bureau, constituted a pattern of containment the country could afford.[15]

[12] Pace to Truman, 22 June 1949, ibid. See also Pace to Truman, 30 June 1949, ibid.

[13] Pace to Truman, 19 May 1949, Truman Papers, PSF-Subject File, box 150, folder: Bureau of the Budget, Budget – Misc., 1945–53 #2.

[14] Pace to Truman, 30 June 1949, and Pace to Truman, 22 June 1949, RG 51, Series 47.8a, box 51, folder: 1951 Budget – Basic Documents.

[15] Unsigned memorandum to the director of the National Security Branch, Budget Bureau, 11 May 1949, ibid., box 50, folder: 1951 Budget Review – Projections. See also Pace to Truman, 10 May 1949, Truman Papers, PSF-Subject File, box 150, folder: Bureau of the Budget, Budget – Misc., 1945–53 # 2; National Security Branch memorandum to Pace, 24 May 1949, RG 51, Series 47.8a, box 50, folder: 1951, Budget Review – Projections; and Pace to Truman, 22 June 1949, and Pace to Truman, 30 June 1949, ibid., box 51, folder: 1951 Budget – Basic Documents.

In effect, Pace and other economizers wanted to safeguard the budget even if it required some retrenchment in the country's military programs and commitments. Because their recommendations were controversial and sure to provoke opposition, Pace urged the president to discuss budget policy with key cabinet officers as quickly as possible. He also wanted the NSC and the Council of Economic Advisers to review the new ceiling with a view to assessing its strategic and economic implications.[16] Shortly thereafter, on 1 July 1949, Pace announced the tentative ceiling of $13 billion on military planning for fiscal year 1951 while Truman met with cabinet officers to review his efforts since 1945 to reduce the national debt, get federal spending on a peacetime basis, and achieve a military program that "could be sustained over a period of time," rather than "a constantly rising program."[17]

The president then set the NSC and the Council of Economic Advisers to work on the tasks that Pace had suggested. In letters drafted by the Budget Bureau, he informed both agencies that mounting concerns about "prospective deficits" required "a complete re-evaluation" of government expenditures in order to bring them within the framework of "a sound fiscal and economic program." He apparently had few doubts that outstanding commitments left little room for cutbacks in international aid or domestic programs, where spending had been held to "minimum levels." Like Pace, in other words, he seemed to believe that substantial savings were possible only in military and national security programs. He noted that military manpower had grown from 1,460,338 to 1,622,324 after the war scare of 1948 and that military spending had increased from $9.9 billion to $14.5 billion in new obligatory authority. He told the NSC that current military programs envisioned expenditures increasing to levels the country could not afford, which is why he wanted that agency, as well as his economic advisers, to assess not only the effects of budget cuts on national security but also the effects of persistent deficits on the nation's economy.[18]

---

[16] Pace to Truman, 30 June 1949, RG 51, Series 47.8a, box 51, folder: 1951 Budget – Basic Documents.

[17] Lawton memorandum of meeting with Truman, 1 July 1949, Lawton Papers, box 6, folder: Truman, President Harry S., Meetings with the President – Agendas and Memorandums, 7/49–7/52. See also Pace to Johnson, 1 July 1949, RG 330, CD 5-1-43.

[18] Truman to Sidney W. Souers (executive secretary, NSC), 1 July 1949, *FRUS, 1949* (Washington, 1976), 1:350. See also Truman to Nourse, 1 July 1949, Nourse Papers, box 6, folder: Daily Diary; and Lawton memorandum of meeting with Truman, 1 July 1949, Lawton Papers, box 6, folder: Truman, President Harry S., Meetings with the President – Agendas and Memorandums, 7/49–7/52.

Within a week Truman had reaffirmed the preliminary ceiling of $13 billion for the military establishment and had established similar limits for the Marshall Plan, the Atomic Energy Commission, the military assistance program, the stockpiling of critical raw materials, refugee assistance, and aid to the Philippines, Korea, and the occupied areas. The total for these programs came to roughly $17.7 billion, down from almost $23 billion in new obligatory authority requested in the budget for fiscal year 1950.[19] Edwin Nourse was thrilled by the president's policy and looking forward to the investigations that Truman had ordered. "The present trend of thought," he said, was "almost literally an application of the analysis" that he had presented in several recent speeches. It showed "respect" for him as a participant in the budget process and "serve[d] notice on the military" that its appropriations would be cut in fiscal year 1951.[20]

In this process Nourse and Truman had a strong ally in Secretary of Defense Louis Johnson, who had succeeded Forrestal in March. In an address to the National War College on 21 June 1949, Johnson admitted that a permanent military establishment had become "a major factor in the fiscal life of our nation," competing for "revenues with measures dedicated to the health, progress, and social welfare of the American people." Given this development, the armed forces had "to provide honest value for the dollars" they expended, because every wasted dollar subtracted from the standard of living that American taxpayers might otherwise enjoy. The challenge, in other words, was to find a level of preparedness that would deter aggression over the long term "without militarizing the nation or bankrupting it in the ordeal."[21] And to meet this challenge, Johnson set out to cut costs and improve efficiency in the Pentagon. He hired a private consulting firm to suggest ways to achieve these goals and urged a similar course on the individual services, which were soon sending the secretary their own plans for better management. He also suggested a force structure that was compatible with the president's $13 billion budget ceiling, and the structure he had in mind would involve a cut in military manpower, a Navy with only four large carriers, and an Air Force of no more than forty-eight groups.[22]

[19] NSC 52/1, Report to the National Security Council by the Acting Executive Secretary, with enclosures A and B, 8 July 1949. *FRUS, 1949* 1:352–57.
[20] Nourse memorandum, 6 July 1949, Nourse Papers, box 6, folder: Daily Diary.
[21] Johnson address before the National War College, 21 June 1949, Truman Papers, PSF-Subject File, box 145, folder: Department of Defense.
[22] Leven C. Allen, Office of the Secretary of Defense, memorandum to Gruenther et. al., 12 July 1949, RG 218, CCS 330 (8-19-45), Sec. 1; Secretary of the Navy Francis P. Matthews to

Not surprisingly, the new budget ceiling and the force structure that Johnson envisioned made it even more difficult for the services to compose their differences. For the Navy in particular the new ceiling and the emphasis on strategic air power seemed to spell disaster. According to Denfeld, the Navy needed a minimum of eight carriers to perform its assigned missions, as well as more destroyers and marine air squadrons to the tune of $110 million in additional funding. Without these increments, he warned, the Navy could not protect the Cairo-Suez area in the event of a war, nor the United Kingdom, the Iberian peninsula, or the northern Mediterranean. The Air Force did not have much to celebrate either. Even though existing war plans gave first priority to a powerful air offensive, the Air Force could not expect funding for more than forty-eight air groups and would not be able to modernize all its aircraft. According to Symington and his colleagues, the Air Force required another billion dollars if it was going to have sufficient strength to defend the United States and perform its other tasks. Anything less would retard the strategic air offensive in the event of war, jeopardize the ability of the Air Force to support ground operations or defend the United Kingdom, and call into question the credibility of the country's deterrent. "I feel strongly that we must work hard as a nation against any damaging over-extension of our economy," Symington argued. But on the other hand, "America will dread the day when the Soviet air arm, backed by the bomb, is ready," especially if it "has allowed much of its effective counter to waste away."[23]

To be sure, both the Air Force and the Navy were ready to accept the ceiling of $13 billion, but only if the sum was properly divided. For the Navy this meant a much greater investment in large carriers than the Air Force thought necessary, and for the Air Force it meant more funding for the B-36 and less for the Navy's air arm. Symington, in particular, wanted some "further consideration" of current plans to give the Navy 39 percent of the money available for aircraft procurement. Eisenhower tried to strike a compromise by supporting four large carriers, about half

Johnson, 22 July 1949, ibid., CCS 370 (8-19-45), Sec. 1; Johnson memorandum for "All Concerned," 10 August 1949, ibid.; Gordon Gray to Johnson, 11 August 1949, ibid., CCS 330.1 (6-7-49), Sec. 1; Johnson to the secretaries of the Army, Navy, and Air Force, and the Joint Chiefs, 5 July 1949, RG 330, CD 5-1-43.

23 Symington to Johnson, 21 July 1949, Symington Papers, box 6, folder: Correspondence File, 1946–50: Johnson, Louis. The Army said it needed one more division and another $33 million for equipment. For more on the needs of the Army and Air Force see Norstad (for Vandenberg) to Bradley and Denfeld, 2 August 1949, Norstad Papers, Pentagon Series, box 22, folder: Official File, 1949–50 (2); Symington to Johnson, 23 August 1949, Symington Papers, box 6, folder: Correspondence File, 1946–50: Johnson, Louis; and Condit, *Joint Chiefs of Staff* 2:274–75.

what the Navy wanted, while admitting that strategic air power, already featured in current war plans, had become even more important in light of the minimum budget available for defense. When *"we cannot have everything we want,"* he advised Secretary Johnson, we must aim first and foremost "at preserving and enhancing" the deterrent power of the country's strategic air arm, even if it meant cutting into other programs.[24]

Eisenhower had managed the grand alliance in World War II, but he could not bridge the differences between the Navy and the Air Force. Service partisanship ran so deep in the Pentagon, as did the commitment to a national security ideology that demanded total preparedness, that every compromise collapsed under their weight. By early August the Joint Chiefs had failed in their principal responsibility. They were unable to send the secretary a recommendation regarding the composition of the armed forces on which to base the allocation of funds for fiscal year 1951, and that failure called into question their competence and credibility, rendered worthless their war plans and strategic guidelines, and left them in no position to defend the budget that would finally go to Congress.

In the end, the secretary of defense had to decide the military budget and the composition of forces, and his opinions were driven as much by economic considerations as by the war plans and strategic guidelines drafted by the Joint Chiefs.[25] The Department of Defense, Johnson explained to the president, "recognizes the overriding necessity of keeping military costs within limits which will not endanger the fundamental soundness of our economy, one of our primary military assets." With this goal in mind, Johnson recommended a budget of approximately $13 billion. He held the Air Force to forty-eight groups, but increased its military manpower. He eventually agreed to ten divisions for the Army and seven carriers for the Navy, which was more than the Air Force had wanted, but he cut other combat vessels, reduced naval aircraft, and shrank marine and naval personnel substantially. The results came close to the compromise that Eisenhower had suggested, though it remained to be seen whether either the economizers or the national security managers would go along.[26]

---

[24] Symington to Johnson, 21 July 1949, Vandenberg Papers, box 41, folder: Budget, 1949–50; D.E. [Eisenhower] memorandum for Johnson, 14 July 1949, RG 218, CCS 370 (8-19-45), Sec. 18.

[25] Norstad memorandum on budget estimates, July 1949, Norstad Papers, Pentagon Series, box 22, folder: Official File, 1949–50 (2); Symington to Johnson, 23 August 1949, Symington Papers, box 6, folder: Correspondence File, 1946–50: Johnson, Louis; unsigned memorandum for Gruenther, 24 August 1949, RG 218, CCS 370, (8-19-45), Sec. 19.

[26] Johnson to Truman, 15 August 1949, RG 330, CD 5-1-43. See also General Omar Bradley, Chairman, Joint Chiefs, to Johnson, 2 September 1949, ibid.; Mark Alger (Budget Bureau)

III

The relative strength of these two groups had begun to shift, even as the next phase of the budget debate was getting underway. As secretary of state, George Marshall had resisted efforts to drive up the defense budget at the expense of Truman's economic priorities. But Marshall had now been replaced by Dean Acheson. A firm believer in the national security ideology, the new secretary tended to see the president's priorities as obstacles to a military posture that was commensurate with the country's international responsibilities, if not his own ambitions. One of the many top policy makers drawn from the Ivy League and Wall Street, or at least from one of the great Wall Street law firms, Acheson was easily the boldest and most hardheaded of the new breed of national security managers that came to center stage after World War II. James Reston of the *New York Times* later described him as "the right man in the right job at the right time."[27] This view assumes a certain affinity for the secretary's policies that may be mistaken, but is correct to the extent that Acheson was without doubt the principal draftsman and master builder of the national security system that took shape in the early Cold War.

Intelligent if not brilliant, witty though acerbic, articulate but often dogmatic, and assertive to the point of being intimidating, Acheson managed to irritate almost everyone on Capitol Hill and many of his colleagues in the administration, some of whom considered the secretary to be much too highfalutin' for their tastes. With his straight-laced demeanor and haughty tone, his bushy eyebrows and imposing mustache, Acheson was almost a caricature of the striped-pants American diplomat who looked more British than the British. Nevertheless, he possessed a broad, geopolitical vision that was remarkably similar to the one articulated by James Forrestal, not to mention a steely fortitude that Forrestal could never muster and that enabled Acheson, in the long run, to put his vision into practice. Indeed, it is impossible to exaggerate the significance of Acheson's appointment as secretary of state, as it gave the national security managers a leader of substantial personal and intellectual weight – the kind of leader that had been lacking thus far.

Another major change occurred in the Budget Bureau, where one of the nation's strongest and most influential economizers, James Webb, had been replaced by the less experienced and less influential Frank Pace. Webb, in fact, had moved to the State Department, where he worked

to Charles B. Stauffacher (Budget Bureau), 13 October 1949, RG 51, Series 39.32, box 75, folder: Army Air Forces Budget Study Staff Memoranda, 1941–1952, and Condit, *Joint Chiefs of Staff* 2:278–79.

27 James Reston, *Deadline: A Memoir* (New York, 1991), 145.

as Acheson's undersecretary, and was therefore on the other side of the debate over priorities. He had become a "renegade from the Budget Bureau," in Nourse's words, replacing his commitment to economy with Acheson's commitment to national security almost as fast as he changed jobs.[28]

Nourse's own influence as an economizer was also on the wane in 1949, in part because he could not keep his own house in order. Instead, Nourse had become involved in almost continuous quarreling with Leon Keyserling and John Clark, his colleagues on the Council of Economic Advisors, neither of whom shared his economic philosophy or his views on how the council should work. Nourse had an ivory tower concept of the council. He saw it as a professional agency that stood apart from politics and the political arena, a nonpartisan agency of economic advice that need not dovetail with presidential policies or congressional opinion. His colleagues, on the other hand, were anxious to involve the council politically. Unlike Nourse, they saw nothing wrong with testifying before congressional committees or with using the council as an instrument of the White House. Its job was not to challenge the president, they said, but to give him expert advice on how to advance his economic policies and political goals.

Nourse and his colleagues also disagreed in their economic views and assessments. Although Nourse did not see himself as a conservative economist, he was inclined to be cautious in his advice to the president and was deeply suspicious of aggressive government efforts to manage the economy. To be sure, Nourse urged new government investment in public programs that had been neglected during the war, but he did not think it possible to have both guns and butter in abundance. The American people had to balance domestic expenditures against spending on defense or risk perpetual deficits, inflationary pressures, and more intrusive government policies, including economic controls that Nourse viewed with a jaundiced eye. Keyserling, on the other hand, was a Keynesian of sorts. A liberal Democrat, he had a more benevolent view of the state and was inclined to ask if government programs were desirable politically as well as economically. He also accepted economic controls as a way to manage inflation, and budget deficits as a way to iron out the business cycle and contribute to a growth rate that made all things possible.[29]

---

[28] Nourse memorandum, 1 October 1949, Nourse Papers, box 6, folder: Daily Diary.

[29] Nourse memorandums, 9 and 13 August 1949, ibid. See also Nourse memorandum, 12 August 1949, ibid.; Hugh Stanton Norton, *The Council of Economic Advisers: Three Periods of Influence* (Columbia, SC, 1973), 1–17; Lester H. Brune, "Guns and Butter: The

Speaking before a crowd of California Democrats in September 1949, Keyserling said that what the country needed was steady growth if it was going to underwrite such desirable social goals as full employment and equal opportunity, not to mention a major military program and ambitious objectives abroad. He bragged about the growth potential of the American economy and said it was possible to increase national output from $262 billion in 1948 to an astounding $350 billion by 1958. That kind of growth would create what Keyserling called "a truly American standard of living." It would guarantee most American families an annual income of $4,000 and generate tax revenues large enough, even at current rates, to underwrite the cost of old age insurance, health insurance, aid to the poor, and other social programs. To Nourse, Keyserling's speech was little more than a political document intended to boost the president's social agenda. Its optimistic assessments, he said, only obscured the tough choices that had to be made and that Nourse's more cautious views brought squarely to the fore.[30]

Nourse had stressed these choices repeatedly in speeches on the defense budget, most recently in a speech of late August on the economic implications of military preparedness. In that speech, Nourse had attacked the idea of military Keynesianism – the notion, in other words, that military spending could prop up the economy. Although defense expenditures created demand, he argued, they also subtracted from government investment in education, health, and social security, kept taxes higher than would otherwise be the case, and thereby constrained private consumption and investment. In Nourse's view, government policy had to combine military preparedness with economic and financial preparedness, by which he meant economic conditions that inspired in the American people "a deep conviction that theirs is a political, social, and economic system that is worth defending."[31]

This combination of military and economic preparedness, of practical policy and moral purpose, was possible through initiatives like the North Atlantic Treaty, the Marshall Plan, the military assistance program, and

Pre-Korean War Dispute Over Budget Allocations: Nourse's Conservative Keynesianism Loses Favor Against Keyserling's Economic Expansion Plan," *American Journal of Economics and Sociology* 48 (July 1989): 357–72; and Ira Katznelson and Bruce Pietrykowski, "Rebuilding the American State: Evidence from the 1940s," *Studies in American Political Development* 5 (Fall 1991): 301–39.

30 Keyserling, "Prospects for American Economic Growth," 18 September 1949, Truman Papers, PSF-Subject File, box 143, folder: Council of Economic Advisers.

31 "Economic Implications of Military Preparedness," Nourse speech, 24 August 1949, Truman Papers, PSF-Subject File, box 143, folder: Council of Economic Advisers.

the Point Four program, all of which, according to Nourse, had made it easier for America's allies to share in the burden of their own defense. Together with airborne atomic power, these initiatives also constituted an "economic pattern of security" that the United States could sustain without wrecking the economic foundations on which American liberties rested. "A defense that is guided exclusively by the most perfect military considerations may be self-defeating," Nourse asserted. It might overlook the nonmilitary measures of national security, underestimate the true cost of national defense, and ignore domestic programs whose success was essential to a productive economy, a happy citizenry, and a healthy democracy.[32]

The debate between Nourse and Keyserling spoke directly to some of the key issues in the national security discourse of the early Cold War. Nourse was asking the same questions that he and other economizers had been asking since 1945. How did the United States want to define itself in the postwar period, and to what purpose should its resources be put? Must the welfare state give way to the warfare state? Must education, health, and other domestic programs give way to international obligations, including the defense of democracy abroad? These questions touched on one of the central themes in the ideology of national security – the theme of national will and sacrifice. National resolve was less of a problem to Keyserling, of course, given his conviction that Keynesian economic policies could expand the economy and alleviate the need to sacrifice on behalf of the country's global responsibilities. To Keyserling, in other words, the American people need not muster the strength of character or the moral resolve to make tough choices or substantial sacrifices. They could have guns and butter both.

But where Keyserling thought that growth made all things possible, Nourse lived in a world of choices. One of "the hard facts of economic life," he liked to say, was that "'you can't eat your cake and have it too.' You can't divert a large amount of materials and manpower to military preparedness and not adjust your domestic economy to that drain."[33] For Nourse, public policy makers were bound to explain these choices to the American people and spell out the sacrifices that national security demanded. In doing so, moreover, they should not ask for more than people were able to give or place unreasonable demands on the country's economic and political system. Doing so would only subvert the system itself, call the policy of containment into question, and undermine the

[32] Ibid.
[33] Ibid.

popular will to sacrifice on behalf of the nation's global role and responsibilities. In light of these views, it is hardly surprising that Nourse framed
his differences with Keyserling as a choice between alternative ways of
life, as well as alternative strategies of deterrence. In his rhetorical formulations, the choice was not simply between a balanced budget and deficit
spending but also between the values and institutions he associated with
those policies, between economic freedom and economic regimentation,
between democracy and the garrison state.

Nourse's dispute with Keyserling came to a head in discussions of the
president's domestic program, especially the so-called Brannan plan for
agriculture, and in debates about the economic effects of national security
expenditures. In addressing these matters, Keyserling's economic analysis yielded a long-run prospect of full employment, stable prices, and
continued growth. He was not concerned about short-term deficits or
increments to the national debt. So long as selective controls curbed inflation and government expenditures promoted growth, revenues would
increase without increasing taxes, the government would be able to balance its budget in 1952, and surpluses would accumulate thereafter. Such
a forecast made it easier for Keyserling to support presidential initiatives,
just as they would make it easier for him to support a massive American
rearmament, but they struck Nourse as unduly optimistic. He was convinced that Keyserling accepted "inflation as a way of life" and was too
easily seduced by economic controls that were likely to be both ineffective and a fundamental threat to individual initiative, private enterprise,
and democracy.[34] In addition, Nourse was not as sure as Keyserling that
the economy would continue to grow at a rate that brought both full
employment and stable prices. As he warned the president in late August, any growth in government expenditures was more likely to result
in larger deficits, more inflation, and a spiraling cycle of wage and price
adjustments.[35]

These differences undermined the council's efforts to hammer out a
coherent response to the questions that Truman had posed regarding the
budget for fiscal year 1951. Nourse and Keyserling ended up presenting
separate responses, which allowed the Budget Bureau to take the initiative with an assessment that split the differences in a way that favored
Nourse and other economizers. Although its budget forecast squared

---

[34] Nourse memorandum, 9 August 1949, Nourse Papers, box 6, folder: Daily Diary. See also
Nourse memorandum, 13 August 1949, ibid.

[35] Nourse memorandums, 22 and 26 August 1949, and Nourse to Truman, 26 August 1949,
ibid.

with Keyserling's in predicting steady or declining prices and a high level of employment and production, the bureau also predicted deficits of $5.7 billion in fiscal year 1950 and $5.1 billion in fiscal year 1951, and therefore urged the president to hold the new budget at or below the level for fiscal 1950.[36]

Armed with the bureau's recommendations and his own views, Nourse was ready to slug it out with his opponents elsewhere in the administration, especially on the NSC, which had also been assessing the effects on national security of the budget ceilings that Truman had established for fiscal year 1951. With the State Department taking the lead, the NSC's deliberations finally culminated in a report that rejected any reduction below $13 billion for the armed forces, ruled out further cuts for the Marshall Plan, and actually recommended an addition of between $1.3 and $2.1 billion to cover the cost of other programs, especially the military assistance program. These programs were essential to national security, it argued, but would not fit under the president's ceiling of $17.8 billion for defense and international programs.

The report trumpeted the new ideology of national security, including America's new responsibilities as the global defender of democracy and the notion that peace and freedom were indivisible in an age of total war. America's security, it argued, as well as American democracy, depended upon its willingness and ability to "establish world conditions under which we can preserve and continue to develop our way of life" against the challenge of Soviet imperialism. It was to this end that the United States had launched the Marshall Plan, negotiated the North Atlantic Treaty, and supported a peacetime military establishment, and it was along this path that it must continue to seek its security. To be sure, American leaders had to take care that security expenditures did not "permanently" impair the economy or compromise "the fundamental values and institutions in our way of life." Deficit spending had to be contained, if only because a strong domestic economy was absolutely essential to the country's military strength and international position. But at the same time, the report turned the economy argument upside down. It argued, in effect, that cuts in current programs would drive up the long-term cost of achieving the country's foreign policy goals, whereas the same programs, if fully funded and carried to completion, would permit the United States to liquidate its outstanding commitments

---

[36] Unsigned memorandum for Truman [undoubtedly a BOB memorandum], 21 September 1949, Truman Papers, PSF-Subject File, box 150, folder: Bureau of the Budget, Budget – FY 1951.

and enable other countries to contribute to their own security. Economic and political conditions would be so improved in areas of interest to the United States that future national security expenditures could be reduced, if not eliminated altogether. In short, the report argued a Keynesian case for short-term deficits that would enable the United States to achieve its foreign policy goals and thereby return to a balanced budget in the long run.[37]

Although the report manipulated some of the same rhetorical symbols and conventions that Nourse had used earlier, especially the notion of an American "way of life," it used them to argue for action that would do more harm than good to the country's basic "values and institutions." At least this was what Nourse told the NSC when it met to consider the report. Together with Acting Secretary of the Treasury Edward H. Foley, another economizer, he maintained that national security expenditures would remain higher than the report suggested. He rejected the claim that military and international programs, if fully funded, would enable the country to reduce its overseas commitments. And he accused the NSC of dodging the consequences of persistent deficits, which to his way of thinking posed the real threat to national security and traditional freedoms.

If the United States was going "to meet the strains of a possible war or an indefinitely sustained defense effort," Nourse reminded the NSC, it had to "maintain economic conditions" that promoted "maximum industrial strength and political and social stability." It must not aggravate the current "threat of nation-wide strikes in basic industries and the menace of Communistic elements in the unions," both of which were "manifestations of the industrial strains" that resulted when "so large a part of the national product" contributed so little "to domestic well-being." Nourse was referring specifically to military expenditures that amounted to a drain on "real wages," drove up taxes, increased operating costs, and threatened the "ability of employers to offer jobs or to expand and improve plant." But in a general sense he was also repeating the point about the nation's democratic character that he had made earlier in his debate with Keyserling. He was arguing, in other words,

---

37 The quoted material is taken from the final version of the NSC report, NSC-52/3, 29 September 1949, *FRUS, 1949* 1:385–93. For an overview see also the documents enclosed in the memorandum from Souers to Webb and others, no date [October 1949], Nourse Papers, box 6, folder: Daily Diary. The documents include Truman's instructions to the council, the proposed ceilings on national security expenditures for fiscal year 1951, the conclusions reached in NSC-52/3, and Nourse's memorandum of 1 October 1949 summing up the council's deliberations on this document.

that excessive spending on defense would not only weaken the economy but would also subvert democracy and undermine the popular resolve to sacrifice on behalf of national security.

To drive his point home, Nourse reminded his NSC colleagues that government had incurred a deficit of nearly $2 billion in fiscal year 1949 and faced a deficit of at least twice that amount in each of the next two fiscal years. Those deficits would virtually wipe out the debt reduction of $7 billion in fiscal year 1948, thereby calling into question "the whole doctrine of a budget balanced over the period of the full economic cycle." Such a development had ominous implications for capital formation, social services, taxation, and labor–management relations, particularly in a democratic country that wanted to avoid the rigid controls by which authoritarian systems squeezed military muscle "out of a lowered standard of living for the masses." American "statecraft," Nourse insisted, must deal with "the economic behavior of free men and how soon and in what ways that free behavior will have to be curtailed if we are to meet the commitments we undertake and at the same time avoid a collapse of the financial machinery, public and private, on which our total security program rests."[38]

Nourse was making the point that budget priorities had something to say about the nation's sense of its own identity, about the nature of the postwar state, about the prospects for democracy when resources were permanently squeezed from civilian investment to military purposes. The logic of his remarks, given his support for domestic expenditures and the Marshall Plan, was that further reductions in the defense budget were in order. But officials from the State and Defense departments, while recognizing the economic risks involved, refused to amend their document or reverse their conclusion that deficits had to be tolerated to underwrite the national security programs they envisioned. As approved, NSC-52/3 recommended an increase of between $1.3 and $2.1 billion in the combined budget ceiling for military and international programs in fiscal year 1951. It targeted most of that amount, between $1 and $1.5 billion, for the military assistance program, which Nourse had wanted to subtract from the budget for the armed forces. The main concession to the economizers was a decision to append a statement of Nourse's

[38] Nourse to NSC, 30 September 1949, *FRUS, 1949* 1:395–96. See also the unsigned memorandum for Truman, 30 September 1949, Truman Papers, PSF-National Security Council Meetings, box 220, folder: NSC Meetings: Memos for the President & Meeting Decisions; Nourse to Truman, 26 August 1949; and Nourse memorandum, 1 October 1949, Nourse Papers, box 6, folder: Daily Diary.

views to the final document, as well as a similar though less aggressive statement by Acting Secretary Foley.[39]

Still, if NSC-52/3 did not recommend the cuts in defense spending that Nourse and the Budget Bureau thought necessary, neither did it recommend increases of the size sought by the Joint Chiefs of Staff. The outcome instead was a compromise that reflected something of a stalemate over national security spending at the end of 1949. Truman stuck to this compromise in his budget proposals for the new fiscal year, although his rhetoric sounded more like that of the economizers than of their opponents. Like Pace and others in the Budget Bureau, Truman downplayed the threat to national security. The "greatest danger has receded," he told Congress, in that Europe and the Mediterranean area had been bolstered against the Communist menace. The president bragged most about the new start his administration had made in various social programs, such as raising the minimum wage and providing low-income housing. He wanted more progress in these areas and continued to argue, along with Nourse, that social investment was one source of the nation's military strength. That strength was "not simply a matter of arms and force," the president said, but of economic growth, "social health, and vigorous institutions."[40]

Truman asked Congress for $40.5 billion in new obligatory authority to support expenditures of $42.7 billion in fiscal year 1951. To be sure, the Republican tax cut made it difficult to invest in domestic programs without adding to the deficit, which new estimates put as high as $5.5 billion in fiscal year 1950, not to mention the $5.1 billion deficit in the proposed budget for fiscal year 1951. Much the same was true of new expenditures for military purposes or for international and security programs broadly defined. As it was, military and international programs, together with veterans' benefits, payments on the national debt, and other indirect military spending, still constituted slightly more than 70 percent of the budget for the new fiscal year. Nevertheless, Truman was confident

---

[39] In addition to Nourse's memorandum of 1 October 1949, cited in the previous note, see minutes of the 46th meeting of the NSC, 29 September 1949, Truman Papers, PSF-National Security Council Meetings, box 206, folder: NSC Meeting #46, 9-29-46; unsigned memorandum for Truman, 30 September 1949, ibid., box 220, folder: NSC Meetings: Memos for the President & Meeting Decisions; Nourse to the National Security Council, 30 September 1949, *FRUS, 1949* 1:394–96; and Nourse to Truman, 26 August 1949, Nourse Papers, box 6, folder: Daily Diary.

[40] Truman annual message to the Congress on the state of the union, 4 January 1950, *Public Papers, Truman, 1950* (Washington, 1965), 2–11. See also Truman annual message to the Congress, "The President's Economic Report," 6 January 1950, ibid., 18–31.

that he could reduce that percentage over time, and not simply because the threat to American security had supposedly diminished. Through the North Atlantic Treaty and the military assistance program, the president was also forging a system of collective security that would be less dependent on American military muscle. Then, too, he had long ago rejected the absolutist thinking that was central to the ideology of national security, favoring instead a program of "relative military readiness" that the country could afford over a long period of time and on which it could build in the event of an emergency.[41]

As Truman viewed it, moreover, the budget for fiscal year 1951 was moving in the right direction. The cost of past wars and current national security programs came to roughly $30 billion, a reduction of nearly $2 billion from the previous year. The president earmarked $1.1 billion of the total amount for military assistance and approximately $13.9 billion for national defense. The latter sum included $13.1 billion in obligatory authority, of which $12.3 billion would be divided among the armed forces. The figures for national defense were considerably less than anticipated a year earlier and barely enough to maintain force levels of 10 army divisions, 48 air groups, and 238 major combat vessels, including 7 heavy carriers.

Expenditures other than those for national security constituted 29 percent of the proposed budget, or $12.5 billion. Although these expenditures still claimed a smaller proportion of the national income than they had in 1939, Truman's new budget would increase domestic spending by $1 billion over fiscal year 1950. This increase would come on top of small increments in previous years and would be followed by additional increments as the economy grew and the cost of defense and international programs declined. The question was "not whether we are doing too much," the president told Congress, "but whether the budgetary requirements of the major national security and war-connected programs have constrained us to undertake too little toward supporting and stimulating the realization of our country's great potential development." The country needed more government investment, not less, in housing, health care, social security, education, and public improvements of all sorts.[42]

Not everyone in the press or in Congress agreed with the choices and the priorities that Truman spelled out. On the contrary, the 1951 defense budget drew more attention from leading columnists than had any of

[41] Truman annual budget message to the Congress, "Fiscal Year 1951," 9 January 1950, ibid., 44–106.
[42] Ibid.

its postwar predecessors, and much of it was critical. To be sure, Walter Lippmann seemed more sympathetic with Truman on budget issues than he usually was on other issues, in large part because he had serious reservations about the growing sweep of the country's commitments around the world and its tendency to rely too heavily on military power to achieve its goals. A leaner budget, in this sense, could help to corral what Lippmann saw as some of the worst aspects of American foreign policy.[43] Other commentators, such as Hanson Baldwin, Arthur Krock, and Marquis Childs, sympathized with efforts to eliminate waste and promote economies in the Pentagon. But they also wondered if Truman and Secretary Johnson had cut the budget too close to the bone and were absolutely certain that further cuts in Congress would drive defense spending below desirable levels and aggravate interservice squabbles. As usual, Baldwin and Krock were more inclined to accept further reductions in domestic spending than in defense spending, while Childs drifted toward the guns-and-butter Keynesianism that Keyserling had articulated.[44]

The most aggressive and acerbic members of this group were Joseph and Stewart Alsop, who devoted enormous space in their weekly columns to a vigorous critique of the defense budget for fiscal year 1951. The two brothers abandoned all pretense of a balanced analysis in favor of a partisan assault on the administration's defense program, notably Truman's budget ceilings and Secretary Johnson's efforts to economize in the Pentagon. In a drumbeat of unrelenting criticism that continued through the deliberations in Congress, they argued that Truman's cuts amounted to a program of unilateral disarmament. This program turned away from the more realistic budget policies that Forrestal had tried to promote, lacked the backing of military experts, especially the Joint Chiefs, and was dangerously foolhardy at a time when the Soviets had just exploded their first atomic device.

It was a "grave scandal," the Alsops said, that realistic "defense planning had been progressively sacrificed to the problem of the budget." As a result, the defense budget added up to little more than "a concealed disarmament program," a "false front" of economy behind which lurked

43 Lippmann, "The National Security," and "The Damnable Obsession," *Washington Post*, 3 April and 1 June 1950.
44 Krock, "Senator Byrd Offers Own 'Budget Message,'" *New York Times*, 11 December 1949; Childs, "Johnson as a Candidate," "Cuts in Foreign Aid," and "Economies and Empire Building," *Washington Post*, 16 and 22 December 1949, and 22 March 1950; and Baldwin, "Pentagon Battle is Far From Over" and "State of Our Defense: An Audit and Appraisal," *New York Times*, 25 December 1949 and 2 April 1950.

"the specter of our eventual defeat in the world struggle with the Soviet Union." The administration, the Alsops argued, had made a mistake in thinking that it was possible to wage the Cold War "with one eye on the budget." Nor was there any need to do so. After all, the country had run substantial annual deficits during World War II and had still emerged from that struggle with its national income tripled and its wealth immeasurably increased. The lesson, according to these Keynesians, was that deficits must be tolerated in the name of national security, and were far "better than slavery or death." Guided by this kind of thinking, the Alsops urged Congress to add up to $7 billion to the defense budget that Truman had recommended, a whopping increase of more than 50 percent.[45]

Arguments in Congress paralleled those in the administration and in the press. Contrary to what the Alsops had recommended, the House subcommittee that considered Truman's budget actually reduced appropriations for the new fiscal year by slightly less than $1 billion. But it still reported "the largest peacetime appropriation bill in the history of the Nation," to quote what had now become an old saw, with an estimated deficit of more than $4 billion. In debating the committee's bill, many on Capitol Hill were ready to discount the old distinction between war and peace, which had given way to a new era of permanent war, or at least of permanent preparedness. It had been a long time since Congress had considered a truly peacetime budget, lamented Congressman Clarence Cannon, a Democrat from Missouri who headed the House Appropriations Committee. It now dealt in "war budgets," for all practical purposes, and these were never balanced. "Everyone knows that a certain type of war is in progress," declared Cannon. It was a "cold war," but it brought "about expenditures in some ways comparable to a shooting war."[46]

Still, as Cannon defined its task, Congress had to keep the gap between permanent preparedness and a balanced budget to a minimum if it wanted to safeguard the American way of life. His subcommittee

45 Alsops, "The Scandal," "The Headwaters," "Johnson and the Chiefs," and "The Cost of Mr. Johnson," and Stewart Alsop, "Cold Wars Can Be Won," *Washington Post*, 11 January, 6, 20, and 17 February and 3 March 1950. See also, Alsops, "Johnson is Very Vulnerable," "Our Fake Defense," "Leadership in a Democracy," "Dimensions of the Deficit," "More American Disarmament," "Retreat from Reality," and "Mr. Johnson's Untruths," and Stewart Alsop, "The Kennan Swan Song," "Mr. Johnson's Untruths," and "The Confidence Trick," *Washington Post*, 19, 21, 24, 28 October 1949, 21 November 1949, 19 December 1949, 15, 24 February 1950, and 6, 10 March 1950.
46 *Congressional Record, 1950* 96:4616, 4617, 6829–30.

therefore felt justified in reducing the president's proposed expenditures on domestic programs – in effect, by eliminating the $1 billion increase that Truman had suggested. To spend more on domestic programs, said Cannon, would increase the deficit, add to a national debt of more than a quarter of a trillion dollars, and thus reveal a "lack of moral fiber and stamina" on the part of Congress. Cannon felt the same way about increasing defense expenditures. Such a course, he said, would play into the hands of the Soviets, who wanted nothing more than to see the United States spend itself into bankruptcy. Nor was it justified at a time when security needs were already being met through an overall package that also included the Atomic Energy Commission, the Marshall Plan, military assistance, and other national security programs broadly construed.[47]

Once the subcommittee's budget reached the House floor, Cannon's line of argument came under assault from two directions. On one side was Congressman Carl Vinson, the Georgia Democrat who led those who wanted to increase defense expenditures, while on the other side was Republican Congressman Richard Wigglesworth of Massachusetts, who was appalled by the size of the budget, the projected deficit, and the damage these could do to the free-market values and national character on which democratic capitalism was founded.

In Vinson's opinion, the threat to American security had actually increased in the last year. After all, the Soviets had exploded an atomic device, China had become a "slave state," and Indochina was in turmoil, all of which amounted to a rising tide of danger with which the defense budget must keep pace. Vinson and his allies also excoriated Truman for impounding funds that Congress had appropriated for air power, and Secretary of Defense Johnson for canceling the supercarrier. In their view, Johnson's efforts to economize had put short-sighted savings ahead of military preparedness, thus running the risk of another Pearl Harbor. Neither Vinson nor his allies expected Congress or the administration to support the kind of defense program they had in mind, including a seventy-group Air Force. But at the very least they wanted additional funds to modernize the current force of forty-eight groups, and they would get these funds, if necessary, by further reducing domestic expenditures.[48]

By 1950, of course, it was commonplace in budget negotiations for Vinson and his colleagues to warn of another Pearl Harbor. Every time Congress took up the defense budget, explained Congressman George

[47] Ibid., 4619, 4685. See also ibid., 4686.
[48] Ibid., 6177–79. See also ibid., 4681–84, 4686, 4689–90, 6180–81, 6187–88.

H. Mahon, a Texas Democrat who chaired the Military Appropriations Subcommittee, "flying saucers begin to sail across the western horizon," "unidentified submarines flit to and fro in the Pacific waters and even our friends" say that "Russia is planning a new Pearl Harbor." He agreed with Cannon that additional expenditures on defense were neither necessary nor desirable, and both agreed with Truman that "absolute and complete readiness for war" would wreck the economy, "destroy our liberties," and bring on a "police state." The best defense in their opinion was to be found in "national solvency," which could not be obtained by "bankrupting the country" and destroying the American "way of life."[49]

This line of argument summoned up the familiar symbol of the garrison state. But this was a contested symbol that meant different things to different people, and thus underscored the contested nature of state making and national identity in the early Cold War. Some used it to fend off pressure for a larger defense budget than the president had in mind, others to claim that even greater defense expenditures would be needed to protect American liberties from the Communist menace, and still others to argue for drastic reductions in all areas of the budget, lest the country be "driven down the road, by taxes and constantly increasing debt, to bankruptcy and dictatorial government." This last warning came from Congressman Wigglesworth, Senator Taft, and other economizers, whose rhetorical strategy continued to associate low taxes, a balanced budget, and a free economy with American democracy, just as they continued to equate high taxes, budget deficits, and government controls with the totalitarian other. They were appalled by a federal budget that topped $42 billion and a federal deficit of more than $4 billion, especially at a time when the national debt had reached unparalleled proportions and when the average American was paying more than a quarter of his income in taxes of all kinds. By their calculations, the tax burden was nearly six times greater than it had been before Pearl Harbor and would lead, unless reversed, to what Taft called a "hand-out state," a "poorhouse state," or a "police state." He wanted to reduce government spending by at least $3 billion, and he would achieve the reduction in part by permitting air–atomic power to carry more of the burden of deterrence.[50]

[49] Ibid., 4688, 4686, 4619, 4785.

[50] Ibid., 4694; Taft to Walter Rogers, 26 November 1949, Taft Papers, Subject File, box 911, folder: 1949, Political, Republican. See also Taft to R.P. Erwin, 19 December 1949, Taft Papers, box 901, folder: 1949, Budget; and Taft to A.H. Thomas, 24 January 1950, Taft Papers, box 915, folder: 1950, Budget.

Some congressional critics traced the rise of big budgets and high taxes to the national security policies of World War II and the Cold War; others started their time line with the New Deal. Republican Congressman Joseph Martin of Massachusetts marked 1933 as the "turning point." That was the first of six years of "pump-priming, "compensatory spending," and peacetime deficits, all of which Truman and the Democrats sought to continue after the Second World War. In Martin's account the real culprit was not defense spending, which had declined sharply since 1945, but domestic spending, which had steadily increased. Congressman Wigglesworth and others agreed with Martin's analysis. Wigglesworth noted that Truman's proposed budget was $8 billion above expenditures in fiscal year 1948. That total included $5 billion earmarked for domestic programs, and that $5 billion, as Congressman Burr Harrison, a Virginia Democrat, pointed out, more or less equaled the current deficit for fiscal year 1950 and the projected deficit for fiscal year 1951. Trapped by the "welfare state," the administration was eroding the nation's economic strength, just as Lenin had predicted and just as the same "blueprint for socialism" had brought Great Britain "to its knees." It was embarked on a course that would eventually undermine America's military strength and position in the world economy, and would produce instead a "dictatorial" regime that destroyed "precious liberties" and turned every citizen into a "servant of the state."[51]

Like Truman and Nourse, congressional economizers were convinced that hard choices had to be made if they wanted to avoid the garrison state and preserve the country's capitalist economy and democratic politics. But just as they saw different roads to serfdom, so also did they favor different avenues of retreat. Although some wanted further restrictions on defense spending and international programs, most believed that the Soviet threat left the American people with little choice but to live "in an armed camp." To be sure, the federal government had to conserve its resources, lest the Soviets "outstay us," but conservation had to come in domestic programs primarily. Social needs had to be met on a local or voluntary basis, and the country had to do without some land reclamation projects and some bridges, dams, parks, roads, and other public improvements, all of which were luxuries in a period of prolonged international crisis.[52]

[51] *Congressional Record, 1950* 96:4853, 4922, 4854, 4700, 4858. See also ibid., 4696–99, 4704–5, 4844–45, 4855–56, 4869–71, 4873–74.
[52] Ibid., 4948, 4923. See also ibid., 4856, 4869, 6176–77, 6512.

In short, each side in the debate feared a garrison state brought on by ballooning budgets and a growing debt that expanded the public sector at the expense of the private. Each side thought that economies were necessary, and each side resorted to rhetorical style that identified its recommendations with the future of democracy, alternative recommendations with the totalitarian other. Whereas Truman and his allies would hold the line on defense expenditures, conservatives like Vinson, Martin, and Wigglesworth wanted cuts in domestic spending, in some cases to free up additional resources for defense. In conservative thinking, the big budgets and big government of the Cold War were linked not only to national security imperatives but also to the New Deal of the 1930s. They were part of a twenty-year trend toward statism, which had to be stopped, if necessary by holding the defense budget hostage to cuts in social spending.

As it turned out, the House of Representatives forced the president into a compromise that gave conservative economizers part of what they wanted. Truman reluctantly supported various amendments adding approximately $385 million to the defense budget, thereby defusing demands for even greater additions. In this sense, he had scored another victory, however modest, in the battle over defense spending. Still, he could not convince Congress to invest more heavily in domestic programs that had been starved for support. On the contrary, gains in these areas were sacrificed to the cost of national security, past and present, and to the Republican party's opposition to a tax increase. In the new budget, for example, the amendments allocating another $385 million for defense fueled a Republican party economy drive that cut nondefense spending by another $550 million.[53]

IV

Even as the House debated Truman's modest defense budget for fiscal year 1951, hard-liners in the administration were arming themselves with the fullest statement yet of the national security ideology that had been forming for several years. Known as NSC-68, it would become an important weapon in their renewed assault on the citadel of sound fiscal policy.

53 See ibid., 6745–6842, for the House debate over various amendments to reduce the proposed budget. The House passed an amendment authorizing the administration to cut $600 million from the final budget. The Senate included a similar amendment in its version of the bill, and the House-Senate compromise authorized cuts of $550 million in areas other than defense. The story is summarized in *Congressional Quarterly Almanac, 1950* 6:113–30.

Aiding the hard-liners as well were further changes in the ranks of top policy makers and a succession of ominous international developments. The period from late 1949 through early 1950 witnessed the successful Soviet test of an atomic device, the collapse of China to the Communists, the continuing spread of revolutionary nationalism in Southeast Asia, and the conviction of Alger Hiss, a former State Department official, for concealing his work as a Soviet spy. Needless to say, these explosive events played into the hands of an increasingly militant group of national security managers who were contemptuous of conservative economizers in Congress, or in the administration, and equally hostile to the kind of balanced strategy that Truman had in mind.

Developments abroad were particularly important because they seemed to portend a dangerous shift in the global balance of power. "During the last six to nine months," Acheson explained in March 1950, "there had been a trend against us which, if allowed to continue, would lead to a considerable deterioration in our position." The Soviet explosion of an atomic device was especially troubling. It meant not only the likelihood of a more reckless Soviet diplomacy but also a weakening of America's atomic deterrent and the need for new measures to make it credible. The same argument reverberated in the Pentagon, where officials missed no opportunity to make the case for additional funds. Symington, in particular, argued relentlessly that Russia's atomic capability, if combined with new techniques for refueling bombers in flight, imperilled "the survival of the United States." To his way of thinking, the administration had no choice but to enhance the American deterrent with a modern, seventy-group air force. This would require "some reduction" in the country's "living standard," he admitted, but "the consequences of inadequate provision" were simply "unthinkable."[54]

The new global developments had occurred too late to influence the defense budget that Truman submitted to Congress in January 1950. The administration had finished the budget in late 1949, before national security managers could fully assess the significance of the new developments or mount a strong campaign for further rearmament. What is more, Truman had managed to deflate the pressure for greater defense expenditures by expanding the stockpile of atomic weapons and moving ahead with the development of a hydrogen bomb. Both decisions

---

54 Acheson memorandum of conversation with Republican Congressman Christian A. Herter of Massachusetts, 24 March 1950, *FRUS, 1950* 1:206–9; Symington to Johnson, 8 November 1949, Symington Papers, box 6, folder: Correspondence File, 1946–50: Johnson, Louis. See also Leffler, *Preponderance of Power*, 323–26, 332–43.

dovetailed with the capital-intensive strategy of defense that had taken shape earlier. They relied, that is, on low-cost nuclear weapons rather than expensive conventional forces to reconcile national security considerations with Truman's concern for the budget.[55]

Although events abroad came too late to influence military strategy or budget making, there is little doubt that they helped to set the stage for a fundamental reassessment of national security policy and its relation to the budget. Much the same can be said of the important changes that occurred in the ranks of top policy makers, one of these being the resignation of Edwin Nourse as chairman of the Council of Economic Advisers and the elevation to that post of Leon Keyserling. Nourse was upset when his pleas for further economy had failed to sway the National Security Council as it debated NSC-52/3. Other setbacks followed when the White House backed a separate program of military assistance, instead of subtracting the cost of that program from the defense budget, and when the president refused to heed Nourse's public warnings about the dangers of a mounting deficit. On the contrary, stung by the public criticism of his policies, Truman decided to find another chairman for the Council of Economic Advisers. The decision eliminated one of the president's staunchest allies in his struggle against the Joint Chiefs and other advocates of a larger defense budget. It was in that sense ironic, though no more so than Truman's subsequent decision to replace Nourse with Leon Keyserling, whose Keynesian optimism would prove so useful to the national security elite.[56]

Another major change came shortly after Nourse's departure, when Acheson asked Paul H. Nitze to head up the State Department's Policy Planning Staff, replacing George Kennan, who would soon leave government service altogether. The change was every bit as important as Marshall's retirement, Nourse's departure, and Webb's move from the Budget Bureau to the State Department. This was so because Kennan, despite his tendency toward alarmist rhetoric, did not believe that the Soviets posed an immediate military threat to American security. To him

---

[55] Rearden, *Formative Years*, 523; Leffler, *Preponderance of Power*, 327–31; Samuel F. Wells, Jr., "Sounding the Tocsin: NSC 68 and the Soviet Threat," *International Security* 4 (Fall 1979): 116–58.

[56] Nourse memorandum, 17 October 1949, Nourse memorandum, 22 October 1949, with attached speech by Nourse, "The March of Progress – *Economically*," 18 October 1949, Nourse Papers, box 6, folder: Daily Diary; Joseph and Stewart Alsop, "The Economic Schism," *New York Herald Tribune*, 17 October 1949; and Anthony Leviero, "President's Economists Entering a New Phase," *New York Times*, 23 October 1949, both in Elsey Papers, box 57, folder: Council of Economic Advisers.

the Communist challenge remained principally an economic and political one, to be matched by economic and diplomatic initiatives like the Marshall Plan.

Not surprisingly, this kind of thinking made Kennan a less-than-reliable ally in Acheson's campaign to defeat the economizers and push Truman toward a more expansive defense establishment. So did Kennan's sometimes oblique sympathy with efforts to balance economic and military imperatives. Given his reading of the Communist threat, he wanted to "maximize" the country's "economic potential," rather than its military might. He was also troubled by the tendency to militarize American foreign policy and had a particular aversion to the country's growing reliance on nuclear weapons. In NSC 20/4, which he drafted in late 1948, Kennan had argued for a level of preparedness that could be sustained over the long term and would be sufficient to meet "immediate military commitments" only. Such views came close to the middle ground that Truman sought to hold. But they were anathema to Acheson, who finally replaced Kennan with Paul Nitze, a successful investment banker turned national security manager who had served on the strategic bombing survey after World War II.[57]

Every bone in Nitze's body ached with suspicion of the Soviet Union. Severe in appearance and even more severe in his outlook, Nitze had spent his college days at Harvard, where he had "studied, almost memorized, Spengler's *Decline of the West*." No doubt Spengler added the philosophical underpinnings to a personal view that was darkly pessimistic and grew increasingly gloomy as World War II gave way to the Cold War. Nitze thought of the Soviet Union as he had thought of Nazi Germany, viewed Stalin as another Hitler, and was convinced that Communist leaders would stop at nothing, even nuclear war, in their messianic quest for world domination. Given Acheson's own geopolitical vision, it is clear that he had picked the right man to join him on the front line of the next battle against the economizers, with their old ways of thinking, and against the president and others who were trying to balance the needs of the welfare state against those of the warfare state without throwing the budget into permanent deficit. If anything, recalled James

57 Kennan's thinking is taken from NSC-20/4, 23 November 1948, *FRUS, 1948* (Washington, 1976), 1:663–69. See also Ernest R. May, ed., *American Cold War Strategy: Interpreting NSC 68* (Boston, 1993), 7–8; Wells, "Sounding the Tocsin," 120–22, Leffler, *Preponderance of Power*, 313, 324, 329; and Paul Y. Hammond, "NSC-68: Prologue to Rearmament," in *Strategy, Politics, and Defense Budgets*, 287–88.

Reston, who was one of Nitze's Georgetown neighbors, the new head of the Policy Planning Staff was "almost too '*hard-charging*' for even his close friend at State, Secretary Acheson," who was no piker when it came to pressing his own worst-case scenarios on the government.[58]

With the Soviet atomic explosion in the background, Acheson and Nitze undertook another review of the country's national security requirements. For this they organized a committee headed by Nitze and composed of like-minded officials, including supporters in the State and Defense departments but none of the economizers who had thrown a wrench into so many previous plans. The eventual result was NSC-68.[59]

As Steven Rearden and Melvyn Leffler have pointed out, NSC-68 recapitulated many of the arguments outlined in earlier NSC documents but gave them a greater sense of urgency and integrated them more fully into a national security ideology. It continued to demonize the Soviet Union as "unlike previous aspirants to hegemony" in that it was "animated by a new fanatic faith, antithetical to our own, and seeks to impose its absolute authority over the rest of the world." Although the Soviets had no plans for immediate war with the United States, or so the document concluded, they did have the capacity to overrun large parts of Eurasia and their military power was growing steadily. They already possessed between 10 and 20 atomic bombs, would have between 45 and 90 in just 2 years, and would possess a minimum of 200 by mid-1954, at which time their threat to American security would reach a point of maximum danger.

In addition, NSC-68 estimated that Soviet officials were spending an enormous proportion of their national wealth on armaments of all kinds. While the United States was investing approximately 6.5 percent of its gross national product in the military establishment and another 13.6 percent in defense-related industries, the Soviet Union was sinking 13.8 percent and 25.4 percent of its gross national product in the same two areas, respectively. As a result, the United States lacked the military power to end the current "diplomatic impasse" with the Kremlin or to advance its own position in the Cold War. Still worse, if the American position continued to deteriorate, the Soviet Union would grow bolder, the United

---

[58] Reston, *Deadline*, 187.

[59] May, *American Cold War Strategy*, 10–11, Wells, "Sounding the Tocsin," 130; and Hammond, "NSC-68: Prologue to Rearmament," 303. Truman commissioned the review to determine the effect of the Soviet Union's atomic capability on U.S. security. See Truman to Acheson, 31 January 1950, *FRUS, 1950* 1:141–42.

States would be thrown onto the defensive, and its allies would retreat into neutrality.[60]

Permeating the document's analysis were some of the central themes in the ideology of national security. There was the usual emphasis on the modern age as an age of "total war," a time when the introduction of atomic bombs and other weapons of mass destruction confronted "every individual" in every country with the "possibility of annihilation." The Soviet-American confrontation was "total" in this sense and in others as well. It was a "permanent struggle," so that the old distinction between war and peace had disappeared, at least until the Soviet system changed in fundamental ways. It also involved not only military but economic, political, and psychological warfare, and not just the armed forces but all elements of society.

Repeating still another theme in the national security ideology, NSC-68 argued that victory in the current struggle required sacrifices, that Americans had to muster the will to make these sacrifices, and that doing so was an obligation of citizenship in a democratic country. "A large measure of sacrifice and discipline will be demanded of the American people," said NSC-68, who may even be "asked to give up some of the benefits which they have come to associate with their freedoms."[61] The notion that freedom was indivisible, another theme in the national security ideology, also found a prominent spot in NSC-68, as did the corollary conviction that Americans had no choice but to rethink the way they saw themselves, cast off their old isolationist habits, and accept their new identity as the champion of freedom everywhere. Indeed, NSC-68, like other such documents, drew the boundaries of America's political identity in a way that tied the survival of democracy at home to its defense abroad. Not only must Americans "fight if necessary to defend our way of life," said the document, they also had to forge global conditions "under which our free and democratic system can live and prosper." From a policy standpoint, such an open-ended obligation had the effect of easing, if not eliminating altogether, any limitation on national security initiatives. Indeed, NSC-68 envisioned a larger arsenal

---

[60] NSC-68, 7 April 1950, *FRUS, 1950* 1:235–92. See also Rearden, *Formative Years*, 531. Nitze had been arguing for some time that the Soviets, armed with atomic weapons, had become more aggressive in their foreign policy and more inclined to take risks. Although they had no plans for a general war with the United States, they were prepared to exploit opportunities and war could come by accident or miscalculation. See the record of the eighth meeting of the Policy Planning Staff, 2 February 1950, and the study prepared by Nitze, 8 February 1950, *FRUS, 1950* 1:142–43, 145–47.

[61] NSC-68, 7 April 1950, *FRUS, 1950* 1:235–92.

of nuclear weapons, stronger conventional forces, additional economic and military assistance to allies around the world, and new programs of civil defense and psychological warfare, as well as other steps not contemplated in the current budget.

As part of the argument for such initiatives, NSC-68 stressed that American military strength was "becoming dangerously inadequate" and that a "sharp disparity" had developed between "our actual military strength and our commitments," not to mention the world conditions that now had to be confronted. This disparity, it suggested, might tempt some Americans to support a surprise atomic attack against the Soviet Union before it gained nuclear parity, and tempt others to adopt a policy of appeasement or to advocate a retreat into isolationism. Such a disparity, in other words, could lead to policies that were morally repugnant and impractical or to policies that would end in the garrison state. This would be the case with any retreat into isolationism, which would leave the United States bereft of allies in a world dominated by the Soviet Union and force American leaders to forge a "regimented system" in order to put all of the country's resources into defense. The "national morale would be corrupted and the integrity and vitality of our system subverted."[62]

As Emily Rosenberg has pointed out on the basis of theories borrowed from Michel Foucault, NSC-68 played on the theme of ideological opposites, of "us" versus "them," that we have seen in other parts of our narrative. It conjured up an ideal American identity, cast it against a demonized version of the Soviet other, and captured the dichotomies in a set of powerful rhetorical symbols: "freedom" versus "slavery," "democracy" versus "autocracy," "tolerance" versus "coercive force," "diversity" versus "monolith," "allies" versus "satellites." As a "free society," the United States valued "the individual as an end in himself," said NSC-68, whereas Soviet socialism reduced the individual to a servant of the state. Whereas American society encouraged tolerance and "freedom under a government of laws," Soviet society envisioned a system of "slavery under the grim oligarchy of the Kremlin." The prison, the jail, and the concentration camp became metaphors for Soviet society. It was a society with an "iron curtain around it" and "iron bars within it"; a society held together by brute force; a "concentration camp" in which "the personality of the individual is so broken and perverted that he participates affirmatively in his own degradation."[63]

---

[62] Ibid.

[63] Ibid. See also Emily S. Rosenberg's assessment of NSC-68 in May, *American Cold War Strategy*, 160–64.

The authors of NSC-68 also relied on various rhetorical strategies to accommodate their recommendations to the older ideology of antistatism and antimilitarism, with its opposition to high taxes, budget deficits, and economic controls, its fear of foreign imbroglios, and its emphasis on a free-willing individualism, rather than a disciplined and ordered community. These strategies tried so far as possible to wrap departures from tradition in tradition itself, as Rosenberg has pointed out, just as they wrapped America's new role as the global defender of democracy in its traditional democratic identity. One such strategy was to claim that active internationalism, rather than isolationism, was the best way to safeguard American liberties against the dangers of the garrison state. Another was to sanction the document's recommendations by reference to traditional authority, namely the Constitution and its democratic purpose. That "fundamental purpose," said NSC-68, quoting from the Constitution's Preamble, was to "secure the Blessings of Liberty to ourselves and our Posterity." This was a pledge that Nitze and his collaborators took seriously and one, in their opinion, that obliged the United States to do whatever was necessary to "foster a world environment in which the American system can survive and flourish."

A third strategy of accommodation, one linked to this talk of democratic purpose, was to emphasize the country's historic identity, not as the frugal defender of democracy in a single state, which is how conservative economizers often defined the United States, but as a great military power and crusader for freedom everywhere. This strategy drew on a traditional cultural narrative and on the discursive tradition that went with it, specifically on a narrative of American exceptionalism that stretched well beyond the wartime rhetoric of the twentieth century to the nineteenth-century ideology of manifest destiny and John Winthrop's seventeenth-century vision of the new world as a city upon a hill. Through this narrative, NSC-68 linked its recommendations to the American past, and specifically to a historic sense of mission that could be invoked on behalf of still another crusade to spread the blessings of American liberty around the world.[64]

Yet another strategy of accommodation was to cast the problem posed by the Cold War as part of a larger historical problem. "Even if there were no Soviet Union," the document argued, "we would face the great problem of the free society, accentuated many-fold in this industrial age, of reconciling order, security, the need for participation, with the

---

[64] Ibid. See also Rosenberg's assessment in May, ed., *American Cold War Strategy*, 160–64.

requirement of freedom." By situating its recommendations in this context, NSC-68 could make them appear less threatening, and the possibility of accommodation seem unavoidable, and could link that possibility to a traditional faith in the potentialities of modern science. Modern science had long been invoked as the new frontier capable of yielding the same combination of material progress and traditional virtue that had been characteristic of nineteenth-century America, and it was now invoked as the best hope for a larger reconciliation of order and freedom, of security needs and traditional concerns about the economy.[65]

Along these lines, NSC-68 appealed explicitly for the mobilization of science, particularly the modern science of economics, on behalf of the nation's security. In essence, the authors of that document used Keynesian theory to bridge the gap between their concern with security and Truman's concern with economy, to explain, in other words, why the United States could expand its national security programs without onerous economic and political consequences. Along with their talk about the short-term sacrifices that would be needed during a period of rapid military buildup, notably in the form of higher taxes, cuts in domestic spending, and economic controls to curb inflation, they argued that in the long run rearmament promised substantial benefits. It would put the nation's unutilized assets to work, the economy would expand accordingly, and the resources required for continued preparedness could then "be obtained by siphoning off a part of the annual increment in the gross national product."

In this kind of thinking, the authors of NSC-68 echoed what Keyserling had been saying in his debates with Nourse. Like Keyserling, they seemed to believe that Keynesian theory would enable the United States to escape the hard choices that Nourse had wanted to confront. Although the balanced budget might have to give way, the new theory made it possible to reconcile the welfare state with the warfare state, to have guns and butter both. And like Keyserling, they cited as authority the lesson of World War II, which proved to their satisfaction "that the American economy, when it operates at a level approaching full efficiency, can provide enormous resources for purposes other than civilian consumption while simultaneously providing a high standard of living."[66]

As Nitze and his coauthors viewed the matter, the real problem was "not so much in the field of economics as in the field of politics." Here

---

[65] NSC-68, 7 April 1950, *FRUS, 1950* 1:235–92.
[66] Ibid.

again NSC-68 spoke to the issue of national will and the need for sacrifice if the United States was going to assume its new identity as a redeemer nation in a troubled world. And here again, it spoke in binary opposites. Soviet leaders headed a totalitarian state: they were not bound by democratic processes; they did not answer to public opinion; they did not wrestle with the problem of dissent. In the United States, on the other hand, people had to see the need to sacrifice on behalf of freedom around the world. They had to be persuaded to live temporarily with lower living standards and government controls that curtailed their economic choices, and they had to forsake some of the other "benefits which they have come to associate with their freedoms." That was the problem. It was the same problem that Nourse had identified, and it had to be solved, said NSC-68, through effective political leadership.[67]

Nitze and his collaborators were especially preoccupied with the problem of leading public opinion, no doubt because they were aware of the extent to which the American people had been unwilling to make the sacrifices that national security seemed to require. After all, economic controls had been trimmed since 1945, taxes had been cut, military spending had been reduced, and resources had been shifted to domestic programs. The need now, Nitze argued, was for a campaign of education "to strengthen the moral fiber of the people," in effect, a campaign to educate them in the new ideology of national security. Acheson agreed, as did Robert Lovett, who had just taken over as undersecretary of defense. The American people suffered from what Acheson called "a false sense of security." They did not realize that the Cold War was "in fact a real war" against a nation that was hell bent on "world domination." Only a strong dose of reality, what Nitze called "the brutal facts," could puncture popular illusions and reconcile the American people to the sacrifices that were necessary. Lovett made the same points. The country was "in a war worse than any we have ever experienced," he argued. It was "not a cold war" but "a hot war," and "anything we do short of an all-out effort is inexcusable." This meant doing away with the "sharp line between democratic principles and immoral actions," which Lovett considered a "dangerous and unnecessary handicap," and fighting the Soviet Union "with no holds barred."[68]

---

[67] Ibid. See also, Guy Oakes, *The Imaginary War: Civil Defense and American Cold War Culture* (New York, 1994), 30–31.

[68] Record of the meeting of the State-Defense Review Group, 27 February 1950, Acheson memorandum of a conversation with Republican Congressman Christian A. Herter of Massachusetts, 24 March 1950, and record of the Meeting of the State-Defense Review Group, 16 March 1950, *FRUS, 1950* 1:168–75, 206–9, 196–200.

The American people had to be given these facts "with no sugar-coating," in the words of one consultant to Nitze's group. They required information "regarding the basic political, economic, and military elements of the present situation" if they were to arrive at an "intelligent" opinion and a "consensus" in support of proper policies. Providing that information was the responsibility of enlightened public policy makers whose first step, as Acheson recounted in his memoirs, was to "bludgeon the mass mind of 'top government'" into resolute action. Once this was done, top government could then launch what public relations expert Edward W. Barrett called a "psychological 'scare campaign'" to mobilize public opinion around the new ideology of national security. The "average American citizen," Acheson said, in his own inimitable arrogance, spent only ten minutes per day thinking about the larger world. To reach him "qualification must give way to simplicity of statement, nicety and nuance to bluntness, almost brutality." The task was not that of "a doctoral thesis." Policy makers had to make their points "clearer than truth" and use what Lovett called "Hemingway sentences."[69]

Still, it had never been easy to "bludgeon the mass mind of 'top government,'" particularly Truman's mind, especially when it came to subordinating economic concerns to military imperatives.[70] Nitze and his colleagues figured that NSC-68 might cost as much as $40 billion per year to implement. But their document contained no such estimate, primarily, as Acheson later admitted, because calculating costs would have drawn economizers from the Budget Bureau into the drafting process, not to mention the Joint Chiefs, who seemed constitutionally incapable of agreeing on the size and distribution of the defense budget. In other words, it would have stirred enormous controversy and might have prevented a final document from reaching the president.[71]

[69] Record of the meeting of the State-Defense Policy Review Group, 27 February 1950, and NSC-68, 7 April 1950, *FRUS, 1950* 1:168–75, 235–92; Dean Acheson, *Present at the Creation: My Years in the State Department* (New York, 1969), 374, 375; Barrett quoted in John Lewis Gaddis, *Strategies of Containment: A Critical Appraisal of Postwar American National Security Policy* (New York, 1982), 108; and record of the meeting of the State-Defense Policy Review Group, 16 March 1950, *FRUS, 1950* 1:196–200.

[70] According to NSC-68, "budgetary considerations will need to be subordinated to the stark fact that our very independence as a nation may be at stake." NSC-68, 7 April 1950, *FRUS, 1950* 1:285.

[71] Paul H. Nitze, "The Development of NSC 68," *International Security* 4 (Spring 1979): 173; idem, *From Hiroshima to Glasnost: At the Center of Decision, A Memoir* (New York, 1989), 96; Acheson, *Present at the Creation,* 374; and Hammond, "NSC-68: Prologue to Rearmament," 318–19.

Excluding the economizers, however, only delayed the inevitable. NSC-68 reached the president in April 1950, right in the middle of the House debate on the administration's skimpy military budget for fiscal year 1951. The administration was determined to defend the budget, whereas NSC-68, in the words of Truman's advisers, threatened to "invite extravagant and well nigh uncontrollable demands by the military services."[72] Under the circumstances, the president reacted as he had so often before: He turned to his allies among the economizers for support against this new assault on his economic policies. To be sure, Truman could no longer count on the Council of Economic Advisers, where Nourse's caution had given way to Keyserling's Keynesian optimism. But he continued to enjoy the strong support of Secretary of Defense Johnson, who had approved NSC-68 with little enthusiasm and who was sticking to the position that future military planning should be based on anticipated appropriations of roughly $13 billion.[73]

Nor was Johnson alone. Several of Nitze's colleagues in the State Department also raised concerns about the military buildup recommended in NSC-68, arguing in particular that it ran the risk of subverting the country's democratic identity for the sake of its global mission. NSC-68, they said, would require something akin to a "full-time war mobilization of the economy," "a gigantic armament race, a huge buildup" that could not be sustained without a "continuing crisis" and would, even then, provoke opposition from those who feared a "garrison state." One of the outside experts consulted by Nitze's group, Dr. Henry Smyth of the Atomic Energy Commission, also warned that a "security minded narrowness" ran the risk of alienating public opinion, while another expert, President Conant of Harvard, drew indirectly on the image of the garrison state to make the same point. Conant told Nitze and his coauthors that NSC-68 had set its sights "much too high." Instead of identifying the "minimum" interests "we must hold outside of the United States," the document envisioned freedom for all the "victims of the Kremlin" as well as fundamental change inside the Soviet Union. It wanted to "democratize everyone," Conant said, and this goal was so ambitious

---

[72] Elsey to Murphy, 10 April 1950, Elsey Papers, box 83, folder: National Defense – Armed Forces Unification.

[73] For Keyserling's thinking see the memorandum by Hamilton Q. Dearborn of the Council of Economic Advisers to the executive secretary, NSC, 8 May 1950, *FRUS, 1950* 1:306–11, Nitze, "The Development of NSC 68," 170–76; and Nitze, *From Hiroshima to Glasnost*, 96. For Johnson's thinking see Rearden, *Formative Years*, 524–25, 534; and Walter S. Poole, *The History of the Joint Chiefs of Staff: The Joint Chiefs of Staff and National Policy*, vol. 4, *1950–1952* (Wilmington, DE, 1980), 25–34.

that it would exhaust the country's economic capacities and erode its democratic liberties. In pursuing "our national destiny" abroad, Conant warned, "we might be risking freedom" at home.[74]

Similar expressions came from the Budget Bureau, where officials were quick to deconstruct the document's supercharged rhetoric. Although the Soviet empire amounted to "a slave world," according to one official, it was "not true that the U.S. and its friends constitute a free world." After all, were "the Indo-Chinese free," or could "the peoples of the Philippines be said to be free under the corrupt Quirino government?" The bureau still considered the Communist challenge to be primarily economic and political, not military. It still believed the Soviet Union to be no match for the United States militarily, and it still rejected defense spending as a necessary or desirable "method of maintaining high employment." The defense budget, it argued again, should never exceed what the country could afford "over an indefinite period" and should always seek to balance the Communist threat to national security against the cost to "our society" of anything like a "large-scale mobilization," including the "cost in terms of the psychology and orientation of our society." As it was, current demands on the government and the rate of economic growth gave little hope of a balanced budget before 1953, and only then if the administration resisted the pressure for greater expenditures on defense and international programs. It must hold military spending to $13 billion a year, the bureau concluded, and must cut the annual foreign aid bill by at least $3 billion if it wanted to fund its domestic agenda without burdensome deficits.[75]

For his part, Truman missed no opportunity to reaffirm his own commitment to the budget before Congress and to postpone action on NSC-68. He asked a special subcommittee of the NSC to review the document from a budgetary point of view and made sure that the subcommittee included representatives from the Budget Bureau, the Treasury Department, and the Council of Economic Advisers. Once the subcommittee

---

74 Charles E. Bohlen (U.S. minister in Paris) to Nitze, 5 April 1950, assistant secretary of state for public affairs to the secretary of state, 6 April 1950, and records of meetings of the State-Defense Policy Review Group, 10 and 2 March 1950, *FRUS, 1950* 1:221–25, 225–26, 190–95, 176–82. See also deputy assistant secretary for European affairs to the secretary of state, 3 April 1950, assistant secretary of state for European affairs to the secretary of state, 3 April 1950, and assistant secretary of state for United Nations affairs to the secretary of state, 5 April 1950, ibid., 213–14, 214–16, 216–17.

75 Memorandum by the deputy chief of the Division of Estimates, Budget Bureau, to the executive secretary, NSC, 8 May 1950, *FRUS, 1950* 1:298–306; Lawton to Truman, 19 April 1950, Truman Papers, PSF-Subject File, box 151, folder: Bureau of the Budget, Budget – FY 1952–53.

met, moreover, it resisted the demands of those pressing for quick approval of the document's recommendations. Symington, who now headed the National Security Resources Board, said the faster the action the better for U.S. security. Given the global situation outlined in the document, Acheson agreed, "we should take extraordinary measures to devote considerably more of our national income to the cold war." Johnson, on the other hand, refused to let the subcommittee be stampeded into quick decisions. He and others thought it would take time to estimate the cost of NSC-68 and determine its influence on the economy. Nor was the president in a hurry. When the budget director told him that some members of the subcommittee had complained about the difficult issues of economy that were being raised, Truman tried to buck him up. He told the director that he and his allies were "to raise any questions that we had on this program and that it definitely was not as large in scope as some of the people seemed to think."[76]

It took the Korean War to break the logjam in the administration. As late as 19 June the Budget Bureau's worst-case scenario still called for a balanced budget. It assumed additional military expenditures of between $1 and $3 billion, offsetting cuts in nondefense spending, and a balanced budget in 1953.[77] But all of this changed after the outbreak of fighting on 25 June 1950. Within weeks the armed services had been authorized to exceed the force levels established in the budget for fiscal year 1951. Symington was soon calling for a new strategic plan and more spending on national security, while Acheson was telling the cabinet that it had to seek a sizable increase in the defense budget, which was then

[76] Unsigned memorandum for the president, 21 April 1950, Truman Papers, PSF-National Security Council Meetings, box 220, folder: NSC Meetings: Memos for the President and Meeting Decisions; Lawton memorandum for the record, 23 May 1950, Lawton Papers, box 6, folder: Truman, President Harry S., Meetings with the President – Agendas and Memorandums, 7/49–7/52. See also Elsey to Murphy, 10 April 1950, Elsey Papers, box 83, folder: National Defense – Armed Forces Unification; minutes of the 55th meeting of the NSC, 20 April 1950, Truman Papers, PSF-National Security Council Meetings, box 207, folder: NSC Meeting #55, 4-20-50; memorandum by the executive secretary, NSC to the Ad Hoc Committee on NSC 68, 28 April 1950, *FRUS, 1950* 1:293–96; unsigned memorandum for the president, 18 May 1950, Truman Papers, PSF-National Security Council Meetings, box 220, folder: NSC Meetings: Memos for the President and Meeting Decisions. Truman told a news conference on 4 May that the "defense budget next year will be smaller than it is this year . . . we are not alarmed in any sense of the word. We are simply maintaining a defense program that is adequate for the defense of this country." See *Public Papers, Truman, 1950*, 286.

[77] See the statement attached to Lawton to Truman, 19 June 1950, Truman Papers, PSF-Subject File, box 151, folder: Bureau of the Budget, Budget – FY 1952–53.

being debated on the Senate floor. If it was "a question of asking for too little or too much," Acheson argued, the president "should ask for too much." Although few saw Korea as an immediate prelude to a global conflagration, the war did lend weight to those who thought that Soviet leaders aimed "to rule the world" and would work toward this end through satellite countries unless the United States responded in Korea. Korea was "the Greece of the Far East," as even the president argued. "If we are tough enough now, if we stand up to them like we did in Greece three years ago, they won't take any next steps."[78]

Viewing the situation in this context, the president and his advisers decided to do more than respond in Korea. They resolved to hammer out a peace treaty with Japan, expand the military assistance program, send American troops to Europe, take other steps to strengthen NATO, push aggressively for Germany's rearmament, and bring both Germany and Japan into the Western system of defense. They also launched the military buildup contemplated in NSC-68. In addition to another $4 billion for the military assistance program and $260 million for the Atomic Energy Commission, Truman asked Congress in July and August for $11.6 billion in supplements to the military budget for fiscal year 1951. Together with the original budget for the armed forces, which the Senate as well as the House had passed by the end of September, the supplementals would make possible an Army of 11 divisions, an Air Force of 58 groups, and a Navy of 282 major combat vessels.[79]

At the same time Truman asked Nitze's group to estimate how much it would cost to implement the security requirements outlined in NSC-68 by mid-1954 – the date of maximum danger, according to the document,

---

[78] Memorandum of conversation by the secretary of state, 17 July 1950, *FRUS, 1950* 1:344–46; Symington memorandum of 6 July 1950 enclosed in Symington to Truman, 7 July 1950, Truman Papers, PSF-Subject File, box 146, folder: National Security Resources Board – Miscellaneous; and Truman quoted in Leffler, *Preponderance of Power*, 367. See also JCS memorandum to the secretary of defense, 5 July 1950, and secretary of defense memorandum to the Joint Chiefs, 6 July 1950, RG 218, CCS 370 (8-19-45), Sec. 25.

[79] Minutes of the 62d meeting of the NSC, 27 July 1950, Truman Papers, PSF-National Security Council Meetings, box 208, folder: NSC Meeting #62, 7-27-50; Secretary of the Army Frank Pace, Jr., to Johnson, 24 August 1950, with attached position paper by the three service secretaries, 23 August 1950, RG 330, CD 381 (War Plans, NSC 68); Truman, "Special Message to the Congress Reporting on the Situation in Korea," 19 July 1950, and Truman to the Speaker of the House of Representatives, 1 August 1950, *Public Papers, Truman, 1950*, 527–37, 564–66; Poole, *Joint Chiefs of Staff, 1950–1952* 4:42; Doris M. Condit, *The History of the Office of the Secretary of Defense*, vol. 2, *The Test of War, 1950–1953* (Washington, 1988), 225–27; and Leffler, *Preponderance of Power*, 371–73.

when the Soviet Union, armed with a large stockpile of nuclear weapons, would pose the greatest threat to American security. A preliminary estimate had calculated the military side of these requirements at $150 billion over a four-year period from 1951 through 1955, plus another $37 billion for such related requirements as military assistance and the Atomic Energy Commission. But Nitze and his group considered these figures inadequate. Their thinking came closer to a more ambitious program suggested by the Joint Chiefs in late September, under which the Army would increase to 17 divisions in fiscal year 1951 and 18 divisions in fiscal year 1954, the Navy would grow to 322 major combat vessels in fiscal year 1951 and 397 in fiscal year 1954, and the Air Force would jump to 70 groups in fiscal year 1951 and then to 95 groups in fiscal year 1954. Working with the NSC, Nitze's committee wrote a similar program into what became NSC-68/1, a document that would require Congress to obligate $214 billion through 1955. But even this was judged insufficient, and further revisions brought the five-year total to $287 billion, including $235 billion for the armed forces and the balance for the Korean War, military assistance, atomic energy, and other national security programs.[80]

Acheson and Nitze saw progress in other directions as well. After the outbreak of fighting in Korea, for example, Truman began to meet regularly with the Joint Chiefs of Staff and the National Security Council, both of which came to enjoy a more prominent place in decision making. The economizers, on the other hand, were now on the defensive and were losing more of their leading voices as well. Frank Pace had by this time left the Budget Bureau to become secretary of the army, following a path similar to the one that James Webb had taken earlier, while George Marshall had come out of retirement to replace Louis Johnson as secretary of defense. Johnson's cavorting with Truman's critics and his incredibly abrasive personality had made him persona non grata in the White House. He was also at odds with the Joint Chiefs, could not get along with cabinet colleagues, especially Acheson, and was under intense fire from some members of Congress who blamed Truman's stingy defense policies for inviting the Korean aggression.

Similar criticism came from key members of the press, and none more so than Joseph and Stewart Alsop. To be sure, Johnson also had his supporters, most of whom blamed the secretary's bully-boy personality

---

[80] Condit, *Test of War*, 228–29, 231, 234; Poole, *Joint Chiefs of Staff, 1950–1952* 4:53–58.

more than his policies for his growing unpopularity. But the Alsops went much further. Their attack on Johnson was similar to the assault that Walter Winchell and Drew Pearson had earlier waged on Forrestal, a deeply venomous and highly personal attack that had helped to discredit Forrestal and drive him from his Pentagon office to his asylum in Bethesda Naval Hospital. Johnson himself nearly broke under the strain of the charges leveled against him, especially by the Alsops, who accused the secretary of everything but treason. He had reduced the country to military feebleness, they said, lied about the dangers inherent in his policies, and given the Soviets an "open invitation" to aggression in Korea. Johnson's policies were also Truman's policies, of course, and the Alsops did not spare the president, either. But Johnson was more closely associated with those policies than any other official in the administration, which explains the special press attention to his role and may also account, at least in part, for the president's decision to assuage his critics by dismissing his second secretary of defense, as he had his first.[81]

Although Acheson, Nitze, and their allies were buoyed by these developments, especially Johnson's dismissal, their triumph was still far from complete. On the contrary, Truman and the economizers had begun to wage a counteroffensive. In late July, the president had told his new budget director, Frederick J. Lawton, that he wanted to take "a pretty good look" at the new budget estimates coming from the Pentagon, "with the idea of not putting any more money than necessary at this time in the hands of the Military."[82] Truman could count on Lawton's collaboration in these efforts, as he could the support of Secretary Marshall, who

[81] Joseph and Stewart Alsop, "The Real Tragedy of Forrestal," *Washington Post*, 9 July 1950. In addition to the sources cited in note 45, see Alsops, "Mr. Johnson's Pearl Harbor" and "Unpreparedness Laid to Johnson," ibid., 19 and 23 July 1950; Stewart Alsop, "In Defense of a Dead Defender" and "Johnson Left Out Some Quotes," ibid., 6 August and 3 September 1950; and Joseph Alsop, "The Guilty," ibid., 8 September 1950. See also, Edwin M. Yoder, Jr., *Joe Alsop's Cold War: A Study of Journalistic Influence and Intrigue* (Chapel Hill, 1995), 24–26; and Robert W. Merry, *Taking on the World: Joseph and Stewart Alsop – Guardians of the American Century* (New York, 1996), 190–95. Arthur Krock was one of Johnson's defenders in the press, though he was not an aggressive defender and may have been motivated in part by his own conservative fiscal views, which Johnson had done much to realize in the Pentagon. See Krock, "Mr. Johnson Answers Some Criticisms," *New York Times*, 27 July 1950. For Truman's decision to fire Johnson see Truman's memorandum on the subject of 12 September 1950, Ayers Papers, box 5, folder: General File – Johnson, Louis, Sec. of Defense, Dismissal.

[82] Lawton memorandum for the record, 22 July 1950, Lawton Papers, box 6, folder: Truman, President Harry S., Meetings with the President – Agendas and Memorandums, 7/49–7/52.

dug in his heels when the Joint Chiefs reported in September 1950 that expenditures for the programs outlined in NSC-68 could approximate $287 billion over a five-year period. Marshall was inclined to agree with one of his top aides, James H. Burns, who expressed strong concern "about the size of the proposed appropriations, their effect upon the American economy and the American way of life and the possibility that these great expenditures will not be supported over the 5 year program by the American people." In Burns's view, it would be better to put a ceiling of $200 billion on the program while officials in the Pentagon sought further economies and submitted new recommendations. This was also the position that Marshall took at an NSC meeting in late September, when both he and Truman approved NSC-68 as a statement of policy, but demanded a further review before approving the program and the cost estimates spelled out in NSC-68/1.[83]

The Budget Bureau could not have been happier. Officials there were convinced that NSC-68 and related documents had been "hurriedly and unilaterally developed by the services." The process had been so sloppy that even Pentagon policy makers called it "Operation Paper Clip." The armed forces had proceeded without regard to production capacity, the availability of manpower and critical raw materials, the normal rhythm of the business cycle, and the need to contain inflation. By contrast, the Budget Bureau still envisioned a program of preparedness that would deter Soviet aggression "without permanently impairing our economy and the fundamental values inherent to our way of life."[84] Marshall shared this goal. He asked his undersecretary, Robert Lovett, to drive the defense budget in this direction, and within weeks Lovett's team had reduced the estimated cost of the five-year program to $190.6 billion, of which $131 billion would be earmarked for the armed forces. According to Lovett, the new plan still contemplated a rapid military buildup in fiscal year 1951, but set more modest goals thereafter, tailored the military buildup to existing resources, especially manpower,

[83] James H. Burns to Marshall, 28 September 1950, RG 330, CD 381 (War Plans, NSC 68). Burns's memorandum was prepared in the form of a statement that Marshall could use in speaking to the NSC. See also James S. Lay, Jr. (executive secretary, NSC) to Truman, 28 September 1950, and minutes of the 68th meeting of the NSC, 29 September 1950, Truman Papers, PSF-National Security Council Meetings, box 209, folder: NSC Meeting #68, 9-29-50; and unsigned memorandum for the president, 2 October 1950, ibid., box 220, folder: NSC Meetings: Memos for President and Meeting Discussions.

[84] G.E. Ramsey, Jr., (Budget Bureau) to the director, 10 November 1950, RG 51, Series 47.8a, box 52, folder: 1952 Budget – Basic Documents. See also Ramsey to Schaub, 26 September 1950, ibid.

and was thus more likely to win support in Congress and across the country.[85]

It is important to recall at this point that top policy makers were debating the cost and timing of a program that had little to do with the Korean conflict. Those involved had estimated the cost of that conflict at approximately $13 billion in fiscal year 1951, and no one quibbled with this estimate. They were arguing instead over the proposal in NSC-68/1 for an additional $274 billion to cover the cost of a five-year expansion of military and other national security programs, as called for in NSC-68.

Marshall was probably the only man in government, other than the president, who could stand up to Acheson's pressure for such a costly expansion, and he could not do so easily. When the NSC reconvened on 22 November, Acheson delivered a blistering critique of the direction in which Marshall and Lovett were taking the Pentagon. He accepted their program for fiscal year 1951, but frankly did not see how "we could carry out our obligations" with current force levels in subsequent years. "Our responsibilities are so great," he said, "that we must be prepared to do several things at the same time." Such thinking won support from Symington, Keyserling, and W. Averell Harriman, who was then serving as special assistant to the president. Harriman stressed the importance of "negotiating from strength" and agreed with Symington that the Pentagon's plan was inadequate to this purpose, especially in light of "the world situation." If the plan had been limited by what the civilian economy could produce, then Symington wanted a chance to "improve on that situation." This was Keyserling's position, too. He had not been consulted about the economic assumptions underlying the Pentagon's plan, doubted their accuracy, and assumed instead that "the economy could stand the job required by NSC 68," so that "no reduction was necessary."[86]

Lovett held his ground in the face of this criticism. While conceding that there was something to "Keyserling's elastic concept of the economy," he argued that there was still the matter of gearing the military

---

[85] Condit, *Test of War*, 232–33, 235–36; Poole, *Joint Chiefs of Staff* 4:63–65. The Joint Chiefs, of course, saw the revised plan as a "compromise" between economic and military imperatives. They endorsed it reluctantly and only after noting that it increased the risks to U.S. security. See the Joint Chiefs to Secretary Marshall, 19 November 1950, *FRUS, 1950* 1:416–18.

[86] Unsigned memorandum for the president, 24 November 1950, Truman Papers, PSF-National Security Council Meetings, box 220, folder: NSC Meetings: Memos for President and Meeting Discussions.

buildup to the resources available. "The danger of producing air frames without engines," he pointed out, required "a phasing of manpower and materiel." Marshall made a similar point. Meeting the production targets and timetables envisioned in NSC-68, he said, would require something like "full mobilization," which the United States had never done "prior" to the start of a general war. A level of military preparedness on which the country could build in case of an emergency was in his view a more "reasonable" goal "than building up a mountain and then sliding off." Others agreed, including Secretary of the Treasury John Snyder and the president himself. Truman worried that anything like full mobilization could impede production for domestic purposes, with deleterious effects on the economy and the military effort both, and could also raise objections in Congress, where conservatives, especially Republicans, were even more concerned about budget deficits than the White House. Truman reminded everyone how difficult it was to get a reasonable military program through Congress, and then instructed the group to focus on the budget for fiscal year 1951. Any subsequent buildup, he said, would have to be discussed at a later date.[87]

As it turned out, this apparent victory for the economizers rested on military conditions in Korea that quickly took a turn for the worse. On 18 September, the UN forces under General Douglas MacArthur launched a vigorous counterattack against the North Korean army, which by that time had come close to overrunning the southern half of the Korean peninsula. By the end of the month, MacArthur's troops had recaptured South Korea and had launched an offensive to reunify both halves of the country under the government in Seoul. With victory apparently in sight, it must have seemed possible to slow the preparedness program, or even anticipate a rollback. Indeed, following the NSC meeting on 22 November, the Defense Department and the Budget Bureau agreed to seek only another $11 billion in supplemental defense appropriations for fiscal year 1951. Down from the original estimate of $20 billion submitted by the Joint Chiefs, the new figure was in line with the idea of a phased military buildup that Truman, Marshall, and Lovett had in mind.[88]

But what seemed possible on 22 November was out of the question three days later, when Chinese forces intervened in the war. Like

[87] Ibid.
[88] Condit, *Test of War*, 237.

MacArthur's army, the economizers were again thrown on the defensive. China's intervention raised the possibility of a longer, wider, more expensive war in Asia and of a Communist opponent even more menacing than expected. Suddenly the rearmament program suggested in NSC-68 no longer seemed as unreasonable as before. Acheson returned to the offensive and this time got almost everything he had wanted. At a meeting on 28 November, just days after the Chinese intervention, the NSC increased the estimated supplemental by $5.8 billion, to a total of $16.8 billion, which was the sum that Truman submitted to Congress on 1 December 1950 and that Congress passed the following month. Then, in mid-December, the NSC decided that a military buildup phased in over four years was unacceptable. The program had to be accelerated so that the goals set for 1954 could be achieved two years earlier.

The discussion in mid-December echoed the NSC's deliberations of 22 November, but with opposite results. Once again, Acheson pointed to the current emergency in Korea and demanded the largest military program in the fastest possible time. "It would not be too much if we had all the troops that the military want," he said. "If we had all of the things that our European allies want it would not be too much. If we had the equipment to call out the reserves it would not be too much. If we had a system for full mobilization it would not be too much." "The danger," he emphasized, "couldn't be greater." Once again, Symington and Keyserling said that the economy could produce whatever the military wanted, as it had done in World War II, without impinging on the "minimum" needs of the civilian population. On the other side, Marshall, Lovett, and Snyder tried to put on the brakes. They thought that Keyserling exaggerated how much had been accomplished in the first year of World War II and slighted how difficult it would be to expand a fully employed economy as compared to the depressed economy of 1941. They still considered it essential to gear the military buildup to the resources available, the demands of the civilian economy, and the morale of the country. In the end, however, the Chinese intervention left the economizers with no choice but to accept a substantial acceleration of the military program, including still another supplemental appropriation, this one of $6.38 billion, which Truman requested in December and Congress approved the following month.

That supplemental brought total defense appropriations for fiscal year 1951 to $42.9 billion, a nearly fourfold increase over the $13.9 billion that Truman had requested in January 1950. Force levels also increased proportionately. Truman's budget of January would have supported an Army of 10 divisions, a Navy of 238 major combat vessels, and an Air Force of 48 groups. But by the end of the year, the Joint Chiefs had agreed to an Army of 17 divisions, a Navy of 322 major combat vessels, and an Air Force of 70 groups. What is more, goals initially set for fiscal year 1954 were to be achieved two years earlier. By the end of fiscal year 1952, the new date of maximum danger, the Army was to grow to 18 divisions, the Navy to 397 major combat vessels, and the Air Force to 95 groups.[89]

V

From 1945 on, Truman had tried his best to reconcile the demands of the warfare state with the needs of the welfare state, the country's new identity as a great military power with its older values and traditions. He had hoped to get the country on something like a peacetime basis while also safeguarding its security and meeting its new obligations as a world leader. He had wanted wartime taxes to continue, but in the interest of a balanced budget and liquidation of the public debt. He had forged a national security organization, but on terms that squared with his commitment to the tradition of civilian leadership. He had agreed to a peacetime military establishment larger than anything the country had known before, but one that it could sustain over the long term and on which it could build in the event of a war. Relying on foreign aid programs and air–atomic power, he had also devised a strategy of deterrence that dovetailed with his efforts to downsize the military, balance the budget, and reallocate resources to civilian investment. The whole program, as Truman admitted, rejected the idea of absolute security. It was based on the notion that certain calculated risks had to be taken if the country was going to avoid a permanent peacetime mobilization, which it could not do without bankrupting the Treasury, draining all

---

[89] Report to the president by the NSC, 14 December 1950, and Marshall to Truman, 14 December 1950, with enclosed memorandum by Bradley to Marshall, 6 December 1950, *FRUS, 1950* 1:467–77; Bradley to Marshall, 13 December 1950, and minutes of the 75th meeting of the NSC, 14 December 1950, Truman Papers, PSF-National Security Council Meetings, box 210, folder: NSC Meeting #75, 12-14-50; unsigned memorandum for the president, 15 December 1950, ibid., box 220, folder: NSC Meetings: Memos for President and Meeting Discussions; Truman, "Special Message to the Congress Requesting Additional Appropriations for Defense," 1 December 1950, *Public Papers, Truman, 1950*, 728–31; Poole, *Joint Chiefs of Staff* 4:69–70; Condit, *Test of War*, 237, 240; Leffler, *Preponderance of Power*, 402–3.

resources from domestic investment, and turning the nation into a garrison state.

But despite his success in shifting resources and balancing the budget in the early years of his presidency, Truman had also confronted obstacles that would eventually undermine his efforts. Conservatives on Capitol Hill had been hostile to the president's domestic agenda, and the Republican tax cut of 1948 and the recession of 1949 had undercut his attempts to balance the budget, trim the national debt, and finance new investment in domestic programs. Over time, moreover, the Joint Chiefs had worked relentlessly to reverse his budget priorities, key economizers had been lost to the cause, the armed forces had gained allies, and international developments had added weight to their claims for additional resources and new priorities. The war scare of 1948 ended the brief era of balanced budgets; the Korean War subverted Truman's attempt to recapture the initiative; and the new military buildup, together with cuts in the Marshall Plan, sidetracked the president's initial strategy of deterrence.

During the Korean War, critics denounced the position that Truman had taken on the defense budget since 1945, arguing that his policies had been penny wise but pound foolish. By putting concerns about the economy ahead of national security, he had supposedly invited the North Korean attack and left the United States militarily unprepared for the war. From what we now know, however, it seems clear that Truman's budget had nothing to do with the North Korean assault. Nor did it preclude an American response to that challenge. On the contrary, Truman had created a mobilization base from which the Pentagon was able to launch a massive military buildup, on a larger scale and at a faster pace than in the early part of World War II. What is more, it was able to do so while devoting only a modest portion of that effort to the conflict in Korea, where American and UN troops nonetheless managed to halt the North Korean advance of June, launch a mighty counteroffensive in September, and stymie the Chinese intervention thereafter.

The myth of unpreparedness in 1950 became part of the new ideology to which national security managers would appeal in the years ahead, just as they had earlier appealed to the lessons of Pearl Harbor. As we will see, their battle against the economizers would continue through the war years, but with a difference. The new ideology now dominated the national security discourse. Indeed, national security concerns became the common currency of most policy makers, the arbiter of most values, the key to America's new identity. On one level, to be sure, fears of the garrison state persisted. The professed aims of public policy were still to reconcile domestic and international priorities, civilian leadership and military authority, traditional virtues and new realities. But defending the American way against Soviet imperialism now took priority over older concerns about the danger that deficit spending, inflation, and government controls posed to economic freedom – just as guarding the nation's secrets often took precedence over the right to dissent and the defense of traditional civil liberties.

8

Semiwar

The Korean War and Rearmament

The military buildup that accompanied the Korean War took place in a highly charged political environment. Although Democrats had sat in the Oval Office since 1933 and had controlled Congress during all but two of the intervening years, a conservative coalition had also taken shape and had worked since the late 1930s to forestall liberal legislation on Capitol Hill. Despite a Democratic party resurgence in the election of 1948, and Truman's surprising defeat of the Republican challenger, Congress was increasingly deadlocked on domestic issues and the political climate had become more poisonous than ever.

The most toxic element in that poison was McCarthyism, named after Senator Joseph R. McCarthy of Wisconsin, a Republican conservative who made his reputation hunting Communist sympathizers in the federal government. McCarthy's brand of witch-hunting had been the stock-in-trade of the Republican right wing since the last years of the New Deal. It had played a prominent part in the Republican party campaigns of 1946 and 1948, and had surfaced again in the violent political battles that culminated in the elections of 1950. One of those battles had involved the so-called McCarran Act, which required Communists to register with the attorney general and authorized the emergency detention of possible spies and saboteurs. Truman had vetoed the measure, but the conservatives had overridden his veto and the battle between them, together with the outbreak of the Korean War and McCarthy's wild charges, had set the stage for a tumultuous electoral campaign that brought substantial gains to the Republican party in Congress.[1]

By that time, moreover, the Truman administration had become a reluctant partner in the anti-Communist crusade. It had established an Employee Loyalty Program under which review panels in virtually every

<hr>

[1] Donovan, *Conflict and Crisis*, 229–38, 395–439; idem, *Tumultuous Years: The Presidency of Harry S. Truman, 1949–1953* (New York, 1982), 295–98; Donald R. McCoy, *The Presidency of Harry S. Truman* (Lawrence, 1984), 66, 162, 242.

government agency were busy investigating the political opinions and personal associations of their colleagues or would-be government employees. The president had tried with little success to moderate the excesses of these investigations, appointing a special commission to examine their fairness and telling a White House aide that he was "disturbed" by what the review boards were doing and wanted to "stop their un-American activities." As it turned out, however, congressional conservatives were unwilling to support a blue-ribbon body that might criticize their work or steal their thunder on the anti-Communist issue. They refused to authorize the commission's appointment and resumed their own efforts to root out Communist influences in the federal government.[2]

Still, it would be a mistake to picture the Republicans as driven by little more than a lust for high office, just as it would be wrong to see Truman as an uncompromising defender of civil liberties. Although Republican conservatives hoped to ride McCarthyism to the White House in 1952, they also drew the boundaries of American identity in a way that excluded certain ideas as un-American, and not just those associated with the Communist party. To their way of thinking a more insidious threat had emerged with the liberal political ideology of the Roosevelt administration, had continued with the national security ideology of the Truman administration, and would lead, unless stopped, to the kind of governmentalism that conservatives associated with the garrison state.

For his part, Truman had to reconcile his commitment to civil liberties with the political pressure being mounted by conservatives in Congress and with his own desire to control an issue that endangered his party. In addition, the president was being pulled from his commitment to civil liberties by the conviction that national security actually required new standards of employee loyalty. Guided by this conviction, he not only established the Employee Loyalty Program, he also instructed the National Security Council to improve the program's effectiveness and then decided, in April 1951, that federal employees could be discharged for nothing more than reasonable "doubt" as to their loyalty.[3]

---

[2] Truman quoted in Donovan, *Tumultuous Years*, 367. See also Truman press release, 23 January 1951, John A. Donaher of the proposed commission to Truman, 17 July 1951, and Truman to Admiral Nimitz of the proposed commission, 26 October 1951, Truman Papers, PSF-Subject File, box 145, folder: President's Commission on Internal Security and Human Rights.

[3] On Truman and employee loyalty see Donovan, *Tumultuous Years*, 366–67. The thinking of Republican conservatives is laid out in the following pages.

The tension between national security needs and traditional values that we see in Truman's thinking permeated the national security discourse after the outbreak of the Korean War. It split the political arena along ideological and party lines, with conservatives, mostly in the Republican party, resisting initiatives favored by Truman and the Democrats. It also divided the Truman administration, as usual between national security managers in the Pentagon and the State Department and economizers in the Treasury Department, the Budget Bureau, and other agencies. At different points the struggle centered on universal military training, the stationing of American troops in Europe, the pace of rearmament, and the new taxes and economic controls that rearmament seemed to require. At issue in these debates was whether American state makers could advance the country's security, not to mention its mission as the military defender of democracy everywhere, without sacrificing its democratic identity and all the values and traditions they held dear. The debates made the last two years of the Truman administration one of the most partisan periods in modern American history, and had much to do with the way the national security state took shape after 1950.

II

After the outbreak of the Korean War, the national security ideology dominated policy making in the Truman administration. NSC-114/1 and NSC-114/2, both approved in 1951, echoed the themes laid out in NSC-68. To be sure, dissenters like Charles E. Bohlen, the State Department's leading Soviet specialist, complained that NSC-68 and its successors presented "the Soviet Union as a mechanical chess player" driven by a preconceived plan for "world domination." In Bohlen's opinion, such simplistic thinking was neither an accurate interpretation of the Soviet Union nor a useful guide to American diplomacy.[4] Nevertheless, major policy papers continued to define America's identity by reference to the Soviet other, as was typical of the national security ideology. They continued to speak in binary opposites of a "free world" and a Soviet slave system, the assumption being that freedom was indivisible and that Americans had no choice but to counter the Soviet challenge everywhere or lose their liberties at home. They still warned of a Soviet "design" for world domination and sounded alarms about the rapid expansion of

---

4 Bohlen to Nitze, 28 July 1951, *FRUS, 1951* (Washington, 1979), 1:106–9. For more on Bohlen's differences with his colleagues in the State Department see ibid., 163–78, 180–81, 172–75.

Soviet military might and the relative decline of American power. They still blurred the distinction between war and peace, claiming that "the United States and the USSR are now, to all intents and purposes, engaged in war." They again predicted a prolonged struggle in which all of the country's resources, not just its armed forces, had to be mobilized, and they again spoke of the discipline and the sacrifices that such a struggle required.[5]

Guided by this kind of thinking, the Truman administration moved quickly after the outbreak of fighting in Korea to counter the Soviet threat in every corner of the world. As Melvyn Leffler pointed out in his sweeping survey of the early Cold War, American leaders worked furiously to rehabilitate the Germans, rearm the Europeans, and strengthen the North Atlantic alliance. They decided to bring Turkey into NATO, underwrite the British position in Iran, and establish a Middle East Command in Egypt. In addition, they negotiated a final peace treaty with Japan and tried to incorporate both Japan and Indochina into the Western system of defense.[6]

Nor do these initiatives tell the whole story. In 1951 the administration again asked Congress to put the draft on a permanent basis and to establish a program of universal military training. Once again, the usual witnesses, including the Joint Chiefs, lined up to support the bill, arguing that selective service would satisfy the military's immediate manpower requirements while UMT created a pool of trained reserves on which the nation could draw over the long term. And once again they claimed that UMT squared with the tradition of the citizen soldier, with the country's historic antipathy toward a large standing army, and with the need for an economical way to mobilize military manpower without busting the budget.[7]

---

5 NSC-114/1 (with appendix), 8 August 1951, NSC-114/2, 12 October 1951, and Joint Chiefs memorandum to the secretary of defense, 15 January 1951, with enclosed review of the current world situation, *FRUS, 1951* 1:127–57, 182–92, 61–75. See also the Joint Chiefs memorandum to the secretary of defense, 13 April 1951, with enclosed supplementary study on the 15 January 1951 review of the current world situation, memorandum by Lucius D. Battle, special assistant to the secretary of defense, 6 July 1951, Joint Chiefs memorandum to the secretary of defense, 17 July 1951, and CIA memorandum, 24 September 1951, ibid., 75–82, 100–101, 104–6, 193–207.

6 Leffler, *Preponderance of Power*, 283–90, 380–83, 411, 426–38, 453–84.

7 U.S. Congress, Senate, *Hearings on S. 1, A Bill to Provide for the Common Defense and Security of the United States and to Permit the More Effective Utilization of Manpower Resources of the United States by Authorizing Universal Military Service and Training, and for Other Purposes* (Washington, 1951), 25–36, 39–234, 244–48, 408–10, 434–38, 552–76, 599, 637–52, 653–65, 700–705, 706–13, 714–18, 726–30, 816–29, 838–61, 1082–83,

In their minds, the distinction between war and peace had dissolved in a view of the Cold War as a permanent state of national emergency. That view, which was central to the ideology of national security, justified the state's decision to exercise emergency powers on a permanent basis, including the power to demand peacetime service from young men of military age. Indeed, it justified a whole "new concept" of citizenship in which the individual's duty to defend the state through wartime service had now become a permanent obligation requiring as a matter of course sacrifices that were formerly considered exceptional.[8]

Other components of the national security ideology also became major themes in this round of the UMT discourse, including the notion that God and history had thrust a new role on the United States and the parallel conviction that playing this part required important sacrifices. The American people had to foot the bill for a permanent military establishment, even if defense spending precluded other public programs; young men had to donate a portion of their lives to military service; and old traditions had to be discarded in the name of national security. "A drastic departure from the anti-militaristic tradition of our peace-loving America is now necessary," argued Democratic Congressman Franck Havenner of California. "We cannot have business as usual," agreed Congressman Carl Vinson, not when the "free world" was "watching mighty America today and wondering if she has the determination to meet the challenge of the times." Senator Lyndon Johnson, a Texas Democrat, made the same point in rhetoric even more soaring. "We shall, we must, with the guidance of God, here embark upon this course to redeem humanity," he said. And with the "righteous strength, which centuries of freedom under God have given us, we cannot fail."[9]

Although many of the usual critics lined up to attack both UMT and the draft, the Korean War drove a wedge between them and set the stage for a compromise similar to the one hammered out after the Czech crisis in 1948. Given the war in Korea, most were ready to admit that selective service had to be continued, at least on a short-term basis. But UMT, they said, was the "capstone of militarism" and would contribute to what Republican Congressman Daniel A. Reed of New York called "the complete garrison state."[10] As Reed's remark suggests, critics also saw the struggle

1121–22, 1126–30 (hereafter Senate, *Hearings on S. 1*). See also *Congressional Quarterly Almanac, 1951* (Washington, 1951), 274–89.

[8] Senate, *Hearings on S. 1*, 1083, 470. See also the sources cited in the previous note.

[9] *Congressional Record, 1951* 97:3219, 1565, 3205.

[10] Ibid., 3204. See also ibid., 3213, 3298, 3303, 3377, 3381; Senate, *Hearings on S. 1*, 778–88,

over UMT as one to define the country's national identity and postwar purpose. While those who defended the measure invoked the tradition of manifest destiny and the vision of America as a "redeemer" nation, critics expressed their misgivings in the metaphor of the garrison state and other familiar figures of speech. They continued to see UMT as "anti-American," as "totally foreign" to the traditions of the republic, and as more compatible with a "police state" than with a free state. To their way of thinking, which they captured rhetorically in these ideological oppositions, the American people could only preserve their democratic identity by remaining separate from the Old World. If they emulated Old World habits, such as UMT, they would "militarize the country," much as had happened in Germany and Japan. They would transform the United States into a "slave state" in which "power-grabbing bureaucrats" decided whom to draft and young men became "the property of the Government," their educations abridged, their family relationships terminated, their careers driven by the dictates of national security.[11]

These were the words of Reed and other critics who were concerned about the corruption of American politics by foreign policy. Indeed, the critics did not hesitate to draw a clear connection between the administration's national security goals and what they saw as a dangerous decline of democratic liberties. To their way of thinking, the country was headed for disaster if it continued "on the road of all-out military expansion and unlimited meddling in the affairs of foreign lands." It was headed for a state of "permanent war," said Republican Congressman Howard Buffett of Nebraska, in which all economic and political liberties would be swept away, as had been the case in Germany, Japan, and Italy, and was now the case in the Soviet Union. Others drew their lessons from an earlier history. Republican Congressman Edgar A. Jonas of Illinois warned that American youth under UMT would be "Hessianized and put on the auction block as was done in the days of George III with standing armies," and Republican Congresswoman Katharine St. George of New York made a similar point when she cited Washington's Farewell Address and warned of the dangers of an overgrown military establishment that rivaled civilian leadership.[12]

For these and other critics, it was clearly impossible to reconcile America's democratic identity with the global obligations that Truman

　　980–82, 1059–67, 1218–21; and *Congressional Quarterly Almanac, 1951* (Washington, 1951), 274–89.

[11] *Congressional Record, 1951* 97: 3213, 3216, 3203, 3204.

[12] Ibid., 3317–18, 3381. See also ibid., 3373–75.

was accepting. They thought it better to tailor the country's military policy to its resources and to insist that other nations share more fully in the common defense. The United States, they maintained, should not squander its limited manpower on "numberless divisions and vast armies," but should emphasize instead its great strength in science, technology, and the production of tanks, planes, and ships. It should also curb its obligations as a member of the United Nations and the North Atlantic Treaty Organization and should give primary emphasis to a defense of the Western Hemisphere.[13]

Although recommendations like these made the critics vulnerable to charges of isolationism, they fought back with a discursive strategy that identified the Truman administration with the foreign other in Moscow and put both beyond the boundaries of America's democratic identity. The "real menace," they said, was to be found not only in Moscow but also in Washington, where a "horrible conspiracy" had been hatched by New Deal internationalists on behalf of domestic and national security programs that overtaxed the nation's resources, threatened the very foundations of American liberty, and played into the hands of the Soviets. The "junta" in Washington, as one critic put it, had just about "succeeded in changing America from a constitutional Republic into a fascistic, militaristic power state."[14]

Criticism of this sort threatened to scuttle the bill and did lead to the passage of two important amendments. One, passed over the opposition of the Pentagon, put a ceiling of 3.5 million men on the size of the active forces. Senators John W. Bricker, Homer E. Capehart, Robert Taft, and other critics were reluctant to give the military a "blank check" to fix the size of the regular forces, in part because they wanted to halt what they saw as a drift from "congressional responsibility" to "administrative policymaking," in part because a military force that cost more than the country could afford would only bring on higher taxes, ruinous inflation, and economic controls – all of which would destroy "the liberty of the people."[15]

Behind arguments like these, critics also rallied to support a second amendment that basically postponed the decision on UMT indefinitely. The draft would be renewed but UMT would become operational only after the Korean War had ended and only then if Congress gave further approval to a concrete training program to be prepared by a National

---

[13] Ibid., 3203. See also the sources cited in the next note.
[14] Ibid., 3395. See also ibid., 3317, 3375.
[15] Ibid., 1996, 1994, 1999. See also ibid., 1998, 2046–56.

Security Training Commission. This amounted to a major triumph on which the critics were able to build in 1952, when they convinced Congress to table the UMT plan eventually submitted.

In effect, those who worried that UMT would cost too much, would regiment the nation's youth, and would give too much power to the military were able to scuttle UMT but not selective service. All sides saw the draft as essential under present circumstances and even conservative critics were inclined to admit that selective service, if not UMT, was compatible with American tradition. A commitment to tradition had thus combined with current necessities to produce a compromise that both sides found acceptable. Much the same was true when leaders in both political parties debated the sweep of the country's commitments abroad and the best strategy for meeting those commitments without inflating the defense budget to proportions that would wreck the economy and bring on the garrison state.

III

The national security ideology, not just the Korean War, drove defense spending after June 1950, with the war itself claiming about a quarter of the Pentagon's budget for fiscal years 1951–1953. The military goals laid out in NSC-68/4 included substantial forces in being, a large supply of war reserves, and a mobilization base on which the United States could build in the event of a global conflict. At first the administration had hoped to achieve these goals by 1954, perceived as the year of maximum danger, but had moved the deadline to mid-1952 after China intervened in Korea. With this speedup in mind, the total defense budget for fiscal year 1951, including several supplemental appropriations, permitted a military buildup that exceeded the pace set in the early days of World War II. The armed forces grew from less than 1.5 million troops at the start of the Korean War to more than 3.2 million a year later. The Army grew from 10 to 18 divisions over the same period, the Air Force from 42 to 72 wings, and the Navy from 618 to more than 1,000 ships and from 9 to 14 carrier groups.[16]

Despite these gains, not one of the services was satisfied. The ink had hardly dried on the budget for fiscal year 1951 when the armed forces began agitating for a defense budget of $82 billion in fiscal year 1952, not counting another $13 billion for military public works.

---

[16] Condit, *Test of War*, 238–42, 509–10; Leffler, *Preponderance of Power*, 374; Poole, *Joint Chiefs of Staff* 4:37–73.

According to the Joint Chiefs, the new sum would enable the military services to achieve by mid-1952 the force levels and mobilization base established in NSC-68/4. But the Budget Bureau, convinced that military goods could not be delivered fast enough to meet the Pentagon's goals, reduced the service estimates to slightly more than $49 billion and triggered another round of interservice bickering over how the smaller sum would be divided. Secretary of Defense Marshall and Undersecretary Lovett finally worked out a compromise calling for roughly $56.2 billion in military appropriations, to which would be added another $4.5 billion for military public works. The total of $60.7 billion would absorb about 20 percent of national production in fiscal year 1952, as compared with 45 percent at the height of World War II. The inflationary effects of such vast expenditures worried Truman, but he nevertheless urged the proposed budget on Congress in April 1951, along with another $6.25 billion in military assistance to America's allies in Europe and elsewhere.[17]

Although military assistance would add to the national security budget in the short run, Truman and other officials were convinced that it was cheaper for the United States to arm its allies than to shoulder the burden of collective security by itself. In the long run, moreover, American aid would enable the Europeans to make better use of their own resources and cover more of the cost of their own defense. Similar considerations also guided Truman's decision to establish military relations with Fascist Spain and Communist Yugoslavia and to support West Germany's rearmament and integration into NATO. One goal was to strengthen the system of collective security while spreading the costs among a larger number of countries. Another was to achieve that strength through a capital-intensive strategy of containment that relied primarily on other countries for military manpower and on the United States for airpower, naval power, and military assistance. "You

[17] National Security Branch, Bureau of the Budget, to Director of the Budget Frederick J. Lawton, 13 and 19 April 1951, and Lawton to Secretary of Defense Marshall, 23 April 1951, RG 51, Series 47.8a, folder: 1952 Budget – Basic Documents; National Security Branch memorandum, "Department of Defense Budget Estimates, Fiscal Year 1952," 19 April 1951, Truman Papers, PSF-Subject File, box 151, folder: Bureau of the Budget, Budget – FY 1952; Truman to the Speaker of the House of Representatives, 30 April 1951, and Truman, "Remarks to Key Officials on the Budget for the Military Functions of the Department of Defense," 3 May 1951, *Public Papers, Truman, 1951* (Washington, 1965), 254–57, 257–60; Budget Bureau memorandum, "Guide Lines Incorporated in the President's Military Budget for F. Y. 1952," 31 August 1951, RG 51, Series 47.8a, box 52, folder: 1952 Budget – Basic Documents; and Condit, *Test of War*, 250–56. On the military assistance program see the sources cited in the following note.

provide the gun but we are providing the man," is how the Europeans described it.[18]

By the time Congress took up the national security budget for fiscal year 1952, the Korean War had settled into a stalemate. Armistice negotiations followed in July and a small band of conservatives, mostly Republicans, began to wonder if such a substantial budget was still necessary. They tried to cap defense spending at a figure well below the president's recommendation, but were easily overwhelmed by a large majority. Most saw the need for continued vigilance as the armistice negotiations dragged on, and some, including conservatives like Taft, found it politically impossible in the current crisis "to criticize or to reduce in any respect the appropriation demands of the Army, the Navy, and the Air Corps." It was much easier to reduce appropriations in other areas of the budget, with the result being a familiar legislative prescription that included more money for air–atomic power as a cost-effective deterrent, less spending for European military assistance, and additional reductions in nondefense expenditures.

The final defense appropriation for fiscal year 1952 came to $56.9 billion, including a billion dollars more than the administration had sought for American airpower. A second piece of legislation appropriated almost $4 billion for military public works, and a third earmarked another $1.3 billion for service expenditures other than military forces and equipment. The total for fiscal year 1952 came to $62.2 billion, an increase of $12 billion over the previous fiscal year and a sum large enough to support an Army of 20 divisions, an Air Force of 80 wings, and a Navy of 1,176 ships, including 16 carrier groups. In addition to the defense budget, Congress appropriated roughly $6 billion for military assistance, mostly to Europe, or about $250 million less than the president had requested.[19]

Given the amount of expenditures involved, it was not surprising that the defense budgets sent to Congress in 1950 and 1951 raised new fears of a garrison state that would overburden the economy and undermine civilian control of the government. "The hand that controls the Pentagon, rules the land," explained one congressional conservative. The

---

[18] The quote is from Condit, *Test of War*, 420. See also Truman, "Annual Budget Message to the Congress: Fiscal Year 1952," *Public Papers, Truman, 1951*, 61–106; and Leffler, *Preponderance of Power*, 383–90, 411–12, 417–18.

[19] *Congressional Record, 1951* 97:11242. See also ibid., 9539–69, 9718–58, 11074–111, 11131–51, 11165–96, 11219–51, 12684–92; *Congressional Quarterly Almanac, 1951* 7:129–32; and Condit, *Test of War*, 257–60, 416–21.

military establishment had taken charge "of our fiscal machinery, of our diplomacy, and of our economic development," said another. For all practical purposes, "we are having our initial experience with the garrison state, in which the conduct of our lives is made secondary to the demands of the Military Establishment."[20] These and similar concerns informed partisan debates over the scope of the country's commitments and the best way to meet them. They encouraged American officials to consider different strategies for harmonizing their national security goals with the country's economic and political values, and they operated in some cases as a brake on how far and how fast the rearmament program could go.

Conservatives, mostly in the Republican party, suggested one such strategy in the Great Debate, as it was called, which expressed again their conviction that America's traditional democratic identity required more freedom from foreign entanglements than the Truman administration thought desirable. President Truman touched off the debate with a decision to contribute several American divisions to a NATO force in Europe and to appoint General Eisenhower to the new position of NATO Supreme Commander.[21] The decision came when Congress was considering the defense budget for fiscal year 1952 and at a time when critics on Capitol Hill were already complaining that Truman had committed American troops to Korea without congressional advice and approval. Senator Taft, former president Herbert Hoover, and former ambassador Joseph P. Kennedy all reacted with statements strongly critical of the president's decision, as did Republican Senator Kenneth S. Wherry of Nebraska, who introduced a resolution that would bar the assignment of American troops to Europe pending a congressional decision on the issue. This resolution, which came in January 1951, shaped the Great Debate for the next four months.[22]

---

[20] *Congressional Record, 1951* 97:9736, 11141. See also ibid., 9748 and 11232.

[21] "Statement by the President Approving an Increase in U.S. Forces in Western Europe," 9 September 1950, Truman "Message to the Secretary of State Designating General Eisenhower as Supreme Allied Commander, Europe," 19 December 1950, Truman to Eisenhower, 19 December 1950, *Public Papers, Truman, 1950*, 626, 750, 754–55.

[22] Joseph P. Kennedy, "Present Policy is Politically and Morally Bankrupt," 12 December 1950, *Vital Speeches of the Day* 17 (1 January 1951): 170–73; Herbert Hoover, "Our National Policies in This Crisis," 20 December 1950, in Hoover, *Addresses Upon the American Road, 1950–1955* (Stanford, 1955), 3–10; and Taft address to the Senate, 5 January 1951, *Congressional Record, 1951* 97:55–61. On the Great Debate see also Ronald J. Caridi, *The Korean War and American Politics: The Republican Party as a Case Study* (Philadelphia, 1968), 126–40; Patterson, *Mr. Republican*, 477–83; David R. Kepley, "The Senate and the Great Debate of 1951," *Prologue* 14 (Winter 1982): 212–26; Gary Dean Best, *Herbert*

The debate focused in part on the military and economic wisdom of stationing American troops in Europe. The Europeans, according to conservative critics, had refused to shoulder a fair share of the common defense, utilize fully their own resources, or contribute much to the cause of containment in Korea. Instead, the burden had fallen disproportionately on the United States, which was bearing the weight of a massive rearmament program, a costly war in Asia, and billions of dollars for Europe's economic recovery and military security. American taxpayers, the conservatives argued, could not afford to defend countries that would not defend themselves. The first order of business must be a strong economy and a healthy standard of living at home, not staggering foreign expenditures that would bankrupt the country and destroy its security.[23]

Although most of the critics would not abandon Asia or withdraw from Europe, they did want the United States to re-tailor its strategy along lines they considered more sensible militarily, more practical economically, and more in step with American tradition. The strategic pattern they had in mind started with the assumption that American military planners could not match the ground forces available to the Communist bloc and should not try to do so. "The first principle of military strategy," argued Taft, "is not to fight on the enemy's chosen battleground where he has his greatest strength." Both Napoleon and Hitler had made that mistake, with results that were as disastrous for them as they would be for the United States. A conventional war in either Asia or Europe, as Hoover explained, would exhaust the United States, which he called the "Gibraltar of Western Civilization," and turn "the quicksands of China, India or Western Europe" into a "graveyard" for "millions of American boys."

Instead, the United States should build a strategic system that was centered on the Western Hemisphere, stretched east across the Atlantic

Hoover: The Postpresidential Years, 1933–1964, vol. 2 (Stanford, 1983), 340–50; Phil Williams, *The Senate and US Troops in Europe* (New York, 1985), 43–107; Ted Galen Carpenter, "United States' NATO Policy at the Crossroads: The 'Great Debate' of 1950–1951," *International History Review* 8 (August 1986): 389–415; and Karen Hunt Exon, "'Fortress America': The U.S. Senate and the Great Debate of 1950–51," (Ph.D. diss., University of Kansas, 1990).

23 In addition to the sources cited in the preceding note see Hoover, "We Should Revise Our Foreign Policies," 9 February 1951, and Hoover, "On Defense of Europe," 27 February 1951, both in Hoover, *Addresses Upon the American Road*, 11–22, 23–31; Taft, "Address Before the Executives Club of Chicago," 26 January 1951, Taft Papers, Legislative File, box 618, folder: Foreign Policy, 1950–51; and Taft testimony before the Senate Foreign Relations Committee and Armed Services Committee, 26 February 1951, ibid., box 844, folder: U.S. International Army and Europe, 1951.

to Great Britain, and stretched west across the Pacific to Japan, Formosa, and the Philippines. Under this system, the United States would arm itself "to the teeth," in Hoover's phrase, but with a powerful navy and a large air force, as Taft had been demanding for years, not an expensive, standing army. Once they had made these initial expenditures, moreover, American taxpayers could reduce defense spending to an affordable level, balance the federal budget, and free themselves "from the dangers of inflation and economic degeneration."[24]

Conservatives viewed their strategy as a realistic way to defend free-dom where it could be defended while safeguarding the economic and in-stitutional foundations of liberty at home. By contrast, they said, Truman's national security strategy, with its indiscriminate commitments abroad, would overtax the country's resources, particularly if added to the cost of the welfare state. Like the Athenians and the Romans, and like the French under Napoleon and the Germans under Hitler, Truman's national security managers were asking the country to tackle more than it could pay for. This was the opinion of Republican Senator George Malone of Nevada, who resorted to the usual rhetorical strategy of in-scribing an American identity that excluded Truman's policies, which Malone associated with the un-American other. If the United States tried to "police the world," he and other conservatives argued, the whole economy would have to be mobilized. Manpower would come under government control and every bit of extra income would be taken from the American family, from farms and factories, from schools and hospi-tals until the "American way of life" was finally destroyed. "Russia could desire nothing more," according to Taft, "than an indefinite condition of economic weakness and inflation, with millions of men taken out of productive work and the inevitable dissatisfaction which will result in turning the United States into a garrison state."[25]

The country's postwar purpose and political identity, particularly the danger of a garrison state, was also the theme when the Great De-bate turned from military strategy to presidential prerogatives, especially the question of whether Truman's decision to commit American troops abroad had eroded the constitutional balance between the executive and

---

[24] *Congressional Record, 1951* 97:58; Hoover, "Our National Policies in This Crisis." See also *Congressional Record, 1951* 97:1122–23, 2652–64.

[25] *Congressional Record, 1951* 97:167, 2986. See also ibid., 2597–98; Taft to Robert Knodel, 24 November 1950, Taft Papers, Subject File, box 917, folder: 1950 Foreign Policy; Taft to C.C. Moseley, 28 February 1950, ibid., box 968, folder: 1951 Foreign Policy; and Taft to Janet Polonsky, 17 March 1951, ibid., box 957, folder: Controls, O-P, 1951.

legislative branches of government. As Taft and other critics saw it, the president could not surrender his constitutional powers as commander in chief to an international coalition or contribute American troops to an international army – at least not without the consent of Congress. Taking such actions meant usurping powers that belonged to the legislative branch and contributing to the development of a "military dictatorship." According to Republican Senator William Jenner of Indiana, Truman's assertion of executive authority was the last round in a liberal conspiracy that began with Woodrow Wilson, ran through the New and Fair Deals, and now aimed at a "world garrison state" dominated by international planning bodies that would destroy the "American way of life." The issue now, said Senator John L. McClellan, a conservative Democrat from Arkansas, was "whether one man is going to send millions of American boys to foreign battlefields or whether the Congress is going to take some responsibility and exercise its constitutional duty in the process."[26]

Conservatives saw themselves defending the nation's traditional political identity against efforts to construct a new one, historic American principles against an overdrawn foreign policy that was more typical of totalitarian than of democratic governments. These principles included the long-standing fears of a powerful central state, standing armies, and government deficits. Included as well was a belief in the value of a strong dollar and a balanced budget and in the primacy of civilian over military rule, of private over public institutions, of state governments over the federal government, of the constitutional balance over "dictatorial power." "We can wipe out all traces of communism in the world," said Senator Bricker of Ohio, "but if we lose the Constitution we are doomed to slavery." As conservatives saw it, moreover, there was a traditional foreign policy that had safeguarded and would continue to safeguard the other traditions they held dear. "We have never wanted a part of other peoples' scrapes," said Kennedy. After all, "what business is it of ours to support French colonial policy in Indo-China or to achieve Mr. Syngman Rhee's concepts of democracy in Korea?" Jenner made the same point when he cited the Monroe Doctrine as a truly "American foreign policy," particularly President Monroe's pledge to resist European intrusions into the Western Hemisphere while abjuring any interest in the internal affairs of the Old World.[27]

---

[26] *Congressional Record, 1951* 97:2873, 2597–98, 3149. See also ibid., 55–61, 1119–20; and Taft to Beatrice Abbott, 3 February 1951, and Taft to Bertha Haven Putnam, 19 February 1951, Taft Papers, Subject File, box 968, folder: 1951 Foreign Policy.

[27] *Congressional Record, 1951* 97:2865, 2973, 2600; Kennedy, "Present Policy is Politically and Morally Bankrupt."

Taft struck a similar note in a major speech to the Senate on 5 January 1951. The traditional goal of American foreign policy, he said to those who would redefine the national purpose, was "to maintain the liberty of our people" rather than "reform the entire world or spread sweetness and light and economic prosperity to peoples who have lived and worked out their own salvation for centuries." The system of defense that he and Hoover envisioned supposedly squared with this traditional purpose, and would therefore protect such American values as a balanced budget, a stable dollar, and the principle of civilian leadership that were otherwise endangered when the country overreached its interests or pursued a provocative foreign policy. War and the constant preparation for war promoted "dictatorship and totalitarian government," Taft argued. Hence, the country should go only "as far toward preparing for war as we can go in time of peace without weakening ourselves . . . and destroying forever the very liberty which war is designed to protect."[28]

On the other side of the Great Debate, numerous senators defended Truman's policy in arguments that resonated with the national security ideology and with their own sense of America's new mission as a great military power and global defender of democracy. Rejecting the military assessments of their opponents, they argued that Europe could not be defended through air and sea power alone, as the Second World War had demonstrated. They defended the European allies as willing to protect themselves and shoulder their share of the common defense, and they defended the president's policies as cautious, not provocative. Truman, they said, was merely containing the Soviet menace, and anything less would amount to "appeasement" and lead to another world war.

Such arguments were part of the geopolitical logic that was central to the national security ideology of the early Cold War. According to that logic, the United States had no choice but to contain aggression in Europe because the nation's security was linked inextricably to that of its allies in the North Atlantic community. "Western Europe is the second greatest industrial complex in the world," explained a Texas Democrat, and this meant that if its labor and industrial power, its markets and materials, came under Communist control they would add to the economic and military strength of the Soviet Union and detract from that of the United States. The same would be true, according to others, if Japan and Indochina or Africa and the Middle East collapsed to communism. The

[28] *Congressional Record, 1951* 97:56.

loss of these areas would also threaten the "economic survival" of the United States and undermine its military potential.[29]

This line of argument led inevitably to other themes in the national security ideology, including the notion that peace and freedom were indivisible, that American power had to be mobilized on behalf of democracy "everywhere," and that tradition had to give some ground to this new responsibility. "We believe that peace is indivisible," said Senator Paul Douglas of Illinois, in an early statement of the domino theory, and "we believe that if aggression" succeeds it will lead to "further aggression." What is more, stopping aggression required permanent preparedness, a military policy that was geared to the country's security, not its economy, and a high degree of flexibility. In an age of permanent struggle, in which war and peace had become inseparable, said Senator Hubert H. Humphrey, a Democrat from Minnesota, "it is hard to tell . . . where war begins and where it ends." And since this was an age not only of permanent war but also of potential total war involving atomic weapons, permanent preparedness must include the ability to respond immediately to aggression. "The days of all the niceties and formalities of declarations of war are past," said Humphrey, in words that expressed his sense of how tradition had to bow before reality. "We are not back in the days of the minuet" but living in a time when Stalin could strike a "deathblow" before Congress decided how many troops should go to Europe. "It is one thing to have legalistic arguments about where the power rests," Humphrey concluded, but another to hamstring the president's ability to deal with a totalitarian state that had the initiative and could act swiftly.[30]

As these arguments suggest, Humphrey and others were ready to tailor both law and the budget to fit a new national purpose – one that embraced not only the country's traditional democratic identity but also its new mission as the guardian of freedom everywhere. In essence, they accused Taft of being penny wise and pound foolish. They wondered what price the United States would pay if it was bereft of allies, and they concluded that in such an event the cost of defense would surely exceed what Truman had proposed, not to mention the other costs that conservatives feared most. "The loss of Europe, Asia, and Africa," as Senator Douglas explained, "would bring an irresistible drive toward isolationism in the United States and the consequent erection of a garrison state.

[29] *Congressional Record, 1951* 97:144, 247. See also ibid., 61, 149, 158, 234–39, 240, 1203.
[30] *Congressional Record, 1951* 97:232, 2854, 3098. See also ibid., 145.

The effort to build an unconquerable bastion while surrounded by a Communist world would bring in its train the suppression of many of our precious liberties. We probably could not avoid the realities of the police state, however we might avoid the name."[31]

The Great Debate resumed in April 1951 when the president relieved General Douglas MacArthur of his command in Korea. MacArthur had repeatedly defied presidential directives and publicly criticized the president's policy of fighting a limited war. He wanted total victory, and to get it he recommended a naval blockade of the China coast, a major air campaign against China and North Korea, and a military partnership with the Nationalist forces on Taiwan. The president responded by dismissing the general and upholding the policy of containment. Like the revolt of the admirals, MacArthur's defiance prompted some to wonder if the Cold War was pushing American state makers down the road to a garrison state in which traditional political values gave way to a dangerous authoritarianism, civilian rule to a military dictatorship.

Truman saw the crisis in these terms at the time and years later, when he devoted several pages of his memoirs to the general's insubordination. His recounting was steeped in a familiar cultural narrative. He told how the American people were descended from men and women who had "fled their native countries to escape the oppression of militarism." He took comfort in knowing that only once before had American voters elected a professional military man to the presidency. He drew a parallel between his action and Lincoln's decision to relieve General McClellan of his command of the Union Army, because the general had ignored direct orders from the White House. He thought the Founders had shown great wisdom in devising a system of government that put civilian over military authority, elected officials over generals, and he saw his action as defending this "basic element in our Constitution." Indeed, he would have violated his "oath to uphold and defend the Constitution" had he allowed MacArthur to "defy the civilian authorities."[32]

Truman's critics turned these arguments upside down. While they, too, defended the principle of civilian rule and conceded the president's right to fire MacArthur, they doubted the wisdom of Truman's decision and argued that his military strategy was more likely than MacArthur's to bring

---

[31] *Congressional Record, 1951* 97:247. See also the whole of Humphrey's remarks in ibid., 243–53.

[32] Truman, *Years of Trial and Hope*, 444. For more on the Truman–MacArthur controversy see also the sources cited in the following note.

on the garrison state. Like MacArthur, in other words, they rejected limited war and containment in favor of total victory through a military escalation of the conflict. For most of the critics, this strategy held fewer risks than a series of indecisive conflicts that would lead to higher taxes, larger deficits, a more powerful military, and, ultimately, the destruction of the country's economic and political institutions. This was a conviction, moreover, to which MacArthur himself appealed. In speeches following his return from Korea, he consistently linked a blistering critique of the administration's foreign policies to a strong denunciation of high taxes, unbalanced budgets, and excessive government spending.[33]

The debate soon spilled over into the nation's press, where national commentators repeated the arguments on both sides. Most were sympathetic with Truman's policies, though not with the president himself. Neither Arthur Krock nor Walter Lippmann had much respect for Truman, and both condemned the president for ignoring congressional prerogatives when he dispatched American troops to Korea and Europe. Nevertheless, both supported the administration's efforts to strengthen the Western alliance and were critical of public figures like Hoover, who were prepared, in Lippmann's words, to "abandon the Eurasian mainland" to the Communists. Lippmann considered Hoover an isolationist whose recommendations added up to "a surrender greater than any Stalin and Mao have ever called for."[34] So did James Reston, Marquis Childs, and other commentators. According to Childs, for example, Truman's critics were the same people who had counseled despair and defeat in 1939,

---

[33] On the Truman–MacArthur controversy see Truman, *Memoirs* 2:442–52; John W. Spanier, *The Truman–MacArthur Controversy and the Korean War,* paperback ed. (New York, 1965), esp. 137–238; Caridi, *Korean War and American Politics,* 141–75; David Rees, *Korea: The Limited War,* paperback ed. (Baltimore, 1970), 264–85; D. Clayton James, *The Years of MacArthur,* vol. 3, *Triumph and Disaster, 1945–1964* (Boston, 1985), 588–655; Burton I. Kaufman, *The Korean War: Challenges in Crisis, Credibility, and Command* (Philadelphia, 1986), 167–78; David R. Kepley, *The Collapse of the Middle Way: Senate Republicans and the Bipartisan Foreign Policy, 1948–1952* (New York, 1988), 116–31; and Michael Schaller, *Douglas MacArthur: The Far Eastern General* (New York, 1989), 241–53.

[34] Lippmann, "The Dewey and Hoover Theories," *Washington Post,* 26 December 1950. See also, Krock, "Sound Basis of Action Begins to Appear," *New York Times,* 19 December 1950; Krock, "The Greatest Issue in Our Foreign Policy," ibid., 21 December 1950; Krock, "Not Much Assistance in the 'Great Debate'," ibid., 9 January 1950; Lippmann, "Mr. Truman and the Constitution," *Washington Post,* 16 January 1951; Krock, "Mr. Douglas Emphasizes Vital Point," *New York Times,* 16 January 1951; Krock, "The Spirit of Concession Tiptoes In," ibid., 18 January 1951; Lippmann, "The Debate Goes On," *Washington Post,* 13 February 1951; Krock, "The Showdown Nears, the Outcome Apparent," ibid., 15 February 1951; and Krock, "Lodge Has Compromise On an Army for Europe," ibid., 18 February 1951.

and were now helping to advance the cause of Soviet propaganda in the Cold War.[35]

The same columnists generally sided with the president during the Truman–MacArthur controversy. Some, like Krock, seemed in awe of MacArthur, while others, like Hanson Baldwin, considered him a "man of unlimited ambition and unlimited ego."[36] The most vigorous criticism of the president came from David Lawrence and others on the conservative wing of the nation's press. Lawrence used the pages of *U.S. News & World Report* to support Republican demands for a reexamination of U.S. foreign policy, to celebrate MacArthur as a symbol of determined anticommunism, and to castigate Truman, the European allies, and the United Nations for practicing appeasement in Korea. The president might have a legal right to dismiss the general, Lawrence conceded, but he did so at the behest of foreign governments who would not allow the United States to bring the full force of its military power to bear on the Korean conflict. The results of such appeasement, Lawrence concluded, could only be a prolonged conflict in Korea, further Communist aggression in both Asia and Europe, and a further erosion of American power.[37]

Although many other commentators were also critical of Truman, they still accepted the president's position on most of the major issues. Columnists such as Marquis Childs, James Reston, Hanson Baldwin, and Stewart Alsop, to name a few, blamed the crisis in part on the leadership vacuum created by Truman's flawed policies in Asia and elsewhere. Nevertheless, they thought that Truman was fully justified in dismissing the insubordinate general and were highly critical of MacArthur's recommendations. Far from ending the Korean War, they argued, these

35 Reston, "Hoover's Speech Raises a Fundamental Issue," *New York Times*, 24 December 1950; Childs, "New Isolationism," *Washington Post*, 27 December 1950; Reston, "Five 'Dubious Assumptions' in the Great Debate," *New York Times*, 7 January 1951; Childs, "President's Powers," *Washington Post*, 10 January 1951; and Childs, "Soviet View of Taft," ibid., 11 January 1951.

36 Baldwin, "Basic Issues Obscured," *New York Times*, 7 May 1951. See also Krock, "Appeal to the Record in the 'Great Debate'," ibid., 22 April 1951; Baldwin, "The Magic of MacArthur," ibid., 23 April 1951; Krock, "M'Arthur's Testimony a Series of Challenges," ibid., 6 May 1951; Baldwin, "Conflicting Views of War," ibid., 11 May 1951; and Krock, "Some Background as a Test of Judgment," ibid., 11 May 1951.

37 See, in *U.S. News & World Report*, Lawrence's "Will Mr. Truman 'Re-examine'?" (1 December 1950): 56; "The 'Defeat' That Means Victory" (22 December 1950): 52; "Quibbling While World Burns" (19 January 1951): 56; "Inviting World War III?" (20 April 1951): 76; "A Salute to Courage" (27 April 1951): 76; "What U.N. Policies, Mr. President?" (4 May 1951): 68; "Civilian Stupidity" (11 May 1951): 132; "1951 – Europe's Last Chance" (18 May 1951): 136; "Old Principles Never Die" (8 June 1951): 72; and "Defeat?" (6 July 1951): 56.

recommendations would actually lead to a wider war with China, risk
Soviet intervention, divide the NATO alliance, and leave Western Europe
vulnerable to attack.[38]

Running through both sides of the argument was a deep concern
that current policies could wreck American democracy and bring on the
garrison state. Lawrence and other conservatives saw this development
emerging from a prolonged state of semiwar that exhausted American
resources, regimented the economy, and led to the loss of economic liberties. Walter Lippmann mounted a similar critique. Echoing his earlier
criticism of the Truman Doctrine, Lippmann accused the administration
of pursuing a reckless globalism that reversed the country's traditional
reluctance to fight a land war in Asia, relied too heavily on ground forces
in Europe, and therefore lacked widespread public support. The country's military resources, according to Lippmann, should not be "scattered
aimlessly around the world" but concentrated in Europe and the Atlantic,
where its interests were greatest, and on air and sea power, where it enjoyed a strong military advantage. Lippmann saw the Korean intervention as the last round in an effort, stretching back to the conquest of the
Philippines, to build an American imperium in the Far East at the expense
of the country's role as leader of the Western democracies and defender of
Western civilization. He did not oppose the stationing of a modest American force in Europe to deter Soviet aggression there, but he was anxious
to withdraw American troops from Korea and was opposed to the creation of a large standing army. Together with hapless military adventures
like the one in Korea, Lippmann told his readers, a large standing army
and the growing prestige of military leaders would place an "intolerable
strain upon our manpower and upon our economy," require regimentation and controls, and spell the end of American democracy.[39]

---

[38] Childs, "Budding Diarist," and Stewart Alsop, "MacArthur," *Washington Post*, 11 April
1951; Lippman, "The President and the General," and Childs, "Martyrdom Vs. War with
China," ibid., 12 April 1951; Baldwin, "The MacArthur Question," *New York Times*,
12 April 1951; Childs, "Storm Over MacArthur," *Washington Post*, 13 April 1951; Stewart
Alsop, "Truman and MacArthur," ibid., 13 April 1951; Childs, "Ridgway's Timetable,"
ibid., 14 April 1951; Reston, "Premise of Our Global Strategy-Strong Allies," *New York
Times*, 22 April 1951; Reston, "Is Red China or Red Russia the Main Issue?" ibid., 29 April
1951; Reston, "MacArthur Offers Congress Policy Based on Hard Facts," ibid., 4 May
1951; Reston, "Great Debate is Marked by Many Paradoxes," ibid., 6 May 1951; Baldwin,
"Basic Issues Obscured," ibid., 7 May 1951; and Reston, "Joint Chiefs' 'Identical' Ideas
Only Apparently MacArthur's," ibid., 7 May 1951.

[39] Lippmann, "Mr. Dulles' Speech," and "Point of No Return," *Washington Post*, 2 January
and 26 February 1951. See also, in ibid., Lippmann's, "The Dewey and Hoover Theories,"

Despite these concerns, the administration appeared to get the best of its opponents in the Great Debate: The MacArthur controversy faded away and the Senate approved Truman's promise of four divisions for Europe. Yet throughout the debate, each side had pushed the other toward policies that embodied a set of shared concerns, notably the desire to safeguard American democracy against the danger of a garrison state. Even while they complained about the president's policies in Korea, conservative critics defended the principle of civilian rule and the president's right to dismiss MacArthur. Even though the military doubled its manpower in the first year of the Korean War, Truman continued to prefer a capital-intensive strategy of defense that emphasized air–atomic power. Even though American troops would be stationed in Europe, the emphasis was on a collective security arrangement that relied primarily on the manpower of other countries. Even though the defense budget jumped to astounding heights, the goal was a national security policy that could be sustained without ruining the economy. And even though the administration spent billions of dollars rearming its NATO allies, the hope was that Europe's rearmament would reduce the burden of collective security on the American budget. Truman, to be sure, was not as cautious as Taft might have been. But his reliance on military assistance, on air power, and on collective security came closer to Taft's strategic design than many realized at the time.

IV

The rapid escalation of defense expenditures raised old questions that were central to the process of state making in the early Cold War: Would rearmament add to the national debt? Would new taxes be necessary? How would the tax burden be apportioned? And what would security cost in terms of social welfare? The answers to these questions would determine the health of the economy, the fate of the defense effort, and the shape of the postwar state. They would decide whether the American people were going to identify themselves with the welfare state or with the warfare state; if they could strike a workable balance between these different visions and the values that each embodied; and if the traditional principles of good government, such as a balanced

26 December 1950; "The Lines of a Policy," 11 January 1951; "A Reexamined and Revised Policy," 5 February 1951; and "A Small Army for Europe," 19 February 1951. On Lawrence's thinking see the sources cited in note 46.

budget, could survive the demands that rearmament placed on American resources.

President Truman said as much in a letter to Senator Walter F. George of Georgia, chairman of the Senate Finance Committee, a month after the outbreak of fighting in Korea. At the time, Congress was considering a bill to eliminate many of the excise taxes left over from the Second World War and to make up the lost revenue by closing tax loopholes and increasing corporate income taxes. The House had passed such a measure under pressure from the Democrats and the Senate was about to act when the Korean War and the big increase in defense spending prompted Truman's letter to George. Under the circumstances, Truman wanted Congress to retain the excise taxes and to increase taxes on corporate and individual incomes. His goal was to raise at least $5 billion in new revenue to cover immediate defense expenditures without adding to the deficit and sparking inflation. Given the crisis, both houses agreed to the president's request and quickly passed a revenue act that came close to what the White House had in mind. Under pressure from liberal Democrats, moreover, Congress followed this act with an excess-profits tax on corporations that benefited from rearmament orders. Taken together, the two measures generated about $9 billion in federal revenue, more than enough to cover the cost of rearmament, which was just gearing up, and still balance the budget in fiscal year 1951.[40]

Over the long term, however, even more tax dollars would be needed to achieve the rearmament targets laid out in NSC-68/4 without wrecking the budget or seriously shortchanging the social welfare programs growing out of the New Deal. This became clear in February 1951, when the president asked Congress to enact another package of new taxes that would put the Korean War and the rearmament program on a "pay-as-we-go" basis, a phrase that captured his continuing commitment to the goal of a balanced budget and to the political and moral values it symbolized. Not surprisingly, given the scope of the rearmament program, Truman was now asking for the largest tax hike in history, a total of $16 billion in new revenue, beginning with an initial tax package of $10 billion to be raised by closing tax loopholes and by increasing individual

[40] Truman to George, 25 July 1950, *Public Papers, 1950*, 545–47; Truman statement on signing the excess profits tax, 3 January 1951, *Public Papers, Truman, 1951*, 1. See also Truman's special message to Congress reporting on the situation in Korea, 19 July 1950, *Public Papers, Truman, 1950*, 527–37; *Congressional Quarterly Almanac, 1950* 6:573–95; and the tax history, "Taxation for Defense," written by L. Laszlo Ecker-Racz of the Treasury Department, Ecker-Racz Papers (Truman Library), box 7, folder: Taxation for Defense.

income taxes by $3.6 billion, corporate income taxes by more than $3 billion, and excise taxes on various consumer goods by another $3 billion. The tax package, Truman said, would not only help to balance the budget but would also "distribute the cost of defense fairly." The progressive income tax would account for differences in ability to pay and would work with corporate taxes, excise taxes, and new efforts to close tax loopholes to curb inflation, with "its grossly unfair distribution of the burden," and to prevent taxpayers from transferring the cost of their security to the next generation.[41]

Almost everyone on Capitol Hill endorsed the pay-as-we-go principle, but Republican legislators, joined by conservative Democrats, refused to move quickly on the president's proposal. They opened a debate that dragged on until October, when Congress finally passed a bill that raised taxes by slightly less than $5.6 billion and did little to close existing loopholes. What is more, a greater proportion of the new revenue would come from individual income and excise taxes, and a smaller proportion from taxes on corporate income, than the president had recommended.

As these results suggest, committee hearings on the tax bill had produced sharp divisions that ran along economic as well as party lines. Business groups generally resisted efforts to tax excess profits, close loopholes, and raise corporate income taxes. They also preferred a uniform sales tax to an excise tax, and they wanted new income taxes to fall most heavily on low-income groups. Labor organizations favored heavier estate, gift, and corporate taxes, which business groups opposed. They also wanted to raise the capital gains tax, close tax loopholes, do away with excise taxes that fell unfairly on low-income wage earners, and provide tax credits to lighten the burden of new income taxes on the same group. In general, labor's position won support from congressional Democrats and liberal organizations, such as the Americans for Democratic Action, while business and banking groups drew support from congressional conservatives, especially in the Republican party, and from such organizations as the U.S. Chamber of Commerce and the National Association of Manufacturers.[42]

When deliberations moved from the committee room to the floor of Congress, class and party divisions often boiled down to a debate over budget priorities. The issue was whether current priorities endangered

---

[41] Truman, "Special Message to the Congress Recommending a 'Pay as We Go' Tax Program," 2 February 1951, *Public Papers, Truman, 1951,* 134–38. See also Ecker-Racz, "Taxation for Defense."

[42] *Congressional Quarterly Almanac, 1951* 7:409–35.

the country's economic and political well-being, and for fiscal conservatives, mostly in the Republican party, pay-as-we-go meant reducing
government expenditures before raising taxes. To hear them tell it, government was swimming in waste, some of it in the Pentagon, where
savings could amount to as much as $2 billion per year, but most of it
in nonmilitary expenditures or in foreign assistance programs. According to conservatives, foreign "give-away" programs added more than $8
billion to the administration's budget, and because much of this was being wasted on socialist experiments, especially in Great Britain, the sum
could easily be cut in half. Similar reductions could be made in what
conservatives called "non-essential" expenditures at home. According to
Republican Congressman Roy O. Woodruff of Michigan, Truman's budget would increase domestic civilian expenditures by $1.3 billion, mostly
for "socialized housing, agriculture, and medicine," not to mention "fed-
eralized education" and other "socialistic programs," all of which could
be reduced by at least $2 billion, bringing the total potential savings to
$8 billion. With such cuts there would be little need to increase taxes
by more than $2 billion, not the $10 billion or more that Truman was
proposing, and the United States could meet the challenge of communism
with a strong and solvent economy.[43]

At the heart of the conservative argument was the familiar rhetorical
strategy of otherness and the equally familiar fear of a garrison state that
would subvert the country's democratic identity and traditional values.
"The truth is that we are slowly losing our freedoms as we move toward the garrison state," said Joseph W. Martin of Massachusetts, the
Republican leader in the House of Representatives. Ever increasing budgets threatened national solvency and stability; ever higher taxes robbed
citizens of the capacity to stand on their own two feet; ever growing
government choked off private initiative and curtailed the private sector.
A citizen was no longer free, argued conservatives, when the government
took one-third of his income in taxes. He had become instead a "ward
of the state" and a lackey of the "smart boys" and the "palace czars"
in the White House whose un-American policies had more in common
with authoritarian regimes than with democratic states. Martin and other
fiscal conservatives were particularly concerned about the "sadistic taxation" of those who had the highest incomes. This "soak-the-rich policy"
supposedly robbed the most able citizens of their incentive to produce,

---

43 *Congressional Record, 1951* 97:6908. See also ibid., 6760, 6893, 6907–8, 6971, 6972,
6974, 12045.

eroded the economic strength that was essential to national security, and took "another step in the direction of totalitarian, socialist control of our national economy."[44]

The last remark highlighted a familiar conservative argument about how communism could win the Cold War: "There's only one way to kill capitalism – by taxes, taxes and more taxes." Together with wasteful government spending, taxes would enable the Communists to take control of the United States without firing a single shot. Such was the view of a Republican congressman from Washington, who said he was quoting Karl Marx, and of other conservatives, for whom Lenin was the principal authority on the subject. " 'We must cause the Americans to spend themselves to destruction.' " Was this not what Lenin had said "before his death?" asked Senator James P. Kem, a Republican from Missouri. Absolutely, answered other conservatives, and that was still the goal of Kremlin dictators and their allies in the Truman administration, who were seeking to drive up the tax rate, the budget deficit, and the national debt until the American dream was replaced by a Communist nightmare.[45]

Liberal Democrats had their own reasons to complain. The bills drafted in both the House and the Senate did not plug existing loopholes or raise taxes, especially on corporate income, as much as Truman had requested. The greater reliance on individual income and excise taxes put more of the burden of national security on average income earners and consumers, as did plans to curb social expenditures in order to pay for rearmament. Democrats made these points repeatedly in the floor debates over the tax bill. They warned that even higher taxes would be needed if rearmament was going to be put on a pay-as-we-go basis, and they rejected Republican claims that high taxes and social expenditures were wrecking the country. "We have grown accustomed to Republican charges of socialism," said Congressman Herman P. Ebertharter, a Democrat from Pennsylvania. "Free enterprise has died a thousand deaths here in the Halls of Congress," agreed Senator Herbert H. Lehman, a Democrat from New York. But in spite of higher taxes and more government spending, personal income and employment were up, the savings rate had increased, corporate profits were running at unprecedented levels, business investment was booming, and so was the economy in general. Nor would liberals like Humphrey let the New Deal take the blame for

---

[44] Ibid., 6982, 6983, 6984, and 6909. See also ibid., 6953.
[45] Ibid., 6761, 11829. See also ibid., 6971, 11940–43.

the national debt or the size of the budget. The debt was a byproduct of
the Second World War, Humphrey said, just as the current budget grew
out of the Cold War and the Korean conflict. What is more, Truman had
earmarked only $12 billion of the 1952 budget for programs unrelated to
national security. Those programs had already been cut to the bone and
any further reductions would "practically destroy the Government."[46]

Because the current crisis precluded substantial cuts in national security
programs, the Democrats saw no choice but a tax hike if the government
was going to meet its global obligations and still balance its budget. They
wrapped the tax package in the ideology of national security, including
America's new role as the defender of democracy at home and abroad.
The administration had not suggested a new tax bill to pay for social
programs, they said. It was not a "socialist tax bill" but a "defense tax"
to deal with a global danger that now threatened the United States "more
desperately than at any time in its whole history." Whereas Republicans
would risk the country's security to reduce expenditures and cut taxes,
the administration, according to the Democrats, sought the financial
means to safeguard the "national interest." Whereas conservatives saw
higher taxes as the first step toward a garrison state, liberals saw them
as essential to a strong defense of the American way. The Republicans
talked about personal liberties, said Senator Lehman, but forgot that
"personal liberty would be destroyed and slavery" would be imposed "if
Communists take over our country."[47]

Arguments like these were enough to pass the Revenue Act of 1951,
which Truman signed in October of that year, but not enough to give
the administration all that it wanted.[48] Although Truman had asked
Congress to "distribute the cost of defense fairly," his own proposal,
which relied heavily on excise taxes, made it difficult to achieve that
goal. Nor did Congress do much to close tax loopholes, provide tax
credits for low-income groups, raise excess-profits taxes, add new estate
taxes, or include other provisions that liberal critics thought necessary
to ease the financial burden of defense on those unable to bear it. What
is more, Congress had provided only $5.6 billion of the $10 billion that
Truman had requested, thereby creating a budget deficit that shifted the
cost of the Cold War to another generation. In effect, the inclination of
the Democrats to pay for rearmament with higher taxes ran up against

---

[46] Ibid., 6966, 11817, 6969. See also ibid., 6990, 11805–6, 11809.
[47] Ibid., 6991, 6991–92. See also ibid., 6904, 6981, 11807, 11817.
[48] "Statement by the President Upon Signing the Revenue Act of 1951," 20 October 1951,
     Public Papers, Truman, 1951, 590.

the limit of what their Republican counterparts would tolerate, and the Democrats decided under the circumstances to accept a deficit as being preferable to a ruthless reduction in nondefense expenditures.

The vast expenditures on war and rearmament, coupled with a tax package that seemed too small to cover those expenditures, put a premium on other measures to manage an inflation that quickly became the principal threat to the administration's goals. If inflation could not be contained, rearmament would cost even more, tax revenues would buy even less, and the financial burden of defense would fall even more heavily on the backs of low- and middle-income earners. Containing inflation thus became a central goal, which the administration hoped to achieve by supplementing higher taxes with a program of production, wage, and price controls. But in this case, too, Truman ran up against the same fears of a government behemoth that had influenced the debate over taxes. And in this case, too, he confronted the same dichotomies that were evident elsewhere in our story – between fears of a garrison state and the requirements of defense, between the old political culture and the new ideology of national security.

V

The Korean War sent the consumer price index soaring. The prospect of shortages and higher prices led to panic buying, which had no sooner tapered off when China's intervention raised the possibility of a long struggle and sparked another round of scarce buying. By the end of 1950, military expenditures were being pumped into the economy at an accelerated pace and plans were being framed for a long-term rearmament program that was bound to put more pressure on scarce materials and prices. Under these circumstances the National Security Resources Board began urging the president to impose antiinflation controls and to mobilize the economy behind the rearmament program. Divisions within the administration ruled out a full-scale mobilization with aggressive wage and price controls, but Truman did ask Congress in July to authorize a partial mobilization with the emphasis at this point on measures to expand defense production, voluntary efforts to restrain prices and wages, and limited use of credit restrictions, tax increases, and government allocation of scarce materials.[49]

---

[49] Connelly, notes on cabinet meeting, 8 July 1950, Connelly Papers, box 2, folder: Notes on Cabinet Meetings 1950 (1/6-12/29); Truman, "Special Message to the Congress Reporting on the Situation in Korea," 19 July 1950, and Truman, "Radio and Television Address to the American People on the Situation in Korea," 19 July 1950. *Public Papers, Truman,*

The president's proposal led ultimately to the Defense Production Act of 1950, but not without a stormy congressional debate over many of the same issues raised in connection with the tax bill. A large group in both houses coalesced around a set of recommendations put forward by Bernard Baruch, the venerable remnant of the country's experiment with economic mobilization in World War I. Testifying before the Senate Banking Committee in late July, Baruch urged Congress to go well beyond Truman's requests to something like a full, wartime mobilization of the economy, including a special agency to coordinate defense production and a comprehensive system of wage and price controls. According to Baruch and his adherents on Capitol Hill, wide-ranging government controls were necessary to facilitate defense production while containing inflation and holding the civilian economy on an even keel.

As in the tax debate, these Cold Warriors wrapped their recommendations in the national security ideology, with its blurred distinction between war and peace, its emphasis on total war and permanent preparedness, its call for constant vigilance and personal sacrifice. The American people, according to Congressman Jacob Javits, a New York Republican, would have to live for many years with the same sacrifices and the same "discipline" they had endured in World War II. They were in a long-term struggle that required a permanent war economy, including powerful mobilizing agencies that could bend all the country's resources to the cause of national security. "Our aim," as Baruch explained, "should be to organize the nation so that every factory and farm, every man, every dollar, every bit of material can be put to use where it will strengthen our defenses." The only alternative was to risk "our way of life" to the dangers of rampant inflation and Communist aggression.[50]

Arguments like these, together with widespread public fear of price inflation, led Congress to add standby wage and price controls to the Defense Production Act. But this addition alarmed conservative critics, led by Taft, who warned again that national security initiatives were

---

1950, 527–37, 537–42; Lawton to Truman, 28 July and 10 August 1950, and Secretary of Commerce Charles Sawyer to Truman, 30 August 1950, Truman Papers, PSF-Subject File, box 144, folder: Defense Production Act; "The Wage Stabilization Program, 1950–53," Records of the Wage and the Salary Stabilization Boards of the Economic Stabilization Agency, Record Group 293 (National Archives), box 1, folder: WSB – ESA, 6/30/53 (hereafter, RG 293); Bert G. Hickman, *Growth and Stability of the Postwar Economy* (Washington, 1960), 79–81; and Paul George Pierpaoli, "The Price of Peace: The Korean War Mobilization and Cold War Rearmament, 1950–1953" (Ph.D. diss., The Ohio State University, 1995), 44.

50 *Congressional Record, 1950* 96:11519, 12151; *Congressional Quarterly Almanac, 1950* 6:624–35.

threatening traditional institutions and values. Taft conceded much to the national security ideology that dominated policy making, including the notion that Americans now faced "a new status" that was neither "all-out war" nor "a state of peace in which we can develop our civilian progress and an increased standard of living." Instead, Americans were living through "a special state of semiwar" that required higher taxes, cuts in nondefense spending, and other economic policies, but must still stop short of what Congressman Jesse P. Wolcott, a Michigan Republican, called the "socialization of America." To the conservative way of thinking, credit restrictions, pay-as-we-go taxes, and cuts in domestic expenditures could prevent inflation and cover the cost of the Korean War without giving government the kind of "arbitrary and dictatorial powers over industry" that would turn the United States from "a free economy country" into a "dictated economy country."[51]

At the heart of the conservative argument was the profound conviction that America's democratic identity would be lost if it went much beyond the demands of the Korean War, which was a limited war and did not require a permanent system of government controls. Liberal Democrats viewed the state in positive terms and were willing to give it extraordinary powers to deal with an extraordinary threat to the American way of life and to the free world generally. As they defined it, the United States had become a great power with a mission to defend democracy and the obligation to make the sacrifices that such a mission entailed. Conservatives saw things differently. As in the Great Debate, they were unwilling to support an ambitious foreign policy and the large-scale rearmament that went with it, because such a course seemed certain to transform the country from a democratic state into a garrison state. If the United States intended to "police the world," said one Republican congressman, then wartime controls would spread until there was nothing left of "our democratic freedoms." That was one problem; another was the willingness of so many on Capitol Hill to let the president decide when such controls would be imposed. To conservatives like Taft, Congress was too willing to abdicate its authority in the name of national security, and thus to destroy the constitutional balance that prevented any branch of the federal government from abusing its power.[52]

For many conservatives, the liberal choice was one between Communist domination and a permanent war economy that destroyed economic and political liberties. Some found the choice so abhorrent that they

---

[51] *Congressional Record, 1950* 96:11514, 12157. See also ibid., 11508–9, 11515–16, 11513, 11611–12, 11613.

[52] Ibid., 11611–12. See also ibid., 11613, 12198.

were ready to contemplate a preventive war against the Soviet Union.[53] Others resisted price controls to the bitter end. But given the popular alarm about rising prices and the emergency in Korea, most were reluctant to vote against a measure that went further than they thought desirable. The same was true of President Truman, who agreed at the last minute to accept provisions he had not supported earlier. So it was that the Defense Production Act of 1950 included standby controls over wages, prices, and rents. Included as well were provisions allowing the government to expand defense plants, restrict credit, allocate scarce commodities, and settle labor disputes growing out of the law. The president signed the measure on 8 September and the next day issued an executive order creating the Economic Stabilization Agency (ESA), which would supervise the work of two important mobilization authorities, the Office of Price Stabilization (OPS) and the Wage Stabilization Board.[54]

Although the Defense Production Act was a significant step toward a peacetime mobilization of the American economy, it still stopped short of the full-scale mobilization that Baruch and others had envisioned. Truman would go along with standby controls, but not mandatory controls, and he resisted pressure inside the administration to transform the National Security Resources Board (NSRB) into something like the War Production Board, which had controlled the American economy in World War II. Instead, the initial emphasis was on higher taxes and credit restrictions to control inflation and on a generally decentralized system of administration. On recommendations from the Budget Bureau, Truman authorized the NSRB to coordinate rearmament policies across the government, with the board's chairman acting as the president's top assistant in mobilization matters. But the president would retain all authority over policy decisions, and operational responsibility would remain in the hands of existing departments and agencies. The National Production Authority, for example, would remain in the Department of Commerce where it would oversee efforts to expand defense production and allocate critical materials, both through a series of industrial advisory committees that brought actors from the private sector into the planning process. This corporative system of mobilization aimed to achieve the goals of NSC-68/4 without creating a command economy dominated by military leaders and national security bureaucrats, and it

---

53 Ibid., 11511–12, 11616–17, 12198.
54 Truman to committee chairmen, 1 August 1950, and Truman, "Radio and Television Address to the American People Following the Signing of the Defense Production Act," 9 September 1950, *Public Papers, Truman, 1950*, 566–67, 626–31.

seemed especially appropriate in September 1950, when MacArthur's Inchon landing gave hope of a quick victory in Korea and a slower pace to the rearmament drive.[55]

In late November, however, when Chinese troops joined the battle in Korea, the situation began to change. Concerns about a garrison state began to recede before another round of price increases, popular demands for more effective economic controls, and the practical need to organize the American economy for a longer war and an accelerated rearmament program. By early December, almost everyone in the administration was urging the president to proclaim a national emergency, freeze wages and prices, and centralize authority over the rearmament program in a powerful government agency similar to the old War Production Board. Much the same was true of the congressional leaders who met with Truman on 13 December. They, too, favored a declaration of national emergency – the only exception being Senator Taft, who was still reluctant to approve initiatives that ran the risk of a garrison state.[56]

Similar pressure came from newspaper commentators such as Arthur Krock, who criticized Truman for ignoring the lessons of the last war, which taught the need for fast action and central direction, and who was sympathetic with Baruch's recommendations and with almost any proposal to curb inflation by reducing nondefense expenditures.[57] For their part, Joseph and Stewart Alsop complained that Truman was not doing enough to control the economy and expand the size of the armed forces, particularly after the Chinese intervention. They were convinced that Communist aggression posed a serious long-term danger and required a vast rearmament supported by a permanent program of economic mobilization. Stewart Alsop, in particular, initially adopted arguments similar to those coming from Leon Keyserling of the Council of Economic Advisors, claiming, in effect, that the American economy could grow fast enough to support both guns and butter so long as the administration

[55] Lawton to Truman, with attached memorandum, 28 July 1950, and Lawton to Truman with attached recommendations, 10 August 1950, Truman Papers, PSF-Subject File, box 144, folder: Defense Production Act; "The Wage Stabilization Program, 1950–53," RG 293, box 1, folder: WSB – ESA, 6/30/53; Pierpaoli, "Price of Peace," 51–52.

[56] "White House Statement Concerning a Meeting with Congressional Leaders to Discuss the National Emergency," 13 December 1950, *Public Papers, Truman, 1950*, 741.

[57] See Krock's articles in *New York Times*, "Another Effort to By-Pass Experience," 21 July 1950; "What Job Will Cost Now and in Future," 23 July 1950; "How Much to Control is Now the Problem," 30 July 1950; "One Independent Agency for Mobilization," 1 August 1950; "Organizing the Administration of Controls," 3 August 1950; and "The Senate Proves it Learned a Lesson," 24 August 1950.

acted quickly to raise taxes and impose controls. The United States might have to become a "garrison state," he wrote in the *Washington Post*, but with proper controls and the right economic policies it could at least become "a prosperous and comfortable garrison state."[58]

Other writers, such as Marquis Childs and James Reston, were less aggressive than Krock and the Alsops but nonetheless convinced that the Korean War amounted to another major turning point in the country's postwar history. The United States was going to have to live with permanently higher defense budgets, less spending on nondefense programs, and a permanent, if partial, mobilization of its economy. "Whether we like it or not," wrote Reston in words that captured the country's new identity as leader of the free world, "we have inherited the role played by the British" of maintaining world peace, and "this role must be organized, not on a temporary, but on a permanent basis."[59]

Given the Chinese intervention and the calls for action coming from almost every quarter, Truman proceeded on 15 December to declare a national emergency and announce plans to increase defense production, reduce nonmilitary expenditures, impose selective wage and price controls, and establish a new agency, the Office of Defense Mobilization (ODM), to provide a more centralized control over the rearmament effort. To head the ODM, Truman appointed the president of the General Electric Company, Charles E. Wilson, who reportedly received a grant of unlimited authority to meet his responsibilities.[60]

These reports notwithstanding, neither Truman nor Wilson envisioned the ODM as a great government behemoth. Neither wanted the new organization to dominate the private sector or run roughshod over the administration. Instead, both preferred an organizational strategy similar to the one that Truman had envisioned in the early debates over

[58] Stewart Alsop, "The Politics of Price Control," *Washington Post*, 25 August 1950. See also Joseph and Stewart Alsop, "We Must Mobilize," ibid., 10 July 1950; Joseph and Stewart Alsop, "The Great Debate," ibid., 12 July 1950; Stewart Alsop, "How Much Control?" ibid., 31 July 1950; Stewart Alsop, "The Politics of Price Control," ibid., 25 August 1950; Stewart Alsop, "The U.S. Economy Can 'Take It,' " ibid., 17 September 1950; Stewart Alsop, "Awful Mess to Offer a Man," ibid., 8 October 1950; Joseph and Stewart Alsop, "What Mobilization Will Mean," ibid., 10 December 1950; and Joseph and Stewart Alsop, "How Much Butter, How Many Guns?" ibid., 15 December 1950.

[59] Reston, "Now U.S. Must Anticipate Many 'Little Wars,' " *New York Times*, 23 July 1950. See also Childs, "All-Out Can Hurt Defense," *Washington Post*, 9 January 1951.

[60] Truman, "Radio and Television Report to the American People on the National Emergency," 15 December 1950, and Truman, "Proclaimation 2914: Proclaiming the Existence of a National Emergency," 16 December 1950, *Public Papers, Truman, 1950*, 741–46, 746–47; Pierpaoli, "Price of Peace," 50.

industrial mobilization, the mobilization of science, and unification of the services – one, in other words, that balanced centralizing and decentralizing impulses in a corporative pattern of collaboration that was compatible with the country's free economy and democratic institutions. Such an arrangement, both men believed, would stop short of the garrison state and protect both presidential prerogatives and established institutions.

With Truman's blessing, Wilson appointed a Defense Mobilization Board (DMB) of representatives from other government agencies to advise him on major mobilization policies. The ODM, he also decided, would not function as an operating agency or usurp responsibilities lodged in existing government departments. Instead, a new Defense Production Authority (DPA) would bring greater order to production planning as a whole while operational responsibilities would remain decentralized in the Commerce Department, the Interior Department, the Agriculture Department, and other government agencies. In addition, these agencies, as well as the DPA, would bring the private sector into the mobilization process through industry advisory committees much like those that revolved around the National Production Authority in the Department of Commerce. The ESA and the OPS would organize a similar network of advisory committees, and the Wage Stabilization Board, which included representatives from labor, industry, and the public at large quickly become the embodiment of this decentralized and collaborative strategy.[61]

If tensions between the fear of a garrison state and the demands of rearmament helped to shape the mobilization setup, they also accounted for sharp policy conflicts over the kind of controls to be established. On the one hand, ESA administrator Allan Valentine had strong objections to mandatory wage and price controls, which he did not think his agency was equipped to administer in any event. But on the other, OPS administrator Michael V. DiSalle argued from the start that price

---

[61] Nathan P. Feinsinger (Wage Stabilization Board) to Eric Johnston (ECA administrator), 4 September 1951, General Records of the Economic Stabilization Agency, Record Group 296 (National Archives), box 5 (hereafter RG 296); unsigned memorandum to Johnston and Michael V. DiSalle (OPS administrator), 11 October 1951, Records of the Office of Price Stabilization, Record Group 295 (National Archives), Records of Joseph Freehill, box 696, folder: ESA Administration, Memos to and from (hereafter RG 295); OPS press release, 16 September 1952, RG 295, Records of Joseph Freehill, box 699, folder: Consumer Advisory Committees; Jack Gorrie (chairman, National Security Resources Board) speech to the Seattle Chamber of Commerce, 16 May 1952, Truman Papers, White House Central File, Official File, folder: 1295 (1951–August 1952); Pierpaoli, "Price of Peace," 75–79.

controls were essential if the government was going to manage the defense effort without overheating the economy. The Wage Stabilization Board, or at least its labor representatives, held views similar to DiSalle's, arguing that mandatory wage and price stabilization was the only way to spare working-class families from bearing the brunt of inflation. By early 1951, the labor representatives had drafted the guidelines for a stabilization plan the board would administer, and by that time, too, the president had declared a national emergency, key officials in Congress were demanding a wage and price freeze, and the administration had decided to invoke the standby controls included in the Defense Production Act. Truman announced as much at a press conference in the first week of January, after which Valentine was replaced by Eric Johnston, president of the Motion Picture Association, who waited only two days before proclaiming a general wage and price freeze.[62]

The general freeze was supposed to contain inflation while the stabilization agencies hammered out a workable system of wage and price controls. As it happened, however, the latter task was fraught with some of the same problems that had marred the mobilization effort from the start. One problem, for example, was labor's dissatisfaction with the Wage Stabilization Board, particularly with its decision to limit negotiated pay increases to 10 percent above wage rates that prevailed at the time of the general freeze. Labor wanted a 12 percent ceiling with exemptions for fringe benefits and for long-term labor contracts that

[62] Marvin H. Bernstein, "Administrative History of the ESA under Valentine," and Herman Kaufman, "The ECA in the Johnston Period," RG 293, box 1, folder: Administrative History of the ESA; "The Wage Stabilization Program, 1950–53," ibid., folder: WSB– ESA, 6/30/53; Senator Joseph C. O'Mahoney to Symington, 6 December 1950, Records of the National Security Resources Board and the Office of Defense Mobilization, Record Group 304 (National Archives), Records of the Office of the Chairman, box 13, folder: Congressional Correspondence, M-Z; Symington to Valentine, 7 December 1950, ibid., box 14, folder: Economic Management Office; Harold L. Enarson (assistant to presidential aide Charles Murphy) to Murphy, 15 December 1950, Truman Papers, White House Central File, Confidential File, box 14, folder: Wage Stabilization Agency; Connelly, Notes on Cabinet Meeting, 22 January 1951, Connelly Papers, box 2, folder: Notes on Cabinet Meetings–1951 (2 January–31 December); Defense Mobilization Board, meeting no. 3, 25 January 1951, RG 296, Records Maintained by the Administrators, Classified General Files, box 2, folder: Defense Mobilization Board Meetings. See also B. C. Roberts, "Wage Stabilization in the United States," *Oxford Economic Papers* 4 (1952): 149–62; Harold Levanthal, "The Organization for Defense Mobilization: Price Controls under the Defense Production Act, as Amended," *Federal Bar Journal* 13 (December 1951): 99–116; and David Ginsburg, "Price Stabilization, 1950–1952: Retrospect and Prospect," *University of Pennsylvania Law Review* 100 (January 1952): 514–43.

allowed wages to keep pace with inflation. On a more general level, labor was also upset when Wilson appointed a number of antilabor officials to top positions in the ODM, when that agency, rather than the Labor Department, took responsibility for manpower policy, and when the Wage Board was reluctant to administer the wage policies it formulated or to settle labor disputes that arose from those policies. Angered by these and other developments, labor first withdrew its representatives from the Wage Stabilization Board on 15 February, and then from all of the mobilization agencies established since the start of the Korean War.[63]

Labor's walkout posed a serious threat to the administration's mobilization plan, which relied on collaboration between key groups rather than coercive government controls to achieve rearmament without work stoppages and inflation. Not surprisingly, the administration reacted in March 1951 by announcing the formation of a National Advisory Board on Mobilization Policy. The new board consisted of representatives from business, labor, and agriculture, and was purposely intended to give labor the kind of high profile involvement in the mobilization effort that trade unions had been demanding. With the board's blessing, the Wage Stabilization Board was then empowered to administer as well as formulate wage policies, much as labor had demanded, and to adjudicate labor disputes that arose under the mobilization effort. These concessions did not involve the 10 percent ceiling on wage increases, but they went far enough to satisfy organized labor, whose representatives rejoined the Wage Stabilization Board in the second half of April.[64]

What pleased labor, however, often had the opposite effect on business. Efforts to curb price increases and to correct various inequities caused by the general freeze led to numerous complaints from business and farm groups. In addition, small business complained that defense contracts favored larger firms, and business as a whole resented the administration's decision to permit the Wage Stabilization Board to adjudicate labor disputes. To be sure, business representatives continued to serve on the board, but it was clear that organizations like the Chamber of Commerce and the National Association of Manufacturers were ready to join

[63] "The Wage Stabilization Program, 1950–53," RG 293, box 1, folder: WSB – ESA, 6/30/53; Roberts, "Wage Stabilization in the United States," 149–67; Donovan, *Tumultuous Years*, 326–27.

[64] Kaufman, "The Economic Stabilization Agency in the Johnson Period," RG 293, box 1, folder: Administrative History of the ESA; Roberts, "Wage Stabilization in the United States," 149–67.

Republicans in an effort to emasculate the Defense Production Act when it came up for renewal in 1951.[65]

VI

In his budget message and state of the union address in 1951, Truman had outlined an ambitious rearmament program, in part to support the military effort in Korea, but mostly to achieve the long-term rearmament goals outlined in NSC-68/4. The program envisioned the production of thirty-five thousand tanks per year, fifty thousand military aircraft, and thousands of jet engines. Reaching these and other goals required aggressive efforts to expand the production of military hardware and essential raw materials. Steel production, for example, had to increase from 100,000,000 ingot tons per year in 1950 to 120,000,000 tons by 1954. Aluminum production had to be doubled, as did electric power capacity, while the production of titanium had to increase by 800 percent.[66] The job of achieving these and other production targets fell to Charles E. Wilson and his ODM colleagues, who encountered one obstacle after another, not the least of which was the opposition to economic controls in Congress and the business community.

In a message of 26 April 1951, Truman asked Congress to extend the Defense Production Act for two years and strengthen its provisions. The government had placed orders for more than $26 billion in military hardware since the start of the Korean War and would order another $58 billion before the end of the fiscal year. Defense production was taking about $2 billion per month from the civilian economy and that amount was expected to double when the rearmament program peaked in 1952. As rearmament peaked, however, so would inflation, unless the government had additional authority to expand production facilities, regulate credit, and control wages, prices, and rents. Hence, Truman wanted greater authority to establish rent controls, regulate bank loans, curb commodity speculation, control credit on the sale of existing housing, and make the price ceilings on agricultural commodities more effective. In addition, he would give the OPS more power to enforce its regulations

[65] Hugh Rockoff, *Drastic Measures: A History of Wage and Price Controls in the United States* (New York, 1984), 180; Levanthal, "Organization for Defense Mobilization," 99–116; Pierpaoli, "Price of Peace," 141–47, 156–58.

[66] Truman, "Annual Message to the Congress on the State of the Union," 8 January 1951, and Truman, "Annual Budget Message to the Congress: Fiscal Year 1952," *Public Papers, Truman, 1951*, 6–13, 61–106; Roderick L. Vawter, *Industrial Mobilization: The Relevant History*, rev. ed. (Washington, 1983), 22, 25–26.

and the ODM additional authority to expand production, including the right to acquire and operate industrial plants.[67]

The president's proposal brought a rush of lobbyists to Capitol Hill, most of whom worked with Republicans to weaken, rather than strengthen, the Defense Production Act. Builders, realtors, and mortgage institutions came out against rent controls and credit restrictions on the sale of existing homes. The meat industry, which was fighting an effort by the OPS to roll back prices, said the best way to control inflation was to increase production. The leading farm organizations, including the American Farm Bureau Federation, opposed price controls on agricultural commodities and wanted to contain inflation instead by cutting "non-essential" government expenditures, raising taxes, and putting more restrictions on consumer credit. Business organizations also wanted to cut nondefense expenditures and abandon price controls in favor of higher taxes and restrictions on credit. According to the Chamber of Commerce, wages need not keep pace with prices, and additional government revenue should come from excise and income taxes rather than corporate taxes.

Support for economic controls came mostly from educational and religious leaders, the Americans for Democratic Action, consumer groups, and trade unions. As in 1950, in other words, the two sides divided largely along economic and ideological lines, with the central issue being the country's postwar political identity and the familiar rhetorical tactic being an effort by each side to associate its opponent with the un-American other. Critics of the Defense Production Act warned again of a garrison state that exercised unparalleled powers and endangered American liberties. Truman's proposal, said William H. Ruffin, who headed the National Association of Manufacturers, would give the president "powers comparable to those exercised by foreign dictators" and would "lead to the destruction of our American economic system." Those representing trade unions and consumer groups stressed the government's responsibility to guarantee "equity of sacrifice." To their way of thinking, workers, consumers, and lower-income groups were shouldering more than their share of the common defense. Rents were too high, corporate taxes were too low, excise taxes were regressive, and prices were going up faster than wages.[68]

---

[67] Truman, "Special Message to the Congress Recommending Extension and Broadening of the Defense Production Act," 26 April 1951, *Public Papers, Truman 1951*, 244–53. See also National Advisory Board on Mobilization Policy, meeting no. 4, 15 May 51, Truman Papers, PSF-Subject File, box 142, folder: Advisory Board on Mobilization Policy, National.

[68] *Congressional Quarterly Almanac, 1951* 7:438–61.

In the floor debates, arguments about equity and fears of the garrison state mixed with strong appeals to the national security. While conservatives denounced economic controls as politically dangerous and un-American, those favoring Truman's proposals claimed that strong controls were needed to stabilize the economy and prevent inflation from crippling the rearmament program. Seen in this light, economic controls became a national security imperative: They would aid rearmament and protect the economic basis of American power. What is more, if government did not have the authority to adjust prices, inequities and distortions in the price structure would penalize some producers while enriching others. The issue in this case was how to apportion the burden of national security fairly, which was the same issue that arose when critics threatened to abandon price controls altogether. According to those who defended controls, such a course would lead to inflation, put more of the burden of national security on the backs of workers and consumers, and erode the economic basis of democracy as well as popular support for the rearmament program.[69]

Although conservatives attacked the president for not imposing controls at the start of the military buildup, when they might have stopped the first round of inflation, they nonetheless rejected efforts to strengthen a system that would change the country "from a free state to a totalitarian state." They argued that controls were unnecessary at a time when shortages and inflationary pressures were easing and when negotiations in Korea gave hope of ending the national emergency. They also claimed that price controls discouraged production and could not deal with inflation in any event. That required cuts in nondefense spending, controls on consumer credit, and a tax plan that absorbed excessive consumer purchasing power through appropriate income and excise taxes. "Since national income is concentrated in the low-income groups," explained one conservative senator, "a tax bill designed to halt inflation should hit [the] broad sources of consumer purchasing power."[70]

When the debate finally ended, the conservatives had scored a major victory. Congress, to be sure, renewed the Defense Production Act, but only for a year and only on terms that denied government much of the authority it needed to control inflation. The revised act restricted price ceilings and limited the government's power to roll back prices. It did not permit the administration to construct and operate defense plants, mostly

---

[69] *Congressional Record, 1951* 97:7108–11, 7219, 7224.
[70] Ibid., 9152, 7201. See also ibid., 7039, 7127, 7200, 7202, 9156.

because conservatives feared government nationalization of the economy. Nor did it extend credit controls to old housing, as the White House had requested, impose rent controls on commercial property, authorize the administration to regulate commodity speculation, or give the OPS new power to enforce its policies. Truman signed the bill on 31 July, but only grudgingly and only after blasting the Republicans for making it more difficult to control inflation. As a result, he said, the cost of living would go up, workers would seek higher pay, and a price–wage spiral would weaken the economy and impede rearmament.[71]

Running through the president's remarks, and those of his allies in Congress, was the familiar theme that national security required vigorous government action to regulate the economy and distribute the burden of rearmament fairly. That argument was sufficiently compelling that Congress extended the Defense Production Act for another year, but it was not persuasive enough to defend vigorous government controls over wages, prices, and rents. On this issue the administration was stymied by a conservative conviction that economic controls were neither necessary nor productive, and that aggressive controls would replace economic liberties with economic coercion. On this issue, in other words, elements of an older ideology of antistatism had put a brake on the development of national security policies and institutions.

That brake continued to operate over the last eighteen months of the Truman administration, as was evident, for example, in the president's famous battle with the steel industry. This part of our story began in late 1951, when the steel industry and the United Steel Workers of

---

[71] *Congressional Quarterly Almanac, 1951* 7:438–467; National Advisory Board on Mobilization Policy, meetings no. 5 and 7, 5 June and 10 July 1951, Truman Papers, White House Central File, Confidential File, box 26, folder: National Advisory Board on Mobilization Policy 1951–1952; National Advisory Board on Mobilization Policy, meeting no. 6, 19 June 1951, with attached "Statement to the President from the National Advisory Board on Mobilization Policy," submitted to the president on 22 June 1951. Truman Papers, PSF-Subject Files, box 142, folder: Advisory Board on Mobilization Policy, National; Steelman to Ted Repplier (president, The Advertising Council, Inc.), 19 June 1951, Paul B. West (president, the Association of National Advertisers) to Steelman, 21 June 1951, Truman Papers, White House Central File, Official File, box 1731, folder: 2855, Feb. 1951–53; Murphy to Truman, 5 July 1951, Truman Papers, PSF-Subject File, box 96, folder: Presidential Appointments File, Daily Sheets, 1951–July; Connelly, notes on cabinet meeting, 6 July 1951, Connelly Papers, box 2, folder: Notes on Cabinet Meetings, 1951, 2 Jan.–31 Dec.; DiSalle to Lawton, 30 July 1951, and ESA memorandum, Defense Production Act Amendments of 1951, 30 July 1951, Truman Papers, White House Central File, Official File, box 460, folder: OF 101-B, Defense Production Act (1951); and "Statement by the President upon Signing the Defense Production Act Amendments," 31 July 1951, *Public Papers, Truman, 1951*, 435–37.

America were unable to agree on the terms of a new contract. Convinced that a steel strike would disrupt the rearmament program and imperil the war effort, Truman asked the Wage Stabilization Board to arbitrate the dispute. In March 1952, after three months of study, a majority of the board recommended higher pay and a union shop for steel workers. The recommendations pleased the union, but not the steel industry, which refused to go along without a substantial increase in the price of steel. The industry had support from ODM director Wilson and the business representatives on the Wage Stabilization Board, but not from Truman, who thought the industry was asking for more than it deserved in view of its record-setting profits and the likelihood that higher steel prices would trigger another round of inflation.[72]

The disagreement drove Wilson from the administration and the prospect of a strike led Truman to seize the steel mills in the name of national security. Truman's decision, which he announced on 9 April 1952, provoked a blizzard of criticism in Congress and the business community. Allies praised his action in "defense of the nation" but critics, who threatened to impeach him, accused the president of "dictatorship" and of raising "the gravest constitutional question since the war between the states." In a ruling of 2 June, the Supreme Court agreed with the critics and declared the steel seizure to be unconstitutional. Thereafter, the government relinquished its control of the mills and a steel strike followed, with no settlement until late July, by which time the controversy had fed widespread concerns that national security was leading to a reckless expansion of executive power, undermining the Constitution, and destroying economic liberties.[73]

These concerns, in turn, contributed to a further weakening of the Defense Production Act. Truman asked Congress to renew the act in February 1952, and congressional deliberations occurred just as the government was seizing the mills. Not surprisingly, Republicans were even more reluctant than usual to extend the government's control over wages and prices, let alone strengthen that control, as the president had

[72] "The Wage Stabilization Program, 1950–53," RG 293, box 2, folder: WSB – ESA, 6/30/53; Donovan, *Tumultuous Years*, 383–84; Maeva Marcus, *Truman and the Steel Seizure Case: The Limits of Presidential Power* (New York, 1977), 54–80.

[73] *Congressional Quarterly Almanac, 1952* 8:320–25; Truman, "Radio and Television Address to the American People on the Need for Government Operation of the Steel Mills," 8 April 1952, and Truman, "Special Message to the Congress Reporting on the Situation in the Steel Industry," 9 April 1952, *Public Papers, Truman, 1952–53* (Washington 1966), 246–50, 250–51; Marcus, *Truman and the Steel Seizure Case*, 80–227; Donovan, *Tumultuous Years*, 384–91; McCullough, *Truman*, 896–903.

requested. Truman argued again that national security required a control program that facilitated rearmament without causing inflation and penalizing those who could least afford it. But it was a hard case to sell, especially at a time when shortages appeared to be easing and inflation seemed under control. Even some members of the National Advisory Board doubted the need for rigorous controls, while the OPS was already lifting the ceilings on certain commodities. Added to these obstacles was overwhelming opposition from business groups and congressional conservatives, who pointed to the steel crisis as proof that government controls were ineffective and a threat to the American way of life.

In the end, Congress renewed the Defense Production Act for another year, in part because of last-minute signs that the economy was again heating up. But at the same time, it exempted a long list of commodities from price control and slashed the ESA's budget, which made it difficult for that agency to enforce the controls that remained. In addition, Congress more or less fired the Wage Stabilization Board for its part in the steel strike. It created another board in its place and denied the new board any authority to settle wage disputes. The ESA predicted renewed inflation, as did Truman when he signed the bill into law. But the administration had little support for a control policy that conservatives considered "un-American," and even the controls that remained kept eroding. The Wage Stabilization Board suspended operations when business representatives refused to participate, the ODM began laying plans to decontrol the economy, and a number of mobilization officials started talking about an approach that relied on indirect controls to curb inflation, at least until another emergency.[74]

---

74 Office of Defense Mobilization, Executive Staff meeting no. 17, 17 September 1952, RG 296, Records Maintained by the Administrators, Classified General Files, box 3, folder: Mobilization Executive Staff Meetings. See also Truman, "Special Message to the Congress Urging Extension and Strengthening of the Defense Production Act," 11 February 1952, and "Statement by the President on the Defense Production Act Amendments," 1 July 1952, *Public Papers, 1952–53*, 145–50, 453–54; ESA Weekly Roundup, 4 March, 3 June, and 1 July 1952, RG 296, Records and Reports of the Secretariat, box 3, folder: ESA Weekly Roundup; OPS administrator Ellis Arnall to ESA administrator Roger L. Putnam, 8 July 1952, RG 295, Records of Joseph Freehill, box 696, folder: ECA Administrator, Memos to and from, Dec. 1951 to January 1952; National Advisory Board on Mobilization Policy, meeting no. 19, 22–23 September 1952, Truman Papers, White House Central File, Confidential File, box 26, folder: National Advisory Board on Mobilization Planning, 1951–52; ESA Executive Staff Meeting, 24 September 1952, RG 296, Secretariat – Classified Files, box 11, folder: Executive Staff Meetings; Disalle report to ESA administrator Roger Putnam, 9 December 1952, and Putnam to Truman, 13 December 1952, Truman Papers, PSF-Subject File, box 144, folder: Economic Stabilization Agency; National Advisory Board on Mobilization Policy, Meeting No. 22, 16 December 1952, Truman Papers, PSF-Subject Files,

VII

The reluctance to support a vigorous control program, the opposition to a pay-as-we-go tax policy, and concerns about the scope and cost of the country's international commitments all combined to influence the shape of the rearmament program. By the late spring of 1951 it was already becoming clear that Congress would pass a tax bill and a control program that fell short of what the administration thought necessary. Making matters worse was a shortage of machine tools and of critical raw materials, which not only hampered the rearmament effort but also drove up the costs of civilian production. Together with higher interest rates, credit restrictions, and the concentration of defense contracts in particular industries, they had led by late summer to serious economic dislocations and rising unemployment in certain areas of the country.[75] Nor were these problems confined to the United States. American leaders had pressed their NATO allies to rearm as well, and their efforts to do so added to the shortage of critical raw materials, unleashed inflation, and threatened to derail the recovery that had begun with the Marshall Plan. Still worse, shortages, higher prices, and other hardships gave powerful issues to Communist trade unions and political parties in Europe, encouraged strikes in the United States, and ran the risk of eroding public support for the rearmament effort across the Atlantic community as a whole.[76]

In the fall of 1951, Eric Johnston, Dwight Eisenhower, and other officials began urging the administration to scale back the rearmament

---

box 131, folder: General File, National Advisory Board, Mobilization; and *Congressional Quarterly Almanac, 1952* (Washington, 1952), 8:304–16.

[75] National Advisory Board on Mobilization Policy, meetings no. 8 and 11, 24 July and 17–18 September 1951, Truman Papers, White House Central File, Confidential File, box 26, folder: National Advisory Board on Mobilization Policy, 1951–52; unsigned memorandum, "Appraisal of the Impact that Could Result from Changes in the Military Program," 12 September 1951, RG 296, Classified General File, box 2, folder: Defense Mobilization Board Meetings; Connelly, notes on cabinet meeting, 21 September 1951, Connelly Papers, box 2, folder: Notes on Cabinet Meetings, 1951, 2 January–3 December; National Advisory Board, meeting no. 12, 15–16 October 1951, Truman Papers, PSF-Subject File, box 142, folder: Advisory Board on Mobilization Policy, National; and Carl Stellato (president, UAW-CIO Local 600) to Truman, 16 October 1951, Truman Papers, OF, box 181, folder: 264 (1951). See also Pierpaoli, "Price of Peace," 151–58; and Vawter, *Industrial Mobilization*, 22–23.

[76] National Advisory Board on Mobilization Policy, meeting no. 12, 15–16 October 1951, Truman Papers, PSF-Subject File, box 142, folder: Advisory Board on Mobilization Policy, National; Johnston memorandum, "The Inflationary Outlook in Western Europe," enclosed in Johnson to Truman, 23 October 1951, Truman Papers, White House Central File, Confidential File, box 17, folder: Econ. Stab. Agency (1951). See also the records of Johnston's interviews with various European leaders in October 1951, RG 296, Records and Reports of the Secretariat, box 2, folder: Johnston's European Trip.

program in order to ease the economic pressure on Europe. Other voices said that a slowdown would be needed to contain inflation in the United States because Congress had refused to go along with higher taxes and more aggressive economic controls. These and other recommendations, when coupled with a wave of labor strikes that disrupted defense production, fed a debate in the administration and in Congress over the pace of the rearmament effort. One result was a slackening of the restrictions on consumer credit, which must have seemed necessary to assist particular industries and sustain public support for the rearmament program. The other was a decision by the administration to stretch out the rearmament goals originally targeted for 1952.[77]

In one sense the latter decision simply confirmed what had already happened. As early as July 1951 it had become apparent that military production had fallen behind schedule and that delivery dates would have to be extended. This development greatly disturbed military officials and their civilian allies. Stuart Symington, for example, thought that the United States was losing the Cold War and that "defensive containment" had to give way to more ambitious policies. The administration, he said, should consider withdrawing American troops from Korea as prelude to a massive air and naval campaign against North Korea and China. It should even consider a preemptive strike against the Soviets before they achieved atomic parity and before the American economy was exhausted through a series of local conflicts, like the one in Korea. Symington wanted the Joint Chiefs to draft a new strategic plan based on this kind of thinking. He also urged something close to a wartime mobilization of the American economy to achieve as quickly as possible the forces in being and the war reserves that such a plan required.[78]

Other national security managers disagreed with much of what Symington had to say, but not with his support for a more aggressive rearmament. They, too, wanted to curtail civilian production to accelerate rearmament in the United States and the NATO countries. Even though the Joint Chiefs found it difficult to agree on how to divide their resources, they had no trouble agreeing that global conditions were growing steadily worse, that Soviet military power continued to expand, and that additional funds would be needed to speed a rearmament program that lagged behind the mid-1952 targets set in NSC-68/4. They suggested

---

[77] In addition to the sources cited in the previous note see Hogan, *Marshall Plan*, 336–38, 381, 393–96, 409–10, 423–25; and Pierpaoli, "Price of Peace," 151–58, 197–200, 201–4.

[78] "Report to the National Security Council by the Chairman of the National Security Resources Board," 11 January 1951, and Symington undated memorandum to Truman, *FRUS, 1951* 1:7–18, 21–33.

a fiscal year 1953 defense budget of $64.2 billion, which would be an increase of more than $7 billion, not counting military public works and other incidentals. That sum would enable the armed forces as a whole to accumulate a substantial stock of war reserves and would permit the Army to grow to 21 divisions, the Navy to 1,191 ships, and the Air Force to 126 combat wings and 17 troop carriers.

As in the past, the Joint Chiefs had support from Dean Acheson, Paul Nitze, and other hawks in the State Department, who had written much of what the chiefs had to say into NSC-114/1 and NSC-114/2. Support also came from the CIA, which shared the Pentagon's assessment of the Soviet Union's intentions and capabilities, and from Leon Keyserling of the Council of Economic Advisers. Along with the NSC, Keyserling was still convinced of the Keynesian notion that economic expansion would permit the country to handle a "substantial security program" without harmful, long-term effects on the domestic economy and New Deal social programs. The issues were political rather than economic, said Keyserling, and they had to do with whether the burdens of rearmament were distributed fairly and whether the American people were willing to live temporarily with the higher taxes, the economic controls, and the limits on consumer goods that rearmament required.[79]

Opposition came from the Office of the Secretary of Defense and from a variety of economic planners and mobilization officials. Robert Lovett thought that a slower-paced rearmament would prevent the accumulation of obsolete weapons, allow the armed forces to take advantage of new technologies, and avoid the economic dislocations and political problems associated with a production program that expanded rapidly to meet immediate rearmament goals and then contracted once those goals had been achieved.[80] Economic mobilizers had related concerns. Unlike Keyserling, Wilson and his ODM colleagues did not think the economy could stand the pressure of a $64 billion defense budget. Labor resources were stretched to the limit and mobilizers could not always invest in the most efficient producers, particularly large firms, for fear of alienating small business and its friends on Capitol Hill. Making matters worse were serious bottlenecks, such as the shortages of critical raw materials,

---

[79] Keyserling statement, 16 October 1951, *FRUS, 1951* 1:230–32. See also the documents by the NSC and Joint Chiefs cited in note 5 at the start of this chapter; the Joint Chiefs to Marshall, 27 July 1951, the CIA's National Intelligence Estimate of 2 August 1951 and its Special Estimate of 24 September 1951, and Nitze to Acheson, 17 October 1951, in ibid., 104–6, 120–27, 193–207, 232–34; and Condit, *Test of War*, 261–70.

[80] Nitze to Acheson, 31 July 1951, *FRUS, 1951* 1:110–12; Condit, *Test of War*, 270.

railroad cars, and machine tools, that made it difficult to accelerate military production. Under these circumstances, achieving the goals favored by the Joint Chiefs would necessarily entail deeper cuts in nondefense spending and civilian consumption than Keyserling contemplated. It would also impose severe hardships on small business enterprises, as defense contracts were shifted to larger, more efficient firms, and on nondefense producers, as military contractors got first claim on machine tools and scarce materials. Eric Johnston thought the Joint Chiefs were absolutely indifferent to the needs of the civilian economy, and there was similar sentiment on the National Advisory Board for Economic Mobilization.[81]

At meetings of the board in August and September, some members wondered if the administration was putting too much emphasis on military strategies of containment while slighting the economic and technical assistance programs that could raise living standards and demonstrate the material advantages of American life. Some were also convinced that a sustained period of large-scale preparedness would weaken and fundamentally alter the American economy, give "military authorities" too much control over "the economic destiny of this country," and thus reverse one of the basic tenets of American democracy – "the ultimate sovereignty of civilian authority over military authority." "Nowadays," explained two members of the board, "the military's take out of the civilian economy is an all important factor in what happens to that economy." With rearmament siphoning billions of dollars from civilian production, decisions about the size and shape of the armed forces came close to being "life and death decisions" about the economy as a whole.[82]

[81] Memorandum for the president summarizing the 93d NSC meeting, 7 June 1951, Truman Papers, PSF-National Security Council Meetings, box 220, folder: NSC Meetings – Memos for President and Meeting Discussions; Canaille, notes on cabinet meeting, 21 September 1951, Connelly Papers, box 2, folder: Notes on Cabinet Meetings, 1951, 2 January–31 December; Enarson to J. R. S. [Steelman], 28 September 1951, Truman Papers, White House Central File, Confidential File, box 26, folder: National Advisory Board on Mobilization Policy, 1951–52; National Advisory Board on Mobilization Policy, meeting no. 12, 15–16 October, 1951, Truman Papers, PSF-Subject File, box 142, folder: Advisory Board on Mobilization Policy, National; Pierpaoli, "Price of Peace," 151–58, 197–200. See also Enarson to J. R. S. [Steelman], 18 September 1951, David H. Stowe Papers (Truman Library), box 3, folder: Formation of National Advisory Board on Mobilization Policy.

[82] National Advisory Board on Mobilization Policy, meeting no. 11, 17–18 September 1951, Truman Papers, White House Central File, Confidential File, box 26, folder: National Advisory Board on Mobilization Policy, 1951–52; Richard E. Neustadt (White House special assistant) to Charles Murphy, 25 August 1951, Truman Papers, White House Central File, Official File, box 1737, folder: 2855-A.

These arguments amounted to a reiteration of what Nourse and the Budget Bureau had said before. They had warned repeatedly that rearmament meant a lower standard of living and less spending on schools, roadways, scientific research, and other infrastructure investments that were essential to the productive life of the nation over the long term. Keyserling, on the other hand, continued to expound an expansionist ideology that would supposedly make it possible to have guns and butter both. To be sure, some short-term sacrifices would be necessary in the name of national security. But through economic growth and an active partnership between government and the private sector, he was convinced that government could meet its obligations at home while also assuming its responsibilities as leader of the free world.[83]

Differences over the rearmament program came to a head at a NSC meeting on 17 October. Acheson said again that a strong foreign policy required a larger defense budget, and Keyserling was still convinced that the economy could handle whatever the military required. Others disagreed. Wilson said that a larger budget would put the country on something like "a full war footing," involve substantial dislocations, and require more aggressive economic controls. Treasury Secretary Snyder declared that more money for defense meant higher taxes, which Congress would not accept, or a burgeoning deficit, which he found unacceptable. The Budget Bureau came to the same conclusion in a statement that also warned against further cuts in nondefense spending, which accounted for only one-fourth of the federal budget in any event. The outcome was a decision that came close to what the economizers had in mind. The council, with Truman present, approved a figure of $45 billion as the basis for further planning in the Defense Department, a sum considerably less than the $64.2 billion suggested by the Joint Chiefs of Staff.[84]

---

[83] Keyserling's thinking is elaborated elsewhere in this chapter, but see also Jerry N. Hess, "Oral History Interview with Leon H. Keyserling," Truman Library, Oral History Interview Collection; *The Economic Report of the President*, 16 January 1952, transmitted to Congress with the Council of Economic Advisers, *Annual Economic Review*, Leon H. Keyserling Papers (Truman Library), box 5, folder: Economic Reports of the President; and Norton, *Council of Economic Advisers*, 1–17.

[84] Memorandum for the president summarizing discussion at the 105th NSC meeting, 18 October 1951, Truman Papers, PSF-National Security Council Meetings, box 220, folder: NSC Meetings – Memos for President and Meeting Discussions. See also Ecker-Racz memorandum, "Budgetary Implications of Major National Security Programs," 16 October 1951, L. Laszlo Ecker-Racz Papers (Truman Library), box 6, folder: 1952–1; "Record of Action by the National Security Council at Its 105th Meeting," 17 October 1951, "Memorandum for the National Security Council by the Executive Secretary," 18 October 1951, and Lucius D. Battle memorandum of conversation, 18 October 1951, *FRUS, 1951* 1:235–37, 237–38, 238–40; executive secretary, NSC, to Truman, 18 October 1951, Truman Papers,

The debate continued as the planning process dragged on into the new year. The Joint Chiefs still lobbied for a budget that exceeded the limit approved by the NSC, while Wilson and others still insisted that resources were spread too thin to accommodate military demands and that doing so would force substantial reductions in industrial expansion, residential construction, and the production of civilian durable goods – all with negative effects on employment in cities that were already hard hit by the rearmament campaign. In the end, Wilson and his allies prevailed, in part because of strong backing from the president. Although the Joint Chiefs won support for the new force levels they had proposed, they had to accept stretched out production schedules, delayed delivery dates, and cutbacks in the accumulation of war reserves. The extension enabled Lovett, the Budget Bureau, and the Joint Chiefs to finally agree on a defense budget for fiscal year 1953 of $48.6 billion, not including about $3.5 billion for such items as military pay raises and public works. Truman gave his consent to the agreed figure, which amounted to a reduction of more than $8 billion from the final budget for fiscal year 1952, and presented the proposed budget to Congress early in the new year.[85]

The NSC meeting of 17 October had ended with general agreement that Congress and the American people were reluctant to make the sacrifices that a more aggressive rearmament would entail. They would not accept still higher taxes, still larger deficits, or still further cuts in civilian consumption. Civilian consumption might be at a "plush level," as Keyserling said, but no one dissented when Commerce Secretary Sawyer concluded that "the country at large" did not share the "sense of urgency" so evident in the State Department and the Pentagon.[86] On the contrary, by the time Congress took up the defense budget for fiscal year

PSF-National Security Council Meetings, box 215, folder: NSC Meeting 105, 10-17-51; Keyserling to Truman, 2 November 1951, *FRUS, 1951* 1:245–54; and Condit, *Test of War,* 272–73.

[85] Defense Mobilization Board meeting no. 19, 14 November 1951, RG 296, Records Maintained by the Administrators, Classified General Files, box 2, folder: Defense Mobilization Board Meetings; Wilson to Truman, 21 December 1951, Truman Papers, PSF-Subject Files, box 147, folder: Office of Defense Mobilization – Misc.; Bradley to Lovett, 4 January 1952, Lovett to Truman, 4 January 1952, McNeil to Lovett, 8 January 1952, and Lovett to the secretary of the army, assistant secretary of defense, and chairman, Munitions Board, 10 January 1952, RG 330, CD 111 (1953); Enarson to Steelman, 24 January 1952, Truman Papers, White House Central File, Official File, box 1737, folder: 2855-A; Wilson to Baruch, 15 February 1952, Truman Papers, Records of the National Security Council, box 16, folder: Mobilization Program, July 1951–June 1952; and Condit, *Test of War,* 273–80.

[86] Memorandum for the president summarizing discussion at the 105th NSC meeting, 18 October 1951, Truman Papers, PSF-National Security Council Meetings, box 220, folder: NSC Meetings – Memos for President and Meeting Discussions.

1953 the pressure to stretch out the rearmament effort had grown even greater. Both political parties wanted a lean budget to their credit in an election year, particularly the Republican party, where conservatives were also disillusioned with the protracted war in Korea and with the American military buildup in Europe and elsewhere. They had reservations about the wisdom of Truman's foreign policy and military strategy, as the Great Debate had made clear, and they were clearly reluctant to support the economic controls and higher taxes that a more aggressive rearmament might require. To their way of thinking, higher taxes and budget deficits debased the currency and fed a "socialistic monstrosity" that would destroy economic liberties. To avoid such a calamity, they and their conservative allies in the Democratic party saw budget reductions and a reshaping of military policy as necessary complements to their actions on economic controls and Truman's tax proposals.[87]

The House of Representatives reduced the president's defense budget from $48.6 billion to $43.9 billion. The Senate approved a figure of $44.1 billion, and the two houses then agreed on a final sum of $44.3 billion. In addition, Truman wound up with only $2.3 billion for military public works and related items. Such a large reduction in the defense budget, coming on top of the reduction negotiated within the administration, required an even greater extension of the rearmament program than had been anticipated. What is more, Congress substituted even more "machinery for men in fighting," to borrow Lovett's phrase, by taking the largest part of its reductions from the Army's budget. In all, Congress had cut Truman's defense budget by a stunning 10 percent, and had earmarked approximately 44 percent of what remained for the Air Force.[88]

Some conservatives had wanted even stricter limitations on the Pentagon's budget, so it would "no longer rule the nation," but had been held in check by the administration and by criticism from commentators like Joseph and Stewart Alsop, Arthur Krock, Hanson Baldwin, and Marquis Childs, all of whom warned repeatedly that a congressional meat axe would endanger national security.[89] Still, if the conservatives

---

[87] *Congressional Quarterly Almanac, 1952* 8:312.

[88] Condit, *Test of War*, 280–84. Lovett is quoted in ibid., 282. See also *Congressional Quarterly Almanac, 1952* 8:97–101.

[89] The quote is from Congressman Frederic R. Coudert as cited in Condit, *Test of War*, 281. See also, Joseph and Stewart Alsop, "Johnson's Ghost," *Washington Post*, 4 January 1952; Baldwin, "Military Budget Spread," *New York Times*, 22 January 1952; Krock, "Only Stalin Could Cut the Budget Much," ibid., 22 January 1952; Childs, "Can We Afford to Reduce Outlay?" *Washington Post*, 9 February 1952; Childs, "Threat to Defense," ibid., 1 May 1952; Childs, "Discord on Arms Budget," ibid., 16 May 1952; Joseph and Stewart

had not prevailed, their concerns had at least shaped the outcome, especially the concern that perceived national security needs were turning the country into a garrison state dominated by the Pentagon and by New Deal social programs that cost more than the country could afford.

VIII

Taft called it semiwar, by which he meant not the Korean War alone or even the possibility it posed of similar conflicts in the future. Speaking at a time when constant crises in Germany, Greece, Turkey, Iran, and elsewhere had the potential to produce total war, he used the term to denote a period of prolonged struggle and constant preparedness in which the usual distinction between war and peace had disappeared. In an age of semiwar, the United States needed substantial forces in being, a large reserve of war stocks, and a mobilization base on which it could build to meet any emergency. All these needs and more, including selective service and measures of internal security, became part of a national security agenda that pointed the American state in a new direction. An older sense of the country's political identity now gave ground to a new global role and national purpose. Elements of wartime policy began to characterize the peace; measures acceptable in periods of crisis became permanent fixtures of American life; the old political culture made room for the new ideology of national security. In such an era, the isolationism of the past had to bow before a new internationalism, and old virtues, such as a balanced budget, had to take account of national security needs. In addition, the principle of civilian rule had to concede a larger role for the military in peacetime policy making; the constitutional balance had to permit a greater degree of presidential discretion; the private economy had to adapt to more government spending and the vast production of military hardware; and the tradition of antistatism had to accommodate the rise of national security institutions, the need for higher taxes, and the resort to economic controls.

These adjustments were not easy, and were never perfectly made. Taft, Hoover, and others who spoke for the older ideology of antistatism and isolationism, for low taxes and balanced budgets, resisted almost every step to the national security state. The turning point came with the

Alsop, "New Lizzie Bordens," ibid., 26 May 1952; Baldwin, "Help Wanted – Congress," *New York Times*, 26 May 1952; Krock, "Some Impulses Behind the Appropriations Axe," ibid., 27 May 1952; and Childs, "An Umbrella Against War," *Washington Post*, 29 May 1952.

Great Debate of 1950–51, in which conservative critics failed to replace the globalism of NSC-68, on which the administration operated, with the more limited strategy envisioned by Hoover and Taft. Once the conservatives had lost on this issue, their gains elsewhere were bound to be minimal. They defeated universal military training, but gave in on selective service. They attacked the president's decision to send troops to Europe, but were unable to reverse that decision. They whittled away at the defense budget and foreign aid programs, but there was no thought of returning to pre-Korean levels of spending. They opposed economic controls and higher taxes, but defense production continued and taxes went up. By the end of 1952 the economy was delivering more than $8 billion in military goods and services each quarter, including one thousand warplanes per month, thanks largely to generous government investment in plant expansion and equipment.[90]

Still, the dissenters had made a difference. Their concerns about the high cost of defense and the stationing of troops abroad encouraged the administration to move even farther toward a capital-intensive strategy of containment that emphasized air–atomic power and toward a collective security system that relied on America's allies to shoulder most of the manpower and some of the financial burden of the common defense. In addition, conservative criticism gave a certain leverage to officials in the Treasury Department, the Budget Bureau, and the ODM who were trying to restrain the insatiable demands of the armed forces and the grand ambitions of national security managers in the State Department. Once Congress had decided against taxes as high as Truman had recommended, or economic controls as strong, the balance of power in the administration began to tilt back toward the economizers. Keyserling, whose expansionist philosophy gave economic soundness to NSC-68, lost ground to those who were convinced that limited resources required the administration to stretch out the defense buildup.

What is more, even though conservatives could not derail the national security state, they had learned to decouple it from the economic and social policies of the New Deal. They voted for new defense taxes, but were reluctant to close tax loopholes, raise corporate taxes, or take other measures that would put the financial burden of national security on those most able to carry it. Nor were they willing to raise taxes high enough to avoid shifting part of the cost of the early Cold War to the next generation. The government ran deficits of $4 billion in fiscal year 1952 and

[90] Office of Defense Mobilization, *The Job Ahead for Defense Mobilization: Eighth Quarterly Report to the President* (Washington, 1953).

more than $5 billion in fiscal year 1953. And while continued growth seemed to indicate that the country could eat its cake and have it too, this was not quite true, despite Keyserling's predictions to the contrary. The Gross National Product increased by 13 percent between June 1950 and January 1953, but the increase, which covered the cost of defense, added almost nothing to the resources available for consumption or for government investment in health, education, and welfare. The average annual per capita income, after adjusting for higher taxes and inflation, increased by barely $40 per year, while wartime budgets reversed the modest growth in nondefense spending that had begun several years earlier. Even Keyserling would concede that such expenditures had to be sacrificed in the name of national security, at least temporarily, and conservatives, who opposed these programs in the first place, took advantage of such concessions by exacting even larger reductions than either Keyserling or Truman had in mind.

Nourse had waged a war against the escalating defense budget so government could invest more in public projects that had been starved since the Great Depression. Taft and other conservatives reversed this strategy. They gave in to national security initiatives, reluctantly in some cases, but viewed cuts in public investment, not higher taxes, as the best way to pay for them. Seen in this light, the rise of the national security state abetted a conservative assault on New Deal social programs and on the notion that such programs were actually essential, not only to the country's democratic mission but also to its long-term military strength. By 1953, national security and other war-related items, such as veterans' benefits and payments on the national debt, accounted for more than 85 percent of the federal budget, and for virtually all of the growth in government spending since the start of the Korean War. Spending in other areas had more often declined, by as much as 9 percent overall in one of Truman's estimates. One result was a budget that looked more like those of World War II than like a peacetime budget. Another was to put an even greater share of the cost of national security onto those who could afford it least. And still another was to transform the nation's postwar identity from that of a welfare state to that of a warfare state.[91]

---

[91] In addition to the source cited in the previous note see Truman, "Annual Budget Message to the Congress: Fiscal Year 1952," 15 January 1951, *Public Papers, Truman, 1951*, 61–106; Truman, "Annual Budget Message to the Congress: Fiscal Year 1953," 21 January 1952, and "Annual Budget Message to the Congress: Fiscal Year 1954," 9 January 1953, *Public Papers, Truman, 1952–53*, 63–117, 1128–64.

9

The Iron Cross

Solvency, Security, and the Eisenhower Transition

Neither Harry Truman nor Dwight Eisenhower had much to say when they met shortly after the election in November 1952. Truman had brought the president-elect to the White House for a briefing by top officials. The briefing had gone well, or so Truman thought, and had given his successor a good tutorial in the difficult problems that confronted the country. Eisenhower had a different recollection. Grim and uncomfortable throughout the meeting, he said little and was convinced that he had learned even less. Inauguration Day saw no improvement. Truman had declined Eisenhower's invitation to return to Missouri on board the presidential plane, and Eisenhower had refused to join Truman for refreshments before the ceremony. According to some accounts, the two men traded insults or sat in stony silence as they rode together to the Capitol. It was a hostile transition, as Stephen Ambrose has said, and a suitable capstone to one of the most vicious political campaigns in recent memory.[1]

Conservative Republicans were unable to get Senator Taft on the ticket in 1952, but they controlled the party's convention and wrote a campaign platform that vilified the Truman administration and the Democratic party as being riddled with corruption, full of Communists, and basically un-American. The Republicans promised to clean up the mess in Washington, get rid of the crooks and cronies and Communists in government, stop reckless spending, cut taxes, eliminate all economic controls, and otherwise reaffirm the country's faith in such old-fashioned virtues as a balanced budget and a sound dollar. A similar emphasis on traditional values ran through Republican party statements on foreign policy. To be sure, the Republicans promised to end the folly in Korea and pay more attention to Asia. But they also promised to reassert the country's traditional independence in foreign affairs, end the give-away programs

---

[1] Truman, *Memoirs* 2:514–21; Stephen E. Ambrose, *Eisenhower*, vol. 2, *The President* (New York, 1984), 15, 41–42; McCullough, *Truman*, 913–14, 921. Eisenhower's recollections of these events are somewhat different. See Dwight D. Eisenhower, *The White House Years: Mandate for Change, 1953–1956* (Garden City, NY, 1963), 85, 101.

abroad, and replace the discredited policy of containment with a more aggressive effort to roll back the Communist tide in Eastern Europe. Through these and other initiatives, the Republicans said, they would rescue the United States from a descent into darkness that had begun with the New Deal and would end in the garrison state.

Though supposedly a moderate, Eisenhower ran hard to the right during much of the campaign, in part to differentiate himself from the Democrats, in part to assuage the conservative wing of his own party, in part because he believed in much of what the party platform had to say. He, too, wanted to get the crooks and the Communists out of government, balance the budget, and cut taxes. An internationalist who was more committed to containment than many Republicans, he nonetheless mouthed the familiar party platitudes about liberating captive nations from the yoke of communism. He also promised a new look at the country's defense and new efforts to eliminate the waste that many Republicans associated with military spending and foreign aid. He talked about the need for solvency as well as security, and to achieve these goals he would reorganize the national security establishment, get the Joint Chiefs under better control, and deliver a formidable defense at less cost to the taxpayer.[2]

Still, in spite of his campaign rhetoric, Eisenhower actually had more in common with his predecessor than either wanted to admit, with the result being that many of his policies were less a break with the past than a further unfolding of initiatives that had started earlier. Although Eisenhower professed the new ideology of national security, he did not want the demands of security to transform the country into a garrison state. Instead, he wanted to end deficit spending, protect the constitutional balance, and guarantee civilian over military leadership. With these goals in mind, he reorganized the Pentagon, harnessed science to the cause of national security, wrestled with the issue of internal security, and promised a defense posture that emphasized air–atomic power rather than a large standing army. In all of these ways he struggled, as Truman had struggled before, to recast the way Americans defined themselves, and to do so by reconciling older values and traditions with the new ideology of national security, the welfare state with the warfare state, the country's traditional democratic identity with its new role as the military guardian of freedom everywhere.

---

[2] Stephen E. Ambrose, *Eisenhower*, vol. 1, *Soldier, General of the Army. President-Elect, 1890–1952* (New York, 1983), 550–72.

In pursuing these goals, Eisenhower also faced some of the same obstacles that his predecessor had encountered. Scientists and military leaders still sought more independence than the president thought desirable; Congress was still leery of reorganizing the Pentagon on terms that centralized more authority in military hands; and interservice squabbles continued to hamper a new defense posture and efforts to contain the budget. In addition, even though Truman had set a course back to the lower budgets of the pre-Korean period, Eisenhower had to squeeze defense even harder if he wanted to appease conservatives and honor his campaign pledges. The death of Premier Josef Stalin in March 1953 and the end of the Korean War in July raised hopes of a new peace and less spending on the military. But on the other side was the successful Soviet test of a thermonuclear weapon in August 1953 and the constant warnings, coming from the Pentagon, that any cuts in defense would spell certain disaster. Like Truman, moreover, Eisenhower spent much of his time in a two-front struggle against congressional Democrats who wanted to invest more in the military, and congressional conservatives, mostly Republicans, who accused the president of not doing enough to reduce taxes and balance the budget.

II

Eisenhower came to office with a set of deeply held convictions about the proper role of government in the modern age, convictions that looked to a middle way between the liberal philosophy of New Deal Democrats and the laissez-faire philosophy of conservative Republicans. Though he believed that government had a role to play in stimulating growth, promoting the public welfare, and aiding those who could not aid themselves, he also believed that Roosevelt and Truman had concentrated too much authority in a powerful federal establishment that was eroding individual freedom, stifling initiative, and hampering the ability of private citizens to run their own affairs. Needed, he said, was a better balance and more cooperation between the federal government and the states and between public officials and private groups.

The same principles influenced the president's view of national security policy. The United States, he argued, had to resist the isolationist impulse, especially if it threatened the constitutional balance between Congress and the president. It had to accept its responsibilities as leader of the free world, maintain a strong military deterrent, and help weaker allies to help themselves. But it also had to do these things without destroying the very freedoms it sought to protect, which was the danger that Eisenhower saw in the policies pursued by his predecessor. He was convinced that Truman had allowed national security to add unnecessarily to the growth of government power, so that military leaders now threatened civilian supremacy, taxes discouraged incentive, economic controls hampered private enterprise, and budget deficits cheapened the dollar. In these areas, too, the president wanted a better balance between the old values and the new, between civilian and military leadership, between solvency and security.[3]

The balance that Eisenhower had in mind was apparent in his struggle to safeguard presidential prerogatives against challenges raised on both sides of the national security discourse. The first of these challenges came from conservative isolationists, led by Republican Senator John W. Bricker of Ohio. Convinced that President Roosevelt had exceeded his authority in the field of foreign affairs, especially with the Yalta accords of 1945, Bricker proposed a constitutional amendment that would curtail the treaty-making powers of the executive. The exact meaning of his amendment was unclear, but there was no doubt in Eisenhower's mind that it would deny him the flexibility that national security demanded. Nor did he doubt that the Founding Fathers had envisioned a separation of powers, which would be destroyed "brick by brick by Bricker," whose amendment would permit Congress to infringe on the president's constitutional rights and responsibilities. Guided by this conviction, which only deepened after he consulted *The Federalist Papers*, Eisenhower devoted an enormous amount of his time to opposing the amendment before finally defeating it in a series of Senate votes that came in February 1954.[4]

Similar convictions guided Eisenhower's efforts to reorganize the national security establishment, an area where he faced challenges from national security managers as well as from Congress. Eisenhower took office convinced that good staff work and sound organization were two of the keys to economic efficiency, to civilian control of the military, and

---

[3] For the best short statement of Eisenhower's convictions and his search for the middle way see Robert G. Griffith, "Dwight D. Eisenhower and the Corporate Commonwealth," *American Historical Review* 87 (February 1982): 87–122.

[4] Eisenhower quoted in Ambrose, *Eisenhower* 2:69, 70. See also ibid., 154–55; Gray W. Reichard, *The Reaffirmation of Republicanism: Eisenhower and the Eighty-Third Congress* (Knoxville, 1975), 60–66; and Chester J. Pach, Jr., and Elmo Richardson, *The Presidency of Dwight D. Eisenhower*, rev. ed. (Lawrence, 1991), 59–62. For the definitive account of the Bricker amendment see Duane Tananbaum, *The Bricker Amendment Controversy: A Test of Eisenhower's Political Leadership* (Ithaca, 1988).

to the president's ability to shape foreign policy. And with these goals in mind, he recruited Robert Cutler, a Boston banker, to reexamine the president's staff arrangements in the field of national security. Cutler converted the NSC's staff into a Policy Board, gave it a more active role in drafting policy papers, and put it under the control of a presidential assistant who would chair meetings of the NSC and track the outcome of its decisions. The new arrangements made for better staff work and more comprehensive planning. They also turned the NSC into an effective instrument of presidential policy, responsible to the Oval Office rather than the State Department and headed by a special assistant to the president for national security affairs – a position that Cutler filled himself.[5]

Besides these changes, Eisenhower encouraged the NSC to wrestle more aggressively with the economic consequences of national security policy and with its implications for the country's "fundamental values and institutions" – a phrase that became commonplace in NSC documents. The council became a forum for such deliberations and for the presentation of competing points of view. It could always count on strong representations from the Joint Chiefs and from Secretary of State John Foster Dulles, the hard-working, evangelical banker who brought to his job a family tradition in foreign affairs and enormous personal experience. To countervail these views, however, Eisenhower also drew the Budget Bureau and the Treasury Department more deeply into the council's deliberations. Both agencies provided an economic perspective on national security issues, and both were headed by staunch fiscal conservatives. Joseph M. Dodge, a Detroit banker, took over the Budget Bureau, while George M. Humphrey, president of the Mark Hanna Company of Cleveland, became Secretary of the Treasury. "If anyone talks to you about money," Humphrey told the president, "you tell him to go see George."[6]

---

5 Cutler memorandum for Eisenhower, 16 March 1953, with enclosed report of the same date, and Eisenhower to Cutler, 17 March 1953, *FRUS, 1952–1954* (Washington, 1984), 2:245–58; unsigned Budget Bureau memorandum, "Implementation of Approved National Security Policy," 7 July 1953, RG 51, Series 52.1, box 77, folder: Organization for National Security and Defense; Robert Cutler, "The Development of the National Security Council," *Foreign Affairs* 34 (April 1956): 441–58; Anna K. Nelson, "The 'Top of Policy Hill': President Eisenhower and the National Security Council," *Diplomatic History* 7 (Fall 1983): 307–26; idem, "The Importance of the Foreign Policy Process: Eisenhower and the National Security Council," in *Eisenhower: A Centenary Assessment*, ed. Gunter Bischof and Stephen E. Ambrose (Baton Rouge, 1995), 111–25.

6 Humphrey quoted in Ambrose, *Eisenhower* 2:23. See also ibid., 21–22; Pach and Richardson, *Presidency of Dwight D. Eisenhower*, 34, 37; memorandum of discussion at the 131st NSC meeting, 11 February 1953, *FRUS, 1952–1954* 2:236–37; and S. Everett

Eisenhower's determination to assert his control over national security policy and to get a grip on the defense budget also led to important changes in the Defense Department. He selected Charles E. Wilson, the president of General Motors, to be secretary of defense, in part because "Engine Charlie" had run the nation's largest corporation and it was therefore assumed that he could also run the Pentagon, which had become the world's largest employer.[7] In consultation with Wilson, moreover, Eisenhower moved quickly to replace the Joint Chiefs with a whole new team. He selected General Matthew B. Ridgway, Admiral Robert B. Carney, and General Nathan F. Twining to head the Army, Navy, and Air Force, respectively, while Admiral Arthur W. Radford, Commander in Chief, Pacific, took over as chairman of the Joint Chiefs. The president appreciated Radford's faith in airpower and his willingness to think differently about grand strategy, particularly his conviction that American forces were currently overextended and that some redeployment was in order. These ideas reinforced Eisenhower's own convictions and gave him good reason to believe that Radford would disavow his "identification with the United States Navy," stand above service disputes, and act as the president's agent.[8]

To complete his reorganization, Eisenhower asked Congress in April 1953 to restructure the Defense Department. His request set off another round in the struggle to balance centralizing and decentralizing tendencies in the national security state that was taking shape. The goal was to protect the constitutional balance and the tradition of civilian control, and the question was whether this goal would be helped or hindered by concentrating more authority in the military arm of the government. As was the case in the unification struggles of 1947 and 1949, both sides in the new debate resorted to a rhetorical strategy that relied on such binary oppositions as civilian or military, coordination or consolidation, centralization or decentralization, democracy or totalitarianism, American or

Gleason memorandum of discussion at the 132d NSC meeting, 19 February 1953, Dwight D. Eisenhower Papers (Dwight D. Eisenhower Library, Abilene, Kansas), Papers as President, Ann Whitman File, NSC Series, box 4, folder: 123d Meeting, February 18, 1953. For Eisenhower's initial assessment of his key appointees see his diary entry of 14 May 1953 in *The Eisenhower Diaries,* ed. Robert H. Ferrell (New York, 1981), 236–40. The workings of the NSC can be followed in the text.

7 Ambrose, *Eisenhower* 2:23.

8 Eisenhower to Radford, 18 May 1953, Eisenhower Papers, Papers as President, Whitman File, DDE Diary Series, box 3, folder: Eisenhower Diary, Dec. '52–July '53. See also Robert J. Watson, *The History of the Joint Chiefs of Staff,* vol. 5, *The Joint Chiefs of Staff and National Policy, 1953–1954* (Washington, 1986), 14–15.

Prussian. Both expressed their fears in these oppositional pairings or in the metaphor of the garrison state, and both claimed to speak for the American way of life, as opposed to the un-American other.

Eisenhower's thinking grew directly out of his postwar experience as army chief of staff and de facto chairman of the Joint Chiefs of Staff. During the great unification battles of 1947–1949, he had consistently favored a single chief of staff, a joint staff under the chief's control, and measures to strengthen the authority of the secretary of defense. To his way of thinking, such reforms would make strategic planning more effective, harness the planning process to budget ceilings, and ensure civilian control of the military. As we have seen, however, these reforms had been largely thwarted in the National Security Act of 1947 and the defense reorganization of 1949, both of which allowed the individual services to retain a good deal of autonomy. Eisenhower was therefore determined to secure what he had long advocated. He brought Wilson into the Pentagon with this goal in mind, and he gave him firm instructions to reduce the defense budget and get better control of the armed forces.[9]

In the background, also, was the endless bickering among the armed services over their respective roles and missions. This feuding had reached new heights during the military buildup that followed the outbreak of fighting in Korea. As usual, the principle culprits were the Air Force and the Navy, although the Army, too, had recently joined the other branches in a major battle to control the development of guided missiles. Each service still had its partisans on Capitol Hill and in the national press, and each was ready to leak information, lobby its supporters, and do whatever it took to gain an advantage over the others. The Pentagon "leaked at the top," Wilson said, and he could not be effective without more control over "the apex of the hierarchy in the Defense establishment."[10]

---

[9] For background on Eisenhower's thinking about defense reorganization see Bryon Greenwald and Clifford J. Rogers, "The Hidden Hand in Defense Reorganization" (in author's possession). See also Condit, *Test of War*, 518–19.

[10] Gleason memorandum of discussion at the 132d NSC meeting, 19 February 1953, Eisenhower Papers, Papers as President, Whitman File, NSC Series, box 4, folder: 132d Meeting, February 18, 1953. See also, for illustrations of interservice rivalry, Finletter to Vandenberg, undated, with enclosed memorandum, Vandenberg Papers, Subject File, box 83, folder: 2A Memos re 138 Wings; Finletter to Vandenberg, with attached memorandum for staff meeting, 17 July 1952, Vandenberg Papers, Subject File, box 84, folder: 8. Selected Memos – Sec. AF to C/S, USAF; Ramsay Potts, Jr., to General Nathan Twining, 23 June 1952, W. Barton Leach to Vandenberg, 21 October and 16 December 1952 and 19 January and 4 March 1953, Leach to Finletter and Vandenberg, 16 December 1952, Leach to Finletter, 16 December 1952, Finletter to Lovett, [December 1952], and Noel Parrish to Vandenberg 12 February 1953, Vandenberg Papers, Subject File, box 84, folder: 7C, Carrier Papers. See also Condit, *Test of War*, 418.

To gain this control, Wilson and Eisenhower asked the so-called Rockefeller Committee to review the Defense Department and make recommendations as to how it might be reorganized. The committee, established to plan a major restructuring of the federal government, was headed by Nelson A. Rockefeller and included a reform-minded group of distinguished citizens. One of these was Vannevar Bush, the wartime captain of science, who had published essays on the subject, and another was Robert A. Lovett, Truman's last secretary of defense, who wanted an organizational reform that concentrated more responsibilities in the secretary of defense, separated the Joint Chiefs from their services, and enhanced the authority of their chairman.[11]

Lovett's views, which came close to what experience had taught Eisenhower, also found support among other members of the Rockefeller Committee. Appointed in mid-February, the committee held hearings through the middle of April, when it released a report that Eisenhower sent to Congress as grounds for his Reorganization Plan No. 6. The plan would abolish the Munitions Board, the Research and Development Board, and other units, and would transfer their functions to six additional assistant secretaries in the Office of the Secretary of Defense. It would also relieve the Joint Chiefs of some of their administrative burdens, thereby separating them to some extent from their services, and would give more authority to the chairman of the Joint Chiefs and to the secretary of defense, largely by allowing them to appoint, dismiss, and otherwise control the Joint Staff.[12]

In recommending the plan to Congress, Eisenhower made it clear that his goal was to strengthen civilian responsibility over the military, much as the Constitution envisioned, while giving the American taxpayer maximum military effectiveness at "minimum cost." His statement struck a balance between the old political culture, with its emphasis on anti-statism, its fear of standing armies, and its concern with a sound dollar and a "solvent" economy, and the new ideology of national security, which envisioned a "perilous" future of neither "total war nor total

---

[11] Lovett to Truman, 18 November 1952, RG 218, CCS 040 (11-2-43), Sec. 9. The Budget Bureau was also looking into the matter and making similar though more far-reaching recommendations. See the unsigned memorandum to the budget director, 15 April 1952, RG 51, Series 52.1, box 78, folder: Defense Department.

[12] Eisenhower, "Special Message to the Congress Transmitting Reorganization Plan 6 of 1953 Concerning the Department of Defense," 30 April 1953, *Public Papers of the Presidents of the United States: Dwight D. Eisenhower, 1953* (Washington, 1960), 225–38 (hereafter *Public Papers, Eisenhower*); James F. Whisenand to Major General James Burns, 14 May 1953, Vandenberg Papers, box 47, folder: Congressional Hearings; and Eisenhower, *Mandate for Change*, 447–48.

peace." As the guardians of freedom everywhere, Eisenhower said, the American people must be prepared militarily, more or less on a permanent basis, but "must not create a nation mighty in arms that is lacking in liberty and bankrupt in resources." If the United States was going to contain communism for the "indefinite future," it must have a defense establishment that was both militarily strong and economical and that was founded "upon our basic constitutional principles" – especially the principle of "unchallenged civilian responsibility," which required clear lines of authority running from the president through the secretary of defense to the military departments.[13]

But what Eisenhower saw as strengthening civilian control, others saw as going in the opposite direction. Their criticism focused almost entirely on the plan's attempt to enhance the authority of the chairman of the Joint Chiefs, in part by giving him greater control over the Joint Staff. Opposition to this reform came from leading figures in the national press, notably Hanson Baldwin, who was widely regarded as the nation's preeminent commentator on military affairs, and Arthur Krock, one of Baldwin's colleagues at *The New York Times*. The trend, Krock told his readers, was toward a "Prussian system" that gave a single military chief of staff the authority to administer and even merge the services, rather than coordinate them. Baldwin went further, claiming that Eisenhower's reform would enable the chairman to "by-pass or neutralize" the Joint Chiefs and "to exercise a balance of power in the office of the Secretary of Defense." It would initiate a "dangerous trend," he said, not only toward military centralization but also toward the concentration of power over military affairs in military rather than civilian hands.[14]

Eisenhower, other critics agreed, would create a "Prussian-type supreme general staff" similar to the German general staff that had crushed democracy and lost two world wars. These critics included Ferdinand Eberstadt and Herbert Hoover, both of whom had been instrumental in earlier reorganizations, as well as retired Brigadier General Robert W. Johnson, a leading Republican and chairman of the board of the Johnson and Johnson Company. Johnson spoke for all critics when he warned of a "well-planned movement" to "expand and entrench the power of the

[13] Eisenhower, "Special Message to the Congress Transmitting Reorganization Plan 6," 30 April 1953, *Public Papers, Eisenhower, 1953*, 225–38.

[14] Krock, "The Plan to Reorganize the Defense Department," *New York Times*, 12 May 1953; Baldwin, "The Pentagon's Changes," ibid., 14 May 1953; and Baldwin, "Airpower Controversy – III," ibid., 11 June 1953. See also, Baldwin, "Shake-up in Pentagon Represents Compromise," ibid., 3 May 1953; and Baldwin, "Airpower Controversy – IV," ibid., 13 June 1953.

military with attendant loss of civilian authority within our Government." At stake, he said, was nothing less than "the preservation of our way of life and our survival as a nation." Opponents in Congress elaborated this argument. Since the start of World War II, they said, the military establishment had become a permanent and powerful force, much different from what the Founding Fathers had envisioned, with enormous resources and influence that extended through "military manpower, education and industrial requirements to the very heart of our national life." Giving more power to the chairman of the Joint Chiefs would only augment this pattern of "creeping militarism" until American democracy gave way to the "military man on horseback."[15]

The president's supporters in Congress rushed to his defense, though sometimes with arguments he must have disliked. Some, for example, defended the president's plan as being in line with the needs of a world power for a strong military establishment, regardless of the cost to the country's traditional values and institutions. A lot of water had "gone under the bridge" since the days of the Founding Fathers, said one member of Congress. American forces were stationed all over the world and military expenditures, both direct and indirect, constituted more than 70 percent of the U.S. budget. Under these circumstances, it was time to "change our ideals" from those of the Founders, who had envisioned little more than an agrarian republic with a militia. It might even be necessary to contemplate less, not more, civilian "meddling" in the country's military affairs, particularly since that kind of meddling had deprived MacArthur of his command and the United States of victory in Korea.[16]

These arguments notwithstanding, most of the president's allies on Capitol Hill saw the concentration of authority in the Pentagon as essential to civilian control and therefore in line with the country's democratic heritage. It would help the president and the secretary of defense to regulate interservice rivalries, eliminate duplication, and put resources to better use, and would thus contribute to a stable dollar and a strong economy. Nor would it give the chairman of the Joint Chiefs too much authority. On the contrary, he would not be a voting member of that body

---

[15] *Congressional Record, 1953* 99:1874, 2447, 1871, 7373, 7377. See also Eberstadt to Taft, 19 May 1953, Eberstadt to Senator Harry F. Byrd, 21 May 1953, and Eberstadt, "Memorandum Re President Eisenhower's Recommendations for Reorganization of the Defense Department Contained in Reorganization Plan No. 6 of 1953," Eberstadt Papers, box 40, folder: 1953 Defense Dept. Reorganization Files. Congressional criticism of the president's plan can be followed in *Congressional Record, 1953* 99:1871–74, 2447–48, 7335–37, 7363–66, 7373–79; and *Congressional Quarterly Almanac, 1953,* 293–94.

[16] *Congressional Record, 1953* 99:7394.

or have the powers of command, and would still be responsible to the secretary of defense and to the president as commander in chief.[17] These arguments finally prevailed, but only by a narrow margin, and only after Eisenhower provided special assurances that he aimed to strengthen, not weaken, civilian control of the military. Armed with these assurances, the president's supporters managed to get his reforms through Congress by the end of June.[18]

Even while he was reorganizing the defense department, Eisenhower was also forging new links between the national security establishment and American science, trying in this area as well to provide himself with reliable sources of information, protect his prerogatives as president, and ensure civilian control of the military. As noted in an earlier chapter, the armed services had developed their own research and development programs and could not be counted on to coordinate their initiatives for the sake of economy or to provide the president with objective advice on military science and technology. To overcome these liabilities, the President's Scientific Research Board had recommended the appointment of a distinguished scientist or group of scientists to advise the White House on national policies, and a similar recommendation had come from the Budget Bureau following the outbreak of the Korean War. Truman had responded by establishing the Science Advisory Committee in the Office of Defense Mobilization (ODM), but a weak chairman, a vague mandate, and a short time line had prevented the new committee from playing an aggressive role in the last months of the administration.[19]

There was good reason to believe that Eisenhower would pick up where Truman had left off. The new president understood the important part that science and technology played in the development of modern weapons. He had helped to launch the Army's postwar research and

---

[17] Ibid., 7173–76, 7362, 7366–73, 7382–86, 7394–96. See also *Congressional Quarterly Almanac, 1953*, 293–94.

[18] Eisenhower's assurances came in a letter to Republican Congressman L. C. Arends, 25 May 1953, *Congressional Record, 1953* 99:7397. See also ibid., 7480–96; and L. A. Minnich, Jr., supplementary notes, Legislative Leadership Meeting, 12 May 1953, Eisenhower Papers, Papers as President, Whitman File, DDE Diary Series, box 4, folder: Staff Notes January–December 1953.

[19] James R. Killian, Jr., *Sputnik, Scientists, and Eisenhower: A Memoir of the First Special Assistant to the President for Science and Technology* (Cambridge, MA, 1977), 60–66; Detlev W. Bronk, "Science Advice in the White House: The Genesis of the President's Science Advisers and the National Science Foundation," in *Science and Technology Advice to the President, Congress, and Judiciary,* ed. William T. Golden (New York, 1980), 245–56; Kevles, "Cold War and Hot Physics," 252–56; and Gregg Herken, *Cardinal Choices: Presidential Science Advising from the Atomic Bomb to SDI* (New York, 1992), 55–57.

development program, and had been won over to a military strategy that relied on America's competitive advantage in nuclear weapons, airpower, and rockets to deter aggression and contain the Soviet Union. By the time Eisenhower took office, moreover, the fast-paced rearmament program was overwhelming the Pentagon's ability to assess scientific initiatives, and the ODM's Science Advisory Committee had come to the conclusion that the need was never greater for a new arrangement between organized science and the White House.[20]

The committee urged the new administration to add a scientist with his own staff to the NSC and to appoint a science adviser to help the secretary of defense evaluate and coordinate the research and development enterprises of the armed services. These recommendations were taken up by Nelson Rockefeller and his committee, and Rockefeller also discussed them with both Eisenhower and Cutler. Cutler was impressed with what the scientists had to say, as were the CIA, the ODM, and Vannevar Bush, who provided a list of qualified experts for Cutler to consider. But for reasons that are still unclear, Cutler eventually decided against adding a scientist to the NSC staff. Bush and his allies saw this decision as a setback for science in the new administration, and they were equally distressed when the Budget Bureau began talking about substantial cuts in the government's research and development budget and when similar talk came from Secretary of Defense Wilson, whose dislike for basic research caused many scientists to despair of his leadership in the Pentagon.[21]

Despite these initial disappointments, however, the administration was soon taking steps to actually strengthen the partnership between science and the state that had been taking shape for some time. Instead of a full-time science adviser, Cutler appointed ad hoc panels of scientists to advise the NSC as the need arose. In addition, Arthur Flemming, who took charge of the ODM, strengthened its Science Advisory Committee through the appointment of an executive secretary who also served as liaison between the Advisory Committee and the NSC. Together with the

---

[20] Damms, "Scientists and Statesmen," 165–66, 169.

[21] For these developments and speculation as to Culter's decision, see ibid., 170–77, 181–84. See also Bush's letter and memorandum to Cutler, both dated 4 May 1953, White House Office Records (Eisenhower Library), National Security Council Staff Papers, Executive Secretary's Subject File, box 17, folder: Special Assistant (Cutler) – Memoranda, 1953; and Dodge to Alan T. Waterman (director, National Science Foundation), 11 May 1953, DuBridge to Cutler, 15 May 1953, and Dodge memorandums on research and development, 9 and 12 June, 1953, White House Office Records, Special Assistant for National Security Affairs, Special Assistant Series, Subject Subseries, box 7, folder: Science and Research – General.

ad hoc panels, this arrangement enabled science and scientists to play a larger role in national security policy making.

Much the same was true of changes in the Department of Defense. Under Eisenhower's reorganization scheme, the department replaced the Research and Development Board with two assistant secretaries of defense, one for research and development, the other for applications engineering. Donald A. Quarles, a former vice president of Monsanto Chemical Company, became the Pentagon's first assistant secretary for research and development. A strong supporter of basic research, Quarles moved quickly to involve civilian scientists in the Pentagon's research and development program through a series of technical advisory panels. At the same time, Eisenhower both moderated Wilson's resolve to eviscerate the Pentagon's research budget and relied on the new partnership with science in dealing with one of the first important defense controversies of the new administration – the debate over the development of an integrated system of continental defense.[22]

By the time Eisenhower took office, the ODM's Science Advisory Committee had already become a leading advocate of continental defense, as had the committee's counterparts at MIT's Lincoln Laboratory, which was under contract with the Air Force to study this and other issues. Both had concluded that U.S. air defenses were inadequate to counter a Soviet attack and would remain so without new antiaircraft defenses and an early warning radar line across northern Canada. Similar recommendations had also emerged from other scientific studies, from a group of consultants working for the State Department, and from a final report to President Truman from Dean Acheson, Robert Lovett, and Averell Harriman. None of those involved thought it possible to erect an impenetrable defense against a Soviet air assault, but they did hope to safeguard America's deterrent power by preventing the Soviets from destroying its nuclear arsenal with a single blow.

These recommendations had produced a stiff reaction from airpower enthusiasts who worried that continental defense would subtract from funds otherwise available for the Air Force. To guide him through this controversy, Eisenhower appointed a special study group headed by the president of Bell Laboratories. The NSC did the same thing, and the ODM's Science Advisory Committee also got involved when the NSC took up the issue in the last months of 1953 – not long after the Soviet

---

[22] Damms, "Scientists and Statesmen," 177–80, 184–89; Kevles, "Cold War and Hot Physics," 259–60; Eisenhower to Wilson, 28 May 1953, Eisenhower Papers, Papers as President, Whitman File, DDE Diary Series, box 3, folder: Eisenhower Diary, Dec. '52–July '53.

Union's successful test of a thermonuclear weapon raised concern about continental defense to new heights. The outcome was a decision that pleased the Science Advisory Committee. To be sure, Eisenhower's resolve to balance the budget ruled out a crash program of continental defense. But the president did stress the need to balance offensive and defensive strategies, which, in his view, required an effective system of continental defense, including a modest increase in spending on an early warning radar line, a better system of air control, and improved anti-aircraft forces. The most dramatic result of these decisions came in November 1954, when the United States and Canada agreed to construct an early warning radar line across northern Canada.[23]

In the debate over continental defense Eisenhower had turned to the scientific community for objective advice he could not always get from the armed forces. He brought scientists into decision making, not as a substitute for his own judgment, but to help him counter pressure from the Air Force and control interservice disputes over the benefits of an offensive or defensive strategy of deterrence. For similar reasons, Eisenhower subsequently instructed the ODM's Science Advisory Committee to launch an even larger study of the connection between science and national security in the nuclear age. In the background was the successful Soviet test of a thermonuclear device, the awesome power of the nuclear weapons being tested by the Atomic Energy Commission, the danger of radioactive fallout, and the ongoing rivalry among the armed forces in the field of military research. All these developments prompted Eisenhower to ask the Science Advisory Committee how best to rationalize the development of military technology and guard against the danger of a nuclear attack.[24]

With these instructions in mind, the committee immediately established a Technological Capabilities Panel chaired by James R. Killian, Jr., who had succeeded Karl T. Compton as the president of MIT. Four months of intense work by over forty scientists followed, after which the panel produced a mammoth report and submitted it to the president in March 1955. Although a detailed summary of the report is beyond the

[23] Damms, "Scientists and Statesmen," 190–99; NSC-141, 19 January 1953, report by the panel of consultants of the Department of State to the secretary of state, January 1953, memorandum of discussion at the 163d NSC meeting, 24 September 1953, NSC-159/4, 25 September 1953, NSC-162/2, 30 October 1953, NSC-5408, 11 February 1954, and memorandum of discussion at the 185th NSC meeting, 17 February 1954, *FRUS, 1952–1954* 2:209–22, 1056–91, 464–75, 475–89, 577–98, 609–24, 624–33.
[24] Damms, "Scientists and Statesmen," 228–36; Robert A. Divine, *Blowing on the Wind: The Nuclear Test Ban Debate, 1954–1960* (New York, 1978), 3–5.

scope of this book, its findings led Eisenhower to accelerate the development of intercontinental ballistic missiles and launch new programs to develop intermediate range missiles, reconnaissance satellites, and high-altitude planes – what became the famous U-2 spy planes. The report also led to a series of presidential decisions regarding the roles and missions of the armed forces in the development and control of ballistic missiles; decisions, or so Eisenhower hoped, that would end the inter-service bickering and make it easier to control the budget. Finally, and most importantly, the panel's performance moved the president closer to the conviction that he needed his own science adviser if he was going to control the Pentagon and inspire public confidence in his military policies. This was particularly true after the Soviet Union launched the first orbital satellite in the fall of 1957. In the wake of the so-called Sputnik crisis, Eisenhower moved the Science Advisory Committee to the White House, where it became the President's Science Advisory Committee, established the new post of special assistant to the president for science and technology, and invited James R. Killian to fill the position.[25]

Despite Eisenhower's growing reliance on scientific advice, the partnership between science and the state operated under a number of important constraints, one of the most important being the president's reluctance to take a stand against McCarthyism or to reverse the loyalty programs launched by his predecessor. In the 1952 campaign, as noted earlier, the Republicans had accused the Truman administration of being shot through with Communists, and Eisenhower had promised to clean house as soon as he took office. Good to his word, the new president ordered the FBI to run security checks on all federal appointees and to make security, rather than loyalty, the test of employment. The new standard substantially altered the loyalty program that Truman had put in place, for it meant that even loyal Americans could be dismissed from government service or denied employment for personal behavior that supposedly made them vulnerable to Communist control. Still worse, the Eisenhower administration eliminated almost every shred of protection against the summary dismissal of accused employees, including the right of appeal and the Fifth Amendment protection against self-incrimination. When it came to security, Eisenhower said, "no doubt can be tolerated."[26]

---

[25] Damms,"Scientists and Statesmen," 227–66, 274–304; Killian, *Sputnik, Scientists, and Eisenhower,* 67–90; Divine, *Blowing on the Wind,* 170–71; Herken, *Cardinal Choices,* 87–89; Kevles, "Cold War and Hot Physics," 261.

[26] Eisenhower quoted in Ambrose, *Eisenhower* 2:45–46. See also Jeff Broadwater, *Eisenhower*

With this principle as a guide, Eisenhower urged Secretary of State Dulles to weed suspicious elements from the State Department. Within weeks Dulles began dismissing scores, even hundreds of employees, often without hearings and often for personal behavior, such as homosexuality, or for political behavior, such as association with the previous administration, the Democratic party, or liberal organizations. With other departments following similar procedures, it was not long before the administration was bragging that it had eliminated nearly fifteen hundred security risks from government service. Not content with this record, moreover, Eisenhower's attorney general also attacked the loyalty of Harry Dexter White, a high-ranking official in the Treasury Department during the Truman administration, and by implication the loyalty of former president Truman. Eisenhower was never able to separate himself from this assault. Nor would he openly oppose McCarthy's vicious investigations into the loyalty of outstanding public servants or the operation of government agencies.[27]

On the contrary, the president often acted to preempt McCarthy's charges by taking steps to drive allegedly suspicious elements from the government. This approach lay behind the purges in the State Department and was also the strategy that Eisenhower adopted in dealing with the Oppenheimer case, which broke when a former congressional aide accused J. Robert Oppenheimer of communism. Oppenheimer was perhaps the most famous scientist in the country. He had led the scientific team that produced the first atomic bomb and was thereafter active in plans to put atomic energy under international control, in the debates over whether to develop a hydrogen bomb, and in the work of the Atomic Energy Commission. Although the charges against the physicist had been investigated and found wanting on several occasions, as Eisenhower admitted at the time, the president worried that McCarthy would use them to discredit the new administration and decided immediately to suspend Oppenheimer's security clearance. He denied Oppenheimer access to classified information, excluded him from meetings of the ODM's Science Advisory Committee, and asked Lewis Strauss, who now headed the Atomic Energy Commission, to conduct a thorough review of the case.

& *the Anti-Communist Crusade* (Chapel Hill, 1992), 85–111; and Pach and Richardson, *Presidency of Dwight D. Eisenhower,* 64.

[27] Ambrose, *Eisenhower* 2:61, 64–65, 80–82, 136–40; Pach and Richardson, *Presidency of Dwight D. Eisenhower,* 64–68; Broadwater, *Eisenhower & the Anti-Communist Crusade,* 54–111.

By that time, Strauss had become a bitter personal enemy of the famous physicist. He deeply resented Oppenheimer's opposition to the development of the hydrogen bomb and the influence he exerted over other scientists, including those associated with the Atomic Energy Commission. Driven by a mixture of jealousy, personal animosity, and ideological zeal, Strauss set out to discredit the scientist by appointing a review panel of conservative cold warriors to investigate the case, marshalling testimony from Oppenheimer's enemies in the scientific community, and using information gathered through wiretaps or from classified government documents. In late May 1954 the review panel declared Oppenheimer a security risk, and shortly thereafter the AEC decided to withhold his security clearance.[28]

Although the conservative press defended Eisenhower's handling of the Oppenheimer affair, more liberal commentators, such as Joseph and Stewart Alsop, wasted no time in denouncing both the president and the AEC, especially Strauss.[29] Similar complaints came from the scientific community, which denounced not only the Oppenheimer affair but a variety of similar cases as well. Scientists were furious when Senator McCarthy, without opposition from the White House, launched a brief but wild investigation of the Army Engineering Laboratories, which had once employed convicted spy Julius Rosenberg. McCarthy found no evidence of treason, but the Army suspended nearly three dozen employees anyway. The ODM's Science Advisory Committee protested the witch hunt as well as the administration's decision to make security rather than loyalty the test of government employment. To its way of thinking, the Oppenheimer case, the McCarthy witch hunt, and the security program were hampering the free exchange of information, alienating large segments of the scientific community, and slowing the development of an active partnership between science and the state in the interest of national security. Their complaints resulted in few changes, however. Eisenhower was reluctant to stand up to McCarthy or to revise the new security policies, in part because he wanted a strong record on an issue that was

---

[28] For detailed treatments of the Oppenheimer case see Philip M. Stern, *The Oppenheimer Case: Security on Trial* (New York, 1969); John Major, *The Oppenheimer Hearing* (New York, 1971); Barton J. Bernstein, "In the Matter of J. Robert Oppenheimer," *Historical Studies in the Physical Sciences* 12 (1982):195–252; and Richard Pfau, *No Sacrifice Too Great: The Life of Lewis L. Strauss* (Charlottesville, 1984), 143–81. See also Lewis L. Strauss, *Men and Decisions* (Garden City, NY, 1962), 267–95; and Richard G. Hewlett and Jack M. Holl, *Atoms for Peace and War, 1953–1961: Eisenhower and the Atomic Energy Commission* (Berkeley, 1989), 44–48, 50–112.

[29] Merry, *Taking on the World*, 254–70.

important to conservatives in his party, in part because he thought that even the shadow of a doubt was enough to remove a federal employee in the field of national security.[30]

Scientists were right to see the administration's security program as a constraint on their relationship with the government, and there were other constraints as well. One of these had to do with divisions within the scientific community, which was not united in its view of national security. Influential scientists had earlier disagreed on the merits of using the atomic bomb against Japan and on the wisdom of developing the hydrogen bomb, just as they later disagreed on the merits of the Oppenheimer case and on the wisdom of security reviews. These divisions inhibited the development of a partnership between science and the state, as did Eisenhower's famous antiintellectualism. The president was more comfortable with business tycoons than with Nobel laureates, whom he sometimes considered impractical, and because of this he often kept his science advisers at arm's length while seeking advice from men like Killian or Strauss, who were really scientific administrators, in the tradition of Vannevar Bush, rather than scientists themselves.

In addition, there were differing visions of the kind of science–government partnership that was desirable. Although many scientists shared Vannevar Bush's notion of a scientific estate exercising an independent role in the formulation of government policy, Eisenhower's thinking was different. The president feared that federally funded scientists would join what he later called a military–industrial complex powerful enough to dominate public policy at the expense of sound democratic and fiscal principles. His own strategy aimed at a partnership with science that would preclude such a development, in large part by involving scientists not as independent actors in public policy but as instruments through which the president could assert greater control over the national security establishment.

Eisenhower's approach, like Truman's, put limits on the influence that science advisers could exert and was the same approach he followed in reorganizing the NSC and the Department of Defense. In all these cases, he was seeking not to undermine his prerogatives as president, but to protect them against new sources of power in American politics, notably the power of modern science and of a military establishment that had now become a permanent feature of American life. By holding these new powers at bay, Eisenhower hoped to guarantee the principle of civilian

---

[30] Damms, "Scientists and Statesmen," 203–5.

control, clear the way for a balanced budget and a tax cut, and thereby reconcile the search for security with traditional values. It was a never-ending struggle, especially when it came to the defense budget.

III

Eisenhower's first defense budget took off from the last budget that Truman had submitted to Congress in January 1953. Work on that budget had occupied much of Truman's last year in office and had involved another NSC appraisal of "United States Objectives and Strategy for National Security." The new document, NSC 135/3, continued the line of argument and the discursive strategy laid out in NSC-68 and similar documents. There was the same resort to a rhetoric of otherness that demonized the Soviet Union, not only to enshrine America's democratic identity by comparison but also its new role as the champion of democracy worldwide. There was the usual emphasis on constant struggle, too, and on perpetual preparedness, the indivisibility of liberty, and the need for discipline and sacrifice, all of which were standard themes in the ideology of national security.

According to NSC-135/3 and supporting documents, the United States aimed to contain the Soviet Union everywhere, which was not an easy task against a "totalitarian state" that was "heavily armed," hostile to any country not under its control, and thrived in an atmosphere of conflict. The Soviet Union, it noted, invested 16 percent of its gross national product in military production, spent another 7 percent on military research and development, and had an army of 175 divisions, an air force of more than 20,000 warplanes, and the capacity to overrun large portions of continental Europe, the Near East, and Southeast Asia. Even worse, it had a stockpile of 50 atomic bombs and was expected to have 100 such bombs by mid-1953, 190 by mid-1954, and 300 by mid-1955. Because of this military buildup, concluded NSC-135/3, the United States was actually more vulnerable than at any time since the end of World War II.[31]

Given this vulnerability, the administration had no choice but to maintain the military strength that was necessary to protect the "free world," prevent a general war, and deter local aggression, such as that in Korea. Although NSC-135/3 endorsed a policy of limited mobilization, those who drafted the document were clearly unhappy with the stretch-out

---

[31] NSC-135/3, 25 September 1953, and NSC-135/1 Annex, 22 August 1953, *FRUS, 1952–1954* 2:142–56, 89–113.

that Truman had ordered. To their way of thinking, the rapid growth of Soviet military power, the war in Korea, and the constant danger in Berlin, Iran, Egypt, and Indochina all highlighted the need to increase the production of selected military items.[32]

As they saw it, moreover, the stretch-out had allowed the economy to catch up with both civilian and military demand, industrial capacity had increased faster than expected, important bottlenecks had been overcome, and it was now possible to accelerate rearmament without overburdening the economy.[33] An ODM analysis supported this conclusion. "We are confronted by a new freedom of choice," reported the director, who urged the administration to increase defense production to "make up for lost time and past slippage." Indeed, the ODM was ready to increase existing programs by 10–12 percent, and by even more if Congress and the American people would accept higher taxes and economic controls.[34]

The question was: What would Congress and the people tolerate? This question touched on one of the central themes in the ideology of national security, namely the notion that sacrifices would be necessary if the United States was going to fulfill its mission as the global defender of democracy, which was how NSC-68 and similar documents sought to cast the country's new identity. Although the Soviet Union was economically inferior to the United States and would have difficulty matching an American military escalation, it was a "totalitarian" state and was thus in a better position than a democracy to curb consumption and restrain economic liberties in the name of rearmament. In the United States, everything depended "on the willingness of the American public to sustain" the burden of rearmament, including the burden of wage and price controls, heavier taxes, and lower rates of consumption. Americans had to see the "value" of such an effort, as one NSC document explained, because only then would they make the sacrifices that national security entailed.[35]

The Joint Chiefs saw the value of this effort, not surprisingly, but they did not have the president's support. Despite a two-year military buildup, not one of the armed services thought it could carry out its assigned tasks in the event of a general war. What they wanted was a force structure and

---

[32] In addition to the documents cited in the previous note see the earlier drafts of NSC-135/3 and various supporting documents in ibid., 73–86.

[33] NSC-135/1 Annex, 22 August 1953, ibid., 89–113.

[34] Undated statement by the director of defense mobilization, ibid., 156–64. See also memorandum for the president of discussion at the 123d NSC meeting, 24 September 1952, ibid., 136–39.

[35] NSC-135/1 Annex, 22 August 1953, ibid., 89–113.

a budget large enough to overturn the stretch-out that had begun the year before.[36] Secretary Lovett opposed this request and engaged the armed forces in a pitched budget battle that ran over several months, picking up support along the way from the Budget Bureau and the White House, where President Truman was reluctant to reverse the downward trend in defense expenditures. When the dust finally settled, the administration had decided on a total budget for fiscal year 1954 that included $41.3 billion in new obligatory authority for the military. This was nearly $8 billion below the president's request of the previous year and $3 billion below the sum that Congress had approved. Although he anticipated a deficit of $9.9 billion in fiscal year 1954, Truman told Congress that the downward trend in defense spending would continue over the next couple of years and would lead, eventually, to a plateau of $35 to $40 billion per year.[37]

Truman talked in his message about bringing the search for security into line with the search for solvency, which was the same theme that Eisenhower picked up when he began his own review of the budget. In the background, too, were NSC papers 141 and 142. In the second paper and related documents, the Joint Chiefs reaffirmed their support for the policies laid out in NSC-135/3 and argued once more that U.S. forces were inadequate to deal with a major military crisis.[38] A somewhat different argument emerged from NSC-141, a report that came to Truman in mid-January 1953 from Secretary of State Acheson, Secretary of Defense Lovett, and Director of Mutual Security W. Averell Harriman, all of whom concluded that current military programs, while fundamentally sound, were barely adequate to the challenge posed by the Soviet threat. They saw the need for additional economic and military aid to the Middle East and Asia, and for substantial investment in a system of continental defense that would protect the country's nuclear arsenal and mobilization base against the danger of a nuclear attack.[39]

---

[36] Joint Chiefs to Lovett, 29 August 1952, ibid., 113–14; Condit, *Test of War*, 290–91, 295–96.

[37] Condit, *Test of War*, 297–303; Truman to the secretary defense, the director of mutual security, the budget director, and the executive secretary of the NSC, 28 June 1952, RG 330, CD 111 (1954); Lawton to the secretary of the army, 9 July 1952, Records of the Office of the Secretary of the Army, RG 335, Office of the Secretary of the Army, General Correspondence, box 111; Lawton to Truman, 19 December 1952, Truman Papers, PSF-Subject File, box 150, folder: Bureau of the Budget, Budget – Military, 1945–53; and Truman, "Annual Budget Message to the Congress: Fiscal Year 1954," 9 January 1953, *Public Papers, Truman, 1952–1953*, 1128–64.

[38] Watson, *Joint Chiefs of Staff* 5:3, 5.

[39] NSC-141, 19 January 1953, *FRUS, 1952–1954* 2:209–22.

When the Eisenhower administration took office, then, it faced conflicting impulses. On the one hand were ongoing demands from the Joint Chiefs for increases in the military budget and new demands for additional expenditures on continental defense. But on the other were the downward trend in defense spending inaugurated by Truman, Eisenhower's own fear of the garrison state, and the tradition of antistatism and a balanced budget evident in Republican pressure to curb spending, cut taxes, and end economic controls. Of particular importance in this mix was Eisenhower's own conception of the country's democratic identity, which included such traditional notions as "individual liberty" and a "freer" economy, both of which required the elimination of the government controls that might be needed to support an accelerated rearmament. The country could live with such controls for brief emergencies, he wrote Bernard Baruch, but over time they would "bring a new conception of the relation of the individual to the state" and change forever the "kind of government under which we live." These convictions guided Eisenhower's decision of 6 February to terminate economic controls, and they also shaped his thinking about the defense budget.[40]

"The great problem," the president told the NSC, "was to discover a reasonable and respectable posture of defense" without "bankrupting the nation" – one, in other words, that reconciled the country's new mission as a global defender of democracy with its historic identity as a nation of free and independent citizens. Eisenhower hoped to avoid the inflationary deficits that drove up taxes and fed demands for economic controls, and he had support in this regard from Treasury Secretary Humphrey and Budget Director Dodge, both of whom encoded the nation's political identity in a rhetorical style similar to the one used by the president. The American people, both were convinced, could not define themselves as "free and democratic" when so much of their money went to the public treasury. Both thought that current government expenditures were "over the limit," and both were pledged to reduce taxes and balance the budget.[41]

---

[40] Gleason memorandum of discussion at the 134th NSC meeting, 25 February 1953, Eisenhower Papers, Papers as President, Whitman File, NSC Series, box 4, folder: 134th NSC Meeting, February 25, 1953; Eisenhower to Baruch, 10 March 1953, ibid., DDE Diary Series, box 3, folder: Eisenhower Diary, Dec. '52–July '53. See also Robert J. Donovan, *Eisenhower: The Inside Story* (New York, 1956), 31–32.

[41] Memorandum of discussion at the 131st NSC meeting, 11 February 1953, *FRUS, 1952–1954* 2:236–37; Gleason memorandum of discussion at the 132d NSC meeting, 19 February 1953, Eisenhower Papers, Papers as President, Whitman File, NSC Series, box 4, folder: 132d Meeting, February 18, 1953. See also the sources cited in the following note; and James

Indeed, almost every member of the new cabinet favored cuts in the government's budget, which meant cuts in national security expenditures. As Dodge explained, Truman's last budget had earmarked only $25 billion for nonsecurity expenditures, and most of that sum would go to mandatory programs, such as veterans' benefits, where cuts would involve "very unpleasant decisions" and could yield no more than a billion dollars in any event. Secretary of Defense Wilson agreed. He told the NSC that very little could be squeezed from Truman's budget unless the administration was willing to reevaluate the "basic objectives of its national security policy" or further "extend the period during which these objectives would be attained." Humphrey, Cutler, and Eisenhower offered similar assessments. Humphrey called for cuts of several billion dollars in the national security budget, Cutler said that nonsecurity expenditures amounted to little more than "chicken feed," and Eisenhower declared that it was time to get the defense "budget back into reasonable limits."[42]

At issue was where to reduce national security expenditures and by how much. To help in making these decisions Eisenhower appointed an independent panel of outside experts and instructed the NSC and other agencies to proceed with their own reviews according to assumptions spelled out by the Budget Bureau in a meeting of 5 March. In this meeting, the bureau began with the assumption that current government expenditures would produce a deficit of more than $43 billion through 1957. If the administration hoped to balance the budget, it had to start by reducing expenditures to $70.8 billion in fiscal year 1954 and to $62.6 billion in fiscal year 1955. And because nonsecurity expenditures could not be reduced by more than a billion dollars in each of these years, the major reductions of $6.8 and $14 billion in fiscal years 1954 and 1955, respectively, would have to come from the military budget and from the economic and military assistance programs administered by the Mutual

Lay to the NSC, 18 February 1953, enclosing Dodge to Humphrey, 13 February 1953, and Humphrey to Dodge, 16 February 1953, White House Office Records, Special Assistant for National Security Affairs, NSC Series, Subject Subseries, box 8, folder: President's Meeting with Civilian Consultants, 31 March 1953 re Review of Basic National Security Policy.

42 Gleason memorandum of discussion at the 132d NSC meeting, 19 February 1953, Eisenhower Papers, Papers as President, Whitman File, NSC Series, box 4, folder: 132d Meeting, February 18, 1953; Gleason memorandum of discussion at the 133d NSC meeting, ibid., folder: 133d Meeting, February 24, 1953; and Gleason memorandum of discussion at the 134th NSC meeting, 25 February 1953, ibid., 134th NSC Meeting, February 25, 1953. See also Gleason memorandum of discussion at the 135th NSC meeting, ibid., folder: 135th Meeting, March 5, 1953; and White House press release, 5 March 1953, White House Office Records, Special Assistant for National Security Affairs, NSC Series, Administrative Subseries, box 4, folder: Consultants – NSC (Feb.–March 1953).

Security Agency. The bureau proposed that mutual security expenditures be held to the 1953 level of $5.5 billion in fiscal year 1954 and be reduced to $4 billion in fiscal year 1955, and that defense spending be cut by $4.3 billion in fiscal year 1954 and by $9.4 billion in the following year. These reductions would trim the deficit in fiscal year 1954 and produce a balanced budget in fiscal year 1955, provided Congress renewed the Korean War taxes that were scheduled to expire.[43]

The bureau's projected reductions prompted a major row inside the administration. The Mutual Security Agency and the State Department predicted that any cuts in economic or military assistance would have "the most serious effects on the security interests of the United States." They would create substantial balance-of-payments problems in a host of countries, and would lead these countries to de-liberalize their import policies and protect their currency reserves through bilateral trade deals. Progress toward multilateral trade would come to a standstill, production would decline, unemployment would increase, and shrinking resources would lead to cuts in defense spending. Nor was that all. Without American aid, the French would oppose Germany's rearmament, and there would be irresistible pressure toward neutralism in Europe or toward some kind of rapprochement with the Soviet Union.[44]

It was hard to imagine a forecast more grim than this, but one was soon forthcoming from the armed forces. The Navy said that cuts of the size contemplated would render the fleet incapable of sustained operations.[45] The Army predicted the forced withdrawal of four American divisions from the Far Eastern Command and one from Europe by the end of fiscal year 1955. The Air Force said that any reduction would doom its goal of 143 combat wings by the end of fiscal year 1955, would eventually

---

[43] Gleason memorandum of discussion at the 135th NSC meeting, Eisenhower Papers, Papers as President, Whitman File, NSC Series, box 4, folder: 135th Meeting, March 5, 1953; Lay to the NSC, 5 March 1953, with attachments, and Deputy Secretary of Defense Roger M. Kyes to the Joint Chiefs, 19 March 1953, White House Office Records, Special Assistant for National Security Affairs, NSC Series, Subject Subseries, box 8, folder: President's Meeting with Civilian Consultants, March 31, 1953, re Review of Basic National Security Policies.

[44] Nitze to John Ohly, 16 March 1953, White House Office Records, Special Assistant for National Security Affairs, NSC Series, Subject Subseries, box 8, folder: President's Meeting with Civilian Consultants, March 31, 1953 re Review of Basic National Security Policies. See also Mutual Security Agency memorandum, "Title I (Europe) Defense Support, Analysis of Effect of Assumed Expenditure Limitations, General Appraisal of Consequences on European Program," ibid.

[45] Secretary of the Navy Robert Anderson to the secretary of the army, 16 March 1953, with attachments, White House Office Records, Special Assistant For National Security Affairs, NSC Series, Subject Subseries, box 8, folder: President's Meeting with Civilian Consultants, March 31, 1953, re Review of Basic National Security Policies.

force a shrinkage to only 79 wings, and would wreck the industrial mobilization base on which its preparedness depended.[46] Under the circumstances, the Joint Chiefs could not guarantee the current level of military operations in Korea or protect American troops there against the buildup of Communist air forces in Manchuria. Nor could they sustain a credible military presence in Japan and Europe or oppose Communist forces in local wars of aggression, except at the expense of commitments elsewhere. The general result, according to the chiefs, would be the "cumulative loss of positions of importance which could in turn eventually reduce the United States, short of general war, to an isolated and critically vulnerable position."[47]

In short, national security planners were convinced that reductions on a scale contemplated by the Budget Bureau would require a fundamental reversal of national policy as outlined in NSC-68 and its successors. It would force the armed services to reduce their commitments and would cripple their ability to deter Soviet aggression, counter local aggression, or deal effectively with a general war. Under worst-case scenarios, in which national security managers tended to specialize, NATO would dissolve, Berlin would be lost, Europe would shift toward neutralism, Indochina would fall to the Communists, and anti-U.S. elements throughout the developing world would grow bolder. These results, according to the Joint Chiefs, would "so increase the risk to the United States as to pose a grave threat to the survival of our allies and the security of this nation."[48]

Eisenhower must have felt like Chicken Little as he listened to these gloomy reports. Their warnings highlighted the conflict between the national security ideology intoned in the State Department, the Pentagon, and the Mutual Security Agency and his own desire to balance the budget

---

[46] Secretary of the Air Force Harold E. Talbott to Secretary Wilson, 16 March 1953, ibid. See also the first source cited in the following note.

[47] Omar Bradley to the secretary of defense, 19 March 1953, White House Office Records, Special Assistant for National Security Affairs, NSC Series, Subject Subseries, box 8, folder: President's Meeting with Civilian Consultants, March 31, 1953, re Review of Basic National Security Policies. See also Director of Mutual Security Harold Stassen to the NSC, 17 March 1953, and Wilson to the NSC, 24 March 1953, ibid.

[48] Bradley memorandums (2) for the secretary of defense, 19 March 1953, White House Office Records, Special Assistant For National Security Affairs, NSC Series, Subject Subseries, box 8, folder: President's Meeting with Civilian Consultants, March 31, 1953, re Review of Basic National Security Policies. See also Assistant Secretary of Defense Frank C. Nash to Stassen, 16 March 1953, ibid.; and Lay to the NSC, 30 March 1953, with enclosed "Summary of the Report of the Director for Mutual Security," Eisenhower Papers, Papers as President, Whitman File, NSC Series, box 4, folder: Documents Pertaining to Special NSC Meeting, March 31, 1953.

The Iron Cross 391

and reinvigorate the values it had come to symbolize. At NSC meetings in March, the Joint Chiefs recapitulated their warnings and the president, who was clearly exasperated, observed sarcastically "that perhaps the Council should have a report as to whether national bankruptcy or national destruction would get us first."[49] At the same meetings, Dodge defended the budget reductions he had outlined earlier, and Humphrey suggested at one point that defense appropriations be cut over the next two years to half the amount recommended in Truman's budget for fiscal year 1954. The country, Humphrey said, could continue the "great security programs" coming out of the Korean War only by bankrupting "the free world," abandoning "its way of life," and adopting "essentially totalitarian methods."[50] Eisenhower made the same point. Americans had to take "the road of disarmament," he argued, if they wanted "butter, bread, clothes, hospitals, schools, the good and necessary things of decent living."[51]

Similar thinking came from the panel of civilian consultants that Eisenhower had asked to study the budget. They urged the administration to tailor its security programs to the goal of a balanced budget, both because "the free world" depended on a strong American economy and because such an economy was essential to the survival of "our fundamental values and institutions." According to the consultants, the current level of expenditure could not be sustained over the long run without higher taxes, mounting deficits, and economic controls – all of which would "impair the incentive system and yield diminishing returns." The administration had to "make certain choices," they said. It had to eliminate wasteful duplications, reduce its stockpile of reserve weapons, concentrate on the development of industrial mobilization potential, and make clear decisions about what areas of the world had a claim on America's limited resources. It also had to take advantage of the country's comparative superiority in nuclear weapons and decide whether nuclear weapons should be used to end the Korean War, if only because such a strategy promised quick savings on the defense budget.[52]

---

49 Memorandum of discussion at the 138th NSC meeting, 25 March 1953, *FRUS, 1952–1954* 2:258–64.

50 Memorandum of discussion at the 138th NSC meeting, 25 March 1953, and memorandum of discussion at a special meeting of the NSC, 31 March 1953, *FRUS, 1952–1954* 2:258–64, 264–81.

51 Emmet J. Hughes diary, 16 March 1953, Emmet J. Hughes Papers (Mudd Library), box 1, folder: Diary Notes of Meetings, 1/12/53–10/15/53. See also Hughes diary, 17 March 1953, Hughes Papers, box 1, folder: Diary Notes of Meetings, 1/12/53–10/15/53.

52 Undated draft memorandum prepared for the NSC, *FRUS, 1952–1954* 2:281–87; and Hugh D. Farley to Cutler, 2 April 1953, with attached memorandum, "Defense Spending and the

Like the Joint Chiefs, Secretary of State John Foster Dulles, CIA Director Allen Dulles, and Director of Mutual Security Harold Stassen clearly had trouble making the choices recommended by the consultants. It was "another world speaking," said Emmet Hughes, Eisenhower's speech writer, it "was a lawyer's answer to a poet."[53] Drawing on the ideology of national security, these officials were convinced that liberty was indivisible and that national security expenditures were the only deterrent to war and revolution on a global scale. The United States, said Secretary Dulles, must hold on to its "vital outpost positions" in Latin America, Europe, Turkey, Japan, Indochina, India, Pakistan, Iran, and elsewhere because "the loss of any one of such positions would produce a chain reaction which would cost us the remainder."[54] Stassen used similar arguments to defend the mutual security program; Allen Dulles thought that any formula for disarmament was a "damn bad idea"; and C. D. Jackson, the president's special assistant, deplored Eisenhower's "PTA approach to the Russians." "Their idiom is totally different," Jackson said, and they would not be "impressed by talk about schools, hospitals," and other things that defense dollars could buy for the Soviet people.[55]

It all came down to Eisenhower. "I'm responsible for this country's goddam foreign policy," he told Hughes, and the national security establishment was "going to have one hell of a time stopping" his efforts to get a better balance between security and solvency.[56] Once again, Eisenhower resorted to a rhetorical strategy that conveyed his sense of the country's democratic values, which he compared to those of the Soviet other, and his conviction that democracy put some limits on what the new administration could do. Because the Soviet Union was a totalitarian country, he told the NSC, its leaders could "assign whatever proportion of national income they desire to warlike purposes." But the

National Budget: Views of the Consultants to the National Security Council," 31 March 1953, Eisenhower Papers, Papers as President, Whitman File, NSC Series, box 4, folder: Documents Pertaining to Special NSC Meeting, March 31, 1953. See also the memorandum of discussion at the 138th NSC meeting, 25 March 1953, and the memorandum of discussion at a special meeting of the NSC, 31 March 1953, *FRUS, 1952–1954* 2:258–64, 264–81.

53 Hughes diary, 16 March 1953, Hughes Papers, box 1, folder: Diary Notes of Meetings, 1/12/53–10/15/53.

54 Memorandum of discussion at a special meeting of the NSC, 31 March 1953, *FRUS, 1952–1954* 2:264–81. See also Hughes diary, 30 March 1953, Hughes Papers, box 1, folder: Diary Notes of Meetings, 1/12/53–10/15/53.

55 Hughes diary, 17 March 1953, Hughes Papers, box 1, folder: Diary Notes of Meetings, 1/12/53–10/15/53. See also memorandum of discussion at a special meeting of the NSC, 31 March 1953, *FRUS, 1952–1954* 2:264–81.

56 Hughes diary, 16 March 1953, Hughes Papers, box 1, folder: Diary Notes of Meetings, 1/12/53–10/15/53.

United States was a democratic country whose leaders must be "dedicated to raising the standards of living" for all people – not just for wealthy corporations, but for the "little guys" who found it hard to carry the burden of taxes.[57]

Guided by these sentiments, Eisenhower threw his weight behind a further downsizing of the national security budget for fiscal year 1954. He endorsed a recommendation coming from Secretary Wilson to cut defense spending, much as the Budget Bureau had suggested, and he supported cuts in the mutual security budget that were deeper than Stassen had favored, though not as deep as Dodge had recommended.[58] Like Truman, he wanted to balance other claims on the budget against the demands of security. And like Truman, he believed in a capital-intensive strategy of containment that concentrated American resources on missiles, airpower, and atomic weapons, not manpower, which was less expensive abroad than it was in the United States. It was far "cheaper," he said on one occasion, "to create and maintain foreign divisions in the field than to go ahead so rapidly in the development of additional U.S. divisions."[59]

Out of these debates over the budget for fiscal year 1954 came NSC-149/2. Approved by the NSC in late April 1953, the document said that a strong American economy was essential to the "survival of the free world" and that a balanced budget and reasonable taxes were the keys to such an economy. In the immediate future, to be sure, the United States had to build strength across the free world, end the war in Korea, and aid the French effort in Indochina, and these commitments would postpone the day when taxes could be reduced and the budget could be balanced. Nevertheless, the administration could make progress toward its economic goals by eliminating waste in the armed forces, developing its nuclear capability, slowing the expansion of NATO forces, and giving up the idea that American military power had to reach an arbitrary level of readiness by a predetermined date. By doing these things, it could reduce military manpower by 250,000 troops in fiscal year 1954, reduce

---

[57] Memorandum of discussion at the 138th NSC meeting, 25 March 1953, memorandum of discussion at a special meeting of the NSC, 31 March 1953, *FRUS, 1952–1954* 2:258–64, 264–81; Hughes diary, 20 March 1953, Hughes Papers, box 1, folder: Diary Notes of Meetings, 1/12/53–10/15/53.

[58] Memorandum of discussion at a special meeting of the NSC, 31 March 1953, undated draft memorandum prepared for the NSC, memorandum of discussion at the 140th NSC meeting, 22 April 1953, memorandum of discussion at the 141st NSC meeting, 28 April 1953, and NSC-149/2, 29 April 1953, *FRUS, 1952–1954* 2:264–81, 281–87, 291–301, 302–5, 305–16.

[59] Memorandum of discussion at the 138th NSC meeting, 25 March 1953, *FRUS, 1952–1954* 2:258–64.

defense obligatory authority to $36 billion, and reduce mutual security appropriations from $7.5 to $5.1 billion. Of particular importance in achieving these reductions would be a temporary curtailment of the Air Force buildup, the major area where substantial short-term savings were possible.[60]

The results of the budget exercise turned out to be much "better than he had hoped for," Eisenhower told the NSC, although it remained to be seen if congressional conservatives would agree.[61] Eisenhower met with Republican party leaders on 30 April and proceeded to give them the good news first: The administration was going to reduce Truman's proposed budget for fiscal year 1954 by at least $8.4 billion. One billion dollars would come from domestic expenditures and the balance from national security spending. The latter would be reduced primarily by replacing the idea of a fixed date of maximum danger, by which American forces had to reach an arbitrary state of preparedness, with the idea of a "floating D-Day," which would permit the armed services to adjust their force levels and budget requirements to changing circumstances. Together with a greater emphasis on mobilization potential, less emphasis on forces in being and a large stockpile of reserve material, the new concept would permit a military posture that could be sustained over the long haul. The bad news was that enormous short-term savings were out of the question. It would take time to complete outstanding commitments and achieve the new posture, and during that time the budget could not be balanced and taxes could not be cut without adding to the deficit.[62]

The reaction took Eisenhower by surprise. Most of the Republican leaders were disappointed that budget reductions were not greater and that taxes had to be continued, but they seemed to understand when Dodge explained that domestic programs had been cut to the bone, that 67 percent of the budget was devoted to national security, and that reductions in that area had gone as far as possible in the current year. The exception was Senator Taft, who could not even "express the deepness of his disappointment" at a program that committed the Republicans to spending as much as the Truman administration had ever spent. The

[60] NSC-162/2 enclosed in Lay report to the NSC, 29 April 1953, FRUS, 1952–1954 2:305–16. See also Iwan W. Morgan, Eisenhower Versus 'The Spenders': The Eisenhower Administration, the Democrats and the Budget, 1953–60 (London, 1990), 50–53.

[61] NSC-149, 3 April 1953, White House Office Records, Special Assistant for National Security Affairs, NSC Series, Policy Papers Subseries, box 4, folder: NSC 149/2 – Basic National Security Policies and Programs in Relation to Their Costs.

[62] "Remarks of the President re National Policies and the FY 1954 Budget," 20 April 1953, C. D. Jackson Records (Eisenhower Library), box 2, folder: Cutler, Robert.

program dashed all hopes of eliminating the Korean War taxes, according to Taft, or of balancing the budget, both of which required deeper cuts in the defense budget than Eisenhower was willing to make. On the contrary, having upheld the principle of economy in arguments with the Joint Chiefs, the president now found himself telling the Republican leadership that "no one should let the budget-cutting principle override national security." His arguments prevailed with most of those present, but not with Taft, who left the White House convinced that his party was on the way to a major defeat in the 1954 elections.[63] It was "one of the worst days I have experienced since January 20th," Eisenhower confided to his diary.[64]

Although Taft would eventually moderate his criticism, Eisenhower still faced a battle on two fronts when his budget reached Capitol Hill. On one, he struggled against other Republicans who were more interested in cutting taxes than in national security, and on the other against leading Democrats who wanted to spend more on defense than the president thought desirable. The major Republican challenge came from Congressman Reed of New York, who still chaired the House Ways and Means Committee. What Eisenhower wanted was progress toward a balanced budget, which he would accomplish by reducing government expenditures and maintaining some of the wartime taxes enacted in 1950 and 1951. He told Congress in a special message of 20 May that he would permit the wartime increase in personal income taxes to expire as scheduled at the end of 1953, but not earlier. Nor would he approve any reduction in the other wartime taxes, and he actually urged Congress to extend the excess-profits tax for six months beyond its scheduled expiration date of 30 June 1953.[65] Reed, on the other hand, sought to reduce taxes wherever he could, even if it led to deeper cuts in the defense budget than Eisenhower thought prudent.

The confrontation began when Reed introduced H.R. 1, a bill that would advance by six months the date when the wartime increase in personal income taxes was scheduled to lapse. Unwilling to sacrifice the revenue that would be lost under the measure, Eisenhower worked with other Republicans to keep H.R. 1 bottled up in the House Rules Committee. The maneuver infuriated Reed and his allies, who reminded the

---

[63] L. A. Minnich, Jr., notes on legislative leadership meeting, 30 April 1953, Eisenhower Papers, Papers as President, Whitman File, DDE Diary Series, box 4, folder: Staff Notes January–December 1953.

[64] Eisenhower diary, 1 May 1953, Dwight D. Eisenhower Diaries (Eisenhower Library), box 1/1, folder: DDE Personal Diary, Dec. 1952–8/19/53.

[65] *Congressional Quarterly Almanac, 1953,* 84–85, 414–15.

Republicans of their campaign promise to cut taxes as well as balance the budget. They wanted to know why Britain and Canada could reduce taxes while the United States could not, and why the American people should cover the cost of foreign give-away programs while their own taxes were oppressively high.[66]

Already upset by the fate of H.R. 1, Reed could scarcely believe it when the administration also proposed to extend the excess-profits tax for another six months. Although Eisenhower opposed the tax in principle, he needed the $800 million in revenue it generated if he was going to finance his national security program and still contain the deficit. "No citizen," he said, favors a tax cut "at the price of essential security." Secretary Humphrey took up the same argument in presenting the administration's proposal to Congress. Containing the deficit, curbing inflation, and safeguarding the dollar, said Humphrey, had to take priority over a tax cut, as did the security needs of the nation. "The danger of an atomic Pearl Harbor is real," he argued in customary hyperbole. Congress would "gamble" with the nation's security if it cut taxes and forced offsetting reductions in the defense budget.[67]

Most Republicans were willing to go along with the administration, but not Reed, who was ready to terminate the excess-profits tax even if it required a $2 billion cut in the mutual security program. When he opened hearings on the administration's bill to extend the tax, Reed stacked the hearings with business leaders who opposed the measure and refused to report a bill for consideration by the whole House. Eisenhower countered with an extensive campaign to win support in the business community and in Congress. He put his own status as a party leader firmly behind the outcome and lined up enough support from Republicans to bypass Reed and get the proposed bill to the floor without action in the Ways and Means Committee. The unusual maneuver forced Reed to convene his committee for a vote on the administration's bill, whereupon the majority overrode the congressman's opposition and moved the bill to the floor, where an ugly debate ensued.

In the floor debate, Reed and his allies once again warned of reprisals at the polls if the Republicans did not redeem their promises to cut taxes and balance the budget by doing away with the foreign give-away programs of the Truman era. And once again they wondered how the

[66] *Congressional Record, 1953* 99:1904–8, 2643–44, 3012–13; *Congressional Quarterly Almanac, 1953*, 422–23.
[67] *Congressional Quarterly, 1953*, 416–22.

administration could favor Europeans with more benefits than were bestowed on American taxpayers. In response, the president's supporters highlighted the economies that had been achieved in the budget for fiscal year 1954. There was progress, they said, and more would follow, but it must not come at the expense of national security. In the end, Eisenhower scored an impressive victory over the conservative wing of his own party: Congress refused to consider H.R. 1 and extended the excess-profits tax for another six months.[68]

The challenge thereafter was to defend the national security budget against Republican economizers who wanted to reduce foreign aid, and angry Democrats who were dismayed by Eisenhower's defense cuts.[69] The Republicans would accept minimal cuts in the defense budget, usually just enough to protect their reputation as fiscal conservatives, but were more aggressive when it came to the mutual security program, which many of them viewed as an ill-conceived effort to buy foreign friends at the expense of the American taxpayer. They refused to accept Eisenhower's recommendation of $5.1 billion for mutual security, demanding instead that the program either be liquidated or capped at no more than $3 billion in new appropriations and no more than $5 billion in new expenditures, including the unexpended balance carried over from previous years. The savings, they said, would help to balance the budget and set the stage for a tax cut in the near future.

The administration and its supporters countered by turning the economy argument upside down. They argued that foreign aid was the least expensive way to safeguard the national security, emphasized the savings they had achieved, and claimed that additional reductions would amount to false economy. Without American aid, they said, certain countries would fall to communism, the United States would be increasingly isolated, and Congress would have to run the defense budget to new heights. These arguments finally carried the day as Congress appropriated $4.5 billion for the mutual security program and reappropriated another $2 billion in carry-over funds from previous years.[70]

Eisenhower also prevailed in his skirmish with the Democrats, who, generally speaking, supported his position on tax cuts and mutual security but were upset with his decision to achieve economies by stretching

[68] Ibid.; *Congressional Record, 1953* 99:7111–13, 7575–81, 8481–518, 8851–77.
[69] Criticism also came from warhawks in the press, such as Joseph Alsop. See Hughes diary, 1 May 1953, Hughes Papers, box 1, folder: Diary Notes of Meetings, 1/12/53–10/15/53.
[70] *Congressional Quarterly Almanac, 1953*, 156–224; *Congressional Record, 1953* 99: 7764–97.

out the construction and purchase of military aircraft. As in the past, the Air Force tried to reverse the president's decision on Capitol Hill, where General Hoyt Vandenberg, who was retiring as Air Force Chief of Staff, said that Eisenhower's budget would leave the United States with the "second best" air force. The Democrats picked up on this theme, with former Secretary of the Air Force Stuart Symington, now a senator from Missouri, leading the charge. Symington attacked the Republicans for doing what they had denounced when Truman was in office: imposing arbitrary budget ceilings and letting "accountants" in the Budget Bureau guide the defense budget. He and others wanted to restore a good chunk of the money denied the Air Force and even demanded that Secretary Wilson resign.[71]

The Republicans fought back. The Air Force, argued Secretary Wilson, had all the money it could spend in a single year, what with new appropriations added to the billions of dollars in unexpended funds carried over from previous years. Other Republicans accused General Vandenberg of the usual "spring war dance" in which the services tried to drive up their budgets by claiming that war was imminent and the Soviets were more menacing than ever. Still others stressed how important it was to get a grip on defense spending if the country wanted to balance the budget and cut taxes. They again quoted Lenin, Stalin, and other Kremlin leaders to the effect that Soviet policy aimed to bankrupt the United States. And they again argued that economic and security considerations had to be balanced if the United States hoped to contain the Soviet Union over the long haul.[72]

Eisenhower's reputation as a war hero, who presumably knew exactly how to build an economical defense, soon became a major theme in the debate. The president was the expert, Wilson said, and had personally approved every item in the budget. Eisenhower also encouraged this strategy and deliberately staked his reputation on the outcome. The Air Force budget represented his "own views," he wrote to one Republican, and had his "personal endorsement." He decried efforts by "service partisans" to seek more money than they could spend, criticized those who sought a "disproportionate" degree of military protection, and argued,

---

[71] *Congressional Quarterly Almanac, 1953*, 136–40; *Congressional Record, 1953* 99:5600. My discussion in the last two paragraphs and in the following paragraphs is based on the floor debates over the defense budget as reported in the *Congressional Record, 1953* 99:5600–5603, 6218–19, 6436–40, 6634, 6932–33, 7237–50, 7730–32, 7803–55, 7932–78, 9452–9514, 9580–9616, 10252–58, 10339–49.

[72] *Congressional Record, 1953* 99:6439, 7933.

as Truman had before, that "total" security was "unattainable" at a cost the country could afford, both economically and politically. Anything like it would bankrupt the treasury and require a "prolonged and total mobilization – which means, practically, regimentation."[73] By August the president had prevailed. Both houses of Congress had passed a bill authorizing about $34.4 billion in new obligatory authority for defense. The amount was $1.3 billion less than Eisenhower had requested, a reduction he had actually encouraged, and included $11.3 billion for the Air Force, which was more or less the amount the president had sought.[74]

In the end, the specter of the garrison state and the danger it posed to American democracy had helped Eisenhower to prevail in the budget battle, as it had in the tax battle. Much like Truman before him, his goal was to contain communism around the world without laying the foundations for economic and political regimentation at home. And with this goal in mind, he had sought to balance the needs of security against those of the economy, the claims of defense against the ideal of a balanced budget and all the values it had come to symbolize. The first step in that effort had come with the revisions to Truman's last defense budget, and the next step would follow six months later when Eisenhower submitted the first budget of his own – that for fiscal year 1955.

IV

Work on the budget for fiscal year 1955 proceeded from the assumption that a proper balance between security and solvency required a major revision of American military strategy, out of which would come Eisenhower's New Look, as the revised strategy came to be called. To a large extent, the New Look would merely bring into sharper focus some of the older elements of military strategy, including aid to allies abroad, a military posture that could be sustained over the long haul, a mobilization base on which the country could build in the event of an emergency, and a capital-intensive containment that relied heavily on air–atomic power. In theory, however, these established elements would be combined with additional initiatives, including a redeployment of American troops, a mobile reserve in the United States, and a new system of continental defense, and the new combination would enable the administration to reconcile the nation's security needs with its "fundamental values and institutions."

73 Eisenhower to Representative Scrivner, 30 June 1953, *Congressional Record, 1953,* 99:7817. See also the source cited in the following note.
74 *Congressional Quarterly Almanac, 1953,* 136–40.

The revised strategy emerged from several major studies and many months of acrimonious debate, during which Humphrey and Dodge could always be counted on to explain the "rude facts" of the budget to their colleagues. If spending continued at the current rate and if taxes were allowed to lapse as scheduled, the Treasury Department and the Budget Bureau expected a deficit of somewhere between $8.7 and $9.4 billion in fiscal year 1955. That "takes us right back to Truman," Humphrey told one meeting, referring to the budget deficit in the last fiscal year of the previous administration. Although the current administration had been elected to cut taxes and balance the budget, the secretary fumed, it "hasn't done a damn thing but go along with the programs and policies of the past Administration."[75] New deficits loomed and the administration was in the embarrassing position of seeking congressional consent to another increase in the nation's debt limit. Even more disappointing was the realization that the armistice in Korea promised no real savings, because that part of the defense budget would be used to maintain American troops in Asia or to train and equip the South Korean army.[76]

The administration was "in a hell of a fix," Eisenhower admitted. The Democrats wanted more spending on defense while farmers, veterans, and other groups complained about reductions in the programs from which they benefited. Henry Cabot Lodge suggested still further cuts in nondefense spending, but Dodge ruled that alternative out. The budget contained less than $25 billion in nondefense expenditures, as Dodge noted, and the controllable portion of these expenditures had already been cut 10 percent below the level for fiscal year 1953, and was actually somewhat lower than in fiscal year 1952. What remained of the nondefense budget went to service the national debt or for veterans benefits, social security, and other programs that were "really untouchable." As a result, said Secretary Wilson, "at least 10 billion more" had to be cut from the defense and mutual security budgets, and a reduction of that

---

[75] Hughes diary, 22 May 1953, Hughes Papers, box 1, folder: Diary Notes of Meetings, 1/15/53–10/15/53; memorandum of discussion at the 154th NSC meeting, 15 July 1953, Eisenhower Papers, Papers as President, Whitman File, NSC Series, box 4, folder: 154th NSC meeting, July 14, 1953. See also the sources cited in the following note.

[76] In addition to the sources cited in the previous note, see memorandum of discussion at the 156th NSC meeting, 24 July 1953, Eisenhower Papers, Papers as President, Whitman File, NSC Series, box 4, folder: 156th NSC meeting, July 23, 1953; Humphrey to Eisenhower, 29 July 1953, ibid., DDE Diary Series, box 3, folder: DDE Diary, Dec. 1952–July 1953; and minutes of cabinet meeting, 27 August 1953, ibid., Cabinet Series, box 2, folder: Cabinet Meeting of August 27, 1953.

size would require more than eliminating waste, promoting efficiencies, and trimming current programs. It would not be enough to "patch up the old jalopy," said Engine Charlie. The administration would have to get out "A BRAND NEW MODEL," the "best damn streamlined model" ever – and would have "to do it in 6 months."[77]

The search for a "new model" had begun with NSC-149/2 and now proceeded through NSC-153/1, approved by the NSC on 10 June. Both documents tried self-consciously to reconcile the country's "fundamental values and institutions" with the new ideology of national security, its political identity as a democratic nation with its new global mission. According to NSC-153/1, the United States faced two major threats: the "formidable power and aggressive policy" of the Soviet Union and the weakening of the American economy that would result from "opposing the Soviet threat over a sustained period." Containing the Soviet menace required a superior stockpile of nuclear weapons, the ability to inflict massive damage on the Soviet Union, and a system of continental defense sufficient to protect the country's mobilization base and nuclear stockpile. Maintaining a strong economy required a balanced budget, reasonable taxes, and a high level of productive activity.[78] By giving apparently equal weight to these military and economic goals, NSC-153/1 carried "water on both shoulders," as Emmet Hughes had said of its predecessor.[79] It set economic against security concerns in a broad statement of policy that lacked specific content on force levels, military strategy, and cost estimates. These specifics would determine whether the need for security and the search for solvency could be balanced, and they were soon forthcoming in two initiatives that got underway as the administration was preparing the budget for fiscal year 1955.

Eisenhower launched one of these initiatives at a conference in the sunroom of the White House in May 1953. Known as Project Solarium, it sought to evaluate the containment policy as compared with more

---

[77] Memorandum of discussion at the 154th NSC meeting, 15 July 1953, Eisenhower Papers, Papers as President, Whitman File, NSC Series, box 4, folder: 154th NSC Meeting, July 14, 1952, and Hughes diary, 22 May 1953, Hughes Papers, box 1, folder: Diary Notes of Meetings, 1/15/53–10/15/53. See also Dodge to Eisenhower with enclosed reports, 28 September 1953, Eisenhower Papers, Papers as President, Whitman File, Administration Series, box 12, folder: Dodge, Joseph M., 1952–53.

[78] NSC-153/1, 10 June 1953, enclosed in Lay report to the NSC, 10 June 1953, *FRUS, 1952–1954* 2:378–86. See also the memorandum of the discussion at the 149th NSC meeting, 11 June 1953, Eisenhower Papers, Papers as President, Whitman File, NSC Series, box 4, folder: 149th NSC Meeting, June 9, 1953.

[79] Hughes diary, 25 June 1953, Hughes Papers, box 1, folder: Diary Notes of Meetings 1/12/53–10/15/53.

aggressive alternatives. One such alternative would roll back the Iron Curtain to liberate the enslaved population of the Soviet bloc, and the other would rely on the threat of a general war to keep the Soviets from expanding beyond their present area of influence. Separate task forces examined these two alternatives and their financial implications, while a third group studied the containment policy. Because containment would continue present U.S. commitments and strategy, it promised no reduction in national security expenditures. On the contrary, the task force that studied containment resisted the notion that national security had economic limits and argued instead that effective containment would cost more than had been allotted in the most recent budget and would never be less than $40 billion annually. The American economy, it said, could handle this burden if tax rates were maintained or increased. It saw the tax question as a political, not an economic, question, and concluded that higher taxes, budget deficits, and a growing national debt did not pose a threat to the American way of life "comparable to the Soviet threat."[80]

The economic consequences of the rollback strategy ran in a similar direction, while the third strategy charted a course more in line with Eisenhower's economic concerns. According to the task force that evaluated the rollback option, this strategy would entail a stronger military posture and new political, economic, and propaganda initiatives to weaken and disrupt the Soviet bloc. These requirements would involve substantial additions to the national security budget, which would climb to roughly $60 billion in fiscal years 1954 and 1955, before leveling off at approximately $45 billion in fiscal year 1958. Such a heavy investment would require higher taxes as well as stand-by economic controls, both options that Eisenhower, Humphrey, and Dodge found difficult to swallow. They were more likely to favor the third strategy, which would counter Soviet expansion with general war, because that strategy would contain the cost of defense by relying more heavily on airpower, missiles, and nuclear weapons, less heavily on expensive manpower, and thus avoiding involvement in an endless series of local wars.[81]

The NSC considered the three task force reports at a meeting on 16 July 1953. Although the minutes of the meeting are brief, they give no

[80] For the reports issued by the Solarium task forces see the undated enclosure in memorandum to the NSC by the executive secretary, 22 July 1953, *FRUS, 1952–1954* 2:399–434. The quote is from ibid., 404. For background on the Solarium Project, see the documents in ibid., 323–26, 349–54, 360–66, 441–42. See also ibid., 388–93.

[81] Undated enclosure in memorandum to the NSC by the executive secretary, 22 July 1953, ibid., 399–434.

hint that Eisenhower and the economizers were ready to abandon their concern for the country's traditional political values to accommodate any of the more costly recommendations coming from the reports. On the contrary, they again reveal their sense of the limits that democratic capitalism placed on what the administration could do. "If you demand of a free people over a long period of time more than they want to give," Eisenhower told the council, "you can obtain what you want only by using more and more controls; and the more you do this, the more you lose the individual liberty which you are trying to save and become a garrison state." With these warnings in the background, the council referred the Solarium reports to its staff for further work and asked the three task forces to consider ways of combining the best of their recommendations.[82]

In the meantime, a second budget initiative had gotten underway at a White House meeting of 14 July, when Eisenhower asked the Joint Chiefs for a complete reassessment of the country's military capabilities in light of its global responsibilities and the need to reduce government expenditures.[83] The president expected the group to balance economic and security considerations within the framework of a new military strategy, which is what it tried to do in a report presented to the NSC in August. The report envisioned a major redeployment of American troops from Europe and Asia to the United States, and the creation there of a mobile reserve that could respond to aggression overseas but also aid in continental defense. To maintain a credible deterrent abroad, indigenous forces in Japan, Korea, and Europe would replace the American troops that were withdrawn, and the United States would increase its air–atomic power and retain its air and naval bases on the periphery of the Communist bloc. It would take time and money to accomplish this redesign, Radford admitted. But its achievement would effect important savings in the defense budget, particularly as ground forces were scaled

---

[82] Memorandum by the special assistant to the president for national security affairs, 16 July 1953, as annexed to the minutes of the 155th NSC meeting, 16 July 1953, *FRUS, 1952–1954* 2:394–98. See also memorandum of discussion at the 157th NSC meeting, 30 July 1953, memorandum by the special assistant for national security affairs, 31 July 1953, and memorandum by the executive secretary of the State Department Policy Planning Staff, 12 August 1953, ibid., 435–40, 440–41, 441–42.

[83] Matthew B. Ridgway, *Soldier: The Memoirs of Matthew B. Ridgway* (New York, 1956), 266–67; Glenn H. Snyder, "The 'New Look' of 1953," in Warner R. Schilling, Paul Y. Hammond, and Glenn H. Snyder, *Strategy, Politics, and Defense Budgets* (New York, 1962), 413; Stephen Jurika, Jr., *From Pearl Harbor to Vietnam: The Memoirs of Admiral Arthur W. Radford* (Stanford, 1980), 317–21.

back and returned to the United States, where they could be maintained at less cost.[84]

Essentially, the Joint Chiefs would build on the capital-intensive strategy of containment that had come out of the Truman administration, and in doing so would take that strategy several steps further. This was true of their decision to rely more explicitly on the deterrent power of nuclear weapons, in effect elevating that reliance to the level of doctrine; of their emphasis on continental defense, an issue that had arisen only at the end of the Truman administration; and of their apparent resolve to withdraw some of the troops that Truman had dispatched to Europe. That resolve was tested at an NSC meeting on 27 August, when Army Chief of Staff Matthew B. Ridgway disputed the need to redeploy and downsize American forces. Ridgway did not believe that airpower alone could pose a credible deterrent. He defended the concept of balanced forces and warned that any redeployment of American troops from Asia and Europe would risk the security of those areas.[85]

Radford and General Twining, the Air Force chief of staff, countered by arguing that current deployments in Korea, Japan, and Germany had always been temporary expedients, pending the development of local forces, and could not be maintained without going to something like a full mobilization. Secretary Dulles appeared to agree, arguing that other countries had to pay more of the cost of their own defense. The administration, he said, was "in no position to extract from our people what tyrannical rulers could extract from their people," and any attempt to do so would "bust" the Treasury and crush democracy. As was so often the case, Dulles had inscribed the country's political identity in a way that ruled out a whole set of policy options as basically un-American, which is exactly where Humphrey entered the discussion. Unless the country downsized its military establishment, he also argued, it would have to live with a permanent draft, mandatory economic controls, and other elements of tyranny that were incompatible with its democratic traditions and system of free enterprise. Because the Joint Chiefs had embraced the idea of downsizing, he considered their report to be a "terrific" document, a way to avoid unmitigated disaster, and easily the "most important thing that had happened in this country since January 20."[86]

Following this exchange, the NSC approved the report on a tentative basis and the president let it be known that he considered it "a

---

[84] Memorandum of discussion at the 160th NSC meeting, 27 August 1953, *FRUS, 1952–1954* 2:443–55.

[85] Ibid.

[86] Ibid.

crystallized and clarified statement" of American national security policy "since World War II." The United States had never intended to build "a Roman Wall" around parts of the world, he wrote to General Alfred Gruenther. The stationing of American troops abroad had always been a "stop-gap operation" and no substitute for the strategic reserve and the mobilization base that were essential to U.S. security. Still, approval of the report did not quiet all concerns about where its recommendations would lead. Some doubted that America's allies were in a position to increase their defense spending to offset reductions on the U.S. side, and there was also the danger that Japan, Korea, and the NATO allies would see America's redeployment as "camouflaged isolation" and retreat toward neutralism or toward a rapprochement with the Soviet Union.[87]

These concerns were shared by Eisenhower and Dulles, whose correspondence on the subject at times seemed to reduce policy options to dreary choices. The more Dulles thought about it, the more he worried that allied leaders would see the redeployment of American troops and the new emphasis on continental defense as "proof of an isolationist trend" in the United States. Collective security arrangements might then break down, the balance of power might shift in favor of the Soviet Union, and the United States might end up spending more, not less, on defense. Dulles wondered if the only way around these problems might not be a negotiated end to the Cold War. Eisenhower was pessimistic about the prospects for such a settlement, but equally unhappy with the alternatives. With the Korean armistice, he told Dulles, the American people were less inclined to cover the cost of current national security programs and more inclined to lower taxes and spend more on neglected public programs, from drought relief to farm supports. Nor was that the worst of it. Eisenhower still believed that the high cost of security could eventually drive the American people to "some form of dictatorial government," or to an effort to protect their liberties through a preemptive strike against the Soviet Union.[88]

The ambivalence apparent in Eisenhower's exchange with Dulles was also apparent in NSC-162, the new statement of basic national security policy that emerged from the Solarium studies and the report of the Joint Chiefs. NSC-162 was the byproduct of intense debate and disagreement

---

[87] Memorandum by the special assistant to the president for national security affairs to the secretary of state, 3 September 1953, ibid., 455–57; and Eisenhower to General Gruenther, 27 October 1953, Eisenhower Papers, Papers as President, Whitman File, DDE Diary Series, box 3, folder: DDE Diary, October 1953. See also the source cited in note 84.

[88] Memorandum by the secretary of state, 6 September 1953, and memorandum by the president to the secretary of state, 8 September 1953, *FRUS, 1952–1954* 2:457–60, 460–63.

on the NSC's Planning Board, which drafted the document. On one level, it repeated some of the familiar themes in the ideology of national security, including the notion of permanent preparedness and the view of the Cold War as long-term conflict with a dangerous and heavily armed enemy. Though basically content with the policy of containment, the board was willing to employ some of the more aggressive tactics suggested in the Solarium studies, including political, economic, and covert measures to divide the Communist bloc and break up the Soviet Union. It also embraced much of what the Joint Chiefs had said in their report of late August, recommending a large arsenal of nuclear weapons capable of inflicting "massive" damage on the Soviet Union, a highly mobile strategic reserve, a strong mobilization base, and a system of continental defense that could protect the country's striking power and mobilization base against a Soviet attack.[89]

But if the Soviet threat suggested no limit on U.S. defense spending, NSC-162 quickly countered with a long analysis of the connection between economic and military security. A sound economy was the bedrock of defense production, it said, not to mention higher living standards and free political institutions. Excessive government spending, even for national security, would lead to budget deficits, inflation, or "repressive taxation." It would undermine the currency, discourage investment, limit growth, and impair the national defense. Not surprisingly, these sections of NSC-162 were drafted by the Treasury Department, the Budget Bureau, and the Council of Economic Advisers, where policy makers also wanted an opening section similar to the one in NSC-153/1. That section would list two equally weighted threats to "the fundamental values and institutions of the United States": The "formidable power and aggressive policy of the communist world," and the "serious weakening of our economy" and "way of life" that would result if national security programs overburdened the country's human and financial resources.[90]

These differences came before the NSC at three difficult meetings in October. The Joint Chiefs still gave the Soviet threat the highest priority, even if containing that threat fundamentally altered "the American way of life." Arthur Flemming, who headed the ODM, took a similar position, as did Dulles, who said that balancing the budget at any cost was "doctrinaire" and had "caused the Hoover Administration to blow up."

---

[89] NSC-162, 30 September 1953, *FRUS, 1952–1954* 2:491–514.

[90] Ibid. See also the memorandum of discussion at the 164th NSC meeting, 1 October 1953, Eisenhower Papers, Papers as President, Whitman File, NSC Series, box 4, folder: 164th NSC Meeting, October 1, 1953.

He and Wilson hoped that economic growth would make it possible to have guns and butter both, but if government expenditures had to be reduced then Dulles wanted to know if it was wise to spend "$2 billion annually for price supports of agriculture," when that money could be used for defense.

Dodge, Humphrey, and Eisenhower took the other side of the argument, using again a rhetorical strategy that differentiated the American way of life from totalitarian policies and identified those policies, not just the Soviet menace, as a threat to the country's democratic ideals. Dodge saw "no hope of balancing the budget" without additional cuts in the national security program; Humphrey said that reductions had already been made in other areas; and all three were convinced that unbalanced budgets, economic controls, and high taxes posed a threat to the American economy and American institutions every bit as great as the Soviet threat. If pushed to its logical limits, Eisenhower said, the position taken by the State and Defense departments "would lead to both general mobilization and out-and-out regimentation." "We could lick the whole world," he continued, only "if we were willing to adopt the system of Adolph Hitler" rather than a democratic system in which popular support for national security had to be voluntary and could not be sustained in the face of economic controls, burdensome taxes, and unrelenting reductions in domestic programs. "We were engaged in defending a way of life as well as a territory," Eisenhower reminded the council, and "recognition of this fact should comprise the first statement in the policy paper."[91]

The final document, NSC-162/2, mentioned in its preamble two basic national security problems: the Soviet threat and the need to contain that threat without "seriously weakening the U.S. economy or undermining our fundamental values and institutions." The economizers had prevailed in the equal weighting of these problems. But the body of the document still listed the Soviet Union as the "primary" threat and Eisenhower rejected language that would mandate a scheduled redeployment of American troops and a progressive reduction in U.S. economic and military assistance programs. Humphrey had wanted to begin the redeployment "reasonably soon" and carry it out over the next few years, the Joint Chiefs had opposed such a timetable, and Eisenhower had agreed with Dulles that redeployment needed to be handled with caution

---

[91] Memorandum of discussion at the 165th NSC meeting, 7 October 1953, and NSC-162/2, enclosed in Lay to the NSC, 30 October 1953, *FRUS, 1952–1954* 2:514–34, 577–97.

and only after European opinion had been prepared. Any other course, he said, would destroy European morale and play into the hands of the Communists.[92]

Both redeployment and the emphasis on nuclear weapons, which were supposed to be economizing measures, continued to be the subjects of bitter controversy in the NSC. This was particularly true at the council's meeting on 13 October, when Wilson presented his proposed defense budget for fiscal year 1955 and Humphrey learned, much to his horror, that it came to more than $42 billion in new appropriations. The total would permit a reduction of barely $2.5 billion below the defense budget that Truman had projected for fiscal year 1955. It would actually permit an increase in military manpower, rather than a reduction, as Eisenhower had hoped, and would contribute to a budget deficit that could run as high as $9 billion. "FY 1955 was *the* critical year," Humphrey told the NSC; either the administration was going to redeem its pledges to balance the budget and cut taxes, or the Republican party was going to "lose the next election."

According to Wilson and Radford, however, the proposed budget was the best the armed services could do until they had solid assurances that nuclear weapons would be used in the event of war. On the surface, the issue was whether nuclear weapons could be launched from bases in allied countries without the consent of the governments involved. But below the surface was the reluctance of the armed forces, particularly the Army and the Navy, to approve a policy of massive retaliation that would save money at their expense.[93] The argument infuriated Eisenhower, who thought the Joint Chiefs had all the assurances they needed and should plan accordingly. He demanded a further reduction of military manpower, and he wanted the reduction to come in support troops, such as the large number of Pentagon lobbyists on Capitol Hill and the high proportion of general and flag officers, which he said was four times what it had been in 1944.[94]

---

[92] Ibid.; and NSC-162/2, enclosed in Lay to the NSC, 30 October 1953, and memorandum of discussion at the 165th NSC meeting, 7 October 1953, *FRUS, 1952–1954* 2:5777–97, 514–34. On the redeployment of American troops also see Dulles to Eisenhower, 21 October 1953, ibid., 549–50.

[93] Memorandum of discussion at the 166th NSC meeting, 13 October 1953, Joint Chiefs to Wilson, 27 October 1953, and memorandum of discussion at the 168th NSC meeting, 29 October 1953, *FRUS, 1952–1954* 2:534–49, 562–64, 567–76.

[94] Eisenhower to Wilson, 30 November 1953, Eisenhower Papers, Papers as President, Whitman File, DDE Diary Series, box 3, folder: DDE Diary, November 1953; and Eisenhower diary, 26 October 1953, ibid., DDE Diary Series, box 3, folder: DDE Diary, October 1953.

Eisenhower also wanted the Joint Chiefs to stop building up "equally all types and varieties of military strength." They had to accept the new emphasis on nuclear weapons, "because it provided some sense of priority for our military planning." He quoted Washington's dictum that a respectable defense posture was the most the country could expect. "We cannot hope for a perfect defense," he said in words that echoed what Truman had said so many times before. Needed was a further "stretch out" of the defense program and a posture geared to "the long pull." When Robert Cutler suggested that the Joint Chiefs might reserve their position on nuclear weapons in the minutes of an NSC meeting, a determined Eisenhower exploded "with considerable warmth" that he would never tolerate a dissent in the record of action. "The Joint Chiefs of Staff were, after all, his military advisers; he made the decisions."[95]

That was that. The council approved NSC-162/2 with the decisions and compromises that Eisenhower had fashioned. It agreed in principle to redeploy American troops from abroad, to a mobile reserve in the United States, to a reduction in conventional forces, and to a military strategy that emphasized the massive retaliatory power of nuclear weapons. Eisenhower subsequently instructed Secretary Wilson to redraft the defense budget and scale back manpower requirements in light of the new strategic design.[96] And when Dodge complained that interservice disputes made it difficult for the Joint Chiefs to establish force levels and budget figures for the new fiscal year, the president again told Wilson that he expected real savings to be achieved, in part by manpower ceilings in each of the services, reductions wherever possible, and a combined figure of no more than three million troops. "We are no longer fighting in Korea," he wrote to Wilson, and the armed services should appreciate this fact and "help us achieve some substantial savings ... without wailing about the missions they have to accomplish."[97] Eisenhower even spelled out how manpower reductions should be accomplished. Meeting with Dulles and Wilson, he decided to begin the withdrawal of American ground forces in Korea and to "skeletonize" some of the Army's service

95 Memorandum of discussion at the 168th NSC meeting, 29 October 1953, and memorandum of discussion at the 166th NSC meeting, 13 October 1953, *FRUS, 1952–1954* 2:567–76, 534–49. See also memorandum of discussion at the 165th NSC meeting, 7 October 1953, ibid., 514–34.

96 Eisenhower to Cutler, 21 October 1953, Eisenhower Papers, Papers as President, Whitman File, DDE Diary Series, box 3, folder: DDE Diary, October 1953.

97 Eisenhower to Dodge, 1 December 1953, ibid., box 4, folder: DDE Diary, December 1953. See also Dodge to Deputy Secretary of Defense Kyes, 17 November 1953, and Dodge to Eisenhower, 30 November 1953, ibid., Administration Series, box 123, folder: Dodge, Joseph M., 1955 Budget.

and support units in Europe. A new reliance on nuclear weapons, the three agreed, would make it possible to "provide necessary security and still reduce the Defense budget" for fiscal year 1955.[98]

Under this pressure, the Joint Chiefs finally came up with a defense budget and force levels that Eisenhower could approve. Writing to Wilson on 9 December, they said that it was necessary to redeploy American forces from abroad to provide a mobile reserve in the United States and an integrated system of continental defense. They called for defense expenditures of approximately $37.5 billion in fiscal year 1955, a decline of more than $4 billion over the previous year, and with these expenditures, they said, military manpower would drop to 3,037,000 troops by the end of fiscal year 1955, and to 2,815,000 troops by the end of fiscal year 1956. Only the Army entered strong objections. The other services seemed to believe that redeployment could be accomplished without any loss of deterrence so long as the United States strengthened the ground forces of its allies and relied more heavily on its nuclear arsenal. But the Army would lose one-third of its manpower under the new plan, and this reduction, according to Secretary of the Army Stevens, would render it unable to perform its basic functions.[99]

Despite such complaints, Eisenhower declared the new budget on track and warned the services, especially the Army, against airing their complaints in the press or on Capitol Hill.[100] One month later he submitted the new budget to Congress. It called for $29.9 billion in new obligatory authority for the Defense Department, which was enough to support expenditures of approximately $37.5 billion in fiscal year 1955. Most of the decline of $4.5 billion from fiscal year 1954 would come at the Army's expense, while approximately 40 percent of the estimated total would be earmarked for the Air Force – a big jump from the previous year but in line with Eisenhower's emphasis on the massive destructive power of nuclear weapons. In addition, the budget envisioned $3.5 billion in new

---

[98] Memorandum for the record by the president, 11 November 1953, *FRUS, 1952–1954* 2:597–98. See also Eisenhower to Dodge, 1 December 1953, Eisenhower Papers, Papers as President, Whitman File, Administration Series, box 12, folder: Dodge, Joseph M., 1955 Budget.

[99] Radford to Wilson, 9 December 1953, Eisenhower Papers, Papers as President, Whitman File, Administration Series, box 39, folder: Wilson, Charles, E. (SecDef), 1953; memorandum of discussion at the 176th NSC meeting, 17 December 1953, ibid., NSC Series, box 5, folder: 176th NSC Meeting, December 16, 1953.

[100] Memorandum of discussion at the 176th NSC meeting, 17 December 1953, Eisenhower Papers, Papers as President, Whitman File, NSC Series, box 5, folder: 176th NSC Meeting, December 16, 1953.

appropriations for economic and military assistance, which, together with carryover funds, would support total expenditures of approximately $5.4 billion in fiscal year 1955.

Altogether, defense, mutual security, and other national security programs accounted for more than 60 percent of the proposed budget and even more if veterans' benefits and other war-related costs were included. Although Eisenhower boasted of the reductions and efficiencies he had achieved in this area of the budget, he still projected a deficit of nearly $3 billion in the new fiscal year. The deficit was not large enough to delay the scheduled expiration of the excess-profits tax, but was more than enough to preclude substantial new expenditures on domestic programs and any further reduction in taxes. Both the excise taxes and the surcharge on corporate incomes that had been enacted during the Korean War were to be continued.[101]

When Congress took up the national security budget, Eisenhower confronted the usual pattern of opposition – from conservatives, especially Republicans, on mutual security expenditures, and from Democrats on defense spending. Together with their counterparts in the Democratic party, conservative Republicans again attacked the mutual security program as a global giveaway that aided international bankers and arms dealers more than it did the United States. It had not worked in India, they said, which received American aid but followed an independent foreign policy, nor in Indo-China, where the Communists were winning the struggle against France. Congress, though, would not kill a program that Dulles, Stassen, Wilson, and others saw as essential to American security, and again the administration and its supporters were able to defend foreign aid as a smart investment that saved money. They reminded Congress that it was much cheaper to help others to help themselves than it was for the United States to contain communism alone. They also pointed to Eisenhower's success in trimming the foreign aid bill by several billion dollars below the amount that Congress had appropriated only three years earlier, a savings that was due in part to a decision by the administration to rely more heavily on private trade and investment to strengthen the free world economically. In the end, Congress appropriated or reappropriated about $5.3 billion for the mutual security program in fiscal year 1955, only slightly less than Eisenhower had requested.[102]

---

[101] Eisenhower, "Annual Budget Message to the Congress: Fiscal Year 1955," 21 January 1954, *Public Papers, Eisenhower, 1954* (Washington, 1960), 79–192, esp. 79–137.
[102] The total of $5.3 billion included $2.8 billion in new funds and another $2.5 billion in

The administration and its allies had a much tougher time when it came to the defense budget, which they sought to defend with arguments already rehearsed in the NSC. They were abandoning the old notion of a fixed D-day, said the Republicans, and replacing it with a floating D-day so that defense spending could be geared to changing international conditions and the capacity of the American economy. They were also reducing reserve stockpiles and standing forces, building up the mobilization base, creating a strategic reserve, and forging a new system of continental defense. These changes, plus greater economies in the Pentagon, the buildup of indigenous forces abroad, and expansion of the country's air–atomic power, would give the United States a more reliable deterrent without burdensome taxes and ever mounting deficits. Indeed, the New Look, as one Republican put it, assumed that sustained military strength was possible only when supported by a strong economy. Again citing Lenin to the effect that capitalism would spend itself into bankruptcy, the Republicans said that absolute security was impossible, that security had to be pursued within the framework of a balanced budget, and that any other course would lead straight to the garrison state. The American people, they argued, must not be chained "to the wheels of a military chariot, driven by a military dictator."[103]

The Democrats, who had supported Truman's decision to stretch out the defense program, would not do the same for Eisenhower. Led by Senator Albert Gore of Tennessee, Senator John F. Kennedy of Massachusetts, and Representative John W. McCormack of Massachusetts, the Democrats fell in behind the Army's critique of the New Look, challenging the decision to stress air–atomic power at the expense of conventional forces and thereby igniting a partisan debate that would continue over the next seven years. Instead of building a strong, balanced force, said the Democrats, the administration was putting too much faith in the kind of "superweapons" and "pushbutton warfare" that had not prevented the outbreak of fighting in Korea or deterred communism in Indo-China. It was permitting the Budget Bureau to write military strategy and putting "tax reductions ahead of the armed strength

carry-over funds appropriated in previous years. See *Congressional Quarterly Almanac, 1954,* 167–69, 275–81. For Eisenhower's emphasis on aid not trade see his annual budget message to Congress cited in the previous note; and Burton I. Kaufman, *Trade and Aid: Eisenhower's Foreign Economic Policy, 1953–1961* (Baltimore, 1982).

[103] *Congressional Record, 1954* 100:5748. See also for the Republican position, ibid., 5688–91, 5743–44, 5747–48, 8324–27. The debate over the defense budget can be followed in ibid., 5665–95, 5741–82, 8321–47, 8418–36, 8440–41; and *Congressional Quarterly Almanac, 1954,* 154–56.

which America, as the leader of the free world, must have in order to inspire the confidence of other free nations." "As between dollars and liberty," McCormack declared, "I prefer liberty." Guided by this principle, Kennedy led an effort to add $350 million to the defense budget to restore the two army divisions that Eisenhower had cut and guarantee "a clear margin of superiority over our enemies." Years later Kennedy would be in a better position to pay any price for national defense, but in 1954 the Republicans easily defeated his amendment, in part by citing the war hero in the White House as their authority on how much defense the country really needed. In the end, Congress authorized $28.8 billion in new obligatory authority for defense, which was actually one billion dollars less than Eisenhower had requested.[104]

As the Democratic critique pointed out, the defense budget and tax policy were inextricably linked: reductions in defense spending would enable the administration to reduce taxes without adding to the deficit. It was this link that held the Republican party together, even while it provoked important questions about how the burden of defense would be apportioned among the taxpayers. These questions arose when the Republicans sought to reduce taxes by several billion dollars, mostly by allowing the excess-profits tax to expire and by shaving a billion dollars off existing excise taxes. Democrats had long championed the excess-profits tax, but not excise taxes, which amounted to regressive consumption levies on such items as alcohol, gasoline, cigarettes, and theater tickets. They wanted to dump the excise taxes altogether, while Eisenhower and Humphrey wanted them continued until there was a better prospect of a balanced budget. The outcome was a compromise. Congress extended some of the excise taxes that were scheduled to lapse, but reduced most of them to a flat 10 percent. Although the reduction cost the Treasury approximately $999 million in lost revenue, the loss was less than Eisenhower had feared and was one he found easier to accept in light of the recession that began in 1954.[105]

A much larger battle ensued over a bill to revise the internal revenue code. Known as the omnibus tax bill of 1954, it was the brainchild of Congressman Reed, who was still smarting from his defeat in the tax battle of the previous year. The bill would provide a tax cut to individuals

---

[104] *Congressional Record, 1954* 100:5685, 8335, 5745, 8436. See also ibid., 8328–29, 8332–33, 8425–38, 8440–41; and *Congressional Quarterly Almanac, 1954,* 153–56.

[105] *Congressional Quarterly Almanac, 1954,* 495–97; *Congressional Record, 1954* 100: 3012–39, 3753–83, 3834–73, 4060–68. See also Morgan, *Eisenhower Versus 'The Spenders,'* 60.

and corporations in excess of $1.3 billion, with most of the reduction going to upper-income groups and business firms. Especially controversial was a provision to cut taxes on the dividend income received by individual stockholders. Democrats denounced this provision as a windfall for upper-income groups who were already comparatively advantaged. They wanted to strike the dividend provision while boosting personal exemptions for individual taxpayers from $600 to $700, or more. According to the Democrats, their strategy would counter the current downturn in the economy, achieve security within the framework of a balanced budget, and put the burden of that achievement on those most able to bear it. The Republicans, on the other hand, defended the dividend exclusion as the best way to encourage investment and stimulate the economy, but denounced an increase in personal exemptions as a measure that would run up the deficit and force deep cuts in the defense budget. Mediating these differences, Eisenhower rejected any increase in individual exemptions as a threat to the country's economic well-being and military security while at the same time persuading Congress to continue the Korean War tax rate on corporations for another year and helping to negotiate a dividend exclusion that was less than he had wanted. The combination, which Congress accepted, kept the revenue loss to $163 million in fiscal year 1955 and precluded deeper defense cuts or a larger budget deficit than Eisenhower thought desirable.[106]

V

The defense budgets for fiscal years 1954 and 1955 established a pattern that remained more or less unchanged through the rest of the Eisenhower administration. The transition to the New Look was complete, although the final results hardly amounted to a sharp break with the past. On the contrary, the New Look built on policies, strategies, and trends already present in the Truman administration. To be sure, Eisenhower turned the emphasis on nuclear deterrence into formal doctrine, addressed the emerging problem of continental defense, and considered the redeployment of American troops as one way to solve that problem and cut costs at the same time. But neither these differences, nor Eisenhower's greater reliance on covert operations, should obscure the fact that both he and Truman were committed to a mobilization base on which the United

---

[106] *Congressional Quarterly Almanac, 1954*, 476–89; *Congressional Record, 1954* 100: 2039–41, 2213–16, 3093–3101, 3223–27, 3311–14, 3335–41, 3418–65, 3516–64, 9150–72, 9267–9310, 9605–19, 12425–34, 12525–50.

States could build in the event of an emergency. Both relied heavily on foreign aid to strengthen allies, and both saw the mobilization base and the mutual security program as cost-effective strategies of containment that were far cheaper than maintaining a large standing army at home or abroad.[107]

Nor do the similarities stop there. Both Truman and Eisenhower were uncomfortable with a large, peacetime military establishment, and with the rivalry, waste, and duplication among the armed forces. Both were appalled by the high taxes and budget deficits that came with war and rearmament after 1950. Both tried to retrench from the peak spending levels reached at the height of the Korean War. Both were convinced that national security claimed too much of the budget, and both understood that expenditures in this area encouraged cutbacks elsewhere, including congressional cuts in Eisenhower's proposals for health care and housing.

Many of these similarities grew out of a shared concern for the country's "fundamental values and institutions," although both administrations were sharply divided over what the major threats to these values and institutions were. Many American policy makers, particularly in the State and Defense departments, found the principal threat in Soviet aggression or Communist expansion. To their way of thinking, which was guided by the new ideology of national security, the United States had entered an era of semiwar against a totalitarian enemy who was hostile to any government not under its control. And because liberty was indivisible, at least to these officials, the United States had no choice but to contain communism everywhere through a global system of collective security, ambitious foreign aid programs, and a large military establishment. Containment also required a new vigilance against internal subversion, the permanent mobilization of essential resources, and a new spirit of discipline and sacrifice as war and rearmament necessarily took precedence over social investment, lower taxes, and a balanced budget.

On the other side were policy makers, particularly in the Treasury Department and the Budget Bureau, who saw the threat to American values and traditions arising primarily from overzealous efforts to roll back the Communist tide. These officials worried that foreign aid and

---

[107] See, for example, Mark J. Gasiorowski, *U.S. Foreign Policy and the Shah: Building a Client State in Iran* (Ithaca, 1991); Mary Ann Heiss, *Empire and Nationhood: The United States, Great Britain, and Iranian Oil, 1950–1954* (New York, 1997); Richard H. Immerman, *The CIA in Guatemala: The Foreign Policy of Intervention* (Austin, 1982); and Piero Gleijeses, *Shattered Hope: The Guatemalan Revolution and the United States, 1944–1954* (Princeton, 1991).

defense were costing more than the country could afford, and by doing so were leading to burdensome taxes and economic controls, to escalating deficits, and to concentrations of bureaucratic and military power that would destroy the traditional balances between the public and private sectors, the legislative and executive branches, the civilian and military establishments.

Eisenhower tried to bridge these differences. As Truman had earlier, he wrestled with the central problem of state making in the early Cold War, which was how to build a national security state without sacrificing the country's traditional democratic identity, and he was not always successful. On the contrary, he secretly recorded many of his White House conversations, used the CIA to topple foreign governments, adopted an internal security program that compounded problems inherited from Truman, failed to take a strong stand against McCarthy's vicious abuse of individual rights, and tried instead to protect himself by asserting a doctrine of executive privilege that his successors would use to hide some of the worst abuses of presidential power.[108]

Eisenhower was more successful in strengthening civilian control of the military, reorganizing the Defense Department, and working out a scientific advisory system to advance his goals. He built on Truman's earlier accomplishments in the latter area and, like Truman, he stretched out the rearmament program to contain the deficit, accommodate tax reductions, and phase out economic controls. He even wanted to divert more resources to housing, social security, and other domestic programs that had been neglected since the Second World War, especially after Stalin's death and subsequent Soviet peace overtures raised hopes that the Cold War might be moderated.

With these hopes in mind, Eisenhower set his speech writers to work on a major address that would highlight the awful consequences of nuclear war and the cost of the arms race in lower living standards, social progress, and basic democratic values. But Dulles, Strauss, and other national security managers were against the idea from the start. The Soviets could not be trusted, they said, and negotiations would be futile unless the United States negotiated from a position of military strength, which required more spending on defense, not less. Even economizers worried, as did Eisenhower, that blunt talk about the nuclear arms race would

[108] Ambrose, *Eisenhower* 2:186–89, 202–3; Arthur M. Schlesinger, Jr., *The Imperial Presidency* (Boston, 1973), 155–59; Ambrose, "Epilogue: Eisenhower's Legacy," in *Eisenhower: A Centenary Assessment*, 249–50.

inspire fear in the American people and actually encourage Congress to increase defense spending at the expense of lower taxes and a balanced budget.[109]

Given the objections and possible problems, Eisenhower's initial proposal devolved into a modest initiative that did nothing to end the Cold War. Speaking to the American Society of Newspaper Editors in mid-April 1953, he warned that current policy envisioned a long and costly arms race that would drain "the wealth and the labor" of the world, the "genius of its scientists," and "the hopes of its children." The cost of one heavy bomber, he explained, deprived the United States of "a modern brick school in more than thirty cities," of two "fully equipped hospitals," or of "two electric power plants, each serving a town of sixty thousand population." The money spent for "a single fighter plane" would buy "a half million bushels of wheat," and that for a single destroyer would build new homes for "more than eight thousand people." As a result of the Cold War, Eisenhower concluded, humanity was "hanging from a cross of iron," with "every gun that is made, every warship launched, every rocket fired" signifying "a theft from those who hunger and are not fed, those who are cold and are not clothed."[110]

Eisenhower clearly understood the terrible cost of the arms race, but his speech held out little hope of ending the Cold War and diverting defense dollars to more peaceful purposes. On the contrary, he used most of his speech to castigate the Soviets for their postwar diplomacy. He laid blame for the arms race at their feet and dared them to accept American peace proposals, such as the unification of Germany and the liberation of Eastern Europe, that were clearly unacceptable. Much the same was true of the famous atoms-for-peace initiative that Eisenhower announced to the UN General Assembly on 8 December 1953. Under this proposal, the nuclear powers would contribute fissionable material to a UN agency for use in such peaceful projects as the development of electrical energy. The proposal grew out of Eisenhower's initial inclination to speak frankly about the cost of the Cold War and the benefits of disarmament. But it

[109] Ambrose, *Eisenhower* 2:91–95, 122–24, 131–35. See also Gleason memorandum of discussion at the 134th NSC meeting, 25 February 1953, Eisenhower Papers, Papers as President, Whitman File, NSC Series, box 4, folder: 134th NSC Meeting, February 25, 1953; and Hughes diary entries, 16, 17 March 1953, Hughes Papers, box 1, folder: Diary Notes of Meetings, 1/12/53–10/15/53.

[110] Eisenhower, "The Chance for Peace," 16 April 1953, *Public Papers, 1953*, 179–88. See also Hewlett and Holl, *Atoms for Peace and War*, 42–72, for Operation Candor and the atoms-for-peace initiative.

was limited by objections inside the administration, had built-in advantages for the United States, and did not appeal to the Soviets.[111]

During Eisenhower's first two years in office, as during the Truman administration, the specter of a garrison state continued to play a role in shaping defense policy. The new ideology of national security had to take account of older values, notably the traditional opposition to economic controls, higher taxes, and budget deficits and traditional commitments to a strong dollar, individual incentive, and civilian control of the military, all of which put limits on how far national security managers could go in pursuit of their objectives. Entering into the policy making process, these older values limited the size of the defense budget, influenced plans to reorganize the Pentagon, and contributed to a military strategy that put less emphasis on forces in being and more emphasis on foreign aid, nuclear weapons, and mobilization potential.

Yet, despite their influence, traditional values had to make room for the new ideology of national security. The United States did not retreat from globalism; defense spending did not return to the comparatively modest levels of the pre-Korean period; budget deficits did not cease to be a feature of federal financing; and the new structures of bureaucratic, military, and scientific power did not disappear from the American system. What is more, national security expenditures stifled any meaningful expansion of the social programs growing out of the New Deal. Although Eisenhower's legislative agenda included more public housing, better health care, and other public services for citizens who could not afford them, most of these proposals were modest and few emerged unscathed from Congress, where conservatives held them hostage to Eisenhower's national security policies and to the Republican party's emphasis on a balanced budget and lower taxes. In this sense, humanity was sacrificed on a cross of iron.

---

[111] In addition to the sources cited in the previous two notes see Eisenhower, "Address before the General Assembly of the United Nations on Peaceful Uses of Atomic Energy," 8 December 1953, *Public Papers, Eisenhower, 1953*, 813–22; and Ambrose, *Eisenhower* 2:147–49.

10

Other Voices

The Public Sphere and the National Security Mentality

The national security mentality reached well beyond the state makers in Washington. National security issues also engaged leaders in other areas of American life, not to mention ordinary citizens, many of whom found ways to register their convictions. This chapter tries to read how people other than policy makers reacted to the Cold War, and especially to the developments described in the preceding chapters. Its focus is on the public sphere rather than on Congress, the presidency, and other agencies in what might be called the political sphere, although this shift in focus does not involve a shift in themes. On the contrary, by moving from a state-centered narrative to one that is decentered, it is possible to determine if the views expressed in Washington reverberated in other quarters and thus to provide a fuller account of the postwar struggle to reshape the state and redefine the country's political identity.[1]

As employed here, the public sphere embraced several groups, including journalists and commentators whose views have been traced in the previous chapters and need not detain us further. Instead, this chapter focuses on Cold War intellectuals and ordinary Americans. Although American intellectuals were not as active in shaping national security policy as they would be a decade later, the early Cold War did influence their thinking and contribute to a national security mentality that is evident in their published work and political activity. Assessing popular views is more difficult. Public opinion polls are less than reliable for the early postwar period and do not give expression to popular sentiment in any event. For such sentiment, this chapter relies on other voices, specifically those evident in popular demonstrations and in letters to the editors of several major newspapers. What we find in these sources is a debate in

---

[1] The idea of a public sphere is borrowed from Jurgen Habermas and is used here to mean a discursive community of citizens, from elite opinion makers to ordinary Americans, who are outside the state but who nonetheless deliberate, debate, and otherwise express opinions about state policy. See Craig Calhoun, *Habermas and the Public Sphere* (Cambridge, MA, 1992).

the public sphere that echoes the political debates in Washington, including a substantial dissent from the direction of public policy and a deep concern that national security needs might alter the basic nature of American life.

II

American intellectuals helped to create a national security mentality that quickly became pervasive in the early years of the Cold War. A preoccupation with totalitarianism was central to this mentality, as it was to the national security ideology, and was stimulated initially by the antifascist crusade and then by the struggle against communism. Eric Fromm's *Escape from Freedom*, published during the war, circulated widely among American intellectuals. So did Hayek's *Road to Serfdom* and Lasswell's studies of the garrison state, and these were soon followed by Hannah Arendt's work on *The Origins of Totalitarianism*, published in 1951. Arendt's book was particularly important, in part because it elucidated key themes in the national security mentality, including a dark view of recent history, an equally gloomy emphasis on man's potential for irrational action and mass violence, and a tendency to see fascism and communism as the evil twins of totalitarianism.[2]

This pessimistic line of thinking, which had started to emerge in the late 1930s, especially among intellectuals associated with the *Partisan Review*, became a dominant motif in historical and political writing during the early Cold War, including the writing on American foreign policy. Hans Morgenthau, Walter Lippmann, George Kennan, and other so-called realist writers shared a conservative view of human nature, which they saw as basically selfish, and a profound sense of the limits that nature placed on individuals and states alike. To their way of thinking, wisdom was to be found in a statecraft that accepted these realities as they revealed themselves in the international system – one, in other words, that was realistic in its ambitions and held the worst aspects of human nature in check. Kennan articulated these notions better than anyone else in his classic study, *American Diplomacy, 1900–1950*, also published in 1951. Condemning the simpleminded idealism that he saw in the history of American foreign policy, especially the naive reliance on legal and moral principles that had inspired one impractical policy after another, Kennan called instead for a diplomacy based on the realities of

[2] Richard H. Pells, *The Liberal Mind in a Conservative Age: American Intellectuals in the 1940s and 1950s,* paperback ed. (New York, 1985), 84–91; Michael S. Sherry, *In the Shadow of War: The United States Since the 1930s* (New Haven, CT, 1995), 161.

power, on the pragmatic calculations of professional diplomats, and on the pursuit of limited goals that would serve the country's interests and security. Running through all of his thinking, and that of other realist writers, was a deep-seated suspicion of popular wisdom, a belief in experts, and a renewed faith in traditional, balance-of-power diplomacy.[3]

Similar themes surfaced in the work of intellectuals like the historian Arthur Schlesinger, Jr., the protestant theologian Reinhold Niebuhr, and the philosophers John Burnham and Sidney Hook. All of these writers discarded a youthful infatuation with Marxism in favor of an unsentimental realism. In *The Vital Center*, published in 1948, Schlesinger celebrated the tough-minded liberalism that had been forged in the crucible of the 1930s and 1940s, with the Great Depression, the collapse of the Communist experiment in the Soviet Union, the Nazi atrocities in Germany, and the carnage of World War II. Schlesinger's book was filled with illusions to the tragic nature of life and the corruptibility of man, insights borrowed from the muscular Christianity of Reinhold Niebuhr, whose thinking also epitomized the tendency of American intellectuals to view the Cold War as a struggle between good and evil, freedom and tyranny, and to replace an earlier faith in reason and progress with a profound sense of the limits that history and original sin placed on human perfectibility.

This point of view, together with a deep, intestinal fear of totalitarianism, had a profound influence on the way liberal intellectuals viewed the state. The conviction that evil existed and had to be controlled established the philosophical and religious basis for policies that would control the worst elements of human behavior, including policies to contain communism. But at the same time liberals like Schlesinger were more inclined than before to eschew the temptations of totalitarianism and to offset an older faith in the state with a new emphasis on the importance of law and the primacy of individual rights. Seen in this light, liberal intellectuals walked a thin line between competing views of the state as the instrument of moral action, on the one hand, and as the fountainhead of totalitarianism, on the other.[4]

---

3 Pells, *Liberal Mind*, 76–77; Christopher Lasch, *The World of Nations: Reflections on American History, Politics & Culture*, paperback, ed. (New York, 1974), 205–15; Jerald A. Combs, *American Diplomatic History: Two Centuries of Changing Interpretations* (Berkeley, 1983), 223–24, 234–42.

4 Pells, *Liberal Mind*, 136; John Patrick Diggins, *The Proud Decades: America in War and Peace, 1941–1960* (New York, 1988), 172–73; Alonzo L. Hamby, *Beyond the New Deal: Harry S. Truman and American Liberalism* (New York, 1973), 18–19, 280–81.

Something similar can be said of the way conservative intellectuals came to view the state in the early Cold War. The conservative movement enjoyed a rebirth after World War II, the beginning of a resurgence that would carry it to power almost three decades later. As George Nash has pointed out, conservative thinking included both the economic libertarianism of Hayek and his American followers, such as Frank Chodorov, Henry Hazlitt, and Leonard Read, and the cultural conservatism of Leo Straus, Russell Kirk, and Peter Viereck. Although libertarians stressed the importance of market economics while their cultural counterparts emphasized traditional values, the two wings of the movement shared a set of common principles. Besides a tendency to associate private property with political freedom, these included some of the same principles that had begun to penetrate the thinking of liberal intellectuals, notably a feeling that progress was not inevitable, a loss of faith in man's basic goodness, a belief in the pervasiveness of evil, a suspicion of mass political movements, a faith in elite rule, and a conviction that totalitarian regimes were globally ambitious and had to be contained. What is more, if these shared principles prompted liberal intellectuals to be more wary of the state as an engine of moral action and social betterment, they led conservative intellectuals to accept the state as a necessary evil in the battle against communism.[5]

Another shared assumption, also evident in the national security ideology, further narrowed the differences between liberal and conservative intellectuals, especially on the role of the state in the postwar world. This was the assumption that isolationism had to be repudiated. The United States had to be prepared militarily and American leaders had to forge a balance of power in the West able to contain Soviet power in the East. This line of thinking, similar to the realism of historians like Kennan, laid the foundation not only for a policy of containment but also for a national security state able to implement that policy. For many liberals, it meant that Dr. New Deal had to make room for Dr. Win-the-War, as Franklin Roosevelt had once put it. For many conservatives, it meant that antistatism had to take a back seat to anticommunism, that the national security arm of the state had to be enlarged if the United States was going to prevail in the global struggle.[6]

This line of reasoning was apparent in the thinking of the philosopher John Burnham, a disillusioned Trotskyite who became one of the most

[5] Nash, *Conservative Intellectual Movement*, 3–83.
[6] Ibid., 125–27. As Nash points out, conservatives sometimes divided on whether the most important enemy was the state or communism.

prominent conservative intellectuals of the early Cold War. Burnham's thinking, which had been germinating for several years, burst into full bloom with the publication in 1947 of his book, *The Struggle for the World*. Filled with bleak predictions of inevitable conflict, the book embraced a hard-boiled geopolitical realism that was almost devoid of moral sentimentality. It included key components of the national security ideology, especially its tendency to obliterate the distinction between war and peace, its emphasis on the total nature of modern war, and its conviction that all of the country's resources had to be mobilized in the battle against communism. It urged the American people to eradicate the Communist threat at home, organize the non-Communist world into an American empire, and use all means available to contain the Soviet Union. In subsequent publications, Burnham even urged American leaders to take the offensive in the Cold War, exploit weaknesses in the Soviet bloc, and move from a policy of containment to one that would liberate the captive people who suffered under Soviet tyranny.[7]

Burnham was convinced that intellectuals had an important part to play in the struggle against communism, as was Sidney Hook, another philosopher who converted from communism to anticommunism in the early years of the Cold War. In April 1949 Hook and other prominent intellectuals took to the streets to protest the Cultural and Scientific Conference for World Peace, a Communist-sponsored peace conference that was held, of all places, in New York's Waldorf-Astoria Hotel. Hook and his allies, including veterans' groups, picketed the hotel's entrance, crashed the conference proceedings, denounced its participants as lackeys of the Soviet Union, and tried at every turn to call attention to the Soviet Union's suppression of civil liberties, particularly for artists and intellectuals.[8]

The Waldorf-Astoria affair demonstrated how American intellectuals, like some American journalists, could operate in both the public and the political spheres, moving from the publication of anti-Communist tracts to active efforts to combat communism on the streets of New York. Nor was it the only example of such activism, or conservative intellectuals its only agents. On the contrary, Burnham and Hook later

---

[7] Pells, *Liberal Mind*, 77–80; John Patrick Diggins, *Up from Communism: Conservative Odysseys in American Intellectual History* (New York, 1975), 319–21; and Nash, *Conservative Intellectual Movement*, 91–94.

[8] *Newsweek* 33 (4 April 1949): 19–22; *Time* 53 (4 April 1949): 21–3; *Nation* 148 (2 April 1949): 377–78; *Life* 26 (4 April 1949): 39–43; *New York Times*, 24, 25, 26, 27 March 1949. See also Diggins *Proud Decades*, 169–71.

A Cross of Iron

joined Schlesinger and other liberal intellectuals to organize the Congress
for Cultural Freedom in 1950 and its American affiliate, the Committee
for Cultural Freedom, in 1951. With help from the CIA, these two groups
sought to contain Soviet influence in cultural circles and to mobilize
Western intellectuals behind the American side in the Cold War.[9]

The revolt against Marxism by American intellectuals had its counterparts in other areas of American life during the early Cold War. More
than one American labor union tore itself apart in bitter internecine
battles between Communist and anti-Communist factions. These battles intensified as the Cold War heated up and as Walter Reuther and
other prominent labor leaders became convinced that labor's progress
depended on their ability to eradicate all vestiges of communism from
the trade union movement. The same kind of struggle unfolded among
African-Americans. The National Association for the Advancement of
Colored People (NAACP) came under the control of vigorous anti-
Communists, backed away from its earlier support for civil rights on
a global scale, and waged a bitter battle against the National Negro
Congress and other radical organizations that were more sympathetic
with Soviet foreign policy. Professional groups and organizations went
through the same ordeal. Congressional investigations, conducted by
the notorious House Committee on Un-American Affairs, divided
Hollywood in an effort to eradicate Communist influences from the film
industry. At the same time, the American Medical Association and the
American Bar Association began to require political tests for membership, as did the National Education Association, which represented a
teaching profession that underwent a national purge during the era of
McCarthyism.[10]

Although the national security mentality pressed relentlessly toward
cultural and ideological conformity, it never achieved that goal and could
even cut a wide swath in the opposite direction. Among Cold War intellectuals, for example, important differences remained between those like

[9] Christopher Lasch, "The Cultural Cold War: A Short History of the Congress for Cultural
Freedom," in Lasch, *The Agony of the American Left* (New York, 1969), 63–114.
[10] On the labor movement see Bert Cochran, *Labor and Communism: The Conflict that
Shaped American Unions* (Princeton, 1977); on the Communist issue among black lead-
ers, see Carol Anderson, "From Hope to Disillusion: African Americans, the United Na-
tions, and the Struggle for Human Rights, 1944–1947," *Diplomatic History* 20 (Fall 1996):
531–63; on anticommunism in the film industry and the professions see Larry Ceplair and
Steven Englund, *The Inquisition in Hollywood: Politics in the Film Community, 1930–1960*
(Garden City, 1980); and David Caute, *The Great Fear: The Anti-Communist Purge Under
Truman and Eisenhower* (New York, 1978).

Niebuhr and Schlesinger, on the one hand, and those like Burnham and Hook, on the other. Niebuhr and Schlesinger helped to found the Americans for Democratic Action and were appalled by McCarthyism, loyalty oaths, and efforts to silence radical opinions, whereas Hook was more tolerant of censorship in the cause of anticommunism, as was Burnham, who ended up defending McCarthy and joining the staff of William F. Buckley's conservative magazine, *National Review*. Differences of this sort also divided the American Committee for Cultural Freedom, eventually disrupting the coalition of liberal and conservative intellectuals on which that organization had been founded. Nor did the retreat from radicalism by American intellectuals mean the end of social criticism, which focused increasingly on the persistence of poverty, the degradation of mass culture, and the impersonal, bureaucratic nature of modern life. There was even a strong critique of American foreign policy coming not only from revisionist historians, who remained fiercely skeptical of the internationalist thrust of American diplomacy, but also from conservative libertarians like Murray Rothbard and Frank Chodorov, who were convinced that current policies were leading straight to a leviathan state that would destroy economic and political freedom at home.[11]

The same dichotomy was evident when it came to social relations in the early Cold War, where the national security mentality contained reform in some directions while advancing it in others. The president's executive order desegregating the armed forces in 1948 grew in part out of perceived national security imperatives, as did the Women's Armed Services Integration Act of the same year, which gave women permanent regular status in the armed forces. Not only was integration necessary if the armed services hoped to meet their manpower requirements, it was also essential if American leaders were going to block the spread of radicalism at home, particularly in the African-American community, and present the United States as the champion of democracy worldwide.

Not all changes were positive, however. As Michael Sherry has observed, some groups, such as Mexican-Americans, gays, and lesbians, were often seen as un-American or as security risks and were denied government employment, purged from the military, or driven from the country. Even women and African-Americans found progress difficult and minimal. Despite the Armed Services Integration Act, women could not engage in combat and were more likely to exercise command over

---

[11] Diggins, *Proud Decades*, 167, 172–75; Lasch, "Cultural Cold War," 63–114; Pells, *Liberal Mind*, 130–261; Combs, *American Diplomatic History*, 204–5; and Nash, *Conservative Intellectual Movement*, 125–26.

other women than over men. And African-Americans, for their part, had to exert constant political pressure to integrate the armed forces, Truman's executive order notwithstanding, and overcome strong opposition from cultural conservatives and southern politicians who were inclined to brand racial reformers as little more than Communists.[12]

III

The public discourse on national security extended beyond organized groups and educated elites to embrace ordinary citizens, who announced their views in public opinion polls, to be sure, but who also gave voice to their thinking in popular demonstrations and in letters to the editors of the nation's newspapers. Although both media provide a window of sorts on the way national security issues were perceived outside the nation's capitol, they actually convey somewhat different messages, as we will see. Letters to the editor were mostly spontaneous expressions. They were prompted by events or by official pronouncements, and they give a sense of how their authors responded to national security policies and whether they "read" those policies as affirming or denying American values. Popular demonstrations can also be read as texts, but they must be read with more caution, as they were typically organized events in which views were collectively expressed and conveyed with considerable prompting. To put it differently, whereas most demonstrations gave some indication of the way official elites sought to mold popular opinion, letters to the editor were more likely to represent a spontaneous and genuine expression of such opinion.

The link between popular and official opinion is evident in the cross-country tour of the Freedom Train, a traveling archive of historic documents that visited more than three hundred cities between September 1947 and January 1949. The tour began with a visit to Philadelphia, where the train was part of a program to commemorate the 160th anniversary of the Constitution, and ended with a visit to the nation's capitol during President Truman's inaugural celebration. Altogether, the Freedom Train traveled more than 37,000 miles across all forty-eight states, revealing its precious cargo to 3.5 million people and prompting community events that engaged another forty-five million.[13]

---

[12] Sherry, *In the Shadow of War*, 144–54.

[13] For the most detailed account of the Freedom Train see Stuart Jon Little, "The Freedom Train and the Formation of National Political Culture, 1946–1949," (M.A. thesis, University of Kansas, 1989). See also U.S. Congress, House, *Hearings on H. J. Res. 84: A Resolution*

Although these numbers would seem to indicate a high degree of symmetry between the political and the public spheres, between official ideology and popular patriotism, the connection was not wholly spontaneous. On the contrary, the outpouring of public sentiment was in part the predictable result of a carefully organized campaign by political leaders who represented what John Bodnar has called the "official culture" of the postwar period.[14] These elites tried to present an idealized and sacred version of the past in order to overwhelm dissent and unify the American people behind the national security policies of the Truman administration. Led by officials in the Department of Justice, including Attorney General Tom Clark, the organizers of the Freedom Train originally envisioned a modest exhibition that contrasted American freedoms with the death of civil liberties in Nazi Germany. The idea was to fix an American identity by demarcating the boundaries that separated the United States from the totalitarian other, which was revealed not simply as a military threat to American security but also as a cultural, ideological, or political threat to the special rights and way of life that Americans enjoyed. Fascism had been conquered, the exhibit would announce, but communism still posed a menace that every loyal citizen had to resist. "There were subversive influences and other problems that seemed to be growing," Clark later told a congressional committee. "We thought that if we could have a program ... of knowing and studying the basic documents and basic principles and ideologies upon which our American way of life was founded, it would be helpful in combatting these various influences that appeared to be on the increase."[15]

Truman liked the idea and gave it his approval, whereupon Clark sold it to friends in the private sector, including the head of Paramount Pictures and other movie executives, as well as Thomas D'Arcy Brophy of the Advertising Council, which had earlier been formed to mobilize public support for the war effort. At meetings in December 1946 and January 1947, those involved drew up plans for the traveling museum,

---

to *Provide for the Acquisition and Operation of the Freedom Train by the Archivist of the United States, and for Other Purposes* (Washington, 1949), 2–3 (hereafter cited as *Hearings on H. J. Res. 84*); "Propaganda: Traveling Heirlooms," *Newsweek* 30 (22 September 1947): 84, 86; "Freedom Train," *Life* 23 (29 September 1947): 49–50, 52; "Freedom Train Tours America," *National Geographic* 96 (October 1949): 529–42.

[14] Bodnar, *Remaking America: Public Memory, Commemoration, and Patriotism in the Twentieth Century* (Princeton, 1992), esp. 13–20, 138–54.

[15] *Hearings on H. J. Res. 84*, 2–10. See also William J. Coblenz, "The Freedom Train and the Story of Its Origins: Our Civil Liberties on Wheels," *Manuscripts* 10 (Winter 1957): 30–34; and Little, "Freedom Train," 8–9.

now limited to American documents only, and for major media and educational initiatives to promote the exhibit and inspire Americanism in communities across the country. In February they incorporated the American Heritage Foundation, a nonprofit, educational foundation, to direct and support the project. Headed by Winthrop W. Aldrich, chairman of the Chase Manhattan Bank, the foundation's bipartisan board of directors, composed of labor, civic, and business leaders, symbolized the spirit of harmony it hoped to arouse in the nation as a whole. Its goal, like Clark's, was to inspire patriotism and stifle dissent, in part by drawing the country's political identity in a way that excluded domestic critics, whose views were branded as un-American and linked to the Communist peril at home and abroad. "Since the cessation of hostilities," the foundation explained, "voices of discord have been all too prevalent on the American scene. Lawlessness and cynicism ... are very much with us. Subversive forces in various guises seek to undermine the democratic structure. ... In this crucial period, we deem it highly desirable that a comprehensive program of education in the ideals and practices of American democracy be launched."[16]

The foundation's first task was a White House conference held in late May to mobilize public support for the project, not only as a symbol of national unity in a time of crisis but also as a call to civic duty in the struggle against communism. In giving their blessing to the Freedom Train, Truman and Clark joined a dazzling array of business, labor, and media figures, as well as politicians from both political parties, in a public display of that unity and patriotism. These "critical times," according to Clark, required an "intensive, dramatic and militant program to reassert the emphatic advantages of American democracy."[17] Truman made the same point in a speech to the conference, while Brophy, noting the attacks on American values by Communists and subversives, told the audience that it was time to sell America to Americans. "All of us know that advertising can sell ideas to the millions just as well as it can sell merchandise and services."[18]

Altogether the Freedom Train enshrined 127 documents, including the Mayflower Compact, the Treaty of Paris, the Northwest Ordinance,

---

[16] American Heritage Foundation, *The American Heritage Program and the Freedom Train* (New York, 1947), 1; James Gregory Bradsher, "Taking America's Heritage to the People: The Freedom Train Story," *Prologue* 17 (Winter 1985): 229–44; Little, "Freedom Train," 10–27.

[17] "Meeting is Called on Freedom Train," *New York Times,* 16 May 1947. See also Bradsher, "Taking America's Heritage to the People," 233.

[18] Brophy quoted in Little, "Freedom Train," 32.

the Bill of Rights, Thomas Jefferson's draft of the Declaration of Independence, George Washington's copy of the Constitution, Washington's famous Farewell Address, Lincoln's Gettysburg Address, the Emancipation Proclamation, and the Charter of the United Nations. These and other documents were housed in specially outfitted railroad cars donated for that purpose by several railway companies and pulled by an electric diesel, christened "The Spirit of 1776," on loan from the American Locomotive Company. The whole train, 800 feet long, was painted a gleaming white with red and blue stripes running its entire length and with a gold eagle or the words "Freedom Train" appearing on alternate cars.[19]

The Freedom Train's visit to most cities culminated a week of patriotic celebration and citizenship training, called "Rededication Week," orchestrated by local elites with assistance from the American Heritage Foundation. The foundation put together publicity portfolios and radio kits, including cartoons, comic strips, and editorials, to help local media arouse public interest in the Freedom Train and Rededication Week. It distributed speech and essay material for training in good citizenship and commissioned a study, "Your Heritage of Freedom," for use in social-studies classes at all levels of instruction. It even commissioned a special song, "Freedom Train," written by Irving Berlin, recorded by Bing Crosby and the Andrews Sisters, and aired by local radio stations across the country.

At the same time, the foundation drummed up support from other media enterprises. At its request, RKO Pictures produced an eleven-minute film, "Our American Heritage," narrated by Joseph Cotton and distributed free of charge to movie theaters and school systems nationally. The film coupled a brief review of how American democracy had developed with a strong appeal for national unity in a time of crisis. In addition, *Look* magazine contributed an illustrated booklet, also called "Our American Heritage," that detailed the documents exhibited on the Freedom Train, while *Reader's Digest* contributed both an article about the Bill of Rights and six Teach-O-Filmstrips illustrating the origins and growth of free institutions in England and the United States.

Leaving no stone unturned, the Heritage Foundation also dispatched so-called area directors to meet with community officials, including the mayor, who had been prompted in advance to assemble a citizens' committee of local elites. Representing the Chamber of Commerce, veterans' groups, trade unions, women's organizations, and education associations,

[19] "98 U.S. Documents to Tour Country," *New York Times,* 24 August 1947; "Freedom Train Here Thursday," ibid., 21 September 1947; Bradsher, "Taking America's Heritage to the People," 233–34.

these committees stood as living symbols not only of the anticommunist consensus but also of a national unity that transcended different groups and interests. They took responsibility for organizing a week of patriotic commemorations, usually keyed to a daily theme, such as Freedom of Religion Day, Freedom of Enterprise Day, American Justice Day, American Family Day, and Good Citizenship Day. These themes were featured in school presentations, church meetings, parades, public speeches, and other ceremonies throughout Rededication Week, which typically ended with the arrival of the Freedom Train. That event was marked by a major public ceremony complete with brass bands, visiting dignitaries, and a public pledge of support for the political and religious freedoms that Americans enjoyed. Composed by the American Heritage Foundation, the Freedom Pledge, as it was called, was usually read aloud by a public official and repeated by those who had assembled for the ceremony or who later visited the train. Those who took the Freedom Pledge promised to uphold American freedoms for "all mankind" and signified their commitment by signing a Freedom Scroll that would supposedly be deposited in the Library of Congress.[20]

The government and private elites behind the Heritage Foundation used the Freedom Train to construct a national identity that was more ideal than real, in part by appealing to a traditional cultural narrative that celebrated consensus and triumphs at the expense of divisions and failures. The Foundation's document selection committee, which included John Foster Dulles, chose documents that conveyed the image of a unified nation bound together by a system of uncontested beliefs that also appealed to people in every part of the world. In this sense, the documents, the Freedom Pledge, and the accompanying literature reinforced elements of the national security ideology, including the notion that freedom was indivisible and the mission of the American people to defend it everywhere. The Foundation also took pains to eliminate any evidence of controversy and conflict, except global conflict, which was generally

---

[20] *Hearings on H. J. Res. 84*, esp. 27–29; Michael Kammen, *Mystic Chords of Memory: The Transformation of Tradition in American Culture,* paperback ed. (New York, 1993), 573–81; Heritage Foundation, *American Heritage Program*; Little, "Freedom Train," 72–75; and in *New York Times,* "Brooklyn Hails Freedom Train," 22 September 1947, "Return Trip Here for Freedom Train," 16 October 1948, "Freedom Program Set," 6 November 1948, "May Rededicates Freedom Train As 8,000 Visit It in Return to City," 26 November 1948, "The Freedom Train in Brooklyn Today," 28 November 1948, "Aides for Freedom Week," 17 December 1948, "Freedom Train Due in City Next Week," 24 December 1948, "Freedom Train Open for Farewell; City Rededication to Liberty Urged," 28 December 1948, "Veterans Gather at Freedom Train," 29 December 1948; "U.S. Tour is Ended by Freedom Train," 9 January 1949.

portrayed as a unifying event in defense of the American way. In this context, the Emancipation Proclamation became a symbol of presidential leadership rather than a byproduct of regional conflict and civil war. Similarly, expressions of diversity were likely to emphasize the union of many people into one nation rather than the bitter struggles for racial equality, worker's rights, or women's suffrage that had marked American history. "It is our policy," as one official put it, "to avoid current controversy and to concentrate our program upon the generally accepted bases constituting the American Heritage."[21]

These shortcomings notwithstanding, the Heritage Foundation drew substantial support from organized interest groups that were anxious to affirm their loyalty in a time of crisis. The major American trade unions contributed to local Rededication Weeks and were represented on the foundation's governing board. Much the same was true of veterans groups, civic associations, and religious organizations. Even African-American leaders backed the enterprise. Although no black leader served on the Foundation's board, Walter White, who headed the NAACP, lent his organization's active support to the Freedom Train. This was especially the case after the foundation announced that it would not permit segregated viewing of the train's precious cargo, and then followed through by cancelling visits to southern cities that insisted on a policy of segregation.[22]

By all accounts, moreover, those who viewed the documents in every region of the country constituted a broad representation of the whole population, including different religious, racial, and ethnic groups as well as social classes. Viewers usually waited in long lines for several hours, often in cold or rainy weather, to spend less than thirty minutes on the train. Although few had time to read more than a line or two of any document, photographs nonetheless revealed awe-struck observers starring reverently at icons of the American past. In Columbus, Georgia, a deaf, dumb, and blind man toured the exhibit with the help of a friend, who explained the documents by tapping signals on the man's fingers. In Trenton, New Jersey, a black woman fainted dead away as she read the Emancipation Proclamation and two older women spent seven hours in line before touring the exhibit, only to get back in line for a second visit. "It gets you," explained a member of the train's staff. "When you see what this country and these documents mean to people – how they'll

---

[21] Little, "Freedom Train," 59. See also, ibid., 53–61, 88–116.
[22] Ibid., 36, 126–34; Bradsher, "Taking America's Heritage to the People," 234, 237–40.

stand out there all day to see the things they feel make the nation great –
you get a lump in your throat."[23]

Indeed, officials often tried to capture popular sentiment through a
rhetorical style that called up images of a spiritual event or religious
procession as the Freedom Train crossed the country. The goal, according
to one source, was to strengthen the "spiritual defenses" of the nation,
reinvigorate the American "credo," construct a "National Shrine," and
host a "revival meeting for American democracy."[24] Winthrop Aldrich
saw the train's journey as a "pilgrimage to reaffirm America's faith in
free men," while another official noted the train's "cathedral effect" on
its visitors. "Everyone," he said, "seems to become reverent and sort
of quiet."[25] Reports in the popular press relied on similar metaphors.
"Inside, one has the feeling he is in church," wrote Gilbert Bailey for
The New York Times. "Parents shush their children and little school
boys take off their caps without being told. People speak in low guarded
tones used by tourists in ancient cathedrals."[26]

By almost any measure, the outpouring of popular support and enthusiasm was nothing short of astonishing. During the course of the train's
pilgrimage, the Heritage Foundation distributed nearly 5 million copies
of its various publications. *Reader's Digest* gave away 3.5 million copies
of its article on the Bill of Rights, *Look* magazine handed out 775,000
copies of its illustrated booklet, "Our American Heritage," and the Advertising Council contributed 1.5 million copies of its pamphlet, "Good
Citizen." Over 15,000 theaters showed "Our American Heritage," at
least one comic book wrote the Freedom Train into its script, and roughly
250 national magazines and thousands of other publications ran stories
about the train and related events – adding up to almost half a million
pages of press clippings.[27]

What is more, approximately 641 people viewed the exhibit every
hour, 9,000 people every day, and one in every three Americans par-
ticipated in the various Rededication Weeks. Almost 100,000 people
toured the exhibit when the train spent inauguration week in Washington,
DC; nearly half the city's population turned out when it stopped in

[23] Gilbert Bailey, "Why They Throng to the Freedom Train," *New York Times*, 25 January
1948. See also Little, "Freedom Train," 38–39, 69; "Freedom Train," *Life* 23 (29 September
1947): 49–50, 52; and "Freedom Train Tours America," 529–42.

[24] Heritage Foundation, *The American Heritage*.

[25] Aldrich quoted in "Freedom Train Tours America," 530; and the second official quoted in
Little, "Freedom Train," 68.

[26] Bailey, "Why They Throng to the Freedom Train," *New York Times*, 25 January 1948. See
also "President Receives Freedom Signatures," *New York Times*, 15 January 1949.

[27] Bradsher, "Taking America's Heritage to the People," 241.

Burlington, Vermont; and thousands were on hand for the parade that climaxed Rededication Week in Dover, Delaware. In New York City, clergymen of three faiths blessed the train during morning ceremonies, after which nearly 7,000 people, most of whom had waited in line for up to four hours, viewed the documents while "Dixie," "Yankee Doodle," and "My Old Kentucky Home" played in the background.[28] In the Borough of Queens, citizens celebrated the train's arrival with the largest parade since V-J Day and a program of community singing at which 2,500 people took the Freedom Pledge. In Brooklyn more than 50,000 people tried to board the train, most to no avail, and over 11,000 signed the Freedom Pledge. In Boston members of the Sons of the American Revolution donned colonial costumes to greet the train, and in Philadelphia citizens representing various nationalities dressed in ethnic costumes to lead a massive rally that welcomed the Freedom Train to that city. The rally took place against a sea of American flags and included a naturalization ceremony, so that the symbolic content of the whole affair remained true to the Foundation's general theme of national unity in the face of international crisis.[29]

At all such events distinguished citizens, often military leaders, wasted no time in stressing key themes in the national security ideology, including the danger of total war, the need for constant preparedness, and the burden of global leadership that both God and history had placed on American shoulders – the last point often driven home with a public prayer that asked for God's help in the struggle against communism. General Courtney H. Hodges, Commanding General of the First Army, warned one rally against permitting the nation to grow "so weak that we cannot defend our rights," while Admiral Thomas C. Kinkaid, commander of the Eastern Sea Frontier, told another group that "we alone are strong enough, actually and potentially, to resist the aggressive forces which are active throughout the world."[30] Following the speeches, parades, and other ceremonies, visitors pledged good citizenship and flocked to sign a Freedom Scroll, while others, who could not visit the train in person, sent their signatures by mail, so that the scroll contained more than three million names and weighed nearly 2,000 pounds at the conclusion of the tour.[31]

[28] " 'Melting Pot' Sees the Freedom Train," *New York Times*, 26 September 1947.

[29] "Brooklyn Hails Freedom Train," ibid., 28 September 1947; "Queens Turns Out for Freedom Train," ibid., 29 September 1947; "Church Freedom Hailed at Rally," ibid., 10 January 1949.

[30] " 'Melting Pot' Sees The Freedom Train." See also Little, "Freedom Train," 74.

[31] "President Receives Freedom Signatures," *New York Times*, 15 January 1949.

The Freedom Train was so popular that it generated several imitations. New York sponsored its own train with documents revealing the state's history and traditions.[32] Montclair, New Jersey, like other communities that were too small to be visited by the Freedom Train, established its own Freedom Week, complete with special school, club, and church exercises, and with a Freedom Truck that toured the community with records that chronicled democracy's development in New Jersey.[33] One group conceived of a Freedom Ship that would tour the Western Hemisphere exhibiting the industrial, cultural, and scientific accomplishments of free people in the Americas, while another group, the Freedom Foundation, organized in 1949, began awarding nearly 150 annual prizes to Americans who had advanced the cause of freedom.[34]

The best know imitation was the Friendship Train, which began its journey outside Los Angeles at a gala attended by Hollywood stars in late 1947, just as the Freedom Train was getting underway at ceremonies on the other side of the country. Conceived by syndicated newspaper columnist Drew Pearson, the Friendship Train was intended to help alleviate the postwar European food shortage, which was widely regarded as one of the most potent sources of communism in countries like France, Germany, and Italy, and to show support for the European Recovery Program that Secretary of State Marshall had proposed in June 1947. After its Hollywood launching, the train rolled through the Central Valley between Los Angeles and Sacramento, stopping at local communities to pick up carloads of everything from dried fruit and vegetables to rice, sugar, and wheat. Those who could not contribute food gave money instead. At Bakersfield more than a thousand people gathered with their offerings. At Oakland another 5,000 citizens met the train, and at Sacramento citizens contributed 7 tons of flour, 15 tons of sugar, 12 tons of assorted foods, and 72,000 cans of milk. Every stop added at least another boxcar to the red, white, and blue train, which headed east for Nevada with twenty five cars, one of which boasted a message in bold blue letters: "From the heart of the American people to our friends."[35]

32 "State to Sponsor a Freedom Train," ibid., 20 January 1948.
33 "Montclair to Hold Local Freedom Week," ibid., 31 December 1947; "Montclair Begins its Freedom Week," ibid., 19 January 1948.
34 "'Freedom Ship' is Planned to Promote Good Will in the Western Hemisphere," ibid., 2 August 1949; "Freedom Awards Raised to $84,000," ibid., 3 August 1949.
35 "Friendship Train Heads East Laden With Gifts of America," *Christian Science Monitor,* 11 November 1947. See also "Friendship on Wheels," *Newsweek* 30 (1 December 1947): 22; "Picture of the Week," *Life* 23 (24 November 1947): 38–39; Herman Klurfeld, *Behind the Lines: The World of Drew Pearson* (Englewood Cliffs, NJ, 1968), 147–61.

By the time it reached North Platte and Kearney, Nebraska, the train had grown to fifty cars, and by the time it left the state Nebraskans had contributed fourteen boxcars of flour and wheat and one of beans, not to mention cash contributions.[36]

As the train moved east to New York, people offered gifts large and small. Pharmacists contributed a carload of medical supplies, a boy's club offered $5 from its tiny treasury, a group of housewives donated jars of canned fruit, and small children emptied their piggy banks for the cause. In one community, college students skipped dinner to give the price of their meals; in another, spectators at a college football game raised more than $1,500; and in still another, a small boy gave the shirt off his back, which was quickly auctioned for $135. Sidney, Nebraska, a town of 10,000 people, raised $12,000 for the Friendship Train, and small farming communities across Iowa, from Boone to Marshalltown to Cedar Rapids, contributed twenty two boxcars and considerable cash.[37]

The train had reached eighty two cars when it arrived in Chicago, where it added another twenty one cars and was split into two parts for the run to New York. Along the way it crossed paths with the Freedom Train near Philadelphia, Pennsylvania, a city that added another twenty two cars of food to the cause.[38] By that time, moreover, a southwest Friendship Train had been formed to bring contributions from Texas, Oklahoma, and Kansas, leading Pearson and his colleagues to more than triple their estimate of the supplies that would be gathered. They now predicted a total of more than 200 boxcars carrying $5 million worth of food, enough to provide approximately 270 million meals to hungry Europeans.[39]

As was the case with the Freedom Train, community elites organized to make the Friendship Train a success. They publicized its visit, raised contributions from local organizations, and arranged parades, speeches, and other festivities to greet the train on its arrival. Schools, police stations, and firehouses became depositories for food contributions, stores

[36] See the sources cited in the following note.
[37] "Food Train Campaign Gains in Momentum," *New York Times,* 13 November 1947; "People's Gifts Swell Relief Train," *Christian Science Monitor,* 14 November 1947; "Iowa Fills 22 Boxcars on Friendship Train," ibid., 15 November 1947; "Kindness Amazes Foreigners Riding on Friendship Train," ibid., 17 November 1947; "Friendship on Wheels," *Newsweek* 30 (1 December 1947): 22.
[38] "Friendship Train Gets Pledges Here," *New York Times,* 15 November 1947; "City Welcomes Food Train Today; Parade, Ceremony to Mark Event," ibid., 18 November 1947.
[39] "Kindness Amazes Foreigners Riding on Friendship Train," *Christian Science Monitor,* 17 November 1947; "Kansas Gifts Top Peak in Relief Train Sendoff," ibid., 26 November 1947.

closed so that people could be on hand when the train arrived, and citizens of French and Italian descent took their place at the head of parades that also included the usual collection of boy scouts, police bands, fire trucks, veterans groups, and assorted dignitaries.[40]

The Friendship Train ended its transcontinental journey in New York City on 18 November. It consisted at that point of 214 cars in four separate sections, and organizers expected New York's contribution to increase the number to approximately 270 cars. Some of the boxcars carried French, Italian, and American flags, while others were decorated with slogans such as "Vive la France," "Viva l'Italia," and "From the Heart of the American People." A mayor's committee organized a large parade up Broadway, which was lined by 100,000 people, to City Hall, where a crowd of 25,000 gathered for ceremonies that included speeches by the mayor, the French consul general, and the U.S. ambassador to the United Nations – all of whom saluted the train as a symbol not only of America's generosity but also of its resolve to safeguard democracy against the menace of communism in Europe. To drive this message home symbolically, thirty three of the boxcars were detached from the train, loaded on barges, and taken on a marine procession around the Statue of Liberty, accompanied by police launches and fireboats blasting tall streams of water into the New York sky and creating a brilliant rainbow that framed the whole event.[41]

The Friendship Train also inspired imitations. These were mostly local or regional initiatives like the New Rochelle Friendship Train organized by the citizens of that city, or the Friend Ship, which carried food and clothing from New Englanders to the people of the British Isles, or the Friendship Caravan of food from Michigan to France. The largest and most successful of these initiatives was a midwestern effort, the Abraham Lincoln Train, which began its journey on Lincoln's birthday, 12 February 1948, in Lincoln, Nebraska. Sponsored by the Christian Rural Overseas Program and backed by the Farm Bureau Federation, the Lincoln Train raised another 150 boxcars of food and clothing for the people of Western Europe.[42]

40 "Friendship Train Gets Pledges Here," *New York Times*, 15 November 1947; "Trains of Friendship and of Freedom Meet," ibid., 18 November 1947; "Iowa Fills 22 Boxcars on Friendship Train," *Christian Science Monitor*, 15 November 1947.

41 "City Hails Friendship Train; Food Total is Put at 270 Cars," *New York Times*, 19 November 1947.

42 "New Friendship Train," *New York Times*, 25 December 1947; "Lincoln Train is Now Being Organized," ibid., 18 January 1948; "Friendship Train Expected to Collect $250,000 in Food," *Des Moines Register*, 8 February 1948; "2 Sections in Lincoln Train," ibid.,

As they traversed the country, the Lincoln Train, the Friendship Train, and the Freedom Train resembled the civic pageants that had been historically popular in America. They proclaimed a conventional cultural narrative, basically a narrative of national greatness, and they harnessed that narrative to the cause of national security. They celebrated the country's generosity, its democratic values, and its mission as leader of the free world; they praised its diversity and pluralism even while stressing the dangers of divisiveness and the need for unity; they stressed the duties of citizenship, including the need for national service and sacrifice; and they relied on a strategy of otherness, both to inscribe the country's political identity and to associate dissent with the communist menace in Moscow.[43]

Much the same can be said of the Loyalty Day parades that were yet another mark of popular engagement with the Cold War. Initiated in New York in 1948, these parades were assembled by organizations that wanted to counter the annual May Day parades that had been popular during the war years and remained so into the postwar period. Billed as an "anti-Fascist procession," the May Day parade in New York City was still drawing thousands of participants as late as 1949 and 1950. Marchers invariably included the leadership of the Communist party, left-wing labor groups, and veterans in uniform, including women and minority veterans on prominent display. They took "an anti-Fascist loyalty pledge," denounced the Jim Crow laws, the Taft-Hartley Act, and the Atlantic Pact, and paraded behind signs that read "Hail the Victories of the Chinese People," "Homes for Vets," and "No Deals with Franco Spain."[44]

In 1948 the Veterans of Foreign Wars decided to challenge the May Day parade in New York with a loyalty parade of its own, and over the next few months a National Loyalty Day Committee, headed by Secretary of Labor Maurice J. Tobin, began asking the governors of all states to issue declarations giving Loyalty Day an official status. Like the Freedom Train, the whole effort was inspired by national and local elites who sought to forge a Cold War culture that was officially sanctioned. The symbolic content of this culture emphasized the triumph of unity

11 February 1948; "Iowa to Load Lincoln Food Trains Today," ibid., 12 February 1948; Drew Pearson, "Carrying Out Lincoln Idea," ibid., 13 February 1948; and Klurfeld, *Behind the Lines,* 159.

43 Kammen, *Mystic Chords of Memory,* 278–80.

44 "Loyalty March Scores Reds; Turnout of Leftists Declines," *New York Times,* 1 May 1949. See also "City to See 2 Loyalty Parades and Left-Wing March Today," ibid., 30 April 1949; and "Two Rival Parades Pack Sidewalks of New York," *Los Angeles Times,* 1 May 1949.

over divisiveness, respect for established authority, and the economic
and political blessings of American democracy. It scripted the country's
democratic identity by comparison with the totalitarian other, which in
turn represented a threat that was internal as well as external, cultural
as well as military, and that had to be contained. Loyalty Day, as Tobin
said, served "as an inspiring demonstration of our belief in democracy
and will greatly assist in combating Communistic tendencies."

New York set the standard with large parades in Manhattan and
Brooklyn in 1949 and 1950. Both parades shared the same theme, "Stand
up, march, and be counted," and both had the blessing of the Democratic
and Republican parties. Governor Thomas E. Dewey proclaimed May
1 to be Loyalty Day and urged "loyal citizens" throughout the state
"to hold celebrations and public assemblies" to counteract the May Day
parades of "disloyal and subversive groups." "In the present state of
international affairs," Dewey announced, "a rededication to the ideals
of our country is most appropriate and desirable."[45] In a symbolic display of national unity, the Brooklyn paraders represented various labor,
fraternal, and civic organizations and the full range of veterans groups,
including the Disabled War Veterans, the Catholic War Veterans, the
Army and Navy Union, and the Veterans of Foreign Wars. Included as
well were 57,000 school children representing the Boy and Girl Scouts,
the Campfire Girls, the Junior Blue Jackets, and the Catholic Youth
Organization.[46]

The Manhattan parade was even more impressive, with Secretary
Tobin serving as Grand Marshal. The paraders, more than 50,000 strong,
marched up Fifth Avenue for three hours while thousands of observers
looked on. The parade included contingents from the Congress of Industrial Organizations and the American Federation of Labor, from the National Guard and various city departments, and from religious, veterans,
and patriotic groups. Boy Scouts carried the flags of all forty eight states
while other marchers hoisted more than one thousand American flags.
A large division of foreign-born Americans marched in native costume,
rededicated their loyalty to the nation, and thus symbolized again how
different groups formed a single, unified nation. The Chinese community

45 "Loyalty Rallies to Rival May Day March Set in 5 Cities, With 100,000 Likely in Event
Here," *New York Times*, 23 April 1949. See also "Plans are Started for Loyalty March,"
ibid., 12 March 1949; "5,000 Call for Ban on May Day March," ibid., 10 April 1949;
"Dewey Proclaims May 1 Loyalty Day," ibid., 25 April 1949; and "Governors Urged to
Proclaim May 1 as Loyalty Day," *Los Angeles Times*, 24 April 1949.
46 "70,000 in Brooklyn Appear in Parade," *New York Times*, 1 May 1949.

was represented by popular dragon dancers who pranced down Fifth Avenue under a terrifying dragon's head. Kilted Scottish pipers were followed by the Knights of Columbus in full uniform, who were followed in turn by the Improved Order of Red Men wearing feathered bonnets, buckskins, and war paint.[47]

Czechoslovakian, Hungarian, Estonian, and Latvian marchers used the opportunity to celebrate their freedom as Americans and to denounce the Communist dictatorships that had brought enslavement and poverty to their former homelands. Indeed, protests against world communism and Soviet expansion dominated the parade. Operators from the telephone company carried a banner that read, "We Don't Like Stalin's Party Line." One Eastern European contingent included women in mourning for their country, wearing black robes and carrying large black flags. The Greek contingent featured a large float of young women standing amidst a ruined temple with a sign that proclaimed: "Communism Spells Destruction." Other marchers carried signs declaring that "The Communists Slaughtered 268 Priests in Greece," or "We licked Fascism and Nazism, Communism is Next." The Hungarians paraded with two draped portraits of Joseph Cardinal Mindszenty, the Hungarian catholic prelate who had been jailed by the Communists; the Irish contingent included a boy in tattered clothes with a sign saying that he had "Just Arrived from the Red Paradise"; and the Lithuanian group marched behind a banner that said "Clean up Eighth Avenue" – a reference to the May Day Parade of left-wing groups that was marching down Eighth Avenue at the same time.[48]

By 1950 the loyalty day parade had become a national movement, with its own organizing committee and parades or other ceremonies in Boston, Buffalo, Chicago, Los Angeles, Philadelphia, Pittsburgh, Trenton, and other locations. In most cases, as in Los Angeles, the parades followed a gubernatorial proclamation of Loyalty Day, on which Americans were "to renew their allegiance to the democratic institutions which have made our country great." Mayors issued similar proclamations and local parade committees, representing patriotic, civic, union, and veteran's organizations, arranged the processions as an answer to the May Day celebrations of local left-wing groups. In most cases, the parade featured popular celebrities, such as Miss Loyalty, or the cowboy

---

[47] "150,000 took March in Loyalty Parade," *New York Times,* 27 April 1949; "City to See 2 Loyalty Parades and Left-Wing March Today," ibid., 30 April 1949; "Loyalty March Scores Reds; Turnout of Leftists Declines," ibid., 1 May 1949.
[48] "Loyalty March Scores Reds; Turnout of Leftists Declines," ibid., 1 May 1949.

actor Gene Autry, who headed the Loyalty Day Parade Committee in Los Angeles, not to mention prominent politicians, high school bands, Gold Star Mothers, winners of the Congressional Medal of Honor, and representatives of nearly every civic, fraternal, and veteran's group in the city.[49] In most cities the Catholic Church also got into the act. In New York, Francis Cardinal Spellman reviewed the Loyalty Day Parade in 1949, and in Los Angles, Loyalty Day ceremonies coincided with "Mary's Hour," a massive gathering of Catholics held under the auspices of the Archbishop of Los Angeles to denounce communism and pray for peace.[50]

Communities that were too small to host a Loyalty Parade conducted other ceremonies, of which none captured more attention than a May Day pageant in the little Wisconsin mill town of Mosinee, population 1,400. Sponsored by the Wisconsin Department of the American Legion, the pageant involved a mock Communist take over of the small community. Local leaders endorsed the idea, which was supposed to give residents a taste of what it would be like to live under a totalitarian government. According to one Legion official, daily life was to be an "oppressive routine of propaganda, rationing, red tape and regulations." In theory, at least, the experience would leave the Mosinee population with a deeper appreciation of their rights as American citizens and with a greater resolve to protect those rights against Communist aggression and subversion. It was an opportunity, editorialized the *Mosinee Times*, "to present a message on Americanism that can be the beginning of an awakening as to the privileges inherent in our way of life" and the need to be ever vigilant in their defense. "It can happen here," was the message that sponsors wanted to get across.[51]

To lend authenticity to the event, the Legion chose Jack Kornfeder, a former Communist, to act as "commissar" on May Day. Kornfeder, who claimed to be a graduate of Moscow's subversive warfare college, had left

49 "Warren Proclaims May 1 Loyalty Day," *Los Angeles Times* 30 April 1949. See also "Thousands to Join in City's Loyalty Parade Tomorrow," ibid.; "Loyalty Parade Set for Tonight," ibid., 1 May 1949; and "Loyalty Day Pledge Taken by Thousands," ibid., 2 May 1949.

50 "150,000 to March in Loyalty Parade," *New York Times,* 27 April 1949; "Thousands to Join in City's Loyalty Parade Tomorrow," *Los Angeles Times,* 30 April 1949; "Loyalty Parade Set for Tonight," ibid., 1 May 1949; "Loyalty Day Pledge Taken by Thousands," ibid., 2 May 1949.

51 "Reds to Take Over Mosinee for a Day," Wausau, Wisconsin, *Daily Record-Herald,* 13 April 1950; and "Our Opportunity," *The Mosinee Times,* 26 April 1950. See also "Mosinee Will Go Communistic For One Day," *The Mosinee Times,* 12 April 1950; "Mosinee's Red May Day Blasted by Real Commies," *Daily Record-Herald,* 27 April 1950; "Mayor's Arrest Really Was a Shock to Him," ibid., 1 May 1950; and "It Could Happen Here," ibid., 1 May 1950.

the Communist party in the early 1930s and had since made a living as a writer and lecturer on right-wing causes. By early 1950 he had become an ally and associate of Senator Joseph McCarthy, whom Kornfeder defended in a press conference shortly after his arrival in Mosinee. He told those present that Communists and Communist sympathizers had infiltrated the federal government, as McCarthy had charged, and that he and the senator would soon ferret them out.[52]

The Red invasion of Mosinee began in the early morning hours with the arrest of Mayor Ralph Kronenwetter and Police Chief Carl Gewiss by Kornfeder, Benjamin Gitlow, another ex-Communist recruited for the event, and members of the local American Legion who were pretending to be armed Communists. Thereafter, the Communist invaders seized city hall and the police station, as well as the local railroad yard, power company, and telephone building. They threw up road blocks around the community, checked citizens for their identification papers and ration coupons, and ordered a mass meeting at which Kronenwetter, a gun to his head, was forced to proclaim the rules and regulations of the "new regime." Private businesses were to be nationalized, trade unions prohibited, churches locked, and all political parties abolished except for the Communist party. Food prices were to be jacked up for the day, restaurants were to serve nothing but black bread and potato soup, the local library and theater were to be purged of unacceptable books and films, and uncooperative citizens were to be thrown into a barbed wire concentration camp that had been hastily erected in the newly rechristened "Red Square." The Mosinee movie house was renamed the Peoples Theater and the town's weekly newspaper, the *Mosinee Times,* whose publisher had helped to organize the event, was retitled the *Red Star,* printed on pink paper, and filled with Communist "propaganda," including a biography of Stalin, a labor code, and a proclamation abolishing private property and civil rights.[53]

---

52 "Ex-Commie Will Be Mosinee Commissar," *Daily Record-Herald,* 24 April 1950; "Mosinee Tense as The Big Day Nears," ibid., 28 April 1950. See also the stories in ibid., 1 May 1950, and in the following note.

53 "Mosinee's Plans for 'A Day Under Communism' Near Completion," *The Mosinee Times,* 26 April 1950; "Mosinee Tense as the Big Day Nears," *Daily Record-Herald,* 28 April 1950; "Reds Set for Mosinee Coup," ibid., 29 April 1950; "Mayor's Arrest Really Was a Shock to Him," ibid., 1 May 1950; "Reds Infiltrate Town in Wisconsin to Deride Mock May Day Seizure," *New York Times,* 1 May 1950; Mosinee, WI, *The Red Star,* 1 May 1950; "Town Deserts U.S. For Day in Soviet," *New York Times,* 2 May 1950; "Commies Call Mosinee Plan 'Police-State Idea' in Attack," *The Mosinee Times,* 3 May 1950; "U.S. Town Stages a Communist Coup," *Life* 28 (15 May 1950): 46–47. See also the stories in the *Daily Record-Herald,* 1 May 1950.

The day ended in triumph, however, with an evening rally in a local park, during which the American flag was again hoisted over Mosinee and its citizens joined in signing the national anthem. They burned the Communist propaganda that had been distributed during the day and listened to patriotic speeches by local officials and legionnaires, most of whom declared divine support for American democracy and urged all those who listened to back every measure, including every military measure, that would prepare the country for the continuing struggle with godless communism.[54]

The Mosinee demonstration, as well as the Freedom Train, the Friendship Train, and the Loyalty Day Parades, were all well-organized events. They were sponsored by the American Legion, the Veterans of Foreign Wars, and similar groups, and by a variety of civic, labor, and fraternal organizations. They were supported by national and local political parties and politicians, from the president of the United States to his attorney general and secretary of labor to the governors of major states to city mayors and other local officials. They inscribed an American identity by linking international dangers and domestic dissent to a totalitarian otherness that was foreign to American life. They put the Communists on trial by featuring Americans of Eastern European ancestry and by comparing American liberties with the loss of freedom under communism. They fostered a spirit of national loyalty, symbolized by the loyalty oaths, and of national pride and unity, symbolized by the naturalization ceremonies and the prominent display of ethnic Americans in traditional costumes. They sought to encourage a sense of national resolve against the Communist menace, and they tried to forge a national consensus behind current policies, from the Marshall Plan to military preparedness.

It is impossible to know if these efforts succeeded. The demonstrations say a good deal about the local and national elites who organized them, about their efforts to conceal social divisions, promote national unity, foster Americanism, and build support for the Cold War and the national security state. But it is difficult to know what went through the minds of ordinary Americans who read the literature circulated by the Heritage Foundation or who visited the Freedom Train, contributed to the Friendship Train, or rallied at "Red Square" in Mosinee, Wisconsin. The large crowds that visited the Freedom Train cannot be dismissed as byproducts of a well-oiled marketing campaign, but neither can they be

---

54 See the stories in *The Mosinee Times*, 3 May 1950. See also "Mosinee's Plans for 'A Day Under Communism' Near Completion," ibid., 26 April 1950.

read as expressions of popular support for current policies or as anything more than tokens of curiosity, national pride, and patriotism.

On the contrary, an undertone of criticism often marked these public demonstrations, despite the pressure for conformity coming from their organizers. As we have seen, the Loyalty Day parades were held against the backdrop of the May Day parades sponsored by radical opponents of American foreign policy. Nor was May Day in Mosinee without irony and criticism. Just before dawn on that day, critics blanketed the little town with flyers denouncing the event and its organizers as "fascists." The Communist Party of Wisconsin later took credit for the flyers and published a letter attacking the spectacle as a fraud perpetrated by the local paper mill management and the American Legion. The charge might have been easily dismissed had it not been repeated by the more mainstream Madison, Wisconsin, *Capital Times*, which said that the citizens of Mosinee should be less concerned about an improbable Soviet invasion than about the dictatorship of monopoly capitalism in a one-company town. The publisher of the *Mosinee Times* ridiculed the charges as Communist propaganda, but he could not deny the leadership role that local elites had played in organizing the event, including officials from the paper mill, the local Republican party, and the state and local American Legion. Nor could he get residents of the little town to take the event as seriously as he wanted or to keep a straight face when surrounded by photographers.[55] One newspaper described the mood in Mosinee as "festive," and another called the Red takeover a "smiling revolution."[56]

That mood ended when Mayor Kronenwetter was stricken with a fatal heart attack just hours after being pulled from his bed by Kornfeder and dragged for the benefit of photographers into a freezing spring morning wearing nothing but pajamas and a bathrobe. A Democrat who had made an unsuccessful run for Congress two years earlier, Kronenwetter did not want the Republicans to get all the credit for the May Day spectacle, but neither was he enamored with the demonstration. On the contrary, he used the news coverage to announce plans to make another run for Congress and to attack Senator McCarthy, whose

55 "Mosinee's 'Red' May Day Blasted by Real Commies," *Daily Record-Herald*, 27 April 1950; "Reds Infiltrate Town in Wisconsin to Deride Mock May Day Seizure," *New York Times*, 1 May 1950; "Commies Call Mosinee Plan 'Police-State Idea' in Attack," *The Mosinee Times*, 3 May 1950; "Different Words, Same Thoughts," ibid., 17 May 1950.
56 "Reds Infiltrate Town in Wisconsin to Deride Mock May Day Seizure," *New York Times*, 1 May 1950; "Smiling Revolution," *Daily Record-Herald*, 3 May 1950.

witch-hunting, the mayor said, was not likely to turn up many Communists in government. Not surprisingly, the *Mosinee Times* was horrified when some commentators, "closely associated with the Communist Party," began to insinuate that the mayor's death was a direct result of his reluctant involvement in the May Day spectacle.[57]

Even the Freedom Train had its share of critics, some of whom gave voice to an alternative reading of American history. Communists attacked the whole idea as a plot by "reactionary big businessmen" and staged demonstrations when the train visited Philadelphia and New York City. Some liberals also saw the train as an example of ideological and class conflict, and specifically as a ploy by Winthrop Aldrich and other wealthy Republicans to promote conservative values over a resurgent New Deal. Some labor leaders complained when the documents did not include the Wagner Labor Act or the executive order establishing the Fair Employment Practices Commission, both of which spoke to the long history of labor–management conflict and racial struggle in the United States. Left-wing African-Americans, including Paul Robeson and Langston Hughes, took a similar position, arguing, in effect, that black leaders could hardly celebrate rights and freedoms that were often denied to minority groups. Writing in the *New Republic*, Hughes captured his suspicions in a devastating poem:

> Can a coal black man drive the Freedom
>   Train?
> Or Am I still a porter on the Freedom
>   Train?
> Is there ballot boxes on the Freedom
>   Train?
> Do colored folks vote on the Freedom
>   Train?
> When it stops in Mississippi will it be
>   made plain
> Everybody's got a right to board the
>   Freedom Train?[58]

---

57 "They'd Despite It!" *Mosinee Times*, 10 May 1950. See also "Mayor's Arrest Really Was a Shock to Him," *Daily Record-Herald*, 1 May 1950; "R. E. Kronenwetter Stricken at Close of May Day Show," *Mosinee Times*, 3 May 1950; "Mosinee Seized By Reds," *Daily Record-Herald*, 1 May 1950; "Mosinee 'Restores' Democracy But Observance Is Marred by Grave Illness of City's Mayor," ibid., 2 May 1950; and "Two Mosinee Men Who Had Key Roles in 'Red Coup' Program are Dead," ibid., 8 May 1950.
58 "Propaganda: Traveling Heirlooms," *Time* 50 (22 September 1947): 23. See also, Bradsher "Taking America's Heritage to the People," 234.

IV

The oppositional voice is even more pronounced if we look at the letters to the editors of major newspapers, an American institution that provided a kind of soap box for popular expressions on both sides of the national security discourse. The expressions that follow come from eight newspapers published in different regions of the country, all of which were examined for public reaction to some of the major issues discussed in the previous chapters. Generally speaking, the critics of American policy felt a stronger need to register their opinions than did supporters, who may have found their views adequately represented by the government itself or by the newspapers, which often endorsed official policy. Nevertheless, the views of both sides are noted below, as are the rhetorical strategies used to convey them. Tone, language, and rhetorical form in general provide important insights into political identity and ideology, in most cases separating the writers into two groups that might be called liberal realists and conservative isolationists. Although writers in the second group were more inclined to communicate with conservative newspapers, such as the *Chicago Tribune* or the *Dallas Morning News*, both groups were represented in every newspaper and in every section of the country.

The arguments conducted on the opinion pages of the nation's newspapers were remarkably similar to those that rang through the halls of Congress. On one level, the debate focused on the Cold War in the United States, namely on the loyalty program, loyalty oaths, and McCarthyism in general, all of which prompted a substantial outpouring of critical letters by writers who were convinced that a hysterical patriotism was overwhelming basic American freedoms. They had good reason to be concerned, moreover, judging by the many writers who thought that Communists and fellow travelers were not entitled to the constitutional guarantees available to other Americans. They were guilty of "organized disloyalty," wrote C. M. Flower of San Francisco.[59] Because they took their orders from Moscow, others agreed, they could not use the Constitution to protect themselves or shield their efforts to overthrow the "American Way of Life."[60] Nor were they entitled to federal

---

[59] Flower, letter to the editor, *San Francisco Chronicle*, 5 March 1947.

[60] W. E. Morgan, letter to the editor, *Dallas Morning News*, 14 May 1949. See also William J. Keenan, letter to the editor, *Boston Herald*, 21 February 1947; H. L. Tewman, letter to the editor, *San Francisco Chronicle*, 25 February 1947; Frank E. Bowe, letter to the editor, *Boston Herald*, 9 April 1947; Arthur W. Blakemore, letter to the editor, *Washington Post*, 9 April 1947; Mrs. A. J. Klein, letter to the editor, *Dallas Morning News*, 1 June 1949; L. S. Scott, letter to the editor, *Cleveland Plain Dealer*, 8 June 1949; Paul C. Von Gontard,

employment, which was a public trust and should be available only to those who would pledge their loyalty to the American government.[61]

"Real Americans," according to this line of argument, had nothing to fear from loyalty oaths and loyalty investigations that would safeguard their liberties against the Communist challenge. Those who had done nothing wrong should even support some restrictions on their freedoms, including the humiliation of being wrongly suspected, in order to weed out the Communist menace that posed a much greater danger. The right of free speech, Chester W. Nichols wrote the *Boston Herald*, would not be harmed by action to remove Communists from the government payroll, "even though some few persons wrongly so."[62]

Such sentiments alarmed critics, who were convinced that loyalty oaths, the loyalty program, the Attorney General's list, and similar measures promised a long "period of persecution, hypocrisy, fear and slavish uniformity disguised as patriotism." "Now begins the purge," one critic wrote of the loyalty program. "Now begins the witch hunt."[63] These critics were most likely to be on the liberal or left wing of the political spectrum, judging by the form and content of their letters. They were inclined to view the anti-Communist campaign as a ploy by conservatives to silence their opponents, who could not utter a single word without fear of being branded un-American.[64] Red-baiting, they said, was being used to discredit labor, intimidate teachers, and attack integrationists who tried to promote racial equality and justice.[65] If government employees could

letter to the editor, *St. Louis Post-Dispatch*, 20 October 1949; Sydney E. Stoliar, letter to the editor, ibid., 4 November 1949; Thomas J. Tanous, letter to the editor, ibid., 4 November 1949; and J. Porter Henry, letter to the editor, ibid., 9 November 1949.

[61] Josephine Powell Beaty, letter to the editor, *Washington Post*, 1 July 1949; Jack Horan, letter to the editor, *San Francisco Chronicle*, 8 July 1949; Edward Barker, letter to the editor, ibid., 12 July 1949; Ellen O'Connor, letter to the editor, ibid., 16 July 1949; A. Mendel, letter to the editor, ibid., 16 July 1949; L. K. Webb, letter to the editor, ibid., 28 November 1950; A. W. Marshall, letter to the editor, *Dallas Morning News*, 6 February 1951.

[62] Frank Johnson, letter to the editor, *San Francisco Chronicle*, 4 May 1949, and Nichols, letter to the editor, *Boston Herald*, 4 April 1947. See also Amy Hobe, letter to the editor, *San Francisco Chronicle*, 6 March 1947; C. A. De Camp, letter to the editor, ibid., 22 June 1949; and Charles F. Martin, letter to the editor, *St. Louis Post-Dispatch*, 3 January 1951.

[63] Charles Merrill, letter to the editor, *St. Louis Post-Dispatch*, 29 March 1947; and "Only One American," letter to the editor, ibid., 30 March 1947. See also David S. Burgess, letter to the editor, ibid., 28 March 1947.

[64] Stanley D. McNail, letter to the editor, *Washington Post*, 9 March 1947.

[65] Hope Wheeler, letter to the editor, *Dallas Morning News*, 7 April 1947; Otis Durant Duncan, letter to the editor, ibid., 9 April 1947; Byron Allen, letter to the editor, *Washington Post*, 19 June 1947; J. Lewis Henderson, letter to the editor, *St. Louis Post-Dispatch*, 19 June 1947; Joseph Facci, letter to the editor, *Washington Post*, 20 June 1947; David C. Fulton, letter to

be dismissed for belonging to a subversive organization, wrote Alvin Guttag of Washington, DC, then all members of the Democratic Party of Georgia should be removed for denying basic constitutional rights to black Americans.[66] Others argued, mockingly, that most federal employees would have to be relieved of their jobs because they favored rent controls, social security, or other programs that conservatives equated with communism.[67]

Both sides employed a discursive strategy that revealed their political identities and ideologies, usually by reference to an un-American other or through oppositional parings that reduced their critics to alien, sick, subversive, or subhuman entities. On the one side, those who defended the loyalty program considered themselves to be "real Americans," denounced their opponents as slavish adherents to the Moscow party line, called liberals fellow travelers, and equated both communism and liberalism with "poison," "termites," "smallpox," or a "cancerous growth" that had to be removed by "radical means."[68] On the other side, critics of the loyalty program reduced their opponents to psychotics or equated them with the Nazis. Instead of protecting traditional rights, they insisted, the loyalty oaths, the Attorney General's list, and other such initiatives would lead to "a Gestapo America" in which citizens subordinated "their speech and opinions to the dictates of the state." They urged their fellow Americans not to adopt one form of totalitarianism in order to defeat another.[69] The defense of democracy against communism, wrote Charles D. Potter of Washington, DC, must not turn the country into a "Fascist oligarchy" with the FBI and the House Committee on Un-American Affairs as "our thought police."[70]

the editor, ibid., 22 June 1947; James C. Brown, letter to the editor, *Cleveland Plain Dealer*, 9 October, 1949.

[66] Alvin Guttag, letter to the editor, *Washington Post*, 1 April 1947.

[67] Harry B. Wilson and E. P., letters to the editor, *Washington Post*, 2 April 1947; S. T. Capps, letter to the editor, *Atlanta Constitution*, 27 June 1947.

[68] Paul C. Von Gontard, letter to the editor, *St. Louis Post-Dispatch*, 20 October 1949; Sydney E. Stoliar, letter to the editor, ibid., 4 November 1949; A. Mendel, letter to the editor, *San Francisco Chronicle*, 16 July 1949.

[69] Pearse T. White, letter to the editor, *San Francisco Chronicle*, 25 November 1950; Stanley D. McNail, letter to the editor, *Washington Post*, 9 March 1947. See also Arvo Josephson, letter to the editor, *San Francisco Chronicle*, 15 March 1947; Arthur Locke King, letter to the editor, *Washington Post*, 28 March 1947; Eugene Sacks, letter to the editor, *St. Louis Post-Dispatch*, 12 April 1947; Rev. Geo. L. Britt, letter to the editor, ibid., 6 July 1947; and Victoria L. Munro, letter to the editor, *Washington Post*, 11 July 1947.

[70] Potter, letter to the editor, *Washington Post*, 31 July 1947. Potter was chairman of the Committee for the Defense of Civil and Religious Liberty in the Americas. See his letter

If a concern for traditional freedoms ran through the debates over the Cold War at home, the same concern was even more evident in the debates over foreign policy. Beginning with Truman's program of aid to Greece and Turkey and continuing through the early years of the Eisenhower administration, critics worried that containing communism in every part of the world would undermine the foundations of democracy at home. They feared a totalitarian state dominated by the military and devoted to military purposes, while their opponents, who generally supported American policy, followed a line of reasoning laid out in the new ideology of national security. They accepted preparedness in an age of total war and saw containment as the only way to avoid the garrison state at home, safeguard basic liberties worldwide, and fulfill the nation's destiny as the global defender of democracy.

Critics were overcome by the futility of war and profoundly skeptical of the global commitments that American leaders were undertaking. To them it was self-evident that nothing good had come of World War II, which they saw as a worthless bill of goods sold to a gullible Franklin Roosevelt by "political crooks in Europe." The war had cost precious lives and treasure and had not brought the new era of world peace and democracy that allied leaders had promised. On the contrary, the wartime alliance had broken down, the postwar world was fraught with danger, and one form of totalitarianism had replaced another.[71]

These developments seemed to prove that no country, not even the United States, could dictate to the world. Asia was too vast to be controlled by the United States and was caught up in a "revolution" that would drive "the white man" into the sea.[72] Nor could the United States do much to help Europe unless the Europeans did more to help themselves. Aid to Greece was useless, according to the critics, so long as it went in large part for military purposes and so long as the Greeks avoided the political and economic reforms that were essential to democratic development and modernization.[73] Critics made the same point

to the editor, ibid., 6 June 1949. See also Marie Reed, letter to the editor, *Cleveland Plain Dealer,* 12 June 1949.

[71] Hay T. Clark, letter to the editor, *Dallas Morning News,* 22 December 1950. See also Chester M. May, letter to the editor, *Boston Herald,* 11 December 1950; James P. Whiteside, letter to the editor, *San Francisco Chronicle,* 26 December 1950; Edwin H. Boyer, letter to the editor, *Chicago Tribune,* 8 January 1951; and James G. Morgan, letter to the editor, *San Francisco Chronicle,* 8 January 1951.

[72] John M. Fisheld, letter to the editor, *San Francisco Chronicle,* 3 January 1951. See also Sigmund Lowe, letter to the editor, *Dallas Morning News,* 3 November 1950.

[73] "American," letter to the editor, *Washington Post,* 14 March 1947; L. P. Chambers, letter to the editor, *St. Louis Post-Dispatch,* 12 April 1947; George L. Payne, letter to the editor, *Dallas Morning News,* 22 April 1947.

about the Marshall Plan and about the military aid programs of both administrations. They complained constantly that money alone could not stop communism and that European leaders were busy making saps of the United States instead of doing what they could to save themselves.[74]

Not only would a policy of global containment be futile, according to the critics, it would also be self-destructive. Among other things, it would cost much more than the United States could afford, an argument that critics made repeatedly in debates over the Greco-Turkish aid program, the Marshall Plan, the military assistance program, and the Korean War. Such initiatives, one critic wrote, would "bleed this country's resources" to a point where it would no longer be a match for the Soviet Union. Lenin, another critic explained, wanted "the United States to spend itself into destruction," which was exactly what American leaders were doing. They were pursuing costly foreign aid programs that would rebuild competitors in the global marketplace and would lead to high taxes, an enormous national debt, and the constant risk of inflation, economic controls, and ever bigger government.[75] Under these circumstances, ordinary Americans would be pauperized and the door would be thrown open to communism or to some other form of totalitarianism.[76]

The case against a policy of globalism had liberal and conservative dimensions. Conservatives relied on a rhetorical strategy that betrayed a suspicion of the outside world, a cynicism about current initiatives, and a conspiratorial view of international affairs. They were likely to see World War II as a failed departure from the nation's isolationist tradition, to complain about the British, and to link foreign aid with New Deal social programs. The Marshall Plan, as one letter writer put it, was a

---

[74] Jos. W. Diebker, letter to the editor, *St. Louis Post-Dispatch,* 23 December 1950; Henry Vantine, letter to the editor, *San Francisco Chronicle,* 23 December 1950; Fred Schreiber, letter to the editor, *Chicago Tribune,* 26 December 1950; Herbert C. Neal, letter to the editor, *Cleveland Plain Dealer,* 17 December 1950; Rex S. Rambo, letter to the editor, *Dallas Morning News,* 6 January 1951. See also Horace G. Merten, letter to the editor, *Chicago Tribune,* 17 March 1947.

[75] "Observer," letter to the editor, *Chicago Tribune,* 30 June 1947; W. E. Lansdowne, letter to the editor, *San Francisco Chronicle,* 14 November 1949. See also Joe McGovern, letter to the editor, *Chicago Tribune,* 19 August 1947; Gust C. Linsenmann, letter to the editor, *Cleveland Plain Dealer,* 24 December 1950; and Edwin Robert Boehmer, letter to the editor, *San Francisco Chronicle,* 27 December 1950.

[76] J. Keller Kirn, Sr., letter to the editor, *Cleveland Plain Dealer,* 9 March 1947; G. M. Schofield, letter to the editor, *Boston Herald,* 16 March 1947; E. W. F., letter to the editor, *Chicago Tribune,* 17 March 1947; "Simple Sally," letter to the editor, *St. Louis Post-Dispatch,* 20 March 1947; John Perrine, letter to the editor, *Chicago Tribune,* 25 May 1947; M. C. Smith, letter to the editor, *Cleveland Plain Dealer,* 20 July 1947; H. F. M., letter to the editor, *Chicago Tribune,* 22 July 1947; Hero Soneberg, letter to the editor, ibid., 9 May 1949; E. Paul Weaver, letter to the editor, *Cleveland Plain Dealer,* 14 May 1949.

"sort of world WPA."[77] This writer and others like him were absolutely convinced that international aid programs subsidized socialism abroad, especially in Britain, and were part of a liberal plot to sustain a powerful federal government at home. Their goal was to eliminate these programs and thus stop "governmentalism" and the "outrageous encroachments of statism."[78]

Liberal critics, on the other hand, were more likely to adopt the rhetoric of realism and to argue that current policies, though well intentioned, were not always well conceived and sensibly implemented. They complained that arms spending consumed too large a proportion of the nation's budget while education, housing, and health care were underfunded – a complaint that grew louder in the early years of the Eisenhower administration. Improvements in these areas would help to create a new generation of responsible leaders in the United States, just as similar initiatives applied globally would eradicate the economic causes of conflict. Liberals were more likely to support the Marshall Plan than aid to Greece or Turkey, and to favor economic assistance to democratic governments rather than unpopular or unrepresentative regimes. They faulted the Republicans for being more willing to support defense spending than foreign aid, and they complained when American officials allowed military programs like the North Atlantic Treaty to crowd out economic initiatives like the Marshall Plan. The real threat to peace, they said, was to be found in hunger, sickness, and other deprivations that could not be addressed through military alliances and arms spending.[79]

Running through these economic arguments was a steady stream of complaints from ordinary citizens who did not always display a clear-cut ideological bent but were nonetheless aware of the economic sacrifices

---

[77] John Balch, letter to the editor, *Washington Post*, 25 June 1947.

[78] W. M. Reynolds, letter to the editor, *Atlanta Constitution*, 8 February 1951. See also D. B. Toley, letter to the editor, *Chicago Tribune*, 4 March 1947; John McCarthy, letter to the editor, *Cleveland Plain Dealer*, 18 September 1949; Curtis P. Nettels, letter to the editor, *Chicago Tribune*, 20 November 1949; and Hugh F. O'Neil, letter to the editor, ibid., 24 November 1949.

[79] Paul Harris Drake, letter to the editor, *Boston Herald*, 10 February 1947; Richard Gregg, letter to the editor, ibid., 13 February 1947; Anthony Russo, letter to the editor, *San Francisco Chronicle*, 8 March 1947; Joseph Peters, letter to the editor, ibid., 5 April 1947; L. P. Chambers, letter to the editor, *St. Louis Post-Dispatch*, 12 April 1947; E. H. Vanderlee, letter to the editor, *Chicago Tribune*, 20 April 1947; Emily Greene Balch, et al., letter to the editor, *Washington Post*, 17 April 1949; P. Schabacker, letter to the editor, *St. Louis Post-Dispatch*, 11 January 1951; Stanton A. Coblentz, letter to the editor, *San Francisco Chronicle*, 13 January 1951; J. W. Fyock, letter to the editor, *Cleveland Plain Dealer*, 11 February 1951; Shelby E. Southard, letter to the editor, *St. Louis Post-Dispatch*, 4 March 1951; James P. Whiteside, letter to the editor, ibid., 12 March 1951.

that national security entailed. "We are having a tough enough time of it," wrote Rubby Smith of Paoli, Indiana, "putting shoes on our children's feet, and paying our insurance, and putting nourishing meals on the table," without giving away billions of dollars to other countries.[80] "Look at the service hospitals," complained W. M. Strong of Cleveland, "filled with the wrecks of what were once superb young men; look at our filthy streets and filthy homes, and say whether we do not have enough to do in the way of rehabilitation and cleaning up after the war without going into another one."[81] "I am for getting out of Europe," wrote A. C. Smith of Chicago, "and reconstructing Chicago, Philadelphia, Detroit, Newark, and, yes, New York City."[82]

Some of these complaints came from writers who conveyed their identity through a pseudonym, such as "White Collar Girl," or by revealing personal details of their lives. John Moore of Chicago wanted to know why he should support foreign relief while being destitute himself. "I am an industrial pipe fitter," he wrote to the *Chicago Tribune*, "with no job, no home, a wife and a 3 month old son – a family I love and can't support" and "also a veteran with three years in the navy."[83] Another man who complained about the Marshall Plan identified himself as one of the many veterans who had left a small business to enlist during the war. "Now, at over 40," lamented Louis J. Leonhardt of Chicago, "I am struggling to build another business, and it's not so easily done under present day taxes and restrictions."[84] Another small businessman, who signed his letter "American For 63 Years," said that he, like the Europeans, suffered "from a dollar shortage." He had been unable to raise his salary in years but had seen everything else, from food prices to his own taxes, go up steadily. He wanted to know what benefits had accrued to him as a result of the Marshall Plan and other international initiatives.[85] Nor were men the only ones to complain. "I am a working girl with a fixed income," wrote a woman who did not have enough money after taxes to "buy a much needed purse in which to carry my hanky and cosmetics." "Could I get a smidgeon of the Marshall Plan before I have to go on relief?"[86]

---

[80] Smith, letter to the editor, *Cleveland Plain Dealer*, 12 November 1950.
[81] Strong, letter to the editor, *Chicago Tribune*, 12 April 1947.
[82] Smith, letter to the editor, *Chicago Tribune*, 28 June 1947. See also J. L. S. letter to the editor, *St. Louis Post-Dispatch*, 12 May 1949.
[83] Moore, letter to the editor, *Chicago Tribune*, 22 March 1949.
[84] Leonhardt, letter to the editor, *Chicago Tribune*, 3 March 1949.
[85] "American For 63 Years," letter to the editor, *Chicago Tribune*, 2 October, 1949.
[86] "White Collar Girl," letter to the editor, *Chicago Tribune*, 1 July 1949.

Buried in many of these complaints was the familiar fear that economic and political freedom would give way to economic regimentation and the garrison state, a metaphor that was almost as popular in these letters as it was in congressional speeches.[87] Critics saw such a development unfolding not only in the higher taxes, the growing national debt, and the threat of economic controls but also in the way power was being concentrated both in the armed forces and in the executive branch of the government. They pointed to the North Atlantic Treaty, under which the president might circumvent the Constitution and involve the United States in a European war before Congress had acted. "With the Atlantic Pact," Edward Wagenknecht wrote sarcastically, "we won't need another FDR to trick us into war."[88] Further proof, if any was needed, came with Truman's decisions to intervene in Korea without a formal declaration of war and to send American troops to Europe without congressional consent. With both decisions, critics argued, the president had usurped congressional prerogatives and undermined the constitutional basis of American democracy.[89]

Although most of these complaints came from isolationists who betrayed a conservative bias in the content of their complaint and in their rhetorical style, both liberal and conservative voices can be heard in the letters dealing with universal military training. As in Congress, the public discourse on UMT focused in part on its military utility in the atomic age and in part on whether it squared with the tradition of the citizen soldier and the country's historic antipathy toward a large, standing army. Beyond these issues, however, lay deep concerns about the threat that UMT could pose to traditional values and institutions. Whereas supporters argued that UMT would improve the physical health and moral well-being of American youth and would educate them in the principles of good citizenship, critics said that all of these functions properly belonged with the home, the school, and the church. UMT, wrote one citizen, was "an

---

[87] J. Murphy, letter to the editor, *San Francisco Chronicle*, 27 December 1950.

[88] Wagenknecht, letter to the editor, *Chicago Tribune*, 9 April 1949. See also Maurice W. Williams, letter to the editor, *San Francisco Chronicle*, 1 April 1949; X. Carson, letter to the editor, *Dallas Morning News*, 2 April 1949; George M. Montross, letter to the editor, 4 April 1949; Rev. J. Paul Cotton, letter to the editor, *Cleveland Plain Dealer*, 10 April 1949; and Helen Dortch Longstreet, letter to the editor, *Atlanta Constitution*, 10 April 1949.

[89] F. O. Richey, letter to the Editor, *Cleveland Plain Dealer*, 5 November 1950; "An American," letter to the editor, *Chicago Tribune*, 16 November 1950; "Outraged American," letter to the editor, ibid., 1 December 1950; Edwin H. Boyer, letter to the editor, ibid., 8 January 1951; Frank Kraemer, letter to the editor, *San Francisco Chronicle*, 8 January 1951; "A Father," letter to the editor, *St. Louis Post-Dispatch*, 9 January 1951; Clifford L. Maklin, letter to the editor, *Chicago Tribune*, 12 January 1951.

open challenge to those of us who still believe the home and the church are the backbone of our country."[90] "The church is capable of looking after moral and spiritual things," wrote another, just as "our universities are capable of instructing without military supervision" and our "voters are capable of raising up their own political leaders."[91] Indeed, these traditional institutions would be dangerously weakened if the military assumed their functions. "With UMT," a veteran wrote to the *Washington Post*, "the church, the school, and the home will lose much of the influence they once had in shaping the character of American society and the ideas of militarism will take their place."[92]

The usual strategy was to draw the boundaries of Americanism in a way that associated UMT with the un-American other, especially with the "Caesars, Napoleons, Bismarks, Wilhelms, Hitlers, Mussolinis, and Tojos" who had subverted democracy in favor of authoritarianism.[93] It was a "European" institution, the critics wrote of UMT, "foreign to the American way of life" and typical instead of totalitarian regimes dominated by the military.[94] "To give the Army control over the minds of youth is the very essence of totalitarianism," wrote Flora Pierson of Omaha, "for the military institution builds the military mind."[95] Would "goose-stepping boys," one writer asked, find a place in American life?[96] Would the "freest nation in the world" choose "its own enslavement to the one course in human history that leads invariably to ruin: the course of militarism."[97] To the critics, in other words, UMT was at war with American tradition and with the democratic identity of the American people, which had been shaped not by the government, let alone by the military, but by such basic institutions as the school, the home, and the church, all of which were now endangered by UMT.

According to conservative isolationists, moreover, the country's democratic identity would be more easily preserved if it followed the advice of Joseph Kennedy, Robert Taft, and Herbert Hoover, all of whom wanted to unite the countries of the Western Hemisphere in an armed camp. This

---

90 T. B. R., letter to the editor, *Chicago Tribune*, 21 April 1952.

91 Alvin E. Houser, letter to the editor, *Dallas Morning News*, 26 June 1947.

92 Veteran, letter to the editor, *Washington Post*, 11 July 1947.

93 P. H. B., letter to the editor, *Washington Post*, 7 March 1947.

94 Wayne F. Buckle, letter to the editor, *Washington Post*, 1 July 1947; Catherine E. Wells, letter to the editor, ibid., 30 July 1947. See also E. Paul Weaver, letter to the editor, *Chicago Tribune*, 17 November 1949.

95 Pierson, letter to the editor, *Boston Herald*, 6 March 1947. See also Dorothy Sage Wyman, letter to the editor, *St. Louis Post-Dispatch*, 22 February 1947.

96 Bob Pope, letter to the editor, *Washington Post*, 5 February 1947.

97 Caroline P. Urie, letter to the editor, *Boston Herald*, 15 June 1947.

was a practical strategy, in part because it was affordable, in part because it played to America's superiority in air and naval power. In operation, moreover, it would supposedly make the United States virtually invulnerable to attack, an "impregnable fortress" of liberty, as one writer put it, and a shining example of democratic government to which the rest of the world could turn.[98]

This line of argument drew implicitly on a traditional cultural narrative that celebrated American exceptionalism and an American sphere of liberty that would grow by example, not by military commitments. According to this rhetorical strategy, internationalism emulated European ways, was incompatible with American principles, and would endanger American democracy. Aid to Greece and Turkey amounted to European "power politics" and would lead to war.[99] Aid to Germany was "playing a game of politics" at the expense of the war dead and the victims of Nazi aggression.[100] The Marshall Plan was still another case of "power politics," as was the intervention in Korea, just as the North Atlantic Treaty was yet another war pact, another case of old-fashioned balance-of-power diplomacy, and would lead to an arms race and world war.[101] The United States, wrote one citizen, could not protect democracy by getting "involved in foreign rackets, secret diplomacy, intrigue, and all the rest of the rottenness of Europe that led our forefathers to come here to seek sanctuary."[102] The "American system is something new, distinctive, and unique," declared another writer during the debate over military assistance to Europe.[103]

For such critics, the emphasis on American exceptionalism went hand-in-hand with the conviction that current policy, with its rush toward globalism, broke with the traditional pattern of diplomacy that had been

[98] Wilfrid Hewitt, letter to the editor, *Boston Herald*, 2 January 1951. See also Herbert C. Neal, letter to the editor, *Cleveland Plain Dealer*, 17 December 1950; and Carl B. Smith, letter to the editor, *Boston Herald*, 18 December 1950.

[99] R. Vollmer, letter to the editor, *San Francisco Chronicle*, 10 March 1947. See also Alan Ramon, letter to the editor, ibid., 12 March 1947; Joseph C. Howard, letter to the editor, *Washington Post*, 18 March 1947; Stanley Chambers, letter to the editor, *Boston Herald*, 7 April 1947; S. H., letter to the editor, *St. Louis Post-Dispatch*, 11 April 1947; and Margaret P. Welch, letter to the editor, *Boston Herald*, 22 April 1947.

[100] Jerome Kirschenbaum, letter to the editor, *Cleveland Plain Dealer*, 31 July 1947.

[101] Joe McGovern, letter to the editor, *Chicago Tribune*, 19 August 1947. See also E. Paul Weaver, letter to the editor, *Cleveland Plain Dealer*, 11 May 1949; M. S. Alderton and M. M. G. Hansen, letter to the editor, ibid., 5 June 1949; Rev. J. Paul Cotton, letter to the editor, *Dallas Morning News*, 17 June 1949; Sheldon D. Clark, letter to the editor, *Cleveland Plain Dealer*, 24 July 1949; and James P. Whiteside, letter to the editor, *St. Louis Post-Dispatch*, 26 December 1950.

[102] Edwin H. Boyer, letter to the editor, *Chicago Tribune*, 8 January 1951.

[103] Curtis Nettels, letter to the editor, ibid., 21 August 1949.

blessed by the Founders and proven itself through the years. No past policies were more frequently cited than Washington's Farewell Address, with its warning against entangling alliances, and the Monroe Doctrine, with its emphasis on separate American and European spheres. American leaders had violated the principles of the Founders, not only by forging alliances but also by interfering in the internal affairs of other nations, particularly those outside the Western Hemisphere, and by aiding corrupt and unpopular regimes throughout the world. One writer compared Anglo-American policy in Greece to the Holy Alliance of the nineteenth century, which had also sought to stymie progressive change. In Greece, according to another writer, the United States was putting its aid behind a faltering British Empire, backing a fascist government at odds with its own people, and thus donning "the armor of Nazism and the mantle of British imperialism."[104] It was taking over the mission of Hitler, Mussolini, and Franco, said another writer, all of whom had justified every manner of sin in the name of anticommunism.[105] What is more, it was asking for trouble by pursuing policies in Greece and elsewhere that undermined Monroe's two-spheres doctrine and invited other countries, including the Soviet Union, to advance their interests in the Western Hemisphere. How would American leaders respond, H. H. Packard asked in a letter to the *Boston Herald*, if the Soviet Union sent military equipment and supplies to Mexico, Canada, Cuba, or the Panama Canal?[106]

The rhetorical strategy in this case again borrowed from a traditional narrative of national greatness, with its emphasis on the two-spheres principle, on old-world imperialism, and on New World exceptionalism. Conservatives used this cultural narrative to argue that Kennedy, Taft, and Hoover were merely reasserting the traditional verities that had separated the United States from Europe and contributed to its democratic identity and record of success. From 1776 until the First World War, wrote Frank Bassett of Chicago, "we kept our armed forces home and

---

[104] S. Bennett, letter to the editor, *San Francisco Chronicle*, 17 March 1947. See also Max Henry Newman, letter to the editor, *Boston Herald*, 6 March 1947; A. C. Little, letter to the editor, *San Francisco Chronicle*, 12 March 1947; Holbrook Bonney, letter to the editor, ibid., 12 March 1947; J. O. Halloway, letter to the editor, *Chicago Tribune*, 13 March 1947; Joseph E. Korvick, letter to the editor, *Washington Post*, 19 March 1947; Valeda J. Bryant, letter to the editor, *San Francisco Chronicle*, 19 March 1947; Ernest T. Weir, letter to the editor, *Dallas Morning News*, 28 March 1947; and Jack Warnick, letter to the editor, *San Francisco Chronicle*, 15 April 1947.

[105] R. V. Wood, letter to the editor, *San Francisco Chronicle*, 19 March 1947.

[106] Packard, letter to the editor, *Boston Herald*, 23 March 1947. See also Harold Allinger, letter to the editor, *San Francisco Chronicle*, 27 March 1947.

stayed out of trouble."[107] This policy had brought the country years of peace and national achievement until "a gang of Napoleons," including Woodrow Wilson and Franklin Roosevelt, reversed course, involved the United States in the affairs of Europe, and wasted both its manpower and its resources.[108] The message was clear: The country had to return to its "historical 'hands off' policy" of mending the "fences in our own back yard."[109] Such a course would not bankrupt the country, which was what the Soviets wanted, destroy its economic and political liberties, or transform it into a garrison state. It was an American, not a European, policy and would create a sphere of freedom to which other nations might be drawn.

These arguments drew a sharp response from letter writers who supported current policy, mostly liberal realists whose rhetorical strategy sought to discredit their opponents as dangerous appeasers and old-fashioned isolationists. Although these writers also looked to the past for guidance, they did not turn to the Founders alone but also to the lessons of the interwar period. They attacked the isolationists and budget-cutters in Congress, claiming that Russia was a threat to world peace, that American security required military insurance, and that anything less would repeat the mistakes of disarmament in the 1920s and appeasement in the 1930s. The United States should have stopped Hitler between 1933 and 1937, argued one writer, and it should stop Stalin now. If the war taught anything, wrote another, it taught the folly of appeasement and disarmament. Appeasement, wrote still others, was the surest road to war, and "brute force" was the only language that aggressors understood.[110]

During the Great Debate, this group of letter writers was quick to brand Kennedy an appeaser who had been wrong before World War II and was wrong again, and to attack Hoover, not to mention Taft, as an "out-and-out isolationist" who would "give up our two touchdowns scored in World Wars I and II, retreat to our 20-yard line, and from there wait to defend our goal against Russian drives."[111] If the American

[107] Bassett, letter to the editor, *Chicago Tribune*, 5 January 1951.

[108] William Spillman, letter to the editor, *Cleveland Plain Dealer*, 31 December 1950.

[109] James W. Smith, letter to the editor, *San Francisco Chronicle*, 27 December 1950.

[110] Philip Marshall Brown, letter to the editor, *Washington Post*, 18 April 1947; Jimmy Hines, letter to the editor, *San Francisco Chronicle*, 3 August 1949. See also Arthur E. Whittemore, letter to the editor, *Boston Herald*, 15 February 1947; "Maryland Veteran," letter to the editor, *Washington Post*, 22 February 1947; Charles H. Coombs, letter to the editor, *Boston Herald*, 10 March 1947; and D. P. Holt, letter to the editor, *Dallas Morning News*, 13 April 1949.

[111] C. Mims, letter to the editor, *Dallas Morning News*, 26 December 1950. See also H. Krunsky, letter to the editor, *Boston Herald*, 24 December 1950.

people had followed Hoover's advice before World War II, one writer argued, "Hitler would now be ruling most of the world and preparing to attack the United States."[112] And if they followed his advice in 1950, it would only be a "short time" before they "woke up and found Uncle Joe living in Blair House."[113] Giving in to Hitler, these writers repeated, had led to World War II, and giving in to Stalin would torpedo the chances for collective security against aggression, alienate the Europeans, and throw them into Soviet hands. It was just the policy that Moscow wanted the United States to pursue and would do more to advance Soviet ambitions than anything dreamed up in the Kremlin.[114]

The lessons of appeasement formed part of the national security ideology that found its way into this side of the popular discourse, as did other elements of that ideology, including the conviction that American leaders had a mission to assert the country's "moral leadership" on behalf of liberty around the world.[115] This conviction also borrowed from an American cultural narrative, notably the narrative of American expansionism, and was used rhetorically to counter claims that current policy broke entirely with tradition and was therefore un-American. It was "this country's duty to lead the world along the path of democracy," wrote one citizen. "We must "boldly accept the challenge now," wrote another, "or world affairs will steadily become worse."[116] Adding plausibility to this argument was the assumption, also part of the national security ideology, that in the modern world democracy and security were indivisible. "The vital interests of the United States are indivisible from those of the other free nations," wrote a group of Bostonians. The American people must therefore "recognize that aggression anywhere threatens our vital interests," and must do whatever was necessary to strengthen their "ties with all people willing to fight for freedom."[117]

The geopolitical arguments that formed another part of the national security ideology also found their way into this side of the public discourse.

---

[112] William Van N. Washburn, letter to the editor, *Boston Herald*, 10 January 1951.

[113] Lawrence Lewis Bierman, letter to the editor, *St. Louis Post Dispatch*, 26 January 1951.

[114] J. H. Morgan, letter to the editor, *Dallas Morning News*, 18 March 1947; Richard Tyler Wise, letter to the editor, *Washington Post*, 8 April 1947; Harry Bloch, letter to the editor, *Atlanta Constitution*, 21 April 1947; Alfred F. Bohn, letter to the editor, *Washington Post*, 27 December 1950; Peter Whitney, letter to the editor, ibid., 28 December 1950; David Caulkins, letter to the editor, *Cleveland Plain Dealer*, 31 December 1950; Elias Jones, letter to the editor, *Cleveland Plain Dealer*, 7 January 1951; William Van N. Washburn, letter to the editor, *Boston Herald*, 10 January 1951.

[115] William T. Long, letter to the editor, *Washington Post*, 24 January 1951.

[116] A. V. Boren, letter to the editor, *Dallas Morning News*, 4 April 1947; Waverly Barker Wright, letter to the editor, *Boston Herald*, 4 April 1947.

[117] Lawrence G. Brooks et al., letter to the editor, *Boston Herald*, 30 January 1951.

These included the argument that the United States, however strong, could not survive in a world without friends and allies, particularly if the rich markets, raw materials, and productive capacity of Europe were lost to the Soviet Union.[118] The idea "that we could get along economically as an island in a 'Red' sea" was ridiculous, wrote Edward Caffery of Biloxi, Mississippi.[119] In such an event, argued Claude Sanders of Paris, Texas, the United States would be "sitting high and dry by herself with no allies, no markets, no American way of life."[120] Such a course would enhance Soviet strength at the expense of American power and would give the Russians the opportunity they were looking for. "The fear of retaliation has kept the Soviets in check," explained one letter writer, "and that fear has been nourished by the existence of bases or potential bases in Western Europe, North Africa and the Middle East, from which atomic bombs can be delivered to Russian cities. To surrender these forward bases would be to destroy in large measure the dike which is containing the Red tide." The "occupation of Western Europe would give the Russians steel making and industrial strength equal to our own," put the United States at a serious disadvantage, and force the American people to live in an armed camp.[121]

For those who defended American policy, as for its critics, the garrison state was a favorite rhetorical symbol, although they were convinced that Hoover's isolationism, not current policy, was the surest route to that destination. If the United States retreated into a "hemispheric shell," they wrote, it would be alone in a hostile world, bereft of friends, and with no choice but to arm itself to the teeth. Unable to share the burden of defense with allies, it would have to divert all of its own resources to this purpose, sacrificing economic and political freedoms in the name of security and transforming itself into a "garrison state." Only a policy of global engagement, in other words, could safeguard liberty at home as well as abroad.[122]

The arguments on both sides reached a fever pitch during the Truman–MacArthur controversy, before dying down in the early years of the Eisenhower administration. MacArthur's supporters saw the war as he

---

[118] Charles H. Taylor, letter to the editor, *Boston Herald,* 27 December 1950; Clyde Looper, letter to the editor, *Washington Post,* 27 December 1950; A. U. Avera, letter to the editor, *Atlanta Constitution,* 27 December 1950.

[119] Caffery, letter to the editor, *St. Louis Post-Dispatch,* 16 February 1951.

[120] Sanders, letter to the editor, *Dallas Morning News,* 15 February 1951.

[121] A. H., letter to the editor, *Washington Post,* 12 January 1951. See also Louis M. Castle, letter to the editor, *Boston Herald,* 23 February 1951.

[122] Elias Jones, letter to the editor, *Cleveland Plain Dealer,* 7 January 1951.

did. They wanted to end the conflict by any means possible, including the bombing of Manchuria and the use of Nationalist troops, and they were convinced that anything less would be a victory for communism. In this case, as in others, their rhetorical strategy betrayed an anti-British bias, a deep-seated suspicion of government, a conspiratorial view of foreign policy, and a tendency to see their opponents as more closely identified with foreign others, including the Communists, than with the United States. They were certain that MacArthur had been hamstrung by irrelevant political conditions imposed by the president and his "lace handkerchief boys" in the State Department, largely at the request of Great Britain and its allies in the United Nations. Whereas Truman would "go down in history as the greatest president of the United States that England and Russia ever had," MacArthur put the interests of the United States and its fighting men first. His dismissal was proof that the American government had been infiltrated by Communists and that Truman had become little more than a British stooge who was willing to abandon the nation's sovereignty to protect Britain's trade with China and its investments in Hong Kong. MacArthur, as one of his supporters summed up, had been "crucified by an incompetent President, a pink State Department, a socialized England, [and] a pussy footing France," and the Korean slaughter would continue until the American people had the foresight to change administrations in Washington.[123]

On the other side of the controversy, the letter-writers who supported Truman also supported the strategic assumptions behind his policies and the rhetoric of realism that marked the national security ideology. The "supreme thing" was "to prevent World War III," they argued, and safeguard the prospects for a united front against Communist aggression.[124] The president's supporters were convinced that MacArthur's strategy flew in the face of these imperatives. It would involve the United States in a large-scale war with China on the Asian mainland – a war that could not be won, that could easily escalate into a global conflagration, and that would drain American military assistance from Europe, weaken the NATO allies, and expose them to Soviet attack. In either

---

[123] George G. Smith, letter to the editor, *Boston Herald*, 14 April 1951; Joseph H. Notbusch, letter to the editor, *Chicago Tribune*, 13 April 1951; G. W. Evans, letter to the editor, *Dallas Morning News*, 15 April 1951. See also Henry W. Forester, letter to the editor, *Boston Herald*, 12 April 1951; Jeane S. Mooris, letter to the editor, *Dallas Morning News*, 14 April 1951; Geo. J. Fix, Jr., letter to the editor, ibid., 15 April 1951; Felix Probandt, letter to the editor, ibid., 15 April 1951; Mrs. E. V. Forsyth, letter to the editor, ibid., 17 April 1951; and Edward C. Jones, letter to the editor, *San Francisco Chronicle*, 21 April 1951.

[124] Delcevare King, letter to the editor, *Dallas Morning News*, 30 April 1951.

460   *A Cross of Iron*

case, MacArthur's strategy would mean a wider war at a time when the NATO countries were not prepared for such a conflict, and would thus drive a wedge between the United States and its allies.[125] "If we ... make the final overt act that touches off" World War III, wrote Edwin C. Clark of San Francisco, "we go alone."[126]

Truman's supporters also reserved much of their fire for a vigorous defense of civilian supremacy over the military. They relied again on a strategy of otherness that placed their opponents beyond the pale of American identity, and they again buttressed their case by citing ancient authority, including the authority embedded in the same narrative of national greatness to which their opponents also appealed. Civilian supremacy had been one of "the major tenets of the United States government from Washington's time on," these writers agreed, and the question was whether MacArthur could "flout and disregard" that basic principle without striking a "death blow" at the "foundation of our democratic institutions." It was a "traditional American principle," explained one writer, "that the military must remain subordinate to the civil if old world militarism is to be kept out of America." To tolerate MacArthur's insubordination, wrote another, was "to lay this Republic open to the dangers of Caesarism" and the kind of militarism that had run rampant in pre-war Germany, both of which would lead inevitably to war and to "the country's downfall."[127]

Under the circumstances, these letter-writers were convinced that Truman had no choice but to preserve the Constitution and protect "free American government" by dismissing MacArthur. As earlier, they sought to strengthen their conviction by appeals to history. They pointed to the collapse of the Roman Republic as an example of what happened when generals took power, compared MacArthur to Napoleon Bonaparte, and

[125] Martha Ward Dudley, letter to the editor, *Washington Post*, 10 April 1951; Chas. C. Boynton, letter to the editor, *San Francisco Chronicle*, 14 April 1951; Henry F. Smith, letter to the editor, *Boston Herald*, 15 April 1951; Publius, letter to the editor, *Chicago Tribune*, 15 April 1951; Eve Walters, letter to the editor, *Boston Herald*, 16 April 1951; Clarence E. Rust, letter to the editor, *San Francisco Chronicle*, 16 April 1951; Edward J. Modest, letter to the editor, *Boston Herald*, 20 April 1951; George T. Cobb, letter to the editor, *Dallas Morning News*, 26 April 1951; and George Clifton Edwards, letter to the editor, ibid., 14 May 1951.

[126] Clark, letter to the editor, *San Francisco Chronicle*, 20 April 1951.

[127] George P. Sayre, letter to the editor, *Chicago Tribune*, 14 April 1951; A. J. Pickett, letter to the editor, *St. Louis Post-Dispatch*, 12 April 1951; Hamilton A. Long, letter to the editor, *Chicago Tribune*, 16 April 1951; Peter H. Odegard et al., letter to the editor, *Washington Post*, 18 March, 1951; William Van N. Washburn, letter to the editor, *Boston Herald*, 15 April 1951. See also the sources cited in the following note.

cited Clemenceau's famous remark that war was too important to be left to the generals. As usual, however, their favorite authorities were those drawn from American history, especially Washington, Jefferson, and Lincoln, all of whom had defended civil over military power and established precedents for Truman's decision.[128]

V

In the letters to the editors, generally speaking, conservative isolationists tended to support the loyalty program while being critical of American diplomacy and the dismissal of MacArthur. Liberal realists, on the other hand, were usually critical of the loyalty program but supportive on matters of foreign policy. Both sides found it helpful to cite history as their guide and to portray themselves as defenders of an American tradition in foreign policy, whether it was the tradition of hemispheric isolation or the tradition of manifest destiny. Both sides were clearly obsessed with the danger of totalitarianism, which they associated with a military regime and captured in the familiar metaphor of the garrison state. Both sides resorted frequently to this metaphor, either to defend an isolationist policy or one devoted to internationalism, and both sides insisted that their policies alone would safeguard the American way of life.

Although Cold War intellectuals were often suspicious of popular opinion and afraid of mass politics, their thinking and the thinking in Washington did not differ markedly from that found in the letters to the editors of many of the nation's major newspapers. Cold War intellectuals like John Burnham borrowed from the national security ideology, with its emphasis on total war, its blurring of the distinction between war and peace, and its theme of constant preparedness. They, too, were concerned with the problem of totalitarianism, a concern made deeper by their profound sense of the limits that history and original sin placed on human progress. Liberal intellectuals were willing to put the containment of communism ahead of the welfare state while conservative intellectuals were prepared to give antistatism a back seat to anticommunism. This development set the stage not only for a policy of containment but also for a national security state that could apply that policy.

---

[128] George P. Sayre, letter to the editor, *Chicago Tribune*, 14 April 1951. See also Peter H. Odegard et al., letter to the editor, *Washington Post*, 18 March 1951; Margaret S. Dermen, letter to the editor, ibid., 13 April 1951; John Robinson et al., letter to the editor, *Boston Herald*, 14 April 1951; Andrew Juvinall, letter to the editor, *San Francisco Chronicle*, 14 April 1951; and J. K. Bukner, letter to the editor, *Dallas Morning News*, 14 May 1951.

Nevertheless, a strong oppositional voice ran through American thinking in the early Cold War. Despite substantial efforts by American elites to squelch opposition and unify the country in a time of crisis, a pattern of dissent began to emerge, in part among left-wing liberals who saw the Cold War scuttling reform at home, in part among conservative libertarians who were convinced that national security needs were adding to the leviathan state that had emerged with the New Deal. A similar pattern appeared in the letters published on the editorial pages of the nation's newspapers. Nor could it be overwhelmed by concerted campaigns to encourage solidarity, such as the Freedom Train, the Loyalty Day Parades, and the Communist coup in Mosinee, Wisconsin. These pageants, to be sure, inspired popular participation and celebration on a sizeable scale, but they were often accompanied by an undertone of criticism that belied efforts to forge an unfractured consensus behind the country's Cold War policies.

11

Conclusion

As the preceding chapters indicate, two broad dynamics were at work in American state making after 1945, one associated with an older political culture and the other with the new ideology of national security. Elements of each dynamic could exist side by side in the same individual, pulling in this direction at one time and in that direction at another. Truman and Forrestal were good examples of this tension, as was Taft, whose thinking on international matters changed considerably in the years after Pearl Harbor. Both dynamics could also be present in the same political party, though each was more likely to be identified with one of the major parties than with the other, and with the views and constituencies associated with that party. One was identified with the Democratic party, the other with the Republican party; one was associated with the executive branch, the other with the legislative branch; one was more liberal, the other more conservative; one was internationally oriented, the other tended toward nationalism, regionalism, or even isolationism.

The tension between these two dynamics tapped into a long history of political controversy over the role of the state in American life, and the role of the United States in world affairs. These controversies can be traced in some cases to the founding of the Republic, in others to the progressive era or the New Deal of the twentieth century, and in others to the antiinterventionism that preceded American involvement in various military conflicts, from the War of 1812 to the Second World War. The conservative critique of the national security state resonated with earlier critiques of the trend toward statism in the modern period; the opposition to UMT drew on a long tradition of popular resistance to conscription; and the critique of American globalism after World War II recapitulated the anti-interventionist sentiments of the 1930s. In these and other cases, the story recounted in this book highlights the persistence of themes in a political discourse that predates the Cold War.

Still, there was something different after 1945. The United States had emerged from World War II as the leader of a "free world" coalition, with global obligations and responsibilities it had not shouldered before. The merits of its postwar foreign policies and the degree to which they advanced the cause of freedom are still subjects of historical debate. But there is no doubt that new responsibilities and perceived threats led to an unprecedented peacetime allocation of resources to the military arm of the state, and to the creation of powerful government agencies that had not existed before. Both developments amounted to major departures from American tradition, both added enormously to the size and power of the state, and both took the state in new directions. The result, in due course, was a peacetime national security establishment that was grafted on to the New Deal state, as many conservatives had feared, and yet challenged the New Deal state, as many liberals had warned.

These transformations provoked a stormy debate over the degree to which national security needs might endanger the basic values and institutions associated with American democracy. Those who defended traditional political culture, notably conservatives in Congress and their allies in the press, were convinced that a powerful national security state would waste precious resources, regiment the nation's youth, and concentrate too much authority in the state, particularly in its military arm. Still worse, at least by their calculations, it would weaken the home, the church, and the school as counterweights to federal authority and would undermine the constitutional balance, first by creating an executive branch strong enough to overwhelm Congress and then by creating a military caste strong enough to overwhelm the president. Nor were these idle concerns in a period marked by dramatic challenges to constitutional authority, as in the admirals' revolt of 1949, Truman's decision to wage war in Korea and send troops to Europe in 1950, and MacArthur's bold defiance of presidential leadership in 1951. Added to these challenges, moreover, was the persistent military opposition to a balanced budget and effective unification of the services, not to mention the largely successful efforts by military leaders to establish for themselves a degree of political authority and independence unmatched in American history.

Concerns of this sort ran through the whole process of American state making in the first decade of the Cold War. They provoked a strong defense of the balanced budget, not only as a hedge against waste and as a symbol of public virtue but also as a barrier against big government and military rule. They inspired a strong critique of Truman's plans to unify the armed forces and create the modern-day Department of Defense. They informed alternative plans whereby authority would be more widely dispersed and a system of checks and balances would be preserved through a decentralized system of decision making. They guided the attack on universal military training, and they influenced plans to give the White House a source of scientific advice independent of the Pentagon. In each case, those involved worried that national security needs would harness the nation's resources to an institutional complex run by military leaders and dedicated to military purposes. Their fear, in other words, was of a garrison state that would undermine alternative centers of authority, destroy democracy, and militarize American life.

On the other side of this discourse were those whose thinking had been influenced by the national security ideology that began to crystalize during World War II. According to this ideology, the United States had entered an era of total war in which the line between citizen and soldier, civilian and military, war and peace, had disappeared forever. The threat of total war required a new degree of military vigilance and a permanent program of preparedness in which all of the nation's resources, civilian and military alike, were mobilized against a ruthless and implacable enemy. According to the new ideology, moreover, it was no longer possible to separate the defense of American liberties from the defense of liberty everywhere. Peace and freedom were indivisible, so that American leaders had no choice but to safeguard the country's security by safeguarding the security of the free world in general. Indeed, this was a mission that God and history had thrust upon the United States, at least according to the national security ideology. The American people had to muster the resolve and make the sacrifices that such a mission required, which is why some officials saw the Cold War as an exercise in national rejuvenation. It was a great opportunity, in Kennan's view, to recapture the moral discipline and the civic virtue that had supposedly characterized earlier periods of American history.

The debate between these two ways of thinking, between the old political culture and the new ideology, typically ended in compromise. The national security ideology abetted efforts to globalize and militarize American foreign policy, and inspired demands for a larger pool of military manpower, for a permanent peacetime military establishment, for the military mobilization of science and industry, and for new agencies, such as the Atomic Energy Commission and the National Security Council, that could bring the resources of the nation to bear in the struggle against communism. At the same time, however, national security leaders could only advance their goals by accommodating such older traditions as antistatism and isolationism, and such older values as a balanced budget and the principle of civilian supremacy. In this sense, the old political culture, including the nation's democratic traditions and institutions, operated as a brake on the process of state making, or at least as a powerful valve that could regulate the process and channel its results in certain directions rather than in others.

When it came to military manpower, for example, the Truman administration at first sought a system of universal training and then settled for a temporary extension of the draft, in both cases because a professional peacetime army was at odds with American tradition and a possible threat to the principle of civilian supremacy. Similar concerns also inspired efforts to guarantee civilian control of atomic energy and to build a system of institutional checks and balances and decentralized decision making into any plans to mobilize science and industry for military purposes. Nor does this exhaust the list of examples. When it came to the budget, as we have seen, both Truman and Eisenhower tried to balance military needs against civilian requirements, the warfare state against the welfare state. And when it came to the defense establishment, both tried to protect presidential prerogatives and the principle of civilian control by centralizing more authority in the Pentagon than many thought desirable.

The policy of accommodation was perhaps most evident in the area of grand strategy, an area that also revealed very clearly the great divide between those who defended tradition and those who spoke for the new ideology of national security. Hoover, Taft, and other conservatives had convinced themselves that Truman's foreign policy, with its expensive foreign aid and military assistance programs, permanent peacetime defense establishment, and troops stationed abroad, would undermine the American way of life as they understood it. It would exhaust the nation's resources and lead to permanently high taxes, economic controls, and ultimately to a garrison state in which economic and political freedoms gave way to regimentation. To avoid this calamity, they wanted to emphasize America's air and naval power, build a fortress for democracy in the Western Hemisphere, and limit the country's military and political commitments on the Eurasian mainland. This strategy had much to recommend it, at least to Hoover, Taft, and their allies in Congress and the press. It squared with American tradition, as embodied in the foreign policy of the Founders and in the Monroe Doctrine, and would tailor the country's commitments to its resources, restrain the growth of state power, and protect the economic and political liberties that made America great.

But if these arguments appealed to Taft, they had little to recommend them to the Joint Chiefs, who were driven by institutional interests to demand ever-expanding defense budgets. To be sure, the Joint Chiefs were trapped to some extent by the aggressive pronouncements coming from the State Department, the White House, and the NSC, all of which opened a gap between the country's global obligations and its military capabilities and made it easier for the military to demand bigger and bigger defense budgets. At the same time, however, the Joint Chiefs subscribed to the same national security ideology that motivated their civilian counterparts, and also tried repeatedly to escape the economic burdens of real unification, counted on additional funds to harmonize their differences, and refused to wrestle with the financial implications of their military recommendations.

Truman, on the other hand, tried to frame a strategy of deterrence that could reconcile military and economic considerations, in part because he and other economizers shared Taft's concern for a balanced budget and all that it symbolized. What is more, the strategy that Truman finally developed had more in common with Taft's thinking than is usually conceded, especially his support for a capital-intensive containment that relied heavily on air–atomic power. Even their differences, as it turned out, were inspired in part by a shared desire to deter the Soviets without wrecking the economy – Taft through a larger Air Force than Truman thought necessary, Truman through manpower policies and foreign aid programs that Taft thought wasteful.

The same concerns also influenced much of what Eisenhower tried to do, including his New Look, which actually evolved out of the capital-intensive strategy of deterrence that Truman had envisioned. The New Look added to Truman's policy an emphasis on continental defense, on the redeployment of American forces from abroad, and on massive atomic retaliation as the first line of defense against Soviet aggression. Like Truman, Eisenhower had been pushed in these directions not only by pressure from Taft and other fiscal conservatives but also by his own concerns for a balanced budget and all that it represented, including a less intrusive state and a high degree of economic freedom. Similar concerns, along with a desire to protect the president's prerogatives and the principle of civilian control, also led Eisenhower to follow through on Truman's efforts to reorganize the Defense Department and strike a partnership between science and the state in the field of national security.

Running through all of these initiatives was a fear of the garrison state, which was just as great in Truman and Eisenhower as it was in conservatives like Taft and Hoover. But where conservatives saw the garrison state arising from an expansive foreign policy, and the costly military establishment needed to support it, Truman and Eisenhower saw the same specter emerging if the United States retreated to a hemispheric system of defense. In their view, such a policy would isolate the country in a totalitarian world, at which point its very survival would demand even larger defense budgets and the kind of government controls and oppressive taxes associated with the garrison state. Whereas conservatives seemed to believe that democracy could only survive behind an iron curtain of hemispheric defense, Truman and Eisenhower tried to devise a military strategy that would allow the country to meet its obligations around the world without leading to economic and political regimentation at home.

As this suggests, the two sides disagreed fundamentally when it came to defining the nation's postwar identity and national purpose. Conservatives expressed their vision in a binary system of symbolic representation that compared the American way to the un-American other. In this system, the metaphor of the garrison state and allusions to the Gestapo, the police state, or the slave state enabled conservatives to summon the image of Hitler's Germany, Mussolini's Italy, or Stalin's Russia, and to compare that image to American democracy – a command economy to a free economy, military domination to civilian rule, the public sector to the private sector, the state to society, the centralization of authority to decentralized decision making. Conservative critics wanted to preserve the country's democratic identity, which they associated with a political culture grounded in antistatism, antimilitarism, and isolationism, and which they said would be lost if the United States emulated Old World habits and traditions, including Old World imperialism and militarism. Instead, the preservation of economic and political freedoms depended in their view on a policy that separated the United States from the outside world, or at least from the world outside the Western Hemisphere, and inspired others by the force of its example.

Truman and Eisenhower often resorted to the same rhetorical symbols as their conservative counterparts, notably the metaphor of the garrison state, and to the same binary oppositions to define the American way by reference to the totalitarian other. As we have seen, however, they did not believe that the United States could survive as an island of democracy in a totalitarian world and called instead for a policy of internationalism. Following the logic of the national security ideology, they argued that such a policy would not bring on the garrison state but prevent it, would not undermine the nation's democratic identity but fulfill it, would not compromise liberty but spread the blessings of liberty to those threatened by Soviet aggression.

II

Truman and Eisenhower were right, in that American democracy did not give way to a garrison state, but the Cold War did enlarge the role of the military in American life and alter the relationship between military leaders and civilian authorities. At a time when American foreign policy began to rely on armed force to achieve its objectives, when the size of the permanent force was so large, and when the military establishment commanded such an enormous share of the nation's resources, it was inevitable, perhaps, that Pentagon policy makers would start to rival American diplomats in the field of foreign affairs, dominate the production of atomic energy, challenge the Atomic Energy Commission, and otherwise assert an unprecedented degree of political authority and autonomy. Indeed, military leaders could no longer be counted on to bow before the principle of civilian supremacy. They demanded a greater voice in decision making, resisted decisions they did not like, and in some cases openly defied civilian authority, including the authority of the president.[1]

From its center in the Pentagon, moreover, military influence extended throughout the government, and from there to virtually every area of American life. Even before the Korean War, commentators had started to notice the increasingly visible presence of military leaders in American government and industry. High-ranking military officials were playing important roles in the State Department, the White House, and other government agencies, and were also taking top positions in science and industry. Some commentators saw nothing wrong with this development, but others were not so sure. Conservative magazines, such as *Business Week* and *U.S. News*, noted with some concern the large number of retired military leaders at the top of American corporations, and liberal journals were even more alarmed. Writing in the *New Republic*, for example, Robert S. Allen complained that the Pentagon sought nothing less than to retain its wartime position as the "directing force in national policy, both domestic and foreign."[2]

---

[1] In addition to the preceding chapters see Arthur A. Ekirch, Jr., *The Civilian and the Military* (New York, 1956), especially 271–77; Russell F. Weigley, "The American Military and the Principle of Civilian Control from McClellan to Powell," *Journal of Military History* 57 (October 1993): 27–58; and Richard H. Kohn, "Out of Control: The Crisis in Civil–Military Relations," *National Interest* 35 (Spring 1994): 3–17.

[2] Allen, "The Big Brass Takes Over," *New Republic* 116 (10 February 1947): 19–21. See also "Military Men in Key Jobs: Shift from U.S. Tradition," *U.S. News* 22 (24 January 1947): 20–21; "Yesterday, High Brass of Armed Forces . . . Today, High Brass of Industry," *Business Week* (5 April 1947): 20–21; "Toward Militarism," *New Republic* 117 (18 August 1947): 5–7; and Ernest K. Lindley, "The 'Military Mind,'" *Newsweek* 31 (2 February 1948): 30.

Nor were these concerns without some foundation. Besides an increasingly visible presence in government, military leaders were exerting an enormous influence over a large portion of American youth, and would continue to do so as long as conscription was on the books. They were also negotiating helpful alliances with friends in the media, in the trade unions, and in the business community, and were using these alliances to safeguard their interests and add to their power. Along with the intelligence community, they were forging a similar partnership with university administrators and faculty, especially scientists, and were taking advantage of this partnership, not to mention the Reserve Officer Training Corps, to establish a substantial presence on American campuses at a time when McCarthyites in government and their collaborators in the university were already creating a profoundly conservative academic environment.[3]

The partnership between science and the state, between university labs and Pentagon policy makers, was particularly important and especially helpful to a handful of elite universities. It helped MIT to sustain its leadership in government-sponsored research, enabled Stanford to break into the front ranks of American research universities, and brought similar gains to other institutions. In most cases, military research made it possible for universities to attract new faculty, build new facilities, and recruit good students, though often on terms, according to Stuart W. Leslie, that compromised the independence of university scientists, allowed the military to establish research priorities, and diverted scientific talent and energy from more productive peacetime purposes.[4]

The benefits of the new partnership between science and the state spilled from the university into the private sector. The partnership between MIT and the Pentagon helped to create the Boston electronics industry around firms like Raytheon and Sylvania, and enabled IBM and AT&T to establish leadership positions in digital data communications and computer technology. A similar partnership between the Pentagon and Caltech undergirded the aviation industry in the Los Angeles Basin, and still another, this one between the Pentagon and Stanford, created the Silicon Valley in California and provided enormous

---

3 For McCarthyism on campus see especially Ellen W. Schrecker, *No Ivory Tower: McCarthyism and the Universities* (New York, 1986). For another view on the partnership between the universities and the national security state see Sigmund Diamond, *Compromised Campus: The Collaboration of Universities with the Intelligence Community, 1945–1955* (New York, 1992).

4 Stuart W. Leslie, *The Cold War and American Science: The Military-Industrial-Academic Complex at MIT and Stanford* (New York, 1993). See also Rebecca S. Lowen, *Creating the Cold War University: The Transformation of Stanford* (Berkeley, 1997), 95–146.

advantages to firms like Sylvania, General Electric, and Pacific Telephone and Telegraph.[5]

These and similar partnerships could also benefit local and regional economies across the country, although the end result was more likely to be a mixed blessing. Military spending helped to revive flagging industries, as was the case with the aviation industry in New England, and contributed to an economic boom in the western states, particularly in California. The federal government invested 62 percent of its budget in defense over the first twenty years of the Cold War, and the western states garnered the largest share of this investment. They received one fourth of all military prime contracts, not to mention a large share of indirect military expenditures by the Atomic Energy Commission, the Veterans Administration, and other agencies. According to James L. Clayton, California alone received more than $67 billion in defense contracts between 1951 and 1965, about 20 percent of the total. Defense spending on this scale raised the average income in the state, contributed to its population growth, and was the largest single factor in the rapid postwar expansion of its economy.[6]

At the same time, however, defense spending could drain resources from productive investment in civilian technologies. Some industries in some areas of the country, notably the old industrial heartland, lost their competitive edge as defense expenditures migrated from states like Michigan and Ohio to the aviation, electronics, and other defense-based industries in what Ann Markusen and her collaborators have called the "gunbelt" – an area that stretched from Seattle down through California across the western and southern states and back up to New England. The social and political consequences of defense spending could be troubling as well, not the least because it provided more employment for white men than it did for women and minorities, and because it increased the political power of areas that were more likely to be conservative than liberal, Republican than Democratic.[7]

Like their university and industrial counterparts, state and local leaders were anxious to take advantage of the largess handed out by the national security state. Building on a tradition of local boosterism, civic

---

[5] In addition to the book by Leslie cited in the previous note see Ann Markusen, Scott Campbell, Peter Hall, and Sabina Deitrick, *The Rise of the Gunbelt: The Military Remapping of Industrial America* (New York, 1991), 82–84. For a contemporary view see Henry Wallace, "Science and the Military," *New Republic* 116 (3 February 1946): 26–27.

[6] James L. Clayton, "The Impact of the Cold War on the Economies of California and Utah, 1946–1965," *Pacific Historical Review* 36 (November 1967): 449–73. See also the source cited in the following note.

[7] Markusen, et al., *Rise of the Gunbelt*, 3–25, 230–34.

leaders in California and other states organized an impressive effort to capture a large share of the defense budget. Without much regard for the long-term consequences of their decisions, they lured the armed forces with generous subsidies and then used the military installations and research labs that followed to attract additional investment from both the public and private sectors. The result was what Robert Lotchin has called a "metropolitan-military complex" defended by powerful politicians, trade unions, industrial leaders, and military officials, all of whom had a vested interest in the arms race.[8]

Slight wonder that local business and civic leaders, particularly in the western states, followed defense spending like hawks. After the outbreak of the Korean War, for example, the *Denver Post* carefully tracked the economic benefits of a government "grubstake" that included more than $1.5 billion to mine the strategic metals of Colorado, Utah, and New Mexico. These expenditures touched off a uranium hunt in the Rocky Mountain states and vastly expanded the production of gold, silver, copper, lead, zinc, and tungsten. They helped to reopen hundreds of mines that had been closed earlier, created new jobs, added to the state's income, and laid the groundwork for new industries. "It's the biggest thing that's happened to the West in many years," said one official, and the benefits would only increase as defense spending went up and government provided other forms of federal assistance, including a measure exempting mine operators from the excess-profits tax.[9]

By the end of 1950, according to the *Post*, Colorado companies were turning out more than $10 million in defense production under government contracts granted since the outbreak of fighting in Korea six months before. The figure for the four Rocky Mountain states as a group exceeded $22 million, and was expected to climb to more than $55 million by the end of the next year. What is more, the figures did not include additional millions to reopen a bomber plant in Tulsa, expand air force facilities in Wyoming and Colorado, develop incendiary weapons at the Rocky Mountain arsenal, and underwrite atomic energy contracts

[8] Roger W. Lotchin, *Fortress California, 1910–1961: From Warfare to Welfare* (New York, 1992). On the role of civic boosters, see also Markusen, et al., *Rise of the Gunbelt*, 37–41.

[9] Robert Hansen, "$1.4 billion U.S. Grubstake to Reopen Empire Mines," *Denver Post*, 5 November 1950. See also in this paper, "Tax Benefits Seen for Vital Mineral Mines," 6 December 1950; Robert Hansen, "Lead Mine Revival Seen in Climax Area," 8 December 1950; "Defense Bill Set at 143.2 million for Coloradans," 12 December 1950; Robert Hansen, "Huge A-Ore Hunt Started in West," 19 December 1950; and Robert Stapp, "Need for Vital Metals Boosts Mining Industry," 27 December 1950.

in Utah and New Mexico. New Mexico, according to one official, was "likely to blossom like a rose due to atomic energy demands." Indeed, a "war born" prosperity started spreading across the western states and local business leaders began organizing to capture an even larger share of the defense budget, which they could use to attract additional industries to the region.[10]

But the wartime buildup had its price. In Colorado, shortages of various raw materials forced state and local officials to abandon earlier plans to increase public services and improve public facilities, including state office buildings and local recreation facilities. Federal matching funds for state and county highway and roadway projects also began to dry up, and the cost to consumers of almost all commodities, especially foodstuffs, started to increase. Even good economic news could produce bad results, as it did in the little "atomic boom town" of Arco, Idaho. When the AEC spent millions to build a reactor testing station in Arco, the town's 500 residents celebrated all night, only to discover two years later that 1,000 new residents and 200 new homes had overwhelmed the local electric system, tripled taxes, and left them short of public health and hospital facilities.[11]

This story repeated itself on a national scale during the war years and in the decades that followed. National security expenditures sustained employment for certain segments of the workforce in certain parts of the country, but drained resources from other areas, kept taxes high, added to the national debt, and diverted a large share of the federal budget from welfare to warfare purposes. By the first year of the Eisenhower administration, the federal government was investing approximately three-fourths of its budget in national security programs, defense spending equaled 18 percent of the gross national product, and defense expenditures accounted for nearly one-third of the nation's business activity. The figures changed from year to year, but during the first

[10] Robert Hansen, "'51 Area War Jobs to Hit $55 Million," *Denver Post*, 30 December 1950. See also in the *Denver Post*, William E. Lowell, "War-Born Prosperity Held Pervading West," 6 November 1950; Robert Hansen, "State Launches Drive for Defense Loans," 24 November 1950; "$70 Million Boom Seen in AF Move," 27 November 1950; "Colorado War Contract Total Hits $10 Million," 13 December 1950; Bob Byers, "$22 Million War Orders Given Four Empire States," 20 December 1950; William Haselbush, "Empire States Swinging Toward Full War Footing," 24 December 1950; and "Engineers Set for Expansion of 2 Air Bases," 26 December 1950.

[11] Pat Munroe, "A-Energy Plant Brings Problems to Arco Citizens," *Denver Post*, 22 December 1950. See also in the same paper, "U.S. Lacks Cash to Aid Rural Roads," 17 November 1950; Bert Hanna, "The War Upsets State Planning," 3 December 1950; and William Haselbush, "Korea Crisis Seen Raising Farm Costs," 10 December 1950.

two decades of the Cold War the federal government invested $776 billion in national defense, an amount equal to more than 60 percent of the federal budget, and more if indirect defense and war-related expenditures are included.[12]

As this brief summary indicates, the national security state had an enormous impact on American life, though it could have been much, much greater. After all, the national security ideology envisioned a comprehensive program of military preparedness and called upon the American people to make the sacrifices that such a program required. Guided by this ideology, powerful voices wanted to further expand the defense budget, add universal military training to the draft, centralize more authority in the hands of military leaders, and give a single government agency the power to mobilize all of the country's resources in the name of national defense. Nor were these military voices alone. They included civilians in the State Department and on the National Security Council, not to mention Bernard Baruch and other private citizens who urged Congress on more than one occasion to put the country on something like a permanent war footing.

This was not to be. While defense spending remained high after the Korean War, it actually declined as a percentage of both the budget and the GNP. Nor did the new agencies of national security, however powerful they became, ever amount to the kind of garrison state that worried Truman, Eisenhower, and others. Both presidents were too astute politically to believe that American voters would shoulder the bigger budgets, economic controls, and higher taxes that would come with a full peacetime mobilization of the economy. Both had their own misgivings about such a course, and both had reliable allies among economizers and budget balancers in the Treasury Department, the Budget Bureau, Congress, and the press. Both devised a military strategy that balanced economic against security considerations, and both faced opposition when they tried to go beyond that strategy, as Truman did when he called for universal military training.

When all is said and done, however, the most important constraint on the national security establishment was the profound fear of a garrison state. Both Truman and Eisenhower worried about the growing power of the military establishment, and both were convinced that constantly

---

[12] Clayton, "Impact of the Cold War on the Economies of California and Utah," 449; and Paul G. Pierpaoli, Jr., "Corporatist and Voluntarist Approaches to Cold War Rearmament: The Private Side of Industrial and Economic Mobilization, 1950–1953," *Essays in Economic and Business History* 15 (1997): 263–75.

expanding defense budgets would exhaust the Treasury, bankrupt the taxpayer, and end in destructive inflation or economic controls. The result, in other words, would be a degree of economic and political regimentation that was incompatible with private-enterprise capitalism and democratic government. It was this possibility that inspired their efforts to contain defense spending, avoid wartime mobilization, strengthen the Office of the Secretary of Defense, and arm the White House with independent science advice – not to mention their support for a capital-intensive strategy of containment that culminated in the New Look of the 1950s.

Put another way, the most important constraints on the national security state were those built into the country's democratic institutions and political culture. To be sure, democracy also took a beating in the first decade of the Cold War, from the loyalty programs and McCarthy's wild assault on civil liberties, from the loss of economic resources to military investment, from the growing autonomy of the armed forces, and from the increasing concentration of power in the executive branch, especially in the armed forces and in the other overt and covert agencies of the national security state. None of these developments should be ignored or slighted. But at the same time, the desire to adapt national security needs to the country's democratic traditions also drove Truman and then Eisenhower to seek better control over military leaders, to protect their own prerogatives, and to worry about diverting too much of the country's resources to national security purposes.

III

If the results could have been worse, could they also have been better? Truman and Eisenhower had tried to balance economic against security concerns, the welfare state against the warfare state, the national security ideology against the values of an older political culture. But under the balance they achieved, the American people had to limit federal funding for housing, education, and other social investments that had been neglected during the war. They also had to live with the intrusion of military influence into civilian affairs, with an increasingly imperial presidency, with higher taxes than most thought desirable, and with persistent budget deficits and additions to the national debt that shifted the cost of the Cold War to subsequent generations. Could more have been done to limit these liabilities and to achieve security at less cost to the American people?

These are not questions made possible by a half century of hindsight. They were asked repeatedly in the first decade of the Cold War, and most dramatically by conservatives like Hoover and Taft, who also provided answers. In the Great Debate, both men argued for a hemispheric system of defense based on air and naval power and stretching across the Atlantic to Europe and across the Pacific to the edge of Asia. Both men included Great Britain and Japan in the hemispheric system, but both were reluctant to station American troops on the Eurasian mainland, which they saw as a death trap for American soldiers. Both were also convinced that a conventional defense of Eurasia was impractical, and both assumed that an army large enough to be effective militarily would be dangerous politically and ruinous economically.

The Truman administration denounced Hoover and Taft as unrealistic isolationists, but elements of their thinking were actually more plausible than critics wanted to admit. After all, the concerns that motivated them also influenced Truman and Eisenhower. Both presidents adopted a capital-intensive strategy of deterrence that relied heavily on air–atomic power, not just to assuage Taft, but because they, too, wanted to contain communism without overreaching the country's resources and destroying its economic and political freedoms. Even Acheson, the most ambitious of the national security managers, had hoped at one point to hold the line against communism along a Pacific frontier that included Japan, but not Korea and the Asian mainland.

Seen in this light, the thinking of conservatives like Taft and Hoover was not as farfetched as it was made to appear at the time. Neither were isolationists, strictly speaking, though both wanted a close fit between the country's postwar commitments and its economic resources. What made their position untenable was their reluctance to protect the country's interests in Western Europe, and not simply their opposition to the stationing of American troops there, which even the Truman administration had ruled out when Congress was considering the North Atlantic Treaty in 1949. Even more serious was their reluctance to back the treaty itself or to support the Marshall Plan and other measures of economic and military assistance, which the administration saw as necessary to revitalize the European allies and enable them to shoulder a greater share of their own defense.

Although this reluctance made it possible for the Truman administration to brand Taft and Hoover as irresponsible isolationists, it was more difficult to level the same charge against Walter Lippmann. Lippmann was one of the country's leading newspaper commentators, a founder of the "realist" approach to the study of American foreign policy, and the most persistent and formidable critic of American diplomacy in the first decade of the Cold War. He was also a man of enormous intellectual gifts who could not be dismissed as easily as Taft and Hoover, both of whom he denounced as isolationists, even though his own thinking came closer to theirs in many ways than it did to that of Dean Acheson and other national security managers.

Lippmann's thinking can be gleaned from his syndicated newspaper columns, from a little book on the Cold War that pulled together some of his most important columns, and from Ronald Steel's excellent biography of the famous journalist. As Steel points out, Lippmann was not always a consistent thinker on matters of foreign policy; his initial reaction to a particular event was often tempered over time and sometimes evolved in a different direction. This was the case, for example, with his reaction to the Communist coup in Czechoslovakia, when he initially gave in to the war scare that swept through Washington, only to conclude later that Soviet foreign policy was less aggressive than he had first thought.[13]

Despite occasional inconsistencies, however, Lippmann's work was marked by several clear and coherent themes which, when taken together, offered an alternative to the policies pursued in Washington. As Steel has pointed out, Lippmann was neither a pacifist nor a believer in disarmament. He wanted the United States to maintain its military strength after the Second World War and was not averse to confronting "power with power," as he once put it. On the contrary, he saw balance-of-power diplomacy as the best way to safeguard the national interest and set the stage for productive negotiations with the Soviet Union. With this kind of thinking in mind, he supported the Greco-Turkish aid bill, the Marshall Plan, the military buildup that accompanied the war scare of 1948, and the deployment of American warships to the Formosa Strait in the early days of the Korean War.[14] It was this kind of thinking, particularly as applied to Europe, that distinguished Lippmann from Hoover and Taft and that allowed him to condemn both men as isolationists.

What Lippmann opposed was a foreign policy based on the new ideology of national security, a policy without the limits and restraints that he thought realistic. This opposition lay behind his devastating critique of the Truman Doctrine and Kennan's famous article on "The Sources of Soviet Conduct," which inspired the columns that he collected in his little book on the Cold War. Lippmann was critical of Kennan and Truman, as he would later be of Dulles and others, who interpreted Soviet

---

[13] Ronald Steel, *Walter Lippmann and the American Century*, paperback ed. (New York, 1981), 486, 450–52.

[14] Ibid., 435–38, 441–43, 450–51, 470.

foreign policy in broad ideological rather than specific historical and geographical terms, who saw Soviet policy, in other words, as driven by the
goal of world domination rather than the search for security along the
Russian frontier. Such views, he was convinced, led the United States to
support policies in Germany and elsewhere that only accentuated Soviet
insecurities, and thus had the effect of actually escalating the Cold War
rather than ending it.[15]

Lippmann also ridiculed the notion, central to the ideology of national
security, that God and history had assigned the United States a new role
as leader of the free world. It was "not leadership," he said, "to adapt
ourselves to the shifts and maneuvers of Soviet policy," which was the
course that Kennan had urged in his article on the sources of Soviet
conduct. On the contrary, such a course actually surrendered leadership
to the Soviet Union, whose actions then determined how the United
States would react. Nor did Lippmann view the United States as the
head of a coalition devoted to democratic principles. He might have
been sympathetic with such a coalition, had it been limited in scope
and restricted to real democracies. But he noted with some irony that
America's free economy was not compatible with the kind of globalism
envisioned in the Truman Doctrine or in Kennan's article, any more than
American democracy was compatible with the weak and corrupt regimes
that American leaders sometimes supported.[16]

But what most disturbed Lippmann was the notion that peace and
freedom were indivisible and that American security therefore depended
upon the security of anti-Communist governments everywhere. This notion, which was another theme in the ideology of national security, had
led Kennan to the conclusion that communism had to be contained
through the "vigilant application of counter-force at a series of
constantly shifting geographical and political points." According to
Lippmann, however, such a policy had no boundaries and would therefore disperse American power too broadly. Eurasia was a big place, he
said, while American power was limited and must be used effectively,
especially when it came to ground forces, where the United States was
comparatively disadvantaged. Any other course would squander American resources, he said, would weaken rather than strengthen the United
States, and would alienate the American people.[17]

[15] Ibid., 426, 431, 433, 437, 443–45.
[16] Walter Lippmann, *The Cold War: A Study in U.S. Foreign Policy* (New York, 1947), 13–14,
    15–17.
[17] Ibid., 18–19. See also Steel, *Lippmann*, 438–39. The quote is from Kennan, "Sources of
    Soviet Conduct," 576.

Lippmann wanted to concentrate American power in areas where the United States had a serious national interest, notably Western Europe, and where American leaders could work with their "natural allies" in the Atlantic Community, a group that included "the British Commonwealth of nations, the Latin states on both sides of the Atlantic, the Low Countries and Switzerland, Scandinavia and the United States." In contrast to the Truman Doctrine, which drew on the ideology of national security, such a policy was informed by "an older American doctrine," which held that "we must not become entangled all over the world in disputes that we alone cannot settle" because "we do not have the power, the influence, the means, and the knowledge to control." What is more, even in areas where American interests were substantial and where power therefore had to be concentrated, Lippmann was reluctant to link the United States too tightly to other countries or coalitions. When it came to the North Atlantic Treaty, for example, he had some of the same reservations as Taft and Hoover, claiming that America's atomic arsenal was the real force for containment in Europe and that NATO was largely useless and would burden American taxpayers unnecessarily. Still worse, the treaty would tie the United States to some countries with which it had little in common politically and whose economic and military weakness would diminish rather than increase American power.[18]

The same kind of thinking influenced Lippmann's view of the Korean War, which he considered a national disaster of monumental proportions. He had been pleased with Acheson's famous speech at the National Press Club in January 1950, in which the secretary drew the American defense perimeter in the Pacific to include Japan but not Korea or Taiwan. American policy makers had never considered the national interests to be worth the risk of a major war on the Asian mainland, and he was convinced that Acheson's defense perimeter squared with this historic policy. Given this conviction, he was appalled when Truman sent American troops to Korea after the outbreak of fighting there. He considered the war a tragic waste of lives and resources in an area of marginal interest to the United States, and he was convinced that fighting in Korea would detract from the country's primary duties in Europe, dissipate its power, disillusion its people, and play into the hands of isolationists like Taft. Given these views, Lippmann did not hesitate to say that American forces should

---

[18] Lippmann, *The Cold War*, 24, 53–54. See also ibid., 25–28; and Steel, *Lippmann*, 458–60. For Lippmann's views on the Truman Doctrine and the policies leading up to it see his column, "Today and Tomorrow," in the *Washington Post*, 7 September 1946, and 6 March, 25 March, and 8 April 1947.

be withdrawn as soon as the situation had stabilized, and to complain bitterly when MacArthur's efforts to unify Korea provoked China's intervention, enlarged the war, and further eroded America's power and authority.[19]

Running through Lippmann's critique of American diplomacy, from the Truman Doctrine to the Korean War, was the conviction that the wrong kind of foreign policy could alter the American state at home. His thinking in this regard was more subtle than Taft's but his concerns were similar, particularly his conviction that an open-ended anticommunism would cost more than the country could afford and more than the taxpayers would support. Lippmann called it "deficit diplomacy," whereby the Truman administration kept expanding the country's global commitments beyond the military resources available to meet them. Yet any attempt to match resources to commitments, he warned, would wreck the economy, lead to political and economic regimentation, and drive American taxpayers toward isolationism.[20]

Nor were these the only liabilities. Lippmann was also convinced that Truman's policies threatened the constitutional balance in the United States by inflating the authority of the executive branch, weakening that of Congress, and involving professional soldiers too deeply in American politics. His thinking in this regard again dovetailed to some extent with that of Taft and Hoover, as was apparent in his reaction to the North Atlantic Treaty, the program of arms aid that followed, and the dispatch of American troops to Europe. Much like Taft, he saw all of these initiatives as vastly expanding presidential powers, including the power to provide arms to any government on earth, to declare war without consulting Congress, and to send troops abroad without congressional consent. The same kind of thinking also inspired his critique of the Korean War, in which case he again faulted Truman for sending troops into battle without congressional approval and for thus bringing on a constitutional crisis over the conduct of American foreign relations. This crisis, in turn, had set the stage for the Truman–MacArthur controversy and for a congressional investigation of American military strategy, both of which, according to Lippmann, saw the "default of civil power" and the "rise of the generals to a place" they should not "hold in the Government of the Republic." The Truman–MacArthur controversy, said

[19] Steel, *Lippmann*, 466–67, 474–76. See also Lippmann's column, "Today and Tomorrow," in the *Washington Post*, 11 December 1950 and 11 January 1951.

[20] See Lippmann's column, "Today and Tomorrow," in the *Washington Post*, 25 July and 22 August 1950, 26 February 1951. See also Steel, *Lippmann*, 460–61.

Lippmann, was "the culminating point" of the "most un-American and most unrepublican evolution in our affairs."[21]

Slight wonder that Lippmann threw his weight behind Eisenhower's campaign in 1952. At last, he thought, the nation would be reunified under a popular war hero who offered an internationalist alternative to Taft's isolationism and who could also end the Korean conflict and control the right wing of the Republican party. But initial optimism soon gave way to disillusionment as the new president continued the policies of his predecessor. Lippmann was unhappy when Eisenhower did nothing to confront the totalitarian menace of McCarthyism, when Dulles resorted to the diplomacy of brinkmanship, when he and Eisenhower tied the United States more closely to Asia, when they continued to militarize American foreign policy, and when they threw their support behind a European defense community that included a rearmed West Germany – and thus solidified the postwar partition of both Germany and Europe.[22]

Following Lippmann's critique, we can extrapolate an alternative foreign policy that went beyond the hemispheric system of defense favored by Hoover and Taft but still stopped short of the globalism envisioned by Truman and Eisenhower. Under this policy, American commitments around the world would be more limited and American power would be more focused and less likely to be enchained in a network of debilitating alliances with weaker countries that had little in common with the United States. This policy would rule out the kind of defense establishment envisioned in NSC-68. Defense would cost less, the military would be less powerful politically, the constitutional balance would be protected, taxes would be lower, and fewer resources would be diverted from the welfare state to the warfare state, from civilian to military investment, from one region of the country to another.

In some ways Lippmann's alternative compares favorably with American foreign policy in the Cold War, though perhaps less favorably with the Truman–Eisenhower policy, the Korean War being a notable exception, than with the policies of their successors, who proliferated the country's commitments overseas, pushed defense spending up, and drew the United States deeper into Asia, Africa, and other quagmires. But maybe history was inevitable. Maybe events had to unfold as they did, or maybe a different policy would have brought results that were

---

[21] See Lippmann's column, "Today and Tomorrow," *Washington Post,* 21 May 1951. See also ibid., 11 December 1950, and 9 January, 16 January, 13 February, and 5 April 1951; and Steel, *Lippmann,* 460–61.

[22] Steel, *Lippmann,* 482–84, 504–10.

worse, not better, than those that actually occurred. Taking this line, one might reject Lippmann's alternative as naive, settle instead for the smugness that came easily to American leaders at the end of the Cold War, and claim that no price was too high for victory over a ruthless enemy. In truth, however, traditional values and institutions had channeled American policy and American state making in some directions while damming them up in others. The American people and their leaders, or at least the best of them, would go so far and no further, lest a reckless abandon destroy the very Republic they sought to protect. And given the limitations they imposed, and the reasons they imposed them, is it not worth asking if victory might have been theirs at less than the price they paid for it?

Selected Bibliography

Primary Sources

Private Manuscript Collections

Library of Congress, Washington, DC

Joseph W. and Stewart Alsop Papers
Robert P. Patterson Papers
Robert A. Taft Papers
Hoyt S. Vandenberg Papers

Seeley G. Mudd Library, Princeton University, Princeton, NJ

Ferdinand Eberstadt Papers
James V. Forrestal Papers
Emmet J. Hughes Papers
George F. Kennan Papers

Dwight D. Eisenhower Library, Abilene, KS

Dwight D. Eisenhower Diaries
Dwight D. Eisenhower Papers (Ann Whitman File)
   Administration Series
   Cabinet Series
   DDE Diary Series
   NSC Series
C.D. Jackson Papers
Lauris Norstad Papers
White House Office Records
   National Security Council Staff Papers
   Special Assistant for National Security Affairs
Records of the U.S. President's Advisory Committee on Government Organization

Harry S. Truman Library, Independence, MO

Eben A. Ayers Papers
Clark M. Clifford Files
Clark M. Clifford Papers

Matthew J. Connelly Papers
L. Laszlo Ecker-Racz Papers
George M. Elsey Papers
Leon H. Keyserling Papers
Dan A. Kimball Papers
Frederick J. Lawton Papers
Charles S. Murphy Papers
Edwin G. Nourse Papers
Harold D. Smith Papers
John W. Snyder Papers
David H. Stowe Papers
Stuart Symington Papers
Harry S. Truman Papers
  President's Secretary's File
  Records of the National Security Council
  White House Central File
    Confidential File
    General File
    Official File
James E. Webb Papers
Oral History Collection
  Jerry N. Hess Interview with Leon H. Keyserling
Records of the President's Advisory Commission on Universal
  Training
Records of the President's Scientific Research Board

Government Archives

National Archives of the United States, College Park, MD

Record Group 51, Records of the Office of Management and Budget, Records of the
  Bureau of the Budget
Record Group 218, Records of the U.S. Joint Chiefs of Staff
  Records of the Administrative Offices of the JCS
  Records of the Chairman
Record Group 293, Records of the Wage and Salary Stabilization Boards of the Economic
  Stabilization Agency, General Records
Record Group 295, Records of the Office of Price Stabilization, Headquarters Records,
  Records of the Office of the Director
Record Group 296, General Records of the Economic Stabilization Agency, Records of
  the Office of the Administrator
Record Group 304, Records of the Office of Civil and Defense Mobilization, Records of
  the National Security Resources Board, Records of the Office of the Chairman
Record Group 330, Records of the Office of the Secretary of Defense

Washington National Records Center, Suitland, MD

Record Group 335, Records of the Office of the Secretary of the Army

Published Government Documents

Director of Defense Mobilization. *Quarterly Report to the President*. Washington, DC: Government Printing Office, 1951–52.

Office of Defense Mobilization. *The Job Ahead for Defense Mobilization: Eighth Quarterly Report to the President*. Washington, DC: Government Printing Office, 1953.

President's Advisory Commission on Universal Training. *A Program for National Security*. Washington, DC: Government Printing Office, 1947.

U.S. Commission on Organization of the Executive Branch of the Government. *The Hoover Commission Report: On Organization of the Executive Branch of the Government*. New York: McGraw-Hill Book Co., Inc., 1949.

———. *The National Security Organization: A Report to the Congress by the Commission on Organization of the Executive Branch of Government, February 1949*. Washington, DC: Government Printing Office, 1949.

———. *General Management of the Executive Branch: A Report to the Congress, February 1949*. Washington, DC: Government Printing Office, 1949.

———. *The National Security Organization: A Report to the Congress, February 1949*. Washington, DC: Government Printing Office, 1949.

Committee on the National Security Organization. *National Security Organization: A Report with Recommendations*. Washington, DC: Government Printing Office, 1949.

———. *Task Force Report on National Security Organization*. Washington, DC: Government Printing Office, 1949.

U.S. Congress. *Congressional Record*, 1947–54. Washington, DC.

———. *Congressional Quarterly*, 1946–47. Washington, DC.

———. *Congressional Quarterly Almanac*, 1948–54. Washington, DC.

U.S. Congress, House. Committee on Armed Forces. *Hearings on H. Res. 234, Investigation of the B-36 Bomber Program*. 81st Cong., 1st sess., 1949.

———. Committee on Armed Services. *Full Committee Hearings on Universal Military Training*. 80th Cong., 1st sess., 1947.

———. Committee on Expenditures in the Executive Departments. *Hearings on H.R. 2319, A Bill to Promote the National Security by Providing for a National Defense Establishment*. 80th Cong., 1st sess., 1947.

———. Committee on Military Affairs. *Hearings on H. Res. 515, An Act to Provide Military or Naval Training for All Male Citizens Who Attain the Age of 18 Years, and for Other Purposes*. 79th Cong., 1st sess., 1945.

———. Committee on the Post Office and Civil Service. *Hearings on H. J. Res. 84: A Resolution to Provide for the Acquisition and Operation of the Freedom Train by the Archivist of the United States, and for Other Purposes*. 81st Cong., 1st sess., 1949.

———. Select Committee on Postwar Military Policy. *Universal Military Training, Hearings and Statements Pursuant to H. Res. 465, A Resolution to Establish a Select Committee on Postwar Military Policy*. 79th Cong., 1st sess., 1945.

———. *The National Defense Program: Unification and Strategy*. 81st Cong., 1st sess., 1949.

U.S. Congress, Senate. Committee on Armed Services. *Hearings on S. 758, A Bill to Promote the National Security by Providing for a National Defense Establishment*. 80th Cong., 1st sess., 1947.

———. Committee on Armed Services. *Hearings on S. 1269 and S. 1843. A Bill to*

Convert the National Military Establishment into an Executive Department of the Government. 81st Cong., 1st sess., 1949.

———. Committee on Armed Services. *Hearings on S. 1, A Bill to Provide for the Common Defense and Security of the United States and to Permit the More Effective Utilization of Manpower Resources of the United States by Authorizing Universal Military Service and Training, and for Other Purposes.* 82d Cong., 1st sess., 1951.

———. Committee on Armed Services. *Hearings on Universal Military Training*, 80th Cong., 2d. sess., 1948.

———. Committee on Foreign Affairs. *Hearings on S. 84, A Bill to Provide for a Department of Armed Forces, and Hearings on S. 1482, A Bill to Establish a Department of Military Security.* 79th Cong., 1st sess., 1945.

———. Committee on Naval Affairs. *Report to Honorable James Forrestal, Secretary of the Navy, on Unification of the War and Navy Departments and Postwar Organization for National Security, October 22, 1945.* 79th Cong., 1st sess., 1945.

———. Committee on Naval Affairs. *Hearings on S. 2044, A Bill to Promote the Common Defense by Unifying the Departments and Agencies of the Government Relating to the Common Defense.* 78th Cong., 2d sess., 1946.

———. Special Committee Investigating the National Defense Program. *Hearings Pursuant to S. Res. 46, A Resolution Authorizing and Directing an Investigation of the National Defense Program.* 80th Cong., 1st. sess., 1948.

———. Special Committee Investigating the National Defense Program. *Report on Industrial Mobilization for War.* 80th Cong., 2d sess., 1948.

U.S. Department of State. *Foreign Relations of the United States, 1946.* Vol. 6. Washington, DC: Government Printing Office, 1969.

———. *Foreign Relations of the United States, 1948.* Vols. 1, 2. Washington, DC: Government Printing Office, 1976.

———. *Foreign Relations of the United States, 1949.* Vol. 1. Washington, DC: Government Printing Office, 1976.

———. *Foreign Relations of the United States, 1950.* Vol. 1. Washington, DC: Government Printing Office, 1977.

———. *Foreign Relations of the United States, 1951.* Vol. 1. Washington, DC: Government Printing Office, 1979.

———. *Foreign Relations of the United States, 1952–1954.* Vol. 2. Washington, DC: Government Printing Office, 1984.

———. *Foreign Relations of the United States, 1945–1950. Emergence of the Intelligence Establishment.* Washington, DC: Government Printing Office, 1996.

U.S. Office of the Federal Register. *Public Papers of the Presidents of the United States: Harry S. Truman, 1945–1953.* Washington, DC: Government Printing Office, 1961–66.

———. *Public Papers of the Presidents of the United States: Dwight D. Eisenhower, 1953–1954.* Washington, DC: Government Printing Office, 1960.

Memoirs, Diaries, and Contemporary Accounts

Abell, Tyler, ed. *Drew Pearson Diaries, 1949–1959.* New York: Holt, Rinehart and Winston, 1974.

Acheson, Dean. *Present at the Creation: My Years in the State Department.* New York: W. W. Norton and Co., 1969.

Adams, Sherman. *Firsthand Report: The Story of the Eisenhower Administration.* New York: Harper and Brothers, 1961.

Alsop, Joseph W., with Adam Platt. *"I've Seen the Best of It": Memoirs.* New York: W. W. Norton and Co., 1992.

American Heritage Foundation. *The American Heritage Program and the Freedom Train.* New York: American Heritage Foundation, 1947.

Anders, Roger M., ed. *Forging the Atomic Shield: Excerpts from the Office Diary of Gordon E. Dean.* Chapel Hill: University of North Carolina Press, 1987.

Baldwin, Hanson W. *The Price of Power.* New York: Harper and Brothers, 1947.

Bissell, Richard M., Jr. "The Impact of Rearmament on the Free World Economy," *Foreign Affairs* 29 (April 1951): 385–405.

Bissell, Richard M., Jr., with Jonathan E. Lewis and Frances T. Pudlo. *Reflections of a Cold Warrior: From Yalta to the Bay of Pigs.* New Haven: Yale University Press, 1996.

Bradley, Omar N., and Clay Blair. *A General's Life: An Autobiography.* New York: Simon and Schuster, 1983.

Bush, Vannevar. *Science – The Endless Frontier: A Report to the President on a Program for Postwar Scientific Research.* Washington, DC: National Science Foundation, 1945.

———. *Modern Arms and Free Men: A Discussion of the Role of Science in Preserving Democracy.* New York: Simon and Schuster, 1949.

Childs, Marquis. *Eisenhower: Captive Hero: A Critical Study of the General and the President.* New York: Harcourt, Brace, and Co., 1958.

———. *Witness to Power.* New York: McGraw-Hill Book Co., 1975.

Clifford, Clark M., with Richard Holbrooke. *Counsel to the President: A Memoir.* New York: Random House, 1991.

Cole, Alice C., et al., eds. *The Department of Defense: Documents on Establishment and Organization, 1944–1978.* Washington, DC: Government Printing Office, 1978.

Correa, Rodolfo A. "The Organization for Defense Mobilization." *Federal Bar Journal* 13 (September 1953): 1–15.

Cottrell, Leonard S., Jr., and Sylvia Eberhart. *American Opinion on World Affairs in the Atomic Age.* Princeton: Princeton University Press, 1948.

Cutler, Robert. "The Development of the National Security Council." *Foreign Affairs* 34 (April 1956): 441–58.

Eisenhower, Dwight D. *The White House Years: Mandate for Change, 1953–1956.* Garden City, NY: Doubleday and Co., 1963.

Ferrell, Robert H., ed. *Off the Record: The Private Papers of Harry S. Truman.* New York: Harper & Row, 1980.

———, ed. *The Eisenhower Diaries.* New York: W. W. Norton and Co., 1981.

———, ed. *Dear Bess: Letters from Harry to Bess Truman.* New York: W. W. Norton and Co., 1983.

———, ed. *Truman in the White House: The Diary of Eben A. Ayers.* Columbia, MO: University of Missouri Press, 1991.

Fleischmann, Manley. "Policies and Procedures for Limited Mobilization." *Annals of the American Academy of Political and Social Science* 278 (November 1951): 110–18.

Friends Committee on National Legislation. *Resolutions Against Universal Military Training, 1945–1947.* Washington, DC: Friends Committee on National Legislation, n.d.

Galambos, Louis, ed. *The Papers of Dwight David Eisenhower*, vols. 7, 8, *The Chief of Staff*. Baltimore: Johns Hopkins University Press, 1978.

Gallup, George H. *The Gallup Poll: Public Opinion, 1935–1971*, vols. 1, 2. New York: Random House, 1972.

Ginsburg, David. "Price Stabilization, 1950–1952: Retrospect and Prospect." *University of Pennsylvania Law Review* 100 (January 1952): 514–43.

Griffith, Robert, ed. *Ike's Letters to a Friend, 1941–1958*. Lawrence: University Press of Kansas, 1984.

Hayek, Friedrich A. *The Road to Serfdom*. Chicago: University of Chicago Press, 1944.

Hoover, Herbert. *Addresses Upon the American Road, 1950–1955*. Stanford, CA: Stanford University Press, 1955.

Hughes, Emmet John. *The Ordeal of Power: A Political Memoir of the Eisenhower Years*. New York: Atheneum, 1963.

Jurika, Stephen, Jr. *From Pearl Harbor to Vietnam: The Memoirs of Admiral Arthur W. Radford*. Stanford, CA: Hoover Institution Press, 1980.

Kaskell, Peter H. "Production Under the Controlled Materials Plan." *Federal Bar Journal* 13 (September 1952): 16–34.

Kennan, George F. "The Sources of Soviet Conduct." *Foreign Affairs* 25 (July 1947): 566–82.

———. *American Diplomacy: 1900–1950*. Chicago: University of Chicago, 1951.

———. *Memoirs, 1925–1950*. Boston: Little, Brown and Co., 1967.

———. *Memoirs, 1950–1963*. Boston: Little, Brown and Co., 1972.

Killian, James R., Jr. *Sputnik, Scientists, and Eisenhower: A Memoir of the First Special Assistant to the President for Science and Technology*. Cambridge: MIT Press, 1977.

Kistiakowsky, George B. *A Scientist at the White House: The Private Diary of President Eisenhower's Special Assistant for Science and Technology*. Cambridge: Harvard University Press, 1976.

Krock, Arthur. *Memoirs: Sixty Years on the Firing Line*. New York: Funk & Wagnalls, 1968.

Lasswell, Harold D. "Sino-Japanese Crisis: The Garrison State versus the Civilian State." *The China Quarterly* 11 (Fall 1937): 643–49.

———. "The Garrison State." *American Journal of Sociology* 46 (January 1941): 455–68.

———. "The Garrison State and Specialists on Violence." In *The Analysis of Political Behaviour: An Empirical Approach*, pp. 146–57. New York: Oxford University Press, 1947.

———. *National Security and Individual Freedom*. New York: McGraw-Hill Book Co., 1950.

———. "Does the Garrison State Threaten Civil Rights?" *Annals of the American Academy of Political and Social Science* 275 (May 1951): 111–16.

Levanthal, Harold. "The Organization for Defense Mobilization: Part II: Price Controls under the Defense Production Act, as Amended." *Federal Bar Journal* 13 (December 1951): 99–116.

Lilienthal, David E. *The Journals of David E. Lilienthal*, vol. 2, *The Atomic Energy Years, 1945–1950*. New York: Harper & Row, 1964.

Lippmann, Walter. *The Cold War: A Study in U.S. Foreign Policy*. New York: Harper & Brothers, 1947.

Millis, Walter, ed. *The Forrestal Diaries*. New York: The Viking Press, 1951.

Monaghan, Frank, ed. *Heritage of Freedom: The History & Significance of the Basic Documents of American Liberty*. Princeton: Princeton University Press, 1947.

Nelson, Donald M. *Arsenal of Democracy: The Story of American War Production*. New York: Harcourt, Brace, and Co., 1946.

Nitze, Paul H., with Ann M. Smith and Steven L. Rearden. *From Hiroshima to Glasnost: At the Center of Decision, A Memoir*. New York: Grove Weidenfeld, 1989.

Reston, James. *Deadline: A Memoir*. New York: Random House, 1991.

Ridgway, Matthew B. *Soldier: The Memoirs of Matthew B. Ridgway*. New York: Harper & Brothers, 1956.

Roberts, B. C. "Wage Stabilization in the United States." *Oxford Economic Papers* 4 (1952): 149–62.

Rossiter, Clinton, and James Lare, eds. *The Essential Lippmann: A Political Philosophy for Liberal Democracy*. New York: Random House, 1963.

Schlesinger, Arthur M., Jr. *The Vital Center: The Politics of Freedom*. Boston: Houghton Mifflin Co., 1949.

Steury, Donald P., ed. *Intentions and Capabilities: Estimates on Soviet Strategic Forces, 1950–1983*. Washington, DC: Central Intelligence Agency, 1996.

———, ed. *Sherman Kent and the Board of National Estimates: Collected Essays*. Washington, DC: Central Intelligence Agency, 1994.

Strauss, Lewis L. *Men and Decisions*. Garden City, NY: Doubleday and Co., 1962.

Taylor, Maxwell D. *The Uncertain Trumpet*. New York: Harper & Brothers, 1959.

Theoharis, Athan G. *The Truman Presidency: The Origins of the Imperial Presidency and the National Security State*. Stanfordville, NY: Earl M. Coleman Enterprises, Inc., 1979.

Truman, Harry S. "Our Armed Forces Must be Unified." *Collier's* (26 August 1944): 63–64.

———. *Memoirs*, vol. 1, *Years of Decisions*. Paperback Edition. New York: Signet Books, 1965.

———. *Memoirs*, vol. 2, *Years of Trial and Hope, 1946–52*. Garden City, NY: Doubleday and Co., 1956.

Warner, Michael, ed. *CIA Cold War Records: The CIA under Harry Truman*. Washington, DC: Central Intelligence Agency, 1994.

Watkins, Ralph J. "Economic Mobilization." *American Political Science Review* 43 (June 1949): 555–63.

Yoshpe, Harry B. "Economic Mobilization Planning Between the Two World Wars." *Military Affairs* 16 (1): 71–83.

———. *The National Security Resources Board, 1947–1953: A Case Study in Peacetime Mobilization Planning*. Washington, DC: Government Printing Office, 1953.

Contemporary Periodicals

Atlanta Constitution
Boston Herald
Business Week
Chicago Tribune
Christian Science Monitor
Cleveland Plain Dealer

Collier's
Dallas Morning News
Denver Post
Des Moines Register
Forum
Harper's
Life
Los Angeles Times
The Mosinee (Wis.) Times
The Nation
National Geographic
The New Republic
New York Herald Tribune
New York Times
New York Times Magazine
Newsweek
Reader's Digest
San Francisco Chronicle
Saturday Evening Post
St. Louis Post-Dispatch
Time
U.S. News and World Report
Vital Speeches of the Day
Washington Post
Wausau, Wis. *Daily Record-Herald*

Secondary Sources

Articles

Adler, Les K., and Thomas Paterson. "Red Fascism: The Merger of Nazi Germany and Soviet Russia in the American Image of Totalitarianism." *American Historical Review* 75 (April 1970): 1046–64.

Amenta, Edwin, and Theda Skocpol. "Redefining the New Deal: World War II and the Development of Social Provision in the United States." In *The Politics of Social Policy in the United States*, pp. 81–122. Edited by Margaret Weir, Ann Shola Orloff, and Theda Skocpol. Princeton: Princeton University Press, 1988.

Anderson, Carol. "From Hope to Disillusion: African Americans, the United Nations, and the Struggle for Human Rights, 1944–1947." *Diplomatic History* 20 (Fall 1996): 531–63.

Auerbach, Lewis E. "Scientists in the New Deal: A Pre-War Episode in the Relations between Science and Government in the United States." *Minerva* 3 (Summer 1965): 457–82.

Bernstein, Barton J. "In the Matter of J. Robert Oppenheimer." *Historical Studies in the Physical Sciences* 12 (1982): 195–252.

The Bird Dogs. "The Evolution of the Office of Naval Research." *Physics Today* 14 (August 1961): 30–35.

Bradsher, James Gregory. "Taking America's Heritage to the People: The Freedom Train Story." *Prologue* 17 (Winter 1985): 228–45.

Brands, H. W. "The Age of Vulnerability: Eisenhower and the National Insecurity State." *American Historical Review* 94 (October 1989): 963–89.

Brinkley, Alan. "The Problem of American Conservatism." *American Historical Review* 99 (April 1994): 409–29.

Bronk, Detlev W. "Science Advice in the White House: The Genesis of the President's Science Advisors and the National Science Foundation." In *Science and Technology Advice to the President, Congress, and Judiciary*, pp. 245–56. Edited by William T. Golden. New York: Pergamon Books, 1980.

Brune, Lester H. "Guns and Butter: The Pre-Korean War Dispute Over Budget Allocations: Nourse's Conservative Keynesianism Loses Favor Against Keyserling's Economic Expansion Plan." *American Journal of Economics and Sociology* 48 (July 1989): 357–72.

Buhite, Russell D., and William Christopher Hamel. "War for Peace: The Question of an American Preventive War against the Soviet Union." *Diplomatic History* 14 (Summer 1990): 367–84.

Carpenter, Ted Galen. "United States' NATO Policy at the Crossroads: The 'Great Debate' of 1950–1951." *International History Review* 8 (August 1986): 389–415.

Clayton, James L. "The Impact of the Cold War on the Economies of California and Utah, 1946–1965." *Pacific Historical Review* 36 (November 1967): 449–73.

Coblenz, William A. "The Freedom Train and the Story of Its Origins: Our Civil Liberties on Wheels." *Manuscripts* 10 (Winter 1957): 30–34, 59.

Combs, Jerald A. "The Compromise That Never Was: George Kennan, Paul Nitze, and the Issue of Conventional Deterrence in Europe, 1949–1952." *Diplomatic History* 15 (Summer 1991): 361–86.

Cuff, Robert. "Ferdinand Ederstadt, the National Security Resources Board, and the Search for Integrated Mobilization Planning, 1947–1948." *Public Historian* 7 (Fall 1985): 37–52.

Davis, Lance E., and Daniel J. Kevles. "The National Research Fund: A Case Study of Industrial Support of Academic Science." *Minerva* 12 (April 1974): 207–20.

Ferguson, Thomas. "From Normalcy to New Deal: Industrial Structure, Party Competition, and American Public Policy in the Great Depression." *International Organization* 38 (Winter 1984): 41–94.

Friedberg, Aaron L. "Why Didn't the United States Become a Garrison State?" *International Security* 16 (Spring 1992): 109–42.

Gaddis, John Lewis, and Paul Nitze. "NSC 68 and the Soviet Threat Reconsidered." *International Security* 4 (Spring 1980): 164–84.

Greb, G. Allen. "Science Advice to the Presidents: From Test Bans to the Strategic Defense Initiative." IGCC Research Paper No. 3, University of California Institute on Global Conflict and Cooperation, University of California, San Diego, 1987.

Griffith, Robert G. "Dwight D. Eisenhower and the Corporate Commonwealth." *American Historical Review* 87 (February 1982): 87–122.

Grose, Bertram M., and John P. Lewis. "The President's Economic Staff during the Truman Administration." *American Political Science Review* 48 (March 1954): 114–30.

Hammond, Paul Y. "Super Carriers and B-36 Bombers: Appropriations, Strategy and Politics." In *American Civil–Military Decisions: A Book of Case Studies*, pp. 465–564. Edited by Harold Stein. Birmingham: University of Alabama Press, 1963.

————. "NSC-68: Prologue to Rearmament." In *Strategy, Politics, and Defense Budgets*, pp. 267–378. Edited by Warner R. Schilling, Paul Y. Hammond, and Glenn H. Snyder. New York: Columbia University Press, 1962.

Jervis, Robert. "The Impact of the Korean War on the Cold War." *Journal of Conflict Resolution* 24 (December 1980): 563–92.

Kargon, Robert, and Elizabeth Hodes. "Karl Compton, Isaiah Bowman, and the Politics of Science in the Great Depression." *Isis* 76 (September 1985): 301–18.

Katznelson, Ira, and Bruce Pietrykowski. "Rebuilding the American State: Evidence from the 1940s." *Studies in American Political Development* 5 (Fall 1991): 301–39.

Kepley, David R. "The Senate and the Great Debate of 1951." *Prologue* 14 (Winter 1982): 212–26.

Kevles, Daniel J. "Scientists, the Military, and the Control of Postwar Defense Research: The Case of the Research Board for National Security, 1944–46." *Technology and Culture* 16 (January 1975): 20–47.

————. "Cold War and Hot Physics: Science, Security, and the American State, 1945–1956." *Historical Studies in the Physical and Biological Sciences* 20 (1990): 239–64.

Kohn, Richard H. "Out of Control: The Crisis in Civil–Military Relations." *National Interest* 35 (Spring 1994): 3–17.

Lasch, Christopher. "The Cultural Cold War: A Short History of the Congress for Cultural Freedom." In *The Agony of the American Left*. New York: Alfred A. Knopf, 1969, 63–114.

May, Ernest R. "The American Commitment to Germany, 1949–1955." *Diplomatic History* 13 (Fall 1989): 431–60.

————. "Cold War and Defense." In *The Cold War and Defense*, pp. 7–73. Edited by Keith Neilson and Ronald G. Haycock. New York: Praeger, 1990.

————. "The U.S. Government, a Legacy of the Cold War." In *The End of the Cold War: Its Meaning and Implications*, pp. 217–28. Edited by Michael J. Hogan. New York: Cambridge University Press, 1992.

Maza, Sarah. "Stories in History: Culutural Narratives in Recent Works in European History." *American Historical Review* 101 (December 1996): 1493–1515.

Moskos, Charles. "From Citizens' Army to Social Laboratory." *Wilson Quarterly* 17 (Winter 1993): 83–94.

Nelson, Anna K. "President Truman and the Evolution of the National Security Council." *Journal of American History* 72 (September 1985): 360–78.

————. "The 'Top of Policy Hill': President Eisenhower and the National Security Council." *Diplomatic History* 7 (Fall 1983): 307–26.

Neu, Charles E. "The Rise of the National Security Bureaucracy." In *The New American State: Bureaucracies and Policies since World War II*, pp. 85–108. Edited by Louis Galambos. Baltimore: Johns Hopkins University Press, 1987.

Nitze, Paul H. "The Development of NSC 68." *International Security* 4 (Fall 1979): 170–76.

Pierpaoli, Paul G., Jr. "Corporatist and Voluntarist Approaches to Cold War Rearmament: The Private Side of Industrial and Economic Mobilization, 1950–1953." *Essays in Economic and Business History* 15 (1997): 263–75.

Pursell, Carroll W., Jr. "The Anatomy of a Failure: The Science Advisory Board, 1933–1935." *Proceedings of the American Philosophical Society* 109 (December 1965): 342–51.

————. "Science Agencies in World War II: The OSRD and Its Challengers." In *The*

Sciences in the American Context: New Perspectives, pp. 359–78. Edited by Nathan Reingold. Washington, DC: Smithsonian Institution Press, 1979.

Rosenberg, David Alan. "American Atomic Strategy and the Hydrogen Bomb Decision." *Journal of American History* 66 (June 1979): 62–87.

———. " 'A Smoking Radiating Ruin at the End of Two Hours': Documents on American Plans for Nuclear War with the Soviet Union, 1954–1955." *International Security* 6 (Winter 1981–82): 3–38.

———. "U.S. Nuclear Stockpile, 1945–1950." *Bulletin of the Atomic Scientists* 38 (May 1982): 25–30.

———. "The Origins of Overkill: Nuclear Weapons and American Strategy." In *The National Security: Theory and Practice, 1945–1960*, pp. 123–95. Edited by Norman Greabner. New York: Oxford University Press, 1986.

Rosenof, Theodore. "Freedom, Planning and Totalitarianism: The Reception of F. A. Hayek's *Road to Serfdom.*" *Canadian Review of American Studies* 5 (Fall 1974): 149–65.

Sander, Alfred D. "Truman and the National Security Council: 1945–1947." *Journal of American History* 59 (September 1972): 347–88.

Sapolsky, Harvey M. "Academic Science and the Military: The Years since the Second World War." In *The Sciences in the American Context: New Perspectives*, pp. 379–99. Edited by Nathan Reingold. Washington, DC: Smithsonian Institution Press, 1979.

Schilling, Warner R. "The Politics of National Defense: Fiscal 1950." In *Strategy, Politics and Defense Budgets*, pp. 1–266. Edited by Warner R. Schilling, Paul Y. Hammond, and Glenn H. Snyder. New York: Columbia University Press, 1962.

Snyder, Glenn H. "The 'New Look' of 1953." In *Strategy, Politics, and Defense Budgets*, pp. 379–524. Edited by Warner R. Schilling, Paul Y. Hammond, and Glenn H. Snyder. New York: Columbia University Press, 1962.

Townshend, Charles. "Militarism and Modern Society." *Wilson Quarterly* 17 (Winter 1993): 71–82.

Walsh, John. "The Eisenhower Era: Transition Years for Science." *Science* 164 (4 April 1969): 50–53.

Weigley, Russell F. "The American Military and the Principle of Civilian Control from McClellan to Powell." *Journal of Military History* 57 (October 1993): 27–58.

Wells, Samuel F., Jr. "Sounding the Tocsin: NSC 68 and the Soviet Threat." *International Security* 4 (Fall 1979): 116–58.

Westbrook, Robert B. "Fighting for the American Family: Private Interests and the Political Obligation in World War II." In *The Power of Culture: Critical Essays in American History*, pp. 195–221. Edited by Richard Wightman Fox and T. J. Jackson Lears. Chicago: University Press, 1993.

Whitfield, Stephen J. "The Cultural Cold War as History." *Virginia Quarterly Review* 69 (Summer 1993): 377–92.

York, Herbert F., and G. Allen Greb. "Military Research and Development: A Postwar History." In *Science, Technology, and National Policy*, pp. 190–215. Edited by Thomas J. Kuehn and Alan L. Porter. Ithaca, NY: Cornell University Press, 1981.

Books

Abramson, Rudy. *Spanning the Century: The Life of W. Averell Harriman, 1891–1986.* New York: William Morrow and Co., 1992.

Adams, Henry H. *Witness to Power: The Life of Fleet Admiral William D. Leahy*. Annapolis, MD: Naval Institute Press, 1985.

Albion, Robert Greenhalgh, and Robert Howe Connery. *Forrestal and the Navy*. New York: Columbia University Press, 1962.

Aliano, Richard A. *American Defense Policy from Eisenhower to Kennedy: The Politics of Changing Military Requirements, 1957–1961*. Athens, OH: Ohio University Press, 1975.

Ambrose, Stephen E. *Eisenhower*, vol. 1, *Soldier, General of the Army, President-Elect, 1890–1952*, vol. 2, *The President*. New York: Simon and Schuster, 1983–84.

Anderson, Benedict. *Imagined Communities: Reflections on the Origins and Spread of Nationalism*. Rev. ed. New York: Verso, 1991.

Andrew, Christopher. *For the President's Eyes Only: Secret Intelligence and the American Presidency from Washington to Bush*. New York: Harper Collins, 1995.

Barlow, Jeffrey G. *Revolt of the Admirals: The Fight for Naval Aviation, 1945–1950*. Washington, DC: Naval Historical Center, 1994.

Barnet, Richard J. *The Roots of War: The Men and Institutions Behind U.S. Foreign Policy*. New York: Penguin Books, Inc., 1972.

Berman, Larry. *The Office of Management and Budget and the Presidency, 1921–1977*. Princeton: Princeton University Press, 1979.

Best, Gary Dean. *Herbert Hoover: The Postpresidential Years, 1933–1964*, vol. 2, *1946–1964*. Stanford, CA: Hoover Institution Press, 1983.

Bird, Kai. *The Chairman: John J. McCloy: The Making of the American Establishment*. New York: Simon and Schuster, 1992.

Bischof, Gunter, and Stephen E. Ambrose, eds. *Eisenhower: A Centenary Assessment*. Baton Rouge: Louisiana State University Press, 1995.

Blum, John Morton. *V Was for Victory: Politics and American Culture during World War II*. New York: Harcourt Brace Jovanovich, 1976.

Bodnar, John. *Remaking America: Public Memory, Commemoration, and Patriotism in the Twentieth Century*. Princeton: Princeton University Press, 1992.

———, ed. *Bonds of Affection: Americans Define Their Patriotism*. Princeton: Princeton University Press, 1996.

Boyer, Paul. *By the Bomb's Early Light: American Thought and Culture at the Dawn of the Atomic Age*. New York: Pantheon Books, 1985.

Bright, Charles, and Susan Harding, eds. *Statemaking and Social Movements: Essays in History and Theory*. Ann Arbor: University of Michigan Press, 1984.

Brinkley, Alan. *The End of Reform: New Deal Liberalism in Recession and War*. New York: Alfred A. Knopf, 1995.

Broadwater, Jeff. *Eisenhower & the Anti-Communist Crusade*. Chapel Hill: University of North Carolina Press, 1992.

Brown, Charles C. *Niebuhr and His Age: Reinhold Niebuhr's Prophetic Role in the Twentieth Century*. Philadelphia: Trinity, 1992.

Bundy, McGeorge. *Danger and Survival: Choices about the Bomb in the First Fifty Years*. New York: Random House, 1988.

Calhoun, Craig, ed. *Habermas and the Public Sphere*. Cambridge: MIT Press, 1992.

Callahan, David. *Dangerous Capabilities: Paul Nitze and the Cold War*. New York: Harper Collins, 1990.

Campbell, David. *Writing Security: United States Foreign Policy and the Politics of Identity*. Minneapolis: University of Minnesota Press, 1992.

Caraley, Demetrios. *The Politics of Military Unification: A Study of Conflict and the Policy Process.* New York: Columbia University Press, 1966.

Caridi, Ronald J. *The Korean War and American Politics: The Republican Party as a Case Study.* Philadelphia: University of Pennsylvania Press, 1968.

Caute, David. *The Great Fear: The Anti-Communist Purge under Truman and Eisenhower.* New York: Simon and Schuster, 1978.

Ceplair, Larry, and Steven Englund. *The Inquisition in Hollywood: Politics in the Film Community, 1930–1960.* Garden City, NY: Anchor Press, 1980.

Chambers, John Whiteclay II. *To Raise an Army: The Draft Comes to Modern America.* New York: The Free Press, 1987.

Clifford, J. Garry. *The Citizen Soldiers: The Plattsburg Training Camp Movement, 1913–1920.* Lexington: University Press of Kentucky, 1972.

Clifford, J. Garry, and Samuel R. Spencer, Jr. *The First Peacetime Draft.* Lawrence: University Press of Kansas, 1986.

Cochran, Bert. *Labor and Communism: The Conflict that Shaped American Unions.* Princeton: Princeton University Press, 1977.

Cohen, Eliot A. *Citizens and Soldiers: The Dilemma of Military Service.* Ithaca, NY: Cornell University Press, 1985.

Coleman, Peter. *The Liberal Conspiracy: The Congress for Cultural Freedom and the Struggle for the Mind of Postwar Europe.* New York: The Free Press, 1989.

Coletta, Paola E. *The United States Navy and Defense Unification, 1947–1953.* Newark: University of Delaware Press, 1981.

Combs, Jerald A. *American Diplomatic History: Two Centuries of Changing Interpretations.* Berkeley: University of California Press, 1983.

Condit, Doris M. *The History of the Office of the Secretary of Defense,* vol. 2, *The Test of War, 1950–1953.* Washington, DC: Government Printing Office, 1988.

Condit, Kenneth W. *The History of the Joint Chiefs of Staff,* vol. 2, *The Joint Chiefs of Staff and National Policy, 1947–1949.* Wilmington, DE: Michael Glazier, Inc., 1979.

———. *The History of the Joint Chiefs of Staff,* vol. 6, *The Joint Chiefs of Staff and National Policy, 1955–1956.* Washington, DC: Government Printing Office, 1992.

Cook, Blanche Wiesen. *The Declassified Eisenhower: A Divided Legacy.* Garden City, NY: Doubleday & Co., 1981.

Cumings, Bruce. *The Origins of the Korean War,* vols. 1, 2. Princeton: Princeton University Press, 1981–1990.

Darling, Arthur B. *The Central Intelligence Agency: An Instrument of Government, to 1950.* University Park: Pennsylvania State University Press, 1990.

Davis, Vincent. *Postwar Defense Policy and the U.S. Navy, 1943–1946.* Chapel Hill: University of North Carolina Press, 1962.

———. *The Admirals Lobby.* Chapel Hill: University of North Carolina Press, 1967.

Diamond, Sigmund. *Compromised Campus: The Collaboration of Universities with the Intelligence Community, 1945–1955.* New York: Oxford University Press, 1992.

Diggins, John Patrick. *Up from Communism: Conservative Odysseys in American Intellectual History.* New York: Harper and Row, 1975.

———. *The Lost Soul of American Politics: Virtue, Self-Interest, and the Foundations of Liberalism.* New York: Basic Books, 1984.

———. *The Proud Decades: America in War and Peace, 1941–1960.* New York: W. W. Norton and Co., 1988.

Divine, Robert A. *Blowing on the Wind: The Nuclear Test Ban Debate, 1954–1960*. New York: Oxford University Press, 1978.

———. *Eisenhower and the Cold War*. New York: Oxford University Press, 1981.

Doenecke, Justus D. *Not to the Swift: The Old Isolationists in the Cold War Era*. Lewisburg, PA: Bucknell University Press, 1979.

Donovan, Robert J. *Conflict and Crisis: The Presidency of Harry S. Truman, 1945–1948*. New York: W. W. Norton & Co., 1977.

———. *Tumultuous Years: The Presidency of Harry S. Truman, 1949–1953*. New York: W. W. Norton & Co., 1982.

Dorwart, Jeffery M. *Eberstadt and Forrestal: A National Security Partnership, 1909–1949*. College Station: Texas A & M University Press, 1991.

Dupree, A. Hunter. *Science in the Federal Government: A History of Policies and Activities to 1940*. Cambridge: Harvard University Press, 1957.

Ehrman, John. *The Rise of Neoconservatism: Intellectuals and Foreign Affairs, 1945–1994*. New Haven, CT: Yale University Press, 1995.

Ekirch, Arthur A., Jr. *The Civilian and the Military*. New York: Oxford University Press, 1956.

Ellis, Richard J. *American Political Cultures*. New York: Oxford University Press, 1993.

England, J. Merton. *A Patron for Pure Science: The National Science Foundation's Formative Years, 1945–57*. Washington, DC: National Science Foundation, 1982.

Evans, Peter B., Dietrich Rueschemeyer, and Theda Skocpol, eds. *Bringing the State Back In*. Cambridge: Cambridge University Press, 1985.

Feaver, Peter Douglas. *Guarding the Guardians: Civilian Control of Nuclear Weapons in the United States*. Ithaca, NY: Cornell University Press, 1992.

Feldbaum, Carl B., and Ronald J. Bee. *Looking the Tiger in the Eye: Confronting the Nuclear Threat*. New York: Harper & Row, 1988.

Ferrell, Robert H. *Harry S. Truman: A Life*. Columbia: University of Missouri Press, 1994.

Flash, Edward S., Jr. *Economic Advice and Presidential Leadership: The Council of Economic Advisors*. New York: Columbia University Press, 1965.

Flynn, George Q. *The Draft, 1940–1973*. Lawrence: University Press of Kansas, 1993.

Fox, Richard Wightman. *Reinhold Niebuhr: A Biography*. New York: Pantheon Books, 1985.

Fox, Richard Wightman, and T. J. Jackson Lears, eds. *The Power of Culture: Critical Essays in American History*. Chicago: University of Chicago Press, 1993.

Freeland, Richard M. *The Truman Doctrine and the Origins of McCarthyism: Foreign Policy, Domestic Politics, and Internal Security, 1946–1948*. New York: Alfred A. Knopf, 1972.

Fried, Richard M. *Nightmare in Red: The McCarthy Era in Perspective*. New York: Oxford University Press, 1990.

Furner, Mary O., and Barry Supple, eds. *The State and Economic Knowledge: The American and British Experiences*. New York: Cambridge University Press, 1990.

Gaddis, John Lewis. *The United States and the Origins of the Cold War, 1941–1947*. New York: Columbia University Press, 1972.

———. *Strategies of Containment: A Critical Appraisal of Postwar American National Security Policy*. New York: Oxford University Press, 1982.

———. *We Now Know: Rethinking Cold War History*. New York: Clarendon Press, 1997.

Gasiorowski, Mark J. *U.S. Foreign Policy and the Shah: Building a Client State in Iran.* Ithaca, NY: Cornell University Press, 1991.

Geiger, Roger L. *Research and Relevant Knowledge: American Research Universities since World War II.* New York: Oxford University Press, 1993.

Gellhorn, Walter. *Security, Loyalty, and Science.* Ithaca, NY: Cornell University Press, 1950.

Gerhardt, James M. *The Draft and Public Policy: Issues in Military Manpower Procurement, 1945–1970.* Columbus: Ohio State University Press, 1971.

Gillis, John R., ed. *Commemorations: The Politics of National Identity.* Princeton: Princeton University Press, 1994.

Gleason, Abbott. *Totalitarianism: The Inner History of the Cold War.* New York: Oxford University Press, 1995.

Gleijeses, Piero. *Shattered Hope: The Guatemalan Revolution and the United States, 1944–1954.* Princeton: Princeton University Press, 1991.

Glynn, Patrick. *Closing Pandora's Box: Arms Races, Arms Control, and the History of the Cold War.* New York: Basic Books, 1992.

Goldberg, Alfred. *The Pentagon: The First 50 Years.* Washington, DC: Government Printing Office, 1992.

Green, David. *Shaping Political Consciousness: The Language of Politics in America from McKinley to Reagan.* Ithaca, NY: Cornell University Press, 1987.

Greenberg, Daniel S. *The Politics of Pure Science.* New York: The New American Library, Inc., 1967.

Greenstein, Fred I. *The Hidden-Hand Presidency: Eisenhower as Leader.* New York: Basic Books, 1982.

Griffith, Robert. *The Politics of Fear: Joseph R. McCarthy and the Senate.* Lexington: University Press of Kentucky, 1970.

Hamby, Alonzo L. *Beyond the New Deal: Harry S. Truman and American Liberalism.* New York: Columbia University Press, 1973.

———. *Man of the People: A Life of Harry S. Truman.* New York: Oxford University Press, 1995.

Hammond, Paul Y. *Organizing for Defense: The American Military Establishment in the Twentieth Century.* Princeton: Princeton University Press, 1961.

Harper, Alan D. *The Politics of Loyalty: The White House and the Communist Issue, 1946–1952.* Westport, CT: Greenwood Publishing, 1969.

Hartmann, Susan M. *Truman and the 80th Congress.* Columbia: University of Missouri Press, 1971.

———. *The Home Front and Beyond: American Women in the 1940s.* Boston: Twayne Publishers, 1982.

Haynes, Richard F. *The Awesome Power: Harry S. Truman as Commander in Chief.* Baton Rouge: Louisiana State University Press, 1973.

Heiss, Mary Ann. *Empire and Nationhood: The United States, Great Britain, and Iranian Oil, 1950–1954.* New York: Columbia University Press, 1997.

Heller, Francis H. *Economics and the Truman Administration.* Lawrence: The Regents Press of Kansas, 1981.

Herken, Gregg. *The Winning Weapon: The Atomic Bomb in the Cold War, 1945–1950.* New York: Vintage Books, 1982.

———. *Councils of War.* Expanded ed. New York: Oxford University Press, 1987.

——. *Cardinal Choices: Presidential Science Advising from the Atomic Bomb to SDI.* New York: Oxford University Press, 1992.

Hershberg, James G. *James B. Conant: Harvard to Hiroshima and the Making of the Nuclear Age.* New York: Knopf, 1993.

Hewlett, Richard G., and Oscar E. Anderson, Jr. *A History of the United States Atomic Energy Commission,* vol. 1, *The New World Order, 1939–1946.* University Park: Pennsylvania State University Press, 1962.

Hewlett, Richard G., and Francis Duncan. *A History of the United States Atomic Energy Commission,* vol. 2, *Atomic Shield, 1947–1952.* University Park: Pennsylvania State University Press, 1969.

Hewlett, Richard G., and Jack M. Holl. *Atoms for Peace and War, 1953–1961: Eisenhower and the Atomic Energy Commission.* Berkeley: University of California Press, 1989.

Hickman, Bert G. *Growth and Stability of the Postwar Economy.* Washington, DC: Brookings Institution, 1960.

Hixson, Walter L. *George F. Kennan: Cold War Iconoclast.* New York: Columbia University Press, 1989.

Hogan, Michael J. *The Marshall Plan: America, Britain, and the Reconstruction of Western Europe, 1947–1952.* New York: Cambridge University Press, 1987.

——, ed. *America in the World: The Historiography of American Foreign Relations since 1941.* New York: Cambridge University Press, 1995.

Holloway, David. *Stalin and the Bomb: The Soviet Union and Atomic Energy, 1939–1956.* New Haven: Yale University Press, 1994.

Hooks, Gregory. *Forging the Military–Industrial Complex: World War II's Battle of the Potomac.* Urbana: University of Illinois Press, 1991.

Hoopes, Townsend, and Douglas Brinkley. *Driven Patriot: The Life and Times of James Forrestal.* New York: Alfred A. Knopf, 1992.

Horowitz, David A. *Beyond Left & Right: Insurgency and the Establishment.* Urbana: University of Illinois Press, 1997.

Huntington, Samuel P. *The Soldier and the State: The Theory and Politics of Civil–Military Relations.* Cambridge: Harvard University Press, 1957.

——. *The Common Defense: Strategic Program in National Politics.* New York: Columbia University Press, 1961.

Immerman, Richard H. *The CIA in Guatemala: The Foreign Policy of Intervention.* Austin: University of Texas Press, 1982.

Inglis, Fred. *The Cruel Peace: Everyday Life in the Cold War.* New York: Basic Books, 1991.

Isaacson, Walter, and Evan Thomas. *The Wise Men: Six Friends and the World They Made: Acheson, Bohlen, Harriman, Kennan, Lovett, McCloy.* New York: Simon and Schuster, 1986.

James, D. Clayton. *The Years of MacArthur,* vol. 3, *Triumph and Disaster, 1945–1964.* Boston: Houghton Mifflin, 1985.

Jeffreys-Jones, Rhodri. *The CIA and American Democracy.* New Haven: Yale University Press, 1989.

Johnson, Robert David. *The Peace Progressives and American Foreign Relations.* Cambridge: Harvard University Press, 1995.

Kammen, Michael. *Mystic Chords of Memory: The Transformation of Tradition in American Culture.* Paperback ed. New York: Vintage Books, 1993.

Kaplan, Amy, and Donald E. Pease, eds. *Cultures of United States Imperialism.* Durham: Duke University Press, 1993.

Kaplan, Fred. *The Wizards of Armageddon.* New York: Simon and Schuster, 1983.

Karl, Barry. *The Uneasy State: The United States from 1915 to 1945.* Chicago: University of Chicago Press, 1983.

Kaufman, Burton I. *Trade and Aid: Eisenhower's Foreign Economic Policy, 1953–1961.* Baltimore: Johns Hopkins University Press, 1982.

———. *The Korean War: Challenges in Crisis, Credibility, and Command.* Philadelphia: Temple University Press, 1986.

Kepley, David R. *The Collapse of the Middle Way: Senate Republicans and the Bipartisan Foreign Policy, 1948–1952.* New York: Greenwood Press, 1988.

Kevles, Daniel J. *The Physicists: The History of a Scientific Community in Modern America.* New York: Vantage Books, 1979.

Kinnard, Douglas. *The Secretary of Defense.* Lexington: The University Press of Kentucky, 1980.

Klurfeld, Herman. *Behind the Lines: The World of Drew Pearson.* Englewood Cliffs, NJ: Prentice-Hall, Inc., 1968.

Kofsky, Frank. *Harry S. Truman and the War Scare of 1948.* New York: St. Martin's Press, 1993.

Kohn, Richard H., ed. *The United States Military under the Constitution of the United States, 1789–1989.* New York: New York University Press, 1991.

Koistinen, Paul A. C. *The Military–Industrial Complex: A Historical Perspective.* New York: Praeger, 1980.

Kolko, Gabriel. *The Roots of American Foreign Policy.* Boston: Beacon Press, 1969.

Kolodziej, Edward A. *The Uncommon Defense and Congress, 1945–1963.* Columbus: Ohio State University Press, 1966.

Koppes, Clayton R. *JPL and the American Space Program: A History of the Jet Propulsion Laboratory.* New Haven, CT: Yale University Press, 1982.

Kuniholm, Bruce R. *The Origins of the Cold War in the Near East: Great Power Conflict and Diplomacy in Iran, Turkey, and Greece.* Princeton: Princeton University Press, 1980.

Lacey, Michael J., ed. *The Truman Presidency.* New York: Cambridge University Press, 1989.

Lasch, Christopher. *The World of Nations: Reflections on American History, Politics & Culture.* Paperback ed. New York: Vintage Books, 1974.

Leffler, Melvyn P. *A Preponderance of Power: National Security, the Truman Administration, and the Cold War.* Stanford, CA: Stanford University Press, 1992.

Legere, Laurence J. *Unification of the Armed Forces.* New York: Garland Publishing, Inc., 1988.

Leslie, Stuart W. *The Cold War and American Science: The Military-Industrial-Academic Complex at MIT and Stanford.* New York: Columbia University Press, 1993.

Lifka, Thomas F. *The Concept of "Totalitarianism" and American Foreign Policy, 1933–1949.* New York: Garland, 1988.

Lotchin, Roger W. *Fortress California, 1910–1961: From Warfare to Welfare.* New York: Oxford University Press, 1992.

———, ed. *The Martial Metropolis: U.S. Cities in War and Peace, 1900–1970*. New York: Praeger Publishers, 1984.

Lowen, Rebecca S. *Creating the Cold War University: The Transformation of Stanford*. Berkeley: University of California Press, 1997.

Major, John. *The Oppenheimer Hearing*. New York: Stein and Day, 1971.

Marcus, Maeva. *Truman and the Steel Seizure Case: The Limits of Presidential Power*. New York: Columbia University Press, 1977.

Markusen, Ann, Scott Campbell, Peter Hall, and Sabina Deitrick. *The Rise of the Gunbelt: The Military Remapping of Industrial America*. New York: Oxford University Press, 1991.

May, Elaine Tyler. *Homeward Bound: American Families in the Cold War Era*. New York: Basic Books, 1988.

May, Ernest R. *"Lessons" of the Past: The Use and Misuse of History in American Foreign Policy*. New York: Oxford University Press, 1973.

———, ed. *American Cold War Strategy: Interpreting NSC 68*. Boston: St. Martin's Press, 1993.

May, Lary, ed. *Recasting America: Culture and Politics in the Age of Cold War*. Chicago: University of Chicago Press, 1989.

McAuliffe, Mary Sperling. *Crisis on the Left: Cold War Politics and American Liberals, 1947–1954*. Amherst: University of Massachusetts Press, 1978.

McCoy, Donald R. *The Presidency of Harry S. Truman*. Lawrence: University Press of Kansas, 1984.

McCullough, David. *Truman*. New York: Simon and Schuster, 1992.

McDougall, Walter A. *. . . the Heavens and the Earth: A Political History of the Space Age*. New York: Basic Books, 1985.

McLellan, David S. *Dean Acheson: The State Department Years*. New York: Dodd, Mead, 1976.

Meilinger, Phillip S. *Hoyt S. Vandenberg: The Life of a General*. Bloomington: Indiana University Press, 1989.

Melman, Seymour. *Pentagon Capitalism: The Political Economy of War*. New York: McGraw-Hill Book Co., 1970.

Merry, Robert W. *Taking on the World: Joseph and Stewart Alsop – Guardians of the American Century*. New York: Viking Penguin Books, 1996.

Meyer, Donald. *The Protestant Search for Political Realism, 1919–1941*. 2d ed. Middletown, CT: Wesleyan University Press, 1988.

Millett, Allan R., et al. *The Reorganization of the Joint Chiefs of Staff: A Critical Analysis*. New York: International Defense Publishers, 1986.

Millis, Walter. *Arms and Men: A Study of American Military History*. New York: Capricorn Books, 1956.

Millis, Walter, with Harvey C. Mansfield and Harold Stein. *Arms and the State: Civil–Military Elements in National Policy*. New York: Twentieth Century Fund, 1958.

Milward, Alan S. *War, Economy and Society, 1939–1945*. Berkeley: University of California Press, 1979.

Miscamble, Wilson D. *George F. Kennan and the Making of American Foreign Policy, 1945–1950*. Princeton: Princeton University Press, 1992.

Montague, Ludwell Lee. *General Walter Bedell Smith as Director of Central Intelligence, October 1950–February 1953*. University Park: Pennsylvania State University Press, 1992.

Morgan, Iwan W. *Eisenhower Versus 'The Spenders': The Eisenhower Administration, the Democrats and the Budget, 1953–60.* London: Pinter Publishers, 1990.

Nash, George H. *The Conservative Intellectual Movement in America, Since 1945.* New York: Basic Books, 1976.

Neuse, Steven M. *David E. Lilienthal: The Journey of an American Liberal.* Knoxville: University of Tennessee Press, 1996.

Newhouse, John. *War and Peace in the Nuclear Age.* New York: Knopf, 1989.

Nieburg, H. L. *In the Name of Science.* Chicago: Quadrangle Books, 1966.

Ninkovich, Frank. *Modernity and Power: A History of the Domino Theory in the Twentieth Century.* Chicago: University of Chicago Press, 1994.

Norton, Hugh Stanton. *The Council of Economic Advisors: Three Periods of Influence.* Columbia, SC: The Bureau of Business and Economic Research, 1973.

Oakes, Guy. *The Imaginary War: Civil Defense and American Cold War Culture.* New York: Oxford University Press, 1994.

O'Neill, William L. *American High: The Years of Confidence, 1945–1960.* New York: Free Press, 1986.

———. *A Democracy at War: America's Fight at Home and Abroad in World War II.* Cambridge: Harvard University Press, 1993.

Oshinsky, David M. *A Conspiracy So Immense: The World of Joe McCarthy.* New York: Free Press, 1983.

Pach, Chester J., Jr., and Elmo Richardson. *The Presidency of Dwight D. Eisenhower.* Rev. ed. Lawrence: University Press of Kansas, 1991.

Parmet, Herbert S. *Eisenhower and the American Crusades.* New York: The Macmillan Company, 1971.

Paterson, Thomas G., ed. *Cold War Critics: Alternatives to American Foreign Policy in the Truman Years.* Chicago: Quadrangle Books, 1971.

Patterson, James T. *Mr. Republican: A Biography of Robert A. Taft.* Boston: Houghton Mifflin, 1972.

Pells, Richard H. *The Liberal Mind in a Conservative Age: American Intellectuals in the 1940s and 1950s.* Paperback ed. New York: Harper and Row, 1985.

Pemberton, William E. *Harry S. Truman: Fair Dealer and Cold Warrior.* Boston: Twayne Publishers, 1989.

Penick, James L., Jr., et al, eds. *The Politics of American Science: 1939 to the Present.* Chicago: Rand McNally & Co., 1965.

Perry, Mark. *Four Stars.* Boston: Houghton Mifflin Co., 1989.

Pfau, Richard. *No Sacrifice Too Great: The Life of Lewis L. Strauss.* Charlottesville: University Press of Virginia, 1984.

Pogue, Forrest C. *George C. Marshall: Statesman, 1945–1959.* New York: Viking, 1987.

Polenberg, Richard. *War and Society: The United States, 1941–1945.* Philadelphia: J. B. Lippincott Co., 1972.

Poole, Walter S. *The History of the Joint Chiefs of Staff: The Joint Chiefs of Staff and National Policy,* vol. 4, *1950–1952.* Wilmington, DE: Michael Glazier, Inc., 1980.

Prados, John. *The Soviet Estimate: U.S. Intelligence Analysis and Russian Military Strength.* New York: Dial Press, 1982.

———. *Presidents' Secret Wars: CIA and Pentagon Covert Operations from World War II through Iranscam.* New York: William Morrow, 1986.

Price, Don K. *Government and Science: Their Dynamic Relation in American Democracy.* New York: New York University Press, 1954.

Pruessen, Ronald W. *John Foster Dulles: The Road to Power*. New York: Free Press, 1982.

Rappaport, Armin. *The Navy League of the United States*. Detroit: Wayne State University Press, 1962.

Rearden, Steven L. *History of the Office of the Secretary of Defense*, vol. 1, *The Formative Years, 1947–1950*. Washington, DC: Government Printing Office, 1984.

Rees, David. *Korea: The Limited War*. Baltimore: Penguin Books, 1970.

Reeves, Thomas C. *The Life and Times of Joe McCarthy: A Biography*. New York: Stein & Day, 1982.

Reichard, Gary W. *The Reaffirmation of Republicanism: Eisenhower and the Eighty-Third Congress*. Knoxville: University of Tennessee Press, 1975.

Robbins, Bruce, ed. *The Phantom Public Sphere*. Minneapolis: University of Minnesota Press, 1993.

Rockoff, Hugh. *Drastic Measures: A History of Wage and Price Controls in the United States*. New York: Cambridge University Press, 1984.

Rogin, Michael Paul. *The Intellectuals and McCarthy: The Radical Specter*. Cambridge: MIT Press, 1967.

Rogow, Arnold A. *James Forrestal: A Study of Personality, Politics, and Policy*. New York: Macmillan, 1963.

Rosecrance, Richard, and Arthur A. Stein, eds. *The Domestic Bases of Grand Strategy*. Ithaca, NY: Cornell University Press, 1993.

Rosenthal, Joel H. *Righteous Realists: Political Realism, Responsible Power, and American Culture in the Nuclear Age*. Baton Rouge: Louisiana State University Press, 1991.

Ross, Steven T. *American War Plans, 1945–1950*. New York: Garland Publishing, 1988.

Rourke, John. *Congress and the Presidency in United States Foreign Policymaking: A Study of Interaction and Influence, 1945–1982*. Boulder, CO: Westview, 1983.

Said, Edward. *Culture and Imperialism*. New York: Knopf, 1993.

Schaller, Michael. *Douglas MacArthur: The Far Eastern General*. New York: Oxford University Press, 1989.

Schnabel, James F. *The History of the Joint Chiefs of Staff: The Joint Chiefs of Staff and National Policy*, vol. 1, *1945–1947*. Wilmington, DE: Michael Glazier, Inc., 1979.

Schnabel, James F., and Robert J. Watson. *The History of the Joint Chiefs of Staff: The Joint Chiefs of Staff and National Policy*, vol. 3, *The Korean War*, Part II. Wilmington, DE: Michael Glazier, Inc., 1979.

Schrecker, Ellen W. *No Ivory Tower: McCarthyism and the Universities*. New York: Oxford University Press, 1986.

Schwarz, Jordan A. *The Speculator: Bernard M. Baruch in Washington, 1917–1965*. Chapel Hill: University of North Carolina Press, 1981.

Sherry, Michael S. *In the Shadow of War: The United States since the 1930s*. New Haven, CT: Yale University Press, 1995.

Skolnikoff, Eugene B. *Science, Technology, and American Foreign Policy*. Cambridge: MIT Press, 1967.

Slotkin, Richard. *Gunfighter Nation: The Myth of the Frontier in Twentieth-Century America*. New York: Atheneum, 1992.

Smith, Alice Kimball. *A Peril and a Hope: The Scientists' Movement in America, 1945–47*. Chicago: University of Chicago Press, 1965.

Smith, Bruce L. R. *American Science Policy since World War II*. Washington, DC: Brookings Institution, 1990.

Smith, Richard Norton. *An Uncommon Man: The Triumph of Herbert Hoover.* New York: Simon and Schuster, 1984.

Smith, Tony. *America's Mission: The United States and the Worldwide Struggle for Democracy in the Twentieth Century.* Princeton: Princeton University Press, 1994.

Spanier, John W. *The Truman–MacArthur Controversy and the Korean War.* Paperback ed. New York: W. W. Norton and Co., 1965.

Sparrow, Bartholomew H. *From the Outside In: World War II and the American State.* Princeton: Princeton University Press, 1996.

Steel, Ronald. *Walter Lippmann and the American Century.* Paperback ed. New York: Vintage Books, 1981.

Stein, Harold, ed. *American Civil–Military Decisions: A Book of Case Studies.* Birmingham: University of Alabama Press, 1963.

Stein, Herbert. *The Fiscal Revolution in America.* Chicago: University of Chicago Press, 1969.

Stephanson, Anders. *Kennan and the Art of Foreign Policy.* Cambridge: Harvard University Press, 1989.

Stern, Philip M. *The Oppenheimer Case: Security on Trial.* New York: Harper & Row, 1969.

Stewart, Irvin. *Organizing Scientific Research for War: The Administrative History of the Office of Scientific Research and Development.* Boston: Little, Brown and Co., 1948.

Stockfisch, J. A. *Plowshares into Swords: Managing the American Defense Establishment.* New York: Mason and Lipscomb, 1973.

Stoler, Mark. *George C. Marshall: Soldier-Statesman of the American Century.* Boston: Twayne Publishers, 1989.

Susman, Warren I. *Culture as History: Transformation of American Society in the Twentieth Century.* New York: Pantheon Books, 1984.

Sussmann, Leila A. *Dear FDR: A Study of Political Letter-Writing.* Totowa, NJ: The Bedminster Press, 1963.

Tananbaum, Duane. *The Bricker Amendment Controversy: A Test of Eisenhower's Political Leadership.* Ithaca, NY: Cornell University Press, 1988.

Theoharis, Athan G. *Seeds of Repression: Harry S. Truman and the Origins of McCarthyism.* Chicago: Quadrangle Books, 1971.

Thomas, Evan. *The Very Best Men: Four Who Dared: The Early Years of the CIA.* New York: Simon and Schuster, 1994.

Thompson, Francis H. *The Frustration of Politics: Truman, Congress, and the Loyalty Issue, 1945–1953.* Rutherford, NJ: Fairleigh Dickenson University Press, 1979.

Treverton, Gregory F. *Covert Action: The Limits of Intervention in the Postwar World.* New York: Basic Books, 1987.

Troy, Thomas F. *Donovan and the CIA: A History of the Establishment of the Central Intelligence Agency.* Frederick, MD: University Publications of America, Inc., 1981.

Vagts, Alfred. *A History of Militarism.* Rev. ed. New York: Meridian Books, 1959.

Vander Meulen, Jacob A. *The Politics of Aircraft: Building an American Military Industry.* Lawrence: University Press of Kansas, 1991.

Vawter, Roderick L. *Industrial Mobilization: The Relevant History.* Rev. ed. Washington, DC: National Defense University Press, 1983.

Watson, Robert J. *The History of the Joint Chiefs of Staff,* vol. 5, *The Joint Chiefs of Staff and National Policy, 1953–1954.* Washington, DC: Government Printing Office, 1986.

Weart, Spencer. *Nuclear Fear: A History of Images.* Cambridge: Harvard University Press, 1988.

Weigley, Russell. *The American Way of War: A History of United States Military Strategy and Policy.* New York: Macmillan, 1973.

Whitfield, Stephen J. *The Culture of the Cold War.* Baltimore: Johns Hopkins University Press, 1991.

Williams, Phil. *The Senate and US Troops in Europe.* New York: Macmillan, 1985.

Williamson, Samuel R., Jr., and Steven L. Rearden. *The Origins of U.S. Nuclear Strategy.* New York: St. Martin's Press, 1993.

Winkler, Allan M. *Home Front U.S.A.: America During World War II.* Arlington Heights, IL: Harlan Davidson, 1986.

————. *Life Under a Cloud: American Anxiety About the Atom.* New York: Oxford University Press, 1993.

Winks, Robin W. *Cloak & Gown: Scholars in the Secret War, 1939–1961.* New York: William Morrow and Co., 1987.

Wise, David. *The American Police State: The Government against the People.* New York: Random House, 1976.

Wittner, Lawrence S. *American Intervention in Greece, 1943–1949.* New York: Columbia University Press, 1982.

Wolk, Herman S. *Planning and Organizing the Postwar Air Force, 1943–1947.* Washington, DC: Office of Air Force History, 1984.

Yarmolinsky, Adam. *The Military Establishment: Its Impacts on American Society.* New York: Harper & Row, 1971.

Yoder, Edwin M., Jr. *Joe Alsop's Cold War: A Study of Journalistic Influence and Intrigue.* Chapel Hill: University of North Carolina Press, 1995.

York, Herbert. F. *The Advisors: Oppenheimer, Teller, and the Superbomb.* San Francisco: W. H. Freeman, 1976.

Yoshpe, Harry B., and Stanley L. Falk. *The Economics of National Security: Organization for National Security.* Washington, DC: Industrial College of the Armed Forces, 1963.

Unpublished Material

Cunningham, Frank Dale. "The Army and Universal Military Training, 1942–1948." Ph.D. dissertation, The University of Texas at Austin, 1976.

Damms, Richard V. "Scientists and Statesmen: President Eisenhower's Science Advisers and National Security Policy, 1953–1961." Ph.D. dissertation, The Ohio State University, 1993.

Eden, Lynn Rachele. "The Diplomacy of Force: Interests, the State, and the Making of American Military Policy in 1948." Ph.D. dissertation, University of Michigan, 1985.

Exon, Karen Hunt. "'Fortress America': The U.S. Senate and the Great Debate of 1950–1951." Ph.D. dissertation, University of Kansas, 1990.

Fousek, John Howard. "To Lead the Free World: American Nationalism and the Ideological Origins of the Cold War, 1945–1950." Ph.D. dissertation, Cornell University, 1994.

Grabavoy, Leann. "Joseph Alsop and American Foreign Policy: The Journalist as Advocate." Ph.D. dissertation, University of Georgia, 1988.

Greenwald, Bryon, and Clifford J. Rogers. "The Hidden Hand in Defense Reorganization."

Seminar paper in author's possession. Seminar in U.S. Foreign Relations, The Ohio State University, 1990.

Harris, Merne A. "The MacArthur Dismissal – A Study in Political Mail." Ph.D. dissertation, University of Iowa, 1966.

Hart, David M. "Competing Conceptions of the Liberal State and the Governance of Technological Innovations in the U.S., 1933–1953." Ph.D. dissertation, Massachusetts Institute of Technology, 1995.

Kepley, David Rodney. "Challenges to Bipartisanship: Senate Republicans and American Foreign Policy, 1948–1952." Ph.D. dissertation, University of Maryland, 1979.

Little, Stuart Jon. "The Freedom Train and the Formation of National Political Culture, 1946–1949." M.A. thesis, University of Kansas, 1989.

McGinnis, John Vianney. "The Advertising Council and the Cold War." Ph.D. dissertation, Syracuse University, 1991.

Pierpaoli, Paul George. "The Price of Peace: The Korean War Mobilization and Cold War Rearmament, 1950–1953." Ph.D. dissertation, The Ohio State University, 1995.

Riggs, James Richard. "Congress and the Conduct of the Korean War." Ph.D. dissertation, Purdue University, 1972.

Rowan, Carl Milton. "Politics and Pure Research: The Origins of the National Science Foundation, 1942–1954." Ph.D. dissertation, Miami University, 1985.

Sale, Sara L. "Harry S Truman, the Development and Operations of the National Security System, and the Origins of United States Cold War Policies." Ph.D. dissertation, Oklahoma State University, 1991.

Ward, Robert D. "The Movement for Universal Military Training in the United States, 1942–1952." Ph.D. dissertation, University of North Carolina, 1957.

Index

Acheson, Dean
  on civilian control of military, 198–9
  on Cold War spending, 304
  criticism of Defense Department strategy,
    309
  criticism of NSC, 309
  demands related to Korean War, 311
  geopolitical vision, 276
  on influencing public opinion, 300–301
  policy of containing communism, 476
  replaces Marshall, 276
  on shift in global balance of power, 292
air–atomic warfare
  Army and Navy position on, 170
  Forrestal's position on, 170
  Joint Chiefs debate over, 170–1
  Nourse's position on, 279
  Taft's strategy based on, 101
  Truman and Eisenhower strategies based
    on, 476
Air Force
  budget for build-up to fifty-eight group,
    183
  growth during Korean War, 312, 322
  Symington as secretary of, 96, 103, 105,
    107, 187–9, 191–3, 203–4
Air Policy Commission, 100
Alsop, Joseph, 55, 177–8, 189–90, 237, 262
  attack on L. Johnson, 307
  on defense budget (FY51), 286–7
Alsop, Stewart, 55, 177, 189–90, 237
  attack on L. Johnson, 307
  on defense budget (FY51), 286–7
anticommunism
  during Cold War, 424
  in postwar state making strategy, 23
  of Truman Doctrine, 117
Appleby, Paul, 77–8
Arendt, Hannah, 420
armed forces

See also Air Force; Army Department;
    Defense Department; Joint Chiefs of
    Staff; Navy Department; War
    Department
  autonomy under National Security Act,
    68, 233, 264
  budget planning (FY 1951), 268–9
  challenge to civilian control of, 184–5
  competition for funds, 97–8, 103–15
  criticism of Eisenhower's budget decisions,
    398
  demands for defense spending (FY 1947),
    77–82
  demands for defense spending (FY 1948),
    83–91
  demands for defense spending (FY 1950),
    268–75
  demands for defense spending (FY 1952),
    322–35
  demands under proposed rearmament
    program (1951), 357–8
  drive for appropriations (1948), 103–13
  efforts to control atomic energy, 234–52,
    263
  efforts to coordinate research activities,
    230–1
  force levels increased during Korean War,
    311–12
  interservice disputes, 96–8, 194
  military research programs, 227–9, 263
  national security ideology in arguments of,
    207
  research and development programs of,
    229–34
  revolt of the admirals, 184–9, 205–6
Armed Forces Special Weapons Project, 168,
    245
armed forces unification
  Army-Navy-Truman agreement, 54–6
  Clifford-Elsey report, 39–40

507